Sacrificing People

Invasions of a Tribal Landscape

"This book deserves to be read for a multiplicity of reasons—by all those interested in re-situating India's allegedly grisly pre-colonial history; by those interested in the gory history of colonialism and the details of how its protagonists came to practise it; those interested in how colonialism perpetuated itself in modern India, especially for tribals and other oppressed sections ; and finally by all those interested in an absorbing read. It is well worth making the sacrifice of time to read it."

Nandini Sundar, *The Book Review*

"The author has examined in detail the attitude of the British officials with enlightening excerpts from official communiques ... describing very colourfully the battles, the clashes and the strategies.... A timely book which should be widely read."

Supriya Madangarli, *Free Press Journal*

"Padel has taken a courageous step towards the acknowledgement and integration of an ugly and little recognized part of the British heritage."

Jeremy Naydler, *Resurgence*

Sacrificing People

Invasions of a Tribal Landscape

New and Updated Edition

FELIX PADEL

With a Foreword by
Hugh Brody

Orient BlackSwan

ORIENT BLACKSWAN PRIVATE LIMITED

Registered Office
3-6-752 Himayatnagar, Hyderabad 500 029 (A.P.), India
E-mail: centraloffice@orientblackswan.com

Other Offices
Bangalore, Bhopal, Bhubaneshwar, Chandigarh, Chennai,
Ernakulam, Guwahati, Hyderabad, Jaipur, Kolkata,
Lucknow, Mumbai, New Delhi, Noida, Patna

First published in India by Oxford University Press, 1995, 2000
as *The Sacrifice of Human Being: British Rule and the Konds of Orissa*

Paperback edition, 2011

ISBN: 978 81 250 4189 4

Typeset in Times New Roman 10/12 by
InoSoft Systems, Noida

Printed in India at
Yash Printographics, Noida

Published by
Orient Blackswan Private Limited
1/24 Asaf Ali Road, New Delhi 110 002
Email: delhi@orientblackswan.com

For the Konds and other tribal peoples

For my parents and wider family

And for the hope that human beings of different cultures
and beliefs will learn to live more harmoniously
on this Earth that we share

Contents

List of Maps

List of Abbreviations

ASI	Anthropological Survey of India
BD	Bajrang Dal
BH	*Baptist Herald*
BMS	Baptist Missionary Society
C	Carberry ed. 1854: Selections from GOI Reports on the suppression of human sacrifice in Orissa
CCO	*Calcutta Christian Observer*
CEC	Central Empowered Committee: Advisory body on forests to the Supreme Court
CIS	*Contributions to Indian Sociology*
CMS	Church Missionary Society (Anglican)
COD	Court of Directors of the EIC in London
CR	*Calcutta Review*
CRPF	Central Reserve Police Force
CSR	Corporate Social Responsibility
CUP	Cambridge University Press
DFID	Department for International Development of the British Government
DKDA	Dongria Kond Development Agency
EIC	East India Company
GBMS	General Baptist Missionary Society
GOB	Government of Bengal
GOI	Government of India

GOM	Government of Madras
GRI	Global Reporting Initiative
HP	Home Department, Public Consultations (Government Archives)
IFAD	International Fund for Agricultural Development
J	GOM 1854: Reports on Jeypore
JASB	*Journal of the Asiatic Society of Bengal*
JRAI	*Journal of the Royal Anthropological Institute*
JRAS	*Journal of the Royal Asiatic Society*
K	Keys ed. 1885: Meriah Agency Reports
LMS	London Missionary Society (Congregationalist)
Mil.C	Military Department Consultations (Government Archives)
MiI	*Man in India* (journal)
MJLS	*Madras Journal of Literature and Science*
Nalco	National Aluminium Company
MMSD	Mining, Minerals and Sustainable Development Process
NGO	Non-Government Organization
NMP	National Mineral Policy
OUP	Oxford University Press
PUCL	People's Union for Civil Liberties
PTGs	Primitive Tribe Groups
R	G.E. Russell 1856: Reports 1832–6
RAI	Royal Anthropological Institute
Rev.C	Revenue Department Consultations (Government Archives)
Rs	Rupees
SC	Scheduled Caste: the untouchable castes variously known as harijans or *Dalits*, which include Pano and Dom, in the north and south Kond areas respectively
SJ	*Salwa Judum*
SPOs	Special Police Officers
ST	Scheduled Tribes: *Adivasis* (aboriginals) or tribal people
SWFA	South-West Frontier Agency (Chotanagpur)
TLS	*Times Literary Supplement*
UNDP	United Nations Development Programme
VHP	Vishwa Hindu Parishad
WM	William Macpherson's book *Memorials of service* of his brother, S.C. Macpherson (1865)

Foreword to this Edition

HUGH BRODY

I first read this book almost ten years ago, not long after having made my own journeys into tribal India—journeys that had brought me into the very centre of debates about human sacrifice. Some of those I met, including one of India's most inspiring and humane social activists who had spent much of his life deep in Madhya Pradesh, had told me in hushed and awed tones, about the sacrificing of children in remote villages in the forests. And others, including First Ministers and senior economists, had told me, in less hushed voices, about the need for some of these villagers to sacrifice themselves and their families for "the good of the nation."

It is impossible to read Felix Padel's work without being drawn into its flow of history, anthropology and profound insights into the way colonial projects have shaped how we see the world in general, India as a nation and tribal peoples in particular. With the help of this book, I was able to interrogate, at least in retrospect, the ideas and beliefs of the famous activist in the forests as well as the economists and politicians. And to see that alongside philanthropy and profound enthusiasm, for the *Adivasi*—'original dwellers', there is a history of colonial misconception in those whispers about human sacrifice—a need to see and to think of the "primitive" as embedded in the forests, savage and awesome in its customs. To sacrifice children to an unseen God, hidden in the wildest territories of both terrain and psyche—there is an appeal to this that has its origins in a particular kind of history. Felix Padel shows that however powerful the sense of elusive mystery, the portrayal of the tribal world in India since the early 1800s has been tied to the need to exploit and, if advantageous to those who exploit, to dispossess it. In this wonderful book, he explores this link between the way the picture gets painted and the destruction of that which is in the picture.

When leaders of Indian government and their eager civil servants, or the sanguine businessmen or sugar cane farmers of Gujarat, insisted to me that the people to be displaced by the Sardar Sarovar dam on the Narmada River must, in the end, make and accept the sacrifice, they did not imagine the donation of human life for the propitiation of gods. They did not think in terms of people dying for the cause, and were not asking for the sacrifice that generals (and politicians) ask of soldiers. Yet loss of land and forced resettlement, especially for the tribal people who sustain themselves in what remains of the remote forests and great river systems of India, is indeed a sacrifice of both livelihood and lives. Many of those who lose their homes and lands find themselves struggling at the edges of destitution. Resettlement and rehabilitation programmes are flawed; compensation money is too little; corruption is too rampant; dislocation is too hard to manage; loss of culture and break-up of family all too easily ensue. Without the protections of land, culture and family, there are many kinds of grim, inescapable vulnerabilities. And there are deaths—from diseases of poverty, from the absence of all that secures health and sustains life. So the sacrifice to development is a human sacrifice, but one that is imposed in absence of mind rather than inherent in the plan. It is in this way, for those who are made to give up their lands and homes to large dams and great mining ventures, that the officials who urge such developments are indeed asking for and then insisting upon human sacrifice. Felix Padel also explores this link between a picture that is painted, in this case of "development", and the destruction of those who are, or should be, at the centre of the image.

I remember visiting some of the villages where the people had been told that they must make the sacrifice, accept that their lands were going to be flooded, and had to move somewhere else. Almost all of those who faced this loss were *adivasis,* the tribal peoples of India who, despite special recognition in India's Constitution and its Fifth Schedule, have so often had to pay the price for developments that are in the interests of others. Many of them lived deep within their lands and their heritage, dependent on subsistence farming, fishing and gathering, speaking their own languages and following their own spiritual beliefs. They did not read and write, did not have radios or televisions, and apart from occasional and often long walks to markets, lived their own lives within and yet somehow far removed from the Indian body politic. I remember group after group of men and women who were facing displacement from this self-sustaining world saying that they would not survive exile—as a family, a community, a culture. And they feared that some would be sure to die. They would say that they could no more move than could the ants and the tigers and their gods that were all going to be submerged. Some said they would refuse to move, that they would rather drown on their lands, with their gods, than go to places where they would not be able to live as they needed to live. Very few, if any, accepted that they were some kind of sacrifice that should be made for the sake of a state called Gujarat or even a nation called India—places from which they neither sought nor received benefits and by which they had never before been given more than token recognition.

At the time of these meetings with villagers in the Narmada Valley, and then, ten years later, when returning to visit western India, I also met with families who had been displaced by both Sardar Sarovar and other dams or their canals. Some lived on plots of land provided by a resettlement package, others lived in makeshift hovels at the sides of city roads. Some had stayed together as families; many had not. All had stories to tell of the terrible hardships they had been through and, often, still had to endure. And many had died who, they said, would have lived if they had not been forced to move. They carried the details of the sacrifices they had made. Their stories were the reckoning of costs in the unreckoned cost-benefit analysis of any such project.

I also remember visiting the construction sites at the Kevadia Colony where the vast concrete wall of the Sardar Sarovar dam was being built. Huge numbers of workers were engaged on this, as also on the digging and lining of canals. There were impressive machines, yet much of the labour was by hand. In particular, the moving of sacks of cement was done by relays of men, stripped to the waist in the heat, carrying these sacks on their shoulders from offload to concrete mixers. The lime-rich cement trickled down onto their bodies, burning the skin, finding its way into their lungs. Presumably it would have cost a lot more to use forklift trucks. Were these men, or those of them who suffered the worst consequences of such work, being sacrificed? Some of them had come from one or other of the thirteen villages that had been completely destroyed to make way for the dam site, and whose population had for decades been denied any form of compensation. How many of them had been sacrificed?

In the wake of the report that the Morse Commission submitted to the World Bank in 1991, in which we detailed many aspects of the Sardar Sarovar projects in the Narmada Valley, the Bank launched its own internal investigation into how many people its projects had displaced. In a 1996 report in which the findings of this investigation were set out, the Bank revealed that in India alone, projects to which the World Bank had made loans, some 10 million had been displaced. Only a very small proportion of these had received resettlement and rehabilitation packages or programmes. The millions of others had been forced to pay the price of development, to make the sacrifice.

It may seem fanciful to suggest that the rhetoric and arguments that explain or justify such large-scale developments—be they the words of politicians, developers or economists who thus obscure the human costs to those displaced and dispossessed—are a kind of superstition. From the point of view of those who are forced into the sacrifices that this book describes, these advocates and defenders of development are seeking or sustaining power through destruction of people. It is possible to see this as a modern kind of devilish mysticism. But this is to anticipate the explorations of this book, and in this foreword I wish above all to emphasize the force, importance and poignancy of the intellectual journey Felix Padel takes us on. A journey that begins and concludes in the domain of the Konds of Orissa. They are just one *adivasi* community that has known what it is to be censured and attacked by powerful strangers who do not speak their language and have minimal and self-deceived ideas about their system of life or links to their lands. Just one of the tribal peoples who now are having to struggle against another, and potentially even more menacing kind of stranger. The journey of the book, like the struggle of the Kond, is from colonial intrusion to developmental destruction.

This is a journey we all need to understand, for we are all implicated. The transformation—be it through flooding to make dams, clear-cutting to make timber and plantations, remoulding and blasting to create open-cast mines—is explained and justified by reference to some greater good. "Greater", this is to say, than the lesser good, which is the harm, that is being done to those who live in and depend on that which the development transforms or destroys. We are this "greater good"—its beneficiaries; the victims are the ones being asked to make the sacrifices of themselves. Yet we the beneficiaries also are being sacrificed. The unthinking development that destroys the lands and lives of the *adivasi* (or of 'original dwellers' in Amazonia, the Arctic, Australasia—all the places where people are defending their lands and rights) also destroys the world that everyone depends on. A world in which there is a balance between global gases that does not push towards catastrophic warming of the planet; a world, this is to say, in which the well-being of forests, rivers and oceans is given priority over their "development". And a world in which the rights of people to live as well as they can in their own landscapes, without needing to sacrifice human life—their own or others'—to some abstract, alien and perhaps self-defeating notions of progress.

These are reflections that many have made, fears to which many give voice. This book is of great importance, however, because it digs far down into the way the idea of human sacrifice has been seen and not seen, misunderstood and exploited. The anthropologist can excavate in ways that others do not, looking into the details of culture and aspects of social and cultural history while also knowing about particular peoples in great and illuminating detail. Felix Padel moves in this way between the close, precise knowledge of a place and a society, and the large historical and global forces that bear down on that place and that society. Yet he also offers inspiration and hope: resistance also must come from the single, small, vulnerable places as well as from those who realize that this resistance is necessary for the survival of us all.

Sacrificing People is a book about a tribe in India and a particular history. It is also a book about everyone and everywhere, and about a moment in time that is now. The Dongria Konds are threatened with destruction of the mountain that they have known, cared for and worshipped since the beginning of their time. By caring for and believing in this place they have ensured the abundance of its forests and plants and creatures, from which cascade the health that they depend on. There could be no more clear example and no more compelling metaphor of that which confronts us and why we have to defy those who are determined to destroy the one mountain, which is the one world, that we have. This is a book that shows what cascades down from the forest that is on the crown of our lands, and takes us to at least one people who know what it will mean if we sacrifice that place, and with it these people. It may be that all societies, in their way, have believed in human sacrifice as a way of saving lives. But no society will survive that believes in sacrificing what it means to be human and what it means to sustain the earth itself.

These are thoughts that this book inspires and develops. I have looked into it to understand the history of India and the challenge that must be issued to unthinking development. Let us hope that it will be read by many, many people—there is no one whose life is not implicated in the stories it tells.

Preface to this Edition

In the fifteen years since this book was written, our world has seen a lot of lives sacrificed in a lot of ways and a lot of wars. A new age of a new kind of war has started, known as the *war on terror*—a concept full of the very contradictions which the book took as its central theme. Who is an innocent victim? When is the taking of human life justified? Who claims the right to take human life? Who is sacrificing whom?

In a way, the war on terror is fuelled by this very clash over the worth or innocence of different human lives, and the validity or otherwise of different ways of inflicting pain and killing. While civilians in the richer countries are outraged by the dramatic terrorist attacks in the world's top cities (New York September 2001, London June 2006, Mumbai November 2008…), the terrorists are outraged at the death and daily terror of countless civilians in countries torn apart by the actions of the most powerful governments in Afghanistan, Iraq, Palestine, Chechnya, Somalia, Sudan, Congo—and at the double standards that count some civilian lives so highly, and others, in poorer countries such as these, at so little.

Fuelled by these rival claims and contradictory victim identities, the war on terror has no end in sight, as those American ideologues who first promoted it warned us: defeating terrorism could take many years. The scale of war is escalating. How can it end? The more we attack terrorists, the more they multiply, fuelled by a martyrdom complex and outrage at the double standards. And what distinguishes counter-terrorists from the terrorists they fight, apart from their greater fire-power and government backing? Both sides use terror, and in many ways, state-backed use of terror and violence is the greater. Often, we (the reading public) do not perceive this because of how our reality and sense of normalcy is constructed through the media—*The Social Contruction of Reality* (Berger & Luckmann 1971) through *Manufacturing Consent* (Herman & Chomsky 1988).

Meanwhile, the military-industrial complex constantly feeds the war on terror with replacement hardware and research that forges new weapons and surveillance systems. Reciprocally, the war on terror feeds the military-industrial complex: the 'aerospace' industry (i.e., arms companies), defence contracts, mining and oil companies, commodity traders, and all the financial institutions investing in these industries. The end result is a state of insecurity for all of us, diminishing our quality of life in the present, as well as sacrificing the future of our planet as we squander its precious resources to feed an insane war-without-end.

Sacrificing People concerns the colonial conquest of a tribal people. Few people outside Orissa know much about the Konds. Even now, Frazer's mention of their custom of human sacrifice in *The Golden Bough* may be some people's only source of knowledge. But deconstructing their conquest by British administrators, which was done in the name of suppressing human sacrifice, has great relevance for understanding our present predicament. Anyone who wishes to penetrate the surface of the war on terror needs to face the *shadow side* of the society we live in. In essence and origins, what this means is: understanding *human sacrifice*. Not (just) as a barbaric 'survival'-custom from humanity's ancient, superstitious past, but as something happening now, that has spread and escalated even in the last fifteen years. Not just in the number of lives being sacrificed in thousands upon thousands of simultaneous tragedies around the world, but in *the sacrifice of human being*—a throwing away of the vast potential we are all born with.

This book has also come into a new relevance locally in Orissa, and in India as a whole. For a start, the whole Kond area—which in colonial times was often called Khondistan—is under a new invasion by mining companies, in pursuit of Bauxite, the ore for aluminium. It so happens that India's largest and best quality Bauxite deposits lie at the top of the Konds' largest mountains, where they form a layer averaging five to ten metres thick, spread over these mountains' distinctive flat summits. But for the Konds, these mountains are sacred entities. To Census officials enquiring their religion, Konds often replied simply 'mountains' (see chapter 9). This is far from some idle superstition. Tribal people have a deep understanding of the ecosystem of their mountains—of how they hold the precious water that falls in the monsoon, storing it throughout the year, and releasing it in perennial streams. In this, Kond religion represents a remarkably sane synthesis of the material and the spiritual, based around the reality of the land's fertility. What mining companies, politicians and financial investors view as *resources* to be turned into money—as fast as possible, regardless of the sacrifice—Konds view as *sources* of life itself.

So a monumental culture clash underlies this new invasion—the subject of a new book, which I have co-authored over the last seven years with Samarendra Das: *Out of this Earth: East India Adivasis and the Aluminium Cartel,* which follows the same mode of analysis that proved so fruitful in analyzing the colonial invasion of Khondistan. The social structure of aluminium companies is highly complex, compared with the colonial roles of administrator, merchant, missionary and anthropologist. Yet beneath the surface complexity of metals traders, hedge funds, credit rating agencies, hierarchies of company officials, World Bank staffers, administrators and politicians, with complex subordinate roles played by NGOs, environmental scientists and the media, lurks a similar simplicity, that boils down to different value systems: seeing Bauxite as dead matter—a resource to be exploited for profit—*versus* a view that combines spirit and matter, seeing it as something that should be preserved inviolate in the mountains to keep the earth fertile and in balance.

The fact that India's richest deposits of Baxite, Chromite, Iron-ore, Coal, Manganese and other minerals are to be found in the East of India, in Orissa and its neighbouring states, recalls the original role of the British in India: the East India Company (EIC). The British entered India through two main centres on the East coast: Calcutta (Kolkata) and Madras (Chennai), and their manipulation of finance, law and politics were what gave rise to the Government of India, unifying the country, but in a colonial mould, geared towards making a profit out of the land's crops and natural resources. Nick Robins' recent book on the EIC terms it *the world's first multinational*—the mother of all companies. So in the remote Kond hills, and the history of scarlet-uniformed sepoys obeying orders from EIC officers, certain trajectories meet of great relevance for all of us.

Kandhamal (Khondmal), the district where EIC sepoys first encountered the Konds and entered their territory, has recently become notorious throughout India for extreme violence and a form of 'ethnic cleansing'. Since Christmas celebrations were disrupted by riots in December 2007, and Swami Laxmanananda Saraswati was assassinated by Maoists in August 2008, an explosion of orchestrated attacks on Christians has occurred on a scale comparable to the violence of the British invasion. Over 50,000 Christians have been driven out of their homes, with numerous accounts of gang rapes and gruesome murders. The burning of their homes and villages recalls dozens of Kond villages burnt under colonial orders, as a tactic to 'pacify' the area in the 1830s–60s. Analyzing the role and words of the first missionaries in Orissa, who targeted this district in particular, is necessary to comprehend recent events.

The role of missionary was not confined to religion. European missionaries saw themselves as supplementing the spread of 'civilization', and this included science, technology, and markets, which missionaries helped propagate in schools and hospitals. The role of missionary was internalized by administrators, school-teachers and engineers. From Keynes onwards, the people who set up the World Bank and ran it saw themselves as missionaries, seeding a new economic order around the world. The role of missionary is everywhere, in each of us—wherever we find the attitude 'we have the truth and it's our role to bring it to people'.

Nowhere is the missionary influence more evident than in the way that 'development' is imposed in tribal areas. The aluminium and dam projects are all justified in the name of development—a development that is extremely one-sided, confined to material constructs, and often masks the looting of land and resources. Big factories and mines, and the companies that build and run them, are thoroughly hierarchical affairs, as closed to learning from or adapting to tribal culture as the most bigoted of missionaries. Development of equality before the law and justice for all, an end to corruption and exploitation, a property ceiling that controls the accumulation of wealth by the few, a system of health and education accessible and accountable to everyone: these measures would count as real development. Orissa's poverty has one main cause: a system of exploitation stretching from the village level to the dissemination of World Bank funds and mining company bribes. Until this is confronted, mining projects may invest millions, but this money will only intensify the exploitation, 'flooding us out with money', as several Konds have expressed it.

One basic problem in the written discourse about *adivasis* is that it rarely quotes what they say, making them into objects, closed to their understanding, which is often enlightened by more intelligence and wit than a library-full of books! *Out of This Earth* draws on the words of many *adivasis* and *dalits*, especially from a documentary film made by Samarendra and Amarendra Das: *Wira Pdika* (in Kui)—*Matiro Poko, Company Loko* (in Oriya)—*Earth Worm, Company Man* (2005).

Running through the film is a commentary about the Kashipur movement against the Utkal alumina project in Kashipur, and the terrible police firing that killed three *adivasis* in December 2000. This commentary is by Bhagaban Majhi, from the Kond village of Kucheipadar, who describes an interaction with the Superintendent of Police as follows:

> I put a question to the SP. I asked him, Sir, what do you mean by development? (*Agya, unnoti boile kono?*) Is it development to displace people? The people, for whom development is meant, should reap benefits. After them, the succeeding generations should reap benefits. That is development. It should not be merely to cater to the greed of a few officials. To destroy the millions of years old mountains is not development. If the government has decided that we need alumina, and we need to mine bauxite, they should oblige us with replacement land. As Adivasis, we are cultivators. We cannot live without land.

Several million tribal people have been displaced by industry. In the new, final chapter we shall see that the proper description of what is happening is not just mass impoverishment, but also Cultural Genocide. The place where these processes of displacement and Cultural Genocide assume their worst form is just west of Orissa in Dantewara district (formerly part of Bastar, in the new state of Chhattisgarh). Since June 2005, a tribal militia formed by politicians and police called *Salwa Judum* ('purification hunt' in Gond language) has displaced an estimated 200,000 *adivasis*, committing uncounted murders and rapes, burning one village after another. This is where the War on Terror has taken root in India. In the wake of the Kandhamal violence, this model is being set up in Orissa, even though it is a recipe for civil war.

This book offers a way of understanding the roots of human violence by understanding ourselves and our place in the structure of power. The main technique presented to anthropology, and to anyone interested in a holistic understanding of the roots of conflict, is to subject a power structure to structural analysis, so that one sees the actions and ideology of different actors in relation to each other: missionaries, government officials, anthropologists, economists, journalists, lawyers, schoolteachers, company directors, *adivasis, dalits*, Hindus, Christians—all of us. Analyzing this in a historical context sheds light on how structures have changed—or endured, shifting their outward form only superficially. In the case of the colonial administration analyzed below, the power structure emerges with clarity from the distance of time, and comprehending it reveals how much of the colonial mindset and system is still in place.

In the case of the aluminium industry, the social structure is considerably more complex, involving engineers, banks, credit rating agencies, PR firms, arms companies, foreign aid and NGO workers, construction contractors, timber mafia, the judiciary and many more. The mountains in Orissa which are capped by Bauxite were named Khondalite by geologists who recognized that they were of prime importance to the Konds, and stood in their territory. Analyzing the aluminium industry starts from another invasion of this territory, that has many parallels with the first, British invasion, but branches out from here to assess the cost of living which involves all of us in a rarely questioned dependence on hundreds of aluminium artefacts. In particular, the costs which the industry *externalizes* onto areas where Bauxite is mined and the metal is manufactured, are beyond imagining, and sacrifice the quality of life of thousands of Konds and Oriyas, now and for centuries to come.

Further historical research has convinced me that the Konds, *Kuinga* in their own language, are basically the same people as the *Kalinga*, whom Ashoka attacked with such violence around 2,270 years ago—an event that stands at the threshold of Indian history, since he recorded it, alongside his repentance for killing 100,000 Kalinga people and enslaving 150,000. The Konds' gradual retreat from the coastal areas of Orissa is recorded in many records (e.g., Cobden-Ramsey 1910). This identification—in fact the whole history of Ashoka's genocidal war waged against the Kalinga—makes the naming of Kalinganagar supremely ironic: an industrial enclave of steel plants, drawing chromite from the Sukinda mines (counted among the ten most polluted spots on earth), and displacing yet more *adivasis*. When police opened fire at Kalinganagar on 2nd January 2006, after a police constable had been killed, shooting dead 14 *adivasi* protestors against a Tata steel plant, the resonance with the ancient story of Kalinga brings this irony to a savage climax. But who has even noticed? Meanwhile, through these ongoing invasions of tribal territory, steel and aluminium from Orissa are feeding the world's arms industry, and therefore its wars.

Moving on from aluminium, a third book is in process—*Transfiguring the Terrorist Within*—which turns the mode of analysis developed in the first two books towards analyzing the War on Terror itself—3,000 years of history leading up to it, and how the war gets internalized in each one of our lives.

Γνωθη Σων (*Gnothi sown*)—*Know Thyself*—inscribed over the entrance to the oracle at Delphi (the ancient Greeks' holiest shrine): this seems the only way that growing conflicts in the world can be resolved. Christians need to understand the intolerance that missionaries brought to Orissa, and to change this pattern. Hindus need to understand that the only forced conversions going on in Kandhamal are by Hindus of Christians, and that the violence and expulsion of Christians pollutes and debases the Hindu *dharma*. People of both religions need to open to the shared truths which underlie both religions. All of us need to learn from other truths, at the centre of *adivasi* religion, whose respect for nature forms the basis for real sustainability. Without returning to this respect, we are a species hurtling to self-destruction from which no gods or science can save us. Kond reverence for mountains has a lot to teach the world.

All the events and situations described above are explored in the new chapter. I am grateful to the publishers for commissioning it, to Hugh Brody for writing the new Foreword, and to Samarendra Das for inside information about the Kandhamal events. My deepest wish is that this new edition will help spread more understanding and tolerance in the world.

Foreword to the First Edition

VEENA DAS

Felix Padel's book on the theme of sacrifice as it organized colonial discourse is one of the most provocative readings of the colonial archive. By showing how sacrifice provided a master trope—tracing its movements between the administrative and the missionary imaginary—Padel opens up an important question, which has been generally avoided since Frazer. Briefly the question may be posed as follows. Frazer thought that many of the customary practices observed in contemporary times such as the burning of an effigy evoke a sense of dread because they recall the practice of human sacrifice. Wittgenstein, in his comments on Frazer, doubted that any historical explanation would be adequate to explain the sense of dread—for what is being burnt is after all not a human being but only an effigy. How do we come to read meaning in ritual practices and what is it that gives depth to what we perceive?

Padel's great accomplishment in this book is to introduce the idea that ritual practices are not about timeless events which embody fundamental human ideas about the meaning of life and death, rather these are framed by concrete historical processes: the meaning we ascribe to such practices is mired in these historical constructions. Like other social practices, rituals also come to be experienced as part of the forms of life in which linguistic practices and social forms are interwined. Thus the dread that we feel at the idea of the taking of human life has also been formed through discursive formations which position us to see it in certain ways.

The Konds, in terms of chronology, were one of the first tribes in India to be brought under British control. According to their own self-understanding the British were engaged in processes of pacification and subjection rather than in a war of conquest. The eradication of the brutal custom of human sacrifice among the Konds was seen as a major reason why these wars against the Kond chiefs had to be waged. An uncritical acceptance of the British official language by many historians and anthropologists positions us to see these events in terms of these organizing images—Padel's achievement is to have blurred this picture. He argues that what was horrifying about human sacrifice to the British was its closeness to judicial execution and capital punishment. Both kinds of customs were, after all, about the taking of human life. It must be remembered in this context that there was a phenomenal rise in the number of executions in eighteenth century England. What is more, the death penalty was freely used for crimes against property. Thus respect for individual property was instilled not because of a new consciousness about the rights of the individual but because of the brutal use of the power of the state to deprive people of their lives. In the colonies, various penal measures including judicial execution were used to inculcate 'respect for the law'—regardless, or perhaps *because*, of the fact that this was a law imposed from the outside. It may also be recalled here that from the sixteenth to the eighteenth century, statutory provisions existed in the United Kingdom for the supply of a number of gallows corpses to the Companies of Barbers and Surgeons for purposes of dissection. This was widely resented among the general population. The Anatomy Act of 1832 allowed requisition of the dead bodies of those who had died in institutions and for whom provisions for funeral expenses had not been made, for purposes of medical training and research. Thus a conflict over the right over death was not only evident in the colonies but also in the home country. In this context, it is interesting to see how the British legitimized the divisions between human sacrifice and judicial executions, law and mere custom.

The discursive formulations around the tropes of innocence and crime were deployed for creating the boundaries between human sacrifice and judicial execution. The former was based on the idea of taking the lives of the innocent, the latter on the idea that the state reinstated the rule of law by taking the lives of the criminals. We have known since Dumezil's pioneering work in this area that judicial executions bear the signs of their birth from sacrifice. Thus the very closeness of these notions required sharp boundaries to be drawn between these two practices. The criminality of the state in taking of human life is hidden by the elaborate creation of procedural rules and rituals that would separate judicial execution from sacrifice. It is interesting to see that there is an ambivalence within the administrative discourse itself with regard to this question: a purely rational calculation would not have justified the tremendous cost of warfare in terms of human lives lost. Padel quotes from a letter from Macpherson to the Governor General laying out the justifications of his proposed coercive measures and testifying to the 'deep regrets which I necessarily feel that every consideration of policy and of humanity appears to dictate the coercive measures which I have been carrying out and those which I now propose ...' (p. 85). Critics within the colonial government were more apt to apply a utilitarian calculus to these coercive measures: 'if we calculate only the sacrifice of life which has attended the Agent's operations during the last years, far greater probably than arising from the Meriah rites in many years, we may pause to reflect whether the cause of humanity would be advanced by such means ...' (p. 85). This debate summarizes the issue: does the taking of human life through sacrifice hold a larger meaning for humanity than the taking of life through wars or through judicial executions? Clearly the creation of boundaries between these different ways of taking life was made to signal the difference between barbarity and civilization.

A second important theme in this configuration is the idea of 'humanity'. It is widely recognized that the late eighteenth and early nineteenth centuries saw the dual revolution of industrial and technological practices on the one hand and political practices inherent in the French Revolution on the other. The transformations of individual disciplines and of the intellectual environments of specific places such as Edinburgh of the late Scottish Enlightenment and Gottingen of the German Enlightenment shaped ideas about the free use of reason in the formation of public spheres. Many have argued that the emergence of social sciences was intimately related to the enlightenment assumptions about reason. Some recent work, however, questions the notion that the two features of modernity, viz. social sciences and nation state can be seen as a continuity of the Enlightenment traditions. Rather, the specifically modern form of polity that emerged during the French Revolution, the modern nation state, provides the backdrop for understanding the ways in which the Enlightenment project was drastically curtailed, including its idea of free public spheres and its commitment to cosmopolitanism.

Padel's formulation on some of these issues adds an interesting dimension to this discussion. For if colonialism was the shadow of nationalism, and both were modern forms of organizing the polity, then it is interesting to see how the idea of 'humanity' provided a justification for the coercive measures used on colonized peoples. In the case of the Konds, human sacrifice provided the master trope for classifying them as people devoid of the capacity of reason. The stereotypes of the Konds assimilated them to animals, hence civilizing them was seen as akin to the domestication of animals. Force was justified against those who had placed themselves beyond the pale of civilization. The appeal to common humanity here served to introduce hierarchies that made reason the dividing line between those with whom one could enter into a conversation and those against whom force had to be used as a matter of necessity. In formulating their own interventions as actions on behalf of *humanity* rather than for any particular constellation of interests, the colonial administration was able to appropriate the category of sacrifice for their actions. Thus despite the formal opposition between the missionaries and the colonial administration, Padel discovers an interesting symbiosis here, for both could be seen to engage in a form of Christian sacrifice. The title of such texts as 'India cries out to British humanity' foregrounds the plight of those who, though innocent, were forcefully deprived of life by 'barbaric' customs such as *sati*, *thugee*, and the rites of Meriah sacrifice by the Konds. The dense formulations of the ideas through which the innocence of the victims, the presumed barbarity of those who took their lives, and the imperative to act to save the victims, created the necessary boundaries between human sacrifice and judicial execution—the latter being premised upon the criminality and presumed guilt of those who were killed and thus separated from the killing of the innocent.

What happened to the Meriah children who were saved, often it appeared, when they were at the brink of losing their lives? Here the record is anything but encouraging—many children died in the process of being rescued, others ran away. Those who were successfully incorporated into civilized life often ended up serving as servants in upper class or upper caste household establishments of British or Indian families. Success cases of British strategies of rescue and re-education of Meriah children, though few in number were aggressively displayed. Such children grew up to be either faithful, valiant soldiers in the colonial army or became the first converts to Christianity and faithful soldiers of Christ. An interesting parallel between British policies in the colonies and French policies instituted in the seventeenth century with regard to orphans may be seen here. As French social historians have shown, a major justification for the investment of the state in saving the lives of orphans by transferring them to state institutions was given on the grounds that orphans would make the most valiant soldiers, ready to die for the country, since they would not be hampered by attachments to family and kin. As in the case of establishing rights over the *death* of its subjects, how the state came to establish rights over their *lives* has fascinating beginnings in both metropolitan centres and colonies. Which populations became the subjects of the practice of these new technologies of power, though, was obviously differentially distributed.

There are other important strands in Padel's argument; I indicate one. In establishing indirect rule over the tribal populations the British administration conceived of the Hindu *rajahs* as having rulership over the tribal subjects. Padel points out that the relationship between the Hindu *rajahs* and the tribal chiefs was of a different order altogether. While Sanskrit texts on statecraft carry advice for the king on how to establish control over tribal populations living at the edge of the kingdom, from the point of view of the Kond chiefs the Hindu *rajahs* were there to serve their needs. Padel gives evidence of the traditional rights of the Konds to appoint or dismiss a *rajah*. Further, the fusion of tribal and Hindu polity seems to have provided several modes of mediation between the tribal chiefs and the Hindu *rajahs*. One of the most striking conceptions is of *rajahs* as those through whom the tribal chiefs 'tasted the outside world'. Consider the statement of a Kond to Macpherson's agent that is quoted to great effect by Padel (p. 132): 'we use the *rajah* as a spoon to taste the food from the fire—that way the spoon gets burnt, but not the mouth'. This relationship was completely misunderstood by the British who assumed that they could proclaim new laws through the mediation of the Hindu *rajahs* whereas the *rajahs* were keen that it should be made perfectly evident to the Konds that they were not acting as free agents when they asked them to hand over the Meriah children to the British officials. This is a very different picture of power and hierarchy than has been assumed not only in colonial literature but also in the anthropological literature on tribe-caste relations. I am not sure that Padel draws out the full implications of his own findings and we often find him resorting to conventional categories of outside domination, or a long common adivasi identity stretching from the Eastern parts of India to Burma and Indonesia. In my reading his book provides considerable evidence that what is seen as quintessential tribal custom, such as human sacrifice, was a result of complex interactions between the tribal polity and its placement within the wider medieval polity and economy. This is how I understand the patronage of the Hindu *rajahs* to the custom as well as the processes of buying and selling through which the Doms managed to procure the children through sale or abduction. Thus instead of the innocence of the Konds versus the capricious nature of the British colonizers, this book showed me that neither stories of progress nor those of complete decline as characteristic of the colonial period would do. Instead it is the tensions, the mistranslations, and the innovations in new technologies of power that were brought in by the British rule which are interesting. Other readers with greater sympathy to ideas of holism or a greater attachment to tradition may draw very different conclusions. It is due to the fidelity to the sources, that Padel maintains throughout the book that others may sometimes read it against the author's own inclinations. In any case, this is a stimulating book on the nature of colonial power and an important contribution to our understanding of tribal communities in history.

Preface to the First Edition

This book is an anthropological study of the structures of power and authority which British rule imposed on a tribal people of Central India. I have not done fieldwork in the usual sense. My field of study is colonial culture. It emerged from the experience of turning the gaze of anthropological scrutiny into a mirror that reflects back onto 'modern' society. I have visited tribal villages not to study them, but to meet and learn from people of a different culture, and I have used this experience to study the world I come from and the ways it has imposed on these people.

My starting point is a paradox, for in order to perceive the essence of colonialism I have chosen the most confronting example possible: British conquest of a tribal people who apparently practised human sacrifice as a ritual of propitiation for the earth. Human sacrifice seems the most inhuman of customs. We tend to associate it with a 'savage', 'barbarian' way of life. Yet it is a practice that at least affirms that a human life is something sacred and of great value. It is easy to see that the level of violence in 'modern' society is actually much higher. The atrocities of the Nazis and those being perpetrated now in Bosnia and many other places, as well as the industry and trade in weapons that feed such conflicts at the same time as creating profit for an elite, not only represent a much greater violence: they utterly negate this sacredness of human life. So in many ways the forms of power and authority that have evolved in Western society and have been imposed on people of other cultures, ostensibly to 'civilize' them, involve a cruelty and inhumanity that go beyond human sacrifice, sacrificing the essence of what it means to be human.

The first chapter introduces the relevant background issues as well as some of my conclusions. The next four enter the world of British officials and the contrasting world of the human sacrifices which they set out to suppress, from the first clash of scarlet-uniformed sepoys with tribal warriors, to the repressive norms of interaction that were soon established by policemen and other junior officials who exploited tribals on a regular basis.

Chapters six and seven examine the roles of missionary and anthropologist. If administrators' and colonists' conquest and extortion represent a basic level of external domination, missionary activity represents another, subtler level of the same process, in the name of 'saving savages' from themselves. Anthropological analysis of tribal culture represents a yet subtler level, by producing a highly 'scientific' but dehumanizing discourse that expropriates or undermines the people's own sense of who they are.

The final chapter is a brief survey of the modern situation of 'internal colonialism'. In some ways modern, independent India has carried the oppressive features of British rule still further, despite the most liberal intentions. The cycles of exploitation established during British rule continue: tribal people are thrown off their land in huge numbers, and their own voices and forms of knowledge are denied by a mainstream population that largely despises them.

This book is a rewritten version of my doctoral thesis in Social Anthropology, which I completed in 1987 from Oxford University, with affiliated status at the Department of Sociology in the Delhi School of Economics, Delhi University.[1]

Now that I have completed my revision of this text, I can see all my doubts and contradictory feelings about it in a clearer perspective. This has been a painful book to write, and much of what I say may seem controversial.

My main aim is to understand what has been imposed on tribal people, by looking objectively at the various groups of people who have imposed on them. By 'objectively', I mean examining their attitudes and behaviour in a wide perspective, in their whole context, taking nothing about them for granted, and looking beneath the surface, behind the mask of their own idealized image of their actions and motives, to reveal their 'shadow' side: their less pleasant or 'unconscious' side, that has affected tribal people more or less destructively. This means that what I write may offend, or be experienced as an attack, by people who identify with these groups. My purpose is not to attack, and I often feel uncomfortable doing this 'unmasking'. In a sense the administrator, the missionary, and the anthropologist are in all of us. Certainly they are roles I am familiar with inside myself, and in exposing their less pleasant side I have put myself through much inner conflict. But this is something that I feel needs to be done, simply to get a clearer understanding of what has been imposed on tribal people.

Secondly, I have taken as my example, a situation that fits the colonial outlook perfectly: British officials imposed their rule in order to suppress human sacrifice and female infanticide, apparently with the highest of motives. My argument is that in fact this involved a *sacrifice of life* as great as took place by human sacrifice, as well as a *sacrifice of human being*—a much greater, yet less visible and much more indirect mode of violence. But the very fact of taking as my example one of the very few tribal peoples who did actually practise human sacrifice runs the risk of reinforcing the very stereotype which I wish to combat—the negative view of tribal people as 'savages'. Human sacrifice is a dangerous subject, yet I feel that there is great value in facing it and believe that a key to many of the horrible situations where human cruelty is on the rampage may lie in trying to understand it. My hope is that this book will give people insight that will in some way help to heal some of the intolerance and cruelty in the world.

Thirdly, in exposing the role of the anthropologist, I am exposing myself. A vast gulf exists between tribal and academic perceptions—a gulf that has rarely, if ever, been bridged. It seems to me that there is something in the academic approach that makes it impossible to actually communicate with tribal people on an equal basis, or genuinely learn from them, except in having them as 'informants'. The 'knowledge' about tribals which anthropologists have created is virtually a closed system, in which tribals themselves have no say, or no authority to question. Behind the mask of objectivity, colonial anthropology defined them in terms that are basically extremely negative, and reinforced the worst stereotypes about them.

Yet in writing this book, I am obeying, more or less, the very academic conventions which I am calling into question, writing something that is 'only for intellectuals' in as much as it is academically correct—a 'meta-discourse', even further removed from a tribal idiom than the colonial discourse which I analyse. On the other hand, in as much as the book questions academic conventions it may seem subversive. I often feel torn apart by these alternatives. I have therefore tried to find a balance between them, writing for scholars at the same time as trying to communicate a difficult subject humanly and openly, for anyone who is prepared to venture into it.

A main part of my method is to let people from a multitude of different perspectives speak for themselves through extensive quotations. I have kept the original spellings in these quoted passages, since the variety of spellings is part of this variety of perspectives.

The main research and series of insights that led to this book took place in Delhi University, so I have a special debt to my two main guides there: to Professor J.P.S. Uberoi, who was my Associate Supervisor from 1982 to 1988, I owe the idea of focusing on human sacrifice, and acknowledge profound thanks for his frank discussions of my work—sometimes traumatic but overall extremely fruitful; and to Professor Veena Das, I owe the idea of analysing administrative, missionary and anthropological discourse as three strands in the colonial power structure, and great thanks for the interest and encouragement she has always shown in my work. I would also like to thank Dr N.J. Allen, my supervisor in Oxford, for his encouragement, patience and helpful criticism, and Professor André Béteille for all he has taught me. The shortcomings of this book, of course, are my responsibility alone. For four years of postgraduate financial support I am indebted to the Social Science Research Council of the UK.

Two friends to whom I feel particular gratitude are Madhu Ramnath, who has supported and confronted me at every stage of my entry into tribal India (a process painfully slow and full of mistakes), and who has taught me much of what I know about tribal life; and Rebecca Oliner, who drafted the maps, and has played a similar supporting-and-confronting role as I completed this book, and helped me to trust myself in giving it out to the world. Among many other people who have given me invaluable help, I would like to thank the following friends and colleagues for their various contributions: Roma Chatterji, Krystyna Cech, Chandrakanta Das, Luis Esparza, Amitav Ghosh, Wendy James, Sophie Johnson, Prashanto Jones, Kusum Gopal, Louisa Gosling, Richard Grove, K. Jayaram, Mukul Kesavan, Chris MacDonaugh, Deepak Mehta, Suleyman Mowat, Jeremy Naydler, Elly Oenema, John and Hilda Padel, Oliver Padel, Ruth Padel, John Palmer, Robert Parkin, Rajendra Pradhan,

Rabindra Ray, Savyasaachi, Hilmar Schönauer, Hari Sen, Keith Skirrow, Lynn Teskey-Denton, Khalid Tyabji, Piers Vitebsky and Punam Zutshi. Without these and other people's support and discussion of the ideas in this book I could not have written it.

I acknowledge great thanks as well to tribal villagers in Central India for welcoming me, and for what they have taught me—which is enough to know that their cultures contain a wealth of knowledge and human contact that most of the literature on them barely hints at, and to show me the huge potential, the mystery, and the humour of what it means to be a human being.

CHAPTER ONE

A Case Study of Colonialism

Nirantali and the Creation of Earth

In Central India there are magnificent forests, heartland of the tiger, as well as leopards, bears, elephants, and many other creatures. The people who live in these forest areas are *adivasis*, India's 'original inhabitants' or 'aboriginals', tribal people who have evolved a way of life suited to the forest over countless generations. The men grow their hair long, wear a short loincloth, and carry an axe or bow and arrows when walking between settlements. Between men and women there is a constant laughter and banter. Dancing to drums and the singing of love songs are at the heart of these cultures.

They differ in significant ways from India's mainstream Hindu culture. To a large extent they are outside the caste system, eating meat and drinking alcohol. They have shamans as well as priests, and practise a religion that is based on a reverence for nature and revolves around the forest and the forces of nature: changes of season, water and fire, fertility and death, disease and healing. There is nothing sentimental about this reverence. It is part of a way of life that involves the killing of plants and animals in a continuous cycle, for food. But this killing is performed with a precise knowledge of nature's laws and limits, as well as a profound respect for the spirit world that manifests through nature.

Among many other tribes there is one called the Konds, who live in the forested, mountainous interior of Orissa. The Konds' chief deities are Darni Penu the Earth Goddess, and Bura Penu the Sky God. Their main culture-hero is a woman, or female being, whom some Konds call Nirantali, who seems to be a human incarnation of the Earth Goddess.[1]

> In the beginning there was nothing but water. Nirantali-Kapantali emerged to the earth's surface at Saphaganna. After her came other gods and the first humans, who were Konds. But how could humans live in all that water? They went to Nirantali and begged her for help. Eventually the water sank down and rock emerged, but there still was no earth, until Nirantali produced it. Some say she got it from her hair, some say she was angry and spat and her spit turned into white ants which excreted the earth, and others say she sent the Konds to search for earth, and when they could not find it, in despair, they besought a mountain of rock and scratched it with their nails, like bears, until it took pity on them and they could excavate earth. They took four handfuls of earth,—black, white, red and yellow—which Nirantali told them to throw in the four directions. Now the earth was spread over the rock, but it still was not firm—when they stepped on it their feet went through. So they set up a bamboo pole and sacrificed a cow, a buffalo and a pig before it, and the earth became hard and dry. The bones of their victims became rocks and the hair became trees and grass. Nirantali created other creatures and plants from beeswax and the dirt on her body.[2]

Every Kond village possesses different myths. To an outsider the variety of characters and versions appears confusing or even contradictory. But some of the main characters and patterns emerge clearly from those which have been collected and published. In particular, the Konds' honour for the earth and sky, whom they take as their main deities, is clear.

Yet many people in India still despise tribal cultures. As with India's other tribes, Kond culture contains much wisdom, and the quality of life in Kond villages is in many ways very high. This quality is being eroded: outsiders exploit *adivasis* and expropriate their land, looking on them with contempt as 'backward' and 'ignorant'. Even taking a positive view of tribal cultures or trying to protect them is often labelled romantic or 'isolationist'. So it is well if I state now that I write this book out of a sense of profound admiration for tribal societies, with the aim of combating prejudice against them, and helping to understand how the present system of exploitation has evolved. I do this by making a case study of the Konds' experience of colonial rule, analysing the forms of power which the British imposed over them.

On the Meaning of Sacrifice

The negative stereotype of tribals stresses their 'savagery' and fastens upon the most violent or incomprehensible features of their cultures. Supreme among these is the Konds' former custom of human sacrifice.

> At first the Konds sacrificed only coconuts to their gods. But Darni Penu was not satisfied with coconuts, she wanted blood. They offered her every kind of animal, but she said "No. Sacrifice a human being to me." The Konds refused—"We'll die rather than do that." But when they refused, she sent a terrible drought that threatened to exterminate all of mankind. It went on and on until, in despair, the Konds agreed to her request. She sent the first victim to them herself. In this way human sacrifice began. The goddess was pleased and gave the people good harvests. And so it continued until Mukman Saheb and Kiamol Saheb came along and stopped it. Since then buffaloes have been sacrificed to her instead.[3]

The British stamped out these sacrifices 150 years ago. Mukman and Kiamol are Kond names for Macpherson and Campbell, the two main officials involved. As they saw it:

> The astounding discovery was....made that we included amongst our fellow subjects a whole people who practised human sacrifice and female infanticide on a scale and with a cruelty which had never been surpassed by the most savage of nations.... The Meriah sacrifices, as they were called, and Kandh female infanticide, may be regarded as amongst the plague spots of the land which have been effectively cured and obliterated by the enlightened treatment and strong hand of the British Government. (Dalton 1872 pp.285–6)

In taking such a tribe as a case to study colonialism, I am conscious of taking the most challenging case possible: if ever a colonial power was right to conquer a tribe, surely suppressing human sacrifice was a valid reason? And yet, I will argue that this 'enlightened treatment and strong hand' involved a greater, more insidious form of human sacrifice.

What then do we mean by sacrifice? In the West we have apparently done away with blood sacrifices of animals, unless we count the 'paschal' lambs still offered at Easter in some rural parts of Europe. Does this mean that we have done away with sacrifice, since we no longer practise it in its classical form (e.g. as Hubert and Mauss defined it, 1898)? As anthropologists we can come up with definitions of sacrifice, but as ordinary people how do we and modern culture in general actually use it as an idea? Obviously the *concept* of sacrifice is still extremely important to us, partly through mainstream religious traditions: we speak of sacrificing ourselves—for our work, or following the example of Christ, soldiers for their country, or parents for their children; and of sacrificing one thing for the sake of another, though usually without formalized ritual, and often without any idea of sacredness.

The *Bhagavad Gita* takes a view of sacrifice that goes far beyond the ancient blood ritual, just as Christianity does.[4] To live, we have to sacrifice. To live fully we have to make major sacrifices; any major decision or action involves the sacrifice of other options or things or beings: sometimes an animal's life, and occasionally, in extreme circumstances, a human life, the upshot of Krishna's advice to Arjuna in the *Bhagavad Gita*, persuading him to initiate the great battle of the *Mahabharata*. Finally, each of us has to give up our life, and some see this, our own death, as a sacrifice.

Hindu and Christian texts speak of different kinds of sacrifice, among which the higher forms involve offering one's work or actions as sacrifice, which could mean simply living one's life making choices conscious of the relative values at stake. At the other extreme are 'dreadful austerities', such as human sacrifice, which the *Gita* suggests are less truly effective forms of sacrifice. As for those who no longer recognize a need for sacrifice at all—do they sacrifice unconsciously? In the secular sense in which the word is often used now, 'sacrifice' often means destroying or throwing away things of great value, including human lives, for the sake of something else which is of less real value, such as immediate profit: an inverted or negative sense of 'sacrifice' that has lost the original meaning of sacrifice as 'making sacred'.

What I am suggesting differs from the definitions of sacrifice in most social anthropology.[5] The decline of animal sacrifices or religious belief does not mean that ideas about sacrifice are no longer an important part of our lives—or that we no longer sacrifice. How can we expect to understand other cultures' modes of sacrifice, if we have not brought our own into conscious consideration? And if we look at the Western lifestyle as creating huge wealth for an elite at the expense of the majority of humans in the world, and at the cost of ruining our natural environment, does it not make sense to understand the costs of this lifestyle in terms of human sacrifice?[6]

To sacrifice an animal to a deity is an action I cannot easily understand, because it is not familiar to me. And yet, from what I have seen, it seems much more respectful and humane than the way animals are killed in slaughterhouses in my own culture. Human sacrifice, as the Konds apparently practised it, is a custom I find extremely difficult to understand. But again, when I look for equivalent expressions of violence in my own culture, I find the arms industry, huge wars, vicious cycles of terrorism and state repression, street violence and murders, as well as the sacrifice of the environment and thus also the sacrifice of future generations of human beings, which is at the heart of our industrial lifestyle. By contrast with this, the Konds' occasional sacrifice of a human life to their Earth Goddess, has the character of a conscious expression of the sacrifice of human life that is intrinsic to other societies at a more unconscious level. Even in terms of numbers, the British probably *sacrificed* more lives in suppressing the practice and imposing 'peace' on the Konds, than were killed in the sacrifices over many years.

The Kond sacrifices sound horrible, and I feel thankful they are over. But the regime which the British set up over the Konds, as over other tribes in India, I have come to see as based on *a sacrifice of human being*—something much subtler and less visible, but more destructive to the essence of human life than the Konds' custom. I am also in a better position to comprehend it, by examining the British culture I come from and its forms of violence, which I feel I can understand to a greater depth than is allowed either by the glorification of the British Raj or the reaction against that. The Kond custom is, to me, an unknown, something that no amount of anthropological analysis would make me able to understand, so I feel unable to judge it.

This is to turn on its head the conventional history of human civilization, in which there is an evolution from savagery and barbarism, characterized by such horrors as human sacrifice, to modern, civilized, largely peaceful society. When we try to understand modern wars and oppression it is evident something has gone terribly wrong with the civilizing process. The Nazi attempt to exterminate the Jewish people is aptly termed the 'holocaust', which refers to a sacrifice where the whole offering is consumed by fire. The massacres in Cambodia under Pol Pot, the present wars in Angola or former Yugoslavia, and numerous other recent conflicts have a similar genocidal aspect. The usual view is to see these atrocities as outbreaks of primitiveness. Instead, what if we see them as the logical conclusion of forms of power that have developed over hundreds of years, whose trend is to dehumanize—to sacrifice the essence of being human?

We may well choose to see rituals of human sacrifice as killing that is cruel and unnecessary, dictated through a bondage to superstition, but at least they affirm the sanctity of the human life that is taken. Modern forms of violence such as those just mentioned, removed from the idiom of sacrifice, deny that sanctity completely. And it is these forms that have been turned against tribal people, again and again. Human sacrifice is thus a subject that takes us to the heart of colonialism, and the study of domination.

Indeed, the negative sense of sacrifice still plays a very important part in atrocities such as 'ethnic cleansing' or genocide. Certainly the idea of self-sacrifice is an inspiring force in most wars. The colonial officials and missionaries we shall meet were undoubtedly motivated to 'give their lives' in pursuit of their duty or the saving of souls. So were many thousands of communist revolutionaries in China and other countries, at the same time as they 'removed dead wood'. Sacrificing themselves, it seems, made them capable of sacrificing people who stood in their way, in the negative sense of exterminating them. For those who sacrifice themselves for some cause, whether for the honour of the group they identify with, or for their religion or ideology, establish power over other people that is to a great extent based in, or justified by, their sacrifice.

So this is a book about power, or the abuse of power: how people of one culture come to dominate people of another, imposing an alien authority onto them. My motive in choosing this subject is my own need to understand human violence and cruelty: its seeds in human beings like you and me, and how it is generated in so many parts of the world, when seemingly normal people become inhuman. Also, because I felt a hidden level of violence and domination in the practice of anthropology, specifically in the way that anthropologists have often written about tribal people in India. This book is my response: an attempt to turn the focus of anthropological enquiry back onto ourselves, and onto the exercise of authority in modern societies. In a colonial setting this appears in stark relief, so it seems a good place to start; also because a colonial regime is a frontier where modern, Western forms of power have been imposed onto another society.

I approach the subject of human sacrifice with considerable trepidation, because it touches on the most negative features of human society, including tribal religion, in which I find much that is of the greatest value. Human sacrifice is not at all typical of tribal cultures, and there are relatively few that are actually known to have practised it—certainly not as openly as the Konds apparently did.[7] More commonly the conquest of tribal peoples has been justified in terms of 'pacifying' them out of 'a state of war'—though this has usually been a much smaller scale of warfare

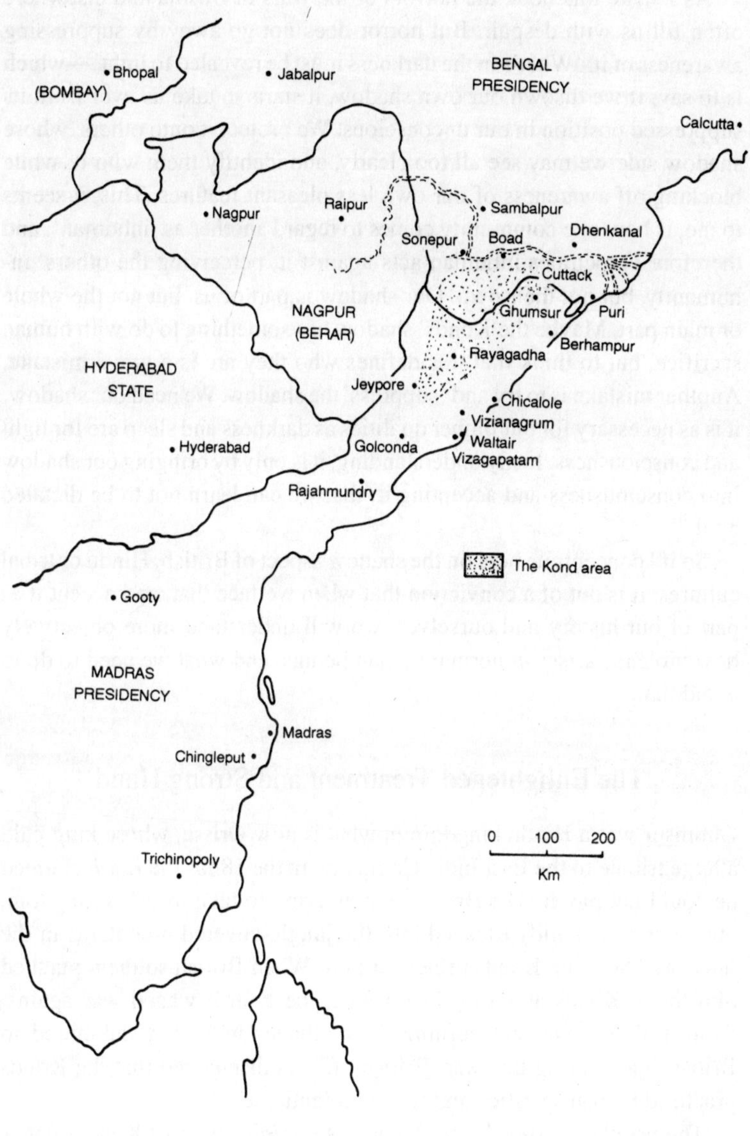

Map 1: The Kond area between Madras and Bengal Presidencies in the 1830s

than the military machine which the colonials turned against them in conquest.

As I write this book the horrors of the wars in Bosnia and elsewhere often fill us with despair. But horror does not go away by suppressing awareness of it. 'What's in the darkness must be revealed to light'—which is to say: if we disown our own shadow, it starts to take us over from its suppressed position in our unconscious. We project it onto others, whose shadow side we may see all too clearly, and identify them with it, while blocking off awareness of our own less pleasant features. This, it seems to me, is how one community comes to regard another as 'inhuman', and therefore perpetrates inhuman acts against it, perceiving the others' inhumanity, but not their own. Our shadow is part of us, but not the whole or main part. Maybe the Konds' shadow has something to do with human sacrifice, but to think that this defines who they are is a grave mistake. Another mistake is to try and 'suppress' the shadow. We need our shadow: it is as necessary for our higher qualities as darkness and sleep are for light and consciousness. In my understanding, it is only by bringing our shadow into consciousness and accepting it, that we can learn not to be dictated by it.[8]

So if I concentrate here on the shadow aspect of British, Hindu or tribal cultures, it is out of a conviction that when we face that, and accept it as part of our history and ourselves, we will understand more objectively how violence arises in normal human beings, and what we need to do to avoid that.

'The Enlightened Treatment and Strong Hand'

Ghumsur was a Hindu kingdom in what is now Orissa, whose king paid a large tribute to the East India Company. In the 1830s the *rajah* claimed he could not pay it. The British sent an army to take over his kingdom, but he and his family escaped into the jungle-covered mountains in the interior, where the Konds protected him. When British soldiers pursued him there, Konds attacked. In revenge, the British waged war against them, killing them and burning their villages until they submitted to British rule. During this war, British officers discovered that the Konds practised human sacrifice and female infanticide.

The people sacrificed were known as *meriahs*. In most Kond villages there were several *meriahs*. Not all were sacrificed. Konds bought them as children from Doms, members of a trading caste who lived among the Konds, and who kidnapped the *meriah* children or bought them from impoverished parents. In some ways they were like serfs, yet often Konds treated them as equals. They married and lived a normal life most of the time, but their children inherited *meriah* status. It was for the priests to declare which *meriah* the goddess wanted on any occasion. So the British began taking the *meriahs* from the villages to save them, though often the *meriahs* had grown up there and did not want to leave. The British demand to give up the *meriahs* became symbolic to Konds, as well as to the British, of a demand to accept British rule. Captain John Campbell was the first officer in charge of these operations. Captain S.C. Macpherson succeeded him, and was put in charge of a special Agency for the Suppression of Human Sacrifice and Female Infanticide in the Hill Tracts of Orissa—the Meriah Agency for short.

At one point Macpherson apparently pressed the demand for *meriahs* too hard, and the Konds of a wide area refused to submit and began an armed resistance. Macpherson sent for a large army and a second war was fought (1846–7). The Government blamed him for causing it and dismissed him, although an enquiry later exonerated him. Meanwhile Campbell had been sent back to take charge of operations. In the following years he and a handful of other officers extended British rule over the whole area where Konds lived, which they estimated as similar in size to Wales.

Macpherson and Campbell disputed the credit for stamping out the sacrifices; as well as the trustworthiness of each other's Indian staff. They also took very different views of Kond religion. Macpherson collected detailed ethnographic material about Kond gods, rituals and myths; as a piece of Victorian anthropology it is surprisingly sensitive, but Campbell did not believe a word of it.[9]

In the 1860s a police force was set up over the Konds. Its administration was left mostly to Indian officers, one of whom, the *tahsildar* Dinobandu Patnaik, held a 'reign of terror' in the 1880s (Bailey 1960 pp.177–8). Konds occasionally took up their weapons again to try and resist the increasing level of exploitation that was imposed on them by the combined forces of Government officials and Hindu colonists, moneylenders and landlords. The Kalahandi rebellion of 1882 was the most potent of these. But the level of Government control increased in the 1930s with the introduction of laws 'reserving' most of their forest, which restricted the Konds' traditional rights to cut it periodically to make fields, and to gather and hunt in it.

Missionaries began their work with the conversion of some of the *meriah* children taken from Kond villages. They made occasional trips to the Kond hills, and set up a residential Mission there in the 1900s. At first few Konds became Christian, but from the 1950s many began converting to the various sects on offer, apparently because Christianity was no longer identified with the Government and offered a defence against Hindu exploitation.

From the time of their conquest, the Konds were given a standard attention by anthropologists in Government publications.[10] The custom of human sacrifice earned them a prominent place in Frazer's *Golden Bough*. Verrier Elwin, the English anthropologist who came to identify his life with tribal India, made several tours of Kond areas. He never published the book he intended on the Konds, so I have consulted his 1940s Kond fieldwork notes, which are in Delhi.[11] More recent anthropological works contain a lot of interesting information and insights into Kond culture, yet between this writing and the way that Konds see and express themselves, there is a massive gulf of understanding.[12] Trying to bridge or comprehend this gulf has been my starting point.

These are the bare bones of the events and situations which I analyse in this book. I analyse them as an exercise in historical anthropology by *deconstructing* them as a colonial myth, looking below the surface, so as to reach some understanding of the unconscious as well as conscious structures. My conviction is that the seeds of the present situation lie in the past, and that seeing clearly what was imposed can give us the insight necessary for healing in the present. My aim is to study colonial imposition on a tribe by focusing on the three main groups of colonials involved, who represent three distinct yet interdependent roles—administrators, missionaries and anthropologists.

So I have chosen a particularly dramatic, seemingly 'perfect' case of British rule at its best: one of the great inspiring myths of British India, like Sleeman's suppression of the *Thugs*.[13] As such, it generated considerable literature, which is highly charged with emotion, not least because much of it was motivated by the differences between the great Mukman and Kiamol Sahebs.

The crucial activity of the three groups therefore occurred at different times. Administrators laid down their norms of interaction with Konds in the crucial first thirty years of British rule. Missionaries started their activities at that time but began to be successful only after the end of British rule, although this success was clearly a product or after-effect of British rule. With anthropologists likewise, I trace the patterns established during British rule into the practice of anthropology since Independence.

This subject arises out of my own feeling of a great need to understand colonial imposition on tribal India in greater depth. To survey the present situation of India's tribal people, is to see, on one side, a range of vital cultures that survive intact in India's remoter areas of forest and mountains; on the other, a mass of 'problems', which largely stem from the systematic oppression and exploitation of tribals by the mainstream population. Two of the most detailed recent surveys of the situation, the 1989 report of India's Tribal Commissioner, B.D. Sharma, and Fürer-Haimendorf's *Tribes of India: The struggle for survival* (1982), reveal this very clearly. A cycle has been recognized of extortion by Government officials, moneylending at impossibly high rates of interest, displacement of tribal people from their land, and conditions of slave labour that they are forced into to survive. In the background is an enormous prejudice against tribal people and their culture, as well as a system of law that has illegalized much of tribal people's forest-based way of life. Added to this, since India's Independence, in one generation, industrial development has displaced vast numbers of tribal people from their homelands to make way for dams, mines and factories.

The Kond Tribe

I feel that my own experience and background put me in a strong position for understanding the culture of British colonialism in some depth. Coming from an intellectual English family, and studying Classics and Social Anthropology at Oxford, I went on to do a degree in Sociology at Delhi University. There, under the influence of friends and teachers, I started to question many things about the intellectual tradition I grew up in. At the same time, I started to visit tribal areas, and to feel at home in three quite different cultures—for tribal India is as different from mainstream India, as that is from Britain, or more so. I have visited tribal villages not as an anthropologist, but as a human being beginning to see the world from the other side.

'Are there Konds in your country too?' When a Kond asked me this question, he made me realize how differently Konds see themselves from the way that the ethnographic tradition defines them—precisely as it defines other tribes, by locating them in a particular area and giving an exact figure for their population. Konds see themselves, quite simply, as one of the main races or divisions of mankind. In their myths, Konds are usually the first human beings to emerge out of the earth, and have a special relationship with the Earth Goddess.

Konds call themselves *Kuwinga* or *Kondho*. This name is probably related to the Telugu word for hill, *konda*.[14] Perhaps in the eyes of their non-tribal neighbours, Konds are the people of the hills. But the name is also probably related to the 'Koya', 'Koitor' or 'Gond'—various names for India's largest tribe who live West of the Konds—and may have some connotation of 'first people' or 'humans', like so many of the names by which tribal peoples call themselves, in India as well as in other countries.

The Konds are Orissa's largest tribe, numbering the best part of a million people.[15] They live over a wide area of southwest Orissa, and speak a language of the Dravidian family like Telugu and Tamil. Two main forms have been officially identified as separate languages, Kui and Kuvi. But though these are not always mutually intelligible (like dialects of Welsh for example), they seem to be close enough to be considered dialects of one language, which possesses a great number of regional dialects.[16] Most Konds also speak some Oriya, the language of Orissa, an Indo-Aryan language like Bengali and Hindi.

Kond villages have a distinctive form, with rows of houses joined under a continuous roof, one row on each side of a wide street—very different from the villages of most other tribes, where households are more separate and dispersed. In the centre of this street there stand wooden poles and piles of large stones which form a shrine of Darni Penu and other village deities. The remotest villages are still sometimes surrounded with stockades for protection against tigers and elephants, as Kond villages were before British rule, when they needed defence against human attack as well. In the more traditional Kond villages, the older boys and girls sleep apart from their parents in 'youth dormitories', one for each sex (or just a boys' one) which are a focus of singing and romance up until the time of marriage. Kond women have patterns tattooed on their faces and arms. Often they wear a mass of heavy metal ornaments, and dress in bright cloth.

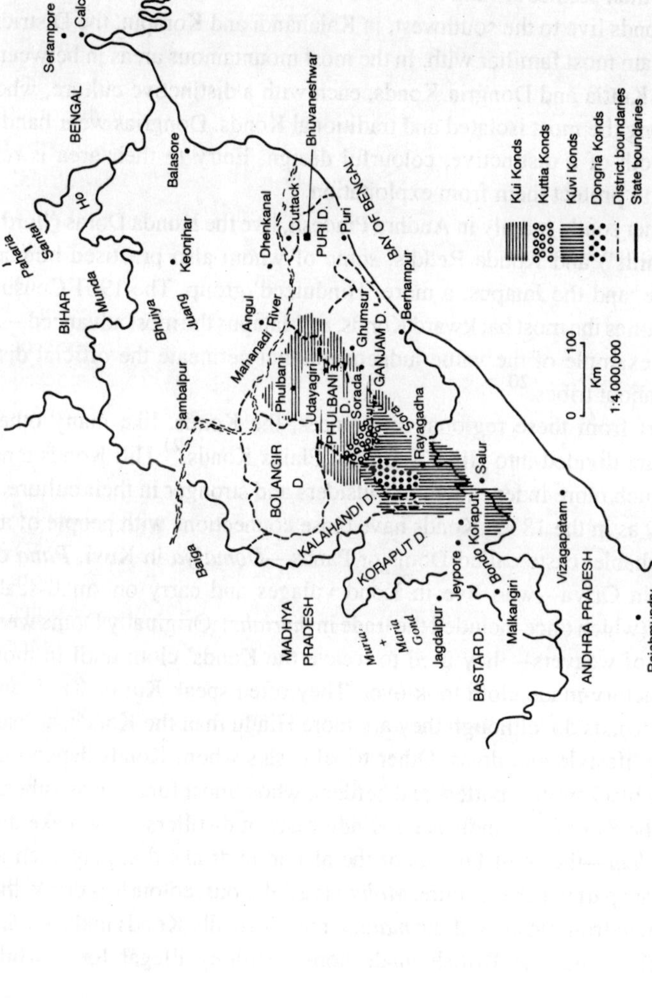

Map 2: The Konds and neighbouring tribes in the districts of modern Orissa

There are many different groups among the Konds. Clans are important in people's identity. Each clan, as well as each section of a clan and each village, has its own territory, and its own ancestors and myths and particular customs or ways of dressing. Apart from this, there are several broader divisions among the Konds, which may have separate origins.[17]

The first Konds to meet the British were the Kui, who are therefore more influenced by the outside world. Some only speak Oriya now. They are concentrated in Phulbani District, where F.G. Bailey and Barbara Boal focused their studies around two of the main administrative centres.[18] The Kuvi Konds live to the southwest, in Kalahandi and Koraput, the District which I am most familiar with. In the most mountainous areas in between live the Kuttia and Dongria Konds, each with a distinctive culture, who are among the most isolated and traditional Konds. Dongrias wear handloom cloth of a distinctive, colourful design. Entry to their area is restricted to protect them from exploitation.[19]

Further south, mainly in Andhra Pradesh, live the Konda Doras ('lords of the hills') and Konda Reddis, some of whom also practised human sacrifice, and the Jatapus, a more 'Hinduized' group. The 1961 Census calls Kuttias the most backward Konds, and Jatapus the most advanced—a typical example of the value judgements that permeate the official discourse about tribes.[20]

Apart from these regional differences, the Konds, like many other tribes, are divided into Hill Konds and Plains Konds.[21] Hill Konds tend to be much more independent of outsiders and stronger in their culture.

Now as in the 1830s Konds have close connections with people of an 'untouchable' caste called Doms or Panos—*Doma'ya* in Kuvi, *Pano* or *Panva* in Oriya—who live in Kond villages and carry on small-scale trading (which once included the trade in *meriahs*). Originally Doms were a caste of weavers—they used to weave the Konds' cloth until in most areas factory-made cloth took over. They often speak Kui or Kuvi, and live as Konds do, although they are more Hindu than the Konds, at least in their lifestyle and dress. Other tribal castes whom Konds depend on include blacksmiths, potters and herders, who almost function as subcastes of the Konds.[22] Sundis are a Hindu caste of distillers; they make and sell *mahua*—the most famous of the alcoholic drinks that play such an important part in tribal culture. *Mahua* is a delicious, colourless drink, that is distilled from flowers of the *mahua* tree. Normally Konds make *mahua* themselves, but the British made home-distilling illegal for a while.

Sundis cashed in on the British licensing laws and used them to exploit the Konds. Today they are still often heavily involved in moneylending at extortionate rates.

Konds also have a close relationship with high caste Hindus. In the 1830s most Konds gave a form of allegiance to Hindu *rajahs*, although this left them largely independent in practice, especially the Hill Konds.

Kond villages, like those of other tribes, show a lot of variety in how far they conform to the non-tribal or modern lifestyle of those around them. When men cut their hair short, this is often a sure sign of conformity, whether to Hindu or Christian norms. In the remoter villages, where men keep their hair long, a way of life continues that has not changed much since the days before British rule.

Several other major tribes are neighbours of the Konds. Each tribe, or section of a tribe, has its own special way of dressing for men and women, its own particular deities and culture heroes, distinctive forms of marriage and rituals of seasonal activities and honour for the ancestors, and different, culturally recognized roles of priests and shamans, male or female. Linguists divide these tribes into those who speak languages of the Dravidian family, as the Konds do, and those whose languages are of the Munda family, which is related to Khmer (Cambodia's main language) and tribal languages of Southeast Asia.[23] Yet for all their differences among themselves, all these *adivasis* share a common tribal culture that connects them, and also links them with tribal peoples further East, from Burma to Indonesia.

The Lanjia Soras live south of the Konds. They speak a Munda language. Many of their fields are elaborately terraced up the sides of mountains, and they erect big stones in memory of those who die. Like Konds, they have female as well as male shamans, and perhaps an even greater interest in the spirit world, although many Soras have converted to Christianity within the last ten years.[24]

The Bondos, or Remo as they call themselves, live southwest of the Konds. They are another Munda-language tribe of only three or four thousand people, who are famous in anthropology (as well as locally) both for their fierceness and readiness to fight, and for the appearance of their women, who shave their heads bald and wear only a tiny loincloth and a great mass of jewelry round their necks. Bondo wives are usually older than their husbands, reversing the norm of most cultures. Near them live the Didayi, or Gataq, another small tribe.[25]

Gadabas live in the same direction. Like Soras, they erect megaliths for their ancestors, as part of a large ritual to honour everyone who has died in the last few years. This ritual involves a sacrifice of buffaloes similar to the Konds' great buffalo sacrifices, killing them by cutting them to pieces with axes. Gadabas are divided into sections with Dravidian and Munda languages—a situation that highlights the uncertainty in the way anthropologists have classified all these tribes.[26] Sora, Bondo and Gadaba women traditionally all wear home-woven cloth made from bark-fibre.

Among the southern Konds live a tribal people known as the Porojas, who speak a Dravidian language quite closely related to the Kond language. Their name apparently comes from the Sanskrit word for 'subject', *praja*, and they are more Hinduized, or acquiescent of outside influence, than some other tribes. But they call themselves by different names, without this connotation of subservience.[27]

The Gonds speak another Dravidian language, having the same word as the Konds for 'god' or 'spirit' (Gond *pen*, Kond *penu*). Some of the headmen of Kond areas are Gonds, who came long ago from the West. Bastar District is the home of the most isolated and traditional Gonds, known as the Muria and Maria.[28]

To the North, across the Mahanadi river, live the Juang, another Munda-language tribe, who have much in common with the remoter Konds, and whose women traditionally wear skirts of leaves instead of woven cloth—or used to, until colonial officials tried to 'civilize' them by making them wear cloth instead.[29]

I shall also refer to several other tribes who live further away from the Konds: the Santals, Mundas, Hos and Paharias to the North; the Baigas and Bhils who live further West; the Todas of the Nilgiri Hills in South India; the Nagas and Abors on India's Northeastern extremity; and the Andaman Islanders.

Tribal Culture

Each of these tribes possesses a distinctive language and culture; but there are also enough similarities to say that they share a common tribal culture. How is this distinct from India's mainstream culture? What makes these people 'tribal' rather than 'Hindu'?

Culturally they have always been part of Indian civilization, on its edge. Unlike most tribal peoples outside India, they have maintained trading and ritual links with city-based, 'civilized' society for well over 2,000 years. Ancient texts on statecraft such as the *Arthashastra* discuss how to win them over as allies. Ashoka's edicts threaten them with punishment if they do not observe his *dhamma* (rule, law). But the Indian situation presents a striking contrast to the European or Christian relationship between tribal peoples and 'civilization': in Europe they were mostly conquered, 'pacified' or 'civilized' into peasantry, and converted to Christianity during the Roman period or soon after. Later, in the 'New World', tribes were exterminated or at least displaced from their land through a stark confrontation between European colonists and aboriginals. Hindu civilization did not on the whole seek to convert or displace tribals, although there was certainly often conflict, and tribes were forced to retreat to the remotest areas: the forests and mountains between Hindu kingdoms.

Tribal religion is not sharply distinct from Hinduism, and was patronized by Hindu *rajahs*, to whom tribes generally gave ritualized allegiance.[30] Tribal myths have clear connections with Hindu mythology. *Adivasis* travel from far around to take part in certain Hindu festivals. The tribes of Central India are similar to castes, in as much as they are described by the same word *jati* (caste or race), and are often ranked by a similar association between status and purity. In these senses, tribal people could be said to be Hindus.

Yet their differences from Hindus are conscious and conspicuous.[31] In some contexts or areas they call themselves Hindus, in others not. One needs to bear in mind that, although nowadays Hinduism is defined in relation to particular texts, rituals, beliefs etc., originally 'Hindu' was a foreigner's word for 'the people who live beyond the river Indus', and thus referred to all the religious traditions in the subcontinent.

The defining features of a tribe anthropologically might be given as a close, ritualized dependence on the natural environment, especially the forest, a strongly egalitarian social organization based more on clans than on class or caste, and a high degree (until recently at least) of economic self-sufficiency and political independence. The difference might be more clearly expressed by saying that Hindus are cultivators and pastoralists, to whom the forest is essentially wilderness, to be cleared or tamed; whereas tribals are hunter-gatherers: people of the forest, for whom agriculture is important as a complementary source of food (more so over the years as Hindu influence has increased and the forest has diminished) but regarded as an irksome chore.

Drums and dancing, music and song are at the heart of tribal culture. Kuvi Konds accompany their songs, of haunting beauty, on a one-stringed percussive instrument called a *dinduna*. Alcohol is something sacred—palm wine and rice beer as well as *mahua. Adivasis* use it with respect, pouring a libation on the ground before they drink, and offering it to the gods. They are not vegetarian, and do not have the same ideals of purity that mark caste society. Their gods are not vegetarian either, unlike the higher Hindu gods, and blood sacrifice plays an important part in their religion. They do not worship their gods in temples or with the aid of *brahmin* priests, but at shrines in the forest. All their deities are closely connected with nature, identified with features of the local environment or natural forces, including diseases. As well as priests they have diviners and shamans, who go into trance to communicate with spirits. It is thus a thoroughly 'shamanic' religion. It was called 'animism' by British anthropologists, because it looks at nature in terms of the spirits (Latin *animae*) that animate it.

Tribal people also dress differently from Hindus, with a shorter loincloth. Among themselves they use a different word of greeting—*Jiwar* or *Johar*. They smoke tobacco (which they grow themselves), but in the distinctive form of a big cigar rolled in a fresh green leaf. They mostly avoid drinking milk, which is of great significance in Hindu culture—'Why take it from the calves?'

Equality is a powerful ideal in tribal culture. Land is usually divided equally among households, unlike Hindu villages which tend to have large divisions between landlords and landless labourers. This is especially so in the remoter tribal villages which still practise shifting cultivation, since each household clears as much land as it can work. This is not to say that they do not have status differences. There is usually a village chief or headman, and a head priest, both of whom belong to particular lineages, although the headman never makes a decision without consulting a council of elders and household heads. Elders carry more weight than young men in village councils, and women do not formally take part, though they may have a decisive influence from the sidelines.[32] On the whole, women are much freer than in Hindu villages. They speak out openly, and are not bound by double standards of sexual morality, as free as men to have love affairs. Divorce is relatively easy and widows as well as divorcees can marry again without any stigma.

This emphasis on equality goes along with tribal villagers' self-sufficiency in fulfilling most of their own needs. They make most of the objects they use—leaf cups, arrow shafts, rope, baskets, and mats, as well as their houses. Certain items they buy from specialists who make them, or at markets, such as ornaments, arrow heads, axe and plough blades, salt, cloth, and pots. Already when they first met the British they had come to depend on potter, weaver, herder and blacksmith castes. Konds' relationship with the Doms is also characteristic of caste relationships in that they will not accept cooked food or water from Doms, for fear of pollution. In other ways Konds and other tribes are outside the caste system, in the same way that Muslims, Christians or foreigners are.

Tribal people see themselves and are usually seen as India's aboriginals, as the word *adivasi* implies. The main view of historians and anthropologists has been that Dravidians were indigenous to India, and that the Aryans invaded India in the second millenium BC, bringing Sanskrit and the Vedic religion. Vedic society called the indigenous, 'black' people, *daasa*, a negative term, which came to mean slave. There has obviously been a long process of high castes incorporating darker skinned, indigenous people as lower castes.[33] In Orissa for example, there is a clear difference of race between high-caste Oriyas and dark-skinned *adivasis*.

British rule in some ways accentuated this difference, by calling them 'wild', 'savage', or 'primitive tribes', and distinguishing them from Hindu castes by their race and customs as well as by calling their religion 'animism'. Also, after the initial period of conquering them, there was a widespread realization among British officials that opening them up to outside influence had made them vulnerable to exploitation. As a result they established Protected or Scheduled Areas, where regular laws did not fully apply, and tribal law was partially recognized.

In the 1930s this policy came under fierce attack by the Congress Party on the grounds that it was divisive. In sociology, G.S. Ghurye set forth the arguments, attacking the very idea that they are India's aboriginals, that they are essentially different from Hindus, and even that they are particularly exploited. Instead, he explained their difference in terms of 'backwardness', claiming that 'The so-called Animists and Aborigines are best described as backward Hindus' (1943 p.24)—and he urged their rapid 'assimilation' into Hindu society. But best for whom? Is this not a very negative way to describe people who are proud of a highly distinctive culture? Surely the way to avoid conflict between *adivasis* and Hindus is not to try and make *adivasis* assimilate to Hindu society, but to encourage the mutual respect that has long existed between them, and prevent the exploitation that inevitably increased when tribal areas were first opened up with roads.

At Independence, *adivasis* were officially defined as Scheduled Tribes.[34] At present nearly 7 per cent of India's population are classified as such, although how a group is classified often depends on political and economic factors, since Scheduled Castes and Tribes are entitled to certain benefits in the form of a quota of reserved jobs etc., while, on the other side, to be classed as a Scheduled Tribe implies a lower social status.

These problems of classification in India reflect a problem in the concept of 'tribe' in anthropology as a whole: what is the dividing line between tribal and other societies?[35] Personally, I find this question of definitions unimportant. The best working definition of 'tribe' seems one that takes account of colonial history and the modern political situation, but essentially follows people's own definition of themselves. In India as elsewhere, the basic popular sense of 'tribe' refers to peoples who live in remote areas and distinguish themselves from mainstream culture, and are distinguished by others, and who (unlike 'peasants', who look to some centre outside for guidance) place themselves unashamedly at the centre of the earth.

In anthropology as well as in popular writing 'tribal' (which in India has become a noun) has replaced pejorative terms such as 'savages' and 'primitives', which earlier anthropologists used. 'Tribal' is not an evolutionist term—it does not (to me at any rate) imply a certain stage on a path of social evolution.[36] Where 19th century anthropologists invariably believed that tribal societies represented a primitive stage of development, modern anthropologists have largely rejected this view.

Some question the usefulness of grouping India's *adivasis* with the native inhabitants of Southeast Asia and the Pacific, Africa and America. To me it seems clear that they possess fundamental features in common: not just in their social organization, economy and religion, but also in their relationship with the natural environment, as well as in the way they have been dominated and marginalized by colonial powers. 'Nature peoples' is what some of them call themselves (Russell Means 1982).

'Tribe' also implies connectedness—a relationship with a much larger whole. In earlier usage it referred to the divisions of Roman or Hebrew society, and came to be used for the divisions of natural species of animals. In this way we could speak of humankind as being divided into innumerable tribes, where earlier writers spoke of 'nations' or 'races'. The Konds, like many other tribal peoples, see themselves as elder brothers to us 'modern', 'civilized' people—a frank recognition of our common ancestry as human beings.

'A Conquest over their Minds'

At first I planned to do fieldwork in a tribal village to try to understand the process of change. But gradually I realized that studying 'social change' makes no sense when so much has been imposed from the outside. Within the last 150 years a large proportion of India's tribal people have lost their traditional freedom and quality of life. The vitality of their cultures has diminished as they have come into the grip of exploitation by non-tribal outsiders, to whom they have to sell their labour in order to live. Reading through the standard anthropological literature about tribes in India, I became intensely aware that many writers do not distinguish properly between changes that are *imposed* on tribals by outsiders, and changes motivated from within. In general anthropologists have concentrated on the internal or indigenous aspect of changes, and ignored, underplayed or taken for granted outsiders imposing changes. The concepts of 'social change' and 'development' tend to blur this distinction. 'Development' is a highly loaded word, and often conceals an elite forcing its own interests on a population.[37]

As I looked deeper into the history of tribes in India and elsewhere, I realized that British administrators assumed that the changes they imposed on tribal people formed part of a necessary process of civilizing them, and that Indian administrators have inherited this tendency. This is how I came to study *the British impetus to impose change*. Where the context is one of outsiders imposing momentous changes in the face of the landscape, in rights to the land, shifting whole populations to make way for a dam or a mine, to try and analyse tribal reactions to the changes imposed on them seems to add insult to injury, and to avoid the root of the problem altogether. Maybe the Konds and similar tribes have been studied enough by outsiders. Certainly my reading makes me painfully aware of how closely related the role of analysing them has been to the role of controlling and ruling them.

So it seems to me vital to distinguish change whose impetus comes from inside the community to change imposed from the outside. Terms such as 'Hinduization', 'Sanskritization' and 'Westernization' describe the diffusion and imitation of high status behaviour, which can be seen as being motivated by 'shame' or 'snobbery'. Features of high class culture which the lower classes adopted during the Middle Ages in Europe so as to claim status or avoid ridicule by their 'superiors' are now diffusing throughout the world. Tribals try to avoid the ridicule of non-tribals through raising their status by adopting high caste or high class customs: using machine-made cloth instead of traditional 'primitive' cloth or leaves; for women, covering their breasts, and refraining from dances; for men, cutting their hair short, or wearing shoes.[38]

Yet in most tribes' histories the world over we find periods of intense imposition by outsiders. British conquest brought Konds into the world economic system, making highland Orissa an 'economic frontier', where several different political systems meet (Bailey 1957, 1960). For Konds as for so many other tribes this introduced an element of *discontinuity* into their history. The whole pattern of their relations with outsiders was transformed in such a way as to undermine their independence. To call this whole process of change 'economic and social development' masks this basic fact (Lévi-Strauss 1978).

Most imitation or diffusion of outside customs is fundamentally a reaction to this imposition. Tribes' reactions to imposed changes can be seen as a mixed strategy of conforming and resisting. There is a long history of tribal rebellions and retreats to the interior; also of passive resistance—telling outsiders what they want to hear so that they go away. Movements to Sanskritize or 'purify' tribal custom seem to be motivated above all by sensitivity to outsiders' ridicule and contempt: even 'internal' changes take place in a context of great external constraint. In other words, ever since British troops invaded tribal areas, the main impetus towards change has come from outsiders. Many studies of social change ignore this break in continuity, along with the whole question of changes in relations of power. My own interest switched to analysing the imposing of change, when the urge to impose changes on others came to seem a more unusual, mysterious and problematic phenomenon than reacting to what others impose.

The reason why studies of social change rarely face the issue of colonial imposition squarely, seems to me to be a fear of confronting administrators' ideas and actions. In fact, the concept of 'social change' virtually blocks off analysis of administrators' culture and actions, by taking a context of change imposed by members of an alien culture for granted. Similarly, historians' interest in tribal India has concentrated on rebellions and their suppression, and neglected, by comparison, the initial imposing of British rule.[39] Yet this imposition was the immediate cause of most tribal rebellions.

So why did the British conquer tribes? How did they justify forcing British rule onto them?

It is a process that began in India in the late 18th century. Before that evidence suggests that tribes all over India maintained a high degree of political and economic independence in tracts on the borders and peripheries between kingdoms. Sometimes tribes assumed the role of guarding the borders of a kingdom. Shivaji for example subdued tribes in the area around Pune, and then set them to guard it for him.[40]

When the East India Company came into conflict with tribes in India, its soldiers began to subdue them in a manner that was completely new—new to India's *adivasis* that is, though it followed patterns that were already well-established by Europeans all over the continents of America and Africa. The first celebrated conquest was of the Paharias, another tribe of 'mountain people' (*pahaar* is Hindi for 'mountain') who live north of the Konds in what is now Bihar. The Paharias were apparently raiding trade and post on the Grand Trunk Road between Delhi and Calcutta, which had recently come under British control. After several years of intermittent raiding between Paharias and British troops, an administrator called Augustus Cleveland was posted to the District as its Collector, who gave his full attention to the problem of governing them. His death in 1784 was commemorated by a memorial stone in Bhagalpur which declared that Cleveland

> without bloodshed or terrors of authority, employing only the means of conciliation, confidence and benevolence, attempted and accomplished the entire subjection of the lawless and savage inhabitants of the jungle territory of Rajmahal who had long infested the neighbouring lands by their predatory incursions, and attached them to the British Government by a conquest over their minds, the most rational as the most permanent mode of dominion.

This language reveals a lot. 'Savage', 'infested' and 'predatory' paint a picture of the Paharias as dangerous wild animals, and the idea that they were 'lawless' serves to justify their conquest. 'Without bloodshed or terrors of authority' glosses over the military aspect of Cleveland's campaign, and his public executions of Paharia chiefs in 1780-82.[41] These words depict British rule as essentially benevolent and rational, and hold up a model of heroism and dedicated service. Most telling is 'a conquest over their minds', which makes us see what was novel about British conquest, for Hindu *rajahs* who had made tribes their subjects did not try to change or convert them, and even legitimized their rule by patronizing their religion.

The pacification of the Paharias, and of the Bhils in Western India, are celebrated in many histories of British India.[42] But the campaign to subdue the Konds created still more sensation, and the extensive body of writings which it left form a fertile field of study, which will occupy us in the next four chapters.

The Colonial Power Structure

The subject of this book then is not Konds' reactions to conquest, but British colonials and their relationship with Konds. The colonial relationship has been amazingly little studied by anthropologists. Evans-Pritchard called for this, though he did not do it himself, at least among the Nuer.[43] Yet in neglecting to study colonial (or post-colonial) rule, anthropology itself remains stuck in a colonial mould.

> Colonial life is a topic neglected by anthropology even though only two generations ago it involved nearly half the world and was witnessed by most anthropologists as part of their fieldwork. At best, anthropologists studied "culture contact".... (Beidelman 1982 p.1)

So what does it mean to study colonials? To me, the first step is to disengage ourselves as completely as we can from the colonial viewpoint, in order to examine the administrators' relationships with each other and the people they ruled with the same 'outsider view' which has been customary in studying tribal societies. This way we can try to understand the administration's effects without being limited to the way administrators understand them. It also makes 'the Government' less of an abstraction, revealing it as a group of individuals with specific cultural beliefs, customs, and myths, as well as formal organization, training and conscious models.[44]

For tribes coming under colonial rule—for the Konds in the 1830s–60s as for the Nuer in the 1920s–30s (when Evans-Pritchard did his fieldwork)—new relations of subordination were introduced quite suddenly and standardized in only a generation or two. This process can only be understood if we analyse it *transculturally*, in terms of interaction between two or more cultures' internal social structures and symbolic systems.[45] This may seem more complicated than a tidy analysis of a tribe's internal social structure, yet it claims logical priority: anthropologists only collect information about another society by entering into such culture contact. Published knowledge about the Konds is the product of interaction between European, Hindu and Kond social structures and symbolic systems. For in the case of the Kond administration, three very different symbolic systems were interacting: those of the Konds and the British colonials were mediated by that of non-tribal Indians, mostly but not all Hindus.

Colonial ideas about native cultures have frequently had the character of rigid stereotypes. For Europeans in the 18th and 19th centuries, these possessed extra force from their place in a hallowed literary tradition, which included 'scientific' definitions of tribal people as essentially primitive. Generations of colonials went out to rule tribals believing they knew what they would find, completely closed to seeing them as anything other than the savages they had read about.[46]

As a social group, British colonials provide certain problems for anthropological analysis. They were exceedingly literate, with an elaborately articulated awareness of who they were and the relationships that connected them. Yet the very fact that the written word played such an important part in their lives means that their writings take us straight to their key values and beliefs. Colonial writings about tribes both reveal evidence about the structure of tribes' relations with outsiders, and form part of this structure. The literature about tribal people is highly standardized, and its basic structure consists of a small number of key concepts and assumptions.[47]

We shall be looking at the written discourse of three groups of people—administrators, missionaries and anthropologists—as three separate discourses, or three strands in a single discourse. Each has its own characteristics, but they are interwoven, so that in each there is a bit of the other two. And in each, unpublished writings often reveal more than what was published.[48] The British legitimized imposing their rule over the Konds, as I shall try and show, from the side of religion as well as science and law. Ultimately they claimed the right to rule the Konds through claiming to know them and to know what they needed better than Konds did themselves.

Many colonial administrators were obviously men of great integrity and high ideals, who honestly believed they were acting in the best interests of tribal people. Their culture and values are familiar to me, and for this reason I feel able to go behind their masks to understand the shadow side of their culture—its huge arrogance and a tremendous urge to control people who are different; often a complete inability to listen to their viewpoint.

In relation to written, 'official' discourse, the Konds are a 'muted group', in that the outside world is deaf to what they say, while the texts I am analysing form a discourse that created power over them. One powerful counterpoise is available from another cultural context in speeches by American Indian leaders.[49] Some of the most powerful techniques that have been developed for dominating tribes are located in language, particularly in written language—from treaties of submission, deeds of landownership, legal documents, the Census, and moneylenders' accounts, to the published writings of officials, missionaries, anthropologists, economists, journalists, and novelists. Since tribals in India have hardly had the opportunity to react in writing to all that has been written about them, it is appropriate to quote the opening of a recent speech by an American Indian leader on the use of writing:

> The only possible opening for a statement of this kind is that I detest writing. The process itself epitomizes the European concept of "legitimate" thinking; what is written has an importance that is denied the spoken. My culture, the Lakota culture, has an oral tradition, so ordinarily I reject writing. It is one of the white world's ways of destroying the cultures of non-European peoples, the imposing of an abstraction over the spoken relationship of a people. (Russell Means 1982).

Writing this book I often feel pulled apart by the incompatibility of different cultures' ways of seeing things, and by the paradox of what I am attempting to do here: writing about tribal people, I believe, has a tendency to 'appropriate' them intellectually; but when I analyse what other people have written about them I enter a level of abstraction even further removed from tribal thought. My solution is to write as directly and clearly as I can, in the conviction that how outsiders have behaved and talked about tribal people calls out for clear analysis; that *deconstructing* the system of power that has been imposed over them and traps them can help many people to see clearly behind the masks. For I believe that the colonial power structure, and its masks, are fundamentally the same as those which we impose over ourselves.

This book is therefore intended as a contribution towards the anthropology of Western society. The classic anthropological studies of Western society are about traditional peasant societies in remote areas of Europe—some of the least powerful, most marginalized members of modern culture. Anthropologists have rarely tackled the West's powerful and influential elites—politicians, businessmen, lawyers, scientists, media people, or academics. I have found the work of Michel Foucault particularly helpful in pointing the way towards a far-reaching anthropology of the West, since he is fundamentally concerned to understand forms of power. His concept of *pastoral power* I find particularly helpful for clarifying the way that modern forms of power developed from the Christian Church's concern to control people by looking after or 'saving' them.[50]

The fundamental structures of Western society, especially its power structure, are particularly clear in a colonial setting. In the very first innovations and institutions which colonials set up (e.g. the first buildings: living quarters, office, factory, courthouse, jail, school, hospital etc.)—there is a pattern that takes us straight to the fundamental structures of modern Western society. Historians of British India have examined the bodies of theory that shaped British policy in some depth.[51] But as Edward Said has commented,

> Imperialism has been defined and studied almost exclusively as a social, political or economic formation. There has been hardly any work on what role culture plays in sustaining imperialism, or, for that matter, in initiating it.... we need closer attention to the verbal, imaginative and ideological overlapping between narrative on the one hand and, on the other, ethnographic reports, travel accounts, political treatises and the like.[52]

Looking at colonial structures of power and authority, knowledge and belief, involves the history of these structures in European society from ancient or medieval times. In other words, what the British brought to the Konds was nothing less than the whole history of Western civilization;

but the clear patterns in their thinking and behaviour offer a way into this huge reality that promises fresh insights.[53]

Since my interest is focused on the colonials, my approach is essentially comparative, in that I compare the administration of other tribes where this highlights particular aspects of colonial behaviour or brings aspects that have an individual shape in the Kond case into a more general focus. My research on Kond history has been complemented by a review of the history of other tribes in India as well as in other countries. This comparison is not of tribal customs or even tribal reactions to colonial rule, but of *colonial administration and discourse*. It is thus comparison on surer ground than that of early anthropologists such as Frazer and Tylor, which removed individual customs from the most diverse societies with no reference to social structure. The Europeans who created colonies and empires abroad were part of a common culture, in terms of religion and literature, as well as forms of authority. For example, the Roman Empire was a model for the Spanish in the 16th century just as it was for the British in the 19th century.

It seems to me of the greatest value to compare what has been imposed on tribal people at different places and times. Much of the contempt which *adivasis* face now in India is an inheritance from Western society. Since their 'voyages of discovery' 500 years ago, Europeans conquered, and enslaved or exterminated tribal people on every continent. Those that survived were herded into reservations or escaped to the remotest forests. Even there they were eventually colonized and constrained by alien laws. All over Africa, America and the Pacific, we find a similar story. For example, if we look at Brazil or other countries in Latin America, we find a continuous history of genocide of the native tribes that has not ceased, starting with wars of conquest in the 1520s against coastal tribes such as the Tupinamba, and the enslavement of the Indians to create a profit for the colonists from timber, precious metals, plantations or factories. African slaves were brought in because slavery was killing a huge proportion of Indians, who succumbed to unfamiliar diseases.[54]

The regimes imposed over tribal people have always had this character of a plunder of the earth together with the violent oppression of human beings. With the growth of industry in the last 100 years this oppression of the earth, as more and more people are starting to see, is damaging the environment to an extent that threatens human survival. The European culture that has introduced an industrial lifestyle over the whole earth has a cutting edge that works out how to create the maximum profit out of the earth and the raw materials extracted from it in the shortest possible time, with complete disregard for long-term consequences. The cutting down of the earth's remaining forests, the damming of rivers, overuse of fertilizers and pesticides, the race to extract minerals and oil from under the earth's surface: the wider effects of these actions are unknown, even to our scientists. By the time they find out, it may well be too late.

Karl Marx offered a devastatingly accurate analysis of the economic system that evolved in Europe—the worship of money and the systematic exploitation of most people to create a profit for the elite. Yet he failed to offer a realistic prescription for a better society. This, I believe, is precisely because he did not understand—hardly any Europeans did at that time—the consequences of the industrial assault on the environment, and the way that this assault is bound up with the oppression of human beings. Marxism thus shares with capitalism a faith in industrial development that is lethally misguided. As Russell Means says (1982), Marxism continues the process of desacralizing nature—it is 'the same old song'.

> All European tradition, Marxism included, has conspired to defy the natural order of things. Mother Earth has been abused, the powers have been abused, and this cannot go on forever. No theory can alter that simple fact. Mother Earth will retaliate, the whole environment will retaliate, and the abusers will be eliminated. Things come full circle, back to where they started. *That's* revolution.

Anthropology Full Circle

In India the story has unfolded differently, in that British conquest did not displace India's native population—they were not exterminated by new diseases like the native peoples of America, so there was no wave of European colonists, just a 'thin white line' of soldiers and administrators, traders and missionaries, 'exiguous to the point of disbelief' (Kirke-Greene 1980). Yet British conquest upset the balance between Hindu and tribal societies by opening up the latter to a much higher level of exploitation by outsiders, who justified their extortion by their contempt. And although some British officials were attracted by tribal cultures, and took steps to protect them from exploitation, very few entered them deeply enough to begin to understand things from their point of view. The negative view was so prevalent that they could hardly even see that tribal people had a point of view, let alone a form of knowledge that did not fit into the 'universal' system of knowledge they had been taught to believe in.

This is the background to the fundamental gulf of understanding between tribal knowledge of the world and university conceptions of knowledge. To attempt to bridge this gulf we need to examine the colonial assumptions that led, and still lead, so many people to believe they know what is best for tribals and that it is their right or even duty to impose it. The gulf between academic conventions and tribal directness often appears unbridgeable.

But in the West, there has been a great opening in the last generation to non-western traditions of knowledge, which includes tribal as well as Hindu, Islamic, Taoist and Buddhist traditions. Simultaneously, the native peoples of America, Australia, and many other countries have made a comeback in political awareness and traditional values, starting to throw off the educational and other structures that were imposed on them.

Tribal and other non-western forms of knowledge, after being denied for generations, are slowly beginning to be incorporated into the mainstream view of things. Inevitably, this is a process that horrifies some people,[55] and those who pioneered this openness to non-western cultures' alternative modes of understaning have had to face a mainstream view that was completely closed. 'New Age' culture is often at the vanguard of openness to non-western traditions. Sometimes this has the appearance of gullibility or superficiality. Yet overall it represents a real opening that is of the greatest potential, and through it, the voices of tribal people are starting to be heard.

Anthropology has been of crucial importance in this opening, by attempting to escape from ethnocentric assumptions and see the world from the radically different standpoint of non-western traditions. Where virtually all Westerners 100 years ago assumed the illogicality of tribal beliefs, most anthropologists now take for granted the richness and coherence of every tribal society—starting with the idea that it possesses a social structure and symbolic system as subtle as our own.[56] Many anthropologists go further now, and affirm that the *quality of life* in tribal societies is as rich as that in 'civilized' societies, much richer perhaps in the sense that each individual possesses a greater variety of skills of work and leisure, and is not dependent on the alienatingly impersonal nature of relationships characteristic of modern society since the division of labour is so much simpler and more human. Certainly, tribes like the Konds present models of the kind of environmental awareness, equality, democracy, and respect for women, children and elders that many people in modern society aspire towards.

Yet anthropology of tribal India still remains largely *evolutionist* in its view of a traditional tribal way of life as 'backward'. It has inherited uncritically some of the key assumptions of colonial anthropology, especially the idea that Konds and other tribes are at a primitive stage of social development. Colonial administrators and anthropologists regarded Kond religion, myth, and knowledge of nature as 'ignorance' and 'superstitious beliefs', by contrast with their own 'scientific knowledge' of the world. In this way, the anthropological tradition can be understood as an assault on tribal knowledge, an attempt to invalidate it.

This book arose out of a perception of some enduring problems in the modern anthropological literature about tribes in India. The language of anthropology, in its abstraction and impersonal formality, could not contrast more with the language which tribal people speak; its similarity to administrators' discourse shows that anthropologists have not fully questioned the social meaning of their studies. There is also a great lack of awareness about the meaning of anthropologists' behaviour as they collect 'data' from 'informants'. I now see this as a problem at the root of anthropology in general. Most anthropologists' models of society do not include their own relationships with those they study. Anthropological understanding emerges from these relations, so an awareness of how they fit into a social structure is peculiarly important. For example, anthropologists collect information in writing about the culture they are studying, and later publish this for other people in their own (the anthropologists') culture to read. This is action only indirectly oriented towards people in a tribal village. It is not work directly *for* tribal people, nor is it even learning *from* them. It involves the idea of studying things and people with 'scientific detachment': a recent, and extremely unusual and strange form of cultural behaviour towards other people.

In other words, a way of writing about tribal people has evolved that is in its essence dehumanizing. What is the relevance of highly abstract analysis of their kinship system or symbolism, when they face genocide? It is the power structure—what has been imposed on them—that calls out for penetrating analysis, but in a spirit of dialogue with tribal culture, instead of always making it into an object of study. This is the origin of my decision to conduct research not about the Konds, but about how others have represented them and related to them. What we can know about a tribal people like the Konds from what has been written about them is actually very little, when we recognize the extent of the bias and cultural arrogance in most of this writing. What we can know about the Konds' British rulers, by contrast, we can understand not just from the historical records, but also from our experience of our own culture, and by looking inside ourselves. Administrators' actions and policies call out for clear anthropological analysis.

In this book I am trying to help bring anthropology full circle. By this I mean—become fully human, and realize the enormous potential of what I believe it could give the world, in terms of understanding our own modern culture, the culture of people who are highly literate, and some of whom wield enormous power. This understanding of who we are, how we relate with each other, where we have come from, the real quality of our lives—anthropologists can give fresh perspectives on these questions by seeing our culture from the outside, from the point of view of other cultures. Anthropologists from non-western cultures—from the 'anthropologized world'—are already starting to study the West—the 'anthropologizing world'.[57]

In the experience of doing fieldwork in another culture I believe we often learn more about our own culture and ourselves than about the culture we live in for a year or two: it is a learning process we could use to question our most basic assumptions. Entering non-western viewpoints gives us the possibility of understanding our own society more objectively. For example, from a tribal viewpoint, it appears astonishing that a culture has evolved where people cannot *feel* their connection with the earth and dependence on it to the extent that they can tear it open and manipulate it for short-term profit, in the way that has become normal in modern society—astonishing that people have evolved who do not realize that they are wounding the earth, and therefore also themselves. Similarly with childcare: the psychologist Jean Liedloff realized from living in a tribal culture over long periods how abnormal Western, or modern, culture is in its customary handling of babies and small children (1986)—e.g. that great emotional deprivation is normal and customary for babies in modern culture in being made to sleep separately from their mothers, in contrast to the custom in the vast majority of other cultures, where babies sleep with their mothers.

One of the first things that needs questioning is therefore the nature of knowledge itself. In the academic tradition, the university embodies an idea of universal knowledge that has been elaborated by generations of philosophers and other academics. Much of the knowledge of tribal societies is not recognized as real knowledge by the standards of this 'universal knowledge', while from a tribal point of view, it might seem that there is very little in what universities teach of the truly essential knowledge of how to live harmoniously with each other and with nature. In other words, this 'universal knowledge' has become separated from what we call wisdom.

So when I speak of 'objective' knowledge I mean this a little differently from how the word is sometimes used. 'Objectivity', to some people, involves delimiting a subject so that all possible variables can be measured, as well as an attempt to avoid bringing one's feelings into the study. To me, 'objectivity' means looking at something from the widest, most 'holistic' perspective possible, to avoid the narrowness of a one-sided view. For how objective is the most tremendous expertise when it completely lacks awareness of larger wholes? To truly know an object, we need to start by understanding our own relationship with it, as well as its context in a much larger whole. We can only know it 'objectively'—free from our own emotions and conditioning—if we also have 'subjective' knowledge—that is, knowledge of ourselves, our motives and the unconscious patterns that generate our feelings and behaviour. Without this a knowledge of objects, however meticulously collected or 'successful', will be essentially flawed, because it will be divorced from our sense of relationship with it.[58] For example, engineers, businessmen and politicians possess great knowledge about mines, dams and factories, but when they act on this without an adequate awareness of their effects on the natural environment, the results can be disastrous. When we write about tribal people divorced from an awareness of our own relationship with them and the effects of what we write, the result is dehumanizing.

As I understand it, the difference between 'objective' and 'subjective' knowledge corresponds to the difference between 'scientific', 'empirical' or 'rational' modes of knowledge, and 'artistic', 'poetic', or 'intuitive' knowledge. Western society privileges the former over the latter, although what we call 'wisdom' is clearly something that involves both and cannot be reduced to the realm of 'scientific' knowledge. Most non-western societies could be said to privilege the latter, or to have more of a balance between the two modes, recognizing the fundamental importance of things that are not susceptible to rational understanding—as shown by the entirely different concerns of Eastern from Western philosophy, or the importance of knowledge that comes from dreams and trance in tribal societies.

The trend of reflexive or critical anthropology, which has increased since the 1960s, goes some way towards healing the dehumanizing nature of colonial anthropology.[59] What I offer in this book is an attempt to take this further by examining our own anthropological customs and beliefs in the light of the unequal power relations inherited from the colonial era.

For this reason I have tried to write this book in a way that is accessible to many different kinds of people. One of the basic divisions within modern Western society is between 'intellectuals' or those with a university education, and 'ordinary people'. There is often intolerance on both sides, but I believe that writing in a way that only other academics will understand or relate to tragically limits the audience we communicate with and reinforces this divide in our own culture: a division that reflects the gulf between rich and poor countries, between 'North and South' or 'first world and third world', as well as the gulf of understanding between Western and non-western traditions.

CHAPTER TWO

Conquest: The Ghumsur Wars

The conquest of the Konds was one of countless 'savage wars' which the British and other Europeans fought against tribal peoples as they extended their empire and colonies.[1] In the Kond case, the British did not call it 'conquest'. 'Subjection' and 'pacification' were the words they used, and Kond resistance they called 'insurgency' or 'rebellion'. Before 1835 the British admitted that they had 'no connexion' with the Konds—except indirectly, through the *rajahs* who paid tribute to the East India Company, and whom the Konds accepted as in some sense their kings. Anyway, to the Konds the British had no rights over them, while to the British the Konds had no right to resist them. This gives the setting for the Ghumsur wars that represent the initial conquest of Konds by British officials.

I shall go over the events in some detail, quoting the officials' unpublished correspondence from the Archives, in order to show how the British saw their actions, before subjecting these events to an anthropological scrutiny. The Kond campaigns have been recounted in several published works, most recently by Barbara Boal (1982). But like previous accounts, hers does not question the official version of events and uncritically reproduces its language. The parts of the reports that were never published reveal the extent of British violence in a clearer light.[2]

In this context I would like to mention two books that made me feel it is very worthwhile to look in some depth into these campaigns. John Prebble's *Culloden* (1961) describes the English conquest of the Scottish Highlands in the 1740s; it brings out the indescribable inhumanity of what was done to the Highlanders through the ordinary accounts of the day-today actions of the soldiers, including what was imposed on them by their officers. Dee Brown's *Bury my heart at wounded knee* is a history of the Yankee bluecoats' conquest of the last independent native Americans in the Indian Wars from the 1860s to 1890s. The records of the soldiers' ordinary activities and words reveal the unimaginable, especially when juxtaposed with what the Indians said and did.

What follows in this chapter and the next is a detailed account of the military campaigns which forced the Konds into the British empire. Personally I find the details absorbing. Readers who find them boring or repugnant may want to skip over some parts. To me it seems that the language which officials used to describe their actions holds the key to understanding the regime they imposed. The pattern of ideas and emotions that structure these texts has a close relationship with the officials' patterns of thought and behaviour.[3] This is why I have peppered my account with quotations from the Britons' reports to each other, bringing to light the dusty secrets that lie hidden in the Archives. For a detailed study of these campaigns reveals a culture which accepted extreme hierarchy and violence as normal.

When tribal people first met European soldiers different universes of understanding came into contact. But they did not meet, because the Europeans were not able to meet a different view of the world. Instead, they imposed their own understanding of order by force.

Central Orissa was divided into a multitude of small kingdoms, each consisting of a core area in the plains under direct control of the *rajah*, as well as more distant, mountain and forest areas, which were inhabited by tribal people and ruled over on the *rajah*'s behalf by Hindu chiefs, *bissoi*, who lived in Hindu settlements, *garh*. Some of these kingdoms were extremely old, such as Sonepur and Boad. The smaller *rajahs* generally gave allegiance and tribute to greater *rajahs* ('*maharajas*').[4]

Muslim soldiers from Afghanistan conquered Orissa in the 1560s, and made it a province in the Mughal empire, so that most of the Oriya *rajahs* gave allegiance and tribute to a Mughal governor at the same time as they gave a religious allegiance to the cult of Jagannath, 'Lord of the Universe', whose great temple in Puri is still at the heart of Orissa's culture. The Hindu *rajah* of Khurda had control over the temple, but co-operated with the Muslim government. In the 1740s–50s Muslim rule in Orissa was ended by the Marathas. According to British sources, which took a very negative view of the Marathas, their rule mostly consisted of periodic invasions and enforced exactions of tribute. But each kingdom was assessed as paying a specified tribute, and the British used these assessments when they took over from the Marathas. In 1803, during the second Maratha war, the British invaded Orissa and took possession of it, which meant direct rule of the coastal area, and indirect rule over the inland kingdoms, formalized through treaties and tribute.

Some of the kingdoms in south Orissa were already tributary to the British, as part of 'the five Northern Sircars'. These had been under the rule of the Nizam of Hyderabad, first as part of the Mughal empire, and later as part of the Nizam's independent territory. In the 1750s the Nizam ceded them to the French, and in the 1760s, on the defeat of the French, they became tributary to the East India Company.

Ghumsur was a kingdom in the Northern Sircars that had a lot of trouble paying its tribute. The French General De Bussy invaded it in 1757, and got bogged down in a jungle war that he could not win. The British invaded it repeatedly to exact tribute, and interfered several times in the royal succession, exploiting divisions within the family. The reigns of the last four rulers were interrupted and resumed at the will of the British.[5] For instance, in 1783, 'Vicrama Bunge having failed to perform his engagement to the Government', the zemindary was made over to his elder brother, Lakshman, who promised to pay double the previous tribute (for each, this was their second period of rule!).

> As usual in those days, the arrangement was made through Soucars, who became responsible for the fulfilment of the terms entered into by the zemindar, and, under that plea were permitted to take the management of the country and the collections of revenue into their own hands.[6]

Sahukars—merchants or moneylenders—probably played a major part in events behind the scenes and embezzled a lot of the tribute themselves.

Lakshman's son Shreekar alternated repeatedly as ruler with his own son, Dhananjay. Shreekar lived a dramatic life as a *sanyasi*-king, usually unable to pay the tribute, and frequently at odds with the British. Once he escaped from a British prison. Displaced for the last time in 1830, after becoming 'a complete devotee', he led the life of a wandering pilgrim for another fifteen years.[7] But Dhananjay was finally unable to pay too, and the British decided to annex the kingdom in 1835.

When Stevenson, the Collector of Ganjam, met him at Aska on 14th August, Dhananjay promised to pay within 12 days. He failed to do so, apparently because his attention was taken up with a war against the rival

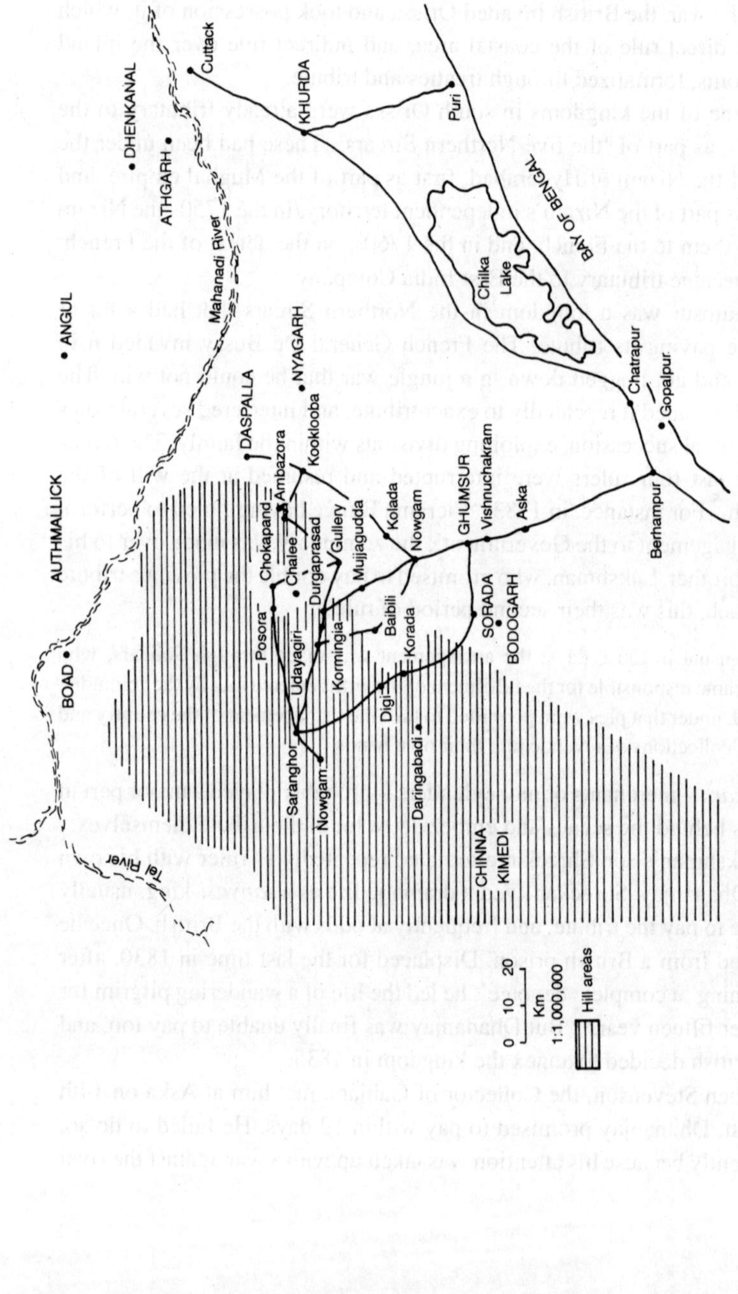

Map 3: The Ghumsur Wars, 1835–7, showing the capital towns of Native States in capital letters

rajahs of Sorada and Bodogarh. On 25th September Lieutenant-Colonel Hodgson joined Stevenson with an army, meeting the *rajah*'s tribute being carried, too late, down to the Collector's office at Berhampore. Negotiations with the *rajah* broke off.

> The zemindar, though he professed anxiety to submit and actually accompanied the Sheristadar from Koladah to Nuttungee....suddenly jumped on his horse and galloped back.[8]

In November the British army invaded Ghumsur and annexed it, proclaiming the *rajah* a rebel. Thus began the Ghumsur wars. The *rajah* and his family fled to the hills and took refuge with the Konds, where the British troops pursued them.

To start with, British troops occupied the towns of Ghumsur and Kolada, which offered little resistance. In the forests beyond Kolada, they came under attack, but continued into the mountains in pursuit of the *rajah*. Hodgson led his troops as far as the fort of Durgaprasad, where he burnt everything he found. In the fighting 16 of his soldiers were wounded and one was killed. Stevenson reported to the administration in Madras:

> Gentlemen,
>
> The reports of the General of Division have probably 'ere this made the Right Honourable the Governor in Council acquainted with the unexpected turn which affairs have taken in Goomsur. The day after the attack on the troops....the force marched through a most difficult country to the Raja's stronghold at Doorgaprasand, which they destroyed, and they have this day returned to Noovagam, 10 miles North of Goomsur.... They have been since entering the hills on 9 November, always fired on by an invisible enemy.... To attempt to hunt the Raja amongst the hills and jungles is a fruitless expenditure of the lives of the troops.... If Government deem it expedient to crush the spirit of rebellion by force, it will be requisite to exert every energy, and to employ a large force to attain the object.[9]

Hodgson's outposts came under repeated attack, killing and wounding more British troops. But his superior, General Taylor, who commanded the Northern Division of the Madras army, did not believe this talk of a large army being necessary.

> There remains no shelter for [the *rajah*]....except in the hilly country inhabited by the Konds, where our troops cannot follow him, and where he will find it difficult to remain.

Nevertheless, he left his headquarters at Vizagapatam to take command of the campaign and reached Ghumsur at the end of November. But the guerilla warfare continued, and malaria started to decimate the troops, increasing greatly within three days of his arrival.[10]

For several thousand soldiers and camp followers, this was no minor war. What was unusual, and made it very costly, was the remoteness of the territory and the prevalence of malaria. Malaria was the Konds' great ally. More Britons, sepoys and camp followers died from it than from the fighting. None of them, it was said, escaped it. More than half the army was sometimes incapacitated by fever, employing the services of a dozen surgeons. Several regiments left the area completely debilitated for the next few years.

Meanwhile Stevenson, as the civil administrator in charge of the whole District, began to argue strongly against annexing Ghumsur. There was no party in Ghumsur that sided with the British yet, so annexation would involve 'great difficulties, expense, and probable loss of life':

> If the district is to be held by Government as a permanent possession it must first be conquered, and this from the nature of the country must prove a most difficult task and one to which the whole energy of the Government must be turned.... In a fiscal point of view, the country is not worth the conquest.... The object of all parties here is to have a Rajah, and unless Government is prepared to establish and maintain its power by force, I at present see little hope of a return to tranquillity but by establishing a Rajah.[11]

Stevenson therefore wrote to the *rajah* on his own authority, offering him the return of his kingdom on certain conditions. For this he was rebuked by the Madras Government, who declared they were determined now to annex and warned him to 'avoid holding out any hope' to the *rajah* of recovering his kingdom.[12] Stevenson had stated that if annexation was the option they chose, they should appoint over himself 'an individual of high rank, possessing the full confidence and authority of Government'.

So it was that The Honourable Mr. Russell of the Madras Board of Revenue set sail from Madras on 22nd December, reaching Ghumsur on 11th January 1836. With his arrival, the initial phase of 'desultory warfare' came to an end.[13] Within days the British took a fort named Rogada, where they captured a chief called Hutteeram, whom they later executed.

By then Dhananjay, the *rajah*, had died. He had actually fallen sick and died only a few days after taking refuge with Konds, on 29th December. Rumour had it that four of his wives committed suttee at his funeral. But at first, the British did not believe the report of his death. In any case, the family continued to fight for their kingdom. By the time Russell arrived General Taylor's army had withdrawn, and 'the enemy' had returned to Kolada under Jagannath Bhanja and his nephew Vurdarauze, Dhananjay's 13 year old son, who was proclaimed the new *rajah*. Jagannath actually wrote to Russell in February, asking him to recognize Vurdarauze Bhanja as the new ruler, but Russell would not agree to this: he was there to annex the kingdom.

On his arrival in January 1836 Russell commanded an army of nearly 2,000 sepoys, under a small number of British officers, deployed in 12 posts.[14] On 10th February he sent his army up into the hills by four routes along jungle footpaths—which were not made for heavy traffic! As well as foot soldiers, this army was accompanied by cavalry and artillery and a host of servants and camp followers, as well as elephants, camels and bullocks to carry tents and supplies.

The detachment under Captains Butler and Campbell followed the direct route of the royal family's retreat to Udayagiri ('Wodiagherry'). Konds attacked them *en route*, killing a camp follower. Two camels were wounded and had to be shot, rice and tents were lost, and the army had to camp on a pass.

> On the 14th [February] the Conds had collected in great numbers, and appeared determined to oppose their further progress. Every effort was made to avoid the necessity of resorting to extremities by explaining our object in ascending the ghauts and assuring them they had nothing to fear. For a time they appeared satisfied, but the evil counsel of Dora Bissye at length prevailed and they assailed our troops, who were in consequence compelled to fire upon them, and make good their way by force.[15]

The next morning however, Konds came to the British camp and 'offered allegiance', explaining they had attacked out of fear and because their chiefs had told them to. Captain Butler 'offered protection' to them in return. The army reached Udayagiri attended by a group of 300 friendly Konds 'who had offered the fullest submission to the Government, with all the Malookoos or petty chiefs'.[16]

Russell joined up with Campbell and the second detachment at Durgaprasad on 22nd February. With him were Sundera Singh, son of the ex-*rajah* of Sorada, Lt Hill of the survey department, and other British officers. The Konds were still friendly, and came to the British camp to barter.

> They came about us without hesitation asking for tobacco and amusing themselves with our looking glasses but would never speak of their chiefs at Huzzagudda.[17]

Russell proclaimed large rewards for the capture of eight of these Hindu chiefs, offering Rs 500/-or 1,000/-, and for Dora Bissoi and Broondawana Bhanja (the late Dhananjay's brother) 5,000/-each. Captain Butler was sent ahead, and managed to capture two of the royal elephants with their attendants, from whom he got information that led him to capture 'twelve females' of the Ghumsur family, and several other prisoners. These were kept under guard at Udayagiri, with the intention of sending them soon back to Nowgam. Broondawana was also captured but escaped a few days later. The main force moved on to Posora, where it met up with the third detachment, which had captured another Hindu chief, Ootan Singh.

Meanwhile all was not well back at Udayagiri. Some sepoys had been stealing chickens and other goods from Kond villagers, sparking off a fight which turned the Konds hostile again.

> The misconduct of some of the men….in forcibly seizing fowls in the village led to a quarrel with the inhabitants which ended in their destruction, and in its consequences, involved us in a war with all the Khondes of the Home Mootahs.[18]

Ensign Wapshire, who had been left in command of the sepoys and prisoners at Udayagiri was attacked by a large force of Konds. Eight of his men were killed by the time 2nd Lieutenant Gibbon arrived from Durgaprasad. Gibbon and another British officer left the next day, 5th March, escorting some of the royal women down the *ghats*. Just after they left an order came from Russell that no one should leave Udayagiri yet.

Too late. An army of two thousand Konds attacked them on their way, killing both the officers and 13 of the 38 sepoys, as well as four of the *ranis* (royal women). Also according to Russell 'a great many private servants belonging to myself and others were murdered'.

General Taylor at once sent three detachments to the rescue. Captain Wight, who led the main relief force, described the scene he found:

> Sir,
>
> I have the honor to report my arrival at Oodiagherry this morning about half past eleven o'clock. I regret to say I found the road strewed with men who had fallen into the hands of the enemy on the morning of the 5th instant.… The number of killed was about twenty with four Ranees and one child, the whole of whom were most horribly murdered and mutilated.[19]

As Captain Wight left this scene, several hundred Konds began an attack on his force from the shelter of the forest, which they kept up until he reached Udayagiri. Here he found Captain Campbell and the second detachment, who had already relieved the British post from the north.

The third detachment was commanded by Major Low, who went to Durgaprasad to arrest the sepoys who had deserted their British officers, and then accompanied the relief force to the scene of the attack. Back at Durgaprasad he reported to Lieutenant-Colonel Muriel:

> My dear Muriel,
>
> I arrived here soon after daylight, without meeting any obstructions on the road. I immediately paraded the Oodhiagherry detachment, reinforced by a Jemadar, Havildar, Naique of Napleton's party and marched them off [i.e. arrested them] …..just as we entered the pass I discovered several men [Konds] sitting upon a rock apparently looking out; we gave them a shell from the little mortar which fell and exploded close to the party and of course made them scamper.[20]

Taylor reported the 'massacre' to Madras, blaming the sepoys for deserting their officers.[21] These sepoys, of the 14th regiment, were given an exemplary punishment for deserting their officers and losing their muskets—though it is hard to see what they could have done against 2,000 Konds. Their arrest twice nearly caused a mutiny of the sepoys in Durgaprasad.[22] Several smaller detachments were also cut down by these Konds soon after—deaths which the British officers calculated in terms of 50 muskets lost to the enemy.

On arriving at Udayagiri, Campbell took revenge on the Konds. His horse was killed in the fighting. General Taylor warmly commended his actions:

> Captain Campbell being on the Hon. Mr. Russell's staff he will not of course report to me, but his gallant conduct on arriving at Oodiagherry on the 7th instant merits approbation; with half a dozen troops [troopers i.e. cavalrymen], a small howitzer, and a few sepoys, he reached Oodiagherry at a most critical moment, found Ensign Wapshire there in command surrounded by at least 2,000 Khonds. This young officer had been harassed by these people for three days—his detachment was nearly worn out with fatigue and himself ill with fever, when this little party came to his relief; the howitzer was discharged without effect, when Capt. Campbell dashed in amongst the enemy, cut down five and drove fifteen into a small hill; this he surrounded as well as he could with the troopers while Ensign Wapshire beat it up with his men and killed six more.[23]

After this he went 'out all day after the rebels and burned many villages.' This kind of violence did not enter the myth of benign British Agents, of which Campbell was to be one of the main heroes. The killing of these two British officers aroused a passionate hatred for the Konds and a desire for revenge among their colleagues, which coloured the rest of the war. From this time countless Konds were killed or taken prisoner. Some were publicly executed. Huge numbers were forced to do coolie service for the troops, carrying their supplies. Their villages and grainstores were systematically burnt under British orders. This was virtually the first British contact with Konds, and led to the subjugation of Konds everywhere else.

The official aims for the next three months were to take the main Hindu chiefs dead or alive, to capture the royal 'treasure', and to recover the muskets and regimental emblems lost to the Konds. In this process Kond chiefs were either killed or forced to make a humiliating submission to British rule. Reporting that Broondawana Bhanja, one of the main Hindu leaders, had just been recaptured, along with the late *rajah*'s widow, General Taylor gave a foretaste of the revenge the British would take on the Konds:

> This succesful capture will no doubt accelerate the restoration of tranquillity, and....we shall be better able to pursue the Konds whose barbarous and treacherous behaviour entitles them to no mercy, for up to the period of the murders in the pass, their villages had been respected and every effort made by presents and kindness to convince them that though necessitated to pass through their Country we came not as foes.

But Dora Bissoi continued to elude capture, and in spite of threats and offers of reward Konds would give no information about the fugitives' whereabouts. Again and again Kond guides misled British troops, to give their quarry time to escape.

Russell himself reached Udayagiri on 11th March to find many of the soldiers down with fever. He left Muriel there in command of 250 men, and made it the advance headquarters of his operations.[24] Then he went off to the lowland forest area between Posora and Gullery, where British troops were attacking villages and being ambushed by Konds, who used the dead sepoys' muskets and wore their uniforms, which infuriated the British. Russell sent Campbell to search out 'and punish the rebel Khondes, who appeared....to be in the habit of insulting our troops by appearing in the uniform of their murdered comrades'.[25]

Meanwhile Major Leggett and Lt Allan marched by night from Nowgam and surprised an enemy hideout near 'Sooroosoomoloo', killing 5 or 6 of the enemy, including one of the proscribed chiefs: 'Some execution has been done among the rebels [for which] we are indebted to Lt Allan's spirit'. A few days later Leggett captured Veerama Soonderay, another Hindu chief, in another early morning raid.[26]

In the same area a few days later Major Walter made a night march from Gullery to attack the *walsas* (hideouts) from which the Konds were making their ambushes. At the first a Kond guard was shot but the guide misled the force and most of the enemy escaped before the British got there. A second was found abandoned. Lt Donaldson, commanding a detachment of about 100 men, was led to the third by a guide whose wife and children were in it. The troops came upon it suddenly, and Donaldson was wounded in the fighting. Again the enemy had got warning: most had already left. The only people who remained were the guide's family. All these places were burnt to the ground, along with large stores of rice which the Konds had brought there for safekeeping.

On 3rd April Lt-Col Anderson attacked Ambazora, where Dora Bissoi was thought to be hiding. He found it empty and burnt it. But on his return via Bodungy he was attacked repeatedly by Konds.

> The rebels according to their invariable custom permitted him to proceed unmolested for a short distance, when they assailed him from the neighbouring heights, and killed two, and wounded six men before he reached the plains.[27]

At his headquarters in Nowgam Taylor held trials for some of the captured chiefs, and sentenced them to death by hanging. These executions, which the local population was forced to witness, were carried out over several days at various places, in order to make the maximum impact on the Konds. In some the corpse was left hanging in chains.[28]

The British were venting on their chosen enemies their own frustration and suffering, largely due to the Konds' great ally, malaria, whose cause was then unknown. The medical situation was dire: 1,350 soldiers were incapacitated by fever, and there was a desperate shortage of surgeons, carts to carry the sick, and medicines, especially quinine. Several more Surgeons were sent from Madras in April, among them Assistant Surgeon Cadenhead, who took charge of Kond affairs under Macpherson nine years later. Taylor listed 197 members of his army who had died so far—154 from fever. Six of the dead were European officers (including a lieutenant-colonel, probably Hodgson, who commanded the first troops that invaded Kond territory).[29] But Taylor wrote that at least 100 camp followers had probably died without record, and Russell mentioned that he had 'been through two sets of private servants' on this campaign: those who did not die outright had to be sent away.

Captain Butterworth commended the good service of the sepoys, since 'their European officers slept in a snug bed under a comfortable tent', and when sick were 'attended with all the care of the surgeon, who considers one Officer's life of more consequence than 50 sepoys'. The majority were Muslims from Tamil Nadu. Many of their wives and children came with them, so those whose husbands died were stranded over 1,000 miles from home. 'As a special indulgence' their commanding officer begged the Commander-in-Chief in Madras for 'some small but immediate assistance' to help them go home.[30]

The war was becoming a very expensive one, and the Madras Army sent its Assistant Quarter-Master General to supervise supplies.[31] Taylor was particularly keen to have more elephants: 'My dear Hanson', he wrote to the Army's Quarter-Master General, 'without the elephants we would never have been able to advance as we have done, and the rebels would have had it all their own way, believe me'.[32]

The war was now spreading to several of the neighbouring kingdoms,[33] while attacks on Kond villages continued. Captain Butler commanded one on the 25th April: four British officers on horseback, including Campbell, led 100 sepoys, surrounding the village at daybreak with their howitzer ready to fire,

> and did a lot of business—ten men of the Conds killed and a good many wounded—our sepoys bayoneted two of them. They took a good many prisoners and burnt the village and drove about 200 head of cattle and other things.[34]

Several prisoners were taken, but Bungo Muliko, who was in the village when the attack began, managed to escape. Several of the belongings of the British officers killed on 5th March were found there. After this, Butler 'did not hesitate to destroy several of the villages within reach', though once again Kond guides managed to save some lives by misleading the troops.[35]

In early May debilitated companies were withdrawn from the front, and the sick were carried laboriously back to the coast.[36] Russell led a force into Chinna Kimedi in pursuit of Dora Bissoi, after receiving information from Sam Bissoi, a local Hindu chief who played a highly ambiguous role in the war; but all they found was the shirt of one of the officers the Konds had killed.

Finally, in the second half of May, the army advanced beyond Udayagiri towards Saranghor, destroying Kond villages as they went, and capturing a fortified village called Nowgam on the 28th. The next day an army of Konds attacked and broke in. Several men were killed and wounded on both sides before they were driven out. When Captain Morgan ventured out with 19 men to search for an elephant that had broken loose in the fighting, he was attacked by an army of 500 Konds 'dressed in their wardress, yelling, blowing horns, beating tom-toms and flourishing their battle axes.' He drove them off by forming his men into a line and firing six rounds, killing several Konds. But they attacked the fort twice more.

The next day Russell arrived, and layed an ambush in a gully—Morgan with 8 men tempting the Konds to give chase. The howitzer was used, but the cavalry disgraced itself to Russell's mortification.

> If the nine troopers who had been ordered to charge as soon as our infantry had fired, had done their duty, they would have made an impression that would have lasted for years, but I regret to state that they forfeited on this occasion, the credit they had so well earned in former conflicts, never having drawn a sword or touched a man who had not been previously knocked down by the officers, although numbers were running in all directions. All they did or attempted to do was to pistol the unfortunate wretches already on the ground.... Notwithstanding these untoward events, the terror produced among the Khondes was so great that they never afterwards ventured in sight of our parties, still less attempted to molest them.[37]

Five Konds were killed in this battle. Russell then had several more villages burnt. In a village which Morgan attacked near Digi he took 18 villagers prisoner (5 men, 6 women, 7 children), and discovered some of the dead British officers' possessions. He tried to negotiate an exchange of the women prisoners for their chief, along with the regimental drum and muskets. A Kond came in carrying the drum, but when he claimed the chief had been killed and the muskets lost, he was seized and made prisoner himself.[38]

Nowgam was the farthest point the British reached in this campaign. The rains were about to start, making army movements in the hills impossible. Not wanting to appear to retreat, Russell left a severe warning.

> I ordered some villages to be destroyed, and left written explanations of my reasons, exhorting the people not to permit their chiefs to bring ruin upon them again by a guilty connection with outlaws, and threatening still more severe measures if it should hereafter be found that the warning thus given had been disregarded. In the low country the destruction of a village involves the punishment of the innocent with the guilty, but above the ghauts every man bears arms and joins the common cause.[39]

This warning he reinforced by a final public execution, the hanging of 'A Khond chief, who led the Khonds in their attack on Lt Gibbon's party and on Wodiagherry'. This was Bungo Mulliko, who had 'surrendered at discretion' on May 29th 'having been so hotly pursued by our troops under Captains Butler, Geills and Campbell'.[40] He was hung at Kormingia on June 22nd, under the supervision of Captain Todd, who led the last detachment of troops down to the plains the same day. This was the 23rd hanging during the war, but possibly the first hanging of a Kond. Taylor intended this execution to reinforce the

> severe retribution....inflicted on the different tribes of Khondes who had been in arms against us, very many of whom had been killed or wounded.... It may be hoped that the example furnished by the fate of this man and others who, like him, have paid the forfeit of their rebellion by an ignominious death, will have a good effect on the great body of the people.

Russell persuaded the Madras Government to pass an Act (No.XXIII of 1836) so that he could condemn prisoners to death with three rather than the usual nine European members; for several times he had wanted to 'make an example' without delay by hanging a rebel leader, including Sam Bissoi, who had admitted deceiving him.

> Though indifferent to blows, the Khondes have a great terror of the gallows, and if I had possessed the power to make an example of one on the spot, the lives and treasure since sacrificed, and still to be sacrificed in the endeavour to effect the capture of the fugitives then at our door would have been spared.[41]

By the time Russell left the hills and ended the first Ghumsur war the British had got hold of most of the 'treasure' of the displaced royal family (Rs 18,544/-and 5 Annas), most of it dug up from where a Kond chief had buried it.[42] Russell sent the long Report of 12th August (which we have been quoting) to Madras with Campbell, who was his personal secretary. This Report contains the first official mention of the Kond customs of human sacrifice and female infanticide. In response, the Madras Government declared it

> very desirable that measures should be taken for procuring the abolition of the practices of infanticide and human sacrifices.... Wherever British influence already prevailed, or could be newly introduced, it should be vigorously exercised for the suppression of these barbarous rites.[43]

During the rains, from June to November 1836, the British army was inactive, holding onto outposts in the core area of the Ghumsur plains. There was not much rain and the harvest was the worst in memory. Kond prisoners were released to carry 'proclamations in the simplest language' (but in Oriya not Kui) to counteract 'false information' among the Konds that the Government intended to collect revenue from them, and to dissuade them from protecting the wanted chiefs.

> It was explained to them that the duty required of them was only that which, according to immemorable custom they owed to the Sircar—namely obedience to the person whom it might appoint Bissoye over them, attendance in arms when their services should be required—the seizure and deliverance of all offenders obnoxious to its authority—and the trifling annual offering or nuzzur, according to their means, in token of allegiance.[44]

This idea of a *bissoi* as an official simply appointed by the Government was certainly new—these were heads of hereditary chiefdoms—but henceforth it was the law. Meanwhile some of the military classes were being won over: Stevenson had been reorganizing the land grants of the local *peons* since May.

From June three and a half regiments were posted in the Ghumsur plains. But over half the army was often down with fever. The number of sick went up to 1,648.[45] They had twelve surgeons to look after them, and a field hospital at Vishnuchakram. To try and check the malaria, which was blamed on the night air, 700 woollen cloaks were sent to the sepoys at the front, and they were made to sleep on wooden cots in barracks with high roofs to allow air to circulate. The cavalry were all sick at Berhampur. Taylor himself obtained a medical certificate and went off to recuperate in Waltair. The advance post, Mujjagudda, was especially unhealthy—three-quarters of the 230 men posted there were in hospital, including the European officers and surgeons. In order to mitigate 'the sacrifice at which it must be held' the three companies of sepoys were reduced to one (i.e. 70–90 men), and local militiamen were installed, who had much more resistance to malaria.[46]

Troops were sent up into the hills again on 20th November 1836, with orders from General Taylor not to initiate hostilities, but only (!) to prevent the Konds gathering in their harvest—'of course, if violence is offered by the Khondes, it must be repelled by force'.[47] However, Konds attacked the two main detachments in strength as they marched up, and 'murdered a couple of washermen in camp' soon after.

> The first blow was thus struck by the Khondes in both quarters, and was shortly afterwards followed by further acts of unprovoked hostility [which] left no alternative but to employ the force at our command to compel that submission which it was now but too plain could not be effected by other means.[48]

This army consisted of about 1,000 sepoys, under Russell, Taylor, Col Alves, Captain Campbell and other officers. This time Taylor made his HQ in the hills at Kormingia. On 26th November Capt. Roberts reported that he had destroyed 4 *walsas* and a lot of grain, and that on his return, when he was only a quarter of a mile from camp, Konds and 'matchlockmen' fired on them. Roberts led the cavalry against them, and killed several of the enemy. A cavalry trooper was killed and his horse captured by the Konds, but

> the man who killed him was followed and cut down by the Duffadar, all of whose party behaved very gallantly. One Doby, a private servant of Lt Luggard, who was following a little in the rear was cut down by the Khonds and severely mangled.[49]

On the same day Captain Byam led a party of 20 cavalry and 20 infantry to surprise a Kond village, where they killed Bourah Naik and six followers, and captured Daddiah Naik, whom they sent as a prisoner to Russell, who tried and executed him under Act XXIII. On the 28th Byam led an attack on another *walsa*, which they 'completely surprised', but because one of the company fired too soon, the enemy put up a defence, and the Kond chief Brae Mullicko instead of being captured was killed 'together with five of his followers, and his body was brought into camp (as he had a little life remaining when taken)'. Four prisoners were taken. The rest escaped.[50]

On 21st December Anderson reported that 'the Gullery peons' (i.e. Ghumsur men now serving the British) had captured two of the main proscribed chiefs, Sooniar Sing and Boliar Sing. Sungram Sing, the chief who had procured their capture was granted a 500/-Rupee reward.

Taylor reported the war at an end on 27th January 1837, after more chiefs had been captured and the muskets lost to the Konds recovered. But Dora Bissoi was still free, having shaken off all pursuit,

> after several hairbreadth escapes….leaving the Khondes to their fate…. [His] elder brother was slain fighting gallantly…. All Dora Bissoye's relations of note have been killed or taken…. He himself is now a wanderer beyond our border without adherents, influence or power….
> [By this time] The military classes who were our active opponents have given the best proof of their submission….by delivering up their own chiefs.[51]

Local chiefs who had served the British were confirmed in their positions and rewarded. Sam Bissoi, who had redeemed himself by helping the British in the second war, was appointed to Dora Bissoi's former position, and new Kond chiefs were appointed to replace those killed or captured.

After the war came more trials and executions. Out of 43 men publicly executed in the second war, at least 20 were probably Kond chiefs. Macpherson wrote that virtually all the Kond chiefs of Ghumsur were executed at this time, and in the words of Campbell (who played a prominent part in the war, as we have seen) 'numbers of Konds were killed like beasts and strung up on trees'. Many more received long sentences in distant jails 'with hard labour'.[52] The executions of Kond chiefs were witnessed by a Baptist missionary, the Reverend William Brown:

> one only of the leaders appeared with a straw in his mouth—a sign of deep supplication; the others shewed no fear: indeed there was a sullen sort of daring manifested at the place of execution by most of these unfortunate men. (*CCO* April 1837 p.164)

Dora Bissoi himself had taken refuge in Angul, and the *rajah* handed him over to the Commissioner in Cuttack in October on condition that his life was spared, receiving the Rs 5,000/-reward for his capture. Dora was seriously ill when he was taken, and a fistula had to be operated on before he could be moved to Chatrapur. There he was tried and sentenced to death, though this sentence was commuted to life imprisonment because of the previous promise. He was sent to the notorious jail in Gooty (South India), where Macpherson interviewed him for his report on the Konds, and took a liking to him.[53]

'Pacification'

We can only imagine Britons' calculated impact on Konds of elephants, camels, cavalry, cannons, sepoys in scarlet uniforms with muskets and bayonets, at attention or firing in line, tents, telescopes, tables and chairs, writing and surveying equipment, and the tight uniforms and boots of the *sahebs* themselves, concerned with an image of tremendous self-restraint and civilized actions they knew appeared mysterious to unfamiliar Indians. Konds showed they were not totally overawed by wearing the uniforms and using the muskets of soldiers they had killed, during attacks on troops—as American Indians and Australian Aborigines also did, in their resistance to white invaders.[54]

And what impression did the British ritual of public hangings create? What did Russell mean when he said they had a 'good effect' on the Konds?

From the British side this was essentially a war of 'pacification', forcing a 'rebel' (though previously uncontacted) tribe into submission. So the concept of 'pacification' makes an appropriate starting point for looking at British words and actions in greater depth. It is based in a paradox, referring to a military campaign that includes a lot of fighting and killing in order to force a submission to British rule, which was defined in terms of a permanent 'peace'—'Pax Britannica'. The Oxford English Dictioary gives the primary meanings of 'pacify' as 'appease' or 'reduce to a state of peace'. In fact this usually means waging war to impose peace. The concept therefore implies a contrast between 'state of war' and 'state of peace', as well as between 'state of war' and 'war to impose a state of peace'.

But what did this British peace consist of? To Britons, 'impartial justice' and 'law', 'protection' and 'security'; but in effect, it seems, *a state monopoly on certain forms of violence*, particularly on the legitimate taking of human life only by British officials acting under authority, in military campaigns or judicial executions. The *Pax Britannica*, like the *Pax Romana* it was self-consciously modelled on, involved a large, complex military machine of professional soldiers trained to kill—to enforce a 'peace' whose essential feature was this monopoly. For even when the direct military violence had ceased, there remained immense physical and psychological violence: the arrest and detention or imprisonment of numerous Konds, countless others being forced to act as coolies, and the high-handed behaviour of subordinate officials.

Yet Britons saw their enforcement of a long-term control as bringing 'peace' and 'justice', as a gift. This idea of wars to enforce a state of peace had powerful Christian associations. Pacifying the Konds, Britons saw as the first stage to 'civilizing' them. As Sir William Kaye put it:

> There are many kinds of war and many degrees of heroic renown, but the highest praise is due to those who, by their victorious arms, have opened new scenes for the civilization of mankind, and overcome barbarians in some important part of the world. (1853, title page)

There is no question of asking the barbarians if they would like to be civilized! For, as we have seen, it involved 'a conquest over their minds', in effect *conversion* to a new order, as when Macpherson spoke of 'the difficulty of converting barbarous men….into peaceful expectants of justice'—a difficulty that had to be overcome, these men believed, by the use of military force, the burning of villages, public executions, 'imprisonment with hard labor in irons' and so on; which is why they frequently mention these harsh actions as having a 'beneficial' or 'salutary effect', and 'making an example'.

The first sign of such a 'conversion' was subordination to British authority: 'obedience', 'faithfulness', 'submission to the will of Government', 'professions of allegiance', 'throwing themselves on the mercy of Government'. For British officials liked to show mercy and 'pardon' people—e.g. the 13 Kond chiefs Russell pardoned at the end of the war—unless individuals had 'placed themselves beyond the pale of forgiveness'. Again and again, Britons justified their acts of violence by pleading 'necessity', 'no alternative', implying their rule was not only 'just' and 'impartial' but essentially 'rational'—even when Konds were forbidden to harvest their crops! (above pp.49–50). The Ghumsur wars thus fitted into a Christian idea of 'a *just war*'.

Fundamentally, British officials were refusing to recognize Kond independence. They conceived of Kond resistance to conquest in terms of 'rebellion', and called the Konds' killing of British officers a 'murder', 'massacre' or 'outrage', while their own killing of Konds was a 'just retaliation', performed 'gallantly'. 'We came not as foes' Russell asserted, but it is hard not to see the campaign in the Kond hills as invasion or conquest.

A particular conception of legitimacy is deeply ingrained in this language: the British Government, with its laws and regulations, was seen as the source of legitimacy and as 'necessarily just', while the Konds were seen as essentially 'lawless'. In effect Britons legitimized their actions through their language. 'Justifying' is too weak a word. Through their language British officials *made their actions legal*, and defined Konds' actions as illegal.[55] The primary right they took away from Konds was the right to take human life, in the specific forms of human sacrifice, female infanticide, and warfare. These were the institutions British officials were first concerned to illegalize, or delegitimize. To Britons they proved that Konds were in need of British peace and justice. 'Loss of life' in a feud was the strongest mark of Konds' 'unlawfulness', and was later punished by taking the offenders' lives.

The idea that the Konds had previously existed in a 'state of war' goes back to Hobbes or beyond. The phrase 'wild tribes' conjures it up (as in the title of Campbell's memoirs, 1864). Macpherson touches on it when he writes about the Konds:

> Peace is their prevailing condition.... Among savage tribes the state of war is universal. At a more advanced stage hostility is limited....by compacts. The Khonds [are in this] second stage'.[56]

The idea of a 'state of war' is perpetuated by modern writers, who describe warfare as 'endemic in the Kond hills'.[57] Was warfare any less endemic in 19th century European or Indian society? It took a very different form certainly—on a much vaster and more centralized scale. But did British soldiers have any less of a 'predilection for warfare' than Konds? There is considerable irony in the British defining their own society by 'peace' and Kond society by 'war'.

Undoubtedly Konds were more or less 'a warrior tribe'. One of their main deities was Loha Penu, 'the iron war god'.[58] On the scale of Kond warfare the evidence is conflicting. Macpherson described a truly catastrophic form, an eyewitness account (which I do not trust) of a clan battle in which 90 Konds were killed and their right arms cut off by the enemy as a 'sacrifice', and the same number died 'from the entire ignorance of the Khonds of the simplest healing processes'.[59] Other evidence suggests that fighting was highly ritualized and casualties were usually low. Campbell wrote:

> I once witnessed two tribes, each numbering about 300 men, drawn up in battle array. On this occasion I prevented any serious results. They had already been three days engaged in the preliminaries of the fight, for many ceremonies are gone through "ere comes the tug of war" (1864 pp.42–3).

Kond wars, he wrote, consisted mostly of war dances and insults, with little loss of life. It is this kind of battle which Cadenhead prevented in December 1844 between the villages of Daringabadi and Grenobadi, when the former Konds

> begged for one more year's war, after which they would be prepared to listen to terms of peace. Finally they pleaded for one grand pitched battle to be fought in my presence, a proposition also made by the people of Grenobadi. (March 1845)

Eighteen years later, Forbes prevented a war between the same two villages, and left a description of Kond warfare in terms of dramatic battles that actually led to very few casualties, which is similar to the form of tribal warfare in many other parts of the world.[60] As British administration became routinized, feuding was regarded as a crime and strictly suppressed. But Macpherson at least was quite clear that Britons were 'giv[ing] Konds justice, not only as an end, but as a chief means of acquiring....dominion over them'.

The Kond armies—or 'mobs' as the British often called them—that faced British troops often numbered one or two thousand men, armed with axes, bows and arrows and a few matchlock muskets, and in impressive wardress.

> When equipped for war, they cover their breast with leather or bearskin, and decorate their heads with cocks' feathers; some of them also wear a slip of bearskin under their chin.[61]

But their casualties were much higher than usual in fighting the British, and their enemy showed them none of the customary respect, especially to prisoners, who were treated most ignominiously. Even the occasional 'mercy' or 'pardon', which to Britons signified their magnanimity, probably seemed the grossest insult to Konds, as to other Indians of that time. 'Why do they fight?' the sepoy Seeta Ram asked about the British. 'Not to kill their enemies, but to have the pleasure of capturing them, and then letting them go'[62]—which conveys the Britons' aim of enforcing a *habit of obedience* to their will.

Britons contrasted their own 'gallantry' with Kond 'savagery'. Their image of Konds oscillates between two polarized concepts rolled into one, 'noble' and 'savage'—like the European image of tribal peoples in general. Konds' nobility lay in their courage and 'hospitality', which was how Britons understood Konds' faithfulness to the Hindu chiefs. Macpherson described a captured Kond who killed himself by tearing out his own tongue, so as not to reveal information. On the other hand Konds were seen as 'wild' and 'cruel', like animals—'the disposition of the Khond partakes much of *animal* suspicion and cunning'.[63] The words used to describe how Konds move, kill or are killed often compares them to animals—'scamper', 'mangle'[64]—while words for British action suggest incisive, heroic performance—'gallant', 'dash', 'hotly pursue'. Which reminds us that this was a war of axes and bows and arrows against bayonets, muskets and cannons. The derogatory image of Konds as 'savages' was the main view, in line with the predominant view of tribal people as 'ignoble savages', from an early period of European expansion (Meek 1976). Campbell's description is typical:

> The Khonds are a degenerate race, with all the ignorance and superstition of savages. (1864 p.15)

The Deadly Pursuit of Honour

To Britons, warfare resembled a sport. As the sepoy Seeta Ram put it,

> the *Saheb log* and the *gora log* [non-officers] like fighting for the sake of fighting; and the latter, if they have but enough of their beloved spirit, are content; it is an amusement, a kind of *khel* (sport) to them (1911 p.44).

In fact, British officers' attitude to war seems to have a lot in common with their attitude to their favourite sport, *shikar*—hunting wild animals. There is the same preoccupation with dominating or subduing. Campbell went hunting with Konds.[65] 'Taking the field', as the phrase for entering a military campaign, also suggests 'the field' in hunting terminology. In hunting, as in warfare, British officers expressed a *habit of control*.

The passages quoted above show a great emphasis on qualities such as 'honour', 'duty', 'service', 'zeal' and 'self-sacrifice'. The British army was extremely hierarchical—great honour was attached to approval by superiors, and promotion depended on it. Russell, as the highest official involved in the war, was honoured by naming the town that grew up around the British base near Nowgam 'Russellkonda'.

The deaths of the two British officers in the Durgaprasad pass were seen as an infringement of *regimental honour*, which had to be regained by the recovery of the uniforms, muskets and regimental drum taken by Konds, as well as the killing of Konds in battles and public executions and the burning of their villages. A similar preoccupation with revenging Europeans killed by tribals with enormous 'interest' is evident in the history of many other tribes—in this as in many other cases, the conquest of a whole tribal people began as revenge.[66] This sense of regimental honour is vividly conjured up in a short story about a subaltern whose 'blooding' took place fighting against the Kachin tribals in Burma:

> He soon learned that the regiment was his whole family. Gradually he absorbed the lessons taught to him by the relics in the officers' mess; and to him every one of them spoke eloquently of honour, devotion to duty, heroic self-sacrifice, and *esprit de corps* as simple as it was magnificent.
>
> He made almost daily pilgrimages round the relics in the officers' mess, and always ended in front of the battle-scarred King's and Regimental Colours. They might hang there in rags and tatters, but they were the outward expression of an inward and spiritual thing that Hawkins could feel dimly surging within him.[67]

From this passage it is evident how allegiance to the regiment, and to the imperial authority it formed a part of, was an extension of family loyalty, and how intimately this was connected with personal honour on the one hand, and Christian sentiments on the other, of 'self-sacrifice', 'devotion', 'pilgrimage' and spirituality in general.

It was above all the impersonal flavour in the British code of honour, associated with abstract concepts of duty and selfless service, that appeared foreign to Indians, as in Seeta Ram's account of a duel between British officers:

> What curious customs the Feringhees have! Here, in this case, revenge was not taken at the time, when the anger was hot, nor was the fight with swords (the sword is a more honourable weapon—Editor). No words were spoken, no abuse given, but the Sahebs were as cool and collected as if on parade. What I did not understand was, the officer attending on the Major [who was killed in the duel] was a great friend of the Captain's, and both the attendant officers spoke to one another, and were friends, as they live in the same house. The English have rules about *izzut* very strict, and if they are insulted they must fight, or they are never again spoken to by their brother officers. (Seeta Ram 1911 p.47)

Seeta Ram's *From sepoy to subedar* (1911), translated from Urdu by a British officer in the 1860s, gives a revealing picture of sepoys' life and training.[68] The book is permeated with notions of honour, loyalty, duty, obedience and service that seem to fuse traditional Indian with British notions of regimental honour and duty to an impersonal Government. Seeta Ram sometimes examines the Britons he served as foreigners with the strangest of habits. The uniform and the parade ground drill he found particularly strange when he first joined up.

> The parade ground was covered by parties of six or eight men, doing the most extraordinary movements I had ever seen, and the orders were given in a language not one word of which did I understand. I felt inclined to laugh, and was lost in astonishment at the sight. However, a violent wrench of my ear by the drill Havildar brought me to my senses. (p.12)
>
> At first I found it very disagreeable wearing the red coat; for although this was open in front, it was quite tight under the arms.... The uniform of the Saheb *log* was very tight, and prevented the free use of the arms and legs. (p.14)

These tight uniforms were in extreme contrast to the looseness of most Indian clothing. Sepoys evidently found them uncomfortable and restrictive—although handsome! The tightness, which prevented free movement and severely constricted breathing was much complained of by even the most senior British officers.[69] Doubtless they had a symbolic aspect, expressing in the physical restraint they put on the soldier's body, the extreme discipline he had to keep constantly in mind. Sepoys, like British soldiers, learnt to perform a parade ground drill of barked commands and machine-like movements in automatic, unthinking response. After the Ghumsur wars, Campbell took some of the rescued *meriahs* and trained them as the beginnings of a Kond *corps*. As Foucault says of the parade ground drill that developed in Europe in the late 18th century, soldiers were made to behave like parts of a machine: they learnt to obey commands automatically and unthinkingly by being drilled in a series of abrupt movements of arms and legs that appeared extraordinary to someone seeing it for the first time (1977 Ch.III). The treatment of sepoys during the Ghumsur wars often seems very harsh. When Britons refer to sepoys as '700 bayonets' and their deaths in terms of '50 muskets lost', this implies the impersonal, machine-like function sepoys were trained to perform.

Butterworth warmly commended the sepoys' service in the first Ghumsur war.[70] Many British officers admired the sepoys they drilled and disciplined.[71] But as we have seen, 'one Officer's life [was reckoned] of more consequence than 50 sepoys', and the terms of sepoys' service were so harsh that a Major had to plead with the Commander-in-Chief in Madras for a special exemption from regulations to give the families of dead sepoys enough money to return home. (above p. 46)

Punish and Reward

The reverse side of this honour was punishment and shame for sepoys deemed to have disgraced their regiment, such as those who deserted their officers and lost their muskets and regimental drum on the Durgaprasad pass, and for the cavalry that failed to charge properly in the fight with Konds at Nowgam. Hence Russell's re-introduction of flogging, to punish sepoys who allowed prisoners to escape; perhaps also those who stole from the Konds, since he recognized that this played a large part in turning the Konds against the British.[72] Yet the beginning of oppression of Konds by lower officials, that soon became routine, was connected with the harsh, hierarchical way these officials were treated by their British officers. The extreme form of hierarchy which sepoys accepted as the basis of their working life was maintained by a balance of honour and rewards with shame and punishments—the same system of controlling people through punishments and rewards that formed the basis of the power structure which the British set up over the Konds.

We have seen the way various punishments were used as 'examples' to make Konds obey the Government's will. British officials seem to have performed at least one public execution in each new area to come under Government control. Russell said that if he had been empowered to execute more, 'the lives and treasure since sacrificed, and still to be sacrificed [in the war] would have been spared', which implies a view of *execution as sacrifice*—the occasional deliberate taking of a human life as an example that will persuade the population to submit, and thus save more lives.

Hanging, though normal in England, was a highly inauspicious form of death for Konds, as for Hindus, in that the soul of someone killed in this way was believed to become a ghost. These executions were intended as spectacles, and were carried out with military precision. In a photograph from the time of the Mutiny, sepoys stand to attention beside the gibbet with its limp corpses (Wurgaft 1983)—a kind of regimentation completely novel to a tribal people, signifying an extreme measure of control, the soldier's body acting automatically, like a machine. Some of the prisoners executed under Russell's regime were hung 'in chains', which means their bodies were to be left hanging for days or weeks to rot.

The punishments imposed in the first period of contact with Konds (1836–7) were particularly harsh (above p.51). At least 32 Konds were among those executed or imprisoned at the end of the second war alone.

Most of these were chiefs, as were the thirteen whom Russell 'pardoned' as a conciliatory gesture to try and gain Konds' goodwill.

Imprisonment was dreaded more by Konds even than execution according to Russell, especially 'transportation' to a distant location, for some of those convicted after the Ghumsur wars were sent to prisons a long way from Ghumsur. Some sentences were for 5–7 years, others were for life. This imprisonment was often 'with hard labour in chains', which means chain gangs of prisoners working on roads etc. This was part of the new system of punishment as *reform* which was institutionalized in the late 18th century (Foucault 1977). Prison life in British India was highly regulated, as a system of re-educating, and inculcating discipline, with techniques parallel to the parade ground drill, but far harsher, including treadmills, a lot of flogging, and clothes and food that were purposefully degrading.[73]

It is significant that some Konds were imprisoned right from the start of British rule. The prison system, because it carried 'a conquest over their minds' to an extreme, played a very important part in making a population accept the novel discipline of British administration. Administrators in India gave a lot of attention to the system in the mid-19th century. Prison routine demonstrated the radical, unprecedented extent of British power and 'rights' over living individuals, just as executions demonstrated the ultimate rights they claimed over human life. This routine propagated European ethics of work and discipline, and demonstrated over selected individuals administrators' intention to 'reform' what they saw as 'social evils'.

All these punishments were balanced by rewards. Officials were always keen to demonstrate that whereas those who disobeyed them would be punished, those who did their will would receive honours and favours as marks of the Government's approval. In effect they got control over the whole of Ghumsur by dividing the population, punishing those who stood up to them and rewarding those who came over to their side. In particular, chiefs who, like Sam Bissoi, were induced to abandon their old allegiances and help the British, were raised to positions of unprecedented power, while others were stripped of all authority.

The large monetary rewards which the British offered for the capture of the 'proscribed chiefs' formed part of this policy. It was a straightforward inducement to throw away allegiance to the old order, and accept service with the British. In his final report on the Ghumsur wars, Russell recommended many such rewards: Rs 1,000/-for several *bissois* who delivered up Brundawana Bunge (who was executed); the *rajah* of Athgarh, whose help was rewarded by reducing his annual tribute from Rs 55,000/-to 52,000/-; several of the Ghumsur *rajah*'s principal servants, who were rewarded with land grants; the son of a *sirdar* who guided British troops and 'fell a sacrifice to the revenge of the Khondes, who murdered him when sent to them with a message'—who was given fifty Rupees, for the sake of both 'justice and policy'; and

> among those of inferior class deserving consideration is Gunga Dora, who, as Duffadar of peons, behaved with great discretion and gallantry on all occasions, and Muddoo Bhera of Patlingia....who can never return to his native village

presumably because he had betrayed his fellow-villagers. *Rajahs* and chiefs were also regularly given presents, from cloth to a horse or elephant, whose cost was carefully calculated and charged to the Government in the Agents' monthly expense lists, starting with Russell, who included Rs 58/-'paid to spies'—a list of 29 men![74]

To Konds, these rewards and presents to chiefs for serving British officials must often have seemed like betrayal. It does seem to represent the co-opting of an elite through rewards, compromising them in the eyes of the general population, and therefore making them dependent on British military power. It was the military classes beginning to come over in 1836 that allowed Britons to win the Ghumsur wars, using one faction of the local chiefs against those who were 'in rebellion'. In Kond eyes, traitors were rewarded and promoted over them, in an alien regime.

One contemporary British view of the Ghumsur war and the Konds was that of Julia Maitland, whose *Letters from Madras during the years 1836–1839 by a Lady,* was a bestseller. Her husband was the Judge of Rajahmundry, not far south of the war zone. But her letter of 15th December 1837 reveals a surprising ignorance of events reported in English newspapers, and demonstrates the power of stereotypes as news gets passed on.

> In your last letter you ask if we have been alarmed by an insurrection of which the papers have spoken. I never heard of anyone being frightened at it, and it is all quiet now. It was 600 miles from Madras, and I never even heard the particulars of it till this gentleman passed through. He had been engaged in helping to quell it. He told me that a new tribe, hitherto unknown, had been discovered among the rebels: a fine, manly, but fierce race, showing many traces of Jewish origin, both in countenance and habits. They worshipped an

> invisible God, but had also one wretched image perched on a tree, which they seemed to look upon as a sort of devil to be propitiated. Unlike the other natives of India, they all live in houses, boarded, floored and ceiled with cedar wood. (p.139)

A different view comes from a missionary, the Reverend Brown, who visited Ghumsur in 1837 to report on the war in the *Calcutta Christian Observer*.

> The destructive ravages of war are still visible: the towns are destroyed and the inhabitants either dead or fled to the woods. This gives the whole a desolate appearance, but the terrible devastation of war extends only to those districts which took a decided part against the Government, and which are generally immediately above the ghats; they will long remember the consequences of this insurrection. Not only are the habitations of Man destroyed, but the harvest of last year, and all the stores for the future have shared the same fate. It is hoped the Government, having chastised them as rebellious subjects, will now pity their helpless state and relieve them. (*CCO* April 1837 p.165)

As he went among the Konds' burnt villages, he gave them tobacco and exchanged some words with them, telling them he 'pitied their helpless and destitute condition', but that he had nothing to do with the war: 'my business is to teach men how they may be happy after death'.[75]

In the next chapter we shall follow the *Meriah* campaigns, that over the next 25 years brought all Konds under British rule. A multitude of voices and different perspectives speak to us through the Government records of these campaigns. British officials often disagreed sharply with each other, and their Reports also contain fascinating evidence on the structures of power and authority that existed between Hindus and Konds before British rule, as well as the way the British changed these structures in establishing a control over the Konds that was more far-reaching than anything they had met before.

In my text I have kept my narrative and analysis as simple as possible, and put into the footnotes many of the quotations and other details that would bore some readers, but which will be rich in insight for someone who knows central Orissa, or for the specialist, or anyone who wishes to get drawn more deeply into this complex 'frontier society'.

But these records give only tantalizing glimpses of how Konds saw these events. Reverend Brown probably cut a bizarre figure to the Konds he met, wandering in tight, black, clerical garb through devastated villages, speaking of Life Hereafter. But what was their impression of the scarlet-uniformed sepoys, and the be-whiskered *sahebs*? And in what language did Brown and the British officials speak with Konds? British spellings of local names show that their ears were not well attuned to local accents. None knew the Kond language yet; few, probably, knew Oriya, and at this date maybe few Konds knew it either, so most communication must have passed through Oriya translators, with the British speaking their 'bazaar Hindustani'. So what of Russell's proclamations? What did Konds understand of the British and their motives beyond their violent 'punishments' and corrupting 'rewards'?

CHAPTER THREE

Suppressing Human Sacrifice: The Meriah Agency

'The Right of the Government.... Did not Admit of a Question'

During the war Russell collected more reports about human sacrifice. Mr. Stevenson and Captain Millar had rescued about 30 *meriahs* (victims).[1] The first impulse of the Madras Government was to order vigorous measures to suppress the custom (above pp.48–9), but Russell warned against using force, or even illegalizing it yet, as this would 'lead to the permanent occupation of an immense territory, and involve us in a war with people with whom we have now no connexion' at a 'fearful sacrifice of life from sword and sickness'. The Madras Government agreed,[2] but nevertheless appointed Campbell to take charge of Kond affairs, to try and suppress the sacrifices peacefully. Meanwhile the custom had also been reported among the Konds in the area that fell under the Bengal Government, and a number of *meriahs* had been rescued there.[3] The matter was reported in newspapers in Britain and India: 'A painful....interest [in these] barbarous customs' was felt by the Government as well as the literary public.[4]

So Campbell returned to Ghumsur after the war as Assistant to the Collector of Ganjam District.[5] In the winter of 1837–8 he made his first tour with a small force: 25 regular sepoys of the 17th Madras Native Infantry and 44 *peons*. These were local men, members of Ghumsur's old militia class, the first members of a corps of *sebundies* ('irregulars') whom Campbell had collected and drilled himself. Wherever he went, he collected the Kond headmen ('*mullickos*') and 'peremptorily ordered them' to bring their *meriahs* in to him. His tour lasted about four weeks, and included the main areas of the Ghumsur hills that had seen fighting in the war. He returned with 100 *meriahs* in his care. Captain Millar had declared that in collecting *meriahs*,

> Force and intimidation were the means I employed, and I do not apprehend any danger from the exhibition of a military force....

But the Madras Government requested Campbell to observe

> the most conciliatory deportment [towards the Konds] and go amongst them as a friend....without risking any steps likely to lead to the necessity of using force.

He was allowed a maximum of 50 regular sepoys, 'exclusively for the protection of his person, and...not...for any purposes whatever of compulsion or violence'. As events proved, this was not realistic: implicitly, Konds were being made to accept British rule.[6]

Meanwhile Mr Bannerman, the new Collector of Ganjam, was trying to convict some of the Doms who kidnapped *meriahs* and sold them to Kond headmen. The first case was reported in November 1837. A man called Lutcheman Bheemoo, who had been kidnapped from Parla Kimedi and sold to a Kond headman in a remote corner of Chinna Kimedi, managed to get a plea for help to his friends; they contacted the local police chief, who sent a party of four *peons*, to which the *rajah*s of Jeypore and Chinna Kimedi added several more. They got the local Hindu chief of Subernagiri on their side. But the Kond headman who had bought Lutcheman 'used violence against the rescue party', and refused to give him up until threatened with punishment. Finally he knocked away the chain that held Lutcheman, but would not release two more *meriahs*. Russell commented that this headman, 'Majee', was innocent, since the Konds had never been taught that human sacrifice was a crime.[7] But of the trader who had kidnapped Lutcheman and sold him to the Konds, 'his act admits of no palliation and his punishment may be expected to have a good effect'. The Directors of the East India Company in London agreed that 'the severest measure of punishment might justly be inflicted' on *meriah* traders. This one had left his own two daughters with the Kond headman as surety until he got hold of Lutcheman, whom he sold for 45 rupees. However, he could not be convicted because the Kond headman could not be made to attend as witness. The same problem came up in future trials.[8]

In the winter of 1838 Bannerman made a tour with a larger force (60 sepoys and 300 *peons*) in order to rescue the *meriahs* who had been left in the *Maji*'s village in Subernagiri. He arrived just as a human sacrifice seemed about to be performed, and laid hold of the *Maji*.

> To the arguments used by me, as to the heinous nature of putting a fellow creature to death, and the folly of supposing that any advantage could possibly result from so sinful an act, the Konds replied that they paid no tribute, and owed no allegiance to us; that the Meriah had always been practised from time immemorial....

The Konds were drunk, and having got the *meriah*, Bannerman took hostages and left, sending to another village 'a small party of *peons*, with a written notification, threatening summary punishment if the [intended] sacrifice took place, with which requirement they thought it prudent to comply', and gave the *peons* seven more *meriahs*—though they found out later that a *meriah* was sacrificed anyway a few days after he left.

Campbell's base of operations was Russellkonda, where a regiment was now stationed. From there he 'ascended the *ghats* [hills]' and made another tour in the winter of 1838–9, in which he ventured into new territory, entering the kingdom of Boad. He found out about three recent human sacrifices—two in Sam Bissoi's *mutah* (territory), and one in Tentilghor.

> All the other Molikos declared that no meriah was sacrificed within their territories, but in the same breath begged permission to offer one victim yearly in each mutah. The refusal did not seem to bother them much.... The more I see of the Khonds, the more is my opinion confirmed that unless we address ourselves to their fears as well as to their better feelings, our steps for the suppression of the meriah pujah will be slow indeed. (15th Jan. 1839)[9]

The *bissois* expressed horror at the custom, yet were 'wholly unable to coerce the Khonds' to stop it. They actually requested the British to issue a proclamation forbidding the *meriah* sacrifice—presumably so that Konds would not blame them for imposing this new law.[10] Campbell recalled that in 1836–7 Sam Bissoi, accompanying Russell through Kond villages, asked not to be released from his chains—presumably so that it was clear to Konds that he was being coerced. During this tour Campbell captured two 'notorious' *meriah* traders. He requested permission to build an outpost of thatched barracks at Udayagiri (which was a Hindu village) for 60 *peons*, so as not to expose his soldiers' health 'to the dangers of the night air'. This became the first permanent British outpost in the Kond hills.

Lt Hill had started a survey of the Kond area in 1838 to discover more about the sacrifices. Like Campbell, he declared that persuasion alone was not enough to make Konds stop the practice, a view he supported with a stereotyped image of the Konds, that reveals how Britons perceived them at first contact.

> This race....is on the very lowest verge of civilization.... The disposition of the Khond partakes much of *animal* suspicion and cunning, and it is to be recollected that the varying ideas of his mind are more nearly allied to *instinct* than to the powers of reasoning, and perception between right and wrong, which are the results of education and civilization. Attempt to reason with a Khond and he refers to the customs handed down from his ancestors; try to persuade him his ancestors were wrong, he looks upon you with dread, and supposes you are endeavouring to entrap him into compromising himself in some fancied manner; but let him know it is positively ordered to do a thing, and let him see before his eyes power, to carry that order into effect, and he will obey. For the suppression of Thugee a strong and almost arbitrary power has been exerted by local authorities, most beneficially for the public good....(2nd July 1838)

Hill made another tour in 1840–1, with a company of the 50th Madras Native Infantry and eight elephants. Unlike Campbell, he went with no demands for the Konds, but was ostensibly surveying for a road to connect Russellkonda to Sonepur. Although his main purpose was collecting information about human sacrifices, 'expediency dictated the absolute necessity of refraining from open allusions to the practice of sacrificing human beings' for fear of alarming the Konds. He visited the kingdoms of Jeypore, Boad and Kalahandi, and gave details of *meriahs* held and human sacrifices scheduled in seven *mutahs*.[11]

Campbell made further tours in the winters of 1840 and 1841, capturing more *meriah* traders and rescuing more *meriahs*, for the trade in *meriahs* continued, showing that 'the intention to continue the sacrifice continues with undiminished force'. In January 1842 he reported that Konds were at last returning to villages they had fled in the Ghumsur wars—with resulting land disputes. Several markets were flourishing, and Brinjaris (a merchant caste) were travelling with bullock carts through the Konds' territory again, and paying a duty on their goods to the Government. Campbell had rescued 125 *meriahs* since January 1838. Of these, 15 had been restored to their relations, 23 had become servants or minor Government employees (including several joining the ranks of Campbell's 'trusty sebundies'), 34 were being supported by the Government, 11 women had been married off with dowries, and no less than 47 had died—which is probably as many as would have died in the sacrifices, or more. The main cause was the unfamiliar climate, but they were also in a bewilderingly new situation, and often tried to escape from British care.[12]

Two human sacrifices had recently taken place in Ghumsur, one of them in Kormingia, 'which mootah is more accessible and more under observation and control than any other part of Khondestan', while Ram Mooliko its chief was 'considered to be better disposed to pull in with the Govt. than perhaps any other of the Khoond Moolikos'.[13]

In the winter of 1841–2 Campbell left Orissa to serve in the infamous 'Opium war' against China. He was succeeded by Captain Samuel Charters Macpherson, who had been employed to make a survey of the Konds during the Ghumsur wars. During this survey, Macpherson's health was damaged by malaria, so he had taken a year's leave in the Cape (South Africa) to recuperate, where his closest servant, Baba Khan, accompanied him.[14] Returning to Madras in September 1840 he continued his Kond survey by interviewing Kond prisoners in their dispersed jails—'I have been listening to and consoling them all, poor souls, to their infinite gratitude' (16th Aug. 1841). Finally he completed a long Report on the Konds of Ghumsur and Boad (1842).[15] He was told that Lord John Elphinstone, the Governor of Madras, 'had never taken so much interest in anything', when he gave him his unfinished paper (2nd March 1839, WM p.141). In Calcutta he conferred with Lord Auckland, India's Governor-General, whose attention was engrossed in a drawn-out war against Burma.

> He went through my long report very thoroughly as did his secretary and chief adviser. He said that before he had not had the most distant idea of the thing, and that all that he had said had been in the most utter ignorance; that he did not see his way in the least; that it was the most difficult subject he had ever contemplated—….a vast social and religious question—….the most impracticable for a Government to deal with.… I told him as I had told the Madras people, that my "instructions" were nonsense, and that as they were susceptible of any one meaning quite as much as of any other, I meant to do what circumstances might prescribe. He requested me to write everything that I did or thought to his secretary and confidant for his information, and said that he would always be glad to help me in any way…. The difficulties I have to contend with—between two Governments looking opposite ways, an imme-

> diate superior [Bannerman] looking a third, foolish orders, rascally public servants, and only my Baba fit for the work—are infinitely greater than I had any conception of before coming here. The other servant, an able brahmin, I should tell you, has just died. The Hindus think themselves polluted by conversation with these Khonds (who, on the other hand, look down upon them), and are dreadfully afraid of the climate.... (16th Nov. 1841, WM pp.162–3)

Macpherson's instructions as Assistant to the Ganjam Agent were to use the surveying of a road as a pretext for dealing with the sacrifices (WM p.159).

His first tour in the winter of 1841–2 was cut short by malaria: over half his men went down with it and two died. After this he set out to win over the Kond chiefs of Ghumsur one by one, for they presided over 'a region 30 miles long by 12 broad, and including four great tribes, divided into nearly 100 distinct branches' (15th Feb. 1844). Human sacrifices were now being performed again openly he wrote in April 1842.

> We have in point of fact established no civil authority here; and you will I think agree with me that the establishment of distinct relations with the Khonds as subjects must precede any attempt to act upon their religious opinions and practices. A missionary might begin at the other end—not, I conceive, the Government.... We have assumed a certain degree of vague authority.... The Khonds most earnestly desire of us justice—not betwixt man and man, which their own institutions can afford, but betwixt tribes and their divisions, which the authority of these institutions is too feeble to reach; particularly since we deprived them of their chief patriarch [Dora Bissoi].... Campbell passed many decisions affecting the most important rights of these tribes. There existed no means of carrying those decisions into effect but the employment of Sam Bissye to see them enforced. Sam has done nothing but plunder every party to every dispute, which the power and the wealth with which we have invested him enable him to do without difficulty. (WM pp.177–8)

The Konds were complaining that their rights were infringed by Sam being 'set over them....a *Hindoo*, the servant of a *single* tribe'. Sam admitted he had plundered them, but said this was necessary to keep them in order. On the contrary, Macpherson declared that only when the Konds realized the British intentions to them were of 'pure benevolence', could the Government 'obtain entire possession of the minds of some section of the Khond people'.

In 1842 he got two of the 'four great tribes' to begin to refrain from human sacrifice. In June the chiefs of Barah Mutah made a promise, which they kept, not to perform any that year. In August 19 of the 21 Kond chiefs of Atharah Mutah came to meet him. In December he reported that four human sacrifices had been performed in Atharah Mutah since then, but that he now 'commanded' 15 of the branches, and these four sacrifices 'were not performed in the usual way, the victims being buried whole and unbroken, without any festivals or assemblies, and by villages, not tribes' (WM p.185).

On his next tour in January 1843, he 'settled above 100 disputes.... So far as I could go, the people are conquered by the sense of practical benefit conferred, and strongly desire to be within our pale'. He brought away 113 *meriahs*, of whom 'one....was rescued from under the knife'. However,

> Many of these victims, instead of being grateful for their deliverance, have to be hunted like monkeys by the Khonds before they can be caught; so that the prospect of sacrifice cannot be so disagreeable as some people imagine after all.[16]

In April 1843 he requested permission to remove Sam Bissoi from the headship of Hodzoghor on the grounds that he had actually authorized three of the recent sacrifices.[17] But Bannerman, who favoured Sam and refused to believe this charge against him, failed to forward this Report to Madras. In October, he still had not done so—at this time he was diagnosed as 'sick in body and mind', and went off to recuperate. In December 1843, under due authority from Madras, Macpherson removed Sam Bissoi for authorizing six human sacrifices. He made a big public occasion of it, and returned a sacred image symbolizing the headship, which Sam had expropriated, to the *Dulbehra*, Sam's rival. As Baba Khan related what happened in a Telugu chronicle of Macpherson's administration,

> Gopee Sing, the Sirdar of the sebundies, proceeded to the village of Sam Bissye, where the deity was deposited, and surrounded it with his guard, who wandered hither and thither unsuspecting and wonderingly, as if they were only going for water to the river. I proceeded by my master's orders, with some sebundies, together with an elephant to impart respect and fear, to see the deity restored. We all slowly brought the deity to my master, who was sitting under a large mango-tree, with Soondera Sing and all the Khonds of Hodzoghor and Tentilghor in a council, relating to them, 'That in former times all nations

> sacrificed, and lived very poorly; but gradually, by their own experience, or that of others, they relinquished the practice, and became prosperous.'[18]

But some of the Konds in Hodzoghor saw Sam as a 'martyr for their religion', and told Macpherson 'We do not want your justice....and we will maintain our religion, and will have for our chief one of the race of its great defender [i.e. a member of Sam's family]' (15th Jan. 1844). In other words, in the eyes of this clan of Konds it was for them, not the Government (or *rajah*), to choose their chief.

Yet after a third tour early in 1844, Macpherson declared 'the whole of the Ghumsur Khond country....is completely conquered, and by the influence of moral influence alone.'(15th Feb. 1844) In July he wrote:

> I now see my way to a beginning of schools among the Khonds, and am deeply engaged in getting up an Oriyah spelling-book, and a First Book of Universal Religion and Morals for them. (Letter of 17th July)

His chief assistant, Assistant Surgeon Cadenhead, began learning the Kond language at this time. Macpherson left him in charge of Kond affairs in 1844 to extend British influence among the Kond chiefs of the female infanticide tracts of west Ghumsur, while Macpherson went to Calcutta again in order to work out the details of a new Agency that would give him authority over all the Konds, who were divided between different administrations.[19]

For the Bengal Government had been making separate attempts to deal with the sacrifices: Mr Mills, as Superintendent of the Tributary Mahals in Cuttack, sent messages to the *rajahs* who had Konds in their kingdoms, asking them to get hold of the *meriahs* and to forbid human sacrifices, and Lt-Col J.R. Ouseley did the same in the South West Frontier Agency.[20] In 1844, Mills made Lt Hicks his Special Assistant for suppressing human sacrifice, and sent him on a tour to enforce these orders. On his first tour (Feb.-May 1844) Hicks met up with a Hindu chief called Noboghon Khonro, who was soon to become a focus of resistance to British rule. On this tour several Kond headmen in Bulscoopa came near to opposing him. Hicks made a second tour in 1845, going through Nyagarh and Daspalla kingdoms. At Raneegunge he came into contact with Madhwa Khonro, the other great chief of the area, who like Noboghon, maintained his independence from the *rajah* of Boad. Hicks 'frightened [him] into propriety', and collected more *meriahs.* One Kond *sirdar* he wanted to punish for the performance of a human sacrifice, but Mills vetoed this, on the grounds that he had never promised to abstain before. Hicks was forced to end this tour when dysentery attacked his camp (Mills 1st & 16th June 1844).

By Act XXI of December 1845, Macpherson finally became head of the Agency for the Suppression of Human Sacrifice and Female Infanticide in the Hill Tracts of Orissa—the Meriah Agency for short. As Agent, Macpherson had authority in Bengal as well as in Madras territory, and reported direct to the Governor-General in Calcutta (rather than to the Government of Madras, as previously).

It was a post full of ambiguity. This goes back to Russell's first reports of human sacrifice, and the Madras Government's comment: '*wherever British influence already prevailed or could be newly introduced*, it should be vigorously exercised for the suppression of these barbarous rites' (p.49 above, italics mine). Is this not a subtle way of ordering the Konds' conquest? 'Influence' is a euphemism for 'authority', which was imposed more or less harshly. Similarly, 'go amongst them as a friend' sounds very nice, but is it not extremely remote from the 'peremptory orders' (or worse) that were already the usual way for the British to approach Konds?

Lord Elphinstone, Governor of Madras, expressed this ambiguity masterfully and grandly:

> It is not by violent measures we can hope to succeed (par.1).
>
> The enormity of the crime and the extent of the misery which it entails, call for our interference.
>
> The complete independence claimed by the hill tribes strike[s] everyone who reads the papers describing them. It appears to me that it is desirable to take every proper opportunity of removing this impression, and of accustoming the hill tribes to look to us as the ruling power, to whom obedience is due. (Minute of 16th March 1841 par.s 5 & 15)

In other words, British officials were 'to remove the impression' that Konds were independent (Russell had frankly acknowledged that they were, above p.64) by 'accustoming' them to a new regime. To Sam Bissoi and a host of local officials who followed him, this 'accustoming' boiled down to extortion and brutality, cowing Konds into accepting their authority.

Macpherson had made it explicit that to stop the *meriah* sacrifice, Konds first had to be made British subjects.

> We have to attempt chiefly, by grafting our authority upon the institutions of these tribes, to give them justice, not only as an end, but as a chief means of acquiring the dominion over them which is necessary to effect our objects. (Report of 18th August 1842)

Lord Elphinstone supported this policy.

> The great omission in the former intercourse with these tribes, seems to have been an acknowledgement on our part, of the duty of affording protection and justice to the Khonds; on their side, of submission and obedience to the Government. In the proposals made to Captain Macpherson by the Khonds of Bara Mootah, which were universally agreed to by them, this omission has been supplied.... at all events, we have now acquired an acknowledgement of our right to interfere, which the tribes cannot dispute.... too much stress cannot be laid on the combination of *measures for the expedient of controlling* the tribes, with our efforts for the suppression of the barbarities which they practise. (Minute of 24th September 1842, my italics)

As Macpherson described this right to the Konds he met:

> the designs of the Government were of paternal benevolence alone, not, as was presumed of hostility, [and] the existence of the rite of human sacrifice was a subject of the deepest concern to the Government, and of horror to all mankind beyond these hills; and that *the right of the Government to suppress it, as a rite, which all mankind concur in condemning, not as erroneous, but as impious and unlawful, did not admit of a question.* (April 1842, my italics)

Indeed, Konds could and did dispute this right to interfere; as they foresaw, suppressing human sacrifice was to be the thin end of the wedge of an alien and extremely oppressive regime.

This touches on another contradiction in the Government's policy—the idea that its authority was to be established, but without using force. Campbell (like Millar and Hill, above pp.65 & 67) declared that it was sometimes necessary to use force, and always necessary to show it. Macpherson was soon calling up a much larger force as he got drawn into a full scale war.

Missionary propaganda played an important part in inspiring the decision to suppress human sacrifice.[21] Ultimately, it was based on the idea that human sacrifice was unlawful, contravening divine law as well as the first principles of human law: 'equally contrary to the laws of God and men' in Lord Elphinstone's words (Minute of July 1841). The idea of a moral necessity for the Government to stamp it out derives from texts such as William Paley's *Principles of Moral and Political Philosophy*

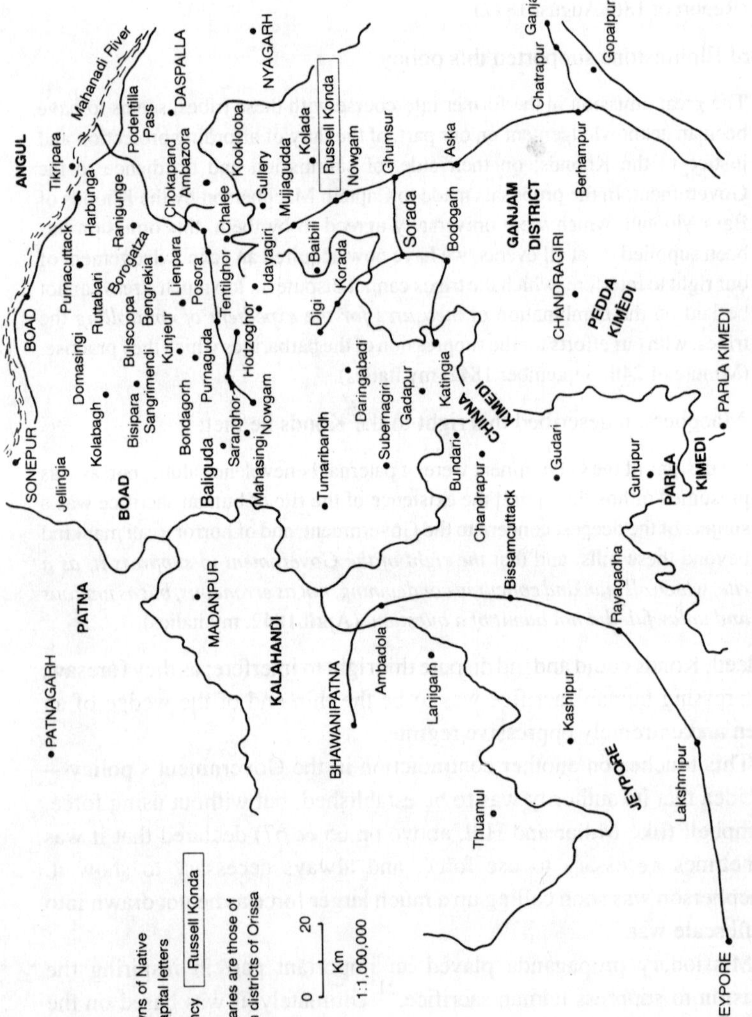

Map 4: The Meriah Agency, 1837–61

(1786), a key text in the East India Office Company's training of its officials. Paley bases Civil Government in the Christian Scriptures and the Will of God, thus deriving British law from divine law. The descriptions of the *meriah* sacrifice certainly emphasize its cruelty and 'savagery', making its suppression appear a self-evident necessity. The fact that it led to the Konds' conquest came to be virtually forgotten. In chapter 5, I will suggest that a deeper reason for this self-evident quality concerns Victorian Christian categories of thought, by which human sacrifice was *anomalous* because it juxtaposed the idea of sacrifice with ideas about the death penalty and public executions: *anomalous* because it was killing on a different rationale from British killing. Suppressing human sacrifice and infanticide was part of the Government's creation of a monopoly on the taking of human life.

Macpherson's War

Macpherson got off to a difficult start as Meriah Agent. His former superior Mr Bannerman was back in Ganjam, and took opposite views on almost everything, starting with the question of who should have authority over the tributary kingdoms of Sorada, Bodogarh and Chinna Kimedi, he or Macpherson?[22] Macpherson claimed the Konds saw the British officials as divided and actually believed that Bannerman permitted human sacrifices! For Bannerman trusted the very set of Hindu chiefs whom Macpherson believed were covertly encouraging them to continue. Macpherson also fell out with a new Assistant, Lt MacViccar, whose close relationship with Baptist Missionaries was arousing intense unease about the Agency's motives among Hindu officials. MacViccar resigned in January 1846.[23]

Macpherson's real trouble began when he tried to take a large number of *meriahs* from a new area outside Ghumsur, in the kingdom of Boad. Wherever Campbell and Macpherson had gone, their main demands were to stop the human sacrifices and to hand over *meriahs*. Many *meriahs* had been born and lived all their lives in Kond villages. It is unclear what proportion were sacrificed, but it seems likely that it was fairly low; *meriahs* worked as serfs for their Konds and a village's prestige was closely tied to the number of *meriahs* there.[24] Be this as it may, handing over *meriahs* became, without doubt, a key symbol to Konds as well as to the British, of Konds accepting British rule.

In February 1846 Macpherson ventured beyond Ghumsur into the kingdom of Boad, reporting that he was trying to get recognition of Government authority from the Boad Konds, who 'had made up their minds to yield....but....offered to the earth goddess one immense valedictory sacrifice, comprising 125 victims' two or three months before (WM p.245).

On 26th February he accompanied the *rajah* of Boad to meet the Hindu and Kond chiefs of his kingdom. The *rajah* seemed distinctly uneasy, and Macpherson thought him devious, declaring 'The Rajah is a stupid sensualist, under total sway of Koortibas'. Koortibas was the *rajah*'s maternal uncle who managed affairs with the Konds, and to whom they apparently paid five rupees for each human sacrifice they performed. Macpherson told the *rajah* to stop deceiving him, and addressed the Konds himself to demand the surrender of their *meriahs*. They collected 172 and presented these to him 'with emulous haste'. But just as he was about to take them away, the chiefs suddenly went off and held secret meetings by themselves, under Koortibas' influence. On 14th March 'a large Kond mob' assembled near Macpherson's camp and demanded the *meriahs* back. They were under 'the exasperating delusion' that the demand for *meriahs* was the first stage of oppression by the Government (the truth as it turned out!). Macpherson accused the *rajah* of complicity; he did not deny it directly but 'to save his honor' asked to take the *meriahs* into his own care, pledging their safety. Macpherson gave them, and retreated three miles over the border into the Hodzoghor territory of Ghumsur, sending for more troops from Russellkonda.

But Sam Bissoi's sons joined Koortibas' cause, and on 19th March a Kond army attacked Macpherson's camp at Kunjeur, which had just been reinforced by three companies. The Konds were driven back, and Macpherson would not let the local 'friendly' Konds pursue them. He marched to Purnaguda and arrested six 'hostile' chiefs, including one of Sam's sons. Two more were at the head of an army of 1,000 Konds which attacked the British again on 1st April. This time, after beating them back, Macpherson fired five Kond villages and authorized the allied Konds to burn three more—actions he deemed 'essential to maintain the prestige of the Government'. Most of the 'rebel chiefs' submitted within a few days, and he left the hill tracts 'in perfect tranquillity' on 15th April.[25]

To me, there are several things about these events that seem very strange or unlikely. For a start, the idea that the Boad Konds had just performed a 'final' sacrifice of 125 *meriahs* seems difficult to believe. Elsewhere there is little reliable mention of more than one person being sacrificed at a time. Apart from this, it is obvious that there were basic misunderstandings between Macpherson and some of the Hindus and Konds, but I am not convinced that Macpherson perceived these clearly. It seems that his demand to surrender the *meriahs* activated rivalries between Hindu chiefs as well as between Kond clans, and that he often took sides, swallowing all that one side told him about the other; also that he failed to understand that the Hindu chiefs' authority over the Konds depended completely on the Konds' consent, which the chiefs guaranteed by patronizing Kond religious rituals, including the *meriah* sacrifice.[26]

The Government in Calcutta certainly found these proceedings very strange. They had not heard from Macpherson for three months, and only learnt about this fighting from the newspapers and some amazed queries in the Madras army.[27] Lt Prinsdale, stationed at Russellkonda, wrote to his commanding officer, Major Bird:

> I am sorry to say that letters from Camp this morning convey the intelligence of another attack by the Khoonds which ended in four being killed and several wounded, they were pursued by the Light Company and Capt.Macpherson's escort,—Capt. Macpherson has now taken to burning the villages and has succeeded in obtaining a few of the ringleaders, whom he has with ropes round their necks to frighten them, as he says, and persuade them to let him know something regarding the rebels. I imagine they [i.e. Macpherson's force] will not be in for some time yet, as in the present state of affairs any retrograde movement would not look well on Capt. Macpherson's part.[28]

Major Bird, who was in Berhampur, also had reports from the military commander with Macpherson, and wrote to the Commander of the Northern Division of the Madras army, who was at Waltair, expressing his anxiety about this use of his troops in the unbelievable policy of burning Kond villages.[29] These reports finally found their way, via Madras, to the Governor-General in Calcutta, with a request for clarification: was Macpherson really allowed to use British troops to terrorize the Konds like this?

After Macpherson 'dismissed' him at Kunjeur the *rajah* of Boad tried to persuade the Konds to disarm without success, and returned to his capital, where he got his closest followers to try. They too failed, apparently due to Koortibas' intrigues. At this point Macpherson saw Koortibas as the main villain, and tried to put him in his place by refusing to meet his officials.[30]

The *rajah* of Boad felt dishonoured by Macpherson's behaviour to him, which had undermined his authority over the Konds, so he wrote to Colonel Ouseley, who supervised the Bengal Government's dealings with him, complaining of this and giving him a very different account of events from Macpherson's.

> I write from Bodh 35th year Monday 10th Cheyt. The state of affairs is thus.... I was going to Juggernauth [Puri] when I received a perwana [letter] from the Commissioner Saheb.... On perusal it appeared to contain the following order: "By reason of your not interfering in the matter of the meriah your country has been taken into the Dakshin Zillah [Madras Presidency]. You are therefore to report to Russelconda and present yourself to the Saheb [Macpherson]."…. He ordered me to go to Biseepara and collect all the Khond zemindars of Bodh. On receiving this order I represented to him that the Khond people did not mind my orders, but if I received some of the sepoys I would go. On this he gave me a duffadar and two chuprassis. [But Macpherson] without consulting me....created great disturbances and seized "*the ploughmen raised at home*".... Then the Khonds assembled and took council among themselves and assembling throughout the night in numbers from 5–7,000 with their arms surrounded the place. The Khonds of Ghumsur....were also with them. The Saheb had only between 100 and 120 coolies and begars [villagers forced to be porters]; from fear they released the meriahs.... he then dismissed me telling me to go and pacify the Khonds and bring in the meriahs. On receiving this order I represented to him that while your [Macpherson's] presence was there I in every way reasoned with those people, how will they mind me now? On this the Saheb repeated the order for me to go and pacify the people. I then agreeably to his orders came to Biseepara and called for all the Khonds but none came.... I reasoned with them in every way, but they would not listen to me but put me under surveillance. I managed however to escape....and came to my own headquarters....[31]

This letter reveals much that Macpherson, it seems, did not understand, and shows what an anomalous position *rajahs* often found themselves in, being expected to exert a kind of authority over Konds which they had not, till then, possessed. On receiving this letter, Ouseley reported on 18th April that 'From what I now learn I fully expect that a general outbreak of the Khoonds is imminent.' Sir T.H. Maddock, President of the Supreme Council, recorded a Minute on 28th May censuring Macpherson, which was sent to him as a letter—'a wig of the grandest' Macpherson called it. Privately, Maddock noted 'There will be no present outbreak among the

Khoonds but Captain Macpherson's failure this season promises little for his future success.'[32]

'Perfect tranquillity' did not last in the hills. It seems that Macpherson's behaviour in Boad had stirred up a spirit of resistance to the introduction of British rule. Fighting broke out in mid-June in Saranghor, near Ghumsur's border with Boad and Chinna Kimedi, in the form of feuding between Kond clans under rival Hindu chiefs.[33] Six or seven villages were burnt by the 'hostile' Konds, and 15 villagers were killed. Macpherson sent Punda Naik, a loyal Ghumsur *sirdar*, with 40 *sebundies* and 100 *paiks* to the rescue, and outlined plans for 'exacting full reparation' next season. He wrote to the chief he considered responsible, threatening him with severe punishment.[34] To the Government he wrote that military 'coercion' would probably be necessary to establish a 'permanent peace'.[35] But on 10th July there was another attack, apparently by the side which had suffered the last time: seven more villages were burnt and two people killed.[36] But the monsoon had started, making it impossible for Macpherson to take any action.

He also threatened the Boad *rajah* with the 'severest' punishment, when he failed to respond to a summons. In fact, the *rajah*'s mother had just died, and he was simultaneously trying to survive a power struggle between different factions in his kingdom.[37] When he did come, he travelled via Daspalla for fear of being attacked by Konds. With him came Koortibas, after threats and 'half under constraint', as well as the *Proraj* and several *bissois*.[38] On 18th August Macpherson arrested Koortibas and sent him under detention to Aska.

> It was quite plain that until he should be removed from hence, his return to power in Boad would be considered possible, and precluded any hope of the settlement of men's minds.... The Proraj I have detained here. The raja and his people and the Khonds now present, are highly satisfied with both arrangements.
>
> [Koortibas] said simply that if I would liberate him and direct him to do so he would as all know he could bring the Khonds to the mind I desired in six days.[39]

A few days later, apparently in retaliation for Koortibas' arrest, more fighting broke out: at least six more villages were burnt by a Kond army estimated at 3,000 in a series of attacks, culminating in one on the large settlement of Tentilghor on 28th August, whose Hindu chiefs got meagre reinforcements just in time to beat off this attack.[40]

The Konds in Boad were now apparently talking of deposing the *rajah* and replacing him with Bir Khonro. They refused all requests to send their *meriahs* to the *rajah*:

> "What reliance can we place on the Rajah? He caused Koortibas to be seized. We shall never go to him on this matter."
>
> "As the present Rajah went to the Sahib's Hoozoor like a thief let him stay there like a thief or if he shall return let us slay him and Madwa Khonro [who had sent in some *meriahs*]."
>
> "At Bispurra we said to the Rajah you are our Rajah come to the jungle with us but he refused to listen to us. If he now wishes to join us let him come to us. We are to set the country in a blaze. If he desires to be Rajah let him bring Madwa Khonro with him and assist us. We all who are Meriah sacrificers are prepared to die but not to give in."[41]

It is clear that the Boad *rajah* had failed to fulfil the obligations he owed the Konds, losing his legitimacy by pleasing the British, instead of taking to the hills with them, as the Ghumsur royalty had done ten years before.

There were warnings that an uprising was imminent throughout August and September. Peace pacts of brotherhood between Kond clans were being formally renounced.[42] Finally on 2nd October an army of about 4,000 Konds attacked the region of Tentilghor, where Sheik Sultan Sing, as *Duffadar*, had a force of only 140 men to defend the main settlement. Ten other villages were burnt, and there were several deaths on each side. Another attack four days later was beaten off more easily, although the day before it Sultan wrote to Macpherson:

> Unless you shall come with two or three companies to our assistance we shall certainly be destroyed (Note by M.—These fears turned out to be purely imaginary). You will never see us again. We cannot hold out. Send companies quickly.[43]

But Macpherson himself was asking the army command for permission to call up 'the four pukha companies' (i.e. of regular sepoys) at Russellkonda, and summoned one company on his own authority immediately.[44]

After the attack on the 6th was beaten off, the news for the rest of October was good. It seemed to Macpherson as if the Konds were accepting the end of human sacrifice to the Earth Goddess.

> The God of Light is believed to have communicated about eight days ago with the tribes of Ghumsur which have relinquished the sacrifice, the first time since the Earth Goddess instituted her rite amongst them. As no-one could behold the Supreme God and live he appeared upon this as on similar occasions in the form of an inferior deity. He and the Goddess of increase together took by the hand a youth of Nilingia in Baramootah as he halted in a stream and commanded him to proclaim to all that there was not the least ground for apprehension that the extraordinary promise of the year [in crops] would be disappointed from the relinquishment of the sacrifice but that they the first deities required every village to offer to them a sheep at one of its gates and a fowl at the other. This revelation has been received everywhere with the greatest joy, and the required offerings have been made in every village.[45]

Macpherson began a long Report of 15th October by explaining that in the Kond view of things:

> The Khonds believe that two divine powers divide the rule of the universe, the first Boora Pennu the God of Light, the supreme being and all perfect and purely benevolent, the second [Bango] or Tari Peṇnu the Earth Goddess, the first creator being his consort.
>
> When the deity formed man the Goddess was offended by the love which he bore to him and introduced evil into the world.[46]

Between Bura and Darni Penu there was perpetual strife. Some Konds already held Bura supreme, and therefore performed no human sacrifices, though instead they practised female infanticide, since they identified women with the evil principle. The majority of Konds held the Earth Goddess supreme, and propitiated her with the human sacrifices to avert her anger. Macpherson claimed, in this Report, to have turned them towards the God of Light, whom he identified with the Christian God, by whose power Konds considered they had been subdued in the Ghumsur wars. The main danger came from a small number of Hindu and Kond chiefs, who were spreading 'delusions' among the Konds that taking the *meriahs* was the first step towards taxes and other infringements of their independence. Macpherson explained he had arrested Koortibas because he was the main source of these 'false rumours', and released a proclamation at this time to dispel Kond misconceptions, defining his purpose as 'an imperative duty to God and mankind' to suppress human sacrifice.[47]

But it is doubtful if Macpherson's interpretation of Kond religion and motives is quite correct. He virtually identified Bura Penu with the Christian God, and the Earth Goddess with evil—a Christian, not a Kond, polarity, that led him to see his work as a religious crusade.

Macpherson suspected the *rajah* of Angul of conspiring against him along with Bir Khonro. So Mr Mills left Cuttack in November, and went to meet the *rajah* at Tikripara on the Mahanadi river.[48] Maheshwar Khonro, one of the main chiefs suspected of leading the Konds astray, also went to meet Mills, and 'sued for pardon' for himself as well as for Bir Khonro, his father. Mills 'guaranteed to him his life and liberty', and wrote to Macpherson on 2nd December that he was sending Maheshwar to him under escort.

But Macpherson, who was a few miles away, had just been attacked, on 30th November, by a Kond army under Bir and Noboghon Khonro. Were they trying to play one *saheb* off against the other? When Bir Khonro came in on 7th December Macpherson put him 'under surveillance' and 'placed him in irons'. Mills was outraged by this arrest, even after he knew of the attack, because he had given his 'most solemn assurance' that Bir Khonro would remain free; the *rajah* of Angul, through whose intercession Bir surrendered, also complained in the strongest terms to Mills of a breach of trust.[49]

The arrest of Bir Khonro, traditional chief of the Boad Konds, served as a signal for armed resistance elsewhere. On 9th December a band of 400 'insurgents' from the hills attacked the Ghumsur plains, killing several merchants in Kolada, and burning several villages nearby, in retaliation for supplying Macpherson's camp. Macpherson said the attackers were only 'low caste Hindus and Benniah Khonds'. Their leader was Chokra Bissoi, who seems to have inherited Dora Bissoi's status of 'great chief' among the Konds of Ghumsur. Macpherson had met him five years previously, and had been impressed by him. From this time he headed Kond opposition to British rule.[50]

The Kond feeling behind this resistance emerges from a letter which a number of Kond chiefs wrote to Mills at this time:

> Sri sri Maharajah the ruler, the Cuttack Govt. Sahib of the Tributary Mahals,
>
> The Mullicks, The Khonros, The Bissois, Dulbehras and all the Khonds send innumerable salutations and in this desire write: About ten years ago wicked men having much engaged in sacrificing human beings, and women having destroyed their young daughters, an order came from the Council (the Sudder

> house of the Sirkar) that these Meriah doings were no longer to be. From that day all have ceased. When Mr Macpherson Sahib, the Govt Agent Sahib, most unjustly called and seized our ploughmen and labourers, whether poor and miserable, or happy, as Meriah children, he gave also rupees as a bribe to those who were afraid, and got men to build a fort of wood (for securing them) during the night and put them in it. The mothers, fathers and brothers of these persons seizing arms and making warlike preparations came in wrath and surrounded the Sahib. The Rajah of the Mahal being afraid caused them to desist. They did not comprehend this but said "Bring and give us our sons and daughters". The Rajah persuaded the Sahib to agree and we received them back. Macpherson Sahib gave them all up and returning from that place remained in Tentilghor, and listening to the advice of Utan Singh Dulbehra made warlike preparations, washed our country with fire, bound our Bir Khonro Bissoee, and took him away into another country. We indeed never outraged the house of the Sahib. We have never committed murder. Had we done so we should have remained in fear and trembling as a tree in the midst of the jungle. Father it is right that the house of the Sirkar should show us kindness and protect us.[51]

Macpherson himself stayed in the Boad hills, remote from the drama unfolding the other side of his Agency, in order to persuade the Boad Konds to submit. He sent Cadenhead back to the plains with a company of sepoys to deal with these disturbances. After a week's march Cadenhead reached Gullery, where he found

> that the principal villages were destroyed; that the whole of the peaceably disposed portion of the community had fled; and that nearly all who bear arms were in open revolt against the Government.[52]

Cadenhead was soon reinforced by sepoys from the Bengal army under Captain Dunlop and Lt Haughton.[53] Bannerman reported to Madras that rebels had burnt about 30 villages, retaliation as he saw it against Macpherson's coercive acts.

> There is in my humble opinion no doubt whatever that these predatory incursions of the hill people immediately result from the course of measures pursued by the Agent.

> No obstruction or molestation was offered to Captain Macpherson's advance towards Boad, but as soon as his detachment had proceeded beyond reach, the depredations were commenced, and continue nearly unchecked.[54]

Bannerman would not support the sending of troops to reinforce Macpherson in the hills, and told his superiors that Macpherson's 'system of coercion on the Khonds....will be disastrous'.[55]

The Government already had serious doubts about the soundness of Macpherson's policy: he had been told not to use force against the Konds, yet fighting had escalated throughout the year, and he was openly advising that more 'coercion' would be necessary. So the Supreme Government wrote to Madras at the beginning of January to say that if Macpherson did not stop the disturbance soon, a senior commander would be sent there with a large force of the Madras army: 'as the hill tribes seem to be devoid of all military resources this object may it is hoped be attained with little sacrifice of life and property'. Major-General Welsh visited the Orissa coast in mid-January and reported that he agreed with Bannerman: 'on the Agent's side all is confusion'. Macpherson was too hard on the troops, supplies were inadequate, and the enemy were killing camp followers at every opportunity.[56]

Meanwhile Cadenhead, joined by Dunlop, had been fighting the Kond rebels in Gullery and Chokapand. By 7th Jan. 1847 they had burnt several abandoned villages, and 32 chiefs had tendered their submission. Chokra Bissoi had retreated, after a fight that left three of his men dead.[57] But Bannerman reported that on the 10th a company under Lt Bell was repulsed in an attack on a fastness in Gullery 'with the loss of tents etc. and some sepoys killed and wounded....the worst kind of thing.'[58] From 16th–25th January Cadenhead and Dunlop moved on to Bengrekia, destroying more villages as they pursued their enemy, who rallied in Kooklooba. On the 28th Cadenhead destroyed a village of the Bengrekia chief Nagson Khonro: he cut down the toddy palms, and distributed the cattle among the allied Konds of Tentilghor. He even encouraged 'friendly' Konds to take into their own hands the defeat of 'hostile' Konds.[59]

The post they had left behind at Gullery came under repeated attack until reinforcements arrived under Lt-Col Green, who had come straight from Calcutta, and took over military command of the '700 bayonets' who had been operating under Macpherson's orders. Macpherson wrote to him on 10th February, advising him to show firmness.[60]

> I am quite confident from our experience both recently and in 1836–7 that as soon as you shall assume the aggressive these insurgents will think only of saving themselves; and that the rest of the population will immediately return to their villages when assured of protection.

Macpherson had sent another 150 men under Lt Pinkney to reinforce Gullery. They went there by forced marches, and Pinkney took three rebel strongholds near Gullery on 12th February, capturing 250 villagers in one, and moved into Ambazora, where Chokra Bissoi was said to be sheltering with 200 followers.

Dunlop meanwhile was in eastern Boad, where more Kond chiefs surrendered on 16th February. Macpherson himself had moved even further away from the fighting into western Boad, against the Konds of Sangrimendi. Pottah Khonro, 'their bravest leader', surrendered to him on the 17th.

Cadenhead was operating to the north: on 10th February he cleared the Podentilla pass, where the enemy had slain merchants and pilgrims. On the 22nd 30 of his men escorted 1,000 Hindu pilgrims through the pass. He got Madras army reinforcements at Purnacuttack, and embarked on a tour to destroy Noboghon Khonro's retreats in the north-east of Boad (18th–25th), receiving at Harbunga the surrender of a chief called Gondo Naik and his followers, though at first Cadenhead 'declined to receive them....and sent them away' because they were armed.[61]

Macpherson wrote to Green on 27th February asking him to send troops against Chokra Bissoi in Challee and Ambazora. To the Governor-General he wrote that he had won over five of the eight tribes of Boad; the other three were still against him under the leadership of Noboghon Khonro.[62] The Ghumsur hill Konds were 'peaceable'; it was the plains Konds of Gullery, Challee and Ambazora that were in revolt under Chokra Bissoi. He expressed 'the deep regrets which I necessarily feel that every consideration of policy and of humanity appears to dictate the coercive measures which I have been carrying out and those which I now propose.' But the Calcutta Government was highly critical of this coercion.[63]

As Sir Maddock saw it, Macpherson had caused the revolt by entangling himself in local politics.

> Leaving out of consideration the great loss of property and the expenses of the employment of troops, if we calculate only the sacrifice of life which has attended the Agent's operations during the last year, far greater probably than that arising from the Meriah rite in many years, we may pause to reflect whether the cause of humanity can be advanced by such means....[64]

But a new commander was on his way: Brigadier-General Dyce, who was appointed to the command of the Northern Division of the Madras Army, and if the Government deemed it necessary, would supersede Macpherson and assume 'full political authority in the Khond districts'. He arrived in Russellkonda on 7th March, and at once summoned Macpherson from

Sangrimendi in Boad, who arrived in two days. Dyce got 'no definite idea' of what was happening from him, but formed the impression that his measures were 'arbitrary and coercive' (Report of 13th March). Macpherson submitted to Dyce his plan for pacification, and they went to Gullery together on the 14th. Dyce let Macpherson direct operations for another week, on the basis of this plan, which was to reinforce Dunlop in eastern Boad and to try and defeat Chokra Bissoi, who was near Gullery, by sending troops against him from two sides—although Dyce 'conceived it both unnecessary and useless'. But an influential chief of Chokapand who was friendly to the Government had just died, making matters harder. The General could stand it no longer.

> I venture to own that under the present local authorities permanent tranquillity will never be restored, and my opinion is based upon the following circumstances. 1st. The extreme hatred manifested throughout these districts against Captain Macpherson and his establishment, the result as is generally stated of the oppression of the Agency towards the inhabitants of these districts. 2nd. The constant and heavy drain upon them both for coolies and supplies. 3rd. The employment of the Somasthan Paiks upon various duties without remuneration contrary to the express stipulation of Govt and above all the harsh and cruel measures resorted to whenever it has been necessary to display the power of the Govt (as it is so termed) against any of these ignorant and deluded people. I have now been at this deserted village for six days and although Captain Macpherson has been likewise here with Sirdar Soonder Sing and another influential man of his establishment not a single creature has returned nor is there a prospect of their doing so, notwithstanding a proclamation has been issued offering pardon to all save the principals in the late outbreak.....
>
> I have seldom walked out without being intercepted by these poor unhappy people [villagers who had not fled?] casting themselves at my feet and entreating me to enquire into their grievances, and from all I have observed as well as from information I have sought I am impressed with the strongest conviction that the feeling of disaffection now so rife and universal in these districts arises from no opposition to the Govt but is solely and exclusively directed against the local authorities....
>
> Whatever information I have acquired whether from the people themselves, the servants of Govt, and from so much of Captain Macpherson's correspondence as he has been pleased to show me, all have irresistibly impelled me to the same conclusion; indeed these latter documents plainly and unequivocally demonstrate that no conciliatory measures have ever been adopted, as they exhibit an almost continuous narrative of burning and plundering villages with occasional destruction of grain, until the entire community—and not "a mob"—have been excited by these inhuman proceedings....

> A large force has been drawn up to this position and scattered over the disturbed districts without either order or system by the Agent and his assistants and employed under their immediate orders in marching about the country and committing acts disgraceful alike to the character of the Army and of the Govt. Although Captain Macpherson can afford no intelligible information of the use to be made of the detachments in their present positions he is opposed to their withdrawal, and...I am...compelled to witness the puerile and supine endeavours of the Agent to restore order and tranquillity at a period of the year which renders it imperative that there should be no delay, and when instant energy and decision are required....
>
> I have therefore respectfully to solicit that if my services can be dispensed with I may be relieved from the anomalous and painful position in which I am placed, or be at once vested with full powers to carry out the objects of Govt by the adoption of such measures as I may find necessary to pursue. (Reports of 20th March 1847)[65]

Dyce finally got his authorization to take over on the 24th. Macpherson was relieved of his post, and Dyce ordered him out of Ghumsur, along with all the officials who had served him. As his own Assistant, Dyce appointed the same MacViccar who had fallen out with Macpherson a few months before. He also made Sooria Narain one of his 'chief instruments', who was behind the opposition to Macpherson in the Ganjam Agency, that had undermined his command. Macpherson remonstrated with Dyce for 'playing into the rebels' hands' by showing the British officers were divided. Dyce replied

> to assure you that in performing a duty painful to my own feelings I have been solely motivated by a deep sense of the paramount importance of the steps I have taken and of my duty to the Government.[66]

Dyce tried, with little success at first, to reassure the Konds who had suffered devastation under Macpherson, and persuade them to return to their villages, while Konds who had recently been regarded as 'friendly' to the British, he punished for looting 'enemy' villages. Allied Konds and enemy Konds suddenly seemed to change places overnight. As a Lieutenant described the situation he witnessed in Chalee:

> We have been here some twelve days now. The first week we were employed in burning and destroying "retreats" etc. and now that conciliatory measures have been adopted we have very little to do. It is a great pity Macpherson's policy had not been changed earlier. I fear now the poor brutes of villagers are much too frightened to return to their villages. On one of our devastating expeditions a poor old wretch was caught because he could not run away; he

> belongs to a neighbouring village and Rose let him go again laden with peace offerings, hoping his exertions would prevail on some of the other villagers to come in; the man himself was settled in his own village and induced one of the Chalee people to come to the tents. Rose had a long talk with him but the poor fellow said that his plough was broken, his cattle carried off and his seed burnt etc. This I fancy must be pretty nearly the case with all of them. We have not succeeded in seeing any of the other inhabitants though from their fresh marks near houses and wells it is evident that they are hiding themselves in the jungles close to their villages—the paiks go about yelling out to them to come in but they get no answer save that of the echo. The other day when our party were proclaiming peace in one village a party of Macpherson's "friendly Khonds" were quietly looting the next village. They were all bound and brought into camp. Their loot was sent back to the villages from which it had been taken and they themselves sent under an escort to Puserah. These rascals have carried off all the cattle they could find in this neighbourhood to their own country and unless these sort of proceedings are stopped I do not see much chance of the villagers returning to their homes. I do not think Macpherson's proclamation will be of much use in this neighbourhood except to light the pipes of some Jettooreedars [?].[67]

But soon these 'enemy' Konds started approaching Dyce for help, and he tried to compensate them for the destruction of their food and homes:

> The enormous plundering which has been sanctioned by the late Agency has ruined many tribes and exasperated them against those who received their goods and cattle....

Dyce 'was greatly astonished to discover that the *Rajah* of Boad has been a prisoner in the Agent's camp for upwards of five months', and set him free, along with Koortibas and Bir Khonro, who was soon 'rendering good service', although long confinement in irons prevented him walking, and he had to be carried back to Boad.[68] Noboghon Khonro himself, no longer considered a rebel, came to meet Lt MacViccar, to complain about his son Bir's seizure by Macpherson, and about how 'Cadenhead burnt and plundered several of his villages and killed some of his people.' Dyce went into Boad to supervise operations, but came down with fever and returned to Russellkonda. Soon after he repaired to the coast to recuperate, leaving MacViccar in charge.

As for Chokra Bissoi, he met Dyce's '*pandit*', Sooria Narain, on 2nd May, but would not formally surrender (which Bir Khonro and Koortibas had promised to make him do), so Dyce was 'driven to adopt measures for his capture'. He sent two companies off in pursuit under MacViccar, having 'the fullest reliance in the talents, tact and judgement of this officer'. MacViccar received the surrender of most of the remaining Boad chiefs at Bisipara: each one brought 'the usual offering of a goat'. MacViccar dismissed them 'after a due caution had been administered to them and they had made the most lavish profession of future obedience.'[69] But he left the hills without catching Chokra.

The Government reprimanded Dyce for failing to effect 'immediate and decisive measures' to restore law and order, and re-appointed Campbell, back from the war in China with the rank of Lieutenant-Colonel, as Meriah Agent. For two weeks there was much confusion, as Dyce thought he was still meant to be in command, until he was formally relieved of it by a letter from the Supreme Government in June.[70] MacViccar continued as Campbell's Assistant, while Sooria Narain and Sam Bissoi were reinstated with full honours to the positions Macpherson had taken from them for aiding human sacrifice.[71]

Chokra Bissoi seemed poised to surrender, writing to Dyce on 5th May:

> I respectfully beg leave to represent to your honor that the Circar in this universe are supporting and taking care of all men from the greatest to the lowest having freed them from all troubles and distress but as my sufferings for my fate are not yet over I am not yet extricated from my troubles and protected. I have addressed four letters to your honor but have not been acquainted with your answers thereto. The order which you were kind enough to issue to me was not conveyed to me and owing to fears I had in consequence entertained in my heart I was unable to [go] to your hoozoor ['presence'] to assist you but when your honor shall be kindly pleased to take my case into your favorable consideration and to extend your clemency to me I can await on your honor for meeting if all the lushkur [troops] is withdrawn from the malia [hills] and if your honor is pleased to proceed with only ten men but not in the event of there remaining in the malia any companies of sepoys armed with muskets. I beg leave also to state that I cannot attend on your honor when Bir Khonro and Kurtia Das baboo stay in your Cutcherry. They should then be absent from thence.[72]

But Campbell went on trying to capture him. In June Chokra's men attacked a village in Chokapand that was under *sebundy* guard, which in Campbell's view 'placed him beyond the pale of forgiveness'. In August he was said to have only 70 Hill Konds with him—so his followers were not only plainsmen as Macpherson had said.[73] Campbell was incensed by another letter which Chokra sent him in August:

> I feel it is my good fortune that you have come to Goomsur country merciful protector. When Macpherson Sahib was the Maliah Governor he burnt all the people's houses, he took away Petamber Deo the Rajah of Boad from his own house and made a prisoner of him, and from all the Mullickos, Bissyes and Khonros money and bribes were taken, all the children whom these people were nourishing were forcibly taken away as Meriahs when they were not so. Macpherson Sahib's servants went inside their houses and behaved ill to the women and the children also and disgraced them, cows, bullocks, buffaloes, grain, and rice etc. were plundered by them. On account of all these great losses all the Maliah zeminderies were plundered and Goomsur Naicks and Paicks of all classes desire the Rajah to come back, or else they had better die. Make Shree Borraja... Deo the Rajah of Goomsur, let Berabur Bissye have his liberty, let Petamber Deo be made firm in Boad, let the Mullickos and Khonds have their lands as in times past and according to immemorial custom, then all will be sacred and well. Great injustice has been done to me Sahib in these Maliahs by those who obeyed the orders of another Sahib and consequently all the Mullickos, Khonros and Dulbehras and all the rest have been driven to the hills and will die to recover what they have lost.[74]

One might have thought this letter was 'honest feedback'. As such, maybe it went against the code of what natives were supposed to say to the British; the idea of restoring the Ghumsur *Raj* Campbell must have considered treasonable, for he at once offered Rs 3,000/-for Chokra's capture 'dead or alive'. The Government made him amend this offer, insisting the reward should be less, and only for the living man: Sir Maddock commented 'It is very strange that an officer of Col Campbell's experience should suppose that the Govt would sanction such a proclamation'.[75]

The district of Chokapand was still 'in rebellion' under Chokra, and Campbell led three columns of troops in November to subdue the Konds there. Meanwhile Bir Khonro and Koortibas spent the entire year from April 1847 in the hills securing the submission of Kond chiefs.[76] Chokra retreated to a remote corner of Atharah Mutah and tried to get the Boad *rajah* to mediate in his surrender, but when Campbell sent MacViccar after him, Chokra fled in the nick of time, leaving writing implements, correspondence, musical instruments and bedding. All the surrounding Kond villages were deserted when British troops arrived.[77]

In April 1848 Chokra had still not been caught. He was said to be sheltering in the nearby kingdom of Sonepur. But Campbell declared the rebellion over.

> The Chokra's influence may be considered at an end; his promise of securing the continuance of the meriah sacrifice was the bond by which he maintained his influence on the Khonds, but that being now broken, he has no longer a party among them. (1st April 1848)

Campbell was still offering Rs 3,000/-for his capture, 'dead or alive', although Lord Dalhousie, the new Governor-General, asked Campbell to 'make it clear that Chokra Bissoi should not be *assassinated*'.[78]

In November some of the Konds in Chokapand were still rumoured to be hiding away 'the supposed son of the Ghumsur rajah'—for this war, like that of 1836–7, seems to have been fuelled by resentment that the British had displaced the royal house of Ghumsur.[79] Other royal houses were soon to go as well. The *rajah* of Angul had been considered guilty of helping the rebels by Macpherson as well as others.[80] In April 1847, when Dyce was taking over from Macpherson, the *rajah* had retreated to a remote fort, where Dunlop went to meet him and listened to him deny any complicity in the rebellion. But in the next few months the Government decided that he was deeply compromised and decided to depose him and annex Angul. Campbell carried this out in a 'brief and bloodless' campaign early in 1848. Lord Dalhousie warmly commended this exploit and welcomed another kingdom into the British Empire:

> We have a perfect right to do with it what we please. It has been justly forfeited and no-one would whisper a complaint if we turned out the whole lot and took it to ourselves.[81]

Not all Konds acquiesced in British rule yet, and fighting between Konds and British troops continued sporadically for a few more months. As for Chokra Bissoi, the British never caught him—although they eventually caught one of his chief supporters.[82] But the *rajah* of Boad was suspected of helping him, which served as a pretext for annexing a large part of Boad in 1855.

A War of Words

When Macpherson was dismissed from his post as Meriah Agent, Dyce ordered him out of Ghumsur, along with Cadenhead, Pinkney and their Indian subordinates. He took up residence on the coast in Gopalpur, accusing Dyce of 'unconscious prejudgement' and demanding an enquiry to clear himself from his charges (letters of 20th and 29th April). These were: that his senior Indian subordinates had extorted bribes (even Dunlop reported on 4th April that this was probably a major cause of the rebellion); that his men resorted to violence unnecessarily, burning villages, destroying orchards and grainstores, and giving 'friendly' Konds the loot; and that he had imprisoned without proper charges Koortibas, Bir Khonro and others, including the Boad *rajah* himself.[83] Macpherson had actually rebuked Cadenhead, writing to 'express the very deep regret which I feel that it should have appeared to you to be absolutely necessary to destroy every hamlet in the tract of Noboghon Khonro, [action] so deeply repugnant to the spirit of these operations' (8th March), and writing again at Dyce's request (9th April) to ask by what authority he had burnt and plundered villages. MacViccar demanded a similar explanation from Lt Pinkney (19th April) for giving away and selling cattle taken from Kond villages he destroyed. Major Rose gave evidence that Macpherson had personally ordered him and Pinkney to burn villages and grain stores (3rd April).[84]

So a senior Civil Servant from Bengal, Mr J.P. Grant, was at once appointed to conduct an investigation into Macpherson's administration. He arrived on the Ganjam coast at Chatrapur in July, and immediately sent off a large order for stationery—including 'ten bundles of red tape'!—explaining that the investigation would take a long time due to the number of witnesses he was to examine. Cadenhead was cleared of the charges first (October 1847), including one charge that he had 'extorted' statements incriminating the Angul *rajah*—in modern terms, that he had extracted confessions using torture. It certainly emerged that he had applied considerable pressure while interrogating prisoners, tying their hands with ropes that left scars, and tying them in stocks in the full sun (Grant's Report 30th October). The enquiry also uncovered many cases of alleged bribe-taking by Indian officials, but not much that could be proved. The enquiry ended in July 1848 by clearing Macpherson of the charges against him, and produced a report running into five huge volumes.[85] Lord Dalhousie conveyed his personal apology to Macpherson saying 'nothing could ever compensate' him for the way he had been treated (WM p.279). After a break in Britain to recuperate, Macpherson continued his career by distinguishing himself as British Resident in Gwalior during the Mutiny.

So were Dyce's allegations against Macpherson's proceedings unfounded? Most commentators have accepted the enquiry's verdict, although one modern historian calls it 'nothing but a farce'.[86] From the evidence we have seen, it seems clear that Macpherson's measures were often, as Dyce described them, 'inhuman'; and that, as Maddock said, Macpherson's over-hasty approach and arrogance, and tendency to take sides, caused a sacrifice of life considerably greater than the number of people sacrificed over many years by the Konds.[87] The corruption and extortion of some of the Indian officials he relied upon seems certain—it is hardly surprising the cases could not be proved!

Opinion was divided at the time for and against Macpherson. The Revd Alexander Duff, one of Calcutta's foremost churchmen, came out as a staunch supporter in his articles in the *Calcutta Review*, where he extolled Macpherson and laid into Dyce:

> The said General, on his arrival in Goomsur, utterly mistaking the *real spirit and intention* of his commission, began officiously, gratuitously and arbitrarily, to intermeddle with matters which in no way whatever belonged to him.... he took it upon himself not only unwarrantably to assume directive control over the agency, but actually in a way the most summary, insulting and despotic, to order it, without any enquiry and in disgrace, out of the country..., Nor did the gratuitous indignity end even here.... The General followed his monstrous decree of banishment, by a string of alleged charges against the agency....[which proved to be] the sheer inventions of some malicious and interested parties, who must have imposed on the General's profound ignorance and all-devouring credulity.[88]

Duff also belittled Campbell's achievements by comparison with Macpherson's.

> With Lt Macpherson's appointment, we consider that the *first era* of comparative ignorance, twilight gropings, abortive but well-meant experiments, and really philanthropic but somewhat disheartening conclusions, terminated; and with his appointment we, in like manner, consider that the *second era* of maturer knowledge, fuller and more steady light, more skilful and successful experiments, and equally philanthropic but more cheering conclusions, commenced.[89]

Campbell was furious. He asked the Government's permission to refute 'the string of misrepresentations and exaggerations' contained in the *Calcutta Review* as well as other journals. This was refused at first.[90] But Campbell persisted: he had 'never deemed it necessary, or becoming, to trumpet my proceedings through the medium of the Public Journals, regarding such a course as incompatible with my position as a servant of the state, [but I did not wish to lose] any credit that may be due to my exertions in a cause sacred to humanity' (14th February 1849). So the Government gave limited permission, and Campbell, or his associates, put together an anonymous pamphlet that refuted Duff's allegations with biting polemic and copious detail (Anon. 1849). This pamphlet produced a mass of evidence to affirm Campbell's achievements: 'to *him* belongs the credit [for suppressing human sacrifice].... the glory of Captain Macpherson as "a propounder of principles and a deviser of plans, and an executor of important deeds" is—mere false glare.'(1849 p.7) The refutation of Duff's articles is introduced as an issue involving 'divine truth, and the divine word', and the same 'Un-Truth' that Luther fought against.[91]

The conflict between Macpherson and Campbell, then, over the apportioning of honour, glory and reputation for succesful service in a lofty cause, was considered very much in terms of conflict over possession of some commodity that can be earned or stolen, a contest for the top place in the history books, or even for credit in God's eyes for sacred work: the Protestant idea of 'good works' that earn, or signify, a place in heaven.

Macpherson and Campbell were highly conscious of their role as heroes for their contemporaries or future generations. Duff's articles influenced Kaye, in his history of British India (1853), to give all the credit to Macpherson, which Campbell considered a great injustice, publishing two editions of his Memoirs to defend his reputation (1861 and 1864, ...*Thirteen years among the Wild Tribes of Khondistan*....). Campbell's version of events offended Macpherson's brother, William, who had been a lawyer in Calcutta. William wrote and complained to Campbell, and published their ensuing correspondence in a Scottish journal, before putting together his dead brother's Memoirs, *Memorials of service*.... (WM 1865). In Campbell's view, 'This bitter controversy was simply a personal matter between Major Macpherson and myself as to whom belonged the chief merit of the suppression of human sacrifice in Goomsur.'[92] It is clear that this obsession with ideas about merit and the infringement of personal honour is closely related to the sense that regimental honour, or British honour as a whole, had been infringed, which led to all-out war against the Konds in 1836.

The 'merit' which these men disputed they felt they had earned by their 'labours in the field' or 'labours under God's blessing': the theme of self-sacrifice is vital, and relates to the reality of their lives, Two younger brothers of Campbell's who joined the Indian Army along with him (1819, 1821) died within a few years (1824, 1827). Several of his children died in India, as did his first wife Eliza at Vizagapatam in 1846, though several other children survived, including two daughters (born 1833 at Vizagapatam and 1838 at Aska, both of whom married Indian Army men). Campbell was born in Skye in 1801 and lived to retire to Edinburgh, before his death in 1878. His father emigrated to Australia in 1821, and John Campbell never met him again, for he died in 1826, though he visited his mother there when he returned to India from sick leave in Britain in 1833 (Duncan Campbell 1925). This absence from friends and relatives was endemic among Indian Army men.

Samuel Charters Macpherson (1806–1860) was the son of the Professor of Greek at Aberdeen University. After studies at Edinburgh and Cambridge, he began training in law, but gave this up because of weak eyesight. His two younger brothers also served in India, as doctor and lawyer. Macpherson's health was permanently weakened by the fevers he picked up in the Kond hills. He fell sick of a liver complaint while Political Agent for Gwalior, where he had served heroically through the Mutiny, and died five days after reaching Calcutta. Apparently he never married. Among his friends was Sir James Outram, who had met him in Egypt, on leave in 1848, and who had 'watched his career with the deepest interest and admiration'—Outram's 'pacification' of the Bhils in western India prefigured the Kond campaigns by a few years. On his deathbed Macpherson 'earnestly urged Sir James Outram (whose own health had now greatly failed) to go home, and not to sacrifice his life by remaining too long in India' (WM pp.348–9).[93]

But the hardships these self-sacrificing officials imposed on themselves, they also imposed on others. We have seen Campbell's early violence, killing Konds from horseback (above p.43). Ironically, when Campbell was in charge of the Kond Agency again, the Government at last sanctioned him to use force as he saw fit, recognizing that British rule could not be introduced without sometimes using it (below p.98). As for Macpherson, published accounts are silent about his violence: his extensive burning of villages, the large number of prisoners he took whom he threatened and kept tied up, and the way that he forced hundreds of Konds into servile coolie work, carrying soldiers' supplies. It is clear that Konds found his behaviour highly oppressive, and felt incited by it to resist the regime he was imposing.

But whether Macpherson was to blame for this war or not, whether he or Campbell laid the foundations of British rule among the Konds, and whose rule was more oppressive or benign, are not such vital issues, for in practice, there seems to have been little to choose between them: their web of accusations and counter-accusations about the Indian subordinates whom both completely relied on, makes it very clear that these subordinates habitually misused their power, extorting bribes and terrorizing Konds. And this violence was something they learnt from their British officers. *En route* for Ghumsur in 1836 Macpherson's 'butler and other followers' tried to extort money from villagers Macpherson had sent them to get milk from, and were roughly handled, on which Macpherson, not believing that his men were the offenders, had the villagers who had stood up to them brought to his tent and beaten, and took them many miles away from their village, only releasing them after they made most obsequious professions of apology.[94]

These norms of interaction were not usually made explicit—whether because they were taken for granted, or because they did not fit with administrators' idealized self-image. One image they publicized was the familiar one of an official seated at his desk in the shade of a tree with Indian subordinates, sepoys or servants standing to attention behind him, and tribal elders squatting in front of him, as Baba Khan describes his master (above p.70). Campbell and Forbes mention an impressive ritual of swearing allegiance on a tigerskin, in which they participated with Konds. Another ritual that Britons laid considerable stress on was the signing of treaties, submissions to British authority, or promises to refrain from human sacrifice or female infanticide. They were evidently less keen to publicize their intimidation of Indians by beatings and whippings, tying up with ropes and 'irons', and threats to kill.

It may well be that the conflict between Macpherson and Campbell had roots in their own Scottish ancestry: there was an old enmity, expressed through a succession of mutual massacres and other outrages, between the Campbells and other clans of Highlanders. At times the Campbells, under the Duke of Argyll, became the instruments of English terror in the Highlands. In fact, the English conquest of the Highlands in the mid-18th century is an episode that has the greatest bearing on the Konds' conquest, as the violent backgound that led to so many Highland Scots being displaced from their homes and serving in the armies that forged the British empire: most of the Konds' top administrators were

Scots (including Dyce, Cadenhead and MacViccar). In the 1730s General Wade 'civilized' the Highlands with military campaigns that involved building 250 miles of roads, so that armies could control the area. After the battle of Culloden in 1745 the victorious English army went on a rampage in the Highlands, burning, looting, and executing, systematically destroying the clans' existence as geographical and political entities. 'The Highland clearances' that followed over many years, were often justified with reference to the Highlanders' supposed 'poverty' and 'backwardness' (Prebble 1967, 1969, MacLeod 1967). So it is no coincidence to find Macpherson associating Kond human sacrifice with poverty, and declaring that he had to be his 'own General Wade' in building roads for military control. Scots in the 19th century, as soldiers and colonists of empire, did to tribal peoples around the world, what the English had done to them. The life-stories of Macpherson and Campbell involve South Africa and Egypt, where they went to recuperate, as well as China, where Campbell fought, and Australia where his father was a colonist.

Campbell's Regime

Back with the Konds, after finishing off the war sparked off by Macpherson's first attempt to take *meriahs* from Boad, Campbell established a no-nonsense regime of touring new areas and taking away large numbers of *meriahs.* While he was still subduing the *rajah* of Angul in the winter of 1847–8, MacViccar, his Assistant, toured remote areas of Boad. Campbell joined up with him in February, and together they collected 235 *meriahs,* which included most of those whom Macpherson had failed to take. Two others had apparently been sacrificed since Macpherson's visit. 'Districts unheard of by Europeans were traversed over, and more gloomy, pestilential regions were rarely seen.' The Konds of Domasingi refused to surrender their *meriahs* at first: 'long and tedious councils were held….', and troops were ordered several times to surround them, but eventually the *meriahs* were given up without a fight. But Campbell did have to fight to capture six Kond Chiefs, mostly from Chokapand, who had performed human sacrifices within the last two years, and aided Chokra Bissoi. The punishment he gave them was imprisonment for 2–4 years outside the Kond area.[95]

The war had effectively enforced British rule over the Konds of Boad. Now it was the turn of Chinna Kimedi, where the Konds were particularly independent from their Hindu *rajah*: 'The people of these maliahs are universally reported to be of a ferocious and intractable disposition; that human sacrifices are offered there seems undoubted.' (Report of 24th June 1848) Campbell worked through the *sirdar* of the Chinna Kimedi hills, who supervised Kond affairs for the *rajah*. The previous *rajah* had been 'an object of peculiar detestation by the hill tribes who accused him of tyrannical conduct', and a few years previously they had invaded the core area of his kingdom, carried him and his sons off to the hills and demanded ransom for them. For this reason 'No open aid can be expected from the Rajah, nor should it be demanded. It would expose him to the severe vengeance of the tribes,' who, when the *sirdar* told them they had to stop the *meriah* sacrifice, 'observed that their forefathers had performed the ceremony from time immemorial and that they would never abandon the rite.' (Report of 22nd July) In other words, Campbell was offering the Hindu chief a chance to establish a much firmer hold over the Konds.

On receiving these Reports Dalhousie declared that the Government was determined to put down the rite steadily now, and that to avoid engaging in another 'little war', Campbell should take enough soldiers on his tours, to impose his will by force whenever he deemed it necessary—a more definite and coercive policy than the 'nonsense' orders Macpherson had been issued.[96] So finally the use of force had been sanctioned—legitimizing retrospectively as it were Macpherson's abundant use of it in 1846–7, when he was under orders to avoid it completely.

Campbell's tour of 1848–9 lasted from November to March, and covered parts of Sorada, Ghumsur, Boad and Korada as well as Chinna Kimedi. On this one, he did not resort to force.

> I am truly happy that such an evil has been providentially averted, and, although we did not altogether escape fever, it pleased God to shield us from severe suffering and to prosper the mission beyond the most sanguine expectations.... I followed my invariable course of procedure with the Khonds, employing an intermediary agency as little as possible, and they began to view me as a much less terriable ogre than their imaginations had worked up.... From the first I openly and in the most plain and intelligible manner proclaimed the chief reason for my appearance among them without any disguise or circumlocution. I told them that the Govt had sent me for the sole and avowed purpose of putting an end forever to the inhuman and barbarous murders yearly perpetrated by them, and if needful, enforce the cession of victims held in possession and destined to die this cruel death. All their other ancient usages I impressed upon them would be strictly respected; the Govt is anxious to befriend them and

> willing to assist them. If any were suffering oppression, redress should be afforded and justice meted out with an impartial hand, but the meriah sacrifice—this inhuman practice—must at once and forever be laid aside. (Report of 17th March 1849)

Campbell took more than 200 *meriahs* from Kond villages, 70 from Boad, and the rest from Chinna Kimedi. He also registered nearly 100 *poosiahs*—*meriah* women with the status of concubines—whom he allowed to remain in Kond villages after taking an oath that they would not be sacrificed.

In Sorada he took measures to prevent female infanticide, declaring that Konds had duped Macpherson into believing they had stopped it. At Campbell's request all the chiefs

> signed an agreement binding themselves henceforward to rear their female offspring.... the best means of stemming the torrent [of infanticide] appears to me to consist in maintaining a constant intercourse and paying occasional visits, always insisting on seeing the children, and visiting with various marks of displeasure the chiefs of those villages [where] the relative number of sexes is so disproportionate as to leave no doubt as to the destruction of the females; while, on the other hand, the preservers of their infants will be specially rewarded, reviving such presents as will plainly evince the favour of the Government.

Campbell also settled feuds between Kond tribes, again through the signing of written agreements.

> They were all, I suspect, right glad to find their feuds terminated, and a written agreement was willingly subscribed henceforward to live in peace and forgetfulness of the past on pain of incurring the severe displeasure of the great Government... The settlement of these long-standing conflicts will prove an incalculable blessing to the whole Khond population of Surada and Chinna Kimedy.[97]

A similar tour in the next season (22nd Dec. 1849–6th April 1850) was commanded by Lt Frye, who had just returned from sick leave in Europe, while Campbell went on sick leave in turn. Frye removed a further 200 *meriahs* from Chinna Kimedi, but registered a greater number of *poosiahs* after 'converting their state of concubinage into marriage', making the Kond headmen pledges for these marriages. The women, he wrote, 'cling to their husbands and Khond associations'. He believed they were safe on the grounds that

> a meriah, once shown to the Government, is considered unfit for sacrifice.... Considering the moral darkness of the Khond, and his extreme poverty, it seems

> only just, in breaking down his prejudices, to avoid, if possible, the infliction of a pecuniary loss.

The *poosiahs* gave the Government 'a foothold....as pledges for the good faith of the people' (Frye's Report of April 1850).

Cadenhead had begun learning the Kond language in 1845, 'assisted by Soonderah Singh, who is remarkably qualified for the task by his perfect mastery of the Khond language, both in its colloquial and its practical forms.' Frye began to learn it in 1848, and in July 1849 he set up a school in Sam Bissoi's village. In 1850–1 he established more schools and collaborated with Baptist missionaries to print some books in Kui for use in them.[98] MacViccar took charge of the Agency later in 1850, and organized a tour to Kalahandi and Patna states, where he met up with officials from the Bengal Government. Frye toured Chinna Kimedi again. Together they removed another 294 *meriahs* from the hills between November and April 1851, and registered 323 *poosiahs,* most of them in Chinna Kimedi. They established a permanent post under Indian officials at Baliguda in the heart of the Boad hills, where MacViccar had suppressed feuding, and built a bungalow at Mahasingi.

Campbell returned to Orissa in October 1851, in time to lead a tour of Jeypore, another large state, barely touched by British rule as yet, from which it was said that flesh from human sacrifices was being brought into Chinna Kimedi. He started by visiting Bissamcuttack, which was known to have performed a human sacrifice recently, and got there in time to prevent a battle between the *that rajah* (subordinate chief) of Bissamcuttack and the Jeypore *rajah,* between whom there was a feud; and also to prevent the Bissamcuttack *rajah* from performing a human sacrifice to the god of war.[99]

From Bissamcuttack, the British went to Ryabaji, and Gudari, where they met Soras, 'less dissipated [than Konds] in their habits and consequently more athletic in their persons' but prone to attack at night. From there they went northeast to Lumbragaum, where 300 drunk Konds attacked them, but submitted two days later and signed the agreement to cease from the sacrifice. From there Campbell went by a difficult path to Sirdapur and Chandrapur, 'one of the strongholds of the Meriah'. The village of Bundari held three *meriahs*; when Campbell approached, its inhabitants fled to the jungle, and 'most reluctantly' Campbell ordered it burnt as a warning, to save the *meriahs.* 'The knife and post smeared with blood are now in my possession.' He returned to base via Sorada, where he arranged marriages between *meriah* women and Kond men of the areas where women were depleted by female infanticide. This year he reported that 'The meriah females have been more eagerly sought after....than formerly.'

On this tour Campbell removed 130 *meriahs* from Jeypore and 23 from Chinna Kimedi: the numbers of *meriahs* removed declined from this year, as most Kond areas had now been penetrated. When Campbell took over from Macpherson and Dyce, he had inherited responsibility for 107 *meriah* children at Nowgam. Some he sent to the Baptist Mission orphanage at Berhampur. Since 1847 how to care for the rescued *meriahs* had been a constant source of concern, for him as well as for his superiors in Calcutta, since at first he found most of them unruly, and unwilling to obey his discipline. Some had escaped. Many had died. The most 'successful cases' were *meriahs* whom he trained as *sebundies,* or who settled down at other 'respectable jobs'.[100]

The Government disapproved of Campbell's burning Bundari and also of his interference in the Jeypore *rajah's* campaign against Bissamcuttack, but sanctioned the present he had given to the Jeypore *rajah* as a token of its goodwill. Two-thirds of the sepoys were down with fever by the end of this tour, and Campbell relied on 'my trusty and hardy sibbundies.' He had to. All four of the other British officers with him came down with fever: two went to the coast on medical certificates to recuperate, one returned to Europe, and one died.

Campbell began his next tour in Sorada in early November by giving beads to parents with female infants, as an 'inducement' to raise them. In the village of Toopungah in Chinna Kimedi he rescued one *meriah* girl aged six, two hours before she was due to be sacrificed. Trying to parley with the villagers, 'the only reply I got was threats of destruction if I did not instantly quit their territory.' He beat off their attack, fired three villages, and received the chiefs' 'unconditional submission' soon after. The Bundari Konds came in too: they were

> anxiously awaiting my arrival.... They soon, however, gained confidence and came to me with their meriahs, throwing themselves on the mercy of the Government.... Before leaving Bundari I was requested by the chiefs to erect a post on the site of the new village which they were about to build as a mark that it was built by authority. I accordingly rode to the site of the old village, but the chief men came to me in haste exclaiming, "Not there, that ground has been accustomed for many years to human blood, and will continue to demand more; we will build on new ground." I followed them and on the spot pointed

> out erected a substantial post amidst the shoutings and rejoicings of men, women, and children. This may appear too trivial to merit relation in an official report; nevertheless such things as these indicate the set of the current of opinion in favor of the renunciation of their ancient rite, which was so generally apparent this season among the Khonds. (Report of 13th April 1853)

Only the chief of Ryabaji, who had performed a human sacrifice the previous year, held off, but Campbell took some of his relatives hostage as surety for the *meriahs* in his keeping. Altogether Campbell took away another 72 *meriahs* from Chinna Kimedi, 62 from Jeypore, and 13 from Kalahandi. The rite seemed at an end everywhere, and Konds were less shy—apparently accepting British authority. 'It afforded me much gratification to see the confidence with which these wild men of Jeypore visited my camp on this my second appearance among them, showing a remarkable contrast to their shyness of last season.' (23rd April 1853)

On his last tour, of 1853–4, Campbell went into Jeypore again as far as Rayagadha. His final report stressed the importance of strengthening the Oriya chiefs' position—indeed, British rule strengthened their grip over the Konds enormously, setting up a cycle of exploitation that still continues.

> It has always been my policy on first entering a new country to conciliate the established Uriya chiefs. Of the 65 Bissyes and Patros of the Khond districts in Boad, Chinna Kimedy, Jeypore and Kalahandi with whom I have come into contact, I have not removed one. All were not equally well disposed to forward my views for the suppression of human sacrifice, for all derived a certain advantage from it in the shape of offerings from the Khonds on the occasion of sacrifice. (Report of 9th February 1854)

The EIC directors in London commended Campbell's 'attitude of firmness without unnecessary resort to forcible measures', and declared that 'germs of an ultimate civilization' had been planted in the Kond country (14th June 1854). Campbell left Orissa and retired to Scotland in 1854. Frye took charge of the Agency for a few months, since MacViccar had gone away to recuperate after an attack of 'fever in its most dangerous form', which he had contracted on his last tour. But within a year, Frye had died of the same malaria.

Lt MacDonald, Assistant to the Ganjam Agent, made a month's tour in the winter of 1854–5, to inspect the schools and police posts that had been set up since 1852 and were being transferred from the Meriah Agency to the jurisdiction of Ganjam District. One of the schools was at

Nowgam in Chinna Kimedi (site of the battle in May 1836), the others at Kormingia and Udayagiri. All three he found in a 'deplorable' state. Only a handful of Kond boys attended them—most of the pupils were Oriyas. At Kormingia all six boys were Konds, but their parents would not co-operate and they had learnt very little; only 5 of the 13 pupils at Nowgam were Konds; and Udayagiri school was all-Oriya. The police posts had been set up as an 'experiment of bringing the hill tracts of Ghumsur under regular police authority'. Neither the Meriah Agents nor Hindu chiefs such as Sam Bissoi approved, but 'circumstances demanded' that police should gradually replace 'the old native system of leaving [the Konds] to the mercies of a hill sirdar'. The main danger was the 'discontent that might be engendered by acts of oppression and extortion on the part of peons and other native officials'—at least this was clearly understood in advance! Infamous stories circulated about Punda Naik, the last *maliah sirdar*, and the first police head in Purnaguda, who had recently been removed for 'misconduct'. But there were no complaints yet against his successor or the head of the other police post at Chokapand. MacDonald had been sent to enquire into feuds in 1851–2, and found that no less than 73 villages had recently been burnt and 16 people killed. 'The misery, confusion and ill-feeling engendered by these feuds was incalculable.'

> Soon after the establishment of the police, a series of these armed affrays attended with arson and loss of life took place, but guards were immediately sent to the disturbed tracts, the ringleaders were apprehended and tried as rioters, and an example made in two mutahs [i.e. they were publicly hanged], since which period not a single armed affray has taken place between any two Goomsur tribes.

Chokra Bissoi's 'robber bands....dignified by the name of rebels in the disturbances of 1846' no longer operated in Ghumsur. The state of peace had led to a great increase in trade, and MacDonald proposed a tax on salt (Report of 31st January 1855).

MacViccar came back and made an extensive tour in the same season, which took him into all three of the British Provinces in India: Ghumsur, Chinna and Pedda Kimedi and Sorada in the Ganjam Agency, and Jeypore in the Vizagapatam Agency were in Madras; Boad and Maji Deso under the Cuttack Commissioner, and Patna, Karcall and Nowgedda in the South West Frontier Agency were under the Bengal Government; while Kalahandi and Bastar were administered by the Commissioner at Nagpur, under the Bombay Government. This was the first British visit to Bastar state—a huge area whose population is predominantly Gond. MacViccar was pleased at the Konds' 'fidelity' in Jeypore in strictly refraining from the sacrifice. But he and Lt McNeill, his new Assistant, investigated cases of *junna* sacrifice by Hindu hill chiefs at Ramgiri, Lakshmipur and Malkangiri, where 'one of these mangled bodies was exhumed, the spot having been pointed out by the chief of the district, when further denial and equivocation were useless.' They registered 100 *toorees* (the Jeypore equivalent of *meriahs*) in Malkangiri, and investigated a case of suttee and five cases of murdering sorceresses (Report of 21st May 1855).

Captain MacViccar resigned in 1855, and Lt McNeill was appointed Agent. The hill area of Boad was annexed the same year, on account of the *rajah*'s lack of control over Konds, and suspected aid to Chokra Bissoi. This area was henceforth called the Khondmals (until more recently it was renamed Phulbani District). McNeill's tour of 1855–6 was mainly in Jeypore, investigating four cases of human sacrifice—two Hindu ones, a sorceress thrown down a well, and one by Konds (Report of 12th June 1856). In Kalahandi, during December, he took around with him, as an example, a Kond chief tied in chains, who had been convicted of performing a human sacrifice. In the same month Kuttia Konds attacked his party, and McNeill's life was saved by a *Jemadar* called Dinobandu Patnaik, who became his chief Indian Assistant. Dinobandu captured Chokra Bissoi's chief lieutenant in 1856, and as *Tahsildar* of the Khondmals from 1855 until 1880 caused great misery by 'his demonic energy and calculated brutality' (Bailey 1960 p.178). A state of rebellion was declared in Parla Kimedi in 1856, led by Chokra Bissoi. It was quickly crushed, though Chokra escaped again—the *rajah* of Madanpur in Kalahandi was accused of sheltering him.

Jeypore was again the focus of McNeill's tour of 1856–7 (Report of 12th May 1857). MacViccar, now a Major, assumed charge of the Agency for a few months again in 1857. The Assistant Surgeon in medical charge of it died of fever in February. Konds were being disciplined into proper subjection by harsh sentences. One was convicted of murdering a Boad *peon* and sentenced to death. McNeill personally supervised his hanging at a village near Mahasingi (below p.162). Several Konds were convicted of practising human sacrifice or female infanticide and sentenced to 'imprisonment with hard labour in irons'. Some Konds from Sonepur served this sentence in Sorada, with a 'salutary effect.... the spectacle of these prisoners working in irons appeared to have a great influence' on the local Konds who had formerly practised female infanticide: men brought their wives to witness the sight. Meanwhile cholera and smallpox were 'making terrible ravages', and many Konds deserted their villages (McNeill's Diary for 14th Jan. 1858). The Agency was 'crippled' and unable to make the usual tour because its elephants had to be sent off at the urgent request of British troops fighting the Mutineers elsewhere in north India. McNeill also sent off some Ghumsur *sebundies* to help them.

In 1859 he investigated a human sacrifice recently performed in Risingia, a cluster of six villages in Atharah Mutah—difficult of access, though not far from the British base at Russellkonda. Two *meriah* girls were rescued. One of the two *molikos* had been arrested in 1854 for planning a sacrifice, but was released for lack of evidence. It came to light that Risingia had performed six *meriah* sacrifices between 1855 and 1858, and Rodingia nearby had performed three more. Four Doms who were convicted of selling the *meriahs*, as well as several Konds, were sentenced to 5–10 years' imprisonment with hard labour. On the whole, Konds had replaced the human victims they offered to the Earth Goddess, with buffaloes. But this year McNeill forbade these buffalo sacrifices too, anxious that they were becoming too frequent, and were a symbol of resistance to British rule. In his view, the Konds had 'pledged themselves to renounce the rites and ceremonies of that pujah' altogether. One reason for the sacrifices McNeill admitted was that 'smallpox had for the last two seasons made terrible ravages in districts and among communities where it was never before known'—which must have had a lot to do with the gradual 'opening up' of the Kond hills by troops and traders since the Agency was set up. In this season he also rescued or registered 19 *meriahs* in Chinna Kimedi (Report of 14th May 1859).

The Agency was smaller now. McNeill did not even have a British Assistant until a Lt Crauford was appointed in 1859. He pleaded unsuccesfully for the transfer of Sorada, Chinna Kimedi and Boad back into his jurisdiction, and wrote that the new police system 'was distasteful alike to Khonds and Hill Uriyas'. On his tour of 1859–60 he visited some new Kond areas, including Gadapur where he stopped a feud, and Lanjigarh on the Jeypore-Kalahandi border, whence he removed ten *meriahs*. Gadapur, in Bori Mutah, was particularly inaccessible, but the Konds there showed no fear: 'my camp was crowded all day with men, women and children, who viewed with awe and astonishment elephants, horses, and tents, all of which were new and strange to them.' But in many areas, smallpox and cholera had reached epidemic proportions. Konds evidently saw it in terms of the Earth Goddess' anger due to the ban on *meriah* sacrifice, and performed buffalo sacrifices to appease her.

> Lt Crauford has brought prominently to my notice that the practice of immolating buffaloes with all the rites and ceremonies of the forbidden meriah has this season been celebrated with unusual pomp in nearly every mutah of Chinna Kimedy notwithstanding the prohibition issued last season by myself. (Report of 22nd August 1860)

In the following season McNeill visited Gadapur again, where he convicted three Konds of practising female infanticide and sentenced each to 3 months' imprisonment with hard labour in chains, 'a lenient sentence', since the Bori Mutah Konds had only 'made their submission' the previous year. He registered or removed more *meriahs* in Kashipur and Thuamul in Jeypore. A few months later, he found nine more *meriahs* who had been concealed in Bissamcuttack, and convicted a Kond in Ghumsur for dedicating a young girl for sacrifice, sentencing him to two years' hard labour in chains (Report of 25th May 1861).

The Meriah Agency was abolished on 18th December 1861, and the Kond districts, duly pacified, came under regular civil and police authority.

As we have seen, handing over *meriahs* was the main demand that officials made on entering a new area. Without doubt, it became a symbol to both sides of accepting British authority. Between 1836 and 1854 nearly 2,000 were removed from Kond villages. In the later years, not all were taken, since they were not in danger of being sacrificed, and preferred to stay put.

Kond chiefs were also asked to sign an agreement to refrain from human sacrifice or infanticide, as well as from feuding, and implicitly to accept British rule. Konds had not met binding written agreements like this before. Did they understand them as the British did? Officials liked to think so. The Hindu chiefs who led Kond resistance in 1836–7 and 1846–7 seem to have been literate; few if any Kond chiefs were.[101] Those who were not, signed with a thumbprint. As with North American Indian chiefs who were persuaded to sign away their land, this signing was a vital symbolic act, that was obviously understood differently by the two sides. To Britons, signing a pledge or treaty implied the acceptance of a whole legal system. They often expressed pleasant surprise at how readily Konds entered into these agreements—for Konds probably saw them more in terms of their own peace pacts and fealty to a *rajah*, than as precisely defined contracts. As contracts, they were very one-sided, for the British wrote what they wanted. When villages refused to submit and declared that the British had no rights over them and should leave their territory, their villages were burnt. It was best to go through the prescribed ritual without objections, and tell the officials what they wanted to hear. To Britons, the signing of these documents also signified a political order of chiefs or headmen distinguished from ordinary men by being able to read and write, and empowered to take decisions on behalf of whole villages or clans, which was not how Kond society worked at all.

In the treaties, as in the proclamations, which were read out or posted up in deserted villages, written presumably in Oriya, the officials emphasized that the Government would not tax Konds or take away their 'traditional rights'. But did Britons really understand what these were? Macpherson and Campbell believed they were supporting the 'traditional rights' of Hindu chiefs and *rajahs*, when in fact they were giving them new rights and powers. They certainly did not recognize Konds' traditional right to appoint or dismiss a *rajah*.[102]

Among other rituals of subjection were the trials, hangings and imprisonment—the chains which McNeill made a 'guilty' headman wear—as well as the coolie service, which Macpherson's lists of expenses show that he forced hundreds of Konds into in 1846–7: the Konds had to carry the soldiers' supplies for several days, for which they were paid in 'batta' (i.e. rice-grain). This is hardly ever mentioned in published accounts, though even Dyce reported that Macpherson had seriously misused his powers imposing this degrading task (above p.86), which shaded into *begar* ('forced service') and remained one of the most oppressive and resented features of British rule, throughout tribal India.

A few years after establishing their right to suppress human sacrifice, and their role as the Konds' rulers, officials started to impose much stricter rules. MacViccar had declared,

> In every case....I hail the immolation of one bullock with more pleasure than the rescue of many meriahs, because it affords incontrovertible evidence that the primitive rite has yielded to the pressure from without. (Report of 26th April 1851)

Yet as we have just seen, McNeill forbade the sacrifice of buffaloes, or any display of the Earth Goddess' insignia, after receiving reports of buffaloes being sacrificed in large numbers in Boad, with dramatic processions.

> Owing to these suspicious circumstances, I publicly and positively prohibited the sacrifice of buffaloes or other animals on ground formerly dedicated to the meriah, and that in no circumstances were offerings in future to be made to the "Dhurni" deity, nor were the "Chutty" and toucan's head ever again to be displayed. (Report of 14th May 1859)

How could the British outlaw worship of a deity? McNeill's prohibition recalls the history of Europe during the Inquisition. It may not have been enforced for long, though ever since there have been occasional bans, or Government restrictions on buffalo sacrifice. Whether human sacrifice and female infanticide took place at all, and whatever their scale, and the scale of local warfare, British rule started by prohibiting the taking of human life in these forms, as a first stage in the process of forcing Konds into 'subjection' and subservience. For with the establishment of police stations, Konds were made to recognize other laws, which restricted their access to the forest, and demanded a duty on salt and alcohol as well as a 'plough-tax', on top of whatever 'gifts' officials demanded. And with the police there also came traders, colonists and moneylenders, who were soon exploiting the Konds, getting them into debt, and taking over their lands.

CHAPTER FOUR

Human Sacrifice as a Kond and Hindu Ritual

The Meriah Rite

So what was the *meriah* sacrifice? Who were the *meriahs*? Did Konds really sacrifice human beings to their Earth Goddess, or was the whole thing a figment of the colonial imagination? The reality of this custom is difficult to understand because it seems so alien. The reality of its suppression is as difficult because it seems so right. My purpose in this chapter is simply to try and look at it in a clearer perspective, before moving on to look more deeply at British actions. What can we understand about it from the written evidence? Can this contribute at all to understanding the nature of human sacrifice in general?

British descriptions of Kond human sacrifice built up a particular image that is highly charged with emotion, and it is hard to approach the subject free from the officials' gruesome stress on 'savagery'. They never witnessed a human sacrifice themselves, of course, although on several occasions they claimed that they arrived just in time to prevent one, or dug up victims' remains; they got their information from Oriya Hindus, among whom were a few key informants, such as Sundera Singh and Sam Bissoi.[1] What it meant to the Konds thus comes to us through a double filter of ideas and language: through Hindu ideas expressed in Oriya or Hindi, influenced by what British officers expected or wanted to hear.

I often wonder whether the Konds practised human sacrifice and female infanticide at all, and whether, if so, the British accounts are accurate.[2] On the whole, I believe that they are, though I believe they represent a relatively superficial understanding. The sources actually agree with each other quite closely on the main outline, whether because they preserve an accurate record, or because they borrowed heavily from each other. Certain differences, particularly in how the victim was killed, seem to be regional variations. Barbara Boal (1982) has brought together and compared the published accounts with more recent examples of buffalo sacrifice.

The sacrifice was performed principally to the Earth Goddess. The older sources call her Tari Pennu, but she has several names, and it seems that her main names, nowadays at least, are Darni, Tana or Bangu Penu. *Darni* and *tana* are words for 'earth', and *penu* means 'deity' or 'spirit', similar to *deo* or *devi* among Hindus and some other tribes.[3] Darni Penu is still the main deity worshipped by most Konds, along with Bura Penu, the Sky God, although she has declined in importance in the Udayagiri area according to Boal. Konds said that the sacrifices were performed in response to Darni's demand for human blood, and to ensure the fertility of the earth—particularly their crop of turmeric: 'they coolly reasoned with me as to the impossibility of the huldee being of a fine deep colour without this shedding of human blood', as one officer put it (Ricketts 23rd Feb. 1837). Most Konds seem to have seen themselves as in some sense the Earth Goddess' own people, with a far-reaching responsibility to perform these sacrifices: 'What fault is ours? The earth goddess demands a sacrifice. It is necessary for the world.'[4]

The victims of sacrifice were called *meriahs*.[5] There were usually several living in a Kond village or set of allied villages. *Meriahs* had to be bought by the sacrificing village: paying a large price for the person helped to cancel the sin of taking their life. But sacrifice was not automatic. Usually *meriahs* seem to have lived in the headman's house, working his fields alongside the headman's sons, with the status of serfs, or of 'ploughmen and labourers, whether poor and miserable, or happy' (above p.83). It was basically the village chief who bought a *meriah*, and the extra labour insured his family's prosperity and ability to play the role of 'givers', for a family's relative status and wealth in a tribal village depend above all on how many pairs of hands make and tend its fields.

In some places a fixed price was recognized for a *meriah* of 40 items (*goonties* or 'lives'), which included a buffalo known as the *duli* buffalo, a bullock, cow, goat, cloths, brass pot and plate, and a large bunch of bananas (Arbuthnot 24th November 1837). Konds bought *meriahs* from Dom traders, who kidnapped or bought them, usually as children and sometimes from their parents, from distant areas, often down in the plains.

Usually they were not Konds by birth, but from other castes—Dom, Lohar (blacksmith), Gauro (herder), or even Brahmin. The Doms lived in Kond villages and managed their trade with the outside world, as well as weaving the Konds' cloth. They apparently pledged their children to the Konds for sacrifice, in case they could not supply anyone else (as in the case cited above, p.65), and these Dom children were sometimes sacrificed after the British removed the intended victim. In the invocation just before sacrifice, the priest disclaimed guilt for taking the person's life on the grounds that the Konds had bought him from his parents—'we bought you with a price, and did not seize you; now we sacrifice you according to our custom, and no sin rests on us.' (Russell 11th May 1837)

A *meriah* chosen for sacrifice could be a child or adult, and of either sex, depending on the goddess' wish. A *meriah*'s children became *meriahs* in turn, so it was sometimes only the second generation who were sacrificed. *Meriah* women who had the status of 'concubines' (i.e. second wives, or mistresses) were called *poosiahs*; as we have seen, British officials sometimes made the Kond men who lived with them formally marry them, to ensure their safety.[6] But on the whole *meriahs* seem to have been well-treated and lived virtually as Konds' equals, until the time of sacrifice approached, when they were sometimes constrained by a rope or chain, at the same time as being venerated and pampered. But the fact that they were hardly ever grateful to their rescuers (above p.70, Campbell 1864 p.112), and that many tried to escape back to the villages they had been taken from, implies that they were not basically oppressed during their day-to-day life.

The *meriah* sacrifice was performed in many ways. The main festival it featured in took place during a full moon in the cold season, usually in January or February.[7] The victim was often dedicated a few days before by having his hair shorn. On the second day of the festival he was fêted and led in a procession around the village before being taken to the sacred grove. A Kond child called the *toomba* garlanded him (Russell 11th May 1837 and WM) and everyone touched his feet, or collected the turmeric paste he was anointed with, as if he was a god, or his identity was beginning to merge with the Earth Goddess. He was offered palm wine and opium, breaking a long fast, and the night was one of dancing and excitement.

Usually he was tied to a wooden post near a pile of stones sacred to Darni and Jakeri Penu, the village ancestor spirit.[8] But there was often a search at night for a place near the village where a chink had opened in the earth, and the sacrifice was performed there (WM p.127). A pole 40 or 50 feet high was erected above the place of sacrifice, on which was mounted an effigy of a peacock. This was in Ghumsur, where a peacock was the royal symbol. In Boad it was a bull; and in Chinna Kimedi, where the royal symbol was an elephant, the victim was apparently tied to an elephant pole which had a cross-bar like a trunk that was whirled round as the victim was cut to pieces.[9] Sometimes the *meriah*'s arms and legs were broken to avoid tying him up, and to keep him passive during the sacrifice. At least he was drunk, or under the influence of opium (WM p.119). In some places, just before sacrifice, he was bound into the trunk of a freshly cut tree, or between bamboo poles (WM, Mills 2nd June 1843).

The priest prayed to the Earth—'O God, we offer the sacrifice to you, give us good crops, seasons, and health' (Russell). Often there were extended invocations or dialogues between victim and priest.[10] The priest then drew the first blood. This signal was often marked by the firing of guns by *paiks* sent by the local *rajah*, to whose representative Konds paid a fee for each sacrifice they performed. At once a crowd of men cut the *meriah* to pieces with axes and knives. The lurid descriptions mention several variations, including burning alive. Campbell's descriptions convey the flavour of British horror:

> The miserable meriah is dragged along the fields, surrounded by a crowd of half intoxicated Konds, who, shouting and screaming, rush upon him, and with their knives cut the flesh from his bones, avoiding the head and bowels, till the living skeleton, dying from loss of blood, is relieved from torture, when its remains are burnt and the ashes mixed with the new grain to preserve it from insects.[11]

Usually the victim's body was cut into pieces and buried at different spots over an area of many miles. In the sacrificing village the main offerings were at Darni's shrines and the village boundaries. Also, a man from each household apparently cut off a piece and buried it at once in his fields. Members of other villages also took part, and ran back to their own villages, to reach their shrines or fields and bury them there before nightfall. The head was kept separate, and burnt or buried later at Darni's main shrine in the sacrificing village. The man burying the flesh always averted his gaze as he placed it in the ground. For several days after the sacrifice, the whole village went into mourning for the person they had killed.

A priest of Darni was called *jani*. *Janis* made a strong negative impression on Britons for being unkempt and drunk, but they possessed great political influence: theirs was a form of authority antithetical to British forms. Macpherson said they were celibate, unlike any modern Kond priests (WM p.106); possibly he misunderstood this, for it is a general custom for tribal priests to remain celibate for a day or more before performing a sacrifice.

The sacrifices were performed by a group of villages in a cycle of three or more years: in one year a village performed the sacrifice itself, in the second and third it got flesh from other villages.[12] At least one sacrifice probably took place at some village in each *mutah* or clan territory each year, attended by members from all allied villages. When Campbell was first exacting promises from Kond chiefs to refrain from human sacrifice, they asked for permission to perform one a year in each *mutah* (above p.66). Apart from the full moon winter festival, the *meriah* sacrifice was also apparently performed on an occasional basis, to avert particular calamities—such as the calamity of British invasion no doubt![13]

Some of the neighbouring tribes closely related to the Konds also practised human sacrifice, although less frequently. Fürer-Haimendorf found evidence that Konda Reddis performed it at intervals of several years on top of a particular mountain (1944), and other tribes seem to have done likewise. The Maria Gonds also probably practised it: three cases were uncovered in the 1930s–40s, and four of the sacrificers were sentenced to death—cases more like murder, involving sudden assault on an unsuspecting victim, whose blood generated fertility (ibid. p.39, Elwin 1943b pp.67–75). Like the Konds, Marias have the Earth Mother as one of their main deities (Elwin ibid. p.16).

The *meriah* sacrifice was replaced most often by substituting a buffalo,[14] along with a plea to Darni to blame the British *sahebs* for the lack of a human victim. But cases of human sacrifice have sometimes come to light since its official suppression: Macpherson believed Sam Bissoi actually patronized several at the same time as he was officially promoting its suppression; and several took place in apparently the most 'subjected' areas (above pp.68, 70, 105). Several Konds told Elwin they had witnessed one.

> I found them still deeply attached to these evil practices. In one village, which I visited in the company of Mr H.V. Blackburn, and where tigers were killing both men and cattle, the Khonds came and told us that if we would allow them

> to sacrifice a human child the tiger-nuisance would quickly abate. "The earth cries out for blood", as a Khond told me. (Report 5th April 1945)[15]

A police officer told me how he investigated a case around 1980, when all the men in a remote village admitted having sacrificed a boy, after everyone in the village, including the boy's parents, had agreed on the need for it.

The buffalo sacrifice too has sometimes been prohibited (e.g. by McNeill in 1859, and during the 1940s, when Elwin says the *rajah* of Chandrapur forbade it because he thought it barbaric), and in some areas it is no longer performed, where a Kond council has decided to stop it under Christian or Hindu influence. It is a dramatic, high-tension event. In the scramble of killing the buffalo with axes men are often hurt, and some consider that shedding this blood appeases the goddess' desire for human blood. Barbara Boal, F.G. Bailey and Hermann Niggemeyer witnessed buffalo sacrifices in Phulbani District, and their descriptions can usefully be compared with the evidence on human sacrifice.[16]

A full cycle of buffalo sacrifice often lasts five years. In the first year, a village dedicates or 'shows' its buffalo to the goddess, sacrificing it in the third (Boal 1982). Kuttia Konds sacrifice two or three buffaloes at a time, once every three years. Like the *meriah*, a buffalo dedicated to the goddess has to be bought from outside (Niggemeyer 1964). At the start of the festival a new post is cut and carved, and dedicated with blood from a sacrificed pig. Several subsidiary posts are used, as well as the long bamboo *satari* pole, which is hoisted above the main post, decorated with strips of pig's flesh, clappers, ropes, cloths, or peacock feathers. Before being sacrificed the buffalo is 'teased'—people hit it, pull its tail and excite it with a din. At other times they honour, feed and soothe it. Bamboo or wooden clappers play an important part, and so do drums, dancing, singing, trance, and alcohol—for a period before the sacrifice, villagers drink while maintaining a fast, and the buffalo is made drunk, just as the *meriah* was. Blame for the buffalo's death and the lack of a human victim is still often placed on 'Mukmol Sahib and Kemel Sahib'.[17] The implements of sacrifice, *mala dupa,* include the *tangi* (ritual axe) with which the buffalo is killed, and are sometimes said to weep for human blood (below pp.118–19). After the sacrifice, the flesh that is not buried or offered to Darni is eaten. The flesh-takers from other villages are pelted with stones and earth as they run off home—as happened in the days of human sacrifice. After the sacrifice, all the villagers purify themselves in a stream before making a feast.

A buffalo sacrifice that I witnessed began with a procession out of the village led by several dramatic figures: 'women' (who were apparently men) dressed in red *sarees*, who wore their long hair loose and carried a sword in each hand (which is apparently how Darni is shown when an image is made of her). They and the men who followed them danced slowly out of the village between the outstretched legs of the women and children, who sat in a long row, giggling. Several men danced through a firetrench just outside the village, while the 'priestesses' went into trance and several goats and pigs were sacrificed. Meanwhile a large crowd of maybe a hundred men charged around with big axes, practising strokes and shouting and creating a highly charged atmosphere. The buffalo was tied up on a distant hillside, and the main crowd of people kept well away. Suddenly several men fired ancient muskets, similar to those used in the Ghumsur wars and fired at the sacrifices in the 1840s. The buffalo was hacked to pieces with axes. Its head was cut off and carried ceremonially into the village.

Female Infanticide

Not all the Konds performed the *meriah* rite. Those who did not told Macpherson that they took great precautions to make sure nobody buried flesh from a sacrifice on their territory, apparently because that would make the local earth demand it too (24th April 1842), much as a tiger that has tasted human blood is said to 'get a taste for it' and become a man-eater.

But most of these non-human-sacrificing Konds apparently practised an even weirder custom: female infanticide. Female infants were exposed in the forest just after birth. Macpherson reckoned that nine out of ten female children were killed; sometimes there were no female children in a village at all. 'At the lowest estimate, above one thousand female children must be destroyed annually'. This in a population estimated at 60,000—a relatively small section of the Kond population, of several clans, that dwelt in the hill regions of Korada, Digi and Gadapur.[18]

The reason villagers gave concerns marriage exchanges. The brideprice or dowry given for women in this area was enormous—about ten times what it was elsewhere. Macpherson said there were only 20 or

30 women in each village, and these apparently came from other areas. What seems certain is that the Konds of this area married women from elsewhere, but would not or could not give women in marriage to men from outside. This group of Kond clans was apparently locked in a system of one-way exogamy, ensuring that wives were taken from other clans but not given in return by killing off most of their female babies. Presumably they claimed the same kind of high status exclusiveness as the Rajputs who practised female infanticide.[19] What these Konds apparently said to Campbell sounds similar:

> that it becomes their manliness to marry the daughters of foreign countries only, but to give their daughters in marriage to others they find degrading; that if they rear daughters, they, at the time of giving them in marriage, will be obliged to give them many presents, which they cannot afford, by reason of their poverty.

Campbell was told a myth of dishonour brought about by daughters and a consequent oath by ancestral brothers never to rear female children.[20]

According to Macpherson the huge brideprices which men paid for their wives were constantly having to be repaid (WM p.133), since there were few women to a village, and women changed their husbands whenever they wished (except when pregnant or nursing a child). The trail of repayments they left in their wake caused great confusion and expense. For instance, when a woman left her first husband, her father had to repay the huge brideprice this man had given him. Women boasted of the number of repayments they had caused. So having girl-children was an expensive business, and the difficulty was blamed on female nature. Like Campbell, Macpherson recorded a misogynist myth that supported the custom, which reflected these Konds' view of the relationship between the 'God of Light' (Bura Penu) and the Earth Goddess: Bura created Tari as his consort, but she was jealous of his love for mankind and became the source of evil.[21] Bura advised his followers to 'bring up only as many women as you can manage' (WM p.113). In fact, women (as Macpherson noted) have great status and influence among the Konds, especially in the areas of female infanticide (where their value presumably went up from scarcity). He believed no Kond area was entirely free from female infanticide. All of this implies a strange ambivalence towards women in Kond culture.

However, Macpherson's interpretation of Kond religion in terms of a 'schism' or virtual war of religion between two rival 'sects' seems farfetched (above pp.81–2, WM p.242). At least he acknowledged that followers of Tari and Bura each worshipped both as their principal deities (WM pp.87–8). How much the British conceptual division of Konds into 'sacrificing' and 'infanticidal' corresponds to the reality of how Konds saw themselves, we cannot be sure. The two customs were suppressed by the British simultaneously, because they both involved taking human life. If they were indeed mutually exclusive customs, then maybe they were symbolically connected for Konds as well, as Macpherson maintained. But did the infanticidal Konds really identify women and Tari Penu with evil? And did female infanticide evolve simply as a reaction to human sacrifice to the Earth Goddess? The economic significance of the huge marriage payments remains obscure; but it implies a high positive value placed on women, which accompanied their freedom to choose and change their partners at will. The written evidence and explanations seem tenuous, and without knowing more about the differences between Konds who practised human sacrifice and Konds who practised female infanticide, these and many other questions remain unanswered. I do not feel I understand the custom at all, beyond the sense that it had a lot to do with these clans' relationship with outsiders, as we shall see was the case with human sacrifice as well.

Macpherson reasoned some families into starting to rear their female children, although when Campbell came several years later, most of these had apparently died. Both officers arranged marriages between 'infanticidal' men and *meriah* women, and by the time Campbell left, he claimed that female children were being reared equally with males.

The Context of Kond Religion

All the British accounts of human sacrifice stress its violence, describing vividly and emotively a scene the officers never actually witnessed. Frazer brought these accounts to a wider public with his description of Kond human sacrifice as 'the best known case of human sacrifices, systematically offered to ensure good crops' (*Golden Bough* abridged version p.434). To him, the sacrifice was primarily a fertility ritual, and he stressed the identification of the victim with the goddess, on his theme of 'sacrifice of the living god'. Frazer's account in turn has been quoted extensively as one of the best documented examples of human sacrifice, in the context of the idea that human sacrifice was virtually a universal feature of primitive society, which is actually how Macpherson and his superiors saw it too.[22]

Does human sacrifice indeed represent a 'barbaric' stage of social development? Or is it a custom that has arisen from particular cultural configurations? Some scholars have seen an original custom of human sacrifice behind all traditions of animal sacrifice (including, for example, the Semitic, as the story of Abraham and Isaac may seem to suggest). Or is it the other way around—that human sacrifice has arisen in particular times and places as an aberrant or extreme form of blood sacrifice? And why among the Konds? Why did this particular people believe it was necessary to sacrifice human beings? And how could they bring themselves to do it?

Many such questions are necessary to shake us out of the illusion that we think we understand such foreign behaviour: the familiar categories of 'human sacrifice', 'primitive tribe', and 'fertility ritual' reinforce the worst stereotypes about tribal people and explain nothing. This is the same problem that Michelle Rosaldo approaches in *Knowledge and passion* (1980): the Ilongot men, among whom she did fieldwork in the northern Philippines, otherwise highly sensitive people, possessed a great longing and nostalgia for their former, suppressed custom of headhunting. Her book is an exploration of the socially constructed ideas and emotions that surrounded this attachment.

Verrier Elwin, in the 1940s, found the Konds similarly nostalgic for human sacrifice—'Even in 1944 the desire for human sacrifice was fundamental to Kond psychology' (1964 p.178). Masks were used as a substitute for *meriahs*, and relics of former victims were kept for use in rituals or as talismans for good luck. Many Konds said that Darni Penu still often asked for a human sacrifice. One *jani* told him,

> twice Darni Penu said to me in a dream, "Give me human sacrifice, and then as of old your crops will be good, you'll get your jungle back: you may cut only a little, but profit will be great. All will be happy. But if you don't you'll starve, elephants will eat your crop and tigers will eat you and Government will take your jungle." I fasted—gave her rice—said "Do what you will, but we can't give a man. It's Government's fault, not ours." ('Notes about Meriah Tribes' Misc. X. 161 p.23)

In another village Elwin was told how Darni's sacrificial tools lamented the lack of human blood.

> Of old when they killed humans, Janni had two axes and a knife in his house—now when they kill mere buffalo, "the axes and knife weep", so when they go dancing to another village for sacrifice, a man fills a hollow bamboo with blood, runs back to [the village] and throws it over Darni Penu, axes and knife. "If we bring them out except at 3-yearly intervals, half the village will die". When the time approaches when they used to get human blood, i.e. the Magh festival moon, they begin to weep, "When will we get our food, our pleasure?" The noise is like *ching ching ching*. But only Janni can hear it.(ibid. p.8)

What is the view of the spirit world, and its relation with humans, that lies behind such statements? Drawing on a wide variety of sources, including Elwin's Kond material—his unpublished fieldwork notes as well as the Kond myths he published—I shall give a brief overview of Kond religion, in the conviction that, with some powerful exceptions, most ethnography gives a misleading account of tribal religion and stays on a superficial level. For the understanding of life given by tribal religion and by the academic tradition could not be further from each other, which means that academic discourse has usually proved a poor medium for describing tribal religious life.[23]

Konds' relations with their gods are a major fact of everyday village life. They come in dreams, they demand certain offerings and respect, causing trouble when neglected, giving great gifts when honoured. There is no limit to their number, and their identities merge into each other in a way that is thoroughly confusing to a Western mind. Elwin admitted that, although Kond myths are highly distinctive and preserve many non-Hindu themes, he could make no sense out of all the different deities and their relationships.[24]

Yet some very clear patterns and themes emerge. The variety does not reflect confusion so much as the fact that each Kond village is the centre of its world, with its own version of how the earth was created, and who the first beings were. Maybe the different deities are not personalities so much as energies—personifications of the energies of nature.

What in their mythology distinguishes Konds from other tribes, to explain why they in particular practised human sacrifice? The first answer is: because they worshipped the earth; they are a people of the earth, and 'the earth needs blood'—even if we simply understand that in the literal sense it needs decaying matter to fertilize it, and that when we die, our bodies return to the earth and its elements: 'dust to dust, ashes to ashes'. For the Kuvi and Kuttia Konds the great female creator and teacher of culture to mankind is Nirantali, who emerged from the earth along with other gods and the first humans. She created animals and plants from beeswax or clay or her own body-grease. Her brother, or consort, or both, is Parumgatti, a great hunter and figure of fun. The myths which Elwin collected only occasionally hint that her 'real' partner, as in Macpherson's myths, is Bura Penu, the Sky God.

Among Kui Konds this female creator is called Ambali Baeli. Like Nirantali, she is a human incarnation of Darni or Tari Penu, the Earth Goddess. In one myth recorded by Macpherson, Tari created the plants and animals when she tried to thwart Bura's desire to create mankind. As he walked he threw clumps of earth behind him. Tari followed him and caught the first four, turning them into plants, fish, birds and animals. For the fifth, Bura held her down to stop her interfering, and it turned into the first humans (WM p.85). Another myth tells how Ambali Baeli cut her finger when slicing vegetables one day. Her blood, falling on the earth, at once made the soil abundantly fertile. When she noticed this she offered herself for sacrifice—but the Konds refused, insisting on a non-Kond victim (WM pp.96–7). In another version about a woman called Karaboodi, she told her sons to sacrifice her, and they did: she became the first victim offered to Tari, her *alter ego* (Boal 1982 pp.126–7).

Another myth collected by Elwin records a primordial act of sacrifice through which the earth came into being, similar to the Hindu myth of Purusha. It tells of Bogi Penu, born at Saphaganna, a being who was all alone, and hanged himself. Bela Pinnu, the Sun God, came down to earth, cut up Bogi's corpse, and scattered it in all directions, forming the hills (Elwin 1954, 1.7).

Nirantali is often coupled with her sister or double, as Nirantali-Kapantali. Kond myths show a great concern with names, and Elwin's collection records dozens of different names given to the first humans—brothers, sisters or couples. Clearly, these are thought of as ancestors of particular groups, clans and lineages. Thus the spirit which a village sacrifices to as Darni Penu is apparently conceived as the spirit of that particular territory, 'ancestor earth', as much as a single deity, 'earth'. She inhabits certain fixed spots—the *darni*-cairns of stones that form shrines, one inside a village, a couple more outside it in the forest. These are also referred to as Jakeri Penu, 'ancestor spirit'—in other words, a village's ancestors are closely associated with its territory, and the cult of Darni Penu has a lot to do with local places and their relationship with people. Konds are clearly not concerned with conceptual consistency, but with 'earth' as an energy that needs to be honoured. The mountain god(s), Horu (or Soru) Penu, are often worshipped alongside Darni Penu as one of the most important of deities. Every hill has its own named spirit that must be honoured in exchange for clearing the hillside for cultivation (e.g. Niggemeyer 1964 pp.149–51). Some are pre-eminent like Neem Raja (Nimgiri), the high peak in the Dongria hills.

Nearly all the Kond myths which Elwin collected (over 250) deal with different aspects of nature. The story they tell of creation is that at first there was only water. This state of flood was brought to an end by the heat of seven suns, which burnt up the water, and created the opposite problem of drought, or bare rock. Some myths tell how the Moon tricked the Sun into swallowing its seven children, by pretending it had swallowed its own children, the Stars, which it had only hidden. The gift of fertile earth to cover the rock is associated with Nirantali; but as we have seen (above pp.2–3), the earth was not made firm and solid until human beings sacrificed to Darni Penu—in some accounts, not until they placated her by human sacrifice.

Bura Penu, the Sky God, is sometimes associated with the sun, Bela or Vera Penu. Several myths tell how the sky was separated from earth by four iron pillars at the four corners of the world, the work of a mighty blacksmith. Niggemeyer records a story of Bura Penu as an archer god who makes his bow and arrows from peacock feathers, and who hung himself after a quarrel with Nirantali, his wife, after which he took up residence in the sky (1964 p.153). Bura has a sister or consort, Pusruli, another female creator-figure, as is Rani Aru (Nirantali's daughter in some accounts). Several other gods are associated with rain and water, thunder and lightning: Bhimenja or Bhima Penu, another archer-god of the sky, whose bow is the rainbow, whose arrows are lightning, and who produces rain; Piju Bibenj, who transforms smoke from funeral pyres into the rain, and divides night from day; and Jaora Penu, a spirit of streams and childbirth.

So who are these gods? How do they affect humans in the present? Trying to order them intellectually as Macpherson did tells us relatively little (WM pp.88–93). They may be non-visible entities, but they are not at all abstract conceptions. They are rooted in natural phenomena and experiences, and their festivals follow agricultural processes and the cycle of the seasons. In a sense they *are* the natural processes. They certainly offer a way of understanding and relating with them—in particular, of coming to terms with misfortune, sickness and death.

There are usually two kinds of priest or ritual specialist in a village, corresponding to two different sides of its spiritual life. Part of tribal religion has to do with the cyclical order of the seasons and the whole village's harmony with the spirit world, expressed through seasonal festivals such as *puni kalu* ('new fruits'). This is the responsibility of the priest, who is variously called jam, *guru* or '*darni*-keeper' (Boal 1982 pp.91–5), and who looks after the village and forest shrines *(darni* or *gudi)*. But a large part of tribal religion is concerned with maintaining health and healing sickness, and this is the field of the shaman. Among neighbouring tribes such as the Gonds, *sira* is the general term. But most Konds call him *kutaka,* or *kuta gatanju.*[25] Female shamans (whom Elwin calls 'priestesses') are known *as bejun* or *gurumai.* The first stage of their work is divining, which they often do by scattering grains of rice using a sickle or winnowing fan. They do this for a child's name-giving ceremony, to discover which ancestor is reincarnating in a child by going through a list of recently deceased ancestors—for Konds, like many other tribal peoples, believe that the soul (or a part of it) comes back within the family (WM p.72).

A more advanced stage is trance, through which 'dialogues with the dead' and other spirits are held.[26] Konds, like other tribes, understand sickness and misfortune primarily as attacks by spirits, who possess or 'eat' people's soul-essence, unless propitiated. Every death is fundamentally the result of spirit attack (as well as whatever mundane or medical causes we might offer). This may be instigated by black magic, practised by an ill-disposed witch or shaman, usually someone within the village. But when someone dies, part of their soul joins whatever spirit 'ate' them, and their identity merges with it. So a dead person may miss a living relative and try to get hold of him or her, instigating the 'nature spirit' with which the dead person has merged to attack the loved one. Through divining and trance, shamans try to discover which spirit is causing the sickness. When a shaman goes into trance, the other people who are present talk with the spirits who possess and speak through him. Discovering what spirits are responsible and what they want is often a highly complex matter. Finally it comes down to a request from the spirit for the sacrifice of an animal such as a chicken or goat. A shaman is helped by his 'familiar'—a spirit of the opposite sex who is 'married' to the shaman and visits him or her in dreams. There is a large range of 'disease'-spirits who regularly attack people.

Shaman-work is difficult and dangerous, and means a life of relative poverty. In stories of their lives, shamans often refused for months or years a demand from the spirit world to become one. But the spirit who was to become their familiar sent them disease and misfortune, often culminating in madness, until they accepted their lot, and started their training. This is partly through assisting elder shamans, and partly through dreams, in which they are taught healing-songs and plant-lore. Shamans are usually poor because they are forced to neglect their fields in order to serve the sick. They are paid little, and only when their cure is effective.

Above all shamans are highly skilled healers, who draw on great knowledge of herbal medicine (over and above the many herbs that are common knowledge to villagers), as well as massaging patients, blowing them with smoke, and chanting spirit-songs—songs learnt in dreams or trance and only sung for healing, some of the most beautiful music I have ever heard. Some aspects of their healing powers are so different from the qualities of Western medicine, that it requires personal experience, or a great leap of the imagination, to even begin to comprehend them. They work at a completely different level from Western medicine: in a sense, a much subtler and more holistic level, that is also effective, but in a completely different way, with different strengths and weaknesses. When tribal medicine effects a cure it goes to the root of the problem, which involves not only patients' physical health but also their relationships with living as well as dead relatives. From what I understand, tribal people keep in close communication with their dead and with the subtle energies of their natural environment, and work through emotional disturbances, much more fully than is common in our society. Trance or 'spirit-mediumship' (which Boal calls 'dissociation'!) is a far-reaching phenomenon, attested in many different cultures. Trance is a healing power at the opposite extreme to the workings of Western medicine: an ability, attended with great physical stamina and often pain, to journey to 'other worlds' and allow 'something else'—something that is non-human and basically unknown—to take over. This 'something else' was interpreted by Christian missionaries in terms of the devil or evil spirits; but tribal culture trusts the phenomenon as part of nature, or part of what it means to be human and to open up to the spirit-world.

Shamans and priests constantly practise various forms of self-sacrifice. Apart from the labour of this ritual work, they have to give up different foods and drink at various periods, as well as abstaining from sex before any ritual. The blood sacrifice of animals is a basic element in humans' relationship with the spirit world. In a tribal view (as in Hinduism and Christianity) sacrifice is far more than simply 'propitiation'—it is an action essential for life.

With this background, Macpherson's idea that Konds considered the Earth Goddess as the source of evil and the Sky God as the source of good, appears highly simplistic. Macpherson felt that his greatest triumph was to have convinced the human-sacrifice Konds that Bura Penu, whom he called the 'God of Light' and identified with the Christian God, was more powerful than the Earth Goddess. He described how Konds were coming round to this belief in his Report just before rebellion broke out (15th October 1846). In his brother's account,

> to find every man believing firmly in the supremacy of the evil principle—to leave all convinced, and acting upon the conviction, that the supreme being is purely beneficient....all this was very remarkable service.... The result was obtained by making the abolition a Khond movement.... they inferred that the evil deity....could no longer hurt them....because in the Deity which the Government professed to serve (the purely beneficient Deity), they recognized a Being whom they already dimly knew, but had not regarded as omnipotent. (WM pp.213–6)

Clearly Macpherson's interpretation of the relationship between Bura and Tari, although the outline of their myths may be correct, is distorted by Christian ideas and terminology (such as 'doctrine', 'sects' and 'schism').

The equation of Bura Penu with goodness, and Tari Penu with evil, goes against the grain of tribal religion. All Konds worshipped both, and there is evidence that Bura Penu also demanded human sacrifice at times (e.g. Elwin's notes, 160 p.346). Some spiritual traditions concentrate on the 'light' and exclude or cut themselves off from the earth, nature or the 'shadow' aspect: the result is a one-sided spirituality and intolerance for what is different or cannot be understood. The American Indian tradition expressed this duality through the image of the forked stick: all opposites have a common root. The Taoist idea of Yin and Yang, female and male, as the opposite but complementary principles behind worldly phenomena, is similar. The evidence suggests that, in Kond thinking, earth (*darni*) and heaven (*darti*) are complementary. When Konds pray, they honour both, along with the four directions (WM p.76, Bailey 1960 p.79). A Kond headman, introducing me to their religion, started by pointing to the earth and to the sky.

Campbell saw Kond religion as superstition without substance. Macpherson showed that there was much more to it than met the eye at first glance. The most sensitive modern enquiry shows that it is much subtler and more complex still—that it is difficult to grasp even an outline of its intricacies because these are so different from the conception of reality that a modern, literary mind is trained in. They are known only to practitioners. Beyond the basic (and perhaps inaccurate or oversimplified) outline I have attempted here, I do not believe that published accounts penetrate the religious meaning surrounding the Konds' human sacrifice, in its internal aspect. But there was also an external aspect. The evidence suggests that relationships with outsiders played a most significant part in the custom, which is worth exploring in greater depth.

The Brotherhood of Clans

I find it difficult to conceptualize the *meriah* system. Were *meriahs* primarily victims of sacrifice, as the British saw them? Were they in some sense slaves, like those kept by some tribes in northeastern India, who were also sometimes sacrificed? Or were they 'ploughmen raised at home'—symbols of a village's prestige, prosperity and power, in their working life as much as in their death?[27] Certainly for the British troops that enforced peace on the northeastern tribes, rescuing these slaves had precisely the same significance as rescuing *meriahs* among the Konds. It was not only self-evident philanthropy: it ended a claim to the tribes' independence. For Konds, owning *meriahs*, as well as sacrificing them, was an impressive demonstration of their power and independence.

Bailey brings out the political aspect of human sacrifice, showing the importance of the cult of the Earth Goddess, Tana Penu, in the Kond clan system: the cult's importance has declined since the British pacification, which 'froze' the system of alliances between clans, but is still important in maintaining relations between clans and lineages.[28] The *meriah* sacrifice probably played a vital part in expressing the solidarity of a clan, or alliance of clans.

Each Kond tribe, or clan, was named after some natural object or totem, and was associated with a particular ancestor or group of ancestors.[29] Each clan was linked through these symbols with a particular territory, whether a whole *mutah*, or several villages within a *mutah*. Alliances of 'brotherhood' were a key feature of Kond political life. In Bailey's model, Kond lineages formed alliances in the idiom of blood-brotherhood, which meant that they aided each other in warfare, and could not intermarry: marriage took place between non-allied, 'enemy' clans. It seems that a *mutah* (or group of allied villages—sometimes part of a *mutah*, or parts of two *mutahs*) performed human sacrifice as a collective unit, in a rotation among the villages within its alliance. At the start of the war against Macpherson, former allies went through an elaborate ritual to end their peace pact, collecting from a large area and firing muskets to free themselves from their former oath.[30]

The cult of Loha Penu, 'the iron god of war', was another important feature of Kond political and religious life, according to Macpherson (WM pp.360–5), who said that Konds considered warfare a sacred activity, where men displayed their courage, although, as we have seen, battles were probably highly ritualized events involving relatively little loss of life.[31] Some of the Kond armies that fought the British in the 1830s–40s consisted of several thousand men, who obviously represented quite large alliances. Since they often fought under Hindu chiefs as well as their own Kond chiefs, one wonders how far such alliances were Kond affairs, and how much they reflected the politics of Hindu *rajahs*. And why did they follow these Hindu chiefs? What was the *rajahs'* hold over them?

The Role of the Hindu *Rajahs*

The local Hindu *rajahs* patronized the *meriah* rite. There is considerable evidence for this: we read of the sacrifices being performed under the royal animal-emblems (above p.112), of Konds paying a tax to the *rajah* for every *meriah* they sacrificed, of *rajahs* sending their *paiks* to fire a salute at the sacrifice; and of Hindu chiefs secretly authorizing the sacrifices long after they had promised the British to help suppress them. MacViccar's informants identified Tari Penu with the Hindu goddess Durga, who was the principal deity honoured by the Oriya hill chiefs (Campbell 1864 p.186).

Is it not probable that Konds' fidelity to their *rajahs* is linked to the *rajahs'* involvement in Kond ritual? One striking feature of the Konds, that emerges clearly in their first contacts with the British, is their willingness to follow Hindu chiefs—but only so long as these chiefs adhered to a recognized code. These chiefs, *bissoi*, Konds addressed as *rajah*, although they were only officers of greater *rajahs* ('maharajahs'). One aspect of this relationship is simply exploitative—as when Konds fled from *rajahs'* officers, who came to demand tribute. But the Konds who lived in remote areas gave an allegiance to *rajahs* that seems part of a strong mutual bond, as with the Konds who sheltered the Ghumsur royalty and aided them against the British.

Other tribes' allegiance to *rajahs* throws some light on this matter. The Muria and Maria Gonds still hold the *rajahs* of Bastar and Chandrapur (in neighbouring Maharashtra) in the greatest veneration, and thousands take part in their Dassehra celebrations.[32] The Bhuiya, in northern Orissa, traditionally had a vital role in the ceremony inaugurating a new *rajah*, in which the *rajah* mounted on the Bhuiya priest's back, and simulated killing him in sacrifice. Konds gave very similar expressions of allegiance: hundreds came in ritual celebration to a *bissoi's* wedding in the 1950s, where Bailey photographed the *bissoi* 'riding' a Kond piggyback, holding an umbrella to add to his dignity.[33] More extreme, and illustrating how this allegiance was expressed in the idiom of human sacrifice, is a custom recorded from the Bhils, whereby an inherited priesthood existed for the purpose of consecrating a new *rajah*: the Bhil priest cut off the tip of his own thumb and anointed the *rajah's* forehead with the flow of his blood.[34] That the *rajah*-tribal relationship has an enduring history is shown in a different way by the tribal kingdoms that flourished at different times throughout Central India, in which tribal kings assumed all the attributes of Hindu kings.[35]

Most Konds gave allegiance to one or other of numerous Hindu *rajahs*, and were incorporated in their kingdoms. Hindus sometimes described Konds straightforwardly as subjects of these kings, and this was the view of things British officers tended to accept, because it suited their own model of authority, and their desire to impose their rule through an authoritarian chain of command. There is also evidence to support the opposite view of Konds as virtually independent of the *rajahs*, entering into alliances with them. The British themselves stressed that the *rajahs'* authority was the result of 'moral habit' rather than 'coercive authority', and often lamented *rajahs'* lack of real control over Konds. Macpherson's fiasco with the Boad *rajah* in 1846 highlights the Konds' traditional right to choose their *rajah*, and to end their allegiance to him if he acted against the code that connected them. The actual extent of Konds' independence is an intriguing problem. What was the relation between Hindu chiefs and Kond chiefs? How did the hierarchy implicit in allegiance to *rajahs* co-exist with the extremely egalitarian spirit inherent in so much of tribal life—as in the great councils, in which Kond elders sat in a circle and reached agreement by consensus? A Kond headman, the early British accounts agreed, did not impose his will, but was *primus inter pares*—first among equals. Macpherson described the paradoxical bond which linked independent Konds with *rajahs*, in terms of alliance rather than allegiance:

> The first Rajahs of Goomsoor established, as the chiefs of Boad appear to have done at a still earlier period, distinct and permanent relations....with a considerable cluster of loosely confederated Khond tribes.... A simple contract arose between them.... The mountain tribes had maintained their territory.... Their political independence was complete. (1842 report pp.21–2)

Apparently two more or less independent systems were linked together: on the one hand the system of virtually independent Kond clans, which Macpherson called tribes, on the other the Hindu kingdom with its outposts of Oriya Hindus in Kond territory. Each *mutah*, as well as each village, within a *mutah*, had its own Kond chief and council of elders. These Kond chiefs were called *abbaya* ('fathers'), *maliko* or *maji*. *Khonro* was apparently the great chief for Konds of a much larger area. But *mutahs* also had Hindu chiefs, *bissoi*, *patro*, or *dulbehra*. It was these Hindu chiefs, as well as the *khonros*, who co-ordinated Kond resistance to British troops.[36]

To me, the evidence seems very strong that Kond human sacrifice to Tari Penu was a ritual central to the political structure of highland Orissa, expressing something essential about Konds' relations with outsiders; and that *rajahs* legitimized their authority over Konds through their patronage of human sacrifice.

Campbell quoted Russell's comment on the Hindu chiefs' ascendancy over the Konds: 'their influence is the moral effect of habit, not of physical power.'(1864 p.59) The study by Kulke and Eschmann (1978 & 1980) of royal legitimation in central Orissa provides evidence on what lay behind this 'moral effect'. There is a Hindu myth that Jagannath himself, 'Lord of the Universe', who is a form of Vishnu and Orissa's principal deity, originated as a tribal deity taken from the Soras. Jagannath is depicted, in effect, as a gaily painted wooden post with a smiling human face and arms.

One could almost say he was the deity of a Kond sacred post, such as Bura Penu, taken over and given a place in their pantheon by Hindu overlords. The Jagannath cult often incorporates Konds in the world of Oriya Hinduism. At a festival of Jagannath which I attended in Bissamcuttack, several hundred Konds from surrounding villages came into town to participate.

As for Tari Penu, the Earth Goddess in Hinduism is Bhumi Devi—a much-neglected deity, although she is still the first whom dancers of Odissi (Orissa's classical tradition of temple-dance) honour before a performance. But the fact that Hindus who lived in the Kond hills readily identified Tari Penu with the goddess Durga when talking to British officials, alerts us to the meaning which the Kond custom held for them.[37]

An examination of how *rajahs* in tribal areas legitimized their rule before the British shows that it was in two directions: in the eyes of the Hindu world they showed their piety through the cult of Jagannath, as well as by making land grants to *brahmins* etc. Each *rajah* built a temple of Jagannath near his palace, expressing his spiritual subordination to Puri, the site of Jagannath's main temple. Towards their tribal subjects, *rajahs* legitimized their rule by patronizing or even taking over the cult of tribal deities, incorporating them into their palace in shrines tended by tribal priests.[38]

Hence the significance of Sam Bissoi's rivalry with the *Dulbehra* for possession of a stone symbol of Bura Penu.[39] When Campbell reinstated Sam in 1847, he was highly impressed at the way he marshalled the Kond warriors.

> His manner of presenting his tribes was, for a man of his educational deficiencies, most remarkable. He marshalled them at a little distance from my tents, and then having arranged them in their order of precedence, he led them successively into my presence, in a most graceful and courtly manner. (1864 p.93)

If Macpherson's suspicions about Sam were correct, this co-ordination with the Konds was achieved by his active participation in human sacrifice.

And if *rajahs* legitimized their authority over Konds through the worship of Tari Penu in royal shrines, and by patronizing the *meriah* sacrifice, this would explain why Britons' orders to the *rajahs* to forbid human sacrifice were not very effective at first: they were being asked to forbid the very custom whose patronage made their rule legal in Kond eyes! To 19th century Britons authority meant the right to impose new laws: a view that could be traced back to the ancient Greek·idea of a ruler as 'lawgiver', and that involves a progressive view of history. In the traditional Hindu view, however, the king's primary duty was to uphold *dharma*—to maintain traditional customs, the antithesis of making new and better laws. For example, the *rajah* of Boad obviously betrayed his traditional duty to the Konds when he tried to get them to give up their *meriahs* to Macpherson; and all the Hindu chiefs asked for it to be made clear to the Konds that the order to stop human sacrifice came from the British, not from themselves.[40]

Thus British rule had the effect of transforming the basis of *rajahs'* power and legitimacy: their involvement in the cult of tribal deities decreased as their military ascendancy over tribals increased. The Hindu legitimation through Jagannath remained constant, but it became less important for them to justify their rule over tribals, at the same time as it became essential for them to legitimize it in the eyes of the British, by upholding 'civilized' laws etc.—otherwise they risked being displaced like the *rajahs* of Ghumsur and Angul.

In fact, there is strong evidence that some of the *rajahs* of highland Orissa performed human sacrifices themselves, mainly to Durga in various forms. Macpherson stated,

> It is acknowledged that they nearly all offered human victims at her shrines one, or at the farthest, two generations ago, and it is difficult to determine when those sanguinary rites were discontinued in each case, or if they have yet finally ceased. The Boad Raja admitted to me that his father….had practised it. It was constantly performed by the father of the late Raja of Goomsur, at the shrine of Bagh Devi at Koladah. (Report of 24th April 1842, C p.53)

According to Campbell the Ghumsur *rajah* performed a human sacrifice in 1835 on the eve of his war with the British; and several *that rajahs* sold *meriahs* to Konds themselves (C pp.121 & 132). In Jeypore and Chinna Kimedi, the British found and suppressed this royal form, which they said was performed regularly at intervals of several years, as well as occasionally, as when the *that rajah* of Bissamcuttack bought a young man to sacrifice when a battle was imminent. In the forest outside Bissamcuttack there is a temple of the local goddess Markoma Ma, who is represented as similar to Durga, riding a lion and killing a buffalo demon. Townspeople tell me that human sacrifice used to take place in front of the temple, where they now sacrifice a goat, and that it actually continued until the 1920s.[41]

So what is the place of human sacrifice in Hinduism? Could the *meriah* sacrifice be, in its origin, a Hindu as much as a Kond custom? Reports of human sacrifice still abound in India. It seems that it is sometimes performed in order to generate psychic power, in 'left-handed' tantric rituals. I have even read a magazine article alleging that a Chief Minister of Orissa was guilty of it in the 1980s. The *Thugs* considered their murders as sacrifices to Kali, and human beings are one category of potential offerings in Hindu texts, from the *Rig Veda's* account of the sacrifice of Purusha, to the story of Nachiketas in the Upanishads—a rejection of blood sacrifice in favour of a higher form of sacrifice.[42] In as much as human sacrifice has survived in modern Hinduism, it is always performed in secret. Whether the Oriya *rajahs* practised it more as a public or secret rite, I do not know, but the fact that they lent their authority to the Kond sacrifices implies their complicity in a ritual that they could no longer practise openly themselves.

The kingdoms of central Orissa represent a fusion that was formed in ancient or medieval times between Hindu and tribal custom and forms of authority. It seems to me likely that human sacrifice played an important part in this fusion. Hindu texts on statecraft mention several ways that a *rajah* could establish control over the tribesmen at the periphery of his kingdom. But from the Kond point of view, it sometimes seems that *rajahs* were there to serve them! The more independent Konds definitely seem to have considered themselves to have the right to appoint or dismiss their *rajah*. One example of Konds' high-handed treatment of their *rajah*, occurred in Chinna Kimedi.

> The late Rajah was accused of tyrannical conduct by the Khond tribes who professed allegiance to him, and they invaded and devastated the low country, carrying the Rajah and his three sons captives to their mountains. After some time, the old man was ransomed for a considerable sum, and his son, the present Rajah, released, because he was supposed to be at enmity with his father. From this it will be apparent that the low-country Rajahs are most unwilling to risk a collision with the hill tribes, which was an important fact to be borne in mind in our attempts to suppress human sacrifice. (Campbell 1864 pp.119–20)

Something similar nearly happened to the *rajah* of Boad when 'not a single Khond would obey his order' to hand over their *meriahs* to

Macpherson.[43] The Boad *rajah*'s relations with Konds had recently deteriorated:

> They have never been induced to submit to the present Rajah's authority as they did formerly, since the death some years ago of the Rajah's mother to whom they were singularly attached.... from disliking the grasping disposition of the present Rajah [they have recently] kept more aloof.[44]

How Konds saw their relationship with Hindu chiefs, was expressed by one Kond to Macpherson's *vakul* ('agent') in Boad:

> "We appointed a Hindu to each Mootah to be a spoon wherewith to try the taste of things without burning our fingers. That spoon has burnt our fingers."

In other words,

> they appointed Hindus to act for them in all external affairs—to manage all business with the Raja etc., and...those Hindus are the sole cause of the present involvement.[45]

Konds made all their major decisions in large open councils. Their chiefs could not make important decisions on their own. Hindu *rajahs* respected the decisions of Kond councils. The Kond village of Toopungah expressed this independent spirit when it contested Campbell's right to forbid a human sacrifice in 1852, threatening to destroy him if he did not leave at once (above p.101). In other words, there was no way that a *rajah* could force his Hill Kond subjects to obey a repugnant order or new law. I have tried to demonstrate the ambiguity of the Kond-*rajah* relationship. The key to understanding it seems to lie in ritual: *rajahs* incorporated Konds' religion into their palace. The legitimacy of a *rajah*'s rule, in Konds' eyes, depended on his correct upholding of Kond custom, and Konds would turn against a *rajah* who betrayed their customs or interests.

As for the Plains Konds—they were usually much more closely under Hindu control, as when MacViccar commented of the Konds in Patna, 'They pay taxes, a fact which speaks volumes for their advancement, and are more under subjection than any we have hitherto encountered.'[46] It seems likely that Kond human sacrifice flourished in a frontier society, and marked a gradual process of increasing subjection and control by outsiders.

The Dom's Child

It is obvious from the evidence so far that relationships with outsiders played a crucial part in human sacrifice: with Konds from allied villages who attended the sacrifice, with the *rajah* who gave permission for it, supplied the *meriahs*, collected a tax or sent his *paiks* to fire a salute, and with the Dom (or Pano) who acquired and sold the *meriah* to the Konds. The *meriah* was also an outsider, captured somewhere distant and bought for a high price.

The *meriah*'s status as 'outsider-enemy' is stressed in an article by Elizabeth Leigh-Stutchbury that compares Kond human sacrifice with suttee (1982). The *meriah*, she argues, was associated with all that was dangerous and chaotic outside a Kond village: 'The jungle and its dangers, including tigers, disease and other Kondhs; and beyond them the plainspeople'—all these disruptive external forces were under the control of Tari Penu (1982 p.51). One clue is that *meriahs* were sometimes referred to as the Doms' children (which sometimes they actually were, above p.65). This implies a deep-seated ritual element in the relationship between Konds and Doms. Macpherson records that certain Dom families had the hereditary duty of supplying *meriahs* to a group of Konds (WM p.65). Campbell, Macpherson, Frye (1860) and Fawcett (1901) all saw Doms as 'corrupting' the Konds. A situation of mutual dependence seems to have built up by the 1830s, in which Doms supplied Konds with cloth and ornaments, and handled most of their other trade, as well as interpreting for them, being bilingual in the Kond and Oriya languages. In a sense Doms lived off the Konds, and in return assumed an inferior ritual status, which involved playing certain prescribed ritual roles, such as musicians and mourners. Elwin commented from the field on the Konds' relationship with Doms:

> Konds use them as a buffer against the world.... They exploit the Konds undoubtedly, but they also save them.... Konds despise the Doms socially as much as they rely on them materially.... (Elwin Papers 161 p.389)

Pfeffer takes a more cynical view of this relationship:

> The "honesty" every outside observer cannot help but notice among the Adivasi of the hills is a direct result of the fact that Doms or others were willing to take over the "dishonest" but necessary jobs of this world.[47]

If Doms handled the turmeric trade too—and all the evidence suggests that they did in the 1830s as they do today (Bailey 1960 p.207)—then everything seems to fall into the kind of sense which anthropologists love. For among the reasons for the human sacrifice, one that recurs is that it was essential to maintain the good quality and full colour of the turmeric crop.[48] Producing good quality turmeric sounds incredibly trivial as a reason for performing human sacrifice. But the evidence is clear that turmeric was an important cash crop, as well as being particularly important symbolically in Kond culture, and in terms of what Konds gave to the outside world. Moreover it was cultivated only by the more independent Konds, since the Plains Konds were described by Macpherson as abstaining religiously from its cultivation. It is striking to discover that a commercial crop was so important to a tribe at this date; and that for the Konds, such ritual attached to a cash crop, reversing the situation among other tribes that cash crops tend to have very little ritual attached to their cultivation.[49]

The evidence I have seen does not take us into details about the connections between Tari Penu, turmeric and the Doms. But it seems likely that Konds were deeply involved with the outside world commercially through the Doms and the sale of turmeric: dependent on Doms for whatever wealth it brought (in the form of jewelry and brass vessels etc.). Financially, Doms must have often made the greatest profit from this trade. But symbolically, at least, the Doms sold their children to the Konds for sacrifice.

> The victims are purchased at from 60 to 130 Rupees each of persons of the Paun or Harree classes, *who sell them as being their own children,* but as there are all classes among those rescued, it is evident that these miscreants steal them, and sell them for slaughter to the Khonds. (Ricketts' Report of 23rd Feb. 1837, my italics)

Doms did actually sell their own children when they could not procure a victim from elsewhere, and Elwin heard stories of Doms who had been sacrificed, or nearly sacrificed, themselves.[50] So symbolically, it seems that Doms sold their own children to the Konds for sacrifice, to demonstrate their subservience—a role which they accepted in return for getting rich at Konds' expense. For they clearly received large payments for the *meriahs* they supplied. This economic relationship continues according to Elwin (1944) with Doms selling Konds the buffaloes for sacrifice, since the same idea prevails that the victim must be bought for a large sum.

Elwin's impression was that Konds often impoverished themselves by buying these sacrificial buffaloes, as well as in fulfilling their 'social duties' to Hindu chiefs and in marriage payments. Two of the first chapters in his projected book on the Kuttia Konds are entitled 'The cost of religious obligation' and 'the cost of social duty'. The 'tax' which Konds paid to the *rajah* or his agent, and the demands for exorbitant 'tribute', are of the same order as the large price they paid to the Dom for a *meriah*. They often said to their victim before sacrifice: 'we laboured hard to buy you'. Thus, Doms had an economic hold over Konds (as over Soras), which was connected with the *rajahs'* political hold over their tribal subjects. Does it not make symbolic sense that Konds sacrificed 'an outsider' in an attempt to ward off the subtle forms of control which outsiders were already enmeshing them in?

Interpreting Human Sacrifice

We can now see various interpretations of Kond human sacrifice in a clearer perspective. Frazer's stress is on the victim's identification with the deity, on the view that human sacrifice represents a 'sacrifice of the living god'. This idea that the *meriah* himself was originally the deity was taken up by E.O. James and Mircea Eliade. Barbara Boal shows its shortcomings: the *meriah* does seem to be primarily conceived as 'food' for the Earth Goddess—the victim's life-blood contains his soul-substance which nourishes her.[51] Boal's own interpretation stresses the continuity of the ritual in the modern buffalo sacrifices; and also the idea that the rite originated in the not-too-ancient past as a 'uniting mechanism' in the face of external pressures.

Hubert and Mauss mention Kond human sacrifice as an example of 'fixing sacredness in the earth' to make it fertile (1899/1968)—which is probably close to how Konds saw it; as Elwin recorded, some Konds trace a decline in their land's fertility and prosperity since human sacrifice was suppressed. Hubert and Mauss give a view of sacrifice as mediation—the victim and his death form a bridge between the human and the divine worlds that generates life-giving sacredness.

But why a human victim? Girard's book *Violence and the sacred* (1977) revives the view of the victim as a 'surrogate', who dies that others may live and prosper, by taking the violence on himself that a community of people could turn upon each other. As Girard suggests, human sacrifice is not, at one level, essentially different from animal sacrifice, since any blood sacrifice offers a life to the gods that is a *substitute* for the sacrificers' lives. At another level, the difference is obviously very great, and poses the question of whether all blood sacrifice originated with human sacrifice, or whether human sacrifice has arisen only in particular circumstances.

Nigel Davies' book on human sacrifice (1981) sees it almost everywhere in 'primitive' or 'pre-Christian' societies—which reflects the early British officials' view of it as a rite 'once universal' that nations have given up as they became 'civilized'. To me this universalizing view seems profoundly misguided: the majority of tribal societies have been free of it, and I will try and show in this final section why I believe it has arisen only in particular contexts, characterized by a high level of domination or exploitation of some (groups of) people by others; in fact, it seems to me a ritual that lies at the threshold of 'becoming civilized', which has so often been a process accompanied by a very high level of oppression, involving large-scale wars and the massacre or enslavement of whole populations. What Nigel Davies and those who take a similar view seem blind to is that some of the most 'civilized' societies practise forms of violence that in some ways go far beyond human sacrifice, where people are killed without any idea of the sacredness of human life.

I have stressed the uncertainty of the evidence on the Kond custom. The interpretations just mentioned take us only so far. Interpreting what it meant to Konds becomes very complex when we understand that all the written evidence comes to us through the double filter of what it meant to Hindus and what it meant to Christian Britons. We are on much surer ground interpreting British ideas and customs, because these can be tested against a multitude of written evidence. It is an enquiry into our own, modern culture. Are we so innocent of human sacrifice? Until we understand our own, more subtle forms, I do not think we have any hope of understanding the *meriah* sacrifice.

Also, I do not believe an authoritative interpretation of the Kond meaning of human sacrifice can be made on the basis of the written evidence. Sacred knowledge is of several kinds in tribal societies. Priests and shamans possess knowledge that they do not share with most members of their village, let alone with outsiders. The British evidence is probably a highly selective and Hinduized version of the common, 'free' knowledge, available to all Konds, while the esoteric, priestly understanding of the ritual has never been written down. Which is appropriate. Konds' understanding of the ritual exists independently of anthropological analysis, and is an important part of their identity as Konds.

Moreover, to interpret Kond human sacrifice is a political act. Awareness of how human sacrifice has been used to reinforce the worst stereotypes about non-western cultures has made me look closely at my own motives in writing this book. Who wants knowledge of what it was, and for what purpose? The interpretation of Macpherson, Campbell and the other administrators is obviously closely connected to their policy of making Konds submit to British authority. Seeing the sacrifice as a savage and impious superstition justified their actions, including their own use of violence, by dwelling emotively on the Konds' more 'savage' violence. To later administrators and missionaries Kond human sacrifice and its suppression had the status of a *myth*, justifying, defining and inspiring them in their colonial roles.

In effect, it seems likely that Kond human sacrifice was intended to avert just the kind of calamity from external dangers that British invasion entailed. Some evidence suggests that the invasion initially led to an increase in the number of sacrifices, just as the British started campaigning to suppress them. Campbell reported an increase in the *meriah* trade in 1838, and in January 1841 he discovered that at least 24 *meriahs* had been bought by Ghumsur Konds the previous year, which proved to him that 'the intention to continue the sacrifice of human victims exists with undiminished force'. Lt Hill's Report of December 1840 also suggests this:

> All my informants agree in stating that whereas it was difficult a few years ago to procure victims for sacrifice; now, (owing to the drought which has prevailed in Ganjam and Calahundy for several seasons past) they are to be had in any number and at a small price, and consequently the Khonds who performed meriah in only one village of a mootah can now afford to have several separate sacrifices.

Cholera and smallpox epidemics as well as droughts affected Konds severely in these years. Konds will in all probability have linked the spread of these diseases to the British invasion, and tried to deal with them, as with any calamity, through blood sacrifice—including extraordinary human sacrifices to the Earth Goddess. It seems likely too that the Konds would have performed extra sacrifices to ward off the threat of British invasion, or gain power from the deity's favour in their resistance to British authority, as the Ghumsur *rajah* did when the British were poised to invade his kingdom. Among the Aztecs and the Ashanti it seems clear that the scale of human sacrifice increased enormously during their resistance to conquest (respectively by the Spanish in the 16th century and by the British in the 1870s), which led the colonial powers to an exaggerated view of its extent.[52] The cholera and smallpox epidemics at least, the Konds may have blamed justly on the British (above pp.105–106), since the British campaigns 'opened up' the Kond hills, introducing a large number of non-tribal traders, soldiers and camp followers, who are likely to have spread these epidemics.

I have drawn attention to the character of the *meriah* rite as 'sacrifice of the outsider', and the likely context of increasing external domination, politically by Hindu *rajahs* and economically by the Dom traders who sold the *meriahs*. The *meriahs'* status as 'serfs' or 'slaves' is analogous to the Konds' increasing 'subjection' to outsiders; and could be understood as a kind of symbolic recompense. The cult of Loha Penu, the 'iron god of war', points to the prominent place which warfare had assumed among the Konds. How does evidence on human sacrifice from other societies fit with this view?

The ritual killings performed by the *Thugs* as sacrifices to Kali, which victimized travellers over a large area of India, and which the British under Colonel Sleeman suppressed just before the Kond campaign, are one of the most infamous examples of human sacrifice in India.[53] But perhaps these too are best understood in terms of a Hindu *reaction* to alien domination. Is it not likely that they evolved during Mughal rule and increased under the British as a secret response to state violence and exploitation, since the victims were often merchants, and sepoys in British pay who were travelling on leave?

Examples of human sacrifice among tribal societies, which one could compare with the Kond case, include several peoples of northeastern India, where head-hunting sometimes apparently extended to 'enslaving' victims before killing them 'in cold blood' in the idiom of sacrifice. More examples involve the Koch and Kachari, where a similar tension seems to have existed between tribal independence and the hierarchy of Hindu kingship. Human sacrifice among the Dayaks in Borneo seems similar, in that the victims were a class of outsider-slaves, captured in war or traded.[54]

The same seems to be true of the cultures of the northwest coast of America such as the Kwakiutl, where the Indians possessed slaves whom they sometimes sacrificed. With certain other groups in America the context of violence or oppression is more obvious, such as the Iroquois, who expanded rapidly, using guns bought from Europeans to commit genocide on other tribes; and the Aztecs, whose human sacrifices seem to represent a high level of domination of surrounding peoples. One could look at other examples—the Tupinamba on the coast of Brazil, one of the country's most 'civilized' tribes who lived in large towns, and whom the Portuguese claimed practised it; Fiji, where it was associated with kingship; and West African kingdoms such as Dahomey and Ashanti, which had evolved in the context of trading slaves to European merchants, and where it shaded into capital punishment. These and most other examples seem to support the view that it was societies that had begun to expand through various forms of domination, such as slavery or kingship, which practised human sacrifice.

But if one looks at the best known cases of the suppression of human sacrifice, one finds that what was set up in its place represents a huge increase in the scale of violence and domination, as in the Roman conquest of the ancient Britons, whose Druids were said to be engaged in human sacrifice; with the Portuguese, who justified enslaving and in effect exterminating the Tupinamba on the grounds that they were guilty of human sacrifice; and with the Spanish conquest of the Aztecs, whose human sacrifices, horrendous though they seem, were soon surpassed by Spanish cruelty.[55] In each case, the soldiers of empire used human sacrifice to legitimize enslaving and massacring a people.

So what is the status of human sacrifice in the societies that evolved in Europe and the near East? By the time we have historical records, the Mesopotamian, Egyptian, Greek and Roman civilizations—from whom we have taken the very concept of 'civilization'—had long been waging genocidal wars against 'enemy' peoples, in which massacre and enslavement of a defeated population on a huge scale was regular practice. It seems that from roughly 3,000 BC relatively peaceful societies gave way to societies built much more on a principle of domination—which included, as well as slavery and a high level of warfare, class domination and the oppression of women. Warlike male gods came to dominate religion in the place of 'the mother goddess'.[56]

As for human sacrifice itself, by the time of historical records, it was little practised, although it occupies a prominent place in the mythology of these cultures. Mesopotamian 'suttee burials' are known from archeology. In Egypt, the symbol of the Pharoah holding a captive enemy by the hair and raising his club to kill him is depicted on temple walls, apparently in the idiom of sacrifice. In Greece human sacrifice was said to survive in a few cults in the classical period. Likewise in Roman society, which provided the example of human sacrifice under the 'golden bough' in the sacred grove at Nemi that Frazer took as his starting point; but in which human sacrifice as a temple ritual no longer existed.

Yet enslaving people had long been regarded as normal. To me it seems clear that the Greek and Roman societies, for example, had actually internalized human sacrifice, and taken it onto another level. The culmination of this trend is the Roman *ludi*, 'games': the gladiator fights in amphitheatres which were put on as spectacles on public holidays. The spectacle of slaves slaughtering each other for public entertainment seems the ultimate in dehumanization. It may seem highly paradoxical that such a sophisticated culture evolved such a delight in cruelty, but this is a paradox central to the history of Western civilization. For if one considers the forms of torture and execution that became regular events in the Middle Ages and Renaissance, against a background of great achievements in science and the arts; if one considers the crusades—the dispensation from sins which the Pope gave in advance and the consequent atrocities, such as the massacre or enslavement of the whole population of Jerusalem and other cities during the First Crusade; if one thinks of the Inquisition and the systematic persecution of 'witches' and 'heretics', in which victims were tortured until they gave false confessions before being sadistically executed in public; one wonders—how did it happen that people who professed a religion of love and peace persecuted victims so viciously, replicating the cruelty of Christ's death by crucifixion?

These Christian killings were technically 'executions' rather than 'sacrifices' of course, though the ritual that surrounded them often had much in common with sacrifice. These forms of execution can be traced back to Celtic and Germanic forms of human sacrifice, in which victims were 'criminals' who were killed in different ways according to their crimes and the gods they were sacrificed to, just as criminals in Christian Europe were burnt alive, beheaded or hung according to whether they were heretics, traitors or common criminals.[57] Thus Christianity, which at first seemed to mark a break away from dehumanizing pagan violence, actually continued it. Europeans' treatment of the natives of Africa and America make this abundantly clear, exterminating them or reducing them to slavery in order to make a commercial profit, on the model of the Romans' imperial conquests and use of slaves in plantations and mines.

The British in the 19th century at first seem innocent of this level of violence: the abolition of slavery and tyranny was an important element in their ideology of empire.[58] But if one examines the way they enforced their rule, one finds an undercurrent of great violence and oppression which existed as part of a deeply held belief in hierarchy. Officially slavery was abolished. In effect their pursuit of commercial gain in India increased it greatly, if one considers the enforced cultivation of opium and indigo, the bonded labour and oppressiveness of *zemindars* who served them, and the many tribal and peasant uprisings, brutally suppressed, protesting against the enormous injustice and domination that British rule entailed. The officials' great concern with legality masked horrendous, but 'impersonal', economic exploitation.

In his book *The civilizing process* (1939/1978), Norbert Elias argues that as the level of violence increased in Europe, its expression became increasingly indirect. Konds' violence in their human sacrifices could hardly have been more open and direct. The violence which British rule replaced them with was in various ways much less open and direct, but more far-reaching: its victims were often spoken of in terms of being 'sacrificed' for the sake of peace etc., but their lives were not held sacred.

From this brief summary, it is apparent that a certain trend in the history of Western civilization, that developed alongside the great achievements we celebrate, was to dehumanize: to dominate and exploit people who are 'different' in a way that disregards their humanity. The Nazi holocaust and other 'crimes against humanity' committed since, in Cambodia and Bosnia for example, represent a culmination of this history. The cult of violence in films replicates the Roman 'games' where people were killed for entertainment. And people are killed for real every day by regimes which are armed with the latest, most sophisticated weaponry, sold to them by the richest nations. Is this not the slave trade in another form, creating wealth for an elite at an inhuman cost?

When we understand the various levels of human sacrifice which modern societies are founded on, maybe we shall see the Kond custom in a clearer light.

CHAPTER FIVE

The Colonial Sacrifice of 'Enlightened Government'

Hierarchy was the basis of the political system introduced by the British. One tribal villager in Koraput District described to me how two white *sahebs* arrived in his village on elephants when he was a boy, and ordered him and others to leave their village immediately and carry the officers' luggage for several days. In its own terms, British rule of the Konds was superbly rational and benevolent, a perfect example of the 'enlightened government' which the British Empire took pride in. Looked at from another angle—from the viewpoint of those it was imposed upon—it was often extremely oppressive, introducing alien and restrictive laws, giving outsiders enormous power over villagers which was abused on a regular basis, and establishing a *cycle of exploitation* that has lasted ever since.

So in order to understand clearly what the British imposed on the Konds—as on countless other tribal peoples—it is necessary to step back and distance ourselves from the terms in which they described what they were doing, for that conceptual framework is an essential part of what they imposed. What do I mean when I say that British rule involved human sacrifice—that it substituted one kind with another? In British terms of reference, such a claim is nonsense. But taking the analysis deeper involves differentiating two basic levels of the social structure of the administration: a fofmal, conscious level at which the administrators ordered and conceptualized their own self-image and relationships, and an unconscious or deep level of implicit norms and patterns, and underlying structures.

The formal structure of the administration consists of an elaborate set of ordered relationships, some hierarchical as between ranks, others horizontal between equivalent units. An elaborate hierarchy is evident in the official chain of command from the Court of Directors in London and the Governor-General in Calcutta downwards. Horizontal relationships are those, for example, between the army and the civil administration, or between the various regiments that made up the army, with their different uniforms and traditions.[1] Or between the Provinces of Madras and Bengal, whose Governments Macpherson described as 'looking separate ways': each had its own 'culture' of traditions and vocabulary—similar to the culture which differentiates Oxford and Cambridge Universities or the leading British public schools, or even the 'houses' within such schools.

The elaborate formal structure of the administration we could call its conscious social structure. Every social relationship was defined by rules, regulations or laws. Every communication and procedure had well-defined channels and forms, including informal structures of clubs and personal life, which also find expression in administrators' unpublished writings,[2] as in Macpherson's comment in a letter that he 'told [the Governor-General] my "instructions" were nonsense' (above p.68)—although what he did not express, because it was in some sense 'unthinkable', is that ambiguity was *necessarily* a key feature of his instructions, since indirectly he was being asked to make a tribal people with whom the British had 'no connexion' recognize British law and sovereignty (above pp.72–3).

This ambiguity at the surface level is an expression of the deep or unconscious part of the social structure, which possesses logical primacy in terms of what was really happening (Lévi-Strauss 1977). On the surface the wars of 1835–7 and 1846–8 were suppressions of rebellions; really they were wars of conquest, consolidating an *expansion* of British rule. Official writings describe these events or the events of the Mutiny as history; but in their symbolic power they have the status of *myths*. For later generations of administrators of Indian tribes, Cleveland among the Paharias, James Outram among the Bhils, and Russell, Macpherson, Campbell and Frye among the Konds had the status of mythic heroes or archetypes, to be honoured in memory and imitated. Published accounts (such as the Memoirs and Carberry's selection of Agency records, 1854) stress Kond violence but omit nearly all reference to British violence and the norms of subordination which Britons established over the Konds.

The many quotations from British discourse which I have given illustrate the importance of a small number of keywords, which are markers for key concepts that generated actions and discourse. There is a *formulaic* quality to the discourse: the set of themes and ideas, which are constantly repeated and which generate 'what is thinkable' for the administrators, is relatively small and limited.[3] In the following three sections we shall explore some of the key themes and polarities (conceptual oppositions or contrasts) which seem to have generated British ideas and actions. For this, we shall look at some of the wider literature which reveals the 'imaginative underpinnings' of ideals and desires that motivated officials to impose British rule on the Konds. The benign image of their rule which they publicized was in many ways a mask.

Saving *Meriahs*: A *Robinson Crusoe* Complex

The focus of the British campaign to suppress human sacrifice was on saving the *meriahs*: finding the villages where they were living and taking them away. Once in British care, they were taken in the officers' elaborate entourage to Russellkonda. Some ran away before they got there, and *meriahs* hardly ever expressed gratitude for being saved. Campbell's expenses for May 1848 show he spent 7 rupees 12 annas 'for marking 124 meriahs with indelible ink'!

The Governor-General took a deep interest in the *meriahs'* welfare.[4] Russell had recommended that the Government should pay for the care and education of the children, mentioning that they had so far been supported by individuals' benevolence (11th May 1837 par.74). He sent the first batch of *meriah* children to Baptist missionary orphanages at Cuttack, Berhampur and Balasore. Between 1836 and 1853 about 300 were sent there, of whom a considerable number died 'from the unfamiliar climate'. Some of the survivors converted to Christianity and joined the Baptist Mission as proselytizers.

By 1845 at least 600 *meriahs* had been rescued. Between 1846 and 1853 Campbell rescued another 1,260. He recorded how he 'disposed of' these, along with 130 he had rescued earlier and 117 inherited from Macpherson in 1846:[5]

Nearly 200 died soon after being 'rescued'
77 escaped

306 were settled as *ryots* (peasants) in 12 villages
About 280 women were married off, many of them to the Konds who had practised female infanticide and were therefore short on wives
About 240 were sent to the Baptist orphanages
167 were 'given for adoption to persons of character'
About 100 were restored to identified relations from whom they had been stolen or bought by Doms to sell to Konds
35 were returned to their Kond owners 'as serfs or adopted children'
About 30 were employed in Government service, some in a *sebundy* corps, and a couple as elephant handlers
32 were being trained in 1849 as carpenters, blacksmiths, weavers, gardeners, and servants
About 40 were employed as servants, or worked to support themselves
23 were supported by the Government as too old to work or blind
A certain number were 'unemployed and unprovided for' (numbering 172 in 1849, and 59 in 1854)

Those who set up as cultivators were provided with a plough and a pair of bullocks. Women were given a dowry of about ten rupees each. Some children were adopted as servants by British officers, including six by Bannerman, and eleven by four senior Indian officials (Report of 6th Jan. 1842). Campbell noted that between 1838 and 1842,

> I brought up seven meriah children under my own roof, six boys and one girl, and they all turned out well. One is a servant of Mr Smith of the Madras army; one is mine—a very good servant, but would never learn to read or write, the girl is an aya to an army wife....(Report of 22nd Oct. 1847)

Campbell was particularly proud of drafting 25 *meriahs* into his *sebundy* corps, which he probably drilled in person (1864 p.133).

> I have drafted 25 promising [meriah] lads into the sebundy corps, and shall strive to interest them in the service to which, at first, they were very averse. The experiment succeeded admirably with a meriah youth last year, whose resistance at first could only be overcome by slight punishment; he is now a smart soldier, fond of his profession, and was of the utmost use to me in the hills as a medium of communication with the Khonds (Report of 19th April 1848).

But the *meriah* children kept at his base in Russellkonda caused him endless problems. From the *meriahs*' point of view, the large number who died or escaped shows all too clearly that his 'care' was terrifyingly alien. Campbell sent the girls to Sorada in order to put many miles between them and the boys, at Nowgam, for fear of sexual adventures—a segregation completely foreign to children from a tribal background! Even so,

> The large number of meriah girls are very unmanageable.... These girls are made to pound rice and prepare their food which keeps them employed, though not sufficiently either to prevent the necessity of the most constant vigilance and supervision, or to remove the grounds of much anxiety regarding them. (19th April 1848)

> The meriah girls at Souradah are becoming very clamorous.... The large crowd [of boys] at Nowgam are most difficult to manage. They constantly quarrel amongst themselves or run away, but generally have either returned or been brought back. (16th June 1848)

He was shocked at the boys' 'wildness and laziness':

> they are well taken care of as far as food and shelter is concerned, but no effort whatever has been made to enlighten their minds....Many of these lads have been for years at Nowgam without deriving any benefit from instruction and training; the important duty of disciplining them into working habits has also been quite neglected....I have unsuccesfully endeavoured to induce some of the youths to take public service as Paiks, Peons, or anything they please but one and all turn away with disgust from the proposal and invariably reply that they desire to till the ground. (5th August 1847)

He had them taught ironwork, weaving and carpentry, and proposed setting up a whole village of rescued *meriahs*. Sir Maddock in Calcutta commented:

> I am disposed to sanction the expensive measures proposed by Colonel Campbell. These children ought not to be brought up in idleness....I fear these children have been pampered and spoiled or we should not hear of their objecting to any particular line of life that might be selected for them.

The top Government officials in Calcutta discussed various plans for educating these 'wards of their benevolence'.[6] Maddock thought many of them could be sent as servants to the towns, to the houses of Europeans or 'natives of rank and undoubted respectability.' To which the Honourable General Sir John Littler objected that *meriahs* should not be entrusted to natives, however respectable: 'They would be apt to consider them as slaves.'

In other words, saving the *meriahs* and elevating them in life were considered important signs of the Government's paternal care. The fact that many died or escaped, or showed themselves extremely averse to the alien discipline imposed on them and the trades chosen for them, was compensated, apparently, by some turning out just as the British wanted, as if they were blank slates or lumps of clay to be moulded into a particular shape. Officials took great pride in the select few who were sent back to 'civilize' the Konds as soldiers, missionaries and schoolteachers, for several ex-*meriahs* became some of the first teachers in the schools which MacViccar set up.

Some of the *meriahs* were apparently rescued in the nick of time, 'from under the knife'. Bannerman, with a force of 300 *peons* and 60 sepoys, surprised a village where the Konds were drunk and the 40 foot peacock pole was in position, in preparation for the sacrifice of a woman. All the villagers fled, but he made the headman a prisoner, and was able to bargain for the woman's release. When she was given up he took hostages and left the village quickly to prevent a fight, since more Konds were arriving for the sacrifice.[7] Macpherson rescued a *meriah* 'from under the knife' in Chokapand in 1843. Frye rescued a girl who was about to be sacrificed in 1850, after which the Konds apparently sacrificed their priest instead. 'These people were afterwards properly dealt with by Captain Frye and sacrifice has never since been practised among them.'(Campbell 1864 p.178) A *meriah* girl called Ootama was saved by Campbell, 'snatched from destruction just two hours before dire superstition had doomed that she should be cut to pieces'. She became the model pupil at one of the Mission schools, and one of their first converts to Christianity.[8]

Enter the District Officer charging onto a scene of human sacrifice alone on an elephant just in time to rescue a *meriah* before a crowd of drunk Konds cut him to pieces. This happens in a novel about British rule of the Konds called *Sacrifice*, which brings into focus the contrast for the British between human sacrifice and Christian ideas of sacrifice.[9]

Where have we met this theme of rescuing victims from human sacrifice by savages before? It is familiar from a children's novel still widely read, and immensely popular in Victorian times: *Robinson Crusoe* by Daniel Defoe. The rescuing of *meriahs* bears such a strong similarity to this narrative that we could diagnose it as a case of a *Robinson Crusoe* complex. It will be useful to look at the similarity quite closely, to see how the saving of *meriahs* was structured by a deeply ingrained English myth.

In Defoe's story, the savages who visit Robinson's island are cannibals, coming from the mainland to kill and eat prisoners captured in war (though he is 15 years on the island before he discovers this as they come to the other end of the island). When he first sees the remains of a cannibal feast, he feels an inexpressable 'Horror of...Mind, at seeing the Shore spread with Skulls, Hands, Feet, and other Bones of humane Bodies', and an 'Abhorrence of the Savage Wretches....and of the wretched inhuman Custom of their devouring and eating one another up'. After two years of fear for his own safety, he begins to plan an attack: 'Night and Day, I could think of nothing but how I might destroy some of these Monsters in their cruel bloody Entertainment, and if possible, save the Victim they should bring hither to destroy'.[10]

At this point Robinson has qualms about 'so outrageous an Execution as the killing of twenty or thirty naked Savages' for the Offence of their unnatural Custom, and questions 'What Authority, or Call I had, to pretend to be Judge and Executioner upon these Men as Criminals.... These people had done me no injury.' Their dreadful Custom was 'nothing but Nature entirely abandon'd of Heaven, and acted by some hellish Degeneracy', and showed them to have 'no other Guide than that of their own abominable and vitiated Passions'. But it was a National Crime, not strictly Murder. It was therefore up to God to punish them, Who 'knows how by National Punishments to make a just Retribution for National Offences.' Robinson's qualms on this and other occasions are similar to administrators' initial qualms about using force to suppress the Kond custom. All the blame for persecuting American natives Defoe puts onto the Spaniards: in spite of the natives' 'several bloody and barbarous Rites in their Customs, such as sacrificing humane Bodies to their Idols', the Spaniards' destruction of Millions of them, rooting them out of the Country, was 'spoken of with the utmost Abhorrence and Detestation, by even the *Spaniards* themselves, at this Time; and by all other Christian Nations of Europe, as a meer Butchery, a bloody and unnatural piece of Cruelty, unjustifiable either to God or Man....'

But six years later Robinson witnesses a cannibal feast on his own side of the island, which changed his mind: he was 'so fill'd with Indignation at the Sight, that I began now to premeditate the Destruction of the next that I saw there, let them be who, or how many soever.' During the next 15 months he remains in a 'murthering Humour'. He also realizes that a rescued victim could help him get away to the mainland.

> I resolved, if possible, to get one of those Savages into my Hands, cost what it would.... I fancied my self to manage One, nay, Two or Three Savages, if I

> had them, so as to make them entirely Slaves to me, to do whatever I should direct them.....

The next time he sees the savages land to hold their cannibal feast, the last victim manages to escape, and Robinson decides to intervene by killing his two pursuers.

> It came now very warmly upon my Thoughts, and indeed irresistibly, that now was the Time to get me a Servant, and perhaps a Companion, or Assistant; and that I was call'd plainly by Providence to save this poor Creature's Life.

With all this build-up to it, Robinson's action of saving Friday stands at the centre of Defoe's story. As Friday approaches, he kneels down every few steps,

> in token of Acknowledgement for my saving his Life....; at length he came close to me, and then he kneel'd down again, kiss'd the Ground, and laid his Head upon the Ground, and taking me by the Foot, laid my Foot upon his Head; this it seems was in token of swearing to be my Slave forever.... [Repeating this later he] made all the signs to me of Subjection, Servitude, and Submission imaginable, to let me know, how he would serve me as long as I liv'd. I understood him in many things, and let him know, I was very well pleas'd with him; in a little Time I began to speak to him, and to teach him to speak to me; and first I made him know his Name should be *Friday*, which was the Day I sav'd his Life; I call'd him so for Memory of the Time; I likewise taught him to say *Master*, and then let him know, that was to be my Name.

He embarks on a programme of reforming or civilizing Friday, teaching him to eat animal instead of human flesh, and salt, to wear clothes, talk in English, fire a gun, and perform the many tasks of agriculture and husbandry by which Robinson orders his life on the island, so that 'never Man had a more faithful, loving, sincere Servant than *Friday* was to me; without Passions, Sullenness or Designs, perfectly oblig'd and engag'd; his very Affections were ty'd to me, like those of a Child to a Father; and I dare say he would have sacrific'd his Life for the saving mine upon any occasion whatsoever....'

Is this not the colonial image of a 'perfect native'? Friday owes his life to his 'Master' and gives him total service in return. When Campbell and his superiors in Calcutta expressed surprise that the *meriah* children would not accept whatever work was selected for them, were they not expecting them to be like Friday? It is significant also that *meriah* children were entrusted to missionaries for their education.

Robinson 'began to instruct [Friday] in the Knowledge of the true God', and about the Devil, teaching him that 'his former Nation's priestcraft was a Fraud and a Cheat, and that if the God the Priests communicated with was not their own Invention, it 'must be…an evil Spirit'. Friday becomes a Christian and Robinson is filled with joy to reflect that by being cast away on the island,

> I had not only been moved my self to look up to Heaven, and to seek the Hand that had brought me there; but was now to be made an Instrument under Providence to save the Life, and *for ought I knew* the Soul of a poor Savage, and bring him to the true Knowledge of Religion, and of the Christian Doctrine, that he might know Christ Jesus, *to know whom is Life eternal*.

Instructing Friday from the Bible,

> serv'd to the enlightening this Savage Creature, and bringing him to be such a Christian, as I have known few equal to him in my Life.

Friday wants Robinson to go and civilize the rest of his people:

> *You do great deal much good*, says he, *you teach wild Mans be good sober tame Mans; you tell them know God, pray God, and live new life.... Yes, yes…you teachee me good, you teachee them good.*

But another band of cannibals arrive with two more victims. Robinson again questions his right to intervene, and wonders 'What Call? What Occasion? much less what Necessity I was in to go and dip my Hands in Blood, to attack People, who had neither done, or intended me any Wrong?' But when he sees that one of the victims is a European, he and Friday attack and kill all 21 of the savages, and save the victims—an action which reflects the reality of countless European encounters with tribal people, that for one European life, revenge was taken by killing many natives, as happened when Konds killed the two British officers in 1836.

After this, Robinson populates his island with shipwrecked Spaniards and English convicts. Returning to Europe, 'my Man *Friday*…proving a most faithful servant upon all occasions', he finds he has become extremely rich from the profits of his slave plantation in Brazil.[11] For Robinson is a slave-trader: his shipwreck occurs when he is on a journey to fetch slaves from Africa. The later history of his island is of wars with the natives, raiding the mainland to get slaves, and exterminating 300 who invade the island; and of dividing the land among the European colonists as plantations, reserving to himself 'the Property of the Whole'.

Among many similarities to the Kond campaign, is the theme of saving and sacrificing lives. Robinson's life is saved several times, and when 'Providence' saves him from shipwreck and places him on the island this gives him the chance to save his own soul.[12] He in turn saves Friday's life—as well as his soul—and a succession of other people, who become, for this reason, his servants and subjects, willing to sacrifice their lives for him.

In many ways, *Robinson Crusoe* is a blueprint for colonialism. The novel has the status of an enduring myth, that encapsulates many elements of the colonial enterprise. We remember the novel above all as an exciting adventure story. But it is an adventure created with the intention of inculcating a particular view of the world and a particular morality. In this sense, it follows on from the book that made Defoe instantly famous as a writer, *The Family Instructor* (1715), which was a manual of proper behaviour and a guide in spiritual matters. The idea of *homo economicus*, 'economic man' is one of the novel's key themes (Ian Watt 1975): the idea of unceasing hard work that combines manual skills with the ingenuity of a rational mind as the basis for prosperity as well as morality. For another theme is of spiritual growth through realization of sinfulness and salvation, in the Puritan or Dissenter tradition of Protestant Christianity. These two themes combine as the Protestant Ethic of faith and profit-making work: the novel is the clearest possible statement of this combination. But it advocates profit-making of a particular kind: mercantile enterprise *abroad*, creating a profit from a distant *colony*.

It is most significant that Robinson's mercantile voyage when he is shipwrecked, is a new, private enterprise of going to Africa to fetch slaves for estates in Brazil. For Britain had just established a monopoly on the slave trade when the novel was published, by winning in 1715 exclusive rights to trade slaves from Africa to Spanish South America.[13] Between then and 1807 when it was abolished in Britain, the slave trade was a major source of British wealth and power. The idea of slavery permeates *Robinson Crusoe*.

By the 1840s the anti-slavery movement had become part of the general ideology of the British empire. But at a deeper level how much had really changed? The idea of extreme hierarchy was still in place, and tribes like the Konds were still required to show a most complete submission and subservience to British officials, who surrounded themselves with a large number of native servants very like Man Friday. Moreover, it was precisely the idea of abolishing slavery that led to the Victorians' assurance of moral superiority and of their right to suppress barbaric customs such as human sacrifice.

Robinson Crusoe presents the negative stereotype of tribal people in its starkest form: as cannibals, who are bloodthirsty, warlike and superstitious, and whose only positive feature is their potential for serving Europeans. This is the image which Friday encapsulates: of the good savage who can be completely remoulded into a useful, faithful servant. Tribal people are either potential slaves, or savages to be exterminated. Being written when the slave trade was expanding to its greatest extent, the novel reads almost as a manual on how to deal with savages, as does its successor *Captain Singleton* (1720), the story of an Englishman who leads a band of Portuguese sailors across Africa, fighting and trading with one savage nation after another.

The idea of savage cannibals on an island was still current in the 1840s: sailors shipwrecked at this time on the Andaman Islands clashed with the 'savages' who lived there, and were 'no doubt cannibals'.[14] The slaver's image of tribals as semi-human, or Africans as descendents of Cain, and intended by God to be slaves to white men, gave way gradually over the 19th century to the view of tribal people as capable of being civilized like Friday, though still needing to be ruled by the Europeans who had saved them from their moral degradation, while they evolved to a higher stage.[15]

So the saving and civilizing of Friday provided a classic model for the era of Victorian expansion, and fits perfectly with Victorians' idea of the benefits the British empire conferred on savages at the same time as the colonies created wealth for Britons.

The popularity and influence of *Robinson Crusoe* can scarcely be overstated. George Borrow called it 'a book which has exerted over the minds of Englishmen an influence certainly greater than any other of modern times.' J.S. Mill recalled that 'Of children's books, any more than of playthings, I had hardly any....: among those I had, Robinson Crusoe was pre-eminent, and continued to delight me through all my boyhood.'[16] From one of the East India Company's top administrators in London, this is significant evidence of its influence, but the novel also gave administrators posted in India their initial inspiration and image of natives.[17]

Teaching is all one way in the novel: Friday apparently has nothing to teach Robinson. In Michel Tournier's reworking of the story, *Friday, or the other island* (1974), teaching suddenly changes direction: the obsessively regulated colony the hero has created suddenly explodes, and instead of imposing his ideas onto Friday any longer, he begins to learn from him: about the sun, and laughter, and work that is not self-sacrificing and does not negate the pleasure of physical sensation. This is what hardly ever happened in the colonial situation: Britons were almost completely closed to the possibility of learning from *adivasis*, because they saw them through stereotypes such as Defoe's. They defined tribes like the Konds in terms of their most 'negative' features such as human sacrifice and war, contrasting these with their own most positive features. What if they had begun to relate to them not in terms of control, but simply in order to exchange ideas and learn? The idea of approaching tribal people as equals, with an awareness that they too have knowledge, however different its nature from knowledge that is familiar from the European tradition—such openness did not exist among the Konds' administrators.

Saving the *meriahs* was the main sign to Britons of the Government's care: their lives were saved, and they were educated and set up in life at public expense. But in another sense, officials saw themselves as saving the Konds in general from a state of 'savagery', by 'giving them justice and peace', and 'elevating them in the scale of civilization'. They did this with immense dedication, at a great 'sacrifice' of British lives and money. But did they not sacrifice Konds' freedom at the same time?

Human Sacrifice *Versus* Christian Sacrifice: The Conscious Contrast

Colonial usage of the word 'sacrifice' ranges between a religious meaning and a secular meaning which sometimes implies simply a loss of life and property. The radical opposite of the Konds' human sacrifice, in administrators' mode of thought, was their own Christian self-sacrifice, which they expressed in terms of 'faithful service', 'devotion to duty', 'dedication' or 'zeal'. For the officers in the Kond hills, this theme of self-sacrifice had a basis in the fact of hard work, sickness and death that was real enough. Macpherson, Bannerman, Frye, Campbell and MacViccar each in turn took a year or so off duty to recuperate their shattered constitutions in the Cape (South Africa). During the fighting of 1836–7 and 1846–7, several European officers and many Indians were killed. Many more died in the Kond hills from the endemic fevers, especially malaria, but also cholera and blackwater fever.

It was usual to speak of death 'in service' in terms of sacrifice. An army historian lamented that 'thousands of lives have been sacrificed in the barracks of India' due to poor sanitation (Mouat 1859 p.33). The Government calculated military action in terms of lives sacrificed. For instance, the Supreme Government recommended using force to end the war of 1846–7, on the grounds that the Konds were militarily weak, so a proper campaign would reduce them to subjection 'with little sacrifice of life and property' (above p.84).

Campbell and Macpherson spoke of their campaign to subject the Konds as a 'mission' or 'crusade', and as 'a cause sacred to humanity', for which they offered their life and labour.[18] This concept of self-sacrifice was more than a matter of language: it involved the deepest beliefs that motivated these officials, and their ultimate model was Christ and His sacrifice. Laying down one's life for the cause of the British Empire and enlightened rule was spoken of as if it was an extension of this. Countless British soldiers and administrators acted this out in India and the other colonies, conscious of this idea of their death as a sacrifice. Among the most famous in the mid-19th century was Nicholson, one of the 'foremost martyrs of the Mutiny', who fell in the siege of Delhi (Wurgaft 1983 p.91). Gordon, it seems, virtually planned his own death in Khartoum as a self-sacrifice, aware that it would force Britain to conquer Sudan: he died as a martyr, 'the perfect archetype of the imperial hero'.[19] For nothing creates power like a sacrificed life. Every Briton who went to serve in India was conscious that duty might well demand him to 'lay down his life'. But a sacrificed life, it seems, demanded 'retribution'. When a British officer was killed in action, a terrible price was often inflicted on those who took it: when Konds killed the pair of young officers in 1836, the British retaliated with an all-out war of conquest.

When Afrikaaners in South Africa today talk of fighting to defend Natal since 'we bought this land with our blood' is this not, in essence, the same idea, of lives 'sacrificed' in war as a kind of economic-spiritual price that buys the right to rule?

The way these ideas are connected in British rule of the Konds emerges clearly in Mrs Penny's novel *Sacrifice* (1910), which draws an explicit contrast between the human sacrifice of the Konds, and the Christian self-sacrifice of their administrators. The novel is set in the Kond hills some years after the abolition of human sacrifice, involving a revival of the custom by a fanatical Kond priest.[20] At the centre of the book is a conversation between Martin Waldringham, Assistant to the Agent in Ganjam, and Krishna Sao, the local Hindu *zemindar,* which revolves around the subject of human sacrifice:

> "It's strange how idolatrous mankind clings to the idea of sacrifice," [Waldringham] observed.
>
> "The idea is not confined to worshippers of idols—in this case there's no idol and never has been one; the deity's unseen—you have it in your own religion," replied Krishna Sao.
>
> "You mean in Christ."
>
> "Yes; yours was a sacrifice of blood, and the victim was a human being. He died, like the meriah of old, that men might live.".....
>
> "He was the only sacrifice, once offered; a sacrifice that is never to be repeated."
>
> "There were martyrs and saints following Him. They died for their faith; were they not also sacrificed?" asked Krishna Sao.
>
> "They were self-sacrificed to the cause of righteousness."
>
> "And as for the present day," continued Krishna Sao, with the deep pleasure a Hindu takes in argument apart from conviction; "You still offer sacrifices to your God; but they're not of blood. Your sacrament, in which you receive a portion of bread and wine, is called by the priest of your Church a sacrifice."
>
> "It's a commemoration of the original sacrifice made by the Saviour.... The idea of sacrifice in the abstract seems to be one point that we hold in common;" said Waldringham. "It is a pity that we cannot make the details of its practice more in accord."
>
> "There is one kind of sacrifice in which we are in accord; that is self-sacrifice. A woman, whether she is of European or Asiatic extraction, will show it as a wife and mother. A man will show it in his patriotism." (1910 pp.110–16)

This point is made again by the policeman's wife, talking to her daughter Rosabelle, who will finally marry Martin Waldringham:

> "Every woman has to sacrifice herself if she would fulfil her mission. She cannot be a good wife without self-forgetfulness, self-less devotion. She certainly cannot be a good mother without constant consideration of another's welfare before her own; and the sacrifice of herself and her inclinations on behalf of that other."

An Indian cuckoo rubs in the point by screeching what sounds to Isabelle like "Sacrifice! Sacrifice! Sacrifice!"

In modern terms we can see how a belief that women should sacrifice themselves for their husbands was at the basis of their own oppression: Hindu as well as European culture sacrificed women's freedom. But the conversation also shows how self-sacrifice on the model of Christ was equated with sacrifice for 'patriotism' or 'honour', and illustrates a deeply-rooted connection between 'sacrifice' and 'saving'. Just as Christ sacrificed himself to save mankind, and saints and martyrs sacrificed themselves for the sake of righteousness, so women sacrifice themselves for their families, and administrators sacrifice themselves to save *meriahs*, and ultimately to save Konds from their savagery. Do we not have here, in its essence, power based on a particular conception of self-sacrifice?

Victorians' ideal of self-sacrifice goes very deep, and has many aspects in this colonial setting. One could almost say that they lived in a culture of self-sacrifice.

One aspect is the imitation of Christ, in which the Church set the standard of moral action. Descriptions of human sacrifice stress Konds' 'wildness' and 'abandonment': it appeared like a drunken orgy of unrestrained evil passions. The aspect of abandonment could not have offered more of a contrast to the Church services which administrators attended. Officials' lives were marked by Church rituals of marriages, births, deaths, and Sunday services that in their complete lack of 'abandonment' and their highly restrained character, were the antithesis of 'frenzied' native rituals. Since this was their standard of a harmonious ritual and a correct expression of religious sentiment, it is not surprising if they judged Kond rituals as unharmonious and evil. Macpherson and others were aware that Ancient Britons were said to have practised human sacrifice, and he exhorted Konds to give it up on these grounds: Britons had become civilized through the Roman suppression of the practice, just as they were now raising Konds in the scale of civilization by forcing them to abandon it.

Another aspect, related to the self-restraint in their religion, is the enormous self-restraint, indeed, the denial of normal human needs, which these officials placed on themselves. Their families, thousands of miles away, they saw only at intervals of many years—or if these lived in India, they often died young, like Campbell's first wife and two of his children (above p.95). Their emotions they learnt to suppress into the 'stiff upper lip' for which the British became famous, as in the inhuman self-restraint of officers in a duel which Seeta Ram wondered at, who behaved 'as cool and collected as if on parade' as they pursued honour to the death (above p.57). This unflinchingness illustrates a less favourable aspect of this culture of self-sacrifice: these men avoided expressing emotion or appearing vulnerable at all costs. Their uniforms were one expression of the constraint they lived by: as a succession of Indian Army administrators complained, they constricted the blood-flow and breathing very tightly, making flinching a virtual impossibility and preventing relaxed movement in general (above p.58). Government rules enforced the same rigidity: 'Regulations and procedures which seemed intrusive and absurd to the native had a magical meaning to the British civilian' (Wurgaft 1983 p.72)—let alone to the British soldier! The cultivation of tremendous emotional and physical self-control is an aspect of their ideal of selfless service and self-sacrifice, that means that, psychologically, these men were enormously repressed (Wurgaft pp.xi & 60–5). In their self-image they were constantly sacrificing themselves: as a result, they were trained to suppress or deny their feelings.

And the constraints they put on themselves were at one with the constraints they placed on each other, their Indian subordinates, the soldiers they drilled, the children and prisoners they 'reformed', and the populations they ruled over. 'Power that sacrifices itself' also sacrifices 'the other'. The officials' anger and violence were all the greater for being expressed indirectly instead of when it was 'hot'. A love of controlling, mastering, disciplining, taming, curbing, subduing, and subjecting other beings (as well as themselves) had become second nature to them, as we see in their passion for the sport of hunting and shooting wild animals, as well as in the way they behaved towards Konds. This 'habit of authority' is the dark side of the high-mindedness, honesty and good intentions which they cultivated and appreciated in their conscious mind—a dark side that only a few British officials of the period were aware of and open about.[21]

The number of Britons present in the Kond hills was very small at any one time. As in other colonial settings, they formed a 'thin white line' of authority.[22] But this small collection of individuals believed so strongly in their own sense of order and morality, that their Indian subordiantes and many others accepted it as reality. They set enormous tasks for themselves and each other, and succeeded in imposing their will over a vast population in one generation. They did this by accepting the role of devoted servants to an impersonal bureaucracy and military machine, believing unflinchingly in the myths they inherited and created through their own actions and writings.

The British in India sometimes referred to their administration as 'a Christian Government', and in many senses it was just that: an exclusive elite in terms of religion as well as race and culture.[23]

Not all officials were necessarily keen to characterize the Indian Government as Christian, aware that this would alienate much of India's population. But even utilitarians with a secular outlook joined evangelicals and missionaries in calling it 'enlightened'—a word which captures the essence of Britons' self-image in India. It retains a strong Christian, or Protestant, significance beyond the connotations of rationality and secularism that have led historians to call the 18th century in Europe the 'Age of Enlightenment'. Administrators' formal separation from missionary activity was full of ambiguity and conflict. In reality administrators and missionaries were deeply interdependent, as well as internalizing each other's roles. Administrators' secular aims were full of missionary intentions; and missionaries cultivated secular aims themselves of benefiting natives through schools and hospitals, partly to gain Government patronage and a hold over the population.[24]

In fact, administrators' most cherished aims of 'reforming' Konds or making 'a conquest over their minds' is very close to missionaries' aim of converting them.[25] They saw their Agency work as furthering God's own purpose, as when MacViccar wrote of 'our labors under God's blessing' (26th April 1851), and Campbell of 'God, whose bountiful harvest so powerfully and mercifully seconded our efforts'! (1864 p.130) This reflects the influence of Paley's 'moral and political philosophy', which was required reading at Haileybury College where officials trained before coming to India (above pp.73, 75), and which viewed Government laws basically as extensions of God's Laws. MacViccar writes of the imposition of British rule over the Konds:

> each minute and isolated portion of a community—a few years ago hardly aware of our existence—is now, by the divine blessing on our labors, united in a common obedience to our will.[26]

Ultimately it was from this article of faith that they were fulfilling the divine will, that the British assumed the role of *judging* their subjects, weeding out those to be punished as an 'example', and choosing a select few to be rewarded, just as their God divided humanity in the same way. This use of punishment and reward is the essence of 'divide and rule'.[27]

This belief in their 'divine mission', and the sense of superiority that went with it, also gave rise to Britons' idea that they had the right and duty to impose laws on the Konds that affected and curtailed every aspect of their life, from their sacrifice of buffaloes and selection of chiefs, to their rights of owning land communally, hunting and cutting trees in the forest, and making alcohol. The starting point, in the Kond case, was the Government's decision that the custom of human sacrifice was 'equally contrary to the laws of God and men'.

The 'sacrifice of life' (as Maddock described it, above p.85) which proved necessary before Konds accepted British rule and human sacrifice was suppressed, was thus for the sake of future generations of Konds: to save them from savagery, if not ultimately to save their souls. Campbell is clear on this:

> When the present generation and, perhaps, their children, shall have passed away, when through the medium of schools and other means of civilisation, such as roads, teaching them improved methods of clearing and irrigating the ground, etc., we shall have been able to change the current of their thoughts and doings, and direct them into a better channel, we shall have some hope of their being as firmly convinced in their hearts of the folly, uselessness, and sinfulness of the meriah sacrifice as they now are of the impossibility of performing it save at a risk which they most wisely prefer to avoid. (Report of 17th March 1849)

Campbell characterized every Kond god as 'always a malevolent being' 1864 p.39) and wrote of 'conquering the Khonds' religious prejudices'. A dramatic example of how he attempted this is his action on discovering 'elephant poles':

> In several villages, I counted as many as fourteen effigies of elephants which had been used in former sacrifices. These I caused to be overthrown by the baggage elephants attached to my camp, in the presence of the assembled Khonds, to show them that these venerated objects had no power against the living animal, and to remove all traces of their bloody superstition. (1864 p.126)

This is an action straight out of the Old Testament idea of casting down false idols. Campbell is demonstrating his Christian 'enlightenment' at the same time as trying to teach the Konds that their religion is based on illusion and 'ignorance'. His act is also a demonstration of British authority. It signifies the end of the old order, an enforced break with the past, and the imposition of a new order of power.

Human Sacrifice *Versus* Public Execution: The Unconscious Contrast

In the idea of 'sacrifice of life' as the price of enforcing peace, we come close to a financial view of sacrifice in terms of 'cost', and when the cost is 'too high', to the negative sense of sacrifice as a 'waste of life and resources' in which the concept is often used nowadays (above pp.4–6): a secular concept of 'sacrifice', which still at this time had strong Christian associations.

The most extreme form of the British 'sacrifice of life' was their use of capital punishment, as a means of enforcing their control through fear. At one level, these executions were completely dissociated from the idiom of sacrifice: they obviously were not sacrifices to the Christian God. Yet as rituals of taking a human life, they have clear connections with the idea of sacrifice, that can be traced back to pre-Christian Europe, when human sacrifice was apparently practised on criminals, and medieval times, when the execution of heretics and witches involved much more of the idiom of sacrifice.[28]

This highlights the two-sided nature of Christ's death on the cross: for Christians it was self-sacrifice, 'the one true sacrifice' of the son of God; for the Roman Government it was the public execution of a dangerous criminal, as an example to others. Human sacrifice was thus an important category in Christian thought (Maccoby 1982), and public execution was the reverse side to self-sacrifice. But because consciously the two were dissociated, Kond human sacrifice was deeply *anomalous* to 19th century Britons, because it conflated sacrifice with the conscious taking of human life, which Britons performed only on people they convicted of crime. The Konds' victims were by definition innocent, as Christ was.

This, it seems to me, explains the particular horror which Britons felt for Kond human sacrifice: it was anomalous because it conflated two categories that had to be separated conceptually. The British Government executed people 'as an example' just as the Roman Government executed Christ. To break this analogy the execution had to be free from any elements of sacrifice or self-sacrifice. Thus on the surface, Kond human sacrifice formed an absolute contrast to Christian self-sacrifice, while at a deeper level, the British in effect *replaced* Kond human sacrifice with their own form of human sacrifice. The Kond custom was also an affront to the British because it was a conscious taking of human life in an alien idiom, and without their permission.

As a ritual, capital punishment presented as much of a contrast to Kond rituals as a Church service did. The victim was tried and proven guilty beforehand in an elaborate procedure of the greatest orderliness. The execution was performed soberly, with extreme orderliness, quite unlike the great 'wildness' of the Kond sacrifice. In photographs from the time of the Mutiny, when the British hanged hundreds of 'rebels', sepoys stand at attention beside the gallows, in a stiff posture of complete self-restraint.[29] And the form of death was hanging: to Britons, the most 'civilized' way of killing someone, but to Konds and Hindus an anathema, since hanging was a form of 'bad death'.

So in a very real sense, British officials replaced one ritual of sacrificing a human life with another, in their own idiom and under their own control. As we have seen, a considerable number of Konds were executed in the war of 1836–7. Most of these were chiefs. Some were sentenced to be 'hung in chains', so that the corpse was left hanging after death, to reinforce the 'example'. Like Kond human sacrifices, though in a different way, public hangings were *political rituals*, which demonstrated Britons' exclusive right over human life, and their power to assert this right.

The first Kond victims of capital punishment were leaders of military resistance. But Campbell soon wanted to make a 'severe example' of some of the Doms who traded *meriahs* (Report of 17th Jan. 1838), and the senior administrators in London agreed (above p.65):

> Whatever circumstances may justify or recommend a lenient course of proceedings towards the Khonds themselves, no palliative considerations can apply to the case of individuals, who may be detected in the horrible trade of supplying victims for sacrifice. Under these circumstances the severest measure of punishment might justly be inflicted. (Court of Directors 24th Oct. 1838—C p.16)

As for Konds who performed human sacrifices, at first they were punished with imprisonment, transportation, and 'hard labour' in chain gangs; only later, when it was clear that they knew it was forbidden by the British, were they executed.[30]

In effect it seems that the British consolidated their rule over each new Kond area that came under their control by performing at least one public execution there. In Jeypore, for example, the British performed no less than 17 public executions in 1863–9, the first six years of bringing it under their control (Carmichael 1869 p.248). It is worth quoting an entire document that describes such an execution to illustrate the way that British officials conceptualized their use of hanging. McNeill officiated at the execution of a Kond who had been convicted of murder, which could also probably be seen as an act of resistance to British rule, on 23rd February 1858:

> Sir,
>
> I have the honor to report for the information of the Hon'ble the President in Council that the sentence of death to "Boyi Khond" was this day carried out at....his native village.
>
> 2. On my arrival at the fort of Mahasingee on the 20th instant, I received information from various sources that the Khonds of the Ballaguddah district meditated an attack on my camp with the view of rescuing the prisoner and thereby washing the stigma which they imagined would attach to them if the prisoner was hanged in their district.
>
> 3. I accordingly summoned the Ooriyah chief of the district and informed him of what I had heard. He at first strenuously denied the truth of my assertions, but I warned him that if any opposition was offered to me in carrying out the orders of the Government, I should hold him personally responsible and would also bring the prisoner in his (the Patro's) villages. This had the desired effect.... As above stated the prisoner was on this day hanged; the sorry thing went off peaceably, though large numbers of Khonds, some armed, and others not, to the number of 600 collected in small groups on all the ground which commanded a view of the execution.
>
> 4. I would not have entered so fully into this case were it not that this "Boyi Khond" is the first person to be hanged in the hill tracts of Chinna Kimedy and the Khonds were prepared by force to prevent the violation, if so it might be termed. But the sorry thing having passed off quietly I am persuaded that this execution will have a most beneficial effect on all classes and will operate most favourably on the furtherance of our operations for the suppression of meriah sacrifices and female infanticide, as the Khonds and others have now had ocular evidence of the determination of Government to uphold its authority in all cases even though unconnected with the immediate spheres of this Agency.
>
> 5. On this latter subject however I will submit in a day or two a few observations for the favourable consideration of the Government.
>
> I have the Honor to be
>
> Sir
>
> Your most Obedient Servant
>
> Lt McNeill, Agent in the Hill Tracts of Orissa.

McNeill later reported that this execution had 'a most salutary effect' and 'inspired great terror into the minds of all the Konds'.[31]

This document evokes the British sense of hierarchy which the hangings expressed: from the Government of India, to which McNeill had 'the Honor to be/ Sir/ Your most obedient servant', down through the Oriya chief who was forced into passing down undesirable orders onto the Konds in his district, to Boyi Kond at the bottom, on whom McNeill visited the wrath of British justice. The extreme control over a human body, which these hangings demonstrated, is clear from George Orwell's vivid account of the hanging of a convicted prisoner in Burma, which he had to officiate at as Inspector of Police:

> Six tall Indian warders were guarding him and getting him ready for the gallows. Two of them stood by with rifles and fixed bayonets, while the others held him, passed a chain through his hands and fixed it to their belts, and lashed his arms tight to his sides. They crowded very close about him, with their hands always on him in a careful, caressing grip, all the while feeling him as if to make sure he was still there.[32]

Public executions were repeatedly said to have a 'beneficial' or 'salutary' effect, in cowing the population into peace and obedience. Konds were made to witness these hangings, which at first they regarded as polluting their territory. Nothing could demonstrate more powerfully how the British enforced the change from the old political order than this displacement of human sacrifice by public execution. As a spectacle of killing someone 'in order to save other lives', were such executions not, in effect, human sacrifices? And for the Konds who witnessed them, can we conceive how they differed from their own open rituals of human sacrifice? Basically, because the killing was in an utterly alien idiom—coldly clinical, instead of in the 'heat' of excitement; and without overt sacredness, instead of as an offering to the deity; and because it was completely out of their control: the executions were the most dramatic statements of British control *over* them, and established that the conscious taking of human life was a monopoly of the British Government.

After the Agency

When the Meriah Agency was abolished in 1861 the Konds were brought under regular administration, which involved greater delegation of power to Indian officials. In the Khondmals 'we...merely...prevent oppression by means of a Tahsildar, supported by a strong force of police' as Hunter put it (1872 vol.II pp.83–4)—although it seems that from the start, this

Tahsildar, Dinobandu Patnaik, who had won British favour by saving McNeill's life, far from preventing oppression, was one of its main perpetrators![33]

The Khondmals was the mountainous portion of Boad, that was annexed and merged with Angul (which did not even neighbour it) into a District of Bengal. The Konds were now divided again between the Bengal and Madras Presidencies, with some under Bombay as well.[34] The main Districts with Konds under Madras were Vizagapatam and Ganjam. 'Vizag' incorporated the 'Hill Agency' part of Jeypore state, which was now taken more firmly under British control with the creation of a police force. Ganjam District incorporated extensive Kond areas, including the hills of Chinna Kimedi, under the control of the Collector and Magistrate of Ganjam, who also had the status of Political Agent of the Hill Tracts.[35]

Gordon S. Forbes was the first to hold this multiple office, from 1861 until 1867. Like the Meriah Agents before him, he made a succession of tours, starting early in 1863, when he visited the hills above Sorada to oversee the construction of another road into the Kond hills, and to check up on the suppression of infanticide. He was accompanied by 200 police constables, commanded by his Assistant, Captain Marshall. In Digi he sent for all the local headmen

> and pressed them a good deal on the subject of infanticide; they strenuously denied that the practice continued among them, and I made them come forward singly and solemnly engage never to permit it.... The Khonds seemed to imagine that they owed obedience to no-one but the petty chief of Koradah (in Sorada). I think however I left them a good deal enlightened on this point.[36]

These words only hint at the great subordination British officials demanded from Kond chiefs, but it is clear that we have come a long way from Russell's frank acknowledgement of the Konds' independence from British rule (above p.64). One Kond couple whom Forbes convicted of practising female infanticide, he sentenced to transportation for life.

At Daringabadi, where he was settling a longstanding feud, his men met some resistance while relaying his orders, so he sent a larger detachment with orders to open fire if necessary. They arrested two headmen as ringleaders of the resistance, in the face of 2,000 hostile Konds. These chiefs, Forbes sentenced to six years' 'rigorous imprisonment'.[37] He established a Sub-Magistrate at Daringabadi to ensure that the Konds there submitted to British authority and gave up their feuds and infanticide.

> These men have never had any means of estimating the power of Government and the Law, no stronger measures than persuasion having ever been used towards them; they have even it is said declared that they will continue to "throw away" female children whatever the Government may say or do to the contrary; but the whole race are apt to be loud and boastful, giving way when it comes to the point.

He set up several other outposts on this tour—not yet all-weather centres, since no European or Indian official would be willing to stay there in the feverish rainy season. The main one was at Udayagiri, where he had a large bungalow built, and appointed Captain Miller Sub-Magistrate. He put a third Sub-Magistrate at Digi.

The new Superintendent of police in Ganjam, Captain R.A. Stuart, enforced some severe punishments, convicting several Konds for murder and sentencing them to death, which he believed 'cannot fail to have a salutary effect'. He set up four police posts for the Kond area, one of them at Sorada with 25 men, and enrolled many of the *sebundies* who had been employed under the Meriah Agency, as police constables. He appointed an official known as a *digalo* from each of 26 *mutahs* to report regularly to the police, giving each one a red sash and turban as a badge of Government service. *Digalos* were always Doms, who had long had the role of mediating between Konds and outsiders. Buffalo sacrifices were now permitted, but only on condition that notice was sent to the police in advance, via the *digalo*, so that they could come and witness the events (Report of 17th Feb.1863). Lt Lys was put in charge of the local police, working closely with Forbes who declared him 'admirably suited by temper and judgement for the duty of dealing with savages' (1885 p.256).

But as the new police force tightened the grip of British rule over the Konds, not everything went smoothly.

> As our police posts were advanced and the enforcement of a general control attempted, resentment and resistance were naturally aroused, and there followed encounters which did not pass off without bloodshed. (Forbes 1885 p.258)

In particular, the Kuttia Konds, who had always been particularly independent, fiercely resented being made to construct roads—a highly degrading job labouring under the critical gaze of an official, that is quite alien to the tribal ethic of work, but which tribal people all over India are still made to perform. A band of Kuttias ('a few hundred Khonds who bore a bad character, as having more debased habits than the rest of the nation' as Forbes described them) attacked the new police station at Tumariband and killed some Oriya villagers, including a headman. Forbes went after them with two European officers and 70 constables. After some fighting, where bows and arrows were once again matched against muskets, the Kond headman came in, and at the insistence of the Kond women present, those who had committed the 'murder' were given up for trial and execution. Forbes made the rest swear allegiance to the *rajah* of Bodogarh, whom, in British terms, their act of resistance had defied (Forbes 1885 p.263).

Forbes wrote up his memoirs after retiring in England, calling them *Wild life in Canara and Ganjam* (1885), after the wild animals he was so fond of shooting, as well as the 'wild tribes' he subjected to British control.

One of his successors was J. MacDonald Smith, who held the office of Special Assistant Agent to the Ganjam Collector 1870–8, with responsibility for Kond administration. He learnt the Kond language and published a Kui grammar in 1876. He was the informant—and maybe the model—for Mrs Penny's novel about British rule of the Konds (above pp.154–5).

By 1882 the administration had further increased its hold over the Konds. The Agent was required to reside in the hills for 7 months of the year, with his headquarters at Baliguda, and about 450 policemen were stationed in the Kond area of Ganjam.[38] That year a great Kond rebellion took place in Kalahandi.

> The Feudatory chief had encouraged the settlement in the state of members of the Kolta caste who are excellent cultivators and keenly acquisitive of land. They soon got the Konds heavily indebted to them for loans of food and seed grain, and began to oust them from their villages…

Konds killed several hundred Oriyas, with great brutality, demonstrating the depth of their outrage at being dispossessed, before British troops arrived to suppress the 'outbreak'. At least one *meriah* sacrifice was performed during the rebellion, which the British punished by hanging.[39]

Several later Kond administrators showed an interest in ethnology: Friend-Pereira, who served there in the 1890s–1900s, wrote learned articles and another grammar (1899–1909), and several presented Kond axes and other artefacts to the Pitt-Rivers collection in Oxford.[40] But the most influential and paternalistic of the Konds' administrators was Ollenbach, who was Magistrate of the Khondmals between 1901 and 1924.

A British family called Mincnin was prominent in Ganjam affairs, especially on the commercial side. J.I. Minchin was Collector and Agent of Vizagapatam in the 1850s–60s. In the 1870s–80s, F.J.V. Minchin, who was a friend of Forbes, owned the important sugar factory and rum distillery at Aska, under the name of Messrs Minchin Brothers and Co., as well as extensive *godowns* (warehouses) on the sea at Gopalpur, and a beautiful house at Rambha, on Chilka lake. He and E.A. Minchin presented several Kond battleaxes to the Pitt-Rivers collection in 1902. A.A.F. Minchin was the officer in charge of the Ganjam forests from 1914. The Forest Department had begun trying to 'conserve' the forests of Ganjam since the 1860s, when it was recognized that timber was a 'valuable commodity', and that too much had been indiscriminately felled by contractors for railway sleepers etc. In 1861 a forest tax was instituted, and a British Conservator appointed, with two *peons* to assist him. In 1864–5 1,000 *sal* trees were felled and sold to the Public Works Department for Rs 3,000/-. Maccaly held the office of Conservator from 1864 to 1878, making depôts at Aska and Gopalpur for export by sea, and enlarging his establishment to 8 *peons*. As commercial profit increased, the local people were forbidden to cut trees in many areas. The Kond custom of 'slash and burn cultivation' was judged wasteful and forbidden, causing considerable conflict. Minchin organized a system in which the forests were 'handed over to the Khonds to protect', in return for the Government supplying them free with wood for ploughs, thatching grass and bamboos, calculating the 'wants of the population' in terms of each village's exact requirements (Minchin 1920)—as if that is something that can be worked out in advance! Such a scheme looks good on paper to someone who knows nothing about tribal life, but when the reality is that people are self-sufficient for supplying nearly all their needs from the forest, and spend a large part of each day gathering materials, how can such a scheme work?

Above all it gives new powers to forest guards, who tour villages checking up on a wide range of petty regulations. For tribal people who do not read, it is impossible to keep track of such rules, especially when they often change. So the forest guard's word becomes law. Elwin describes how Kond villages were approached by forest guards in the 1930s–40s who had orders to demarcate 'Reserved Forest', to be owned by the state and not to be felled for making fields. In almost every case, the forest guard demanded bribes, and if villagers refused to pay, he designated forest which they habitually used (unpublished notes on the Konds).

The history of British relations with Konds from the 1860s exemplifies the rationalizing and routinizing of British rule. It is largely a matter of statistics of increase as roads were built, schools were set up, and civil, police and forest officials were stationed in the hills for longer periods at more posts, enforcing more laws. These included forbidding access to the Reserved tracts of forest, forbidding Konds to distil their own liquor, regulating disputes of land ownership and theft, as well as (supposedly) protecting them from oppression. Certain areas were 'excluded' from the normal operation of Indian Law by the Scheduled Districts Act of 1874. This classified certain tribal areas, including most Kond areas, as 'Scheduled Districts and Backward Tracts', making the selling of tribal land to non-tribals illegal, in an attempt—largely unsuccessful—to protect tribals from the cycle of indebtedness and land-grabbing by moneylenders and colonists.[41]

Indian Intermediaries: Old and New Elites

Within weeks of Britons' dispossession of the royal house of Ghumsur, the traditional elite gradually began taking service with the British.[42] The Oriya chiefs and soldiers who came to serve as Britons' immediate subordinates made the transition from the old elite to the new one by playing the Britons' game, accepting British rewards instead of seeking Konds' approval. It is clear that in the old system of authority and power, Hindu chiefs and *rajahs* had to win Konds' acceptance by patronizing their traditional customs, and that Konds played a vital role in the appointment of a chief, and often had the role of his allies rather than 'subjects' (above pp.126–32).

But British officials refused to recognize authority based on the Konds' consensus, which was established through numerous councils with a minimum of status distinctions. As far as Britons were concerned, the duty of chiefs and headmen was simply to obey or relay their orders, just as British officials considered it their duty to observe their superiors' instructions. Oriya chiefs had always depended on cultivating Konds' goodwill. Kond chiefs took no decisions without consulting their fellow tribesmen. The British thus placed both in a novel position—indeed, throughout their empire they sought chiefs and headmen to rule through, even where no such role had existed before.

In this way the new political order was extremely hierarchical—much more so than the old Hindu order, whose *rajahs* recognized Konds' consensus. The members of the old Hindu elite who kept their positions under British rule therefore gained far more power over Konds than they ever had before (above p. 107 etc.). Indeed, Britons demanded they do so, in a sense, by the very fact of relaying orders to them. Campbell at first held 'long and tedious councils' with the Konds, but in general, 'it has always been my policy on first entering a new country to conciliate the established Uriya chiefs'—for he made them his 'instruments' for ruling the Konds. So when officials proclaimed to Konds that they would respect their traditional rights and customs, they did nothing of the kind, disregarding in particular their right to choose their *rajah*. At first, co-opting the chiefs and increasing their authority was the backbone of British policy. Later, in areas taken directly under British rule, the old system of authority was removed as police were established, instead of relying on the *bissoi* and his *paiks* to maintain the peace. McNeill and some members of the Meriah Agency did not approve of police taking over this role—a similar matter of controversy as took place between the famous Lawrence brothers in Punjab at this time.[43] But either way, Britons strengthened the Hindu elite enormously over Konds.

This *paik* class of Oriyas already had a certain deep-seated contempt for Konds, and a tendency to oppress them when they had the means: 'the Wooriah population is generally of the paik class (matchlock-men) by whom the Khonds and Gonds are kept in abject servitude'; in Patna and Kalahandi the Konds were already 'kept in complete restraint by the Wooriahs, [whose] chiefs are well-disposed to the Europeans' (Hill's Report of 2nd July 1838).

The *rajahs* found themselves in a particularly ambiguous position in this shift of power (above pp. 129–32). They had already lost much of their former authority, since their treaties with the EIC surrendered the exclusive right to take life in the British Government, withdrawing *rajahs*' right to execute criminals or declare war. British interference was usually justified on account of small wars, murder, suttee—or failure to pay tribute. For several states the Meriah campaigns were the decisive stage in their loss of independence.

As we have seen, the whole way that *rajahs* legitimized their authority changed drastically under British rule, although imperceptibly in the sense that British officials saw themselves as merely supporting their traditional authority. Yet in the first years of British presence, officials repeatedly said that *rajahs* had 'no proper control' over the Konds. British rule gave them this control, making them dependent on British military power to enforce a new hold over the Konds. Now there was little need for *rajahs* to legitimize their rule in tribal eyes by patronizing the cult of tribal deities, which had been essential before. What was essential now was to win British approval and respect, with grand palaces, an English education, and a willingness to try new methods of increasing their revenue. The 'superstitious practices' of tribal religion were the last thing that would impress British officials!

Yet something of this ritual element the British actually used themselves, as when Forbes made the Konds who had 'rebelled' in 1864 swear allegiance to the *rajah* of Bodoghar (above p.166):

> Before the conference closed...an oath of fealty to the Bodogudda Rajah was sworn. The Rajah had been afraid to accompany me, and his headman represented him. A bit of earth, a squirrel's skin, and a lizard were placed on the tiger's skin, together with a dagger, and the oath was pronounced over these symbols. (Forbes 1885 p.265)

Here a British official is self-consciously setting up a traditional ritual of authority, using it to bolster the power of a *rajah* who is afraid to meet the Konds personally, because he has become dependent on British force of arms: his authority has become a cover for the British power that enforces it. A letter from the *rajah* of Authmallick to Macpherson exonerating himself from a charge that he had helped Chokra Bissoi makes this point even clearer:

> Sir, By the favor of the Government I am a Rajah. The chiefs of this zemindery are extremely ill-disposed persons. Their practices are known to the Superintendent Sahib. Had I after having eaten the food of the Commissioner acted in the manner described, I should be the greatest villain in the world. In this zemindery there are two chiefs Bala Biswal and Balaram Garotta who for four or five years have not obeyed me and are well known to have behaved treacherously to me....but as we are under the Company's rule I am not afraid of them.[44]

'By the favor of the Government I am a Rajah....' This is what *rajahs* had come to: their authority derived from British approval, which they gained by learning to say to *sahebs* what *sahebs* wanted to hear.

When Britons praised *rajahs* it was for 'intelligence', 'faithfulness', 'enlightened policy' and the like. They were honoured and rewarded with presents when they did as they were told. When they did not, the attitude of British officials was one of extraordinary arrogance or contempt. Campbell echoes a very common sentiment when he writes that the *rajahs* are 'in truth an abjectly degraded class....the fact is, that these hill potentates seldom, never perhaps, act under the inspiration of reason, but simply as impulse dictates; and the result is certain—they are defeated and dethroned' (1864 pp.26–28). 'The Rajah of Jeypore is an old imbecile creature' MacViccar wrote (21st May 1855), and Macpherson described his first interaction with the *rajah* of Boad in a way that reveals this double message of honour and contempt:

> I explained to him the views of the Govt respecting the hill population of his zemindery, and required him to exert his utmost influence to induce the chiefs to conform to them, inviting him at the same time, to become the chief instrument of my work, to the advancement of most of his interests....The Rajah of Boad bears the character of a stupid sensualist who takes no part in public business which he can avoid.[45]

As the *rajah* described their interaction, Macpherson behaved with great arrogance, threatening and refusing to listen to him (above pp.76–9). When a *rajah* made a good 'instrument' he received an outward show of honour from the British. In a few cases, an official genuinely saw a *rajah* as 'enlightened'—which meant he had learnt to take a British view of things. For this reason, *rajahs* were urged to give their sons an English-style education.[46] Hunter approved highly of the *maharajah* of Dhenkanal, whom he visited in 1870, as representing 'the highest point of culture, moderation and justice which any of the chiefs has attained under our surveillance' (1872 vol.II pp.119–20). He could speak Hindi fluently, possessed 'a really interesting armoury', had his palace built 'on the plan of the Commissioner's Circuit House at Cuttack' so that it had 'the look of a very strongly built Italian villa', and was engaged in Anglicizing his kingdom. Significantly he was *au fait* with the principles and details of British law:

> On my turning our talk to the Administration of Justice, he had out his law books, particularly the latest commentary on the Indian Penal Code in Uriya

> and Bengali, and I found that he really understood the legal points which the annotators discussed. He does justice in public sessions to his people, and keeps his prisoners hard at work upon the roads. In the afternoon we went together to the jail.... Next day the Maharaja took me to his school and his charitable dispensary, both formed on the model of our own Bengali institutions of the same kind.... About noon arrived a band of jungle people [Juangs], whose national dance the Maharaja wished to show me. (ibid. pp.104–11)

The *rajah* was also trying to resettle his tribal subjects and get them to clear permanent fields out of the jungle, a similar policy to the Kalahandi *rajah*'s encouragement of more 'efficient' Oriya colonists, who were taking over Kond lands at this time, which was to cause the rebellion of 1882. The *rajah* of Dhenkanal had just met with similar opposition: in 1868 20,000 Juangs had taken up arms against the harsh changes taking place in his territory and in neighbouring Keonjhar; a rebellion that was swiftly and bloodily suppressed by British officials, who executed six Juangs and imprisoned 100, without enquiring too closely into the cause of their discontent.[47]

The *rajahs* were acquiring status symbols that would impress Britons as well as Hindus through harsh taxation. They learnt what won British officials' approval, internalizing a British scale of values, with its concepts of 'progress' and 'justice', becoming 'enlightened reformers' and 'efficient' collectors of revenue. They remained good Hindus, but no longer based their rule on tribals' consensus or patronage of their religion, but on British recognition and the military backing that went with it. In this process the tribals within their territory became alienated from their rule and came to be heavily exploited: the *rajahs* became figureheads of British rule and 'sucked the blood' of their Kond subjects for their own aggrandizement.

When the British imposed their rule directly onto Konds, they relied heavily on a few Indian intermediaries, some local, others from elsewhere, who had already been promoted to positions of influence through the system of rewards and punishments that characterized British service.[48] For instance, Macpherson asked for gold medals, inscribed with their names, to be presented 'in testimony of the appreciation by the Government of their meritorious and important services' to his two main Indian assistants in 1844 (WM p.210): Sundera Singh, son of the ex-*rajah* of Sorada, who had been brought up in a Kond village and could speak Kui, which he later taught Cadenhead; and Baba Khan, a Muslim from Hyderabad who had been Macpherson's closest servant throughout his

Indian career, and whom he appointed Head *Munshi* (scribe) and chief interpreter in the Agency—even though he did not know the Kond language, as Campbell (or someone writing on his behalf) pointed out.

> This "Head Moonshee" was an ignorant Mussalman, who, possessing a certain degree of low cunning and tact, had acquired a fatal influence over his Master. Baba Khan was a few years ago, a menial servant, in Captain Macpherson's personal service, and, by some means or other, suddenly rose to the rank of "Head Moonshee", though unable to write or read one word of Hindustani, Persian, or Oriya.... We hesitate not to say, that this man did no small mischief in Khondistan by his corrupt and disgraceful practices. (Anon. 1849)

Macpherson was equally scathing about Sooria Narain and Sam Bissoi, whom Campbell and Bannerman relied on. Which were the guiltier of extortion and oppression towards Konds is impossible to tell now.[49] As George Orwell commented, 'no British officer would ever believe anything against his own men' (1949 p.3). But the evidence clearly shows that such individuals acquired great political power, essentially by *learning the sahebs' language,* which included saying what the *sahebs* wanted to hear: learning precisely how they judged situations—how, in a sense, they constructed reality in the foreign environment onto which they were imposing their laws—and making their *sahebs* dependent upon them.

The accusations show how, from the start, some of the Indian officials used their position to extort bribes when their British superiors were not around. This was not an occasional or accidental by-product of British rule: it was one of its regular, enduring features, a key element of the social structure of interaction between Konds and administrators—a norm that was never made explicit, but from the beginning was as much a characteristic of this imposed normality as the laws and regulations by which Britons defined their rule. Doubtless it cowed people into accepting British rule, as well as building up the resentment that occasionally gave rise to armed resistance.

McNeill and his successors clearly had the same kind of close dependence on Dinobandu Patnaik as Macpherson and Campbell had on those just mentioned (above pp.104, 164), and which both placed on Punda Naik, who also acquired a reputation for extortion (above p.103). Dinobandu's harshness and corruption were not one man's aberration, as Bailey implies. Indian officials did more than just mediate British rulers' relationship with Konds: in effect they controlled it, through their understanding of both cultures and monopoly on translation. The more extortionate norms of interaction were, of course, usually formed in the much more frequent contact they had with Konds away from the eyes of the British, who could not, or would not, check up on them effectively. In the early years of British rule a few British officers made a great show of listening to and reasoning with Konds in their councils, and fraternizing with them, as Campbell did by taking them hunting with him. But as Britons' right to rule came to be taken for granted, in terms of orders communicated downwards rather than the agreements settled through councils that had been customary before, most interaction with Konds was delegated to Indian subordinates, who seem to have projected the same inferior status onto Konds as Britons did onto them, and made similar or even greater demands from them for subordination and subservience. For instance, a Baptist missionary who accompanied a Government survey of Kond districts in 1862, described the degrading way that Konds were forced to carry supplies for the party by an Indian official:

> A number of coolies were required to convey to the next village the apparatus and baggage of the topographic survey. The chuprassi (native official) who was in charge, instead of going to the proper authorities in the village, seized the first men he could lay his hands upon, no matter what their engagement or employment, and drove them like wild beasts before him. (*GBMS Report* for 1862 pp.13–14)

This kind of behaviour may or may not have been habitual in Britons' presence. In their absence, there seems little doubt, it was normal.

The sepoys who sparked off the first fighting with Konds (above p.42) were from a distant part of India. Most native officials were soon being recruited locally. Campbell was proud of his 'trusty and hardy sibbundies', some of them ex-*meriahs*. He drilled them himself, and could rely on them, just as James Outram could rely on the Bhil soldiers he trained, to carry out his will on their fellow tribesmen. In the 1860s these *sebundies* were drafted into the police force, and by the 1880s a number of the police constables were Konds, although not all British officials viewed them so favourably:

> As active and intelligent police officers they are perfectly useless, and they are no more to be trusted to abstain from bullying their own country people than are the ordinary low country constables; their enlistment is allowed because the number of applications is few and they are very useful for communicating orders and the like to their fellow Khonds. (NB: A recent

order of Government directs that they be enlisted as Police as much as possible.) (Maltby 1882 p.92)

To encourage Konds to join the police seems 'enlightened' enough. But it also created a novel hierarchy among Konds, an elite of Government servants with separate interests from the main part of their people, who often abused their power. Britons might deprecate police brutality and extortion when it came to their notice, but a large part of this brutality was what they had taught, and actually relied on to gain ascendancy over an unwilling population. It was a regular feature of the *Pax Britannica* quite as much as any positive role the police played. When the Gonds in Bastar took up arms against the administration in 1910, the British Lieutenant-Colonel who suppressed them admitted that police behaviour was one of the main causes of rebellion: 'The police are badly paid and badly supervised. The usual forms of police oppression are therefore rampant' (E.C. Smith 1945 p.253). Apart from extortion and beatings, one of the most insidious forms of police oppression that was rarely brought into the open as a major injustice until recently, is rape, which Chokra Bissoi implied that Macpherson's men were guilty of in 1846, at the start of British rule in Boad (above p.90).

I am stressing the shadow side of the British, as well as of their Indian intermediaries, with the aim of bringing to light the prime causes of the cycle of exploitation that still haunts India's tribal areas. The other side is a great integrity of many officials, Indian and British, *rajahs* as well as policemen, motivated by notions of honour and service that were a composite of British and Indian ideas. The trouble is, this composite also involved negative stereotypes of tribal culture, and the idea that tribals were to be cowed or awed into a servile obedience by imposing a far-reaching hierarchy over them. The officials' honourable uprightness and 'enlightened' fairness thus existed side by side with great oppression and exploitation, concealing or masking it.

The 'corruption' of many Indian officials in relation to Britons' 'honesty' has a lot to do with British exclusiveness: Indians' social and kinship ties were with the local people; those of British officials were with families thousands of miles away. They thus formed a *ruling caste* that erected an impenetrable social barrier between itself and Indians with the rigidity of *apartheid*, reckoning a British soldier's life 'of more consequence than 50 sepoys' (above p.46). The colonial official in India was a more absolute example of '*homo hierarchicus*' than *rajah* or *brahmin*.[50]

'Caste' is a European word and concept (from Portuguese *casta*, pure), with different connotations from the Indian words *varna* and *jati*. To a great extent it seems that British rule actually reinforced the caste system, by creating a fusion between a hierarchy based on class or race, and caste hierarchy: a fusion that Indian society internalized during the Raj.

A British official's 'native establishment' exemplifies this, with its elaborate hierarchy of functions, from the top officials such as Sundera Singh and Punda Naik, who were paid Rs 80/- to 120/- a month; down to the cooks, washermen and sweepers, who got between one and three rupees.[51] This hierarchy corresponded quite closely to the caste system: the *paik* militia were mostly Oriyas from a warrior caste, while the sweepers and washermen were from castes with this function. As for officials' private servants, whose extraordinary number and variety amazed newcomers to India, their inferior status is clear in Russell's comment that within a few weeks he had 'been through two sets of private servants' (above p.46), meaning they had been killed or made useless by fever. Officials, as well as their wives and families, depended on a highly standardized array of Indian subordinates and servants. Britons evidently found caste congenial in many ways, for it made ruling India easier. Playing on Indian notions of honour and status they developed among Indians who served them a sense of authority, law, class, race, loyalty etc. that often appears more British than the British, producing an ideology of British rule that made it virtually impregnable. Maybe India's great rebellion of 1857 failed because *rajahs* and sepoys had internalized this ideology so deeply that they could not effectively free themselves from the British sense of right and wrong, as much as for military reasons.

In other words, the hierarchy and discipline which Indians experienced in British service were in many ways more extreme than in the old order, and the subordination and subservience which Britons demanded from them, they demanded with interest from Konds. The tribal situation was not nearly as stark as the genocidal confrontation with Europeans faced by the native peoples of America or Australia. The fact that British rule in tribal India made use of non-tribal Indians who had a long history of interaction with tribes such as the Konds, made it comparatively lenient—at first. Indian officials evidently extended their control over Konds a great deal, but were not yet motivated like their British superiors by a desire to 'reform' them, in terms of 'conquering their minds' or 'uplifting' them.

But gradually, as this control became more repressive, and non-tribals began to colonize tribal lands, large numbers of Konds lost their land and all traces of their former independence. Many became 'bonded labourers' in conditions of virtual slavery.

Baba Khan recorded Konds' amusement at Sundera Singh's grand ways:

> One morning, on a sunshiny day, while Soondera Sing was coming on his palanquin to see my master, one of [the Konds] remarked, with astonishment and laughter, "See! that palanquin was made in the low country; it is very beautiful, painted with colours, fixed with boards, lined with cloth, and iron fixed to it; how well it looks!" Another said: "The senses of the low-country people are not worth a cowry. How many men must have taken how much trouble in making this palanquin! They felled wood, sawed it into planks, placed them together, and formed them into a palanquin; and then it is only comfortable for one individual, and great wastage of money, while on account of one person many suffer much labour. If that man was to walk and go, he would save his money, and not give trouble to others." (WM pp.207–8, note)

The Sacrifice of Life, Land and Liberty

There are several levels then of colonial sacrifice. Firstly, a sacrifice of human life, from the more or less spiritual sense in which British officials 'sacrificed themselves' for 'a cause sacred to humanity', or to defend the honour of their flag; to the 'sacrifice of life' in a more secular sense, for the sake of order and peace—the Konds they killed in wars of 'pacification' and executions: throughout the Victorian era 'the Pax Britannica was being introduced at the cost of many lives' into India's tribal areas (Simcox [1920] p.31). One of India's top administrators reckoned that the last year of Macpherson's rule caused a 'sacrifice of life' greater than the *meriah* sacrifice had accounted for over many years (above p.85).

There is also the sacrifice of villages burnt, and countless Konds imprisoned, beaten, forced into coolie service, and ultimately into bonded labour. For beneath the surface image of 'enlightened government' the British imposed their 'peace' over the Konds with great violence. Their model of authority was based on 'suppression', producing order through fear: a 'pressing down' of human sacrifice and armed resistance that pushed violence underground to find expression in the cycle of exploitation and the enormous resentment this bred. 'Suppression' can be seen as a particular form of colonial sacrifice, and one aspect of the great *op*-pression and *re*-pression which British rule initiated or intensified throughout tribal areas.

This idea of 'peace at a cost' in a colonial setting epitomizes the secularization of the Protestant idea of *sacrifice*. Bourdillon considers the modern concept of 'calculated sacrifice' to be sacrifice 'only by metaphor' (Introduction to Bourdillon & Fortes 1980). If so, it is a metaphor that has had momentous consequences, which are clear in a colonial situation such as the imposition of British rule over the Konds, where we have observed the interplay between 'spiritual' and 'financial' concepts of sacrifice, and the key role these played in officials' self-image and motivation.

But it was not simply a matter of lives that were sacrificed for 'peace'. Konds' political and economic independence, self-sufficiency, self-determination—their freedom to live as they used to—were gradually sacrificed as well, along with their customary rights of land ownership and access to the forest. From an initial position of suppressing human sacrifice and warfare but 'preserving customary rights', British rule started a process of sacrificing a whole way of life for the sake of economic profit and 'progress'.

We can see that the initial motive for abolishing human sacrifice and bringing Konds under British rule was Christian rather than economic. But economic motives were never far away. The British war against Ghumsur started over tribute, and Konds in Boad feared that British rule would bring an increase in taxation; although Macpherson assured them it would not, this fear proved all too well-grounded, in terms of the 'voluntary plough tax' introduced in the 1870s, and duties on alcohol and salt, not to mention extortion by Government officials.

From Russell onwards, Britons realized that one of the surest ways to establish power over Konds was through trade.

> The civilisation of the wild tribes, with which we have now for the first time become acquainted, will be an object no less interesting than important. Dependent as they are on their lowland neighbours for salt and salt fish, of which they are very fond, as well as for all but the coarsest kinds of cotton manufactures, they will view with satisfaction the change which places these things within their reach.... There is perhaps no race of people who take more delight than the Khondes in silk and coloured, particularly red, cloths.... The revival of the fairs formerly held at Sooradah, and Codundah, and the establishment of similar marts at Kolada and other places favourable to the purpose, where they will have opportunities of seeing articles from all over the world,

> will tend greatly to promote their intercourse with us, and by *giving them new tastes and new wants will, in time, afford us the best hold we can have on their fidelity as subjects, by rendering them dependent upon us for what will, in time, become necessities of life.* (Report of 12th Aug. 1836, italics mine)

Russell is echoing the language of political economy as well as that of Cleveland's memorial inscription, and outlining a programme of increasing Konds' economic dependence, as a way of controlling them by manipulating their desires: 'with the extension of this commerce, their wants will encrease....' as Lord Elphinstone put it.[52] Eighteen years later, in 1855, MacDonald noticed

> a great increase in the number of persons who resort to these hills for the purpose of traffic [as a result of pacification by the police]. The civilizing effect which must be produced by the opening of these hills to the traders of the plains is so obvious that it seems very desirable to encourage this traffic as much as possible.[53]

Opening up Kond territory by building roads and enmeshing Konds in the wider economy meant, it is now generally realized, exposing them to manipulation by Hindu traders and moneylenders. Money was new to Konds, and they often got into debt, which is the story behind the great uprisings such as that in Kalahandi.[54] The monetary system non-tribals manipulated had the sanction of Government law behind it, while laws to protect tribal lands from being mortgaged and sold to non-tribals were never very effective. Once land ownership came to be defined permanently and individually in monetary terms, a new kind of inequality was introduced into Kond villages, as some families grew richer and others poorer, and many lost their land to outsiders.

Gradually British rule introduced a scale of values that defined land and forest in monetary terms as economic assets and sources of revenue.[55] Forest was cut and sold off or 'reserved' on the basis of a kind of financial value that had not existed before. We have seen how some *rajahs* were trying to make their tribal subjects settle in permanent villages, and extend cultivation more 'efficiently' by clearing the jungle to create permanent fields, instead of the Kond system of shifting cultivation. Paradoxically, the British put a lot of the blame for deforestation on shifting cultivation, when from a tribal perspective, one could say that it has been the tendency to create permanent fields that destroys the forest, and that shifting cultivation tends to preserve it, by rotating the growing of crops with the forest's continual regeneration. Minchin's monograph *The Sal Forests of*

Ganjam (1920, above p.167) reduces the Konds' forests to statistics and techniques of 'timber consumed', 'utilization of the product', 'schemes of fellings', 'bamboo extraction' and the like. There is no mention of what the forests meant to Konds, or their protests against the 'reserving' of forests for Government gain. The Kuttia Konds who practised 'slash and burn cultivation' suffered severely in this way, as did the Baiga tribals, west of Orissa, whom officials tried to force into permanent villages, where they had to use ploughs and grow cash crops. In the 1870s–1890s 'the marketable value of forest produce rose in something like geometrical proportions' (Elwin 1939 pp.111–23).

The 'reserving' of forests hit at the heart of Kond life:

> The people feel strongly because Government has taken possession of the forests. They can point to the fact that no other ever did so before. They ask "Who made the forests? For whom did He make them? For the Government or for the people?" (*BMS Report* 1895 p.30)

Government appropriation of the forest followed from a refusal to recognize Kond customary land rights as regards access to forest, as well as communal ownership of village land. Land came to be conceived in terms of private or state property, rather than in terms of territory that a village held in common, each family clearing as much as their labour could cultivate. Hunter compared Kond with Scottish traditional land rights, in which 'the individual nowhere appears', and asserted that the principle of individual ownership was the most radical aspect of the changes which British rule imposed:

> It is by what we have implanted in the living people, rather than what we have built upon the dead earth, that our name will survive. The permanent aspect of British rule in India is the growth of Private Rights.... By a wise limitation of our state ownership we have raised up a permanent Proprietary Body, composed of mutually hostile classes; but each of which, from the great seigneurs down to the Resident Husbandmen, holds its lands under documents issued by British officials. (1872 vol.II pp.201 & 277)

But tribal people, being non-literate, rarely got the ownership deeds to the land they had long cultivated, that was theirs by right. The settlement records tended to pass them by, and the irregularities by which non-tribals acquired the title to tribal lands are well-known. In the process, many tribals came to be classified as 'encroachers on Government land', on the basis of which they are still being expelled from land that has been theirs for generations.[56]

Dramatically alien British notions of individual land ownership had been introduced throughout India ever since the Permanent Settlement of 1793, as R. Guha has shown in his *Rule of property for Bengal: An essay on the idea of permanent settlement* (1963). The reserving of forests from the 1860s represents an extension of the tendency to make land as profitable as possible and limit public access, that had been worked out in Britain with the Enclosure Movement and the Highland Clearances. The huge estates in Scotland that were increasingly cleared of their human inhabitants, who had lived there for centuries as crofters, were filled not only with sheep, which gave a bigger economic profit, but also with deer and game birds for aristocrats to hunt.[57] A very similar pattern characterizes the British in tribal areas of India, for the passionate hobby of countless officials was hunting, a 'sport' that shows their motivation at a deep level. The animals and birds they shot in such numbers, with such bloodlust, are a potent symbol of the habit of control they imposed in their working life over the forest and its human inhabitants. If one considers the huge tracts of forest which the British felled for profit, as well as the countless animals which they shot for fun, one could say they were engaged in a sacrifice of wild-life, or of nature itself, which helps to explain the assault on the forest that has taken place since then.

Along with the curtailment of tribal self-sufficiency and rights to the forest, went an assault on their independence at other levels. As we have seen, the buffalo sacrifice was soon forbidden or strictly controlled (above pp.106–8 & 165). The making of alcoholic drinks, that form a vital part in tribal social and religious life, was also suppressed: a ban on home distilling was introduced in 1870, which forced Konds to buy their *mahua* from sundis (men of the 'distiller' caste), who doubled as moneylenders and landlords, and got rich at Konds' expense. In 1910 Ollenbach banned this liquor trade, but still curtailed home distilling.[58] A particularly drastic interference in tribal life occurred when British officials, who disapproved of the scanty leaf dress which Juang women wore, made them exchange it for cotton sarees.[59]

'Enlightenment' is the concept that encapsulates Britons' view of their purpose towards their tribal subjects (above p.158). They defined it along with 'knowledge' and 'civilization' in opposition to tribal 'ignorance' and 'superstition': a conceptual opposition that is one of the most fundamental elements of British discourse, which reduces *differences* to hierarchy on a scale of 'advancement'.[60]

> It is only by the European mind, free from prejudice and ignorance, and capable of fostering the nascent desire for improvement, that the people can be brought forward and their condition ameliorated. The first impulse has been given, but the same force which communicated motion must be applied to continue it, unless indeed abolition of sacrifice rather than general *development* of resources and advance in the path of civilization, be regarded as the *ultimatum* of our efforts.... Roads, bungalows, and schools are amongst the very best means—subordinate always to those divinely appointed for the recovery of our fallen race [i.e. missionaries]—to elevate and improve the Khonds. (MacViccar's Report of 26th April 1851)

The Directors of the EIC in London commended Campbell and his staff when he retired in similar words:

> They have....opposed rational conciliation to popular prejudices and error.... It is obvious that germs of an ultimate civilisation have been planted in the country, and we may entertain a confident hope that the advance of the population towards a higher social condition will be in an accelerated ratio of progress. (14th June 1854)

These are classic statements of social evolutionism. The words 'development', 'progress', 'advance', 'civilization', 'improve', 'ameliorate', 'elevate' and 'higher' mask the *imposition of unwanted change*. Administrators believed that they knew what was best for Konds, and that it was their Christian duty to impose it on them. In the process they believed Konds' former liberty had to be sacrificed for the sake of 'civilizing' them.

Schools played an important part in this 'civilizing process'. Macpherson saw his way 'dimly to a beginning of schools amongst the Khonds' in 1844, when he composed a 'First Book of Universal Religion and Morals for them' (above p.71). Frye, MacViccar and Campbell put the idea of schools into effect, despite Kond hostility.

> The opposition was most intense. Words can scarcely convey an adequate idea of the scorn and contempt manifested, especially by the elders of the tribes. This was to be expected; their eyes had grown dim in their old delusions.... These men had passed their lives in darkness, and in darkness they wished to die. (Campbell 1864 pp.178–9)

This image of the Konds as essentially 'ignorant', of spiritual matters as well as the means to material prosperity and all scientific or rational knowledge, has been extremely persistent—in the words of a modern historian:

> The Khonds resisted the spread of education in the hill tracts on several grounds of superstition and blind faith.... Even the prospect of employment did not attract the attention of parents for sending their children to schools. The Khonds totally failed to understand the importance of education; their aggressive [!] refusal to send their children to schools forced [!] the Government to deploy police force to collect students for schools. (Behara 1984 p.76)

But why was the Government so keen? Apparently because administrators saw schools as another means of 'conquering Konds' minds' and creating a Kond elite to rule through. Schools were also a tangible proof to Europeans of Government 'care' and 'benevolence'. The fact that Konds did not want schools was considered irrelevant, and in 1863 a tax was levied for them. It is significant that the unwanted introduction of schools in Bastar was given as an important cause of the 1910 rebellion there.

Thus on the one hand, British rule involved a lot of well-meaning but utterly insensitive innovations, based on the unspeakably arrogant idea that 'we know what's best for them'; on the other, it gave a new kind of power over Konds to a large range of officials, who despised and exploited them in collusion with local moneylenders and landlords. Gopinath Mohanty's novel *Paraja*, written during the last years of British rule about the Poroja tribe, neighbouring the Konds in Koraput District, is an accurate representation of how this cycle of exploitation functions: a forest guard makes extortionate demands, causing a family to get into debt to a moneylender, who works a system of compound interest from which a debtor can never get free and is forced into bonded labour, a state which, though illegal, was (and still is) widely prevalent.

Realizing the adverse effects of 'free trade' on tribal areas, the British passed laws to protect tribals from exploitation (above p.168). The resulting policy that developed of separating tribal areas off from the mainstream legal code, exemplified in the Backward Tracts Act of 1919, was attacked by Indian nationalists as an example of 'divide and rule'. Ghurye wrote *The Aborigines—"so-called"—and their future* (1943), attacking the whole idea that tribal people have a distinct identity, and arguing for their 'assimilation' into the Hindu mainstream (above pp.19–20). In support of his argument he quoted British officials' most reactionary comments on tribal life—e.g. that the Konds are 'thriftless, ignorant, and prone to self-indulgence and choose to get into debt and lose their lands'.[61]

Thus evolutionism and negative stereotypes about tribals from the colonial era have merged with Indian ideas to produce a disdain for tribal culture that is almost universal among the non-tribals who live near *adivasis* and have power over them. It allows them to be displaced in huge numbers from their land for 'development projects' such as dams and mines, where they are given labouring jobs in conditions of slavery, in addition to the gradual displacement that has taken place since British rule was first imposed. The deepest and most pervasive aspect of the colonial sacrifice was thus a gradual, accumulative assault on tribal people's quality of life as a whole.

Tea and coffee plantations in Assam and South India were the first large-scale projects that cleared forest to make way for commerce. It is significant that hundreds of Konds and other *adivasis* went to Assam to work in these plantations from the 1850s on. They were taken there by contractors, whose activities were only regulated in 1901, and generally stayed for several years, or even settled there. About 3,000 Konds were living in Assam in 1902.[62]

Fitzgerald's *Kuvinga bassa* (1913) is a Kond grammar 'written from a Tea-Garden point of view, for Tea-Planters', for dealing with Konds in Assam. Fitzgerald includes a few comments on Kond ethnography: from their skin colour to their 'devils', and the inconvenient fact that they were 'much addicted to strong drink' and had 'a most inordinate craving for beef flesh'. The phrases he lists suggest a great deal about how *sahebs* spoke and behaved to Konds in general:

Bring my horse	Put out your tongue
Beat the dog	Bury the corpse
Give her a rupee	Drink the medicine properly
Sing a song	Don't annoy the bear
Finish the work	Don't dance all night long
Listen to me	Be silent! Let me sleep
Don't wear dirty clothes	You're a very lazy person
Don't drink too much liquor	I am not pleased with you
Don't cough so much	How many goats has your father got?

The village headman did not come when called

He has done better work than you

The Sahib had given him two days' leave, therefore he had gone to Doom Dooma

CHAPTER SIX

'Soldiers of Christ'

The role of the soldier-administrators who 'reduced the Konds to subjection' under the British flag was complemented by the role of the missionary. Formally separate from the Government, missionaries took over the task of 'conquering the minds' of tribal people to draw them into the empire and 'civilize' them more thoroughly than administrators could.

It is difficult to write about missionaries objectively, because of the dualism that is inherent in the missionary enterprise. Missionaries' self-sacrifice is often extreme and their benevolence, especially in education and medicine, seems beyond question. But there is a fundamental bias in their outlook which polarizes people, in the idea that Christianity is superior to other religions and that only Christians can be 'saved'. Behind a mask of meekness there is thus an enormous arrogance and violence in the missionary enterprise: a fundamental closedness and prejudice against other cultures and religions. Part of being objective, then, is to expose this bias.

And yet, as with anthropological analysis of any social group, one needs to enter into the missionaries' point of view to try and understand it from the inside, as well as to examine their ideas and actions from the outside, within a social context that included other Europeans and Hindus as well as Konds. I shall therefore build my argument around numerous quotations from missionary writings, in order to recreate the way they perceived their actions. But my aim is to go to fundamentals, beyond missionaries' self-representation, by analysing what they said as well as what they did, in order to understand how the missionary system worked as a whole. One monograph I have found useful is Beidelman's *Colonial Evangelism* (1982), an anthropological study of an Anglican Mission to a tribe in East Africa. Another, *Is God an American?* (Hvalkof 1981) exposes the destructive impact of evangelical missionaries of the Summer Institute of Linguistics (alias Wycliffe Bible Translators) on Indians of Latin America. My appraisal of mission work, like these, may appear unsympathetic, since I do not share missionaries' negative judgement of tribal religion or their desire to uproot traditional beliefs and customs. Yet the missionaries we shall meet 'gave their lives for the Konds' in years of devoted 'service', and many of them died 'in the field'.

Missionaries became involved with Konds at the same time as Government officials. Some of the first *meriahs* whom British soldiers 'rescued', they sent to Baptist orphanages to be cared for and educated. During the Ghumsur wars, Reverend Brown visited the scene of the war and wrote two articles in the *Calcutta Christian Observer*, which played an important part in generating the public opinion that persuaded the Government to take action to stamp out Kond human sacrifice. We have already seen the significance of Alexander Duff's publications, eulogizing Macpherson's role (above p.93). Duff was a High Church Anglican clergyman. Brown was a Baptist missionary, and from the start it was Baptists who were involved most closely with Government officers in Kond affairs, for which reason we shall be focusing mainly on them.

Baptist missionaries were among the first Protestants to evangelize in India. William Carey came out in 1792, as the first missionary of the Baptist Missionary Society (BMS), which was founded in London that year. He was the prototype of a new kind of missionary: a very 'low church' Protestant, 'humble' in outlook and dead against the elaborate hierarchy and ritual of Catholic missionaries, and also much stricter on rules that reflected a literal obedience to the words of the Gospels, which these missionaries propagated in thousands of printed pamphlets and translated into every possible language.[1] Carey made his base at Serampore in Danish territory, since the British Government did not allow missionaries to work in India until 1813, for fear of disturbing Indians' religious sensibilities and hence endangering Britain's commercial interests. After this date, missionaries from a wide variety of Christian sects came, and the Government gradually allotted them different 'fields', parcelling India up between them.

An Orissa Mission was started in 1822 by Bampton and Peggs of the General Baptist sect—the first missionaries to be sent out by the General Baptist Missionary Society (GBMS). They came via Serampore, whence they brought over 4,000 religious books and pamphlets printed by Carey in English, Bengali and Oriya: 'We go forth bearing precious seed' Peggs declared (1846 p.151). Both men came with their wives, like most of the missionaries who followed them. Peggs' wife gave birth to three children in as many years, who all died in infancy. Peggs went home, seriously ill himself, to become a missionary propagandist, writing pamphlets denouncing capital punishment, Britain's opium trade, and the maltreatment of *lascars* (Indian sailors in Britain), as well as a series about 'social evils' in India which he called on the Government to abolish. These were published together as a book called *India's cries to British humanity* (2nd ed. 1830), that was widely influential.

Bampton visited Puri, whose cult of Jagannath was a prominent focus of missionary criticism. He took to wearing a *dhoti*, unlike his colleagues, who disapproved of this experiment with native attire, and wore sober, close-fitting black suits that made them stand out wherever they went. Bampton died in Cuttack in 1830. But several more missionaries carried on the work in Cuttack and Berhampur, setting up the orphanages that took in *meriah* children. One missionary, who retired early after his wife died and his own health was undermined, named his nephew John Orissa Goadby in memory of his unfinished work. This nephew joined the Mission in 1857 and was its first missionary to the Konds, visiting them in 1859–63 before dying of blackwater fever in 1868.

The next Baptists to visit the Konds were three missionaries who came in 1891, when the GBMS was merged with the BMS. All three died in the 'Kond field' of fever or smallpox, one almost immediately. Abiathar Wilkinson translated St. Mark's Gospel into Kui, and died on a tour of the Kond hills in 1897, just after returning from sick leave in England. Arthur Long survived until 1909, after establishing a long-term base at Russellkonda. Alfred Ernest Grimes from Australia joined Long in 1906 and served as a missionary to the Konds until 1937.

Soon there was a steady stream of recruits to the Kond Mission, until its base at Udayagiri was the largest BMS station in India. Oliver Millman 'masterminded' this expansion between 1908 and 1929, building the all-season centre at Udayagiri, setting up schools, and printing textbooks for them in Kui. Edward Evans served there betwen 1911 and 1948. A woman he married in 1915 died within weeks of coming to Orissa. He went as chaplain with a detachment of Kond soldiers to Mesopotamia in the first world war, after which he married again. Winfield served at the Mission 1917–27, after which he published a grammar and vocabulary of Kui (1928–9), and went on to become one of the top BMS administrators in London. Other missionaries were doctors and nurses, and in 1935 a hospital was built, which is still flourishing today. In its heyday between 1930 and 1970 the Mission consisted of a European staff of, on average, five couples and five single women. One of the latter was Barbara Boal (serving there 1950–60), who published a Kond ethnography in 1982. India passed a law against missionizing in 1968, and the last European left Udayagiri in 1973. But by then their Church was self-perpetuating: from the first Dom priest and his family whom Millman baptized in 1914, the number of 'baptized believers' grew to 400 in 1930, and in 1963 was up to well over 5,000, with a further 15,000 in the 'wider Christian community', who had not yet been baptized.[2]

For Baptists were stricter than other missionaries. In terms of the number of converts, Roman Catholics did much better. A Catholic Mission was based at Sorada from 1850: French missionaries of the order of St Francis de Sales, who came as part of a 'second spring' of Catholic Missions in India.[3] By 1875 they claimed 800 conversions, though many of these lapsed ('apostated'). In the 1880s they made outposts in the hills, at Digi and Katingia, and went on tours of remote Kond villages. By 1902 they estimated a Christian population around Sorada of 3,200 (Neill 1985 p.299). In 1908 the Baptists admitted, 'It may be said that the Roman Catholics are extending their influence much more rapidly, and have recently sent five new priests to their section of the field.'[4] In 1923 the Sorada Mission was taken over by Spanish missionaries from Madrid of the order of St Vincent de Paul. They were evidently stricter, and found only 100 'genuine Catholics' in their new flock.[5] The first 'native priest' was ordained in 1947, and in the 1950s the Catholic Mission began an expansion among the Konds greater than that of the Baptists. Their missionaries were 'celibate, and thus more mobile', and their discipline was less oppressive. In 1986 three retired Spanish missionaries were still living in the area, in Sorada and Gopalpur.

A third sect to be allotted a share in 'the Kond field' was a German Lutheran Mission, which operated among southern, Kuvi-speaking Konds in Jeypore state (the modern Koraput District). This was the

Schleswig-Holstein Evangelical Lutheran Mission, founded in 1876. By 1890, they had four Mission stations in Jeypore.[6] The Revd F.V.P. Schulze, at Salur (just south of Koraput District), wrote the first grammar and vocabulary of the Kuvi dialect. In the 1900s the Mission expanded to the predominantly Kond area in the east of Jeypore state, establishing more stations in Gunupur (1902) and Bissamcuttack (1910). By 1931 their total number of converts was over 21,000. But the German missionaries were repatriated during the First World War; and afterwards the Mission was divided (like Schleswig-Holstein itself) between Germany and Denmark, with Danes taking over the Kond area in 1928, as the East Jeypore Mission. This grew in the 1950s to be as large as the Baptist Mission, and built a similar Christian Hospital at Bissamcuttack, which is highly respected today. Three elderly Danish women who had been part of this Mission were still living in Koraput District in the 1980s.[7]

In all Missions, the first converts, as well as a large proportion of later ones, were Doms, to whom Christianity offered equal status with Konds. Only in the 1950s, after India's Independence, did Konds begin to convert to all three sects of Christianity (and more) in large numbers.

We shall be looking at this trend: a dramatic turn to Christianity that represents the fruit of missionizing begun under British rule a century before. Christianity offers a strong support system, including the skills of literacy and an ideology of justice and equality, that helps to counteract exploitation by non-tribals. Since these, including the majority of Government officials now, are mostly Hindus, Christianity offers an alternative identity that has a powerful appeal. The price is the giving up, or sacrifice, of many features of traditional Kond society, and particularly a new divisiveness between Christians and non-Christians (or between Christians of different sects), which stems from the idea that Christianity alone is 'true' and only Christians can be 'saved'.

Complementing the Administration

On the surface missionaries were independent from the Government. Sometimes they came into conflict with it. There was a longstanding tradition of missionaries who championed basic human rights overseas, from Las Casas and others who stood up for the Indians in Latin America and denounced the worst excesses of soldiers and slavers, to the campaign in Britain that led to the abolition of the African slave trade. But the same impulse that led missionaries such as Carey and Peggs to campaign against slavery and even capital punishment, also led them to proselytyze. So the other side of this conflict is the Government's suspicion of missionizing, that led to the banning of missionaries from India until 1813. But there was a lot of liaison too, and at a deeper level a mutual dependence and division of labour evolved: in return for its patronage, missionaries extended the Government's hold over Konds in various ways. Administrators and missionaries were both anxious to stress their formal separation of powers and independence. Protestant missionaries valued their independence from Government and contrasted it with Catholic colonies, where civil and missionary spheres were not properly differentiated.[8] At the same time, they tried to influence Government officials and draw them into their Church.

All British officials in India were professed Christians. Whether this meant that they represented 'a Christian Government' though, was not generally agreed.[9] And officials were sharply divided on whether the Government should involve itself in missionary efforts or not. As an article in the *Calcutta Christian Observer* on 'the Government Religion of British India' put it:

> Whether the British Government ought, or ought not, to aid in the direct conversion of its Mohammadan and Hindu subjects to Christianity, is a question on which our editors agree to differ. (*CCO* May 1836 p.258)

Some administrators, in India as well as in London, were more or less hostile to missionary activity, and the predominant attitude considered it vital that they should distance themselves from missionaries as much as possible, in order to show India's inhabitants that the Government had no intention of making them convert to Christianity. For instance, when the President of the Bengal Government let Campbell send *meriah* children to the Mission orphanages, he was anxious to make it clear that they were not being sent there to be converted (Minute by Maddock, 2nd Sept. 1847).

There was a marked difference between administrators and missionaries in terms of class and education. Missionaries tended to be more working class, and often evoked Anglican or High Church hostility to their 'Non-Conformist' evangelizing and demonstrations of piety. On ships to India, missionaries often isolated themselves or seemed ridiculous to the rest of the ship's company.[10] Similarly, when Peggs and Bampton arrived in Cuttack in 1822, their missionary zeal offended most of the officials (Peggs 1846 p.197):

> At first most of the Europeans attended the English preaching....but after a time, some little offence was taken at the faithful exhibition and application of Gospel truth, and but few attended.

However, some administrators became wholehearted allies of the missionaries. Certainly this is true of the Kond Agency, where a conflict on this matter between Macpherson and MacViccar led MacViccar to resign, making a passionate avowal of his spiritual and ideological allegiance to the Baptist missionaries (below pp.195–8). So when he took office in the Agency after Macpherson's dismissal, the Agency became identified more closely with the missionaries. The complete independence of Government and Missions is thus not as clear-cut as it seems at first.

It was widely believed by Britons in the mid- and late 19th century that the enlargement of their empire was actually part of the same historical or even natural process as the spread of Christianity, guided by 'Providence'.[11] So the interests of missionaries and soldiers coincided, and the spread of Christianity was often identified with, or held to justify, the spread of empire. It seems to have been almost taken for granted by missionaries and many administrators, if not by most ordinary churchgoers in Britain, that 'the flag and the cross' should advance together.

To understand how missionaries inspired and legitimized Government actions towards the Konds, it is worth quoting in some detail Reverend Brown's two influential articles in the *Calcutta Christian Observer* (April & July 1837, mentioned above p.62):-

> If brought under the civilizing influence of education, and the softening and elevating influence of Christianity, [the Konds] would make the best subjects, and the most manly and devoted Christians in India. (p.157)
>
> The condition of the people with regard to civilization is the lowest almost which can be imagined, with the single exception that they are not cannibals.... Like most savages, they destroy without mercy: neither age, sex, guilt or innocence is spared. They war to exterminate, not subdue; for revenge, not honor. Many instances of their cruel and bloody disposition have occurred during the late contest.... Where this wretched race now wander, let the Missionary of the cross enter. (p.158)
>
> A nation of drunkards, they are addicted to many of the vices attendant on drunkenness.... I saw an officer pour the remains of a bottle of brandy into the mouth of one of these unscrupulous people, and it was difficult to say which

manifested the more satisfaction, the Khund or the officer.... [On religion] their minds appear to be exceedingly contracted. (pp.159–60)

One intended victim, rescued during the march of the army, I now have staying with me in Berhampur.... Several persons intended as victims have been rescued besides the one with me. There are several children at Chutterpur plucked as brands from the burning. They are now under the protection of Mr Stevenson. May they return again another day to these "hills of darkness" and teach these wretched savages the way of eternal life. (pp.160–1)

It is said that these people are in the utmost terror lest the Government should interfere to prevent human sacrifices, supposing that from thence, the earth would again become unfruitful, unstable, and sink under them.... Will this infernal practice be allowed to go on? Surely it cannot be said that the Government have no right to interfere. The Government have interfered, and have hung many of the Khund principal men by sentences of courts martial for taking up arms. Surely it is as just to punish for abduction and murder as for rebellion. Shall *satis* be prevented and the infernal *meria puja* be allowed? (pp.161–2)

The country is capable of much improvement by the application of labor. (p.165)

The Collector very kindly took me to see a part of the country where the ravages of war had not reached. (p.167)

Baligar Singh, a man of Gullery, who headed the party that murdered the two young officers, Bromley and Gibbons, was executed at his native town. (p.168)

If "the battle of the warrior and the garments rolled in blood" be the harbinger of civilization, literacy, and finally Christianity itself; we will be thankful to Him of whom it is written, that though "clouds and darkness are round about him, yet justice and judgement are the habitations of his throne". (p.338)

Let the friends of Christianity, of education, of moral improvement pray for and *determine* on the destruction of these horrible sacrifices; and the inhuman wretches, who for selfish purposes now support the practice, will be confounded, and this horrible iniquity will hide its head. The cry of British humanity has caused the fire of the *sati* to be forever extinguished. The same wonder-working power, the detestation of a Christian and powerful people publicly expressed, will shortly penetrate these desolate hills and secluded valleys, and innocent blood, till now shed with impunity under the awful sanction of a cruel superstition, will forever cease to flow. Truth and mercy will triumph over deception and cruelty; thus through the breadth of the land shall be spread the knowledge of the Lord, and the terrible *Meria Puja* be exchanged for the holy institutions of the religion of the Bible, and the blessings of civilized life. (*CCO* 1837 p.340)

This gives a foretaste of the stereotypes which missionaries spread about Kond 'heathens'. The point to note now is the way that Brown, as a missionary, takes on the role of exhorting and legitimizing the actions of Government soldiers; while at the same time claiming a complete lack of involvement or responsibility for Government actions. As he went among the burnt villages, giving out tobacco,

> I told them I pitied their helpless and destitute condition, but that I had nothing to do with the war or this world's knowledge: my business was to teach men how they may be happy after death. (ibid. p.344)

Similarly in 1841 the *Friend of India*, a Christian weekly magazine in Calcutta, publicized the Baptist missionaries' appeal to Christian principles to call on the Governor-General to allow the use of force to rescue *meriahs*:

> "Auckland! with tearful eye and bended knee, These children breathe their earnest prayers to thee!"[12]

In 1854 an article in the same magazine (28th Sept.) glorified Campbell's 'almost entire suppression' of human sacrifice, commenting: 'All over India the warfare against the darker crimes is everywhere proceeding, everywhere successful.' In other words, the conquest of the Konds was a 'Christian war', instigated and justified by missionaries.

Campbell (1864) made clear his faith in missionaries, to carry further his own work of 'civilizing' the Konds:

> I have not alluded to the great precursor of Civilisation—the Gospel—not because I am insensible of its fitness for these wild tribes (who have no predilection for Brahmins) but simply because it is not within the province of the Government of India to introduce any agency of the kind. I may, however, express the hope that in due season these savage Konds will be visited by the teachers of a higher and purer wisdom than that of men.

Macpherson too saw missionaries as potentially complementing his own work:

> The establishment of distinct relations with the Konds as subjects must precede any attempt to act upon their religious opinions and practices. A missionary might begin at the other end—not, I conceive, the Government. (A letter of 1842 in WM p.177)

As we shall see, Macpherson differed vitally from the missionaries on some points. But Pearce Carey's book on the Baptist Mission to the Konds,

Dawn in the Kond hills (1936), glosses over these uncomfortable differences—as well as British violence—and contributes to the mythic image of Macpherson and Campbell as 'Captains of wisdom', who were 'stern but benefic precursors of Christ'.

> The colonel's [i.e. Campbell's] indebtedness to the orphanages filled him with a deep regard for missionaries and their labours. Moreover, he vividly realized that what the law and the Government could not do by reason of human frailty, could only be accomplished by the evangelism of Christ.
>
> The colonel's successor, Major MacViccar, advised that Russellkonda should be the base of such a mission, which should give its utmost attention to those parts of Kondistan which had known most of "Britain's power and Britain's mercy." Surely it was significant that officers of the British army, administrators of the Indian Government, should thus invite the uplifting arm of Christ for the people of the Hill Tracts. (1936 p.30)

Surely it was! Beneath a formal independence and separation of powers, a deep and complex interdependence evolved; while this kind of eulogy from missionaries served to legitimize imperial expansion and reinforce Government myths and versions of events, in a shared ideology of empire.

From their side, missionaries followed the army's lead, relying on soldiers to 'open up' or 'pacify' new fields for evangelism: it was axiomatic that the cross should follow the British standard.

> Wherever our soldiers and sailors can go, our Missionaries *must* go also; it is not a question of policy or possibility, but of Duty.....[13]

In the case of the Konds, missionaries saw themselves as relying on Government officials to effect an initial pacification by force, 'opening a way for the missionary, who otherwise could not have penetrated through those dense jungles.'[14]

One area where the complementarity is clear is in the setting up of Kond schools. As Pearce Carey says, Macpherson and Campbell were 'both zealous for the establishment of schools'. In 1854 Mission schools all over India decided, after considerable debate, to accept Government subsidies: a sure sign of missionaries and administrators working more closely together. Structurally, they were deeply dependent on each other by then: a dependence that operated on several levels, and contradicts the official, surface model of independence.

For instance, Millman's Kui school system and textbooks were accepted by the Government in at least 70 Kond schools in the 1930s, despite their explicitly Christian message. And missionaries sometimes worked directly under the Government. Evans accompanied Konds overseas in the first world war, and was awarded an MBE; in the second world war Dr Stanley Thomas did likewise; and in 1936 the Government appointed Revd Grimes of the Baptist Mission to be 'representative and spokesman for the Hill Tribes' in the new Province of Orissa: tribals' interests were to be represented by a missionary.

Macpherson gave his favour to Mission work by patronizing the marriages of three *meriah* girls in the orphanage at Berhampur in 1844, at which

> all seemed to strive to make it as much unlike a Hindu marriage as possible. Captain Macpherson made the girls a present on their wedding day of ten rupees each.

He promised the same for another ten girls (Peggs 1846 p.279). But the depth of missionary influence on the Government is shown by officials' attendance at their services, which evidently led one or more to convert to the Baptist faith.[15] In December 1845 Captain Frye, in Berhampur, 'had the humility and the courage to be there baptized'. In other words, he became a Baptist, and the missionaries hoped he would leave the Government and become a missionary himself:

> A circumstance very promising to the missionaries at Berhampur, has been the interest taken in their work by a young officer. He was educated at one of the English universities, but is stated to be in principle, a Baptist.... He makes great sacrifices, it is stated, to serve the cause of God and the mission. Ought not the friends of the mission to pray that one promising so fair for usefulness where eternal interests are concerned, may be rendered willing to sacrifice his worldly prospects, and to devote himself wholly to advancing the cause of Immanuel? (Peggs 1846 p.280)

Frye declined this offer, but worked closely with the missionaries, bringing out his own lithographic press, on which he printed translations of Christian texts in the Kond language, which were displayed in the Great Exhibition of 1851, and used in the schools that he and MacViccar set up.

So some of the officials identified closely with missionary aims. The conflict between Macpherson and MacViccar is highly significant in this context. MacViccar seems to have been baptized a Baptist around the same time as Frye.[16] He and Campbell may have had a Presbyterian background similar to Baptist Christianity, whereas Macpherson's open interest in Konds' religion and identification of their 'God of Light' with the Christian God evidently extended to Hinduism, and differed much from missionary attitudes.

Some GBMS missionaries were touring the Kond area at the beginning of 1846, and put up camp close to the administrators' HQ at Nowgam. MacViccar (who may have instigated them to come) wanted to go to their Sunday service, but Macpherson asked him not to, on the grounds that

> The sensitiveness of the Hindu population of this part of Orissa on the subject of the identification of the European officers of Govt with the proceedings of the Missionaries resident in it, is, from various causes, at present very great.... If a belief in the virtual identification of the officers of the Agency with the Missionaries shall once arise our indispensable public servants will no longer place the necessary degree of confidence in them, while even if they should do so, their services would avail us nothing as the Hindus whom we must influence through them would not confide in them as persons leagued with the virtual subverters of their faith.[17]

MacViccar went to the Sunday service anyway, leaving a note offering his resignation if this embarrassed his superior. It did:

> His act elicited expressions of feeling on the part of our public servants which proved to me and to my principal assistant Dr Cadenhead, that we had even underrated their sensitiveness, and the strength and distinctness of the popular feeling on the subject of the identification of the officers of this Agency with Missionary proceedings.

So MacViccar wrote justifying his action and again offering to resign.

> My Dear Captain MacPherson,
>
> ....Were this a civil question the most implicit obedience and the most faithful and zealous adherence to your directions, would be my exclusive, though it might be my unpleasant duty, but the question at issue placed in any conceivable form, resolves itself into this, am I or am I not to purchase the confidence of the natives at the price of my conscience, and in direct violation of the commands of God? (12th Jan.)

Macpherson replied in a letter which he intended to be unofficial (16th Jan.):

> My dear MacViccar,
>
> I am so anxious that your mind should become reconciled to what I conceive to be the requirements of this service, on the point of the connexion of the officers engaged in it with the missionaries of these districts, that I must beg you to allow me notwithstanding our long conversations and the decisions to which you say that you have come, to restate those requirements and the

grounds for them and to request your most deliberate reconsideration of them. I assure you that there is no arrangement compatible with the accomplishment of the work entrusted to me, which I will not gladly make to meet your views.

I can only….express the hope that you may in the end, determine, that with reference to the very peculiar and extreme exigencies of our anomalous work, you are free to adopt the line of conduct which appears to all engaged in the work to be essential to its accomplishment….

This elicited another letter from MacViccar (20th Jan.) that is remarkable for its uncompromising, moralistic sense of religious conviction, which is clearly modelled on the language of Luther and the Protestant martyrs:

Sir,

I have had the honor to receive your official letter of the 16th and suffer me to assure you, before entering on my reply, that it was not without the fullest and most anxious consideration, that I arrived at the conclusion which I have already communicated to you. My wishes and my interest conjointly would have led me to think lightly of any personal sacrifice, to meet your views, and those of your native servants; but a wilful deviation from the revealed will of God, a virtual denial of my faith and a departure from the truth, which I hold to be betrayed by *evasion,* are conditions to which I feel assured you would never desire me to assent, and yet I believe these very conditions, though I deeply regret you fail to perceive it, are involved in the assurance you require me to give and without which you cannot hope to retain the confidence of your native servants.

….I informed you that I proposed going over on the following day, Sunday, to see my friends who were Missionaries, and near at hand; you mentioned to me that you were in great fear of being identified in any way with Missionaries, but you did not clearly point out what identification meant, and a very long conversation on the afternoon of that day still left the question of identification undetermined. I did not fail plainly to state that no fear of man would ever make me omit a positive duty to God; you left me however to decide in foro conscientiae, whether or not on the succeeding day I should visit the Missionaries; after bestowing the deepest thought of which I was capable on this important matter, I felt that my duty was clear, that I should be dishonouring God if I shrank from going where I could join with others in His worship, and that if I *evaded* so doing with the sole object of deceiving the natives, I should be little better than an hypocrite…. I returned the same evening. On the following morning (Monday) there was no longer any difficulty in determining the meaning of "identity" for I was told in express language, that your Cutcherry were alone to be made judge of what identity was, that they chose to designate a simple visit as "identity" and therefore I was to give the assurance of not repeating this specific act until the Cutcherry interdict was removed….

> I submit with much deference that if ever the principle were admitted of allowing the native servants to dictate to me, when, where, and in what manner I shall worship my God, and with whom in religious matters I shall associate, there is no height to which it may not be carried; the first fruits and the full harvest are *alike* in quality, the difference only being in the quantity. I cannot see and do not feel the force of the argument, so often presented to me, that the good work in which we are engaged would justify the concessions required. Most respectfully, but earnestly, would I point out that no unfaithfulness of mine, though it may serve in the end to magnify or to advance the cause or truth of God, would be thereby palliated if I knowingly offend against His Law; though his wisdom may lead to a good result, I am not the less evil.
>
> In conclusion I would add that all I have ever asked is liberty of conscience (while you have demanded from me assurances that would reduce me to a time serving, waiting upon God); which assurances I will never give; and therefore tendered my resignation. "A secret belief which shuns an open avowal of Christ is removed but one step, and that a very short one, from an absolute and positive unbelief and open denial."

MacViccar's appointment as Macpherson's Assistant ended thus after only a few weeks. But after Macpherson was dismissed in March 1847, he became Campbell's chief Assistant, and Agent himself in 1855-6, so his wish for closer relations with the missionaries was undoubtedly fulfilled. In any case, after the Mutiny, missionaries were evidently in a stronger position, able to rely on more open support from Government officials.

So under Campbell and his assistants the Agency became essentially Baptist in outlook. The missionary ideal and ultimate aim of converting Konds to Christianity became a strong part of the officials' personal motivation. Administrators' reluctance to be directly involved in proselytizing is thus at the surface level. Even Macpherson aimed to 'convert' Konds into 'peaceful expectants of justice'. He was clearly delighted to be influencing them towards 'the God of Light', away from the 'evil' Earth Goddess; and like later officials, he supported a school syllabus which openly propagated Christianity through Frye's Gospel texts. Indeed, many administrators saw Christian conversion as the logical sequel to the changes which they were imposing: the civilizing process they began by pacifying the Konds, missionaries were to complete. It was thus in Christian evangelical terms, in the language of Brown's articles and Peggs' *India's cries to British humanity,* that administrators seem to have conceived their role and believed in their own 'mission' of abolishing human sacrifice and bringing Konds into the centralized economic and political system of British rule. Their duty to God and the Government was one.

These close relations between Kond administrators and Baptist missionaries continued in the following years. Goadby formed a close friendship with Captain MacDonald, and was clear about his dependence on the Government to 'open the way' so that he could penetrate 'the blue hills, the great barrier which Nature had upheaved between the plains and Kondistan' (Pearce Carey 1936 p.34). After the Meriah Agency was terminated in 1861, with Konds duly 'pacified', Goadby announced that:

> the way is clear for the heralds of the cross to go up and achieve nobler triumphs for the Prince of Peace. The secular power has nobly given the aid that was necessary, and without which no European could safely have entered the country: upon its retirement it is most fitting that the opportunity should be embraced to attempt the spiritual subjugation of the people. The spread of the Gospel among the Khonds will be the most effectual security against any desire for a recurrence to their former murderous practices, as well as the means of promoting their present and eternal well-being. (*GBMS Report* 1862 p.20)

And if administrators were motivated by missionary ideals, missionaries saw themselves as 'soldiers of Christ'. Such was Goadby's sense of purpose when he embarked for India:

> At his ordination in crowded Woodgate in 1857 his father gave him the charge: "Be strong my son.... When at Waterloo the Imperial Guard was overpowered, and bidden to ask for quarter, they proudly made answer: 'The Imperial Guard do not ask for quarter: they die'. And they fell in their ranks." It was Mutiny-year, and the *Agamemnon*, in which he sailed, was crowded with soldiers. He also meant to be a soldier—but of Christ. "I am in the path of duty," he wrote to his mother from the ship. "Our heavenly father is leading me; do not be afraid." He was the first European to be going to India purposed to give his life for the Konds. (Pearce Carey 1936 p.33)

'Giving his Life for the Konds'

So what did it mean to these men and women to be a missionary, drawing people of other faiths to Christianity? What was this identity based on? Clearly, on following Christ's example and message of love and salvation. But there was also a great emphasis on the idea of sin, especially by Baptists, for whom an 'inner conversion' consisted of the realization of one's sinfulness, followed by a renunciation of sin. The missionary message was thus often aimed at persuading people of their sinfulness and appealing to their fear of damnation. As a result, a dominant theme in missionary discourse is a contrast between their own self-sacrificing Christianity and the sinfulness of various other groups—pagan Konds and Hindus, as well as Christians of other sects.

Thus the missionary outlook tends to exaggerate differences into stereotypes in a way that is extremely dualistic or divisive. Missionaries' stereotype of Konds, like that of Government officials, stresses the ideas of 'savagery', 'superstition' and 'ignorance', but goes further with connotations of 'sin' and a 'fallen' state under the influence of evil.

The idea of self-sacrifice is central to the conceptual framework of mission work; a missionary is, almost by definition, someone who gives, dedicates, consecrates, or sacrifices him- or herself. This is not just a matter of language. It derives from a basic Christian concept of sacrifice: for Christians, Christ's sacrifice, which they celebrate in the Mass and Eucharist, provides the model for their life. The saints, as well as the Protestant martyrs, sacrificed themselves in imitation of Christ's sacrifice; and so did generations of missionaries who died spreading his words, some of them 'martyred' by the pagans they were trying to convert. Self-sacrifice is a persistent theme in the writings of the Baptist Mission to Orissa:

> The Committee received an application from Miss Kirkman, to consecrate herself to the spiritual welfare of the female population of India.... The Committee *unanimously and with much pleasure* accepted Miss Kirkman's offer of herself. Her estimable parents, in a spirit of consecration to the cause of Christ, like that of their beloved daughter, much as they feel the sacrifice, cheerfully resign her.[18]

A martyr complex was expected of these missionaries. The theme of self-sacrifice was certainly based in a high death rate. Four of the first five missionaries who came to Orissa died there; of the first nine, two more had to leave to save their health, and at least three lost their wives there. As for their children, a large proportion died, starting with Peggs' infants:

> PARENTAL affection desires to rescue from oblivion, the names of the following dear children, who, for a short period, solaced the minds of the missionary family in India. They, like Abraham's beloved wife, Sarah, by right of Sepulture, have taken possession of the land of our inheritance in the East. They were born and are buried at Cuttack.

> FRANCES SMITHEE PEGGS, born May 14, 1822, died August 17, 1822.
> ELIZABETH SMITHEE PEGGS, born Sept. 2, 1823, died July 28, 1824.
> MARY SMITHEE PEGGS, born Nov. 25, 1824, died May 14, 1825.
> "*Verily Thou art a God that hidest Thyself.*" Thou destroyest the hope of man; but "Thou doest all things well".... these painful events shall best promote thy purposes of mercy to Orissa. May angels watch the dust of these infants! May myriads of saints slumber with them! And in the morning of the resurrection, may multitudes of Oreah Christians congratulate them on the first fruits to God of the dust of Orissa. (1846 pp.362–3)

All four of the first Baptist missionaries to the Konds also died in Orissa (above p.187). John Orissa Goadby's aunt had been one of the early missionary wives who died there, and throughout his boyhood in Loughborough, where his father was a Baptist minister, the Konds caught his imagination.

> At every missionary meeting in his circle, in every missionary report, in almost every issue of his father's magazine, he was reminded of the woes of Kondistan. (Carey 1936 p.32)

Reporting on one of his first Kond tours Goadby announced 'The path that lies before us has not been trodden by a missionary.... The Gospel day for these wild tribes is dawning.' (*GBMS Report* 1863 pp.25–6) During his tours, 'more than once he had to be rushed down to Russellkonda in a high fever.' (Pearce Carey 1936 p.37) He died in Cuttack helping in relief work during the famine of 1866–8. After his death, it seemed to later missionaries

> incredible in this period that no-one volunteered to be "baptised for the dead", and to give himself in Goadby's stead for the evangelization of the Konds. (Pearce Carey 1936 p.41)

But in 1889 the appeal went out for a Kond Mission that called the next three:

> May the love of Christ constrain some, who read these lines, to say "Here I am send me". (*BMS Report* 1889 pp.27–8)

Thomas Wood died in Udayagiri within weeks of arriving there, expiring 'in Long's arms' in the Magistrate's house. 'To Long the loss was tormenting.... the two seemed made for double harness....' When Long died, two decades later, his tombstone commemorated him as

> pioneer missionary BMS to the Khonds, who for twenty years laboured with unselfish devotion and fervent zeal for their welfare and lived to see the desire of his heart realized in the establishment of the Khond Mission. (Pearce Carey 1936 p.46)

As a writer expressed it in the volume to commemorate the centenary of the BMS, on the self-sacrifice of missionaries in general:

> It all seems so strange. There must be a sacrificial joy.... Their noble self-abandonment....will be held in honour by thousands of churches.... (Myers 1892 pp.18–19)

Five of the first Lutheran missionaries to the Kond area also died in the field (Federation of Lutheran Christians in India, 1931). When Oliver Millman's daughter died, four months old, in 1914, she was buried in

> Russellkonda's little God's acre, already sacred as the resting-place of Wood and Wilkinson and Long, and of many a British soldier who had died of jungle-fever when suppressing the Meriahs.

I found a tiny fragment of her tombstone in 1986 when I visited this graveyard, which is small, tightly-packed, and enclosed by a high wall, but half-ruined.[19]

There was also the isolation and loneliness. In terms of family life, this took a different form from the isolation of administrators, who rarely saw their families. Nearly all male missionaries were married, either immediately before departure or soon after becoming missionaries. The exception was Wilkinson:

> No wife through the years shared his loneliness, nor ministered to his comfort. He had sought a woman's hand, but she was destined for another. So he ploughed his lone furrow. (Pearce Carey 1936 p.47)

The three missionaries whose wives died in the early years of the Orissa Mission all remarried the following year. Hasty remarriage is a recurring pattern in these missionaries' lives, as it was evidently considered important for the men to be married. Women played a significant part in mission work: in fact, in the duration of the Kond Mission from 1908 to 1973, there were twice as many women as men. Virtually all the men were married, but half of the women remained single. The missionaries' sacrifice in their personal life was therefore significantly different from that of Government officials. It consisted of a high rate of female celibacy, a high mortality for missionary wives and children as well as men, and also a social isolation greater in some ways than that of the administrators. As a result, missionaries' bungalows and routines were comforting oases of European culture, more or less divorced from the native culture that surrounded them.

In later times, children who survived infancy were sent away to England, where they grew up away from their parents. A touching letter from Mrs Evans, on the point of her final departure from India, illustrates this, and gives a sense of life on a Mission station, where a few Europeans formed a closed-in, isolated community of set routines:

> We are expecting Mr Wakelin (taking over from us) and leave two weeks later. I do hope we do not all strike him as "dead old" and "quite impossible". We are used to each other now, more or less, but you never know how a youngster will look on us!! For his sake I hope he finds both staff and country fairly congenial, and that he soon makes friends with the Konds.... The Evangelist and a number of the children from Russelkonda have just been in and had tea with us. They pay a visit about once in five years.... It will be good to see Alex again, though the change in her is going to be rather a shock, especially to her Father. It doesn't matter how much one tries to prepare oneself, the actual reality, and the poignancy of all the years one has missed that comes when one sees a child is like a blow. But we are very keen to see her all the same.[20]

Baptist training colleges such as Harley and Regent's Park inculcated a very different outlook from administrators' education. Missionaries based their life on an intense 'inner conversion', publicly 'confessed'. Just before departure, a missionary went through an emotional 'ordination' that formed one of the most important rituals in their lives. As Peggs described the ordination in 1838 of one of the first missionaries to go to Orissa:

> Mr Wilkinson's account of his religious history, excited much deep feeling throughout a crowded and numerous congregation. His conversion from sin and infidelity was connected with circumstances of a singular kind, and strikingly displayed the power of divine grace.[21]

This kind of personal 'confession of sin' and declaration of faith were taken as evidence of an inner salvation and missionary calling. Missionary language is therefore less intellectual, and much more sentimental and emotional, seeking continually to stir up the reader's emotions of pity, admiration or horror:

> Long bathed himself in the biographies of immortal pioneers, and felt himself "a pigmy, a snail, a hanger-on in comparison with the Judsons, and a mere shadow alongside of Paton, the immovable oak". (Pearce Carey 1936 p.44)

This image of heroic self-abasement is a recurring figure in descriptions of missionary identity. It is decidedly passive by contrast to the vigour and vividness in many administrators' writings; probably because suffering in itself has a strong positive value for missionaries. There is none of the delight in knowledge about India or appreciation of local culture that characterizes some administrators' writings, such as Macpherson's.

In a way, missionaries lived closer to 'the natives' than Government officials did. In another way, they were more completely closed to the possibility of learning from them. This shows particularly clearly in accounts of Long's hero, Adinoram Judson, an American Baptist who went to Burma as a pioneer missionary in 1813. For the first three years, he lived there alone with his wife, Ann, enduring great hardships, and descibing Burmese culture in the most negative possible terms. In Ann Judson's words,

> We now see a whole populous empire....sunk in the grossest idolatry; given up to following the wicked inclinations of their depraved hearts, entirely destitute of any real principle, without the least spark of any true benevolence. (quoted in Trager 1966 p.82)

In other words, of the Judsons' discourse,

> The total effect is a scarcely relieved, most unflattering portrait of the Burmese, a prime example of nineteenth century national and racial stereotype. (ibid. p.81)

Judson disapproved of a missionary who had come on a temporary basis:

> How can we, who are devoted for life, cordially take to our hearts and councils one who is a mere hireling?.... Missionaries need more trials instead of less.... (ibid. p.51)

Later, when a colleague died on tour he made it into a heroic event:

> He fell gloriously at the head of his troops, in the arms of victory; 38 wild Karens having been brought into the camp of King Jesus.... Such a death, next to that of martyrdom, must be glorious in the eyes of heaven. (ibid. p.52)

The missionaries' sufferings were real enough, and their dedication and sacrifice sincere, but also showed an immensely arrogant attitude. Often it seems that missionaries sought suffering, masochistically. And it is largely because they were not open to learning from natives and sharing with them that they experienced their life abroad as hardship at all: they were not prepared to adapt to the native lifestyle, in matters of housing, clothing, food or medicine that suited the local scene, but clung to a cocoon of Western ways, and suffered accordingly, intent on converting the natives instead of learning from them. As a missionary historian rationalizes these missionaries' obsession with their suffering and negativity about the Burmese:

> these men and women who served in Burma had to endure numerous and unending trials and discouragements. It is impossible to understand the degree of their dedication and the extent of their sacrifice unless some small part of the story of their struggle and suffering entailed in the missionary enterprise is explained.... Their portrayal of Burma and the Burmese therefore reflects.... their many problems of adjustment in what must have been for them a very strange land indeed.... In physical terms, their deep frustrations produced a consequent verbal aggression against the unresponsive Burmese.... Major catastrophies and minor irritations were borne year after year with incredible fortitude and devotion to their chosen vocation. As Ann Judson wrote immediately on arrival, "it was in our hearts to live and die with the Burmese".... The early missionaries to Burma literally committed themselves to the far-off task for life. (Helen Trager 1966 p.31)

Konds, like the Burmese, were the 'chosen field' for missionaries who had 'dedicated their lives for saving them' yet were quite closed to a reciprocal relationship with them. Konds did not actually kill any of the missionaries who came to their land, but nor did they ask them to come. Nevertheless, missionaries who died there had the status of martyrs, and their self-sacrifice imposed an unasked-for debt. Peggs apparently saw his dead children as 'pledges', that 'took possession of' Orissa: a missionary sacrifice that put Orissa into their debt (above p.200–1). Pearce Carey wrote of Arthur Long's death in 1909, 'The Konds will always be in his deep debt for pre-eminent service.' Missionaries' 'altruistic' sufferings give them an authority difficult to question. Their sacrifice assumes the figure of a gift that needs repaying. In other words, they were setting up a system of authority based on 'power that sacrifices itself'. Foucault's insight about the Christian origin of modern forms of power is particularly revealing in a missionary setting.

This is highlighted by the way missionaries contrast themselves with Konds. Of John Orissa Goadby,

> He must ever be remembered as the *first apostle of Kondistan.* "He delighted to penetrate into the solitary places of the Kond hill tracts, and there, amidst the dirt, the drunkenness and destitution of the people, to do what lay in his power for their welfare, and for the softening and enlightening of their savage natures." (Pearce Carey 1936 p.40, quoting Dr David Smith, Gov. Sanitary Commissioner)

Goadby's wife 'was spared. She also had played her part as a sacrificial pioneer.' Missionaries sacrificed themselves for Konds they saw as savage, depraved, and usually unappreciative. By doing this, and preserving the memory of each other's sacrifice, they were staking a claim, which won them support from Government officials, as well as from parishes in Britain; and perhaps the eternal gratitude of future generations of Indian converts.

The positive features of Christianity are clear, but evangelical Christianity often has the appearance of a religion of intolerance and hypocritical self-righteousness, that could not be further removed from Christ's teaching. The idea that people are either to be saved or damned and that only true followers of Christ can be saved, has led many Christians to divide people into 'good' and 'bad', and to become completely closed to other spiritual traditions. This is particularly true for missionaries.

Missionary Dualism

A contrast between how missionaries saw themselves and how they saw those they came to convert is thus at the basis of their thinking. If they idealized their own sufferings and benevolence, their image of various groups of 'others' is basically a negative stereotype. This dualistic outlook is closely related to the theme of self-sacrifice: missionaries 'gave their lives' to save 'depraved' Burmese and 'savage', 'ignorant' Konds.

A martyrdom complex is intrinsic to much of Christianity. Both Baptists and Catholics, much as they differ in other ways, have it in high degree. Tracing it back to early Christianity, one can discern a marked difference on this matter between the sect in Rome that became the established Church and what came to be known as the Gnostic Church. Apart from many other differences in doctrine and practice that were declared heretical, such as reincarnation and women priests, many of the Gnostics lacked this martyr-impulse. When the Roman authorities made Christianity illegal, provincial governors interrogated suspected Christians and asked them to dishonour Christian symbols and make obeisance to the emperor. Christians of the established Church made a point of openly confessing their faith, and taking the consequences that followed of torture and execution in the arena. Gnostics were willing to conceal their faith in order to survive. As a result mainstream Christians turned their wrath on the Gnostics, and when they came to power, hounded them out of existence (Pagels 1979). This illustrates how a martyrdom complex came to dominate a large section of Christianity, and gave rise to a deep intolerance for people who do not believe in this sort of self-sacrifice.

The martyrdom of the Catholic saints, many of them courting death at the hands of the Roman authorities, is well known. As for the Baptists, persecution by Catholics figures large in the early history of their Church. Baptists are one of the main Dissenting or Non-Conformist sects of Christianity that developed in Britain in the 17th–18th century, along with the Congregationalists, Presbyterians, United Reformed Church, Quakers, and later the Methodists. The distinctive feature of Baptists was their refusal to baptize infants: they baptized adults only, and insisted someone could only be baptized after going through a personal inner conversion. The baptism itself was by full immersion, not sprinkling. In this and other matters they claimed to represent the authentic tradition of Christianity, and an immediate spiritual ancestry that included the radicals of the Reformation who had been burnt as heretics and 'protestants', in particular the Anabaptists, who were persecuted especially viciously.[22] In the 1520s Zwingli's regime in Zurich issued edicts to enforce the baptism of children and make adult baptism a capital offence. The first victim was a minister who was executed by drowning for disobeying this. In Britain several Baptists were executed for treason during the reigns of Charles II and James II, as members of the other Non-Conformist sects were also, but Baptists were especially targeted as they were considered particularly radical.

At first Baptists were divided into Particular or Calvinistic Baptists and General Baptists. Particular Baptists, who were much more numerous, believed that 'Christ died only for the elect', whom they believed they represented, while the vast majority of mankind was predestined to damnation. General Baptists on the other hand believed that 'Christ died for the salvation of every man'. In the 18th century General Baptists were discredited by the 'taint of socinianism' or unitarianism—'the heretical doctrine of Christ's humanity'—until a 'New Connexion of General

Baptists' was formed in 1770, which gave rise, within fifty years, to the Orissa Mission.

Baptists therefore regarded their former persecutor, the Roman Catholic Church, as their main enemy. They carried this 'almost innate prejudice against Catholics' with them to the field.[23] In fact, Baptist missionaries' hostility to Catholics and to Hindus was almost the same: both they saw as idolaters, hardened against receiving the truth, who should be combated by propaganda, 'deluging benighted lands' with printed books and pamphlets. The BMS maintained a small Mission in Rome itself, to combat the Catholic 'contagion' at its source. In Orissa, the Baptists were shocked to discover that Catholic converts called prayers *jop*, the commandments *mantras*, worship *puja*, and festivals *jatra*. Their polemic against Catholics fastened on this assimilation to Hindu custom and language, attacking the tolerance which had been Catholic missionary policy since Francis Xavier, the first Jesuit missionary in India and China. Protestants also claimed Catholic conversion was superficial, because it was not preceded by thorough instruction and exams. The number of Catholic converts was often much greater, because they were baptized without being made to undergo a long, strict education in Christian doctrine.[24] In the Kond field too, Baptist missionaries called their Catholic rivals 'sheepstealers' because they asked a much less radical change of Kond converts.

> A confession of faith which at first demanded fewer changes from the old life and its ways—especially regarding liquor-drinking—as well as their more colourful form of worship, proved attractive not only to non-Christians, but to Protestants smarting under Church discipline for the most common reasons of drink or adultery. (Boal 1982 p.187)

Baptist missionaries who passed through Sorada on one of their tours, avoided contact with the Catholic missionaries who had their headquarters there, but interviewed their servants, and examined their buildings.

> The so-called cathedral is a very plain structure, and would not contain more than 300 people; and the success of the priests is, to say the least, of a very questionable character.... We were painfully struck with the fact that Popery here had assimilated itself as much as possible to heathenism.... What an accursed thing Popery is! In Christian lands it is bad enough, but in the lands of the heathen it is ten times worse; and while we earnestly seek the downfall of idolatry, we ought devoutly to pray that this mystery of iniquity may come

> to an end. May the Lord consume it with the spirit of his wrath, and destroy it with the brightness of his coming. (*GBMS Report* 1862 pp.14–15)

At first, the Baptist Mission to Orissa was aimed at Hindus—Konds became the prime focus much later—and the Baptist missionaries who came to Orissa were already deeply prejudiced against Hinduism from the propaganda they had been exposed to throughout their training, for Baptist literature went even further than that of other Protestants, which was often incredibly biased:

> Of all the systems of false religion ever fabricated by the perverse ingenuity of fallen man, Hinduism is surely the most stupendous.[25]

When Peggs and Bampton chose Orissa, they saw themselves as attacking Hinduism at its heart, since Jagannath's temple in Puri is one of the most important Hindu ritual centres. Its annual 'car festival' drew (and still draws) tens of thousands of pilgrims. A few, as an act of extreme self-sacrifice, threw themselves under the wheels of Jagannath's enormous 'chariot' (whence the modern concept of 'juggernauts' as huge lorries, heedless of what lies in their path, that came to the English language through this missionary propaganda). Peggs saw his Orissa Mission as

> destined, it is humbly trusted, to undermine the idolatry of Juggernaut and to blot out his atrocities for ever. (1846 p.147)

Bampton and later missionaries conducted a 'sacred warfare' in Puri:

> At the great festival in 1838, no less than *seven* brethren were employed in diffusing the gospel light among the myriads of benighted pilgrims. (ibid. p.266)

The festival was a key focus of missionary polemic in the 19th century. The EIC made money out of it through a tax on pilgrims. Missionaries called the Government 'the wet-nurse of Jagannath' for tolerating the festival at all.[26] The tirade against this form of Hindu self-sacrifice is a significant parallel to that against Kond human sacrifice. The two together made Orissa an infamous province in missionary eyes:

> "One dark night of sin and sorrow, cruelty and misery, overspread the land. Idolatry and vileness everywhere met the eye, assailed the ear, and grieved the heart. The whole land was emphatically the region and shadow of death."[27]

In actions, as in words, the missionaries showed little respect for Hindu custom. William Bailey, on the tour that went through Sorada, entered a temple without taking his shoes off. When the priests asked him to do so,

> I quietly told them that sahibs did not pander to such prejudices, and retained my seat. (*GBMS Report* 1862 p.12)

Missionaries on tour often visited *rajahs* to try and convert them. Those who showed a diplomatic interest were judged enlightened. Those who would not play the game, came in for severe criticism. On a tour in Dhenkanal,

> the Mudpore Raja's residence was visited: we found the Raja at home, and had an opportunity of making known to him the claims of God, of righteousness, temperance, and judgement to come. The behaviour of the Raja was very unbecoming; he displayed a lamentable amount of ignorance, superstition and levity. In his estimation, the evil doings of the gods constituted their chief glory. A large festival was being held near his residence. He was opposed to our speaking to the people: heedless of his wish to the contrary, we went among them, and laboured in making known the truth and circulating tracts as long as our strength would permit. (*BMS Report* 1873 p.14)

In their negative stereotypes of Hinduism, which strangely included the idea that Hindu women were all promiscuous, Baptists were in general much harsher critics than Anglicans or Catholics, and showed none of the appreciative interest in India that so many other Europeans did. Their closest allies were utilitarians, who worked in a secular frame of reference, such as James Mill, whose *History of British India* poured scorn on the depth of Hindu religion and philosophy revealed by William James' researches.

Missionaries often contrasted tribals with Hindus, and considered them more open to conversion. This is a persistent theme, starting with Bishop Heber in the 1800s.[28] The same contrast is evident in the writings of the first Baptist missionaries in Burma, who found Buddhists difficult to convert since they already had an elaborate religion. Karen tribals were considered much more amenable, on the theory that they lived in a 'religious vacuum'.

> So the Sandwich Islander, so the Karen receives the truth, the benefits of a written language, and instructions in books, and the elevation that follows, as favours conferred; and as there are no stains of ancient superstitions, they are better Christians than converts from heathenism. When I say no stains, of course comparatively is meant. (A female missionary quoted in Trager 1966 p.84)

The Konds too were at first thought of as ripe material for conversion on the grounds that they were 'clean slates', having almost no religion of their own. Goadby considered them 'not as keen as the Red Karens of Burma' to receive Christian truths, although in a similar state of 'savagery', 'ignorance' and habitual drunkenness:

> The Kond is grossly ignorant and his mind enveloped in the thickest darkness. Yet there are rays of light which pierce that darkness, and reveal a pathway to his understanding, by which medium his heart may be impressed.... The Meriah rite, though nothing less than murder, and inhuman in its details, embodies his mysterious faith in the virtue of the most precious of oblations, human blood, and shows his twilight gropings for that great 'Salvation purchased by the sacrifice of Jesus.'....
>
> The heart that beats within a Kond is dark and ignorant, a very wilderness like the trackless waste in which he hunts his game. In the latter the rankest vegetation grows up unobstructed; so in the former the lowest passions, with no purer thought to check them, are free from all restraint. This moral jungle must be levelled, the soil prepared to receive the seed, and the early and latter rains must fall thereon. (*GBMS Report* 1863 p.26)

The theory here is that Kond religion consists of ignorance and the free expression of savage passions. The metaphors are of combating darkness and clearing the jungle, to 'elevate the Kond' by impressing his heart, subjugating his spirit, or conquering his mind: a set of images and stock phrases that recur in missionary writings.

The use of singular instead of plural in these passages is significant. It isolates the individual, just as in practice missionaries isolated individuals through teaching and conversion. 'The Kond' is a hapless, demonstrably ignorant specimen of scientific study and missionary persuasion. Perceived as isolated individuals, Konds lost their threatening image as a mutually supportive group, who confronted missionaries with complete confidence in their alien culture.

Like administrators, missionaries saw Kond society in terms of wildness, disorder and anarchy. For Goadby, the evils in their society were due to their having lived 'age on age in savage freedom' (*GBMS Report* 1863 p.25). His later analysis was even bleaker:

> The gross ignorance of the people which more intercourse with them has revealed, has at times, I must confess, saddened and depressed my spirits. Darkness indeed "covers the land, and grossest darkness the minds of the people". (*GBMS Report* 1865 p.20)

On the whole, missionaries referred to Kond religion as 'animism', although Goadby asserted that 'Among the lowest Konds pantheism more or less prevails' (*GBMS Report* 1863 p.27). They saw Konds as fundamentally ignorant—of 'medical facts' as well as of Christian truths. Yet the early missionaries, as these comments reveal, were remarkably ignorant of Kond religion, speaking of it in terms of 'demon worship', and evil human passions given free rein. The first engraving of human sacrifice, in Peggs' *History of the Orissa Mission*, is entitled 'female infanticide in Goomsur', and evidently conflates the quite separate customs of human sacrifice and female infanticide. It shows Konds as archetypal savages, dancing with knives around a child tied to a stake. After Goadby's time, 'animism' became more respectable among missionaries as an object of ethnographic study. Missionary ethnography has tended to fasten on beliefs and doctrines, as if these were standardized and clear-cut, and represented the heart of tribal religions, in the same way that the 'Credo' is fundamental to Christianity. For instance, Schulze opens his book on Kuvi Kond religion (1912) with an amazingly simplistic statement of 'fact':

> The Kond believes in the existence of one good God and many evil spirits.

On the positive side, if Konds were simply 'ignorant', this gave great potential for converting them. And the missionary concept of 'pagan but possible to save' (Fabian 1983) is closely related to the administrators' concept of 'primitive, but with potential for development'. For the idea of salvation was gradually becoming secularized in the 18th and 19th centuries into the idea of saving backward peoples materially, in terms of economic, educational or medical advancement and welfare. But underlying both concepts is the idea of an essential primitiveness: the evolutionist paradigm.

On the surface, this seems to conflict with Alexander Duff's view of Konds as having 'degenerated' from some pristine state. He looks on them not as primitive or unevolved, but as degraded—in a state of regression:

> The readers of the [*Calcutta Christian Observer*] do not require to be told at any length what the Bible account of this subject is. A few sentences may be sufficient to remind them. Originally created holy and innocent, just and right—
>
> "Sufficient to have stood, though free to fall,"—
>
> Man abused his freedom,—broke the command,—incurred the threatened penalty,—contracted a sense of guilt which speedily issued in confirmed alienation from the true and living God, and a consequent fabrication of idol-deities instead,—and entailed on himself, considered individually, and nationally, a *tendency* to decay, degeneracy, dissolution and death, through

> every department of his physical, intellectual, moral and religious, being.... In this view of the subject, the present condition of the Khonds may be regarded as *somewhat more than midway down* from the lofty tableland of Noahchic civilisation to the dead level of savage barbarism. (Duff 1842 p.585)

Yet missionaries reconciled this 'degenerationist' view with the evolutionism of all 19th century social scientists, and adopted the evolutionist view wholeheartedly themselves, since their conversion of pagans accompanied those pagans' material advancement as they were brought under British rule.

According to Barbara Boal (1982 pp.79–81), one of the key debates in missionary theology at this time was between 'monogenists' and 'polygenists'. Polygenists believed in the separate origin of the world's religions. Monogenists believed in a single origin, and that most religions were debased forms of the original, true religion, yet contained some survivals from it. This was Alexander Duff's view of the Konds, as well as that of his hero, Macpherson. It was the view of many Baptists too, such as Goadby, when he writes of 'the Khond', that 'He has religious legends which have become fainter and fainter by transfusion through successive generations, but are not utterly devoid of truth.' (*GBMS Report* 1863 p.27) This relatively generous monogenist theory lost ground to the polygenist view in the later 19th century, which is apparently why missionaries neglected the Konds in this period. The polygenist theory was clearly a parallel in theology to the growth of racism as a theory favoured by a large proportion of social scientists as well as medics and biologists at this time: the theory that the different races of mankind were fixed, different in origin, and different in intellectual potential, and represented a hierarchy with whites at the top and negroes at the bottom. Racism and polygenism were linked through the idea (popular e.g. in the southern states of America) that negroes were descendants of Cain, blackened by his crime, and ordained by God to labour for whites.

Christian thinkers have often compared 'backward races' with children who have not yet evolved into adulthood. The missionary view of tribals tends to stress both evil and childlike innocence more than the administrator view, which polarizes around the themes of lawlessness and bravery, or savagery and nobility. Missionaries perceived a tribal as 'half-devil and half-child' (Kipling's phrase). They compared tribals to children in their concern for the present rather than the future, presumably because Christian theory tends to value an afterlife above this life and the present moment, just as modern economic theory evaluates a situation in terms of future profit and growth.

> Interest in the present rather than the future is paramount among the traditionally-minded. (Boal 1973 p.110)

Missionaries tended to focus their efforts on children, who could be most easily influenced, as with the *meriah* children. They learnt to keep their distance from unconverted Kond elders, who were not generally appreciative of their efforts. At least one elder spoke his mind to Goadby on a preaching tour:

> Once a village headman was roughly abusive, blaming the Christian religion for the suppression of the Meriahs, and this for the cholera, which had smitten his district. (Pearce Carey 1936 p.38)

Sometimes Goadby behaved more informally, as he describes during the evenings on his tour of 1864–5.

> Having dined, I took my wicker stool, and joined the group sitting around the fire, and on these occasions I had some of the most pleasing and interesting opportunities for conversation enjoyed during the entire tour. (*GBMS Report* 1865 p.24)

But this informal contact, on an equal basis, was rare. In general, missionaries' behaviour involved keeping a great social distance from local people. They certainly behaved like *sahebs*, with a strong element of hierarchy, since they employed a large range of coolies, cooks, and personal servants, and brought in a whole new range of material goods, from tents and chairs to solar topis and forks, and eventually bungalows and cars. We can see this in photographs of missionaries on tour. In one of 1907 they recline in deck chairs at table, while their servant stands erect behind them. The way they organized space and the material objects they used all stressed missionaries' separateness from the Konds they lived among, and implied the 'superiority' of their culture.

This is illustrated by the way that German Lutheran missionaries talked to Konds, as shown by Schulze's *Kuvi-Kond vocabulary* (1913 pp.26–30), which is laid out virtually as a Kuvi phrasebook for missionaries:

> Build a basin for water.
> Bring me nails.
> Make me a fan.
> Where is the key for the door?

> It is good to wear badices [*sic* i.e. bodices, for women].
> Do not buy so many jewels.
> Take my trousers away.
> Put your belt on.
> You must put a cap on.
> A sluggard is a sinner.
> I never drink toddy.

The missionaries' heavy-handed morality is clear from this (on 'decent clothing', alcohol etc.), as well as the way they 'talked down' to Konds and ordered them around like servants ('Take my trousers away', 'You must wear a cap'), and the importance they attached to introducing items of Western material culture—from washbasins, nails, fans and keys to bodices, trousers, belts and caps—which they surrounded themselves with and propagated along with their religion.

Behind the sense of brotherhood which they projected, missionaries thus operated with considerable hierarchy. This was so even among themselves. The BMS leadership formed a clique, presenting a united 'front' that was often a considerable distortion of actual circumstances. One revealing inside view comes from Alexander Innes, a missionary who left the BMS, after being posted to the Cameroons in the company of a famous but brutal and self-seeking missionary called Alfred Saker, who embezzled funds.

> The Baptist Society have been very unfortunate in their leaders; as a rule they have been composed of men who have no regard for the truth .... They have been a despotic body from the days of William Carey to the present time.... Of recent years they have had Edward Bean Underhill as Pope.
>
> ....the Baptist clergy....never acknowledged William Carey, he not being a college-trained minister, but a shoemaker....in 1816 'the committee' wrote to William Carey, stating that he must now consider himself the servant of the London committee.... All these facts are kept out of sight in the Centenary volume.[29]

Innes' book is an attack on a centenary volume for the BMS written by Revd J.B. Myers, who was the secretary (1879–1912) immediately after Underhill (1849–79). Innes describes how the Central Committee refused to listen to his own and others' complaints about Saker, and tried to stop him speaking out. As he says, Myers' book as well as the BMS Reports gloss over every conflict, presenting a sentimental, idealized picture of missionary life. Missionaries emphasized the idea that they were 'brethren', but were run by a clique who sent orders from London; women had an important, but strictly subordinate role; and the same is true of Indians employed as catechists and evangelists.

The contrast missionaries drew between themselves and people of other faiths, whom they tended to stereotype, is one symptom of the dualism that pervades their thought. Their conceptual world was dualistic to its core. This dualism was the filter through which they perceived the Konds and their culture—as well as everything else. We can schematize some of their key conceptual oppositions, and the way these connect with each other, as follows:

Heathen, pagan, Hindu, animism, idolatry, demon-worship, spiritism	Christian, Christianity
Roman Catholicism, Popery	Protestant, Baptist
Satan, demon, evil spirit	God, Jesus
Evil, sin	Goodness
Hell, damnation	Heaven, salvation
Darkness	Light
Savage, warlike, bloodthirsty, cruel, barbaric	Peace, mercy, pity
Human sacrifice and female infanticide	Self-sacrifice, martyrdom
Rituals as orgies	Restrained rituals
Uncontrolled human passions	Self-discipline
(Religion of) Fear	(Religion of) Love, Peace
Lazy, indolence	Hard-working, labour
Addicted to drink	Sober
Naked	Well-dressed
Promiscuity, infidelity	Faithful, chaste
Independent, self sufficient wild, uncivilized	Obedient, civilized
Ignorant, uneducated, preliterate	Educated, enlightened
Ignorance, superstition	Truth, knowledge, science, facts

Anthropologists have studied the systems of complementary opposition that characterize tribal as well as ancient societies, since Hertz' essay, 'The pre-eminence of the right hand: a study in religious polarity' (1909, in Needham 1973). Missionary dualism is both more abstract and more total than the systems of dual classification that form the basis of most other cultures' value systems. For its premise is a division of the world according to the principles of Good and Evil: a concept essentially foreign to tribal religions, which tend to see good and bad as opposites that need each other, similar to darkness and light, or two branches of a single tree (above p.124).

Missionary dualism is similar to administrators' conceptual framework, and obviously influenced it. Administrators do not actually describe Konds as 'sinful', but their view of them and their *meriah* sacrifice in terms of bloodthirsty superstitions often implies the concept of sin. 'Original sin' was among the most basic ideas that motivated the missionaries: if there was no hell to save the Konds from, there would be no need to convert them. They thus approached Konds with the assumption that they were sinners, and this 'fact' was the first thing they tried to teach them. 'Original sin' is a universalizing theory that applies to all human souls, ever since 'the Fall'; and from the missionary viewpoint, it amply justified the Government's conquest of the Konds that had allowed them to come and work for Konds' salvation.

One set of keywords describes how missionaries modelled their behaviour to Konds on Jesus' and God's behaviour towards mankind:

Preach, teach, heal
Save, salvation, confer benefits, benevolence, welfare
Self-sacrifice, dedication, labour of love, martyr
Punish, forbid, suppress, spiritual subjugation, discipline

Another set of words was used for Konds who came under missionary influence—words that were antithetical to the stock phrases used for describing unconverted Konds:

Anxious, afraid for their souls
Obedient, humble, with the spirit of martyrs
Literate, educated, hard-working, sober
Hating superstition and idolatry.

In the section on religion in Schulze's *Vocabulary* (1913 pp.66–8), a series of phrases is listed which illustrates missionaries' preaching discourse, and the simplistic dualism they offered the Konds:

In each church is an altar.
This man is excommunicated.
God is holy.
God knows all things.
God is everywhere.
Wherever you are he sees you.
God made everything.
We cannot see God.

We are sinners.
We shall not sin.
Sinners shall be punished.
Idol worship is stupiditiness [*sic*].
Do not make an image of God when you are believing in him.
Do not worship idols.
Jesus Christ is our saviour.
Repent your sins.
We pray to God.
Kneel down before God.
Pray evening and morning.
Our soul never dies.
Virtue is better than vice.
Remember your death.
After death is heaven or hell.
Bible is God's word.
I believe in Jesus.
Do not believe spectres [*sic*].

The vision of life on offer is a frightening, black and white affair: Konds must be shown that they are sinners, under threat of eternal damnation, from which their own gods cannot save them, since 'Idol worship is stupiditiness'! An intensely dualistic view of the world underlies nearly all the missionary quotations and behaviour cited in this chapter. As any reading about Missions elsewhere reveals, it is a view that has been propagated extremely widely.

School and Hospital: Diffusing Christian Knowledge

Schools and hospitals were central to the way missionaries established a hold over tribes such as the Konds. These seemingly secular institutions won missionaries great support from the Government, as well as from churchgoers back at home. They embodied a secular idea of 'saving' and 'conferring benefits' by helping natives to 'advance' at a material level, but also incorporated Christ's role as a teacher and healer. Unlike preaching, educational and health work are widely considered to be disinterested and unquestionably beneficial. They are also more effective than straightforward preaching in beginning the process of 'conquering minds'. To people that have never encountered them before, schools and hospitals represent novel, mysterious forms of authority and power.

Schools supposedly broaden children's horizons, opening their minds to knowledge of the world and rational thinking. Yet the essence of the school system which missionaries established seems to have been to teach 'facts' that invalidated Kond knowledge: for missionaries perhaps there could be no such thing, and it was self-evident that Konds who could not read or write were ignorant. For they assumed that Europeans' Christian or scientific knowledge and rational, 'enlightened' attitudes were superior in some absolute sense to Konds' 'superstition of ages'. Science therefore complemented Christian doctrine, in the minds of missionaries and Government officials alike. It was the secular counterpart of specifically religious teaching, and the proof of the superiority of European forms of understanding. From the 1830s, when Macaulay wrote his famous Minute on education in India, missionaries allied themselves with Government plans for education, in the belief that Western science would undermine pagan beliefs. In a familiar metaphor, missionaries believed that 'Western science would undermine Hindu superstition, clear the jungle, and produce an open field for the proclamation of the gospel.'(Neill 1966 p.106)

So schools were not just a secular addition to Mission work: they were central to it, and it seems that the fundamental aim of Mission schools was to undermine traditional beliefs and inculcate a reformed pattern of behaviour and attitudes, preparing the ground for conversion, and creating a missionized elite among the population, who would see the world as missionaries wanted them to see it, separated from their fellows by many symbols. This small, school-educated elite provided a way into the culture for the spread of Christianity.

The first Konds under missionary influence were the *meriah* children sent to the orphanages from 1836. The idea was to use Mission-educated *meriah* converts as the first evangelists to the Konds, with a kind of poetic justice (e.g. above p.192). Frye and MacViccar used them as teachers in the first Kond schools they set up in the 1850s; Goadby was accompanied on tour by one, who read Frye's Kui translations of Christian texts to assembled Kond villagers. Goadby was keen to establish schools in the vicinity of Kond villages.

> They would not only give the missionary increased influence over the parents of the children, but over the people generally.[30]

He was unwilling to send Kond children to Mission schools in Berhampur since so many of the *meriahs* had died in the orphanages—'they die so quickly in the plains' (*GBMS Report* 1866 p.17). But he did establish a school in Russellkonda which several Kond children attended. Wilkinson did some school teaching in the 1890s, and printed some new textbooks in Kui.

A more systematic phase was initiated by Oliver Millman, whom the BMS sent to Udayagiri in 1908 with explicit instructions to establish Kond schools. He did this quickly and influentially. In 1911 there were nine teachers there, with 25 Konds training to be teachers at a Government training college in Phulbani; and the first permanent school buildings were going up:

> Beautiful is the situation of our new houses. They may be seen from every point of a broad valley.... To us these buildings mean the permanent occupation of the Khond Hills. To the people also they have the same meaning, for when they see the brick walls they say, "Aba has come to stay among us." (Millman, in *BMS Report* 1911 p.81)

In 1912, two new Mission houses were

> an object of the greatest wonder to the hill tribesmen, who come from near and far to see them. (*BMS Report* 1912 p.92)

From this year, Millman edited a new series of textbooks in Kui, using the Roman instead of the Oriya script, which Frye and Wilkinson had used—an innovation that seems almost designed to accentuate the separateness of Konds they educated from the Oriya culture that surrounded them. But as Millman said:

> The great difference between the Mission School and the (Government schools) is that the children in the Mission School are instructed in their own tongue. (*BMS Report* 1914 p.125)

The Bengal Government was following his lead though, having just sanctioned the use of three of his Kui readers (two of them arithmetic books), and the Madras Government was starting to recruit Konds as teachers. His school had a Government grant-in-aid of Rupees 300/-. In 1915 a boarding school was going up, and the Mission school was the only school in Phulbani District teaching to the 5th standard. By 1917 all 70 Government schools in the District had adopted his principles, and some of his pupils had gone on to Government high schools. Government schools, such as those started in the 1850s, were not popular (above p.183), but according to Millman, his own were:

> Government officials say the Khonds do not want schools, yet week after week we have requests from distant villages for teachers to be sent out to them. (*BMS Report* 1910 p.64)

Missionaries were candid, at first, about using schools as a means towards conversion. Amos Sutton wrote of the orphan school in Cuttack, just before the first batch of *meriah* children was sent there in 1837: 'Of course, the Bible and elementary religious books are used in this school, in addition to the usual branches of a native education.' (*CCO* p.250) Similarly, the *GBMS Report* for 1860 declares on the subject of the girls' asylum in Berhampur: 'But whilst endeavouring to expand their minds by the communication of secular knowledge, prominence has been given to that by which faith shall make them wise unto salvation.' (p.30) At the LMS orphan school in Berhampur, 'The orphans enter school at 6, breakfast at 10, and are employed in a workshop till 4pm.... At sunset prayers and a sermon....conclude the day.' (*CCO* 1838 p.678) Millman's school does not sound very different:

> our schools are the only Protestant schools in the district. Every morning they are opening with prayer, singing, and a Bible lesson. Such influence is telling in a remarkable way, and will tell in future still more. (*BMS Report* 1914 p.126)

The school day began with a singing of hymns in Kui, which Mrs Grimes taught:

> Her singing to the people in their own language has been an attraction, as well as a source of wonder, especially to the women and girls. (*BMS Report* 1912)

At one level, what missionaries taught in their schools was 'the three Rs'—Reading, wRiting and aRithmetic: the fundamentals of European knowledge. Textbooks included works on maths, astronomy, natural history and history (e.g. one called *Daybreak in Britain*). But more than half the titles are of Christian tracts and translations. Textbooks in Kui started with Frye's translation of the story of Joseph and a Psalm (1851), and continued with Wilkinson's *Gospel of Mark* (1893), Long's *Life of Christ* (1907), Hebelet's *Way of Salvation* and *Exodus* 1–20, Millman's *Gospel of John* (1916) and *Acts of the Apostles*; as well as hymn books, catechisms (1912 & 1925), and Kui primers and readers, whose passages for reading practice were mainly from Christian texts.[31]

So when Konds' language was 'reduced to writing', missionaries made sure its first texts were Christian texts. The same has happened with the vast majority of tribal languages in the world. The avowed aim of modern evangelical or fundamentalist mission societies such as the Wycliffe Bible translators (Summer Institute of Linguistics) and the New Tribes Mission is to translate the Gospels into every extant language, 'reaching new tribes until we've reached the last tribe.'(Hvalkof and Aaby 1981)

Missionaries are therefore very often linguists, writing some of the first grammars of tribal languages. They have often complained at a lack of abstract nouns in these tongues (as Government linguists did also, below p.257), which is problematic for introducing Christian concepts. Schulze and Winfield published grammars and vocabularies of Kuvi and Kui (1911/1913 and 1928/1929 respectively) which set out the language on the model of Latin grammars. Although Schulze calls Kui and Kuvi two dialects of 'a very fine language' (1911 p.8), he takes a dim view of Kond mentality, as well as Konds' hold on their own grammar!

> Most of the Kuvis are not talking grammatically.... The Kuvi-Konds as a whole appear to be somewhat stupid. (1913, preface)

Winfield describes Kui as having 'a power of expression that is terse, vivid and adequate for mundane affairs, but poor for philosophy', because of this paucity of abstract nouns. Barbara Boal is more explicit:

> There is an absence of abstract nouns which all but prohibits western methods of teaching Christian doctrine at depth, but probably does not inhibit the basic proclamation regarding God and man. Kui Christians may be nearer their Hebrew forefathers-in-the-faith when, e.g., they speak their religion in direct verbs active in voice. (Boal 1973 p.71)
>
> As conduct is judged in terms of its effect on the wider group, quite logically there is no noun in the traditional vocabulary for the abstract ethical concept of goodness or badness. (ibid. p.188)
>
> There is no word in the Kui language to express forgiveness. (ibid. p.190)

Similarly, to a missionary who wrote a book about the Juang tribe, it was a fact that 'love was unknown' to them.[32]

Going back to Goadby in the 1860s, we find an impression of Kui as a 'barbarian tongue', and understand why missionaries paid it so much attention.

> Many of the words are sweet and musical; others are gifted with a clicking, harsh, heavy pronunciation peculiar to all barbarian tongues .... The majority of the sounds are uttered by the tongue, the throat and the teeth, and by the gnashing of the latter he ['the Kond'] punctuates his sentences when completed.... The ability to preach to them in their own native language will be of no mean importance and worth striving for. The words of one's mother-tongue

> are sweeter to the ear, easier to comprehend, sink deeper, and go nearer to the heart than any in another language, however well acquired. (Quoted in Pearce Carey 1936 p.35)

Missionaries placed the greatest value on literacy, taking it as the defining feature of being civilized, as in Boal's definition of Konds as 'pre-literate' (1973). Peggs' book about the Orissa Mission (1846) has engravings of its first Hindu converts to Christianity. They are shown standing in their native landscape, holding books and reading: reality, in the missionary view, is no longer to be found in experience of the outer world or nature, but only in The Book. Literacy was a skill at the heart of Protestant Christianity, with its emphasis on the Bible as the source of spiritual knowledge. Hence the significance of MacViccar and Goadby taking a Mission-educated *meriah* on tour and getting him to read out to Kond villagers. And since schoolchildren learnt to read by reading Christian stories, they imbibed Christian ideas and images at the same time as they acquired the ability to read and write.

Mission schooling was an experience that set people sharply apart from their fellow villagers. It left them with new ideas and skills, and gave them possibilities of Government as well as Mission employment. For the first thing a complex education does, is create status differences. As Boal admits, even of the Konds who are now Baptists,

> The present position of the Church could be summarised thus: a very limited number of well-educated men, who have assimilated Christianity as it has been presented to them during years of schooling and professional training and through close contact with missionaries. The vast majority, however, accept Christianity as a way of life involving certain beliefs and principles which replace traditional rituals, without necessarily challenging the traditional world-view. (1973 pp.12–13)

This segregation begins with the construction of schools that are spatially very separate. Millman sited his boarding school a mile out of Udayagiri to separate children from unwanted influences. Hence the significance of orphan schools, beyond the idea of caring for the most deprived members of society: orphans are children who could be removed completely from their traditional social context, and moulded into the vanguard of a new elite. We shall find the same pattern in the segregation of Christian converts. For the moment, let us stress that Mission-educated Konds from the start formed a separate class, with a new set of values, often eager to find employment with missionaries or the Government, and alienated from other Konds by their European 'knowledge' of science, history, geography, and religion that, in effect, contradicted traditional Kond knowledge. They tended to consider themselves too highly-educated to work in the fields. This is more than an 'education gap' (Boal 1973 p.56). It is the invasion of class into a classless society.

Discipline was a prominent part of what missionaries taught and virtually a subject in its own right. An elaborate system of rewards and punishments was a vital element in Mission schools. It was inculcated through rules and exams, and a high value placed on submissiveness and obedience. One of the first Oriya converts, on his death-bed, expressed his happiness that his own children at Mission school,

> did not have the will or the power to 'run wild' as he did at their age. (Peggs 1846 p.361)

In 1899, Kond schoolchildren were already responding, though not yet with the desired alacrity, to the school drill of

> 'Sit! Stand! Walk!' (*BMS Report* p.25)

The set of values inculcated in the classroom is clear from Schulze's Kuvi vocabulary (1913 p.71):

Next day will be examination.	Take your slates.
Why have you been absent?	Sit down.
Don't make such a noise.	Stand up.
I got a good certificate.	Go out.
This boy failed.	

Through schools, missionaries introduced a system of authority quite alien to tribal culture—a more thorough-going version of the submissiveness and obedience which administrators demanded from Kond elders.

Linked with this, is missionaries' concern with sexual morality. From the start, this was an issue with the *meriah* children (above pp.145–6). Once in missionary care, they were segregated completely: an implicit denial of the close contact between the sexes that is encouraged in Kond culture. Freda Laughlin, in charge of the girls' hostel near Udayagiri, wrote in 1933 that the dormitory was now enclosed and its access guarded by the matron's room, so there was less danger of 'night visitors.... The girls had never been used to discipline, and it was rather hard for them....'(Pearce Carey 1936 p.108) Miss Laughlin taught them laundry, sewing and hygiene.

In this way, Kond schoolchildren picked up elements of European material culture along the way, which had a powerful symbolic value, and paved the way for conversion. The dual values of productive labour and the Sabbath as a day of rest from that labour, uniformity of dress, short hair, and soap were all vital elements of the Mission school system. As Boal put it (1973 pp.57–61):

> through Middle and High School education, they are gaining some vision of a world greater than their own, and a certain code of discipline and obedience, much valued for them by their parents; they are more accessible to medical advice and attention; and they learn by experience the value of good wells and simple sanitation. Those living in hostels are assured regular good meals, often of a better standard than at home though, like most institutional meals, lacking the interest of the unexpected relish....
>
> Illiterate parents do not realise their children's need of better clothing and personal necessities, and school equipment.

In short, missionaries used schools as a means towards social, as well as religious change, with a view to undermining and combating pagan beliefs and customs. The idea that tribal societies might have their own system of education, of a much less authoritarian nature than school education (as was often stressed by Elwin, who started out as a missionary until he was 'converted' to the tribal way of life)—let alone that Konds might possess their own forms of knowledge—such a possibility did not enter the missionaries' horizon.

The same is true of medical work. 'Send us a doctor and we will make him a god', Macpherson wrote, imagining that Konds had no form of medicine. But the alliance between Christian doctrine and medical science for invalidating Kond ritual knowledge, seems as complete in the 1970s as in the 1840s:

> When in addition to low standards of general health, traditional belief in uncleanness during menstrual periods prevents a woman from even touching cooking utensils....the relevance may clearly be seen of *preaching a salvation that includes a Christian approach to physiology*. (Boal 1973 pp.304–5, italics mine)

Medicine is the pre-eminent example in popular thought of non-western peoples being in need of Western knowledge, and medical work is the most powerful advertisment for missionary work, proof to most people of missionaries' disinterestedness. Similarly with their great emphasis on hygiene, cleanliness and neatness, which impressed many Hindus too.

S.C. Roy, in *Mundas and their country* (1912), showed contrasting photographs of neatly dressed Christians and unkempt pagans. Only recently have a few anthropologists and others questioned the idea that tribal people are destitute of effective methods of healing (above p.123). Livingstone recorded a revealing conversation he had with an African witchdoctor, who conceded Western pre-eminence in matters of clothes and guns,

> [but] God has given us one little thing, which you know nothing of. He has given us the knowledge of certain medicines by which we make rain. We do not dispute those things which you possess, though we are ignorant of them. You ought not to despise our little knowledge, which you are ignorant of.
>
> *Livingstone:* I don't dispute what I'm ignorant of; I only think you are mistaken in saying that you have medicines which can influence the rain at all.
>
> *Witchdoctor:* That's just the way people speak when they talk on a subject of which they have no knowledge.... I always thought white men were wise until this morning. (Jan Morris 1973/1979 p.321)

Missionaries in India, certainly, were on the whole completely ignorant of tribal methods of healing, which involve great knowledge of plant medicines, as well as more spiritual practices which have a greater affinity with accounts of Christ's healing powers than with the approach of missionary doctors.

As with schools, the missionaries were frank in regarding their Moorshead Memorial Hospital in Udayagiri as a direct aid towards conversion. Pearce Carey ended his book on the Kond Mission (1936) with the statement:

> There is no pulpit so influential as a hospital ward, and no pew where the heart is so receptive as in a hospital bed.[33]

The *BMS Report* for 1950 (p.xiv) describes how, in the Hospital

> The Gospel is faithfully preached according to a syllabus planned to bring the plan of salvation before the patients each month.

On the eve of departure of the last missionaries from Udayagiri in 1972, they declared that

> The hospital has played a leading part in the proclamation of the gospel in the Kond Hills, for which we thank God.... (*BMS Report* p.4)

Missionary institutions—bungalow, chapel, school and orphanage, hospital and dispensary, printing press etc.—form an enduring pattern, in which a Western material culture is implicit, as well as the dualistic conceptual structure I have outlined of self-sacrifice and stereotypes, discipline instilled through punishment and reward, Christian and scientific knowledge *versus* ignorance and superstition, and so forth.

The way these key themes are associated with missionary institutions into a theory of social change is clearly visible in an article in the *Sunday Statesman* published shortly before Indian Independence (Keith Little: 'The Khonds of Orissa', 21st April 1946). Hindu civilization, it argued, was antithetical to the Konds, and had driven them to the hills. In Kond religion, 'Nature, the unpredictable, was to be feared exceedingly, and propitiated unceasingly.'

No wish to change

> You can see the aborigine today, in all essentials, exactly as he was before there was any civilization at all on earth. You can see him in Australia, in Equatorial Africa, in India and in Burma. Here is a man who has not changed—a man who has no wish to change—who is content with the same life as his father and his forefathers lived before him. His music is still the beginning of music, his dancing is the leaping and gambolling which mimics animals and the hunt....

He is 'fearless and frank', but extremely ignorant—a few agricultural skills are 'all he needs to know' for this simple life. With the arrival of British civilization in Orissa,

> The Khond had to be administered into a more reasonable way of life—human sacrifice at least had to stop.
>
> A Baptist Mission with headquarters at Udaigiri, practically in the heart of the Khond hills, is working hard and with encouraging success, to civilize this people, which had been static for centuries. It is striving to make them into persons fit to take a worthy place in the world of today. The orgies of drunkenness are ended; the dancing has now nothing to its discredit; the animist religion, with its fears and horrors is slowly giving way before education and Christianity, and the Mission Hospital is usually full. The Khond is beginning to realize that he is not self-sufficient and is at last—at very long last—beginning to take advantage at least of the medical aid, so freely offered, which is part of a neighbouring culture and civilization.

As these words imply, missionaries' aim was to 'civilize' the Konds—to transform their way of life, following the Government's lead. School education and medical work they saw as the first stages in this transformation. Many schoolteachers and healthworkers carry on the missionary role today when they approach *adivasis* with the attitude that their traditional religion and knowledge are based on 'superstition' and 'ignorance' and that they should exchange their self-sufficiency for dependence on outside 'experts'.

Conversion: A Religion of Fear

The next stage is conversion. In many ways conversion involves a theory of social change, based on the idea that one set of beliefs is right, and another wrong. Christianity, in its extreme forms, claims a monopoly on truth at the expense of other religions, as A.D. Nock has shown in his book tracing the history of this idea (*Conversion* 1933). The Jesuit 'Reductions' provide a particularly clear example. These were Mission stations established in South America from the 16th century, into which Indians were collected after their conquest. Here they were protected from slave-traders (the aspect highlighted in the film 'The Mission'), but also brainwashed into accepting a way of life that contradicted their former one in every way. More recently Roman Catholic missionaries have often been more tolerant of traditional customs than Protestants, and nowadays some are willing to admit that a religion which a forest-dwelling culture has evolved over centuries, may be better suited to their environment than Christianity.

So what persuades people to convert?

Preaching is the definitive missionary role. School and hospital, orphanage and boarding school are ideal places for it, providing a captive audience. But missionaries also preached in markets and on tours of remote villages. Goadby was the first to make regular tours of the Kond hills. In December 1859 for the first time he 'entered the wild forest, of which we had heard so much before leaving Berhampur'. By 1863, 'Mr. Goadby has....been diligently studying the Khond language, and has made his first attempt at preaching in it.' He did not travel alone, but with assistants and a large retinue of camp followers, who carried his supplies on the backs of bullocks along the narrow jungle paths (*GBMS Reports* 1860, 1863, 1865).

When they brought their 'sacred warfare' to an unfamiliar audience, of Hindus or Konds, missionaries were often laughed at or shouted down (above pp.210, 214)—'obscene abuse' that they almost seemed to revel in. But by the 1920s, the missionaries based in Udayagiri preached regularly at several of the weekly markets which Konds attended. In 1927 three women missionaries who paid a visit to the Kond area, witnessed Evans preaching to a crowd of 5,000 in Tikkavalli market.

> When he preached, his grip on the people and his wooing of them were wonderful. Crowd keenly interested and responsive. (Pearce Carey p.101)

The first converts clearly reinforced missionaries' sense of purpose (K. Mazumdar 1984 p.114). They took great care to ensure that the 'enquirer' fully understood what he or she was converting to, since if they 'lapsed' this would be a setback for further conversions. The first Hindu convert of the Orissa Mission was a *brahmin* called Gungadhor—one of the readers engraved in Peggs' book, and later, perhaps, an officer in the Ghumsur wars (above p.61). As the missionaries described him, 'not a single stain rested on his character. His hatred of idolatry was intense....'(*GBMS Report* 1872 p.42) A description of Gungadhor shortly before his conversion in March 1828 gives a vivid impression of how the missionaries thought and preached, to Konds as well as to Hindus:

> I invited Gungadhor, a brahminical inquirer, to accompany me to the bazar, and he gladly acceded. He sung a geet, the "*Jewel Mine of Salvation*" to a great number of people, who were astonished to hear such things from a brahmin. This piece exposes the ten incarnations of the Hindoos, and introduces Jesus Christ, as the saviour of sinners; and speaks very feelingly of his sufferings and death.... Having finished the poem, I put the catechism into his hands, when he read over the *Ten Commandments*, and made some severe remarks from them upon the moral conduct of the Hindoos, as, "God here commands you to worship himself alone, and you have all worshipped wood and stone;—not to commit adultery, but you have all committed uncleanness with your neighbours' wives.... Will God endure this disregard of his commandments? Nay, but he will not my brethren; and we have all sinned. But hear, Jesus Christ died to deliver us from the wrath of God, and let us believe on him: his is the true salvation."
>
> While we stood and heard these things from an Oreah brahmin with such feeling and effect, we could not withhold the tears of pleasure, but tears involuntarily flowed from our eyes. We have all experienced feelings not known before, and surely angels hear; and if ever they weep for pleasure, it must be to witness scenes like these. O that this dear man continue steadfast unto death:—should he do so there is no doubt of his abilities as a preacher.... After this opportunity the people were almost mad for books: "Give me the Ten Commandments, Give...." was the cry from all sides.... Went out with us boldly in the evening and preached the Gospel. Sat with him afterwards till about 11 o'clock, talking upon a variety of subjects. Giving up his cast and

> connections is a most serious obstacle, and it requires much prudence to lead him on. I could not encourage him to do so till he is better established in his mind, for in the event of his forsaking us afterwards, the loss of his cast would produce a most unfavourable effect on the mind of the public. (Quoted in Peggs 1846 pp.356–7)

Another of the early Hindu converts, Paul Singh, described the sense of fear that led to his conversion:

> A sermon, preached by Dr Sutton from Hebrews ii.3, "How shall we escape etc.", deeply impressed his mind, and led to his giving his heart to the Saviour. Referring to this sermon, he said, "as I heard this discourse, I felt increasingly anxious about my soul, and on returning from worship, I read the verse, and thought of the instruction I had heard from the lips of the sahib, and I felt that I was a neglector of the great salvation. From that time I could no longer trifle, but I went to the sahib and related to him the exercises of my mind. From that day I felt myself to be a sinner, and forsaking sin, I believed in Christ. I had also evidence in my own mind, that Christ was truly the Saviour. Steadfastly believing this, I was baptized on the 5th of September 1847." (*BMS Report* 1888)

One of the great success stories of the orphanages that took in *meriah* children was the girl Ootama, whom Campbell had rescued 'from under the knife' and sent to be educated at a Baptist orphanage in the 1850s:

> She is naturally very quick, clever, and amiable, but since she has learnt to love the Lord Jesus, her disposition has become more lovely and tractable. The change which dear Ootama professes to experience shows itself in every way. Her voice and manners are more subdued, and she, with several of her companions, have established a meeting amongst themselves to pray for the conversion of their schoolfellows and the heathen around. (*GBMS Report* 1860 p.30)

Converts, then, were 'more subdued' and 'tractable'—willing to do and be as the *sahebs* wished—like Man Friday. They were also persuaded of their sinfulness, and 'anxious about their soul', in fear of 'the wrath of God'. On children, especially children separated from their families, the fearful effect of these ideas can be imagined. In 1872 some missionaries reported of one of the orphanages,

> we were gratified to learn that four of the orphans were really anxious about their souls, and had been of their own accord to the native preacher to converse about things which belong to their everlasting happiness. (*GBMS Report* 1872 p.20)

It seems that the main theme of preaching was the threat of eternal damnation, contrasted with the hope of salvation, that lay only in admitting one's sins and accepting Christ. This concept of sin as something intrinsic to human nature is quite alien to tribal religions. Missionaries focused therefore on the task of persuading Konds that they were sinful and in mortal danger. For instance, as Goadby described the sermons he gave on preaching tours of Kond villages:

> I was more than once exceedingly gratified with the seriousness which pervaded the minds of my hearers. Many of them appeared to be quite startled by the new and awful ideas I gave them of the character of the unseen God, and when I referred to sin, its certain punishment, the impossibility of fleeing from the power and presence of their Maker, even though they hid thmselves in the densest jungles or the darkest cave in their mountains, and the certainty that all their actions and thoughts were known to Him, the remarks produced a deep impression. (*GBMS Report* 1865 p.23)

It seems clear, from this, that the missionaries' religion was in many ways precisely what they described the Kond religion as—a religion of fear. Fear was the first emotion they sought to arouse when they preached, and fear of damnation was the first stage towards Konds' conversion. Later, among converts, fear of rebuke by Church authorities, and ultimately fear of excommunication, served to maintain discipline, and keep them on the 'straight and narrow path' to salvation.

In their own terms of course, the Christianity which missionaries propagated was a religion of love and joy; though its basic emphasis was on sobriety and discipline, and the wildness and abandonment of pagan rituals, including the shamans' state of trance, had no place. The ritual of baptism that marked entry to the Church illustrates this. It is a highly public ritual out in the open, evidently modelled on John the Baptist's baptism of Christ, and involves full immersion in a river or village tank. Often 20 or 30 individuals are baptized at once, witnessed by a large crowd, 'separate groups of Christians and animists watching from the bank'. Photographs show the minister entering the water with the 'candidate' up to waist height, and placing his hands on the candidate's head and heart.

Evans' description of his first conversion of a Kui-speaker, who was in fact a Dom, whom he baptized in 1916, gives an impression of the way later missionaries conceived of the whole process of conversion and baptism.

> I am sending a short account of the Kond convert who was baptized with his wife on New Year's Sunday. It will interest people at home to know how Christ is working in our midst.
>
> Twelve months ago a man accosted me in the market place at Udayagiri, and told me that he had accepted Jesus Christ as his Lord. He was trusting Him for salvation.... week by week he had listened to our preaching, and felt what we said was true. It was so unlike the Kond religion, with which he was dissatisfied. I questioned him.... Jesus was his all. He believed that Christ had done for him what he had been seeking to do for himself, by sacrifices and offerings to the Kond gods. Christ had died to release him from the burden of sin....
>
> He began morning and evening to worship in his home.... He has been a true disciple from the beginning, bringing others to the services and giving his testimony at all times as he seeks to win his friends and neighbours for Christ.
>
> Many are the difficulties he has encountered. His village people mocked him and laughed at him. They told him he was an ignorant man.... [His] mother was opposed.... [During an illness] he was tempted to sacrifice to the Kond god. He was sorely tried, but he prayed to his God, and came for medicine.... His integrity of character, and the reality of his change in life, is testified by his own neighbours.
>
> It is not surprising that such a man should desire to witness before his people and follow Christ through the waters of baptism. The happy event took place on New Year's Sunday. A joyous and blessed day it was for us here. What rejoicing there must have been in heaven! Gupinath being desirous to witness before his own people, the baptism took place at Courmingia, 4 miles from our station.... We formed a procession on arriving at the village and sang hymns as we processed to the tank. It was a very peaceful spot, surrounded with jungle. A very large crowd from the villages all around had gathered to see the ceremony. We had a short service, and an address from Mark xvi.16 was given. After Mr Millman had prayed, Gupinath witnessed a good confession, before the people who knew him. We then went down into the water, and amid a deep reverence and silence I baptised Gupinath and his wife. (*Missionary Herald* April 1916 pp.105–6)

Before baptism can take place, a correct hold on Christian doctrine, as well as a personal inner conversion, are necessary. These are tested through an oral examination of questions and answers, and a public confession of past sins and assurance of salvation. The process of conversion thus takes a considerable time, which is why Baptist congregations are divided into separate groups of baptized 'communicants', and 'learners' or 'enquiring candidates', who cannot take communion yet—and why, despite their head start, Baptists had a slower conversion rate than other denominations. During the 1950s, Boal found that more than half the candidates failed the exam. She gives the example of a Kond chief who failed it three times.

> Painstakingly simple instruction by the theologically trained Area Superintendant followed these baptismal exams, but it served to confirm that facts about Jesus Christ could not apparently be retained at this stage, even after three repetitions of teaching. (Boal 1973 p.230)

This way of describing the process, and the whole idea of basing entry into the Church on an exam, demonstrate the authority structure that missionaries were imposing over Konds, and shows how they saw their religion as reducible to doctrine, conceived almost scientifically as 'knowledge' of 'facts'. Hence Schulze's simplistic account of Kond religion, as if it could be reduced to some comparable body of doctrine (above p.212). And hence Boal's comment that 'Many local churches show a marked decline in interest and personal standards within three or four years', because Konds find the Mission's 'basically mental approach to God' dull (1973 p.247).

Dividing the Community

As an expression of their dualistic philosophy, missionaries segregated their converts as far as possible from unconverted pagans. From the 1830s, converts from Hinduism were collected into Christian villages or 'colonies'.

> It is a pleasing state of progress in a Mission where the converts "come out from among the ungodly and be separate," and like Israel of old "dwell alone and not be reckoned among the nations" of Idolaters around. The report of the Society for 1832 gratefully refers to this event. The first village to which reference is made is CHRISTIANPORE. (Peggs 1846 p. 296)

By 1844 there were seven villages, containing 54 households.

> "Christian natives must form themselves into colonies and separate communities. They have no possessions when they embrace the Gospel, and they are not permitted to mix with the population of the country...." (Quoted ibid. p.304)

Orphanages and schools separated Kond children from their communities in many ways. Conversion to Christianity carried this much further, dividing a village with a host of values and symbols.

> To be a Christian in these hill tribes is still on the whole to gain prestige, though joining a local congregation undoubtedly leads to fragmentation within the village. (Boal 1973 p. 231)

What sets Christians apart most immediately are rules they have to observe. For a start, 'Liquor drinking is prohibited by Church rule.' (ibid. p. 29) Dancing likewise. In the 1950s (and probably still), a Kond male was required to cut his hair short as soon as he became a learner—a powerful symbol of difference in a culture where men are proud of their long hair. Women are required to wear a tight bodice over their breasts, and are forbidden to tattoo their daughters. Missionaries did what they could to make Konds consider bare skin indecent:

> Clothing will continue to remain at a minimum until contact with wider communities is of a sufficient strength to cause a feeling of need (whether for reasons of climate or status) and gives the knowledge that the need can be met. (Ibid. p.55)

Sexuality is a major issue. Premarital and extramarital sex are considered grave offences. Youth dormitories, and taking a second wife after admission to the Church, are forbidden. Divorce is difficult under Church law. Boal speaks of a resulting 'conflict concerning premarital sex-experience' (ibid. p.26):

> Sexual misconduct among the more educated young Christians has become one of the insistent problems in the Kui Church today. [Traditionally] Sex is regarded as a good and joyous gift. (Ibid. p.40–1)

> Into this tradition of sexual freedom outside marriage, the Church comes with a new *suju* [taboo]. It speaks from a background of European values which (until the present "new morality" at least) insists on premarital virginity and legally ratified monogamous marriage.... When the new convert finds that premarital intercourse is a punishable offence by Church Law, and that a legal rather than a socio-economic seal on marriage is required, he is bewildered. (Ibid. p.197)

The Church did seem to create a community preoccupied with rules, even to some of those who set it up.

> Unfortunately, through cross-cultural misunderstanding, all too soon in new Christian communities gospel is introduced as law; the Good News is imprisoned in rules of conduct and fixed forms of discipline. Now, since the arrival of western Victorian ethics, as in many other lands, the issues are confused for the Kui Christian. A Christian may sin according to community-

> understanding without reprimand, yet within his new church life, "law has intruded into this process to multiply law-breaking." (Romans 5.20) (Ibid. p.200)

> Not all aspects of Church discipline have...helped the Kui convert to understand the meaning of penitence. As in most Protestant churches, the concept of discipline is usually punitive; and over the past half-century the Kui church has formulated the rules defining the behaviour required by its members. (Ibid. p.285)

Boal sees these difficulties as a 'creative tension'.

> Though the downright "No" may sometimes be required of Christian communities when belief and behaviour make explicit denial of the Lordship of Christ, yet there are surely areas of awareness in Kui culture which so far have been denied by the western approach to Christianity. (Ibid. p.154)

The communities which missionaries established were regulated by, even based on, an elaborate set of rules and forbidden activities. Discipline was maintained through penalties, which included fines as well as various grades of exclusion from the church service. Exclusion from communion was one of the severest. It was virtually the outcasting of an outcaste, since converts to Christianity were already outcaste to their pagan fellow-villagers.

Prior even to the rules concerning liquor, dress, dancing, sex and marriage, are those that forbid participation in non-Christian rituals. This in itself entails a complete dividing of the village community: religious ritual ceases to be something that unites the village, for the ceremonies of Christians and pagans become mutually exclusive. Boal is willing to discover certain insights in Kond cultural attitudes to death, but adds,

> True, certain pre-Christian concepts concerning the ancestors would need to be cleansed. (Ibid. p.294)[34]

Since ancestors play a vital part in tribal religion, and their approval is constantly sought, were Christian converts not being asked to cut themselves off from their pagan forefathers, and thus, from their roots?

In other words, the missionary Church established a system of authority, one that contradicted and differed fundamentally from traditional Kond authority. The Church undermined chiefs' authority in many areas. Boal writes of a village chief with more than one wife,

> Even though he may be the natural leader of the village, he may never become an elder in the local church nor represent it at wider gatherings, for the Union follows the apostolic teaching: "Let deacons be husbands of one wife" (I.Tim.3:12). This is quite incomprehensible to the village community. It appears as some inexplicable Christian taboo, to be observed if one wishes to belong. (Ibid. pp.29–30)

Missionaries therefore created a new kind of community superimposed on the old village and clan-based community. The Church community of fellow-communicants was defined by its members' regular sharing of communion, and by their acceptance of a list of rules, which were established by a hierarchy of missionaries or Church councils: an authority system based, for the BMS, in London; and for other Missions in Rome or other foreign cities.

As a system of authority, the missionary Church creates a direct hold over the individual's conscience. Responsibility rests on the individual, without reference to the family or village community.

> An apparent failing of the Kui Christian is his refusal to accept *personal responsibility*. (Ibid. p.34)

An individual is therefore punished by his pastor: the village council has no say in the matter. He is put in a direct, exclusive relationship with the Church hierarchy. His membership of a Church rests not only on his own observance of Church rules, but on the state of his mind and soul—what he as an individual believes and understands. In this respect, missionary Church organization recreates the 'individualizing and totalizing' power system of the modern Western state (Foucault 1982). Pastoral control over each individual is very clear in this tribal setting, because of the conflicts Boal mentions, that arise when Church ministers bypass as if they do not exist the traditional authorities of a Kond village: councils, family heads, chiefs and priests. In a Protestant Church, one could see this form of control by the minister over every individual in his congregation as a development out of the authority structure of the Catholic Church, and the practice of confession.[35]

In 1931 the Kond Hills District Church Union (KHDCU) was formed at a great meeting near Udayagiri, attended by 800 Kui-speakers who came from surrounding districts and camped for three days, submitting to a new form of discipline: 'at 10.30 : "lights out" was heard throughout the camp'. They left, according to Mrs Evans, with

> a new understanding of the largeness of the fellowship, and of what the Christian Church meant in the Kond hills, and a deeper realisation of their own personal need for the Saviour. (Pearce Carey 1936 p.106)

In 1950, when there were about 50 Churches affiliated to the Udayagiri Mission, the KHDCU got a constitution and instituted annual meetings (Boal 1982 p.185). At this stage most converts were still Doms: Konds only began to convert in large numbers after 1956. By 1966 there were 180 affiliated Churches. But as a rapid expansion set in, new differences of opinion arose within the Church, which perhaps challenged the Europeans' supremacy. One major decision the Church Union made at this time, which produced a split among Baptists in Orissa, was to join the Church of North India, which was represented in Orissa by the bishops of Cuttack and Sambalpur.

> After a period of rapid expansion and many conversions, the churches have entered a difficult phase, with many tensions, clashes, strife and party spirit which has virtually paralysed any effective activity. Adult education work and the revision of the Kui new Testament have come to a standstill with no immediate prospects of restarting it.... Many of these troubles are the almost inevitable result of the rapid growth of the church and the rise of Kui leaders to take over work initiated by missionaries. The change from "outsiders" to local people must come, but the change often uncovers problems and needs which were not obvious before. God is raising up new leaders. (*BMS Report* 1972 p.5)

To compound missionary difficulties, India passed the Freedom of Religion Act in 1968, which made attempting to convert someone to a new religion a criminal offence. Several of the English missionaries at Udayagiri were arrested the same year, and although they were soon released, they reduced their village tours greatly the next year, 'to avoid trouble with government officers'. The last to leave were five single women. In 1973 only one remained:

> Miss I.V. Wright, the Nursing Superintendent, courageously stayed at her post until August, when she was the last BMS missionary to leave. (*BMS Report* 1973 p.5)

But by then, Christianity was self-perpetuating among the Konds, in a number of different Churches, which appear to replicate the European legacy of religious dividedness.

When we see the authority structure which these Churches embody, the recent trend among Konds and Soras to convert to Christianity becomes clearer. Missionary authority was separate from Government authority, yet complemented it. Since India's Independence, Church authority has become more of an 'alternative' system, as its rules are markedly different from Government laws as well as from the norms of mainstream Hindu society, which have become identified as the forces of exploitation. It is not simply that Christianity offers an ideology and form of organization that aid resistance to oppressive landlords and merchants—this was already so for the Mundas who began to convert in large numbers in the 1850s. From the present Government's point of view, Christianity is potentially subversive as it never was under British rule, when missionaries' ideology was intertwined with that of administrators. The present Government is in no way a 'Christian Government'; relatively few Government officials are Christians now. Churches also often remain a source of direct contact between Westerners and tribal Christians, through organizations based outside India.

This is probably a large part of what makes Missions so suspect in Government eyes, for foreign missionaries remained the ultimate authority for Kond Christians until well after Independence. Kond churches still refer back to the BMS in London, although Christianity can expand now with a minimum of help from abroad, since first or second generation Kui converts as well as Christians from other parts of India have become evangelists themselves. Government hostility to missionizing may actually increase the attraction of the Church for tribals. In Nagaland, where the vast majority of Nagas have converted to Christianity (especially to the Baptist Church) one sees the tendency for a Christian identity to form a rallying point against Hindu or mainstream Indian oppression, taken much further. In its ideology and system of authority, Christianity offers *adivasis* a measure of independence from the local elite—though at the sacrifice of a strict and alien discipline, and the dividing of communities.

It is beyond doubt that the missionaries we have been discussing 'meant well', and 'dedicated their lives for the Konds', and I hope what I have written here will not cause offence to missionaries or Kond Christians, but will be taken as constructive criticism that can be helpful in looking more deeply into what it has meant to introduce Christianity into a tribal society. One aspect that is often stressed is the way that communities are divided. Rituals of sowing and harvesting and of respect for the ancestors that once united a village cease to do so, and Church authority negates the traditional authority of the elders. Some of the Christians I have met in tribal areas have an intolerance for other religions reminiscent of the missionary attitude at its most extreme, describing tribal or Hindu deities as 'false gods' or 'evil spirits'. Many converts today appear to have internalized a missionary view of tribal religion that looks down on the unconverted as 'sinners' in the grip of 'evil'. Christians who take this view are trapped in an attitude of false superiority that separates them from people who have different beliefs. It is all too similar to that of fundamentalist missionaries from Europe or America who are still active today in other countries, especially in Latin America and Africa, such as the New Tribes Mission, whose missionaries believe that tribal religions are 'motivated by superstition and fear', being 'generally a spiritist form of worship which is energised by satanic forces'.[36] Apart from different religious affiliation, Christianity has tended to introduce class and hierarchy into Kond society through an educational elitism, that has little or no respect for traditional forms of knowledge.

One could also say that Christianity introduces a divorce from nature or the forest. At the end of her book on the Konds, Barbara Boal describes how a village that converts to Christianity cuts down its sacred grove, and destroys the forest around the village, which had been left before out of respect for Sora Penu, the Hill God (1982 pp.235–7). In many of the missionary quotations, we have seen imagery equating the jungle with moral darkness, and clearing it with light. Nature, to some Christians, is no longer sacred.

In their initial impact, missionaries inspired the military campaign to suppress human sacrifice without taking responsibility for it (above p. 193), and began the process of changing Konds and transforming their way of life, in order to 'save' them. At another level, I would argue that Christian conversion has been a model for how administrators and economists plan for social change. From 'pacification' and 'conquest over their minds', how far is it to development plans that take no account of tribal values or feedback, and interpret tribes through stereotypes and monolithic theories of development?

In all these ways, the missionary impulse sacrifices traditional beliefs, values and customs, as well as communities' former cohesiveness which was based around a religion of respect for ancestors and nature. Missionary 'care' has a tendency to sacrifice the *spirit* of tribal culture. We have seen how Kond Mission schools regulated every aspect of children's lives through rules and institutional norms, in which dinners lacked 'the interest of the unexpected relish' (above p.225). It seems that the aim was to *re-form* Kond children into a particular image of how 'good' children should be, by breaking the independent 'wildness' of their spirit. Is this not a subtler level of the same *sacrifice of human being* that colonial administrators initiated?

In the United States of America, when the 'Indian wars' were over, and the native tribes had been forced onto reservations, a more total, but much less famous, form of oppression began, comparable to the missionary influence on the Konds, but more extreme. It shows more starkly how the missionary role takes Government control much further by establishing a system of authority based on absolute standards of 'right' and 'wrong'. The US Government parcelled Indian tribes and reservations among missionary sects, just as the British divided India (above pp.186, 188). These missionaries presided over a process of indoctrination, which involved removing children by force from their parents, whom they often were not allowed to see for several years, and taking them to boarding schools, where every aspect of their life was regulated in a way that was intended to root out old beliefs and instil new values, forcing Indians to 'assimilate' to the lifestyle of white society.

> Their hair was cut short; they were forbidden to speak their own language, to wear their own clothes, and to maintain their own customs. They were given English names and compelled to undergo religious training by designated Christian sects.[37]

As Lame Deer, a modern Lakota medicine-man, describes the draconian school regime he was raised under in the 1910s–20s:

> In those days the Indian schools were like jails and run along military lines, with roll calls four times a day.... We were forbidden to talk our own language or to sing our songs.... The teacher said "Stand," "Sit down!" He said it again and again until we caught on.... We also had a lady teacher.... For many weeks she showed us pictures of animals and said "dog" or "cat".... To the Indian kid the white boarding school comes as a terrific shock. He is taken from his warm womb [of his family] to this strange, cold place.... The schools are better now.... But in these fine new buildings Indian children still commit suicide, because they are lonely in all that noise and activity. I know of a ten-year-old who hanged herself. Those schools are just boxes filled with homesick children. The schools leave a scar.... My mother died of tuberculosis in 1920, when I was seventeen years old, and that was our family's "last stand".... But in 1920 they wouldn't even allow us to be dead in our own way. We had to be

> buried in the Christian fashion. It was as if they wanted to take my mother to a white boarding school way up there.[38]

One of the most telling responses to the missionary impulse came from Chief Joseph of the Nez Percés, who explained, before the onset of this missionary phase, why he did not want schools or churches for his tribe:

> They will teach us to argue about God. We do not want to learn that. We may quarrel with men sometimes about things on this earth, but we never quarrel about God. We do not want to learn that.[39]

CHAPTER SEVEN

Merchants of Knowledge: Anthropologists in a Social Structure

A Gulf of Understanding

In the colonial power structure that imposed a new order over the Konds, the roles of administrator and missionary are complemented by another role—that of the anthropologist, the expert who supposedly understands or has knowledge of tribal culture. Anthropology was a vital element in British rule of the Konds, not least because it legitimized British rule from the side of science by defining Konds as a 'primitive tribe' who stood to benefit from 'enlightened government', just as missionaries legitimized it from the side of religion and ethics.

When I started to study anthropology, I was thrilled by the prospect of learning about different cultures in depth, and made the customary fieldwork plans. But when I began meeting *adivasis*, and when I got to know the anthropological literature about them in more detail, I found realities that do not meet. Between the reality of India's tribal cultures as they are lived and anthropologists' accounts of them, there is a chasm—a gulf of understanding.

The issue came to a head when I visited a tribal village in 1982, and around a fire in the evening announced my plans for fieldwork. The men roared with laughter at the idea that I would understand their society by living there for a year. 'And what good would it do us?'—a question to which I found I had no satisfactory answer.

I still feel torn apart as I re-write this chapter, between the anthropologist in me, and the *adivasi*, who hates this academic style of writing; between the need to question radically the way that anthropology has been carried out, as my own first step towards bridging this gulf of understanding, and the disapproval this provokes, inside myself, let alone among others. What gives me the conviction to present this chapter nevertheless, is an answer which Karl Jung gave when asked whether he thought the atom bomb would ever be used—that it depended on how many people were able to stand the clash of opposites inside themselves: if many people learnt to do so, there would be no need to use the bomb.

Studying social anthropology opened many doors for me in understanding human society, and my own place in it. But after the freshness of these insights wore off, and I began to enter into non-western cultures in some depth for myself, I began to sense the limitations of the purely intellectual forms of understanding which anthropology concentrates on. As I started to spend time with tribal people and enter into their forms of understanding, the project of analysing their culture for intellectual consumption by people in my own society gradually lost its appeal altogether. I came to feel there was something fundamentally acquisitive in my own initial fieldwork plans, as well as in much anthropology that I read. And when I looked at the anthropological literature about the Konds and other tribes in India, I realized that it forms an essential part of the discourse of power that was imposed on them. It denies them a voice, and denies their reality, by defining and categorizing them in a way that is fantastically, incomprehensibly alien.

Briefly, then, my argument in this chapter is as follows. Victorian anthropology produced a highly impersonal way of writing about tribes such as the Konds, that defined them as 'primitive' in every domain of life. It thus gave out as a 'scientific fact' what was essentially a negative stereotype. The underlying theory is what we call 'social evolutionism' (below pp.255–6)—which, officially, most anthropologists have rejected. Yet it persists in India now in a slightly different form, in the idea that *adivasis* are 'backward' or 'in need of development', and thereby legitimizes imposing momentous restrictions on them or displacing them from their land in the name of development. Thus the inheritance from colonial anthropology, in underlying theory as well as in behaviour 'collecting data in the field', has yet to be confronted and repudiated.

Only Verrier Elwin and a handful of other anthropologists have written in a way that bridges this gulf a little, and their work is often dismissed as romantic, subjective, or unsystematic.[1] This is disturbing, because mainstream anthropological writing diminishes the human quality of tribal life so thoroughly, and still assumes an attitude of gross superiority.

Colonial anthropology about the Konds, and countless other *adivasis*, has had a huge impact on them, especially by reinforcing the negative stereotype. The quality of human contact in a tribal community, which lives through eye contact, a constant open humour, the grace of movement in activities around the village—anthropological convention sacrifices this aliveness for the sake of an impersonal objectivity. Without that human touch, anthropology creates the corpse of a culture.

It is my own sense of shock at the persistence of this gulf of understanding, and its place in the enormous continuing oppression of tribal people, that led me to study colonial domination in the first place, so it is the problem I start from here, and I present this chapter as an anthropologist's exploration of the inhumanity in anthropology.

This is not to deny the positive features of anthropology, such as its role in opening people's minds to non-western perceptions, or the fact that it is sometimes anthropologists who speak up most strongly for tribal people. But in its colonial form, anthropology represents, as I see it, a further level of domination beyond the more obvious forms so far discussed; a level that is subtler and less visible, and which persists in modern professional anthropology today. As such it is a form of orientalism,[2] and has created a discourse that in its abstruse impersonality, objectifies or dehumanizes people by turning human *subjects* into *objects* of study, and their relationships into abstractions.

Obviously, the number of anthropologists who have studied the Konds and published about them is quite small, and there is no way to measure the influence their writings have had back on the Konds. But for all the years that separate them, not to mention their personal differences and variety of theoretical affiliations, these anthropologists have worked from a common culture of assumptions and behaviour that is in many ways extremely uniform. So in order to understand what anthropology has imposed on Konds, it is necessary to take a fresh look at this *anthropological culture* itself, since it has somehow avoided scrutiny of the kind that it practises on other, less powerful or 'educated' societies. And since it is a culture that has interacted with all known tribal cultures in broadly similar ways, I supplement the Kond experience with material from other tribes. As in the previous chapter, I also extend the focus into the period after British rule, to demonstrate ways in which colonial forms of domination have continued until today.

Anthropologists are experts at conceptualizing the structure of social relationships in tribal societies. Yet, as I have stressed, they have often neglected relationships *between* societies, not least colonial relationships, and as part of that, their own relationships with the people they study. How do these fit with their relationships in their own societies? Since the pattern of anthropologists' relationships makes up the filter through which they experience and write about people of another culture, if they do not understand this pattern, what is the status of their data and studies? How can we understand other cultures unless we understand our own culture as well as its relation to those others, and our own place in this?

I am therefore reversing the customary perspective here to make the ethnographic relationship itself into an object of study—an anthropological study of anthropologists. My interest is not in the anthropologists themselves so much as the ways of thinking and behaving which they take to the 'field' and put into their writing. This means studying actual social relationships through the language of those who initiated them and their underlying conceptual structure, as in previous chapters. There has been an increasing tendency among anthropologists to reflect critically on their traditions, or on their personal experience of fieldwork.[3] However, there has been little attempt to apply the concept of 'social structure'—so basic to social anthropology—to anthropological relationships. To correct the distortion of knowledge implicit in 19th century anthropology we need to conceptualize ourselves and our intellectual ancestors inside a social structure for a change.

For one thing, this means looking at anthropologists' behaviour towards tribal people in the context of the behaviour of various other groups of outsiders who have also initiated contact with the people concerned, particularly administrators and missionaries. Just as the roles of administrator and missionary interweave and incorporate elements from each other, so too with this role. Certain key concepts play a significant part in all three roles, such as 'going to the field', and ideas about 'self-sacrifice' and 'saving'—for anthropologists, this often takes the form of putting oneself through maximum culture shock in a quest for the truth—to discover some part of the riddle of mankind, or to collect and 'preserve' certain vital pieces of information 'before it's too late'. But how conscious are we of the collective ideas we draw on here?

In the 19th century most anthropology was a sideline practised by certain administrators and missionaries—in fact all of them, when writing about tribal culture, tend to adopt this role of the expert who has 'objective' knowledge about tribal society. Strictly it is ethnography, 'culture writing', that these Victorians practised—an apparently straightforward level of description of a culture based on the collection of detailed information about it. Anthropology, 'science of man', referred to a more theoretical level, that drew upon ethnographic studies in order to compare different societies.[4] Nowadays, it is often recognized that the distinction is not so simple, since it is difficult, if not impossible, to describe a culture without bringing in one's theories. For this reason, I shall focus on underlying beliefs, theories, attitudes and behaviour much more than on content. For although Kond anthropology obviously tells one a fair amount about Kond society, it obscures or distorts a lot as well, and arguably tells one as much, or more, about the anthropologists who wrote it, and their culture.

Is it possible, in fact, that what tribals understand about us when we go to study them may be as much or more than what we are learning about them? It often seems a tragedy that out of all the labour of anthropologists' encounters 'in the field', their books give so little of the insight that many people read them for. Of tribal knowledge, or even recognition of its existence, they are still usually more or less empty.

In sum, my purpose is anything but polemical, though the very fact of subjecting other anthropologists, dead or alive, to the same kind of anthropological scrutiny as they have subjected tribal people to, may take on the appearance of attacking them. If so, this will draw attention to the destructive side of anthropology—the way that it has often attacked the essence of tribal cultures, but remains largely unaware that it has done so. What I attempt here is thus a *deconstruction* of anthropological discourse, an examination of its internal contradictions or 'sub-texts', grounded in the perception of intellectual distortion just mentioned, as well as in my own feelings of profound disquiet when I read these texts—a disquiet which I have found difficult to define or come to terms with. This chapter is my struggle to do so.

The tribal view of anthropologists is put more earthily than this by an American Indian medicine-man.

> The anthropologists are always after us, wanting to know about Mister Indian's sex life...."aboriginal sexual patterns".... Some folks have fun with these anthropologists, telling them wild stories, playing games with them. The game works like this.

Anthropologist: "How's your sex life?"
Indian: "Fine. How's yours?"
Anthropologist: "Do you always have the same position?"
Indian: "Yes. I've been an ambulance driver for twenty years."
Anthropologist: "You have a taboo about your organ?"
Indian: The only guy around here with an organ is the Catholic priest. You should see him working it."
Some of our people are very good at this kind of thing.[5]

The Conquerors as Anthropologists

The first ethnographic writing on the Konds emerged from Britons' initial encounter with them in the Ghumsur wars, and its authors were some of the officials who forced Konds to accept British rule. The Government showed an anthropological interest from the start—when Lord Elphinstone requested more information about the Konds and their customs from officers in the field (9th Sept. 1836), he enquired in the same breath whether they had a taboo on eating dogs! The anthropological interest may have seemed to honour the Konds, but its focus on the custom of human sacrifice created an image of Konds as 'savages'. It also appropriated them intellectually, and diminished them, by giving out as 'facts' about them a kind of information that was so superficial and full of stereotypes as to be extremely distorting.

Several scholarly articles were published during or just after the wars, apart from Revd Brown's missionary writings in the *Calcutta Christian Observer* (above pp.191–3). The *Madras Journal of Literature and Science* published a series of pieces based on notes sent in by some of the officers who took part in the wars. Its editor, Revd Taylor, commented on 'the deep but melancholy interest' which Kond affairs had aroused, stating that 'The Khoonds are clearly in a state next to entire barbarism.' Maxwell, one of the surgeons who served the British troops, set the scene by describing the 'stagnant, suffocating and impure atmosphere' of the Konds' forests—he recommended the introduction of English vegetables, using the Konds to cut the forest back!

> The Khonds are absorbed in the grossest ignorance and superstitions; and practise that most horrid and ancient of rites, human sacrifice, by the perpetration of which they consider they propitiate the earth, the great object of their wild and frantic adoration, and procure fertility.[6]

Stevenson and Sooria Narain, Ganjam Collector and *Tahsildar* of Ghumsur, also sent pieces to Taylor. Stevenson made a list of some 400 Kui words and phrases and gave the following questions and answers, with Kui translations:

> How many people do you sacrifice in one month?
> Who is your God?
> How many gods have you?
> How do you pray to the God?
> Amongst the Khonds how many castes?
> Do you kill the women in your country?
> Yes, they kill any person they can get.
> Before killing how long are they kept?

Quite a phrase-book! One imagines the administrator greeting Konds with these questions: 'How many people do you sacrifice in one month? Who is your God?....' Stevenson commented:

> After making out the list of words and questions, I took every opportunity of interrogating any Khond whom I met, and it was amusing to see his astonishment when I spoke to him.

He also sent a translation of a Telugu document (by Sooria perhaps) on 'the customs of the race of people called Codalu', which discussed Kond culture under the headings of marriage customs, childbirth, funerals, death by tiger, the castes of the mountains, the gods honoured and the manner of sacrifice to each, human sacrifice, and oaths. On the basis of this, Taylor compared the Konds with other tribes (Gonds, Bhils, Paharias), remarking too on 'the more than accidental resemblances to South Seas human sacrifice' (a topic in Pritchard's recent *History of Man*).[7] Along with Taylor's learned comparison of Kui with Tamil and Sanskrit, this served to place the Konds on a conceptual map of the peoples, customs and languages of India and the rest of the colonized world.

So did two more articles in the journal. 'Meteorological experiments made on the Goomsoor Mountains' (October 1838) was by a Lt John Campbell who had been employed in the Ghumsur wars to survey the country that British troops were entering for the first time.[8] Its purpose was 'to show the approximate height of these mountains' and to demonstrate the progress of meteorological science in 'the relation between the wet bulb thermometer and the dew point [barometer]', as well as the older dry thermometer, which it does through tables of measurements by each technique, with a list of places and dates of the experiments.

As a piece of 'pure science' it has no direct connection with the Konds; yet measuring their mountains seems a potent symbol of the British conquest. The other article was also the result of a scientific survey, Macpherson's 'Report on the Goomsoor, Duspallah, and Boad Zemindaries', his first publication (April 1838). It is a geographical and geological survey of the Kond country, from its latitude and longitude to an account of its river and mountain systems, its forest ('These great sylvan glades....of considerable extent and remarkable beauty....'), vegetable products, General Geological Characters ('The great gneiss deposits' being the fundamental rock, with 'infinitely diversified superficial aspects'), and two routes through the forest which he and Lt Campbell had surveyed. Macpherson promised a second article on the Konds themselves in the journal, but this was not published, since he fell ill and left India at this time, and published the material later in another form.

This early series of articles on the Konds was therefore linguistic (Taylor) and geographical (Maxwell, Lt Campbell, Macpherson) as well as ethnographic.[9] In effect it incorporated the Konds and their country into European 'scientific' knowledge, and by defining them as savages, closed off the possibility of any kind of openness to or acknowledgement of whatever knowledge the Konds might possess. A tribe entering British consciousness for the first time was to be put in its place conceptually, with the same assurance with which British soldiers 'reduced it to subjection'—a preliminary definition that left no space for Konds' idea of who they were and what they knew about the world.

Macpherson was one of the first administrators in India who took a serious interest in a tribe's ethnography. Lord Auckland, the Governor-General, honoured him by paying for his Report on the Konds to be published.[10] Macpherson also published two articles on the Kond religion in the *Journal of the Royal Asiatic Society*, of which he was a fellow (1843 and 1852).[11] He evidently intended to write an elaborate book about the Konds, since he employed an artist to paint the portraits of 40 Kond chiefs, and kept a diary that he filled with information about the Konds. The portraits were lost at sea—they would have been a unique record that might have preserved a vivid impression of the Konds as Europeans first encountered them, similar to the famous portraits and photographs which white Americans made of the Indian chiefs they negotiated with—and the diaries were destroyed in a fire during the Mutiny:

> I am sorry to say that all my Khond diaries—my private ones—are burnt by the rebels; so that I can never, as I intended, tell the tale of their religious conquest. (Letter of 1859, WM p.340)

Macpherson died in 1860, so it fell to his brother to publish his ethnography in a more accessible form, in the book he wrote to defend his brother's reputation against Campbell's allegations (WM—*Memorials of Service....* 1865).

A striking feature of Macpherson's ethnography, when compared with later Government ethnography, is its emphasis on Konds' political relations with Hindu rulers, as well as with the British Government. The 1841 report makes this its central theme: it is explicit that the Government was in the process of imposing its will on tribes whose 'political independence was complete' (1842 p.21). While painting a grim picture of Kond warfare (above p.54), he admitted that 'peace is their prevailing condition' (1842 p.41), and that their own 'Government of society' was admirably uncoercive:

> The system of society...is...purely patriarchal.... It is based almost exclusively on the principle of family.... The spirit of equality pervades its whole constitution—society is governed by the moral influence of its natural heads alone, to the entire exclusion of coercive authority. (Ibid. pp.27–8)

He does not gloss over the British violence which followed the Durgaprasad 'massacre', and the coerciveness of British rule:

> the Khonds refused with the most admirable constancy, to bring their natural heads, or their guests, bound to our scaffolds. The country was laid utterly desolate. The population was unceasingly pursued by our troops.... The Khond chiefs of Baramootah were condemned and executed almost without exception.... Our authority is acknowledged, in any degree, in the Khond districts of Goomsur alone, which our arms reduced. (Ibid. pp.80–81)

But Macpherson's identification with the Government is complete. He thus combines the roles of ethnographer and administrator, using his ethnography to recommend a policy of 'pacifying' the Konds, in order to 'establish relations with them as subjects' before abolishing human sacrifice.[12]

Macpherson analyses the Kond political system as a whole by examining relations with *rajahs* and British administrators—in a way that, as I have remarked, even Evans-Pritchard fails to do in *The Nuer* (above pp.24–5). But the ambiguity of the role he played, as well as the accuracy of his analysis, is demonstrated by the war he got drawn into soon after writing it. For there is a great discrepancy between his demonstration that only Konds conquered by force had recognized British rule, and the idea that 'giving them justice' would make them 'spontaneously yield'.

His interest in Kond religion is unusually open for its time. He acknowledged its richness and complexity, highlighting its multitude of deities and their association with places, natural forces and diseases, as well as the idea of several distinct 'souls' or elements of personality—features corroborated by the most detailed recent anthropology of Central Indian tribes.[13] In this, his ethnography is evidently based on careful enquiry, sifting information from a number of different people. He even compared what he found positive in their religion with Christianity; though as we have seen this led him to divide Kond religion into two great warring 'sects', between which was a 'schism', and to see his administration as a 'religious conquest' for the God of Light (above pp.81, 124). He also—like future generations of anthropologists!—imposed his own highly artificial hierarchy of categories onto the Konds' 'pantheon', as he admitted himself.[14]

Campbell fastened on this admission to ridicule Macpherson's whole account of Kond religion—though, as Boal points out (1982), Macpherson's information is much the more reliable.

> The author of this report represented the Khonds as a refined people, overflowing with the most ingenious ideas. This was very much at variance with the notorious fact that they were without a written language, and that their religious ritual was as simple as it was savage....
>
> The mythology attributed to the Khonds of Orissa by the author of the report I have alluded to must be considered marvellous, when their present state of semi-barbarism and gross ignorance is borne in mind. They are furnished with a pantheon in which there are deities of various degrees of power, in a kind of railway classification....[T]heir beatified souls...possess a certain amount of influence as intercessors for the restoration of lost relatives....The festivities of the Khonds usually terminate in universal drunkenness, for which I have never known them show the least signs of penitence or remorse....
>
> According to this narrative, the priest much resembles the medicine man of the North American Indian, seeking to discover, by certain ritual tests, the cause of the malady he may be called upon to cure, which he usually attributes to the displeasure of some god, or the magic of some enemy whom the patient has offended.
>
> According to this authority, there is a particular form of worship to every god, with particular traditions respecting him or her, all of which are given in detail, as well as ceremonials for different seasons....

> My own experience was considerably greater than that of the writer, and my assistants were neither prejudiced nor careless observers....[Frye] says very little respecting [Khond religion], simply because there is very little to be said. He gives four short lines in the Khond language as their creed, and describes their ceremonial in half a page. (Campbell 1864 pp.160–8)

What is interesting in Campbell's complete dismissal of Macpherson's account (whose accuracy is clear even in Campbell's outraged ridicule) is his assumption that there *cannot* be much to say about Konds' religious beliefs, that these must be extremely few and simple because of 'the notorious fact' that Konds are savages, in 'a state of semi-barbarism and gross ignorance'.

In other words, Campbell's evolutionism determined completely what he saw. This is also true to a lesser extent of Lt Frye in his article 'On the Uriya and Kondh population of Orissa' (1860). Like the earlier crop of articles, Frye introduced the Konds by defining them as 'quite uncivilized' (below p.256). He contrasts 'the wildest and poorest part' of Kondistan with 'Those portions under the real control of the Uriya chieftains [which] wear a more favorable appearance', thereby equating 'wildness' with poverty, and Hindu domination with prosperity. He starts out with geography and political relations between Konds and Hindus, stressing the *rajahs'* involvement in Kond human sacrifice and the evidence that they practised it too; but unlike Macpherson he does not go into the Konds' political relations with the British. After this there are sections on seasons and crops, markets and trade, dress, money, food, drink, weapons, music, song and dance, language, and diseases, before introducing human sacrifice as 'a rite which deluges the land with social evils'. As ethnography, his account was taken by later writers as more reliable than Macpherson's, lacking as it does Macpherson's great detail which Campbell called into question. It also mixes some careful observation and enquiry into what Konds and Oriyas say, with the usual extreme negative stereotype of Konds as ignorant and superstitious.

From the 1860s, ethnography of the Konds—as of India's other tribes and castes—began to be incorporated systematically into large compilations of administrative knowledge: Gazetteers,[15] the Census,[16] Hunter's huge set of writings on rural Bengal,[17] and several encyclopaedic works that enumerated and compared India's tribes and castes, starting with Dalton's *Descriptive ethnology of Bengal* (1872).[18] In particular, Risley's *Tribes and Castes of Bengal* (1891, in six volumes) analyses Konds among all their neighbouring peoples in the light of the latest European anthropology, as well as a huge survey of physical measurements, which exemplifies the practice of anthropometry ('man-measuring') which Risley effectively introduced to India.

The trouble is, this anthropology's knowledge about tribal people is deeply flawed, above all by being expressed in an idiom that could not be further removed from the reality of tribal life and tribal perceptions, since its idea of 'scientific' knowledge is so alien to *adivasis'* ways of talking and understanding. The customary arrangement of Konds side by side with all the other tribes and castes of a given area defines them and 'puts them in their place' intellectually (through comparison or typology), in a way that is analogous to the process of their incorporation into the British empire. The urge to standardize and catalogue, which permeates this encyclopaedic body of writing, sacrifices the aliveness of Kond social life by giving out as primary 'facts' the most superficial or misleading pieces of information.

Another administrator, Friend-Pereira, published some new ethnographic data on the Konds in the form of three articles (1899–1904) and also wrote a Kond grammar (1909). His first article is a translation of four Kond songs,

> composed in a rude and often ungrammatical language; they are loosely constructed and carelessly worded.... But yet they possess a peculiar charm of their own. They are eminently true to nature; and their crude and half-developed thoughts, struggling through a mist of faulty expression, occasionally afford a glimpse of high imaginings, of tender feelings, and of fanciful imagery.... (1899 p.1)

The fourth of these songs is a 'Hymn to the earth-god', in which 'the names of the zealous officers Captains Campbell and Macpherson who worked so hard and successfully to put down the human sacrifice that was rife among the Khond tribes are immortalized'. It is likely that this was extemporized for the sake of the visiting *saheb*, for Elwin (1944) found other songs, much less flattering to Mukman and Kiamol *sahebs*! Friend-Pereira's next article, on marriage customs, includes photographs of Kond men and girls; one of the girls is at a market and gives a hard look at the *saheb* photographing her. The third article tries to set straight the ethnographic record: 'It has been hitherto believed that the Khonds, in strange contrast to the other Dravidian tribes....are not totemic.' His enquiries elicited evidence that their religion was originally a form of totemism. He lists the data he had collected of ancestors and totems associated with Kond septs, from which he concludes: 'This is something more than animism. It is pure totemism.'

Several administrators sent Kond artefacts, including brass figurines from a shrine, to the Pitt-Rivers Museum of ethnology in Oxford between 1880 and 1930 (above pp.166–7). The pride of this collection is a group of about twenty Kond battle-axes, extremely impressive for their size, elaborate workmanship and formidable blades in various designs—some with two, three or even five points. When we see this collection in the light of the British suppression of Kond warfare and human sacrifice some years before, as the *Pax Britannica* was enforced, it gains special significance. The custom these axes represent was stamped out by administrators, the predecessors of those who collected the axes. The axes' place in glass cases in the museum signifies the control that Britons had acquired over Konds. These axes are victors' trophies, in a scientific idiom. The same applies to a *meriah* post that had been taken from a Kond village and erected in Baliguda police station, before being sent to the Madras Government Museum and put on display there. Thurston, who was Superintendent of the Museum, published a photograph of it (1906) and records how some Konds who saw it there 'became wildly excited when they came across this relic of their former barbarous custom' (1909 pp.371–2).

In the 1900s the Konds and other Central Indian tribes were safely under British rule and anthropologized. The tribes of Northeast India, however, represented a new frontier, for British soldiers as well as anthropologists.

Hence the series of monographs by administrator-anthropologists on the Nagas and neighbouring tribes written from the 1900s to the 1930s by Hodson, Hutton and others, at a time when no monograph was written on the Konds. Konds had been reduced to subjection long ago and were therefore of comparatively little interest, while the Nagas were still to be properly subjected. They were still 'practising headhunters', and therefore represented a new bloodthirsty superstition to suppress in the role of administrator, as well as fresh data to record in the role of anthropologist. These monographs are again like trophies of conquest: anthropology incorporates them into British knowledge of the world to signify their satisfactory incorporation into the British Empire.

'The Kandhas do not Take any Thought for the Morrow'

All this ethnography was evolutionist to its core. Social evolutionism is essentially the theory or belief that societies evolve through a fixed series of stages from 'primitive' to 'civilized'. Darwin's theory of the evolution of natural species was applied to society by a number of 19th century theorists. In Frazer's version, societies evolve from magic to religion, and from religion to science. In Marxist theory, societies evolve from 'primitive communism' to feudalism, to capitalism, to communism proper.

In Darwin's theory of natural selection, every species evolves in relation to others, but along its own particular path, to assume a unique form of its own. What is so simplistic about most social evolutionism is the idea that every society evolves through the same stages, in the same direction. Tribal societies are seen as 'primitive' or 'backward', as if they are less fully evolved than our own society, without understanding that their evolution has had a different emphasis, towards a sophistication of oral culture and the skills of living close to the earth for example, rather than towards the centralization and materialism that are basic to most 'civilizations'. British colonials saw Kond society as 'stuck in a primitive stage', and their own as the height of civilization; and associated with these stereotypes, as part of the same set of beliefs, saw it as their right and duty to hasten Konds' 'advancement' by subjugating them. In this way, social evolutionism goes hand in glove with colonialism, by legitimizing the imposition of unwanted change.[19]

This explains why Government anthropology analyses every domain of Kond social life basically in terms of judging it as primitive, fabricating a set of negative stereotypes that had the status of science. The topics in this ethnography are already set—clan organization, assemblies, chiefs, marriage, birth and death, music and dance, material culture, warfare, religion, and so on. Of course there is much detail of the greatest human interest; but the way it is presented is profoundly dehumanizing, alienating the customs from their human meaning. Each domain defines the Konds in an evolutionary scheme: their clan organization places them at a primitive stage of political evolution; their agricultural practices are extremely backward; their religion consists of superstitious beliefs and taboos and interesting 'totemic survivals'; their sexual *mores* are lamentably backward; they still go about virtually naked; their songs have 'half-developed thoughts'; their language is rudimentary; and above all, they are completely 'ignorant'.

This idea is already fixed in the first writings about the Konds, which place them at the lowest imaginable level of civilization (Revd Brown), 'in a state next to entire barbarism' (Revd Taylor), and 'absorbed in the grossest ignorance and superstition' (Maxwell). Campbell expressed this particularly strongly, projecting European stereotypes of savages in their bluntest form onto the Konds:

> a race *sunk* in the depths of ignorance, superstition and sensuality. I know they have been styled [by Macpherson] "a clear-minded and truthful people," but how or where they can have inherited these rare and precious blessings is very far beyond my conception. Why the Khonds should be different from all other savage and barbarous nations I know not. Between the New Zealand savage who regales himself on human flesh and the Hill Khond who pitifully immolates a human being there is nothing to choose; the one has not outstripped the other in civilization, nor have either (except in a few favored spots) yet had the opportunity of emerging from their barbarisms. (Report of 16th April 1848)

In this view, ethnography is unnecessary: the Konds' religious beliefs are bound to 'illustrate the awful effect of ignorance and superstition on the human mind' (ibid. p.153), and their rituals are simply 'orgies'—an 'abandonment' of reason to the bloodthirstiness of unrestrained human passions. Ethnography is an element in Campbell's discourse, but evolutionism—the idea that the Konds are uncivilized—determines all the details.[20] Frye is similarly scathing of Kond culture:

> There are remote glens.... Placed beyond the pale of communication with the plains, the tenants of these hills are necessarily buried in ignorance, superstition and prejudice.... The Kondh is quite uncivilized; ignorance and superstition are universal.

The Hill Oriyas he defines as 'degenerate', although 'when compared with the Kondhs as a race [they] may be esteemed the less degraded of a deeply debased people' (1860 pp.2, 7, 9).

Macpherson also describes the Konds in evolutionist terms, according to their degree of advancement along a set course,[21] but he is much less insistent on Kond 'savagery'. If anything, he tends towards the 'noble savage' view, in contrast to the far more prevalent view of tribal people as '*ig*-noble savages' (R.L.Meek 1976). He also describes them as 'exactly similar' to the Soras, Gonds and Todas in that different segments 'exist both unchanged, and at every stage of assimilation to the more civilized people' (WM p.19). Campbell's evolutionism, then, is very much more sweeping than Macpherson's, and led him to be more closed and negative towards Kond culture. Yet for both, the primitiveness which they projected onto the Konds was what justified—or 'necessitated'—the imposing of British rule. Each incorporated the role of ethnographer—the expert who 'knew' Kond society—as well as the missionary role—crusading to abolish the Konds' evils and convert them to 'peace'.

Later Kond ethnography relies heavily on these older sources, which it accepts as authoritative. It supports in every way the idea of Konds as 'primitive' and the negative stereotype of every aspect of their culture. For instance, on the subject of sexuality, Maltby's *Ganjam District Manual* gives out a judgement and stereotype that had already become a major theme in the discourse on tribals:

> Chastity is not known, or at least practised by the Kuttiya girls. They go naked till marriage and the unmarried men and girls sleep together in a house set aside for the purpose in some villages; in others, by invitation of the girl, any man she may fancy visits her at her parents' home. (1882 p.74)

Similarly, Hunter introduces his section on tribal ethnography in *Annals of rural Bengal* with some typically derogatory remarks on tribal people:

> Of such inferior races, a great variety survives in the Tributary Estates. Some of them have reached the lowest stage of human existence. In Dhenkanal the Maharaja had a party of wild jungle people [Juangs] brought in to me, among whom the women wore not an inch of any woven garment.... (1872 p.68)

In his Kui Grammar Friend-Pereira made a harsh judgement on the Konds' level of thinking, taking particular offence at their large number of words for baskets:

> The Kandhs might well have exercised their ingenuity in a higher direction and evolved distinct names for the various mental acts as "wisdom", "intelligence", "reason", "judgement", instead of being content with the single vague term *elu*. That they have not done so only shows that their intellectual condition remains in the same rude and undeveloped stage in which it was in primitive times. Dr Caldwell, in discussing the prae-Aryan civilisation of the Dravidian people says—"....they had a word for 'thought', but no word distinct from this for 'memory', 'judgement', or 'conscience'; and no word for 'will'." This remark aptly sums up in a word the present mental condition of the Kandhs and the state of their language. (1909, introduction p.xi)

This assumption that a lack of abstract words means an inferior level of thinking runs through all grammatical studies on the Konds.[22] Against this one could cite Russell Means (above p.26), who is outspoken on the opposite, non-literate viewpoint: that in its extreme abstraction European thought tends to separate itself from nature and lose touch with reality altogether.

This whole tradition of writing about Konds and other tribal peoples, can be seen as a massive attempt to incorporate tribal culture—something essentially alien and incomprehensible to Europeans—into Europe's 'universal' system of knowledge, in a way that, as these quotations show all too clearly, reinforced and spread the worst stereotypes about tribal people, and did so in the name of science.

These administrator-ethnographers based their writings on the ideas of the leading social theorists of their day. Lord Elphinstone cites Hume; Taylor cites Pritchard's *History of Man*; Friend-Pereira cites Andrew Lang's *Myth, ritual and religion* and Frazer on totemism. But Risley is the keenest to place his work in the context of the latest social theorists.[23] He gives first place to the anthropometrists' studies of race, dedicating the first two volumes of his work—which consist entirely of anthropometric measurements of the heads and bodies of tribal 'specimens'—to Topinard, Professor of anthropology at Paris, who had pioneered this approach. Risley introduces the Konds as the closest approximation to MacLennan's

> local exogamous tribe.... A fortunate combination of circumstances has preserved for us in the Kandhs....a singularly perfect specimen of a tribe divided into local septs, each inhabiting the area from which it derives its name.... Contiguous septs were always at war with each other; wives were captured, female infants were slain, and all the incidents of primitive society as sketched by Mr McLennan were in full force....[24]

This kind of cross-referencing between administrators and anthropologists shows the same kind of interdependence between academic anthropologists and Government administrators as we saw between missionaries and administrators in the previous chapter. The anthropologists drew on administrators' writings to support their largely evolutionist theories of culture, while administrators drew on European social theorists to give their writings on tribes, and their image of tribals as 'uncivilized', scientific status, thereby legitimizing their rule as the only conceivable method of 'civilizing' them.

Since the 'armchair anthropologists' back home drew on the administrator-ethnography we have been quoting, the idea of tribals as uncivilized was in effect a circular argument. Tylor cites the Konds as a good example of polytheism, quoting Macpherson's description of their elaborate pantheon (1871 pp.170 & 264), and we have seen how Frazer gave the Konds a prominent place in *The Golden Bough* as 'the best known case of human sacrifice systematically offered to ensure good crops....' (above p.117).

Entwined in all this social evolutionism are strands of other theories which on the surface may seem contradictory. One is the idea that Konds were 'degenerate' or 'debased'. This is not necessarily incompatible with evolutionism, since the idea that Konds or others like them had 'regressed' or 'sunk' to a lower level from a previously higher 'Noahchic' or Hindu level, made it even more of a duty to help them 'advance' or 'rise' again in the 'scale of civilization'.[25] It is similar with the openly racist theory of superior and inferior races, by which, even if tribes like the Konds are never going to rise to Europeans' level, they should still be civilized and helped to evolve as much as possible. Meanwhile, as 'subject races', their labour can profit 'superior races', and their own development will benefit from this contact and be hastened. The exploitative aspect of this theory, which was being formulated by some of the leading anthropologists of the mid-19th century, is all too clear.[26] Racism is implicit in Dalton's work, as when he describes Doms as 'the low bastard Hindu people called Pans' (1872 p.299), but the theory of racial difference as an expression of hierarchy reaches its climax in Risley's measurements of all the tribes and castes of Bengal.[27]

Compared with this, social evolutionism represents a relatively liberal viewpoint, in its idea that tribal societies at least had the capacity to advance 'to the same level as us'. However, the whole debate on whether tribes like the Konds were inferior racially or because of their lack of intercourse with the civilized world, hardened the assumption that they *were* inferior, by defining the parameters of what was in question. It was not in question to anyone at the time that *adivasis* were stuck in a primitive stage of development, or that British rule would hasten their development.

Evolutionism was thus the dominant model through which Britons perceived the Konds to an overwhelming extent. The writer who comes nearest to escaping it is Macpherson, whose enquiry into Kond religion is refreshingly free from preconceptions about what he would find, and is one of the few pieces of 19th century ethnography that gives any impression of the wealth of tribal people's religious life—and sober ethnographers of the next generation, such as Risley, followed Campbell in dismissing it as probably false for this very reason. Campbell's issue with

Macpherson demonstrates the limits of what was *thinkable* by administrators and anthropologists about the Konds. For Campbell there is hardly anything to write ethnography about, while Macpherson is interested in the Konds in their own right. Later ethnography veered between these views, and ossified a 'scientific' representation of Konds as 'uncivilized'. Thurston's or Friend-Pereira's ethnography reads like footnotes to the earlier accounts: the Konds have already been 'put in their place' in the scale of the world's peoples; a place that defines who they are and what they believe; it remains only to correct or add a few details.

Thus later administrator-ethnographers approached Konds with their minds and eyes completely closed to seeing anything that lay outside their preconceived ideas. For example, Ollenbach (1908), the Konds' main administrator in the 1900s, was willing to affirm the Konds' truthfulness against the stigma of lying which Campbell had cast on them, but added, 'It is, however, true that the Khonds were, and still are, very superstitious and ignorant, and addicted to drunkenness.'

Government anthropology has been extremely resistant to the more sensitive insights of academic anthropology. For example, Henrika Kuklick (1978) has shown how in British Africa between the first and second world wars, Government anthropology remained overwhelmingly evolutionist, virtually uninfluenced by the functional/structural tradition developed by British academic anthropologists at that time, which was giving rise to a much more sympathetic understanding of tribal societies.

In India this style of Government anthropology did not end with British rule. Considering the colonial heritage it is hardly surprising to find that social evolutionism has continued to dominate mainstream social theory as well as popular thought about India's tribal peoples. The reason that I have dwelt at some length on this aspect of colonial anthropology is that it disseminated a highly negative stereotype in the guise of science which still dictates the way that most outsiders perceive tribals.

An example of this tendency published shortly before India's Independence is L. Sahu's description of the Konds in *The Hill tribes of Jeypore:*

> The Kandhas do not take any thought for the morrow. They have very little idea of property. They have very little foresight.... They are addicted to drink. Both men and women dance and become happy and in their dances males and females come into contact with one another and erotism is not rare.... Superstitions they have many. For instance, when any body falls ill, it is believed

> that it is the work of some evil spirit and they try to exercise [*sic*, i.e. exorcise] it by means of incantations, etc. But after all what are superstitions? They are the sincere beliefs of those who hold to those superstitions. It is only others who have got newer and real knowledge about those things and can apply their minds to new methods that call the previous imperfect knowledge superstition. Therefore in order to bring them up to our level, we must feel that we have a heavy responsibility on us to look to their education and enlightenment.
>
> Many people aver that these hill tribes are contented on account of their ignorance and in their own way of life. Why disturb them? The fact is that they have been disturbed by our inroads. Therefore [!] they should not be left where they are. As for ourselves, so also for them, divine discontent is a necessity which will prompt them to go higher and higher up in the scale of civilisation and progress. (1942 p.43)

The expression here is more informal, but the inheritance from colonial discourse is very clear. This is as absolute a statement of social evolutionism as one could find: differences between societies are reduced to a matter of levels or stages of development. It is noteworthy that Sahu's book was published at the Baptist Press in Cuttack, for the similarity of this passage to missionary discourse is striking (e.g. above pp.227–8). Its basic emphasis is on the idea that Konds are 'ignorant' and 'superstitious', as well as on the missionary impulse to change them. 'Heavy responsibility' implies the associated theme of self-sacrifice, and the final sentence implies an idea that it is necessary to *sacrifice the present to the future*. This is an expression of pastoral power, imposing 'care' that has not been asked for, and seeking to incorporate Konds conceptually and materially into the mainstream culture.

Ghurye's book on tribal India (1943/1959), also written just before Independence, occupies a central place in Indian tribal anthropology, influencing the style as well as the basic assumptions of later anthropologists. It is a classic statement of the evolutionist perspective. The essence of his argument is that Central Indian tribals should be 'assimilated' into mainstream Hindu culture, since they are 'backward Hindus' and no more 'aboriginal' than the rest of India's population, so that even the best of their culture is a degenerate form of Hindu culture (above pp.19–20):

> Science and history do not countenance the practice of calling these tribes aborigenes. (1959 p.13)
>
> Under the circumstances, the only proper description of these people is that they are the imperfectly integrated classes of Hindu society....they are in reality backward Hindus. (Ibid. p.19)

The conquest of the Paharias to Ghurye was an attempt to 'raise them from their backward state' (ibid. p.16). However,

> In view of the fact that these tribals were sullen, and on occasions violent, the main purpose of British policy was to secure peace and not necessarily to help the people to advance on the road to progress either by integration with the plains Hindus or otherwise. (Ibid. p.79)

This is a highly distorted interpretation of British policy. It is true that, from the 1870s, there was a general policy to protect tribal people from exploitation by trying to limit access to certain tribal areas (above p.168). But this had followed the 'pacification' and 'opening up' of these areas in the first place, for which one of the main motives was the impulse to give tribal people 'the benefits of civilization'. We have seen how Russell and other officials did all they could to enmesh Konds into the mainstream economy (above pp.178–9). Ghurye follows the same scale of values, viewing economic contact between tribals and Hindus as necessarily beneficial, even when it is blatantly exploitative:

> H.B. Rowney, writing in 1882, appreciated the role played by the money lenders and the spirit-sellers who went among the tribals to ply their trade. About the effects of the contact thus established he says: "Their contact with them is generally held to have deteriorated their character, but their only hope of civilization rests on such communion becoming closer day by day". (Ibid. p.30)

If 'communion' with Hindus leads to an end of tribal dancing, this too is beneficial, as it will 'chasten the sex morals of the community'! (Ibid. pp. 60–8) With shifting cultivation likewise: Ghurye endorses British attempts to suppress it in the 1870s, citing Forsyth among other officials who condemned it. Ghurye is therefore critical of a change in this policy that took place in the legislation of 1919:

> The acknowledgement of the right of the so-called aborigines to their traditional pursuits, like the practice of shifting cultivation, without any reference to the needs of the welfare of the general community, was the most dangerous doctrine endorsed by the Commissioners, especially when....the practice of shifting cultivation is condemned as very obnoxious by most competent authorities. (Ibid. p.111)

The 'competent authorities' whom Ghurye cites, on this as on other matters, are the colonial officials who took the most negative view of tribal practices. His sociology thus inherits colonial anthropologists' worst stereotypes about tribal society, along with the evolutionist paradigm that incorporates these stereotypes as if they were 'scientific facts'. In a similar way, it seems clear that much of the modern discourse about 'the tribal problem' supports and legitimizes oppressive Government policies.

For Government imposition on tribes is still legitimized in evolutionist terms. The language has changed, but only slightly. Instead of seeing Konds as a 'primitive race' who need to be 'helped to advance', they are now defined as a 'backward tribe' who need to be 'brought forward'. Social evolutionism persists almost unchallenged in modern Indian anthropology, which maintains the same interdependence between Government officials and social scientists as characterized British rule of the Konds. Where colonial discourse labelled *adivasis* 'wild', 'savage' and 'ignorant', they are now called 'backward', 'underdeveloped' and 'uneducated'. This 'backwardness', like Victorian anthropologists' 'primitiveness', is assumed to apply to all areas of their social and economic life.

A Hierarchy of Knowledge

At the same time as British anthropologists were establishing a 'scientific' image of Konds as a 'primitive tribe', the British Government was laying claim to most of India's forests in order to manage them on a basis of 'scientific forestry', exemplified by Minchin's *Sal forests of Ganjam* (1920, above pp.167, 179–80). The aim of 'scientific forestry' was to combine the aim of preserving the forests with the creation of revenue or commercial profit out of them. The main concern of this science was clearly with how to 'manage' the forest so as to turn it to maximum short-term economic profit (Gadgil and Guha 1992 ch.4):

> As a system of knowledge about nature, [scientific forestry] is weak and inadequate; as a system of knowledge for the market, it is powerful and profitable. (Vandana Shiva, in Ashish Nandy ed. 1990 p.239)

Botanists' classification of forest species is very impressive in one way, but for subtler levels of understanding, *adivasis* such as the Konds possess a much vaster body of knowledge. Nowadays, with our awareness of ecological issues, it may be obvious that this is so, and one can see all too clearly that 'scientific forestry' led to a great increase in deforestation during British rule. But it is striking that British foresters as well as anthropologists showed little awareness that this tribal knowledge even existed. The whole approach of anthropology in effect denied its existence: if tribes were ignorant and superstitious, there was nothing to be learnt from them—it was only they who could learn from us.

It is in this way that the hierarchy which the British established over Konds comes down to a *hierarchy of knowledge*. British ideas about nature or about tribal people were seen as knowledge; tribal ideas as ignorant superstition. Colonial discourse allowed no relationship between the two, or only a one-way relationship of power. At the heart of this hierarchy there is thus a sacrifice—the sacrifice of mutual learning, or of mutual relationship.

In assuming that people who base their society on unfamiliar principles are 'inferior' and in making such people into objects of study there is a sacrifice of being human.

Looking at the early phase of Kond anthropology, it is possible to identify certain key ideas and customary ways of behaving, which underlie the whole discourse: an urge to define and classify people; the idea of subjecting people to detached scientific study, which laid great emphasis on counting and measuring them; the collecting, recording or preserving of 'data' or 'specimens'; the exhibiting or publishing of these; and connected with all of this, ideas about saving and sacrifice, that are perhaps as important in the motivation of anthropologists as we have seen they are for missionaries and Government officials. Throughout all of this runs a deep sense of hierarchy, which was expressed in hierarchical behaviour 'in the field', but whose essence is this hierarchy of knowledge.

The scientific status claimed by Kond ethnography lay to a great extent in its emphasis on counting and measuring, which, increasingly in the 19th century, came to be seen as essential for accurate knowledge of tribal people. The Census was one expression of this, and it caused consternation among tribal villagers all over India, for whom being enumerated is highly inauspicious. Campbell came up against this fear when he tried to make a census of Konds in a village affected by infanticide:

> I tried hard to establish a registry of the men, their wives and children, but was compelled to abandon the attempt. On discovering my intention the people fled in great alarm, asserting they were sure to die if I persisted in my design of numbering them. (1864 p.144)

The Census, as well as most ethnographic writing, begins by defining the Konds in exact numbers. The idea of such accuracy in relation to a vast population whose members are constantly being born and dying, and who on closer inspection elude or fall between the exact categories of the Census Commissioners, is a fantasy. Yet the effort to get such figures exactly correct has been great on the part of Census officials, as well as by the anthropologists who quote these figures. It derives from the idea that 'scientific knowledge' depends on accuracy of measurement, on the model of a scientific experiment. The latitude and longitude of their homeland, the population figures for each District and subdivision, for males and females, for speakers of Kui and Kuvi, for animists and Hindus—these pieces of information were, and still are, taken as defining and classifying the Konds numerically, and therefore as the most basic or reliable 'facts' about them. In this, the contrast with tribal forms of understanding could not be more extreme. Maybe the villagers who fled when they found themselves being counted, were sensing accurately something that was essentially alien and hostile to their culture: the collecting of a kind of knowledge that was geared towards controlling them.[28] What *was* the kind of power over people which the Government established by counting and categorizing them?

This tendency to try and define tribals through numbers reaches its peak in the practice of anthropometry. It was established as a 'science' by Bertillon in France around 1880, as a development from the earlier 'science' of phrenology.[29] Risley applied it in India on a grand scale, presenting his ethnographic data on the Konds and other tribes as a mere 'glossary' to the first two volumes, which contain his measurements of tribal 'specimens'. As he put it,

> Anthropometry may be defined as the science which seeks by measuring certain physical characters, such as the stature and proportions of the head, features and limbs, to ascertain and classify the chief types of mankind, and eventually by analysing their points of agreement and difference to work back to the probable origin of the various race-stocks now traceable. Like ethnography and ethnology, it forms part of the circle of studies grouped together under the head of anthropology.
>
> Looked at merely as a scientific experiment, an anthropometric examination of even a small fraction of the people of India promised to reveal results of no ordinary interest. (1891 p.xxvi)

Anthropometric studies soon became a standard part of ethnographic practice. For example, in 1901 the Royal Anthropological Institute published an administrator's anthropometric study of the Doms in its first issue of the journal *Man*, which demonstrates the arrogance and contempt behind this custom of measuring people with callipers:

> The Dômbs are an outcaste jungle people.... I am informed, on good authority, that there are some Dômbs who rise higher than this but cannot say whether they are, or are not, crosses with superior races. Most likely they are: for most of the Dômbs are arrant thieves.
>
> It was this propensity for thieving, in fact, which had landed some hundreds of them in the jail at Vizagapatam when I visited that place lately, and gave me the opportunity of recording their measurements, and of making some notes of their customs, and these measurements and notes I now submit for what they may be worth, as bearing on the Dravidian problem of Southern and Central India....
>
> [Colour of the skin:].... Of the total number, 34.9 per cent were between numbers 28 and 34 of Broca's colour-types…
>
> [General characteristics:....hair:] ....Number 19, in particular, was abnormally hairy in the armpits, and rather thickly covered on the abdomen and legs. But he was fair of colour and probably a cross. All had, like the [ordinary Madras] Pariah, a very strong and unpleasant odour. They were an ill-made and poor-looking lot of men, one only, out of 25 being really well-shaped and sturdy. (Fawcett 1901 pp.34–6)

Apart from the implicit theory of racial difference and 'crosses', what is striking in this passage is how a derogatory stereotype is reinforced by the use of scientific measurement and numbers, and how this measuring and enumerating distances the writer from the men he is studying, as if they were animals or inanimate objects. It is clear that the *saheb* who wrote this behaved to the men he studied with the same superiority and contempt that he put into his writing. He gained his 'knowledge' about them by measuring them, not by asking them who they are. Number 19 has no voice. His hairiness and bad smell are held up for critical study by men of science all over the world. Making people into objects of scientific study through the demeaning ritual of man-measuring is obviously related very closely to the process of making them subjects politically—in this instance, it came as an extension of the demeaning prison regime to which these men were being subjected.

In other words, anthropology played a significant part in administrators' attempt to incorporate people whom they were unable to understand into their control. The practice of measuring people in this way is the profoundest declaration possible of the cultural superiority which those who study tribal people customarily assume. It is nothing less than an attempt to incorporate them into an alien system of knowledge, which implicitly denies their own knowledge and their sense of who they are. Tribals measured in this way are the epitome of a 'muted group' (Ardener 1975 pp.xi–xii).

Early anthropology had a preoccupation with measuring people, dead or alive. Dalton's *Descriptive ethnology* grew out of a scheme for an Ethnological Congress to be held in Calcutta in 1869–70. At first the idea was to exhibit a collection of skulls and material artefacts, but later, more ambitiously, to exhibit a collection of 'living specimens':

> specimens of the hill tribes, typifying the races of the Old world, for scientific study. (Dalton 1872, preface).

George Campbell, Chairman of the Asiatic Society of Bengal, supported this idea enthusiastically at a meeting in 1866:

> All, or almost all, the tribes and castes of Hindustan would be represented without any difficulty....Bhooyas and Khonds, and others yet unclassed.... they have much engaged the attention of a very scientific man, Colonel Dalton, the Commissioner....
>
> Without in any way degrading men and brethren to the position of animals, opportunity should be given for studying man at least to the extent to which animals are studied.... In this way I think that a commencement might be made of such a scientific study of man, as has never yet been attempted. (George Campbell 1866 pp.87–91)

In this speech George Campbell went on to recommend the collecting of skulls when 'their owners....no longer have a use for them'. He mentioned a widowed Andaman woman who was induced 'with great anxiety' to part with her dead husband's skull, worn round her neck, 'by a bribe of one rupee'. Beneath this humorous plea to further the cause of science, we can observe a distinct custom: the collecting, preserving, measuring and displaying of human skulls, more particularly of non-Europeans' skulls, by European men of science. Indeed, the current Manual of Ethnological Enquiry devoted its first and longest section to 'physical characteristics', and declared that the most important task of a would-be ethnologist on coming into contact with a primitive race was to measure and weigh them. 'Human skulls should be collected, and care should be taken to take away such specimens as truly represent the people.' (*Journal of the Ethnological Society of London* 1854, section 1, note 6) This custom certainly involves an attitude to death every bit as bizarre as headhunting or wearing a skull around the neck, and maybe considerably stranger: one marked by an absence of respect or mourning. The Andaman woman's anxiety is mocked as her customary expression of mourning is undermined.

And how were ethnologists expected to get skulls from tribes like the Konds who did not conveniently wear their relatives' heads round their necks? Dig them up? Cut the heads off corpses before the funerals? Get them from 'specimens' who died in prison? A deep psychological dissociation is apparent in the custom of collecting a subject people's skulls for scientific study, and the idea that it is reasonable or straightforward to do so.

The Government would not grant permission for the exhibition of tribals in Calcutta, and George Campbell began arranging for it to be held in Jabalpur in the Central Provinces. Colonel Spence, the main official in charge of the Baigas, objected to the request to send in some 'Baiga specimens' on the grounds that the tribe was 'wild and naked, and they are so suspicious that they would be sure to think we must have some suspicious object in view'. But Sir Richard Temple, his superior, who was already distinguished for his interest in ethnology and was keen on the plan, commented in a letter to George Campbell:

> I have told him to get the Exhibition Committee to see whether a little lucre may not tempt these wild creatures to come into the station and be clothed, and shewn off for the edification of their more civilized fellow-humans. (George Campbell 1866 p.188)

In more recent anthropology, this tendency towards a scientific idiom has, if anything, greatly increased. When *Man In India* started in 1921 its subtitle was *A quarterly record of anthropological science*.... Through this hardening of the scientific paradigm, it has become customary to describe tribal societies with a level of abstraction and jargon that is even more impersonal, and even further removed from tribal idiom, than the writings of colonial anthropologists. The dehumanizing result is especially apparent in physical anthropology, which still relies heavily on 'man-measuring'. S.C. Roy published a text book on physical anthropology in 1920, D.N. Majumdar studied it at Cambridge, and their monographs on tribal peoples contain tables of anthropometric measurements in appendices, as does Grigson's monograph on the Bastar Gonds (1938). A general claim to scientific accuracy and respectability seems to be a principal reason for the inclusion of this kind of data. B.S. Guha standardized Risley's work and extended it to cover the whole of India in the 1930s. A more recent *Reference manual of somatological studies* (Gupta and Dutta

1966) contains 373 pages densely packed with human measurements to cover all India, compiled from hundreds of anthropometric studies of tribals that have been published in books and articles since 1947. It seems that following British anthropologists' inauguration of the practice, man-measuring has become an entrenched custom in social relations between middle-class Indians, or Indian anthropologists, and tribal people.

For example, a couple of articles in the journal *Eastern Anthropologist* by Gautamsankar Ray in 1949–50 describe Konds' 'physical characteristics' and their kinship terminology. The first of these starts by complaining that 'no-one has yet studied them from the cultural or from the physical standpoints', and proceeds to give a set of anthropometric measurements, from which he draws the enlightening conclusion that

> The majority of the Kondhs studied are bright tawny in complexion with wavy hair and with prominent cheek bones. They are between short and below medium in stature. The mean st. is 159.96 cms. They are mainly dolichocephalic (mean C.I. is 73.57) mesorrhine (mean N.I. being 77.15) people.

Krishan Sharma's book *The Konds of Orissa: An anthropometric study* (1979) compares the measurements of three Kond villages in Kalahandi. One purpose is apparently to aid racial comparison between different ethnic groups, in the tradition of Risley:

> The technique of anthropometry has been used so as to find out the ethnic affinities of the Konds with neighbouring tribal populations like the Bastar tribes and the Bhils of Rajasthan. (pp.10–11)

Sharma also uses his measurements in order to calculate Konds' state of health and nourishment.

> Anthropometric measurements with callipers and tape are very handy because they can be obtained with ease and rapidity, and such measurements are used so as to establish body fat, body muscle, and the weight of the lean body mass. (p.12)

He interviewed members of 51 households through an interpreter.

> It was rather difficult to convince them about the aim of the study.
>
> The other problem was when measurements of female subjects had to be taken. Only twelve adult women agreed to co-operate in this respect. (p.22)

Through calculations based on the average food that Konds ate each day he 'proved' that they were malnourished, though this was difficult to work out because of the unfortunate fact that 'Konds have very irregular food habits'.

> The average calorie intake of an adult Kond is 1708.9 and this has been calculated from the staple diet of the Konds.
>
> These figures indicate conclusively that Konds are under- or malnourished with respect to the calorific value of food articles. (p.44)

The chapter on 'somatoscopy' (i.e. 'examining bodies' without measurement) contains tables, from which, for example,

> It is seen that male Konds show predominance of straight forehead (58.49 per cent) followed by slight slope of forehead (9.43 per cent).
>
> 90.91 per cent of female members of the tribe manifest straight type foreheads, and 9.09 show medium forehead slope. (p.75)

This correlates with 'predominance of medium width of forehead (100 per cent)'. The anthropometry proper proves that, like the Bastar tribes, 'The Konds are predominantly dolichocephals with a tendency towards mesocephaly'; that 'Konds predominantly manifest broad nose *i.e.* platyrrhine (52.83 per cent)'; and that 'The majority of Konds fall in the category of under-size stature' (p.94). Sharma's book ends with some depressing conclusions:

> The Konds are a malnourished people. They manifest malnutrition signs like dental caries, night blindness, tingling and numbness of feet, anaemias, anorexia, and gum bleeding. Hospital records show a high incidence of diseases or disorders like Avitaminosis and other deficiency diseases, Pellagra skin diseases, eye diseases, G.I. tract diseases and infectious diseases. These diseases are the result of malnutrition, and poor hygiene.
>
> Fertility and mortality rates of Sagada range are higher than those of Bhatguda village. High fertility is associated with mortality.
>
> The Konds fit into the proto-Australoid racial type of Guha with considerable Mongoloid admixture. Konds manifest a predominance of under-size stature, wavy or curly hair, broad face, dolichocephals, broad nose *i.e.* platyrrhine, alveolar prognathism, distinct epicanthus fold, scanty beard and moustache.
>
> Konds are underweight with respect to their stature.

The whole Kond people is thus sweepingly defined as 'malnourished' from a study of three villages. This kind of study has no place for dialogue. The scientific idiom precludes any possibility of hearing Konds' sense of their own situation. They are not even asked what they think about their own health and diet—let alone what they think of outsiders' physical or mental health! Do these Konds feel themselves to be malnourished? And if so, from what causes? Or are such questions better avoided by the 'scientific researcher', in case they uncover something of the systematic exploitation that has given rise to such symptoms?

By giving such a depressing, semi-medical diagnosis, this study confirms a most negative view of tribal people, in words that appear to call for the introduction of unasked-for programmes of health-care and hygiene, regardless of Konds' understanding of whatever problems they face, and irrespective of their wishes. Key features of colonial anthropology are implicit, such as the value or emphasis placed on racial difference and the custom of measuring with callipers, which imply the absolute hierarchy that forms the basis for anthropologists' interaction with *adivasis*. Again, it is clear that this comes down to a hierarchy of knowledge: Konds' knowledge has no place in assessing their health compared to the 'objective knowledge' of 'scientific evidence' obtained by measurement.

The impulse to collect and exhibit was channelled towards items of tribes' material culture to create anthropological museums (Ames 1992). The first collection in India was made and turned into a museum in Calcutta in the 1850s–60s, and formed a background to the Jabalpur exhibition of 'living specimens'. In addition to their collections of tribal artefacts and skulls, anthropological museums incorporated the idea of exhibiting an array of tribals for comparative study, by making life-sized models or sculptures of tribal people. These are still to be found as the main attraction in the anthropological collections of several Indian museums. In Bhuvaneshwar Museum, the anthropology gallery is filled with large glass cases displaying life-sized models of Orissa's tribal peoples, to show their physical features and social setting. The Kond family group, like the others, has an exceedingly 'primitive' appearance, suggesting a 'caveman' stereotype. Their label reads:

> The Kondh is a most numerous tribe of Orissa, inhabiting the Koraput, Ganjam and Phulbani districts, divided into four sub-groups like Kutia, Desia, Penga and Dongaria. They have short stature, thick nose, flat face, dark to yellow colour. Linguistically they fall into Dravidian group—speak "Koi" dialect.

This summary of Kond anthropology and the group itself could hardly give a more demeaning introduction to the Konds. They reinforce the worst stereotypes about Konds under the guise of 'scientific facts'. Similar life-sized, stereotyped models of tribals are also to be found in fairs that tour India.

The Konds who saw the *meriah* post in Thurston's museum (above p.254) had been 'brought to Madras for the purpose of performing before the Prince and Princess of Wales'. This custom of taking troupes of tribals around India to entertain VIPs by dancing for their entertainment became widespread in British India, and continues today, as degrading as ever (Chattopadhyaya 1978). Is there not a deep connection between such dances and the collecting and exhibiting of skulls and 'living specimens' in the 1860s? The dances and the museums exhibit *adivasis* to the popular view in a way that confirms the stereotype of tribal people as primitive and exotic; they also turn tribal culture into a commodity.

Dalton's photographic prints of tribals form part of the same tendency: they are a permanent version of the exhibition of live tribals. There are several photographs of Konds, but one of the most telling is of two young and beautiful Juang women who stare hard at the *sahebs* who were examining them. Their caption reads:

> Mr Peppé had immense difficulty in inducing these wild timid creatures to pose before him, and it was not without many a tear, that they resigned themselves to the ordeal.

Anthropological photography is now a well-established practice. We can trace British images of Konds from Macpherson's lost portraits of Kond chiefs, the prints in Campbell's and Macpherson's memoirs, the collection of photographic 'portraits of the wild races' which Carmichael includes in his *Manual* (1869) and the elaborate photographic collections published by Dalton (1872) and Watson and Kaye (1875), to numerous recent publications.

As a symbolic act, photographing tribals can be seen as closely related to the practice of measuring them with callipers, in its use of Western science and technology to incorporate them into our system of knowledge or into our power (Edwards 1992). Alienation, a sense of loss, a surreal relation with time and death are implicit in the very act of photographing (Sontag 1979, Barthes 1984). They are especially deeply involved in the photographing of tribal people, because the act juxtaposes different cultural notions of space, time, and image, and interposes an alien machine into a relationship. It removes people from a particular, real moment in time and space, and puts their image into others' possession in an alien environment, where it has effects that cannot be calculated. For instance, photographs like Dalton's of the Juang women verge on the pornographic when they are published in cultures where women customarily conceal their breasts and thighs in public, and undoubtedly contributed to the current association in popular thought of tribal people with 'free sex'.

The recording of ethnographic data can be seen in a similar light. Whatever the positive aspect of the interest that Macpherson or Friend-Pereira showed in Kond culture, their ethnography accompanied or directly followed the British subjugation of the Konds: recording the culture in writing was part of what Britons customarily did after they had brought a tribe under their authority. It preserves a memory of Konds as they were at the time of first British contact, just as the Pitt-Rivers Museum in Oxford preserves Kond war-axes. Collecting to preserve in this way is a motivating force in anthropology, and its value often appears unquestionable. But who is the preserving for? For posterity? For the sake of academic knowledge? For the sake of 'the truth' itself, to preserve an accurate record? For the sake of future generations of social scientists? For Konds who may become social scientists like us at some future period? Or 'for the edification of their more civilized fellow-humans' (above p.268)?

The value of anthropological collecting and preserving may seem self-evident. However, when interaction with tribal people is reduced to a matter of acquiring objects for museums or 'data' from 'informants', a major sacrifice is involved: an opportunity of unusual value for communication and learning between (instead of just about) human beings is sacrificed by being subordinated to the collecting of new information or the making of a career.

Increasingly, some anthropologists have been prepared to take a stand on behalf of the tribal peoples they study, and depart from this attitude of 'detachment'. When tribal communities are being 'sacrificed' to make way for 'national progress' by being moved off their land to make way for a dam, mine or nature reserve, it is often anthropologists who object.

Yet the greater tendency is still to try and 'save' tribal societies symbolically or at an abstract level, by preserving information, photographs, recordings or artefacts of their traditional culture.[30] This makes tribal culture into a commodity, as if its 'social facts' could survive in the abstract, without the human beings to whom the culture belongs. There is an aspect of this 'preserving' that is as detached and impersonal as scientists who preserve animal specimens in jars, or administrators who try to preserve forests by evicting their *adivasi* inhabitants.

Of course, anthropologists often attempt this rescue job of preserving a record of tribal culture with the best of intentions:

> The Mundas say, that he who sacrifices a human being, is obliged to worship the victim's spirit during the rest of his life, to compensate him for the worship he would have received from his own descendants, had he been allowed to live his normal life. I am convinced that the Aryans are mainly answerable for the impending extinction of the Munda race.... It is therefore a duty incumbent upon our race, that some member of it should try to give as faithful a picture of [the Munda] civilization as possible, and therefore keep alive at least the memory of that, which has been so ruthlessly and senselessly destroyed. (Hoffman 1930 vol.I [letter A] p.ix)

The Revd Hoffman thus introduced his *Encyclopaedia Mundarica*, the largest work of ethnography on an Indian tribe ever attempted, as a labour of love, to save a detailed memory of a culture that is being sacrificed.

S C. Roy touches on the same theme in an article about Kond human sacrifice in the second issue of *Man In India* (1922), in which he makes a plea to save Government Archives that contain ethnographic data about the custom:

> I would recommend to Government with all the emphasis I can command, to make arrangements for rescuing these valuable materials from decay and disappearance. Though in respect of many of these obsolete customs themselves their decay and disappearance is indeed to be rejoiced at, the decay and disappearance of the old papers recording those customs is, however, to be greatly deplored—all the more so because of the disappearance of the customs they record. (1922 p.81)

In other words, the Konds' custom of human sacrifice has happily been sacrificed, but the ethnographic record of these sacrifices should be saved. In the same issue of *Man In India* Hira Lal has an article on 'The Aboriginals of Central India', in which he takes issue with Risley and argues from an analysis of nine Indian tribes that Dravidian tribes represent the indigenous population of India and did not enter India after the Kolarians (Munda-speaking tribes). He ends with the comment that the problem remained to be satisfactorily established by future researches:

> In the words of Professor Turner of Benares University, the path of knowledge is laborious, the road is long and difficult. It calls for high endeavour and the nobility of sacrifice. But this reward awaits the traveller. (1922 p.32)

Hira Lal, like Hoffman, is referring to a specifically anthropological notion of self-sacrifice; though it is also clearly part of a general idea of self-sacrifice in the academic pursuit of knowledge; and is also related to missionaries' and administrators' self-sacrifice. For whom, or for what do anthropologists labour alone in 'the field', with its discomforts and dangers? For the sake of tribal people? As part of an academic search for some ultimate truth? Or to further their own careers?

Also in *Man In India* for 1922, Roy appealed to the Government for anthropology to be put back in the Indian Civil Service exams on the grounds of its usefulness to administrators. This was done the following year. In other words, the product of anthropologists' self-sacrificing labour needs to be understood in terms of its contribution to the exercise of power over *adivasis*.

The first professional anthropologists who carried out independent fieldwork in India worked closely with administrators, such as Rivers (1906) among the Todas, and Radcliffe-Brown (1922) among the Andaman Islanders. Some of the main Government anthropologists became some of the first professional ones, such as A.C. Haddon and T.C. Hodson, who was dismissed from the Indian Civil Service after shooting and killing a coolie in an argument (Morrison 1984 pp.29–30). These men were D.N. Majumdar's teachers in Cambridge in the 1930s.[31] Thus from the start, Indian tribal anthropology inherited its conceptual structure from British administrator-anthropology, along with a tendency to regard the writings of Western social scientists as authoritative.

Ghurye also studied anthropology in Cambridge, under Haddon and Rivers. We have seen how he attributes the same 'ignorance' and 'backwardness' to tribal cultures as British writers did, and assumes the same right and 'necessity' to impose upon them as a result. To support his argument that tribals should be 'assimilated' into mainstream society and that 'the welfare of the general community' should dictate the forest policy, he cites the most reactionary 'authorities' such as Forsyth and Rowney, for whom there was no point in attempting to protect tribals from outsiders because 'legislation has never yet enabled an inferior to stand before a superior race' (1959 p.83).

The way that colonial anthropology hardened negative stereotypes about tribal people and reinforced the most outrageously hierarchical forms of behaviour towards them, and the way that modern Indian anthropology has inherited these features, have hardly been commented upon. But is it not up to anthropologists to try and correct the distorting effects of colonial anthropology, and to insist that tribal societies are *not* backward, superstitious or 'underdeveloped'?

If we survey anthropological writings on the Konds of the last 50 years, we find much of human interest, but rarely get a sense of the culture's aliveness. The conventional mode of expression is an academic, quasi-scientific idiom which abstracts or alienates Kond culture from the Konds. What does it mean to write in such an academic style about people whose lifestyle and outlook are as far removed from academic life as any on earth? As I have tried to demonstrate, it creates, or perpetuates, a gulf of understanding between tribals and non-tribals, and prevents any acknowledgement that Konds have knowledge of their own. It gives out a relatively superficial level of understanding of the Konds as if these 'data' were primary facts about them.

Elwin's anthropology of the Konds (unpublished apart from his 1944 article and Kond myths) is some of the most human, for it is an expression of his belief that 'to study a people is to love them, and to publish your studies is to make them widely loved' (1943 p.31). He stresses the place of the *kutaka* (shaman) that was missed by most previous Kond anthropology; and with this, the importance of dreams, and the manner in which the Earth Goddess and other deities press their demands on the Konds. Yet his Kond fieldwork was based on short tours rather than any long stay, and rarely goes very deep, as his view of Kond mythology as hopelessly confused suggests (above p.119). For example, he gives little indication of the huge knowledge that Konds (and other tribes for that matter) possess about the plants of the forest and their uses. But his fieldnotes make up for this to some extent by a much earthier and vivider description than that of most published anthropology:

> Boys and girls rampage up and down in each others' arms; best girl dancers wriggle their bottoms in singularly seductive manner.... Beautiful pose of girls & shape of head with hair fluffed out to side so attractive. Blow nose onto hand and wipe mucus off on any convenient post. (Notes on the Konds p.13)

In 1944–5 as 'Honourable Anthropologist to the Government of Orissa' he toured Kond areas intensively, and laid great emphasis on Konds' exploitation by outsiders, as well as their own destruction of the forest.

> The destruction of fine forests makes you catch your breath.... for miles you walk through the graveyards (or rather cremation grounds) of magnificent trees. (1945 Report par.11)

This destruction was obviously related very closely to 'the wholesale robbery and extortion' of Konds by various classes of outsiders, including Government officials.

When we come to the Census, we find a different world—one that embodies the idea of objective knowledge as what is measurable, reducing the elementary 'facts' about people to figures of population, employment, cash income and literacy. The 1961 Census also published a monograph on a Kond village, which presents information of human interest alongside tables of statistics, and a concluding comment that the village's advancement in matters of social awareness, education and hygiene call for 'a herculean task' (Ahmed 1961)—the same negative view of traditional culture as characterized colonial discourse, and the same idea of a need for outsiders to sacrifice themselves in order to bring unasked-for changes.

The Anthropological Survey of India (ASI) continues the British tradition of Government anthropology. K. Sharma's anthropometric study of Konds is one of a series of monographs published by the ASI. Another is S. Banerjee's *Ethnographic study of the Kuvi-Kandha* (1968), a detailed account of a Kond village that documents its social life under the usual headings: material culture, kinship system, life-cycle rituals, economy (again with an emphasis on statistics), and religion. As with so much ethnography, the aliveness and human interest of Kond culture is sacrificed to 'objectivity', and one needs to ask: what is the purpose of this? What kind of relationship was made to gain this information? And what kind of relationship does the book create between Konds and the outsiders who will read it?

The same can be asked of the three main monographs on the Konds published by Western anthropologists in the last 35 years. F.G. Bailey's *Tribe, Caste and Nation* (1960) is a work of wider anthropological significance. It tackles the question of Konds' relations with Hindus and the administration, making clear the context of interaction between several political systems, though it falls short of providing a clear analysis of the pervasive reality of exploitation. As an example of structural-functional analysis it is often highly theoretical, analysing village and clan organization with abstract concepts that convey a somewhat misleading impression of Kond social life.

Barbara Boal's ethnography, *The Konds: Human sacrifice and religious change* (1982), centres on a survey of the existing data on the *meriah* and buffalo sacrifice, and adds some more. This anthropological study follows her earlier books, which have a more explicitly missionary perspective (1966, 1973). More recently she has been collaborating with the Government of Orissa to produce a series of handbooks on tribes that will give administrators a less stereotyped view of them.

Niggemeyer's *Der Kuttia Kond* (1964, in German) is probably the most detailed Kond ethnography to be published. Yet the impersonal presentation begs the same set of questions as the previous works. So do his conclusions, which seek, once again, to impose a definitive conclusion on the Konds about who they are:

> The Kuttia....do not represent the original culture of the Kond, as it has sometimes been said. It is much more likely that the Kond people, with a population of more than three quarters of a million, has grown together from heterogeneous tribal groups who took over the Dravidian Kui language, and that the Kuttia represent one of them. This hypothesis still needs support by (a) further ethnographical investigations of other Kond groups, (b) a comparison of their dialects, and (c) the re-examination of the physical anthropological data. (1964 p.245, from the summary in English at the end)

This is a call for more ethnographic and linguistic studies, and more anthropometric studies with callipers. What or who is it all for? When producing thorough linguistic and racial surveys or studies of tribal kinship or religion becomes an end in itself—an academic norm or custom—do we know how much of our behaviour is oriented to an idea of truth that has become dissociated from reality, and how much is motivated by desire for academic prestige, making a career or emulating others' competence? Western as well as Indian anthropologists still seem to perpetuate the highly alienating features of colonial anthropology, in which tribal people are abstracted and objectified, and real communication with them is *sacrificed* to an impersonal communication with posterity, for the sake of preserving data about them or fitting them into our categorizations of the world.

A parallel to anthropology is found in the way that tribal languages have been analysed by linguists. T.W. Burrow helped to set a model for the study of tribal languages that is now in general use, and with S. Bhattacarya published a study of Kuvi (1962–3). This grammatical study and a more comprehensive one by Israel (1979) are no doubt excellent examples of linguistic analysis. But the underlying assumption of a need to define and analyse these languages in a scientific idiom that is completely alien to Kuvi-speakers needs examining. As with anthropologists, one needs to ask: through what kind of relationships do linguists obtain their data? The statement by Burrow and Bhattacarya that they 'decided to spend some time interrogating Kuvi-speakers' (1962–3 p.231) implies the hierarchy of knowledge, and the accompanying hierarchical mode of interaction and its 'scientific detachment', that are implicit in their work. Their academic style of presenting the Kond language makes their work completely inaccessible to Konds (as well as to other non-academics), and thus attempts to establish an expertise about it that is removed from Konds' control and 'above their heads'.

The Sacrifice for Science

From the first articles about Konds in the *Madras Journal of Literature and Science* to Ghurye in the 1940s and much recent writing, a negative view of tribal culture is given out in the name of 'science'. In Victorian times anthropology already claimed the status of science, and it is the idea that Konds were essentially primitive taken as a 'scientific fact' that gave British rule its impeccable air of legitimacy, and made administrators believe it was their right and duty to impose their will over the Konds.

Anthropometry was seen as the scientific edge of anthropology. Risley saw his survey of measurements of Indians as 'a scientific experiment'; Dalton was considered 'a very scientific man'; and both aimed at a 'scientific study' of tribal 'specimens'. 'The science of culture' forms the first chapter of E.B. Tylor's *Primitive Culture* (1871).

What did these people mean by calling their studies scientific? Few if any of today's anthropologists would say that much of this early anthropology was objective—it is so clear to us how preconceptions determined what was observed and described. Modern professional anthropologists and sociologists may acknowledge the unscientific nature of Victorian anthropology, and do not push their own claim to be scientists in the same way; but they are still classed as 'social scientists', along with economists, whose method, being more 'scientific' in that it depends more on measurement, appears to give them higher status. The highly abstract models and concepts and convoluted, specialized jargon which anthropologists use to interpret relationships in a tribal society, are markers of a scientific status or method. It seems to me now that the very idea of studying tribal people more or less 'scientifically' has brought in a highly invidious form of domination that has worked alongside the administrators' and missionaries' forms already discussed.

A lot of violence has taken place in the name of science since Dalton's time, as a recent series of essays by Ashish Nandy and others point out (1990). It is easy to see what was inhuman in Dalton's idea of an Exhibition of 'living specimens'. It may be harder to see this inhumanity in more recent anthropological writing, if one is accustomed to it.

To be objective or scientific is thought to involve a 'detachment' or 'dissociation' between the researching subject and the object of study, as in experiments in the natural sciences. Results obtained from 'the scientific method' are thought to yield an absolute, or universally valid, knowledge (even though many scientists would not make such a claim). The word 'science' derives from Latin *scientia* meaning 'knowledge'. The phrase 'scientific knowledge' is thus tautological—what does it refer to, if not this idea that knowledge obtained 'scientifically' is in some way more reliable or 'real' than other forms of knowledge?

Whatever the status of this detachment when an experiment is performed on inanimate matter, when experiments are carried out on animals, taking their lives and causing them pain are considered acceptable by the experimenter and the scientific community in general, for medical reasons—because the research will save human lives or train doctors to do so—or for the sake of academic truth, or for economic reasons. In this way, should we not regard scientific experiments that involve vivisection as, basically, a form of sacrifice? Has vivisection evolved out of the secular concept of sacrifice in Western society? Looking dispassionately at vivisection, would it not be true to say that 'modern society' performs animal sacrifice on a greater scale and with greater cruelty than any previous society?

For the experimenter aims to kill without feeling, and cultivates a complete detachment from the animals' pain, perceiving them in consequence as objects, with which he has no connection. The 'knowledge' which experiments create does not aim to include knowledge of the scientists' relationship with the animals they experiment on, or the animals' connection with those who sponsor or benefit from the experiments. Any question that the animals are perceiving subjects that experience great pain is laid aside, because it is considered unprovable as well as irrelevant to the specific topics of research.

And from vivisection how far is it to scientific experiments on human beings, such as those that Nazi doctors carried out on the inmates of their concentration camps, or those that the US Government carried out on various groups of people after the War to discover the effects of radiation?[32] Some aspects of this behaviour appear to be quite closely connected to the activities of Victorian anthropologists who measured and collected tribal 'specimens', dead as well as alive. Shiv Visvanathan, in his essay 'On the Annals of the Laboratory state' (in Nandy ed. 1990), investigates this theme of experiments on human subjects. The inhuman killing of the Nazis' concentration camps, as he says, was a direct application to human beings of the procedures of 'normal science'. In a sense the very notion of 'scientific detachment' can open the door to abuse by separating a scientist from his wider awareness of and responsibility for the effects of his actions.

Bruno Bettelheim wrote his book *The informed heart* (1960/1986) in an attempt to come to terms with his own experience as an inmate of a Nazi concentration camp in 1938–9 by making an objective psychological study of inmates' behaviour. The book arose from his sense of 'how difficult it is to try to comprehend these phenomena, to come to terms with man's inhumanity to man.... It also shows that mastering the emotions which such inhumanity arouses can easily require a life-long struggle....'(p.xiii) He wrote from his 'conviction that to withstand and counteract the deadening impact of mass society, a man's work must be permeated by his personality', as well as by objectivity (p.4). For objectivity without an 'informed heart' threatens to replicate the violence of the Nazis. One of Bettelheim's most significant experiences he relegates to a footnote (p.118 note 6): 'It is now of minor interest that from 1939 to 1942 I met disbelief and criticism when I spoke of the German concentration camps as serving important purposes for the Nazis.' Psychoanalytic journals rejected and declined to publish his psychological findings, in the belief that they represented a former prisoner's 'loss of perspective'. In this kind of suppression lies the inhumanity of much 'scientific' discourse, that aids oppression by refusing to face it.

Similar ideas about 'scientific detachment' are implicit in much anthropology and sociology. At times anthropology offers the deepest sense of what it means to be human, through an exploration of other societies that are based on different, often much gentler, principles than our own.[33] At other times it sacrifices the essence of being human, as colonial anthropology did on the whole, by broadcasting negative stereotypes in a scientific dressing. For example, Frye, Friend-Pereira and Fawcett claim a scientific status for their writings on Konds and Doms through the impersonal way they present their 'data', and the fact that they do not mention their relationship with Konds, or how they obtained this data. They thus dissociate or detach their information from how they collected it. We can see that their view of Konds is far from objective; but its extreme subjectivity seems to arise from their very belief that they were writing objectively.

One example where this custom of scientific detachment is carried to an extreme is *The Mountain People* (1973) by Colin Turnbull, otherwise one of the most human of anthropologists. In his fieldwork in a remote corner of Uganda, Turnbull studied and photographed the Ik as they starved to death. A major reason for the famine among them was their recent exclusion from their former hunting grounds, which had been incorporated into a nature reserve. Turnbull's interpretation of the Iks' inhuman behaviour to each other as they starved to death is celebrated, but what of the anthropologist's inhumanity, as he witnessed and recorded it? He even ends by recommending the tribe's forced removal from its mountain territory, on the grounds that this would save the lives of its last members, and that their culture was beyond saving.

I can only point out this tendency within anthropology to sacrifice the essence of being human because I am conscious of this tendency in myself. At an earlier stage I wrote about tribal people in a way that, in an attempt to be detached and objective, cut me off from my feelings and from a wider awareness of what it means to write about tribal people in a conventional style that was established by anthropology several generations ago—a style that I would now say is fundamentally hierarchical and arrogant. If anthropology is the 'science of humankind', the gravest error, it seems to me now, is to practise this science without bringing in one's humanity: a study of people that is not human involves the sacrifice of *anthropos*—the sacrifice of man as a subject who seeks to know himself.

To convey a sense of this sacrifice in terms of an anthropologist's actual relationships: every piece of anthropological writing about Konds involves social relationships between outsiders and Konds. Yet it is the custom to abstract tribal cultures into a discourse not easily intelligible to *adivasis*. The preserving of anthropological data about tribal culture usually involves translation into a scientific idiom that could not be more alien to tribal culture. It is in this sense that the old style of anthropology alienates knowledge *about* Konds *from* Konds. There is no room in this anthropology for whatever knowledge Konds have of themselves or of us or of the forest they live in. As a result, the actual relationships through which outsiders gain their knowledge about them disappear, *sacrificed* to the pursuit of a universalized, 'scientific' knowledge. Anthropologists sacrifice tribal people by making them into objects of scientific study; and they sacrifice their own relationships with them for the sake of 'objective analysis'.

Several contrasted relationships are evident in the practice of anthropology: with 'informants' in the community studied, with Government officials who permit the research, and with the people who listen to or read what an anthropologist writes—colleagues and teachers as well as the anonymous literary public. An anthropologist's work thus implies a contrast between 'informants' from whom he gets his data in its raw form, and readers who receive it in a highly interpreted form. Both are absent while he writes. As with photography, there is no way to calculate the effects of an anthropologist's writing. It communicates impersonally, and survives his death, preserving his memory, as well as a memory of the people studied. His writing puts readers into a relationship with tribal people, an imaginative relationship that will have real but unknowable effects, a relationship mediated by the anthropologist's actual presence in both cultures at different times.

This involves tribals in a novel kind of impersonality in a relationship, which they meet in the anthropologist's behaviour towards them, recording or preserving their conversations or actions in writing, or by taperecorder or camera. Such behaviour subordinates human interaction to the search for fresh information or interpretation. For an anthropologist's first loyalty is usually to his discipline or department, and to his project or career, which depend on the quality of his data and arrangement of it. Some anthropologists actually describe extracting secret information—a secret name or choice religious or sexual 'data'—by lying, or playing off one informant against another. But even without this, anthropological custom demands a sacrifice of present contact for the sake of a future, impersonal end, that is more or less incomprehensible to 'informants'. Even if an anthropologist does not measure tribal people with callipers, this quest for data, which he writes down or taperecords and takes away with him, makes tribal culture into an object, and tribal people into means to that object. Often informants are paid for giving valuable data, like the Andaman woman's one rupee or the 'little lucre' for tempting Baigas to become exhibits so that 'men of science' can study them. The 'data' are paid for again when someone buys the anthropologist's product. In this way, there is a tendency for anthropologists to turn tribal culture into a commodity that is sought after and packaged, bought and sold. In doing this they assume the role of *merchants of knowledge.*

A Human Anthropology?

When Dalton was sent to visit a previously uncontacted section of the Abor tribe in Assam, his party listened to a long speech by an elder,

> which proved to be an inquiry as to what possible object we could have had in visiting them. It was not easy to persuade them that there was nothing premeditated, no *arrière pensée* [hidden motive] in the assurance that the visit was solely intended to inspire confidence and friendship. (1855 p.162)

But was this the Britons' only intention? Not many years later, they used force to make Abors accept British rule. When Britons first visited Kond villages they said they came 'as friends' as well (above p.65). Do anthropologists know the answer to the question we are invariably asked—'Why have you come here?'

Tribal people are often described in stereotyped terms as being dictated by a blind superstition, or limited by irrational taboos. Are we really so aware of our own customs and why we observe them? Is it possible that a lot of that image of tribal people is a projection of our own lack of freedom from our own constricting customs? Colonial culture is certainly full of the strangest taboos. If we make these, as well as our own anthropological values and customary forms of relating, an object of anthropological enquiry, maybe we can create a more human anthropology.

Behind anthropologists' customary 'detachment', is there not in fact a deep *attachment* to entrenched forms of understanding and behaviour from our own culture? Could we cultivate a detachment from these instead, that would allow us to visit tribal people and describe what we learn there free from preconceived ideas or acquisitive motives? The kind of objectivity that we could seek—and which some scientists as well as anthropologists seem to be turning towards now—is one that incorporates, or is not detached from, subjective perception.

In this chapter, I have considered the content of Kond anthropology very little, focusing instead on the parameters of anthropological discourse: our social relationships, and the overarching conception of the difference between 'civilized' and 'primitive' societies. If my interpretation of anthropological practice concentrates on its most negative aspects, this is because its positive potential seems so great. Anthropology has played a vital part in challenging the ethnocentrism of the West, by revealing the richness of non-western cultures. I believe that there is still much to be learnt through anthropology in freeing ourselves from a narrow view of what it means to be fully human. This is the dream that attracts many people to anthropology.

I hope my analysis of Kond anthropology has gone some way to exposing the reasons why anthropology so often fails to fulfil this quest.

I would suggest that a paradox lies at the heart of anthropology. The urge is to discover and learn about 'the other'. But however much we learn about it, 'the other' will always remain, finally, an enigma, unknowable. Rather than accept this, the anthropological tradition has constructed ways of 'knowing' and defining people of other cultures that are profoundly limiting—on them (since it has an effect on them) as well as on ourselves. Is the urge to collect, enumerate, classify, define or even interpret tribal people not at some level an attempt to have control, at least in our own minds, over people who live in a way that is at a very deep level different from how we live?

So what would a truly human anthropology of Kond society look like?

The first prerequisite would be that it leaves the Konds free, by not imposing anything on them or appropriating their culture—an anthropology that would not tell future generations of Konds what to think of Kond culture. For this we need to look closely at our motives—are they 'a non-acquisitive pursuit of philosophy'?

Secondly, the context of Konds' relations with outsiders needs to be our starting point. Since most of their external relations have been characterized by gross exploitation and hierarchical dominance, we need to have some understanding of these transcultural relations simply in order not to fall into or add to that tendency. Most anthropology of tribal India is still enmeshed in assumptions inherited from colonial anthropology or Government ideology, and fails to analyse the actual structure of power and authority that has been imposed over tribal people. To do so means to question a hierarchy of knowledge that we may take for granted, as well as our own motives and the way we approach a tribal village.

When we come to look at relationships within an *adivasi* community, what do the people themselves want to show us? Can anthropology become to some extent a vehicle for transmitting *adivasi* knowledge? Some of the best recent anthropology, which explores the coherence of a tribal people's key concepts and values and shows how these differ from our own, does this incidentally.[34] Such works go some way towards bridging the gulf of understanding with tribal people, though the academic presentation still often limits the human meaning of what is communicated. If we still want to go as anthropologists to people such as the Konds, what does it mean to observe and describe them as full human beings and without hierarchy? How do we free ourselves effectively from the older ethnographic custom of collecting and describing dehumanized data? Instead of 'what can we learn about them?', perhaps the best focus is: 'what can we learn *from* them?' If we are conscious of the inequality and intolerance in our own society, and the calamitous effect of our lifestyle on our environment, is there anything which they can teach us on these matters? How come they are able to live, on the whole, so much more harmoniously with each other, and to take from their natural environment without destroying it?

This is not to idealize tribal life or play down its negative features and internal conflicts, but to say that colonial anthropology put all its emphasis on these, which created enduring negative stereotypes and denied the existence of *adivasi* knowledge, from which we and our society could learn a lot.

With the treatment and behaviour of children in *adivasi* society, we can observe the combination of security and freedom they are given. Parents and relatives give their children a well-rounded education without the alienating features and restraints of most school systems, that impose a heavy-handed authority over children and disembody knowledge from experience. Jean Liedloff's comparison of upbringing in 'modern' and tribal societies calls attention to the depth of emotional deprivation in modern child-rearing, and highlights the tendency to impose alien ideas about what is good for them onto our children.[35]

With marriage and kinship and the position of women, instead of focusing on exotic-seeming rituals or the algebra of kin-terms or systems of 'cross-cousin marriage', if we look at the freedom of choice which partners exercise, the way they complement each other in work, and the daily diplomacy that makes it possible for so many close relatives to live so close to each other with comparatively little strife, there is a lot we can discover which most anthropology has barely touched on.

With old people we see a society based on principles that could not be further from modern ideas about retirement and passivity in old age. Elders in a tribal society grow into a freedom full of humour, and exercise an authority that is real, because it is based on a lifetime of knowledge accumulated through experience.

Adivasis' relationship with nature is based on a body of knowledge that has evolved over many generations, about plant and animal species, wild as well as cultivated, how to take from them without diminishing them over time and use their gifts to make a huge range of foods, medicines, tools and other objects. To think of preserving the forest without drawing upon this knowledge, as the Forest Department as well as some environmentalists do, appears shortsighted in the extreme.

And when we look at *adivasi* religion, instead of seeing it as a jumble of meaningless superstitions, or excitingly exotic symbolic structures, what if we try and understand it as a real and sound way of relating to all that is unknown in the natural environment, and in misfortune or death? The work of shamans and priests deals with forms of healing that go beyond the mental understanding which our own culture has become so expert in; and in coping with death, it offers scope for a fuller and more expressive mourning than most of us have any experience of. Part of being human is to be open to the unknown: no amount of 'scientific knowledge' diminishes the effects on us of pain or death, or the wonder at life's mysteries—at worst, it tends to numb our sense of this. Perhaps tribal cultures have developed a more harmonious relationship with what is unknown or unknowable in human life.

CHAPTER EIGHT

In the Name of Development

Cycles of Exploitation

This book would not be complete without a comment on the situation now. For colonialism has not come to an end. The structures of power and authority which British rule imposed over the Konds and India's other tribal peoples are still in place.

To start with, it is beyond question that a high scale of oppression and exploitation of *adivasis* has continued, if not greatly increased, since British rule came to an end, despite the formulation of policies for tribal welfare and protection. This is clear, for example, from B.D. Sharma's Report as Commissioner for Scheduled Castes and Tribes (1989). Industrial development has compounded the situation enormously by completely displacing many thousands of *adivasis* from their land to make way for dams and mines—a process of displacement which carries much further what the British began by 'reserving' large areas of forest and carving others into coffee and tea plantations. On the one side there is thus great exploitation, on the other an ideology of 'development' that imposes unasked-for changes. Overall, the present situation in tribal India has aptly been called *internal colonialism*.

This chapter is only a sketch of how it seems to me this whole subject needs to be approached—an attempt to arrive at a more balanced or objective understanding of the present situation by looking at it as a whole, from the perspective of having analysed the imposition of British rule onto the Konds. As in the previous chapter, I am broadening the focus outwards from the Konds to look at the situation in tribal areas of India generally. Each tribal area has its own local complexities and political subtleties, yet it is clear that what has been imposed on *adivasis* in different areas is essentially the same pattern—the same techniques of control imposed through the same colonial roles. The non-tribals who come to a tribal village today act out a similar range of roles to those that existed 100 years ago. It seems that what Europeans imposed on Indians as a whole, certain classes of Indians continue to impose on *adivasis*.

If one sees the situation basically in terms of what outsiders bring or impose on the Konds, then to go to the root of this process means examining this culture of imposition, rather than simply its effects. So I shall not go into much detail here about the effects of change; nor about the relation between changes which outsiders impose directly and changes within Kond society, many of which are in response to outside pressure or the lure of an image of power or success offered by the outside world, and which accentuate acquisitiveness and divisiveness. Suffice it to say for now that, in contrast to popular ideas that equate remoteness with poverty, remoteness tends to be the best insurance against poverty—except where moneylenders use it as a cover for their extortion. Konds, like most other *adivasis*, still have inaccessible core areas, which the outside world views as the most 'poor' and 'backward'. But these remoter Konds, who still dwell in areas of full forest in villages that can only be approached by a footpath, have on the whole a much richer quality of life both because of their access to the whole range of products which the forest offers them, and because they are relatively free from the attentions of exploiters or of *sahebs* who come there to tell them how they should live. At the opposite extreme, where the forest has been cut down and there is regular road access, there tends to be a much greater level of interference and exploitation; as a result, there is often the deprivation of basic needs that can justly be called poverty. Most Kond communities probably exist somewhere between these two extremes.

The cycle of exploitation that enmeshes so many *adivasis* is quite widely understood by many who live in tribal areas. *Adivasis* are cheated, money is extorted from them, they get into debt, enter the status of bonded labourers, and lose their lands. This cycle is repeated with endless variations throughout India's tribal areas. The more sensitive officials frankly admit the corruption and exploitation and do all that they can to stop it, which is some compensation for the notorious extent of other officials' habitual extortion.

Yet this cycle has been little studied by social scientists.[1] Why not? Partly, there is the obvious difficulty of getting reliable data about bribes and illegal land deals, combined with the falsely 'scientific' tendency to ignore things that cannot be proved with 'hard evidence' in the form of quantitative data. If the reality is that bribes to Government officials are often one of tribal people's main expenses—or even *the* main expense—then by definition 'hard data' will be concealed, yet economic studies are meaningless if they ignore this fact. Added to this is a fear of contentious issues, of studying or offending those with power, questioning their perception of events and cultural bias: a fear that needs to be faced.

A lot has been written on 'the tribal problem', most of it apparently sympathetic to tribal interests. The truth is, it is not tribals who are the problem, it is outsiders and their customary behaviour in approaching tribal villages in the role of *saheb*, that asserts a higher status, combining caste hierarchy with the attitude: 'I'm civilized, you're not'. Outsiders go in towns-clothes, their smart shirts, pants and shoes, wristwatches and short hair all assert this superiority. An outsider usually sits on a 'cot' or chair, while villagers sit around him on the ground, addressing him as *saheb* or *maharaj* ('great lord'), while he talks down to them patronizingly or orders them to serve him with curt barks. *Adivasis* have evolved a customary response of appeasing *sahebs* to try and get them to be less intrusive and demanding; a false persona of inferiority that confirms *sahebs'* stereotypes and protects *adivasis* from conflict by not revealing their full vitality.

At the root of outsiders' customary behaviour, are the negative stereotypes of tribal culture, whose history I have examined in previous chapters—the idea or belief that tribals are dirty, naked, promiscuous, lazy, addicted to drink, superstitious, and essentially 'ignorant' and 'backward'; at the best they are seen as 'like children', and 'straight'. Thus outsiders talk down to *adivasis* in various ways, which explains why *adivasis* tend to take a dim view of outsiders' powers of comprehension. As a saying of one of the Poroja tribes expresses this:

> *Poraal paataa paapkul paataa okti.*
> 'Outsider talk is baby talk.'

Hence the *gulf of understanding* which marks nearly all communication between *adivasis* and outsiders. Most of what has been written and published about *adivasis*, as I have tried to show, actually widens this gulf, because it is in a language so far removed and abstracted from the way tribal people speak that it makes no sense in their language, and because there has been so little attempt to interact with them on an equal basis or to learn from them. Hence the pervasive lack of any recognition that *adivasis* have their own form of knowledge. Most outsiders who deal with tribal people on a regular basis know and appreciate their culture very little.

The modern background to this negative stereotype is an extremely widespread belief in 'development'. 'Development' is, of course, a concept of the greatest value and importance. We all believe in it, or say we do. But what do we mean by it? Is it not very often used as a cover for gross exploitation and the imposition of unasked-for changes? Is the popular belief in 'development' in India actually very different from Victorian Britons' belief in 'progress'? Is it any less naive and all-encompassing? Sahu's description of the Konds' 'ignorance' exemplifies this (above p.261). It is clear, from the quotations presented in the previous chapter, that the negative stereotypes which outsiders hold about Konds, and which form the basis of their interaction with them, are essentially a hangover from British colonialism. At its most extreme, they allow people to look on tribals as if they were animals. 'They live like cats and dogs' a contractor told me in Bastar of the lorryload of tribal women he was delivering to their worksite.

The Colonial Roles

I have approached this study of colonialism by taking the dominant colonial roles of administrator, missionary and anthropologist, because these separate roles seem to contain the essence of colonialism. A whole culture or sub-culture lies behind each one, yet in their separateness, even when they conflict, the assumptions and ways of behaving of each role reinforce a general pattern of domination. A fourth role of colonist, trader or moneylender completes this pattern of domination. As the Government 'opened up' tribal areas, this increased local non-tribals' ascendancy over tribals and accelerated a process of taking over and colonizing their land. So this fourth role is often the most directly exploitative.

These colonial roles are still being acted out. In some ways they have changed only superficially since India's Independence. Each embodies a kind of domination which can be understood as a distinct level of the sacrifice of tribal culture, or of tribal people's quality of life.

The roles of colonist and trader are often blatantly exploitative, especially that of the moneylender, whose inhuman rates of interest are at the heart of the exploitative cycle, by forcing tribals into debt, loss of their land, and 'bonded labour'—the status of *goti*, well documented e.g. by Patnaik (1972) and Mohanty (1945/1987). I remember one moneylender whom I met in a Kond village, who showed first a highly artificial friendliness before putting on a great show of anger, shouting at everyone when his demand for payment could not be met, and waving an enormous wad of 50 Rupee notes in the middle of the village.

In America, whites played this role of the direct exploiter and displacer, as well as the other roles. The merchants who sold guns and liquor to the Indians, the colonists who took over Indian land and turned it into private ranches, and the gold miners, were all whites, from the same race and culture as the administrators and missionaries. In India, the roles of colonist/merchant and administrator were mostly quite separate, since the colonists who began to take over tribal lands during British rule were Indian non-tribals, mostly Hindus. Before the Mutiny of 1857 though, some Britons formed revealing plans of colonizing India's tribal areas with poor white settlers, who would help to clear the forest and 'civilize the natives'.[2] And whenever the Government extended its rule to a remote tribal area, it aided 'communion' between Hindus and *adivasis* as a means of undermining tribal independence—as Russell advocated for the Konds (above pp.178–9). The roles of colonial administrator and colonist of tribal land thus went together and complemented each other.

Nowadays, the towns and administrative centres in tribal areas that are linked by asphalt roads and buses have the character of frontier towns, where Hindu and tribal cultures meet, on a most unequal basis. The forest is receding further from these towns year by year. Every day there is a slow procession into them from the surrounding countryside of tribal men and women carrying loads of firewood on their shoulders and heads to sell for small amounts of cash. What is the economic necessity that drives them to cut down their forest to sell to townspeople, except the cycle of exploitation? Many Hindus wear the tooth or claw of a tiger or bear around their neck—a symbol of the ascendancy they aim for over the forest areas that surround them, which one could compare with the stuffed heads of animals which British *sahebs* kept on the walls of their houses.

In fact, the first role of the British in India, in the days of the East India Company, was that of merchant. The EIC gained territories for the sake of the tribute that could be raised from them. The Ghumsur wars for example were initiated over a matter of tribute (above pp.37, 39). The fact that the most senior administrator in a District is still called the 'Collector', after his role of collecting taxes, is a survival of this mercantile motive, where revenue was the first priority. Minchin's timber company is another example of the top end of the merchant role (above p.167). Modern developers and industrialists, who build mines, dams and factories in close collaboration with the Government, represent an extension of this role. Some of the topmost players are not in India at all though: they are the people who run the foreign banks and companies that support such projects, and put pressure on India to make a quick profit to repay foreign debt, and they affect tribal areas impersonally: few of them go there, and those that do have no need to interact directly with the tribal people they are displacing.[3]

As regards the role of administrator, we have examined its formation under British rule. At its best, the present Indian administration offers great stability and protection, with a strong ethic of service and care; especially when compared with Europeans' behaviour to indigenous people all over the continents of America, Australia and Africa, and with the elites of other recently independent countries, such as Burma, Bangladesh, Indonesia and Sudan, whose tribal populations are still frequently terrorized and massacred on the level of genocide.[4] In parts of Northeast India the Government often plays a much more oppressive role, comparable to these other regimes as well as to British soldiers' 'subjection' of the Konds 150 years ago, with a similar burning of villages, but heightened by the modern bitterness of a clash of ideologies and an extensive if not systematic use of torture and rape to terrorize people, that recalls the many hangings which British officials performed in Kond areas to produce the 'salutary effect' of order through fear: a 'peace' based on repression. As a result, it is not surprising that a large proportion of the Nagas are now quite alienated from India and refuse to accept the legitimacy of the Indian Government.

Yet quite apart from Nagaland and other sensitive frontier regions, the present administration of India's tribal areas, as Sharma's report suggests, is characterized by a profound split between policies that are often based on the best intentions, and an implementation of these policies that is often non-existent. Hence Sharma's urgency and frustration at a complete divorce between what is supposed to be happening according to official policy and the Spirit of the Constitution, and what is actually going on. The split is due in part to the ubiquity of corruption—the fact that it has become normal and customary among many of the lower level policemen and forest guards to demand large bribes from tribal villagers. The top administrators thus say one thing, while lower officials do the opposite, because basic patterns of behaviour and stereotypes remain unchanged. Officials entering a tribal village assume the role of *saheb* in a way that creates enormous distance and hierarchy between them and tribals, and is highly inconsistent with their role as 'public servants', leading to a great lack of free communication and trust. Instead of protecting tribals from exploitation, they often initiate the cycle of exploitation themselves.

This frequent divorce between what administrators say and what they do can be traced back to a basic ambiguity at the start of British rule (above pp.68, 72–3, 168–9), when the normality of extortion was almost certainly established, as we saw through Campbell's and Macpherson's accusations against each other's subordinate officials. It was there after the Agency period during Dinobandu's 'reign of terror'; it was there when forest guards 'reserved' the forest which Kond villagers customarily used for their basic needs unless bribed to do otherwise (above pp.167–8); and it is all too prevalent now.

Anthropologists and sociologists have shied away from studying administrators: it is virtually a taboo—despite Evans-Prichard's recommendation (Johnson 1982a), and a start made by Gluckman (1971). To form an understanding of the administration that is objective, in the sense of being free from administrators' own ideas, it is necessary to study these ideas as a belief system that is linked to set patterns of behaviour. A good starting point for conceptualizing the social structure of the administration is thus the contrast we used in chapter 5 (above pp.142–3) between an elaborate formal or conscious organization with its hierarchy, departments, laws and rules, etc., and the structure as it actually works: the norms of behaviour; values and beliefs; stereotypes; conflicts and rivalries between departments, personalities or ideologies; and motives, acknowledged and unacknowledged, to do with honour or prestige and financial gain.

Before British rule, it was the *rajahs'* duty to uphold *dharma*: the law was custom sanctified by tradition. Of course, the *rajahs'* officials were often highly exploitative, but their impact was much less intrusive on the whole simply because their ideology was conserving, rather than trying to change, the order of things. The modern conception of law as something that is very precisely defined but keeps changing according to a belief in 'development', as well as the decisions of a remote group of people in power (the *sarkar*) is very alien. Local officials use this contradiction by assuming the status of small kings (like the forest guard in Mohanty's novel), with the power to decide who shall prosper and who shall suffer according to their whim, playing on the older conception of law as something that stays constant but is imprecisely defined: everything depends on the *marzi* (the wish or pleasure) of the officials, which is to be gained by a bribe or grovelling or some other favour, exacted as if it was tribute. In this context, the act of writing often functions as a symbol of officials' superior power and status, and they make the most of its mysteriousness to tribals: a family can lose its land with the stroke of an offended official's pen.

The administration has increased hugely since Independence, and the administrative centres, as the largest 'frontier towns', are in many ways similar to the 'fort' towns that established European power over American Indians (such as Fort Dallas) and Scottish Highlanders (such as Fort William). The expansion in the administration has brought a huge increase in bureaucracy that often ties the hands of the best-intentioned officials, as well as creating large 'colonies' of people who serve the administrators.

The role of *contractor* is an essential element in this expansion, and involves a mode of behaviour that is the epitome of the *saheb* role. It is a common sight in any tribal area to see a contractor, in 'civilized' shoes, shirt and pants, standing by the roadside or at a construction worksite supervising a team of tribal men or women, whom he orders around with indescribable harshness and contempt as they labour to mend a road or erect a building.

Many officials see their presence in a tribal area as a 'punishment posting' whose only advantage is the bribes with which they customarily supplement their low pay. The hierarchy that they impose over tribals is a reflection of the hierarchy that is imposed over themselves, which pervades the system inherited from the British. Some of the senior officials from the IAS (Indian Administrative Service) cadre, with its elite exams and training, have the best of intentions, but there is such a gap between them and the lower officials in terms of status and education, that to really confront the issue of corruption requires the greatest courage and integrity.

As the corruption grows, so does the alienation of tribal people from the Government and from mainstream Hindu society. Hence the danger of a violent tribal-Hindu split, as in Assam. Christianity offers one organized alternative. The Naxalites offer another: terrorists whose violence is a reflection of the state's violence. In areas of Central India where they operate, the Naxalites confront the corruption and domination of oppressive landlords and policemen, although fundamentally their Marxist-Leninist ideology is as arrogant and uncaring towards tribal culture as the mainstream, with its own practice of tyranny and sacrifice of lives.[5]

In other words, the administrative system needs examining afresh, by Indian scholars and officials. For in the eyes of many *adivasis*, the system established by the British is often nothing but institutionalized extortion. As another saying of one of the Poroja tribes expresses it:

> *Sarkaar theen parkaar:*
> *Narpitaanaa, Adeithindaanaa, Jiyam noypitaanaa.*
> 'The Government has three qualities:
> to frighten, demand food, and make the heart ache.'

As for the missionary role: the foreign missionaries have gone, but Christianity is self-perpetuating now among Konds, and much of this Christianity 'on the frontier of paganism' is very evangelical and intolerant of other religions. Many Christians in the Kond area still talk of Hinduism and the Kond religion as the worship of 'false gods' and the road to damnation. Konds are thus divided into traditionals and Christians, and the latter into Catholics, Baptists, Lutherans and other sects. There is obviously great value in Christ's example and message of love and equality before God, but to take the Bible as the only source of truth creates a terribly narrow, closed and divisive society, reminiscent of the time in Europe when Christianity was enforced by law and 'heresy' was punished by death. Many Christians nowadays no longer see themselves as having a monopoloy of truth, and recognize the paradox that much of what has been imposed in the name of Christ is highly oppressive—the very antithesis of the radical path of freedom and love that Christ taught. But how far have first and second generation converts inherited the missionaries' intolerance?

Also, just as colonial administrators internalized some aspects of the missionary role (above pp.153–9, 198–9), so in many ways modern schoolteachers, health workers and 'development workers' or NGO (Non-Government Organization) activists carry on the missionary role by seeking to 'educate' and 'care for' *adivasis*. It is significant that a large proportion of development projects that work with Konds are run by Christians, quite a few of them from South India, and that as yet very few of the numerous NGOs that have been set up to help Konds within the last ten years are run by Konds. Many of these non-tribal activists and development workers, who devote their lives to trying to help *adivasis* and do much to support them and protect them from exploitation, actually hold similar negative stereotypes about tribal culture as the oppressors whom they confront, and approach Kond villages in a similar *saheb* role, of someone from a superior culture who claims to know what is best for Konds. The best of these activists are careful to avoid being patronizing or making any show of superiority, but this in my experience is quite rare, simply because the assumption that tribal culture is inferior or 'backward' is so pervasive in the mainstream culture.

Perhaps the missionary role and its concept of 'conversion' is at the root of the whole idea that tribal people should change or 'develop' to come 'up to our level': the idea that 'we alone have real knowledge/education/civilization/development' has evolved from the same set of ideas that Christian missionaries expressed when they claimed that they alone had the truth.[6]

The projects started by missionaries have turned into (supposedly) secular organizations that aim to benefit the Konds, especially (like Mission centres under British rule) in the fields of education and medicine. Schoolteachers in tribal villages, who are mostly non-tribals, very often show a striking arrogance and insensitivity towards those they teach. An assumption that tribal culture is backward and inferior is intrinsic to much of what they teach and how they teach it. This assumption can be traced clearly back to the school system which missionaries set up among the Konds (above pp.218–28).

> No one could deny the value of real education, that is, the widening and enrichment of knowledge. But today education has become something quite different. It isolates children from their culture and from nature.... modern schooling acts almost as a blindfold, preventing children from seeing the

> context in which they live.... School is a place to forget traditional skills and, worse, to look down on them. (Norberg-Hodge 1991 pp.110–11)

This comment on modern schools in Ladakh applies equally to schooling in Kond and most other *adivasi* villages. A 'highly educated' person, rather than being someone who thinks for himself or herself, is thus all too often someone who has rejected one set of values for another set that is alien, and therefore sets the person apart from his or her village community. As in the early missionary pictures of converts who learnt to look for truth or reality in a book instead of through experience (above p.223), Kond schools tend to substitute abstract concepts for traditional knowledge and a direct awareness of nature.[7] 'You are ignorant, that is why people exploit you; you need to become educated and aware', is a recurrent theme of many of the education and health schemes which have been set up for Konds, instead of supporting Kond culture the way it is and going to villages willing to relate as equals, open to learning from Konds as well as teaching them.

This involves giving recognition to tribal knowledge and accepting that having a very different form from our own knowledge does not make it inferior; that, without schools, tribal societies nevertheless possess their own extensive system of educating children; and with this, that we do not know what is best for them, that our knowledge of life is not necessarily superior or more extensive than theirs, and that we are not necessarily more educated or civilized than they are—let alone wiser! If we see *adivasis* as ignorant in specific areas that lay them open to manipulation by exploiters, of course we can help them by teaching things they do not know about the outside world. For instance, as many development workers stress, illiteracy lays tribal people open to manipulation by moneylenders and other exploiters, so there is a strong case that introducing them to literacy and numeracy helps them to protect themselves. But this needs to be balanced by an awareness that there is at least as much for us to learn from them as for them to learn from us.

Obviously, 'modern' society is much more highly developed in certain areas than traditional Kond society, such as the skills of literacy and technology, but are there not corresponding areas where their society is much more highly developed than ours? Can we appreciate the positive features of non-literacy, hinted at in Russell Means' speech (above p.26)—the directness of human communication, the power of memory, and the art of improvising? And how many of us non-tribals can make our own house, grow our own food, or practise a range of skills and techniques of self-sufficiency comparable to those of the Konds? A lack of material goods or comforts that we outsiders take for granted does not mean that *adivasis* live in poverty. In as much as they have lost their land and freedom and been forced into a position of inferiority, poverty is something that outsiders have imposed upon them.

The missionary perception of Konds as 'ignorant' and 'in need' also focuses especially on medical care and hygiene. Medicine is often the crucial issue on which it seems obvious that outside intervention is called for, especially in the treatment of diseases which tribal medicine does not cure, but most potently in the area of infant mortality, whose rate among Konds may be higher than among Oriyas, who have greater access to hospitals. I once met some Oriya students who were studying the Konds' 'IMR', or Infant Mortality Rate, which previous studies had shown to be higher than among the neighbouring non-tribal population. They were visiting about 50 Kond villages, filling in questionaires, for which they asked a range of highly sensitive questions which not all villagers were happy to answer. It seems that some Konds visit hospitals for certain conditions when they can, or appreciate outside instruction in midwifery, and that others want nothing to do with this. But in comparing mortality levels, other factors need taking into account. Modern society's attitude to medical intervention is that saving every possible life is always desirable; but in ensuring a high quality of life for every human being who is born, modern society is in some ways most uncaring, e.g. in the inequalities of wealth and the many kinds of oppression which it allows. In a tribal society, if the infant mortality rate is higher, this means that to some extent natural selecton still operates among the population so that the fittest survive, and the relationship of people to land stays balanced, which makes for a different kind of health.

To give *adivasis* the choice of recourse to Western-style medicine is obviously desirable. But if a high infant mortality rate seems to require outsiders setting up programmes visiting, checking up on and 'educating' Kond villagers, this is clearly an extension of the state's exclusive right over human life that carries much further the monopoly over taking human life that British rule established when it suppressed human sacrifice and female infanticide (above pp.161–3). Certainly it introduces a dependence on outsiders who have taken on a 'caring' role, but who enter villages and interact with Konds as their social superiors.

Tribal healing operates at levels we are not accustomed to (above p.123), and rests on a concept of health that is very different from that of Western medicine: it includes spiritual well-being and a full vitality. Maybe if one looks in the streets of a city or town, many of the people one sees are alive only in a relatively small part of their being; health for *adivasis* means the kind of vitality that allows a family to be self-sufficient through the work of their own hands, from building a house and creating fields out of jungle to the whole process of growing crops and the nights of dancing that express the flowering of this vitality. Is it possible that a concept of health as something that has to be checked and safeguarded by outside professionals is something that saps this vitality?

Of the anthropologist role, we have seen in the previous chapter how it tended to give 'scientific' validity to the changes which British rule imposed on the Konds. In modern Indian anthropology, the British are sometimes blamed for having kept tribal people in an isolated and deprived state. But the continuing trend to impose unasked-for changes barely comes under scrutiny, and recognition of tribal knowledge is as lacking as it was in colonial discourse. For example, Vidyarthi (1977) writes on British policy:

> Since Independence, India has been actively thinking for the uplift of her tribal people. (p.411)

> The policy of isolation by the British Government was largely effected by their deliberate efforts not to develop communications in the tribal areas, which as a result, remained cut-off from the rest of the population. (p.413)

> During the pre-Independence period, it was the policy of the British Government to let tribes live in isolation and maintain their *status quo*. However, after Independence, in 1947, the national leaders undertook the programmes of tribal welfare as a top priority. (p.461)

To perceive British rule of the Konds in terms of an absence of such 'development' implies the enormous increase in the scale of imposition that has taken place since Independence.

A similar concept of 'development' runs through Sengupta's book *Applied anthropology: Meaning and necessity* (1977),[8] which starts from the problem that despite a necessity for 'raising the backward conditions' in tribal areas,

> The development of the weaker sections is not attaining the expected level, because non-economic factors are working as the factors of resistance to it. (p.iii)

> ....resistances to innovations are cropping up.... (p.1)

Tribal resistance to innovation is 'based on cultural or social factors'—what colonial anthropologists called 'superstition' and 'ignorance'. To overcome this resistance, Sengupta calls for schools: 'Educational development is a prerequisite for social and economic development'. He adds that 'The education must flow from their traditional roots' (pp.2–3). But if it did, would not their traditional roots be likely to support them in resisting many of the 'innovations'? Tribals are excellently educated in traditional knowledge by their own parents and relatives, in the informal manner customary in their society. If 'education' means schools that disseminate mainstream society's system of knowledge, this is usually an implicit rejection of tribal knowledge, and hardly a process that can flow from their traditional roots. The underlying assumption of most educational schemes (as well as many other innovations introduced by outsiders) is the missionary belief that there is only one system of correct knowledge, so that either people are educated and have this knowledge, or they are uneducated and therefore ignorant.

Sengupta sees tribal communities as exploited by outsiders, though he does not mention the problem of bribe-extorting by Government officials, or the local vested interests that perpetuate the exploitation. Instead, he sees the basic problem as 'underdevelopment' or 'poverty' (citing Myrdal 1971); a 'backwardness' that stems from tribals' 'ecological and social isolation'. The Government's system of Tribal Development Blocks and 'programmes for bringing the Scheduled Castes and Tribes to the level of the main population' go unquestioned, and the anthropologist's role is simply to study tribals and advise administrators, practising 'applied anthropology':

> The basic need is to study the Indian *rural communities* for overall development of the backward parts of the country. (p.1)

> The anthropologists with their conceptual framework of their discipline and methods can supplement knowledge concerning tribal societies provided they have interests for development of the people (Mair 1968). This can easily be done concentrating upon the study of facts and processes which have bearing

> on the problems of application. The planners and the administrators can handle these facts finally, for uplifting the quality of life of the people. (p.19)

Sengupta conceptualizes administrators' range of actions by distinguishing between two kinds of necessary controls, 'direct' and 'dependent': '*direct* control means the ruthless imposition of our value system on the tribals'.

> However, in both the *dependent* and the *direct* controls, it is noted that a full knowledge of the tribal culture is indispensable. (Ibid. p.20)

The modern Indian anthropologist, then, seems to be as firmly committed to the role of supplying the administrator with 'knowledge' as he was in the 19th century, and takes the nature of this knowledge as much for granted.

The modern literature on 'tribal development', situated within anthropology and sociology as well as economics, is very extensive. The predominant assumption throughout is that tribal societies are 'backward' and in need of 'uplift' (above pp.260–1). They are portrayed as 'islands of deprivation' (Joshi 1984), in need of discipline and education (Pareek 1977), 'promiscuous' (K. Sharma 1979 p.19), and 'underdeveloped' in every way. Indian anthropology has thus inherited from British colonial anthropology the idea that tribal culture is 'primitive' or 'backward', along with an implicit denial of the existence of tribal knowledge. It has also inherited the total hierarchy through which colonials constructed their 'knowledge' about tribal societies, and with this, the assumption that outsiders know best who tribals are and what they need.

This role of the expert who 'knows' tribal society thus extends to different disciplines of study, such as economics and health care, as well as to the extensive 'fact-finding' studies undertaken to assess the socio-economic impact of dam projects and so on. The abstract jargon and disembodied discourse frequently add insult to injury, and sacrifice being human to an unreal, pseudo-scientific image of truth.

Also related is the role of the tourist: increasingly, tourists in Orissa are offered trips to tribal villages where they photograph people and watch dance performances, but have no real communication with the villagers. Such contact tends to reinforce tourists' stereotypes, and makes tribal culture into a commodity which tourists buy.

All these roles thus have a tendency to dehumanize: to alienate people from their humanness, and to sacrifice their quality of life.

Yet the problems that plague tribal India can only be solved by building on the positive aspects of these roles, starting with the Konds' first administrators' avowed aim of preventing human sacrifice and warfare as well as exploitation. I have dwelt on the negative aspects, because I believe that it is only through an awareness of these that the positive potential can be realized: Hindu tolerance, Christian love and peace, the tradition of faithful service in the Indian administration, and the anthropological insight that has laid foundations for giving outsiders a more accurate sense of tribal life and thus for bridging the gulf of understanding.

Sacrificing the Present for an Unreal Future

In his pamphlet entitled *The Aboriginals* (1943), Elwin commented on the *loss of vitality* that follows as tribal culture is gradually eroded, and *adivasis* are drawn into mainstream society, where they assume an inferior status, and from seeing their society as the centre of the world get drawn towards outsiders' view of it as a peripheral backwater.

Films play a significant part in this process, and so does television, which the Government has sometimes stated that it intends to introduce into every village in India. In most tribal villages, people still do not feel on the periphery: where they are here and now is the centre, and they create their own sense of order through rituals and their self-sufficiency—which includes energetic, vitally alive arts of entertainment such as dance and improvised songs. By contrast,

> Having the rest of the world through TV in your living room may not be as enriching as we tend to think. It may have just the opposite effect, in fact. The idealized stars make people feel inferior and passive, and the here and now pales by comparison with the colourful excitement of faraway places. (Norberg-Hodge 1991 p.134)

Recently I witnessed the impact of films on tribal life at a great buffalo sacrifice in a fairly remote Kond village. After the buffalo had been killed and its head was carried into the village, the resident traders took over and set up a huge screen in the middle of the village. They had promised to honour the festival with a showing of Hindi films. It turned out a most ambiguous honour. From dusk until dawn they showed a continuous series of violent films, at an amazing volume. After a while few Konds watched them and Doms formed the main audience. No one could sleep, but etiquette prevented the films being stopped. The harmonizing of village life that normally takes place after a major blood sacrifice was effectively prevented: sacred violence gave way to modern, profane violence, manufactured for entertainment by people elsewhere.

Ghurye's book, *The Aborigines—"so-called"—and their future* was written as a reaction to Elwin's argument about the erosion of tribal vitality, and focused on a contrast of attitudes towards tribal people: that of 'isolationism' or 'protectionism', which is how he characterized British policy-makers in general and Elwin in particular, and the attitude which he shared in that the sooner tribals were 'assimilated' into the Hindu mainstream the better. The trouble is, 'assimilation' is based on a completely negative appraisal of tribal culture and an intolerance for difference, as in the USA, where the term was coined for the policy of drawing American Indians into white society. In India it means accelerating the process of 'Sanskritization' or 'Hinduization', since un-Hindu features of tribal culture are seen as undesirable symptons of backwardness that disappear as tribals are absorbed into mainstream Hindu society. Ghurye's attack on Elwin for wanting to 'keep tribals in zoos for anthropologists to study' has been repeated countless times in Indian anthropology, although it could not be a greater distortion of Elwin's argument—which was, that tribal people need protection from exploitative outsiders; that remote tribal villages are extremely highly developed and sophisticated in their own way; and that it would be well if outsiders gave them the choice of remaining so, at least until we non-tribals have made some progress in eradicating our own grave faults and corruption. It is the merchants and moneylenders, industrialists and Government officials, contractors and schoolteachers who need reforming. What is the real nature of 'development' that sacrifices peoples' vitality?

Ideas about sacrifice, self-sacrifice, and saving are implicit in all three roles of missionary, administrator and anthropologist, as I have shown. In my exploration of these ideas throughout this book, have I been reading too much into a few words, and their metaphorical usage? I do not think so. If one says that the secular use of 'sacrifice' is 'only metaphorical', the metaphors we express our thoughts in often reveal our deepest attitudes and beliefs, and the values that motivate us. The concept of 'sacrifice' arouses patterns of strong feelings whose roots lie deep in Western as well as in Indian culture. People who idealize self-sacrifice, and do constantly sacrifice themselves, as we have seen colonial administrators and missionaries did, also sacrifice others. It seems to be a psychological consequence of constraining oneself that one will also constrain other selves—people, animals, or the natural environment. One could say that British administrators conquered the Konds because they had cultivated a 'habit of authority'. They sacrificed the Konds' lives and freedom, because they were sacrificing their own.

Tribal people are highly skilled at living here and now in the present, rather than always working towards distant goals. Of course they also plan carefully for the future, e.g. for the food they need throughout the coming seasons, but this does not stop them from living very fully in the present moment, and getting the maximum enjoyment from whatever situation presents itself. The contrast with the capitalist ethic of building up credit and accumulating wealth as an end in itself is very strong. Linked with this tendency to live fully in the present is an acceptance of life's difficulties along with its pleasures. If actual happiness was something that could be measured—by the quality of people's smiles and laughter for instance!—I believe that one would find that on the whole there is a much higher level of happiness to be found in tribal societies than in 'modern' societies, where the majority of people live in a state of constant longing for things they have not got and cannot get, starting with economic wealth.

It seems that many of the people who impose changes on the Konds, as well as those who exploit them, are motivated by a belief in 'development', or use that belief as a mask to justify their actions. It is clear that this is a modern form of the 'evolutionist' set of beliefs that was the motivating force behind the British empire and its attitude to tribal peoples such as the Konds. These beliefs leave no room for the possibility that different societies develop in different ways, or that only Konds know what they need. Thus 'development' often sacrifices the present to an unreal image of the future. The modern lifestyle based on commerce tends to sacrifice present happiness for the sake of an illusory future that promises material prosperity for all, but which never comes (or for which there is little capacity for enjoyment when it is present). For this prosperity is measured in terms that have little relation with the actual quality of human life. Much of what is called 'development' is thus the opposite: a diminishment in the quality of life.

'Development' is a concept that holds an enormous power over us and is an integral part of ideas about 'modernity', so that it requires considerable effort to free ourselves from the evolutionist assumptions discussed in the previous chapter and look at a tribal society without bringing in the assumption that it is 'less developed' than our own. The modern concept of 'development' grew out of a biological usage referring to the natural growth of plants and animals. During the 18th–19th century its meaning in science gradually extended

> from a conception of transformation that moves towards the *appropriate* form of being to a conception of transformation that moves towards an *ever more perfect* form. During this period, evolution and development began to be used as interchangeable terms by scientists. (Esteva 1992 p.8) [9]

We have seen how British rule of the Konds justified itself through the concept of 'evolution' or 'development' in the sense of 'rising higher in the scale of civilization', on the theory that colonial rule hastened the rise of subject peoples. But the nationalist reaction against colonialism incorporated the same concept towards sections of a nation that had been judged as 'backward'. This involved a further convolution in the concept of 'development' that took place during the 1940s–50s, when the US Government under Truman first used the term 'underdevelopment' to refer to the majority of the world's peoples: 'third world' countries were henceforth defined as 'underdeveloped', and gradually since then as 'developing nations'—i.e. as not yet 'fully developed' by contrast with Western countries! The American discourse on 'underdevelopment' incorporated aspects of Marxism and a reaction against the type of direct colonialism represented by British rule in India, to establish a deeply conservative and expansionist ideology. Newly independent nations such as India took up this view of themselves, along with the idea that in order to be 'modern' it was necessary to follow a similar path of development as Western countries (Esteva 1992). This involved 'foreign aid' that has gradually led India and many other countries to become indebted to financial organizations based in the West, which in turn has allowed Western financial leaders to dictate vital aspects of India's economy.

Hence the definition of India's tribal peoples as 'underdeveloped' by many social scientists. As with 19th century evolutionism, this view reduces differences between societies to a matter of stages along a single path, on the assumption that there is only one proper way to develop, which is basically the way of economic primacy taken by the West, or the path set by India's mainstream society. This view gives rise to a set of dichotomies similar to those which characterized colonial views of tribal people:

'civilized'	*versus*	'uncivilized'
'developed'	*versus*	'underdeveloped'
'advanced'	*versus*	'backward'
'modern'	*versus*	'primitive'
'literate'	*versus*	'illiterate'
'educated'	*versus*	'uneducated' or 'ignorant'

It is significant that 'development' is often not seen as a process arising from within a tribal society at all, but as something they need to be guided into. The view of tribal societies as 'in need of development' implies the transitive use of the verb 'develop' that is sometimes actually used: 'we must develop them'. It is in this way that 'development' often serves as a euphemism for imposed and unasked-for change.

Social science also tends to see development as something that can be measured by economic criteria, or statistics of schools, road building or electricity supply, which make up 'the standard of living', and by which most tribal people 'fall below the poverty line'. 'Development' is often a shorthand for 'economic and social development' in which economics is put first and the 'social' element comes a poor second: an adaptation to economic circumstances.

This reflects the increasing primacy of economic values in modern society, where productivity and the creation of a profit are given an importance that tends to override other considerations. Undoubtedly the main impulse towards changes imposed on tribal people comes from the profit motive. In many ways the whole concept of 'development' has been hijacked into a one-sided, economic process, modelled on the West's path of development via industrialization, and geared towards making an immediate financial gain.

This faith in the forces of economic and industrial growth has led to a massive displacement of tribal people in the name of development, to make way for dams, mines, quarries and factories. When Nehru performed the opening ceremony for one of India's first large-scale dams in 1954, he called these dams 'the temples of modern India'. In many ways, they *are* the temples of a religion, whose main set of beliefs revolves around a particular idea of development that offers prosperity to all but creates it only for an elite; while the thousands of people who lived on the land that is flooded are *sacrificed*, their lives destroyed for the sake of other people's profit and prestige. At the same time the wider environment is also harmed, with long-term consequences for the lives of countless other people. The great controversy at the moment concerns the dams on the Narmada river.[10] On the popular level the project is motivated by a belief (which appears to be tragically misplaced) that the dam will alleviate the great drought in Gujarat. Behind this is the huge profit which such projects create for the elite of technicians and politicians involved. The kind of thinking that supports the dams is revealed very clearly in some comments of senior politicians in Gujarat about the *adivasis* who are threatened with eviction from their land:

> 'I do believe that tribal culture should be preserved, but it should be in the museum and not in their real life.'
>
> 'We do not want the tribals to remain in the jungle. It is the biggest shame of this generation that tribals are living like this, like a "jungli jat" away from the benefits of civilization.'
>
> 'What is this great culture people are talking about? These tribals live in nakedness, in illiteracy, in hunger.'[11]

The negative stereotype combines in these comments with development-speak—'Ask them—they want the fruits of economic progress.' But no one does ask them if they want the dam, and if they want to be taken away from the forest. At present, by refusing to move out of their villages they are making the strongest statement in their power that this is not what they want. The project authorities justify evicting tribals from their land on the grounds that at present they 'live in poverty', and that 'resettling' them will 'raise their standard of living': as part of this they offer the displaced tribals employment in building the dam, reserving a quota of the lowest labouring jobs for them—reducing people who lived freely on their own land to a condition of virtual slave labour, building in effect their own tomb.

The role of the World Bank in financing such projects is significant indeed: it perpetuates foreign colonialism in India, since the economics of foreign aid to the third world means that the West is still actually gaining much more than it is giving, and reinforces the *internal colonialism* of India's industrial elite. Even in attempting to ensure that displaced people are given adequate compensation, the Bank generates a discourse that distorts people's humanity, by referring to well-adapted tribal villages as 'below the poverty line', all those who are to be moved as 'oustees', all who lack title deeds of their lands (which includes a large proportion due to the haphazard keeping of land records) as 'encroachers on Government land', and the process of moving them as 'Resettlement and Rehabilitation' ('R & R' for short).

Similar though much less well-documented projects affect many Konds. The building of a dam on the upper reaches of the Indravati river, which has also been funded by the World Bank, threatens a large number with displacement. Recently the unfinished dam collapsed, killing some of the labourers. A large railway is being built through Kond land from Koraput to Rayagadha, in order to export iron that is mined at Baladila in Bastar more quickly. This mine has displaced many thousands of Maria Gonds, and has been built in collaboration with Japanese industrialists. There are several other mega-projects in the Kond area, including a bauxite mine and aluminium factory near Koraput built with Russian collaboration, and the Upper Kolab dam between Koraput and Jeypore, which has been completed with French assistance.

It is clear that development on the Western model means unsustainable growth, a great lack of balance with the natural environment, and for tribal people, their culture denigrated, their knowledge denied, and oppression of many kinds, that reaches its peak in this process of displacement from their land. Such projects as these dams and mines mainly benefit those who are already rich; the poor they mostly make poorer still.

For one result of this one-sided 'development' is that, as the Konds' first British administrator intended, 'their wants will increase...' (above pp.178–9). With the lure of ease, money, power, and external goods, comes a huge inequality—the laws of Capitalist economics with which the West has eroded innumerable cultures from the inside by dividing them against themselves, introducing many tribal societies for the first time to the whole division into rich and poor. Even the richest are haunted by a longing for what others elsewhere have got; and when people accept a view of themselves as 'underdeveloped' and everyone wants what they have not got, does this not in itself contribute to a decrease in the general level of happiness? It seems that the West has invented a style of life which it sells by advertising and commerce, and which by its own logic of 'the laws of economics' makes a few people richer and most people much poorer.

Behind the development-speak is another idea: why should a few tribals, a minority, sit on so much land and stand in the way of progress and the interests of the majority? Even if this displacement causes them enormous suffering and destroys their culture completely, is that not the *sacrifice* which someone has to make for the nation's overall prosperity? This is where we come back to human sacrifice in its modern form, in the idea that a nation's development depends on the 'national sacrifice' of its tribal minority.[12]

Is sacrificing people like this really development? And is India's majority really benefited at all? Or is the benefit simply the creation of further economic wealth for an already privileged elite? And can we say we know the relative values of what is gained and what is destroyed? Do we fully comprehend what is being sacrificed when tribal peoples' culture and quality of life are destroyed?

What is Real Development?

Since Independence, the administration of tribal areas has been defined in terms of the concept of 'development'. A Development Block is a unit of administration, under a Block Development Officer, or BDO. The Dongria area, which is restricted to outsiders as a safeguard against exploitation, is called the Dongria Khond Development Agency. On one level, this is a very positive way of defining the Government's role—although it carries the danger just mentioned that outsiders will impose their own ideas about development on tribal people. But when we look at actual changes that have taken place in the Kond area in the last 150 years, and are taking place now, we see huge changes at a material level of roads, administration, markets, towns, dams and mines, and at the mental level of implicit ideas and laws. But at a deeper level of the structures of power and the cycle of exploitation, how much has really changed at all?

So what do we mean by development? What does it mean to believe in development? What is real development?

Drawing on the original biological meaning, one can view development as, most fundamentally, the process of coming fully into life and reaching a full potential. One aspect of this lies in following natural laws and natural cycles, which are continually present at many levels: the processes of conception, being born, growing, maturing in several senses, and dying or transforming, as we see with plants and animals as well as with individual human beings. Another aspect deals with the final stage of transformation, which one could see as a rising above or getting free from restrictions inherited from the past. So what does it mean for a society—a collection of human beings—to develop?

One may contrast two very different views of development that highlight these two aspects: the cyclical view of change that is broadly characteristic of tribal societies, and the linear view of development as advancement along an established path of set 'stages' which we have characterized as 'evolutionism', and which has a major place in the ideology of modern society. A traditional tribal society places as much value on the continuation of ancestral custom as modern society does on change. The status of old people brings out this contrast especially clearly. In the West, and increasingly in modern India, old people get left behind by the generation gap that results from rapid change: after retirement their value diminishes and their authority declines. In a tribal society, where values and knowledge change relatively slowly from one generation to the next, elders remain an esteemed authority. Is there a kind of development that bridges the contrast between these two modes?

It seems that the linear idea of development often seeks transformation without a respect for the full natural cycle of stages that come before. An idea of 'development' that ties it down to an economic and material meaning produces a highly one-sided, imbalanced development that is not really transformative at all, in terms of leading to an increase in happiness or freedom. If 'development' means the kind of growth that has emerged in the Western tradition of economics and commerce, has this not always involved expansion at other people's expense and to the detriment of our natural environment? Is this not an unsustainable line of development that ultimately threatens all life on earth, sacrificing in the meantime most people's happiness and well-being for the sake of short-term profit for a few? 'Development' in this sense is often, as we have seen, a euphemism for exploitation or for change that is imposed over people. If development is essentially something that happens from within, and each culture, like each human being, has its own unique path of growth, then real development is not something that can be imposed at all. Trying to impose development interferes with an organic process and prevents free choice. History is full of peoples imposing on each other, and one can see a tendency for history to repeat itself in people wanting to impose on others what was imposed on themselves. Hence the exterminating extent to which 'civilized' people have already imposed on tribal peoples throughout the world. What would it mean to allow societies to develop in their own way, and to have a real choice?

It seems that development is often seen as a process of 'rising above nature', which has had the effect of divorcing us from nature. In Colombia, a pre-Colombian civilization has survived by cutting itself off from the outside world, its inaccessibility still assured by mountains and forests as well as the banditry of drug traffickers. Like tribal people in India, the Kogi see themselves as elder brothers to those 'younger brothers' who developed the modern lifestyle. Kogi priests believe they have the special role of safeguarding the health of the earth through ritual. Like Konds, they take Mother Earth as their main deity. Recently, noticing changes in their natural environment brought about by the increasing pace of industrialization all over the earth, they broke their isolation to get a message of the greatest urgency to the outside world: the earth is sick, and the younger brother's treatment of the earth, if it continues, will destroy us:

> We are the Elder Brothers.
> We have not forgotten the old ways.
> How could I say that I do not know how to dance?
> We still know how to dance.
> We have forgotten nothing.
> We know how to call the rain.
> If it rains too hard we know how to stop it.
> We call the summer.
> We know how to bless the world and make it flourish.
>
> But now they are killing the Mother.
> The Younger Brother, all he thinks about is plunder.
>
> The Mother looks after him too, but he does not think.
>
> He is cutting into her flesh.
> He is cutting into her arms.
> He is cutting off her breasts.
> He takes out her heart.
> He is killing the heart of the world.
>
> When the final darkness falls everything will stop.
> The fires, the benches, the stones, everything.

> All the world will suffer.
>
> When they kill all the Elder Brothers then they too will be finished.
> We will all be finished.[13]

'Sustainable development' is not by any means a novel concept: it formed the religious basis of innumerable non-western societies. But the fact that 'sustainable development' is much talked about now is a sign that environmental awareness is increasing at many levels in modern society (though it sometimes seems that the companies that talk most about it remain the worst polluters). There is also more talk now of 'indigenous change' and 'self-determination'—concepts which recognize that tribal people's development is a matter that needs to be entirely under their own choice and control. Of course, there are already many development schemes that genuinely validate *adivasis'* choice and power, such as small-scale irrigation projects, co-operatives, and a sustainable harvesting of forest produce.

If by 'development' we mean something more than the biological sense of fulfilling a natural cycle, or the possibilities held by past custom, then it is vital to ask: to what extent is the motivating desire for any change basically acquisitiveness and greed, and to what extent is it a desire for freedom and real happiness? What are we choosing to sacrifice? How can societies re-learn a kind of development that is really sustainable, in the sense of not cutting themselves off from nature, either by polluting it irredeemably or by exhausting its resources?

The poverty and deprivation which one sees in the low quality of tribal peoples' lives in areas of India where there has been heavy industrialization result from a one-sided 'overdevelopment': an elite's push towards wealth or a Western lifestyle that inevitably pushes other people under and causes their *underdevelopment.* In a broader view, the *underdevelopment* of 'third world' countries results from the *overdevelopment* of the West. But in the West itself, an increasing number of people are turning to older philosophies and traditional cultures in order to find a balance between modern advances and a healthier, less destructive way of life. This amounts to

> a rediscovery of values that have existed for thousands of years—values that recognize our place in the natural order, and our indissoluble connection to one another and to the earth. (Norberg-Hodge 1991 p.192)

Can we plan for our own and other people's future without sacrificing the traditional knowledge that has sustained Hindu as well as tribal cultures since ancient times? Can we draw from this knowledge and find a way for it to co-exist with modern forms of knowledge, and modern desires?

The first prerequisite for real development for tribal people is thus protection from exploitation. Without this, money can be poured into tribal areas, but most of it will go into the hands of contractors and others who perpetuate the cycle of exploitation.

In order to free Konds and other *adivasis* from the stranglehold of exploitation, it is necessary to undo the negative stereotype that mainstream society still holds of them. This will involve educating administrators and others who visit tribal villages into a respect for tribal cultures, to understand that they are ancient civilizations of great subtlety and contain much wisdom.

It also means giving recognition to tribal knowledge: accepting that it exists, is not something easily learnt, and that it has a very different form from the knowledge we have learnt in schools and universities, though fundamentally it is not irreconcilable with this. If we start to take it into account and learn from it, we shall strengthen all that is best in tribal societies, and at the same time revitalize our own lives by discovering more human and joyful kinds of development.

CHAPTER NINE

Questioning the Sacrifice: A Postscript

Different Levels of Human Sacrifice

Nobody knows where they are gone. Nobody would have known that they were ever here, had it not been for the wizened old priest of Bisam Katak....[1]

Alora (*Unwanted*) is a little-known short story by Gopinath Mohanty about the Dongria Konds, based on the idea that Bissamcuttack would one day become a huge city by exploiting the Bauxite deposits on top of Niyamgiri's 5,000 foot mountains, whose thick forests would disappear into an industrial wasteland along with every trace of the tribal people whose name is synonymous with Niyamgiri. Another short story Gopinath wrote about the Dongria, *Tadpa*, gently mocks the plans of a group of administrators and anthropologists for the tribe's development, when they get lost in the Niyamgiri forest and meet a Dongria youth, who guides them out and confounds their ways of thinking. But Gopinath knew about the Bauxite, and in *Alora*, he confronts the genocidal impact which mining this ore is likely to have. Even as I write this postscript, a London-based mining company called Vedanta/Sterlite is trying to build a road up the mountain to mine it, while Dongria and others are trying to stop them. Just recently (7th January 2009), in a scene reminiscent of the confrontations with British-led troops outlined in the early chapters of this book, 800 Konds started collecting at 3 a.m., and blocked the road against construction vehicles, sent by the London-based mining company Vedanta to start building a mining road up the sacred mountain in the middle of the night, backed by police.[2]

When tribal people are displaced by dams, mines and factories, they are invariably promised a better life, even though their standard of living invariably drops drastically in every dimension. Sometimes though, when tribal people are displaced by industry, their loss of homes, land and community are described more frankly in terms of a *sacrifice* these people are making—the 'price of progress'.

People are fascinated by the Kond custom of human sacrifice—for a start, did it exist or not? Several people are convinced one way or the other. This book has looked at the evidence and left that question open. It makes no difference to the main argument, which is that the colonial idea of human sacrifice was used to justify imposing a system onto the Konds that embodied an even worse kind of human sacrifice—but one much harder to see, because it was, and is, so widespread.

If the original meaning of sacrifice is to 'make sacred', modern usage is often the opposite, with an implication of throwing something of great value away, even desacralizing it.

This book puts forward the hypothesis that human sacrifice is a ritual that lies at the threshold of what we call 'civilization'. There is evidence it was practised in various forms in ancient Egypt, Mesopotamia, Thrace, and among the Celts. Many features of Minoan civilization appear idyllic, and their elaborate ritual centres or 'palaces' are unfortified, but more recent excavations have unearthed evidence of human sacrifices, in line with the Greek myths about Minoan Crete (Castleden 1989).

The Greeks and Romans expressed abhorrence for the custom, which they believed their remote ancestors had practised. But various kinds of violence that they considered normal already show a transition from an actual ritual of human sacrifice to a whole system which institutionalized the sacrificing of human life. Both societies practised extreme, 'genocidal' forms of warfare, in which the norm was massacre and enslavement for a defeated population. The Romans took this further, with the slow death by torture of crucifixion for people judged guilty of certain crimes, and the *ludi* —the gladiatorial games for which the Colosseum and hundreds of other amphitheatres were built—in which people killed people and animals in front of huge audiences for sport. Significantly, the origin of the *ludi* is usually traced back to a form of human sacrifice through combat that formed part of the burial rites practised by the Etruscans, forebears of the Romans.

There is evidence that several of the ancient civilizations of Peru also practised human sacrifice. Recent research from Bolivia and Peru suggests that ancient forms 'went underground', and that mafia bosses still practise human sacrifice for wealth and power, capturing victims from the poorest of the poor (Tierney 1989). Reports in Indian newspapers illustrate a similar degeneration of tantric custom. In Orissa and neighbouring States, such as Chhattisgarh, stories of human sacrifice surround every major construction project, and local people are frequently on edge against people trying to capture their children as victims. This was the case with Vedanta's Lanjigarh refinery, where villagers' minds saw a continuity between the large number of deaths that took place during construction and actual human sacrifices. Some scholars see these stories as an enduring 'myth' (Parry 2007). But an Oriya anthropologist is on record as saying that no major industrial project starts up in Orissa without a human sacrifice. Tantrism was very likely born in Orissa, but is thought to have degenerated in medieval times into a quest for power through human sacrifice and occult arts, so that in popular usage now, a tantric is a practitioner of black arts who gains power for himself and clients through killing people. The power of tantric priests commands widespread currency, not least among the mafia community.

Whatever the reality of macabre human sacrifice 'survivals' like this, these stories of human sacrifice for industry stand in for the large-scale sacrifice of human lives laid down in the process of industrialization, which perpetuate and compound the ancient story. For example, the Hirakud dam in northwest Orissa, where Nehru laid a foundation stone in the 1950s, calling dams the 'temples of modern India', has a stone monument commemorating by name about 200 workers who died during construction. Over 100,000 people displaced by the dam find no memorial. Nor does any such monument memorialize workers killed in more recent dams, such as the Upper Indravati project, where several hundred people are said to have been killed in a single accident on 28th July 1991, when an earth dam gave way and water flooded a tunnel, killing all the workers inside—deaths never properly recorded. An estimated 50,000 people (mainly *adivasis* of the Jhoria, Kond and Pengo tribes) were displaced by this project during the 1990s, and remain very bitter that even the electricity promised to their villages has never been given.[3]

The sacrifice of tribal people's lives for industry often appears massive in scale. Indeed, why was Chhattisgarh created as a new state out of Madhya Pradesh, in the year 2000? Events have shown that the interest of mining companies was of paramount influence. Since June 2005, parts of the 'tribal paradise' that was Bastar district have been engulfed in a 'manufactured civil war'. The day after the state government signed a deal with Tata for a major new iron-ore mine and steel plant project on tribal land, a state-sponsored tribal militia called *Salwa Judum* was launched to fight the Maoists or Naxalites, with another major iron and steel project signed with Essar Steel a few days later. Since then, over 600 tribal villages have been burnt by *Salwa Judum*, thousands of people have been raped and killed by both sides, and an estimated 200,000 tribal people have become refugees. The situation amounts to civil war, since many Maoists are also *adivasis*, from the same clans and families as those conscripted into *Salwa Judum*.[4] Yet this model is presently being copied in Orissa, especially in the very district whose colonial history is outlined in this book: Khondmal or Kandhamal.

A song sung by *adivasi* children from families displaced at Lanjigarh to make way for Vedanta's alumina refinery, brings the sacrifice theme out in the open. This was taught to the children in their Vedantanagar school, and performed in front of Commissioners visiting the area on behalf of the Supreme Court, in mid-2005:

> This country, this earth, is our mother.
> We will sacrifice ourselves in service of it,
> and make our nation proud of us.

Adivasis who refused to be displaced see the situation very differently. The company has showed no respect for their customs and deities, especially *Dharni Penu* and *Sora Penu,* their Earth and Mountain deities, and is 'flooding them out with money'.[5]

The term 'National Sacrifice Areas' was coined by the US Academy of Sciences in 1973 for the Four Corners region of the US Midwest, which had been devastated by toxic waste 'owing to relentless corporate stripping of its coal, oil, gas and uranium reserves.'[6] Uranium mining has affected several native American reservations. As Russell Means puts this (of the Lakota tribe, quoted in chapter 1):

> Right now, today, we who live on Pine Ridge Reservation are living in what White Society has designated a 'National Sacrifice Area'. What this means is that we have a lot of uranium deposits here, and white culture, not us, needs this uranium as energy production material. The cheapest, most efficient way for industry to extract and deal with the processing of this uranium is to dump the waste products right here at the digging site—right here, where we live. This waste is radio-active, and will make the entire region uninhabitable forever. This is considered by industry, and by the white society that created this industry, to be an 'acceptable price to pay' for 'energy resource development'… The same sort of thing is happening down in the land of the Navajo and Hopi, up in the land of the Northern Cheyenne and Crow, and elsewhere. 30% of the coal in the west and half of the uranium deposits in the U.S. have been found to lie under 'Reservation Land', so there's no way this can be called a minor issue. We are resisting being turned into a 'National Sacrifice Area'. We are resisting being turned into a 'National Sacrifice People'. The costs of this industrial process are not acceptable to us. It is genocide to dig uranium here and drain the ground water… (Means 1980/1982)

Konds take a similar line with the mining of their mountains for Bauxite. The base rock of these mountains was named Khondalite by geologist T.L.Walker in 1900,

> in honour of those fine hill men the Khonds in whose mountain jungles Khondalite is better developed than in any region hitherto described. (1902 p.11)

Gopinath Mohanty's autobiography recalls a conversation he had with a Census official in 1941, who narrated how Konds answered his enquiry 'What is your religion?' with the answer 'Mountains', which the official found hilarious.[7] But Kond religion is based on a profound understanding of the web of life. Their mountains are sacred entities of prime importance because they store monsoon water and release it in perennial streams, full of minerals, ensuring the land's fertility. Mine the mountain, and the constant supply of water ends forever. Mining a mountain's minerals sacrifices its ecosystem and the tribal culture that has utilized and channelled this for hundreds of years, to create short-term profits through the metals trade.

Colonial Roots of the Modern Sacrifice [8]

In other words, the colonial system of exploiting and displacing tribes such as the Konds, instead of disappearing at Independence, has gathered pace. The large-scale felling of timber in colonial times, and the displacement of Konds to make way for cultivators such as the Koltas in Kalahandi, who cultivated the land more 'efficiently', have given way to the displacement of people and forest on a vaster scale than the East India Company ever conceived of. British geologists studied India's mineral deposits, and started extracting them, but on a small scale compared to what is happening now.

Industrialization has already displaced an estimated 60 million of India's villagers within the last 60 years, 3 million in Orissa alone, around 75% of whom are *adivasis* and *dalits*.[9] Very few indeed have been properly compensated, let alone improved their standard of living. So for most of them, as they say themselves, these projects have been the opposite of development. Often even more painful than the poverty these projects have reduced them to, is the erosion of their cultural values and traditions, which invariably accompanies their separation from the land which they and their forefathers always cultivated. Land is acquired using the notorious Land Acquisition Act dating back to 1894, with its concept of Government's 'eminent domain'. The hierarchies of power in the law courts, police and administration were all put in place in British times. Hunter's comment that the biggest influence of British rule would be the growth of the concept of private property (above p.180) is bearing fruit now in a huge land-grab—a Highland Clearances of tribal people off their land. To add insult to injury, far from preventing this encroachment onto tribal territory, it is tribal people who are classified as 'encroachers on government land', wherever they have failed to get officially registered title-deeds (*patta*) to their land.

Money lending is still one of the main ways that tribal people lose their lands, despite a set of laws meant to prevent the sale of tribal lands to non-tribals. But the 5th Schedule of India's Constitution, which established Scheduled Areas where tribal people predominate, is circumvented in many ways, especially using a loophole which allows the taking of tribal land for industrial projects where 'national interest' dictates, and this is where the 1894 Act is used to force-buy tribal lands at well below their real cost. The Samatha Judgement at India's Supreme Court (1997) was a landmark case, protecting tribal land against the interests of mining companies in Andhra Pradesh, affirming the principle that tribal land cannot be bought up by non-tribal persons, and insisting that mining companies count as this. Since then, the governments of mineral-rich states have found elaborate ways to circumvent this Judgement, by earmarking 5% of profits for 'tribal development', and using public sector companies to partner private companies, exploiting another loophole.

Expropriation of land through money lending finds parallels at the state and global level. The fact that Orissa is one of India's most highly indebted states is undoubtedly linked to it being one of India's most mineral-rich states. 'Orissa is poor but rich in minerals' is a mantra taught at schools throughout the state. The World Bank, Asian Development Bank, IFAD and many other foreign agencies have lent huge sums to the Orissa Government for building infrastructure—especially the big dams, roads and railways essential for the mining industry. The new National Mineral Policy (NMP) introduced in 1993 (when India as a whole faced a balance of payments crisis) allows higher proportions of foreign ownership of mining and metals projects, while Orissa's repayment difficulties allowed the World Bank, along with the DFID (Department For International Development of the British Government), to use 'conditionality' clauses for future loans to force-start a privatization program of Orissa's electricity and other assets—another benefit for the foreign mining companies, increasingly active in exploration and deals. Another NMP that has gone through several forms from 2006–8, is geared towards streamlining the procedure to speed up mining projects that bring in foreign investment—even though the annual clearance of India's forests to make way for mining and other industries is already increasing annually. It is apparent that frustration by the world's biggest mining companies, such as Rio Tinto, lies behind this new policy, that is geared to attracting Foreign Direct Investment and allows 100% foreign ownership of projects.[10]

What this means is that foreign companies and banks are starting to gain control over some of India's prime natural resources, while the interests of tribal farmers are sacrificed to an even greater extent than they were in colonial times. A struggle between mining companies and the governments whose natural resources are exploited is a constant feature of the history of mining. Invariably, the companies get the lion's share of profits, but the struggle marginalizes the people who have lived for centuries in symbiosis with the resources of mountains, forest and rivers, despite the promises always given at the start of a project, that they will get the fruits of development.

The pattern of power wielded by mining companies and politicians who facilitate the deals needs laying bare, just like the colonial system this book has analyzed. In many ways, the East India Company, whose system of power we have seen at close quarters in its impact on the Konds, was the world's first multinational company (Robins 2006). The Ghumsur War, and therefore the Konds' initial subjection to centralized rule, came about as part of a system of maximizing the revenue (or 'tribute') from hundreds of *rajahs*, each of whom was put under increasing financial pressure, that they passed on to their subjects. Today's conflicts are caused by the government's attempt to further the aim of a host of private companies to make a lot of money by maximizing a country's (or state's) resource potential. In the case of mining companies, this means permanent extraction of deposits, and large-scale pollution by metal factories, with an eye on the profits to be made through increasing the consumption of metals in various sectors, and through metals trading. As the speed of extraction increases, it is apparent that mining companies make use of a manipulation of law and finance structurally similar to the techniques used in the EIC's takeover of power in the 18th–19th centuries. The result is an undermining of India's real Independence, especially its economic independence. The 2008 NMP reduces the role of government to that of 'facilitator' for companies and their projects. As a result, the government has receded from its former responsibility for people's well-being. This retreat facilitates a mining company such as Nalco or Vedanta in taking over tribal land along with responsibility for people's health and education, making villagers dependent on pleasing the representatives of the very companies that dispossess them.

A mining company, just like the East India Company, embodies an extreme form of hierarchy, from the directors, shareholders, and ranks of highly-paid officials, down to the labourers hired on a contract basis, whose living, safety conditions and pay are kept extremely low, and the people displaced from their land. In many ways, beneath the veneer of modern technology and jargon, this hierarchy replicates the colonial hierarchy analyzed in the pages above.

The notorious Land Acquisition Act is a symptom of a far wider malaise in the law-courts, where tribal protestors against a project are trapped in false cases, while companies evade laws that are meant to control pollution etc., with impunity. The case concerning Vedanta's right to mine Niyamgiri at the Supreme Court exemplifies these double standards, excluding tribal interests from the case, while glossing over numerous illegalities which the company was guilty of, according to the court's own advisory body on forests, the Central Empowered Committee.[11]

Where British colonials cut forests for company profits, and hunted tigers and leopards as a sport, this space is now occupied by extensive, well-organized and ruthless timber and tiger mafias. Mafia elements are also visible alongside major mining and construction projects, yet they form no part of the discourse on a project, even though it is known that the timber and hunting mafia are often the first to make use of roads opening up a tribal or forest area. Earmarking 5% of profits for tribal development and 'wildlife management' ignores the evidence that—far from benefitting tribals—most of what is called tribal development is notorious for its corruption (Sainath 1996). The difference between what is promised and what is delivered amounts to a *reality gap* at the heart of development discourse (Padel & Das Dec. 2008).

The pattern of internal colonialism in evidence now needs to be understood in terms of structures inherited from the colonial past. For example, a number of police firings into crowds of tribal demonstrators have taken place in recent years. These follow an infamous pattern of firings: above all the firing ordered by General Dyer at Jallianwalla Bagh in Amritsar, 1919, that killed hundreds of unarmed civilians, but also a number of police firings that took place during the Quit India Movement in Koraput and other districts of Orissa in August–September 1942, which culminated in the hanging of Lakhman Naik a year later. Among the largest were shootings on crowds of tribal protestors *gherao*-ing the police stations at Pappardahandi and Mathili. About 30 people were killed in these two firings alone. Among the dead at Mathili was a forest officer called Ramayya, whose death was wrongly blamed on Lakhman, who was leading the agitation against the police (Pati 1993). The movement he was leading in Koraput was basically against widely prevalent forms of exploitation and displacement, in which police and forest guards were complicit—the system of exploitation laid bare in Gopinath Mohanty's *Poroja* (1945/1987), which is basically as prevalent today as it was in the 1940s.

Police firings on tribal protestors against the Utkal alumina project at Maikanch village in Kashipur, that killed three and wounded a dozen (December 2000), and against Tata's planned steel plant at Kalinganagar, that killed 14 and wounded about 60 (January 2006), have clear roots in this colonial model. When one hears members of Orissa's elite or middle class justifying such use of force 'to teach them a lesson', this brings back painful memories of the widespread support which General Dyer enjoyed among the British for his 'decisive action' at Amritsar.

Even the *Salwa Judum* militia, and its recent counterpart in Kandhamal and other Naxalite-affected districts, has a colonial heritage in the tribal troops trained by Cleveland among the Paharias, Outram among the Bhils, and Campbell among the Konds—'my trusty sibbundies' as he called them (above pp.63, 174). Recruiting tribal youths as SPOs (Special Police Officers) to fight against other tribal youths inducted into Maoist ideology, is a recipe for civil war.

The colonial roots of the Kandhamal disturbances go back to events not just in the Ghumsur and Meriah Wars (1830s–40s), but also in the following decades, where research on British records reveals more about the colonial-Kond conflict that influenced the regime set up in the Khondmals. Recent research gives more details about the insurgency of Chokra Bissoi, that lasted intermittently from 1846–56, going through various stages as the British authorities put pressure on the *rani* of Sonepur, and the *rajahs* of Baud, Madanpur and Patna, while the surrender of the last surviving claimant to the Ghumsur throne, Pitambar Bhanja, is said to have particularly shocked Chokra (N.R. Patnaik 1992).

When McNeill became Agent in 1855, he arrested a Kond chief named Rindo Majhi, of Borikiya in Kalahandi, on the charge of practising human sacrifice. It was this chief whom McNeill led around in chains on his tour in December 1855 (p.104), along with Rindo's son Palaso, as an example. The Borikiya Konds attacked McNeill's party on 10th December at Orladhoni, apparently to try and free their leader, and some days later they attacked again, combining with a large army of Kuttia Konds—an attack which seems to have succeeded in freeing Rindo, though he was later executed. This attack was blamed on Chokra Bissoi as well as the *rajah* of Madanpur. McNeill's life was saved by Dinobandu Patnaik, who brought him all the way to Russellkonda. In return, McNeill made him *Tahsildar* of the Khondmals, where his 'reign of terror' lasted about 25 years. The Konds of Baud rebelled in 1860, and the Khondmal Konds rose up against Dinobandu in 1862. The next year, Konds in the area around Digi and Daringabadi rebelled. When Lt Lys was pursuing the arrest of men judged guilty of practising female infanticide, his party was attacked twice in November. Captain R.A. Stuart (Superintendent of Police) brought reinforcements from Russellkonda, joining Lys at Daringabadi on 1st December. The fighting left at least 20 Konds dead, and at least six villages burnt, with 300 cattle and over 1,000 weapons confiscated, to induce submission.[12]

December 1865 saw another uprising of the Kuttia Konds against their Oriya and Pano exploiters, with attacks on Tumudibandh and other towns (above pp.165–6 & N.R. Patnaik), and by 800 Konds on Captain R.A.C. Marshall, who was sent to suppress the disturbance, which he did with the help of one Dervish Ali, who had also been instrumental in enforcing British rule in 1863, and with more public executions. In 1869, another Kond rising in the Zemindary of Patna was viciously repressed by the *rajah* there (Cobden-Ramsey 1910).

These uprisings may, or may not, have been motivated partly by adherence to the customs of human sacrifice and female infanticide—this was an interpretation the British favoured wherever possible. British officials were often candid that these uprisings were primarily against increasing exploitation, and it is abundantly clear that British rule introduced major changes in the order of power that exacerbated the system of exploitation. This is the continuity with today's situation. The system of exploitation has changed its form only superficially, and has diminished little if at all. The uprisings in the 1850s–60s were not rebellions so much as attempts to repulse a new order, that demanded submission to a regime under a central Government of India that controlled the lives of Kond villages more closely than ever before and trampled on their customary rights—the colonial power structure.

Conflict in Kandhamal

During 2007–9, Kandhamal has witnessed worse conflict than any violence since the years of British conquest and tribal rebellion described above (1835–65). Once again, the burning of villages has been one of the main forms of attack. This time, though, the strife has taken the form of a Hindu-Christian clash on one side, and tension between the Konds and Panos on the other. The two overlap, since a large number of Kandhamal's Christians are originally from the Pano (Harijan) community. Many have been Christian for several generations, and the district has easily the highest proportion of Christians of any in Orissa. Religious intolerance has a long history, and in Kandhamal we saw some of its roots in the writings of the first generation of missionaries who came to Orissa. Nevertheless, the present intolerance is from both sides, and to some extent, religion is a smokescreen in a traumatically complex situation, where a number of different levels need unravelling.

The first violence erupted on Christmas Eve 2007, when the 82-year old Swami Laxmanananda Saraswati alleged there was a threat to his life, after pressurizing Christians to remove Christmas decorations in the village of Brahmanigaon, causing a riot which swiftly spread. This swami led a campaign in the district since 1969 to reconvert Christians to Hinduism, and is known to have used highly provocative language against Christians.[13] Christmas Day and the next week saw thousands of homes burnt—mostly Christian homes, but also in certain areas, Christian mobs burnt Hindu homes.[14] Five people were officially listed as killed, though the number may have been many more.

Among other causes was the demand of a large section of Kui-speaking Christians, originally from Pano families, who had lost their Scheduled Caste (SC) status by becoming Christians, to be given the status of a Scheduled Tribe (ST), which enraged many Konds. Many Panos speak Kui, and as far back as 1916 missionaries sometimes wrote of them as if they are Konds (above pp.231–2), but when an application for 'Kui' to be registered as a new ST was made by an organization called Kui Jana Kalyan Sangho in 2002, this was done out of public view, and the official announcement of a new Kui tribe, in September 2007, was taken as an affront by many Konds, and was a major cause of tension.[15]

The violence in December 2007 opened the wound of violence between Konds and Panos that had flared up in 1994, leaving at least 20 people dead in the district. Then on the night of 23rd August 2008, Saraswati and four of his followers (one a woman) were murdered in an attack on the ashram where he was staying at Jalaspeta, near Tumudibandh. The attackers left a note identifying themselves as Maoists, and blaming the swami for inciting the Christmas-time violence as a reason for killing him. What followed was an orgy of violence that has shocked the whole of India. The swami's funeral procession across the district to Chokapand (or Chokapada, site of his first ashram) was rerouted at Nuagam by his followers, and along the way hundreds of Christian homes were burnt and Christian men and women were hounded out of villages and attacked. At least 50 people were killed (some sources estimate over 500), many women were raped, and at least 50,000 refugees fled to the forests. Most eventually found their way to 14 refugee camps that were hastily set up.[16] Six months later, an estimated 12,000 of these Christians remain refugees in the camps, but uncounted thousands more have dispersed outside Kandhamal into Bhubaneswar and other cities, as well as to states outside Orissa. Christians have been told repeatedly by former neighbours that they cannot return to their homes and land unless they reconvert to Hinduism, and even those who do this feel extremely unsafe.

The violence and reconversion campaigns have been orchestrated by the VHP (Vishva Hindu Parishad). This time the violence against Christians was not limited to Kandhamal. There were horrific attacks, including burning of churches, mob murders and rapes in other parts of Orissa, and in several other states throughout India. Within Kandhamal, the violence continued even after large numbers of the CRPF (Central Reserve Police Force) had been posted. For instance, a Kond mob estimated at 2,000 burnt down several Christian buildings on 13th September, including a church at Kurtamgarh, near Jalaspeta, and when a CRPF force fired into the air, they were shot at, and fired on the crowd, killing between two and five people and injuring a dozen. In retaliation for this, a mob of about 500 Konds attacked and burnt Gochhapara police station on the 15th, killing a constable who could not escape.[17]

In the wake of this violence, the reactive diatribes between Christians and Hindus (in evidence not just in Orissa, but all over India) are all too understandable. Yet in many ways this flare-up between religions is a contrived, manufactured thing, part of the polarizing tendency inherent in the colonial ideology analyzed in earlier chapters. Moreover, each religion carries a huge shadow, as well great beauty and truth. This simple equation gets lost in the intolerance.

The shadow of Christianity is a belief that 'only we have the truth, the others worship false gods'. We have seen how the first wave of European missionaries spread this attitude during the 19th century. The result is that Christians held themselves separate and propagated a derogatory view of other religions. Long before it came to India, Christianity carried a terrible history of intolerance, with wars of religion and vicious persecution between Catholics and Protestants—the antithesis of the love which Jesus taught. We should remember too that Jesus never founded a Christian Church or wrote the Bible, which is a selection of texts made several centuries after his death, that excluded important writings such as the Gnostic Gospels and included some by followers with a much narrower vision than that of Jesus. On the other side, it is clear that in Kandhamal now and for many years, the only forced conversions going on are of Christians by Hindus. Conversion to Christianity has given thousands of people in India respite from the cruelties of caste, and a more personal relationship with God.

Hinduism too carries a great shadow too, more complex in a way. We all know about the cruelties of caste hierarchy. Organizations such as the Bajrang Dal and VHP, of which Saraswati was a leading member, represent a great narrowing of the universal truths so evident in earlier writings, such as the *Upanishads*, where the quest is not fixed into a dogma. *Neo Vedanta and Modernity*, by Bithika Mukerji (1983/2008) shows one aspect of the way that Hinduism has tended to narrow itself into a rigidly defined religion of conversion and set beliefs, like Christianity, and also to undermine the great critique of materialism that lies at the heart of *vedanta*, bringing Hinduism into line with Western materialism.

When people are cruel to others in the name of religion, they demean themselves and their religion. The cruelties perpetrated in Kandhamal on such a massive scale spell great danger for India. When the Maoists killed Saraswati, they acted out of stupidity and their own belief in violence. When the VHP and BD reacted by systematic ethnic cleansing this showed the same kind of diabolical planning evident in Gujarat in 2002, and the same transgression of all that is good in Hinduism. The state authorities' failure to curb or punish those responsible for the ethnic cleansing makes them appear to tacitly condone it. Many critics maintain that this stems from an election-oriented reluctance to anger the mainstream community, and undermines the rule of law. There are many similarities between the assault on Christians in Orissa and ethnic cleansing of Muslims in Gujarat and Rajasthan, such as the orchestration of tribal people to commit violence against non-Hindus, and the whole connection between stirring up communal tensions between communities, and the growth of the fascist power of corporations (Hardiman 2007, Shubh Mathur 2008).

The perpetrators of the violence felled trees to block the approach roads into the district, and for ten days there was no effective administration. Critics of the Orissa Government ask whether the contingents of police who tried to enter were really incapable of removing these felled trees, and point to countless accounts of police standing by while violence took place, and senior administrators who, when called on to act, said that their hands were tied. Just as Narendra Modi allowed three days of anti-Muslim violence in Gujarat, critics say that the Orissa Government allowed events to take their course for ten days—an accusation strenuously denied by the ruling party, which claims they have made at least 500 arrests.[18] Yet a dozen or so individuals from both communities who played a leading role in fanning the flames remain free. No one who knows Kandhamal, and was there when the violence erupted, has any doubt that political parties played a very dark game in the district, which fed into the complex and ugly patchwork of communal violence.

Part of the violence can be traced to a split in the grassroots organization that all Konds in the district gave allegiance to, the *Kui Samaj Seva Samiti*, whose late president, Kumud Chandra Mallick, while critical of the influence of missionaries, helped to keep peace between the communities. After he died in June 2003, an influential section of this body broke off and made an alliance with the VHP, partly to counteract what is seen as a widespread takeover of Kond land and influence by non-tribals.[19] This alliance with the forces of Hindutva assumed a virulent form in 2007–8, fuelled by the Kui tribe issue, and culminating in the huge dispossession of Christians—an 'ethnic cleansing' comparable to terrible episodes that have taken place in other countries in the last 15 years. Former Yugoslavia, Chechnya, Rwanda, Congo, Darfur: what has happened in Orissa has a complex relationship with even worse 'ethnic cleansings' in distant countries. But also in the neighbouring state of Chhattisgarh, where systematic atrocities have been used to force an even larger number of tribal people from their homes in the *Salwa Judum* civil war.

This more hidden aspect to what is going on in Kandhamal, with parallels in other parts of Orissa and neighbouring states, is a 'resource war'. For example, six weeks before the swami was killed, in July 2008, the Orissa Government announced the discovery of a new Bauxite deposit, on the mountains in the Kuttia Kond area, near Tumudibandh (though this is known to have been surveyed at least six years before).[20] The idea of a new Junagarh-Angul rail line through Kandhamal has been promoted since the violence, to end the district's isolation, and has been added to a list of demands by the Kond leaders. The real reason is undoubtedly to facilitate access to this Bauxite, as with the Rayagada-Koraput railway built in the 1980s.[21]

To astute observers, the tragedy of what is happening in Kandhamal is that the two most disadvantaged communities, namely the Scheduled Castes and Scheduled Tribes (*dalits* and *adivasis*), have been incited against each other, by political and fundamentalist forces. Closely related to these are the corporate interests whose goal is the district's exceptionally rich resources—land, forest, water, minerals.

Since August 2008, the Orissa Government has announced that the '*Salwa Judum* experiment' in South Chhattisgarh is to be tried in five districts of Orissa particularly affected by Maoist violence: Kandhamal, Gajapati, Rayagada, Koraput and Malkangiri.[22] This comes in the wake of a series of high profile Maoist attacks in Orissa, preceding that on the Jalespata ashram. Already about 500 tribal SPOs (Special Police Officers) are being recruited in each of these districts.

The trouble is, human rights organizations have raised fundamental questions about *Salwa Judum*, bringing evidence that SPOs have committed violence on a massive scale. Maoist atrocities are not in doubt, but the SJ's burning of hundreds of tribal villages with systematic torture, murder and rape committed by SPOs on thousands of villagers just for refusing to join SJ is attested by thousands of witnesses. In a recently highlighted incident, SPOs killed 17 tribal people in Singaram village (under Gollapalli police station) on 8th January 2009. The bodies were photographed by journalists from Andhra, and included four women (two of them naked). As in other cases, Maoist guns and uniforms were almost certainly planted. Villagers say these 17 were taken to one side and shot after the SJ attacked the village, angry that they would not join SJ.[23] Several well-researched human rights reports have highlighted SJ's appalling rights abuses, and the impunity with which they are perpetrated, without minimizing Maoists' atrocities. Unfortunately a report by the National Human Rights Commission (staffed by ex-police), called for by the Supreme Court, has whitewashed the SJ, which is protected by a state-level Security Act that bans independent reporting of the conflict (Balagopal 2008). The imprisonment of Binayak Sen for over 20 months—a doctor who has spent years serving the people, and was a leading critic of the SJ as a prominent member of the People's Union for Civil Liberties (PUCL)—is widely seen as a blot on India's tradition of freedom and democracy.

In this context, to promote the model of *Salwa Judum* in Orissa seems a recipe for spreading conflict and displacement even further. As with the wider war on terror, repression as a response to terrorism pushes ordinary people towards extremism in frustration and outrage. What gets covered up in the mayhem is then a land-grab and a looting of resources. Kandhamal has been lucky in one way. Thanks partly to the sympathetic administration of Ollenbach during the 1900s–20s, the district has preserved some of the best expanses of *sal*-forest in Orissa, which will be in danger if the railway is built.[24] The idea promoted by Hindutva forces that *adivasis* are *vanvasis* represents another kind of Cultural Genocide, 'purifying' the culture of *adivasis* to convert them into Sanskritized 'backward Hindus', in a denial of their indigenous ancestry and ancient non-brahmanical traditions.

Mining and Cultural Genocide

The mining projects being imposed and planned involve dispossessing thousands of farmers, tribal and non-tribal, whose culture represents one of the most ancient and balanced layers of Indian civilization. Yet few non-tribals have much understanding of tribal culture, and many show it gross disrespect. The very act of mining a mountain violates the order of life which tribal culture has preserved and lived harmoniously with since history began. There is a clash of belief systems here more fundamental than the conflict between religions.

The sacrifice theme is clear in a 1980s study commissioned by the National Aluminium Company (Nalco) of tribal people, mainly Konds and Porojas, displaced by their refinery at Damanjodi (Koraput district):

> The Government of Orissa as well as the NALCO have taken the view that the homesteads lost by the tribal families were practically of no value as they were small mud huts. As no compensation could be paid for loss of such homesteads, durable houses (partly pucca) could be constructed for them at the cost of NALCO. Secondly, the concept of rehabilitation was based on the fact that it was necessary for NALCO alumina project to create certain amount of community relationship with those who have lost all their assets in the larger interest of the nation, by offering them various types of employment opportunities as well as social support… by way of health, medical and educational facilities.
>
> It has been established that marginalization of displaced tribals is largely due to payment of compensation in cash which they quickly spend away in conventional luxuries. To a certain extent it was also due to their being duped by non-tribals by involving them in various types of non-profitable transactions. It is well known that the tribal culture and ways of living have no future orientation. Naturally, sudden influx of money into their hands [p.5] induces extravagance in them. Of course the amount of compensation paid to them for loss of their land was rather small because of third-grade land possessed by them. In order to insure against repeating mistake of this type, NALCO has taken the initiative in drawing up a plan of action. In this process,

the displaced tribals themselves would be the active participants in their own rehabilitation. The action plan envisages provision of a house and some land, though much smaller than what they had lost, for cultivation, which was their way of life. In this context, it is necessary to operationalize their plan in a way that all elements of an integrated pattern of living are provided.

This plan is not only an engineering venture, but also has several social and psychological dimensions which cannot be totally comprehended within an engineering framework. These could only be tackled by an interdisciplinary approach to tribal rehabilitation and planning by psychologists, sociologists, economists, agronomists, and area planners, who have to pool their experiences and build blocks of information which in totality could provide the full structure of the plan. The NALCO, therefore approached the National Institute of Rural Development (NIRD) to undertake a study in order to find out the ways which would enable them to lead a new life supported by gainful employment in agriculture, animal husbandry, poultry, vegetable cultivation, rural and cottage industries and salaried employment in NALCO alumina plant. It was comprehended that the needed action programmes are to be worked out and implemented so that people who were happy peasants enjoying fruits of their labour amidst natural surroundings yesterday are not rendered homeless and unemployed today leading the life of destitutes because of their sacrifices in the national interest." (Mutthayya 1982 p.1 ff., emphasis added)

This passage illustrates the negative stereotypes about tribal people that are still embedded in mainstream discourse. As local tribal people say in interviews: their resettlement at Damanjodi was humiliating and substandard, under asbestos roofs, while their villages used to be beautiful and fertile; company promises guaranteeing employment were soon betrayed, and people have to beg or give large bribes for even the most degrading jobs: 'Nalco is death for us.'[25]

Nearly always, in India and worldwide, displacement of tribal people leads to a massive drop in their standard of living: 'projects meant to reduce poverty are the ones adding to the numbers of the poor.' According to World Bank and other international standards on involuntary resettlement, if a project really constitutes 'development', then 'the first rule is that all parties to the project should be better off.'[26] Resettlement & Rehabilitation (R & R) policies formulated by the World Bank, DFID and UNDP, as well as the Governments of Orissa and India, insist that people's standard of living should go up, not down. It is generally acknowledged that this hardly ever happens in practice (Mathur 2008 p.179).

This exemplifies a reality gap at the centre of R & R policies. Between what is supposed to happen and what actually happens there is often no correlation at all. Since most projects have no Social Impact Assessment, since displaced people are not made part of the decision-making process, and there is no proper check on the success of R & R, or even proper ways to assess this, let alone any disciplinary action against officials responsible for failure, this reality gap remains almost completely outside the approved discourse on R & R (Padel & Das Dec. 2008).

Part of the problem is that most of the discourse on tribal people, and on R & R, barely quotes tribal people's voices at all. Even a large segment of the Left perpetuates the 'primitive' stereotypes formulated under colonial rule, dismissing any positive view of tribal culture as 'primitive romanticism' that tries to 'preserve tribal cultures in a museum'.[27] The museums set up in Orissa actually form an intrinsic part of the process of Cultural Genocide. Tribal people visiting them become grim and subdued, saying 'these things are for other people, not us'. Most of the objects in the tribal museum set up in Koraput during the 1980s were actually acquired from over 60 tribal villages that were obliterated by Nalco and the Upper Kolab dam.

In the late 1970s, the category of 'Primitive Tribe Groups' (PTGs) was formulated in India. Out of 70 groups identified, 13 are in Orissa. Special Development Agencies were set up to give these groups 'all-round development', such as the Dongria Kond Development Agency (DKDA) for the Niyamgiri area. The 2007 issue of *Adivasi* is devoted to PTGs, accepting the category uncritically: 'the Dongria Kondh is a primitive and backward section of the Kondh tribe.'[28] Calling other cultures 'primitive' has long been considered deeply offensive in the 'developed' world—a hallmark of the earliest, most primitive stage of anthropology, that aided the colonial conquest of tribal peoples (above, chapter 7). In the present Dongria situation, it serves to justify Vedanta's takeover of their mountains. During 2007–8, the DKDA channelled central government funds to build huge tarmac roads into the heart of Niyamgiri, ostensibly for the sake of the Dongria, but dovetailing with Vedanta's plans. Dongria informants say that the first people to use these roads in a big way were the timber mafia, who within a few months have denuded huge areas all around the roads. Roads often seem an obvious, unquestionable benefit, but when one examines who promotes and funds them and what actually happens as soon as they are built, they are a central means of exploitation and domination going back to Roman times.[29]

The term 'Genocide' was first used in 1944–5, to describe Nazi treatment of Jews. What is classed as Genocide now is often a sensitive political issue: while most people class Turkey's slaughter and mass displacement of its Armenian population in 1916, and Sudan's ongoing slaughter and mass displacement of Darfur's population as cases of Genocide, this is hotly disputed by the governments of those countries. However, the classic model of Genocide, applied to countless tribes that were exterminated all over the continents of America and Australia, is not in dispute.

'Genocide' means killing (Latin *caedo*) a people, race or tribe (*genus*). Examining what was involved in the genocide of America's indigenous tribes, it is evident that there are two levels to what was killed: the physical extermination, and the killing off of cultures. Contemporary accounts show that members of those tribes often preferred to die rather than survive physically without their land and culture, and the same applies to tribal people resisting displacement in India today, who often say 'Our blood may flow, but we won't leave our land'. Actual killings, as at Maikanch and Kalinganagar, may be quite few (though in the *Salwa Judum* war they are not few), but they symbolize a violent sacrifice, and a psychic death for *adivasis* that non-tribal people rarely understand. Underlying the Cultural Genocide is the invaders' total lack of respect for tribal people's traditions and connection with the land. Mainstream culture ceased a long time ago to be rooted in the soil. As land prices shoot up, collective attachment to the land that a village has worked over successive generations, has no value in the incomers' eyes, which focus only on profits they hope to generate.

The US policy from the late 19th century was to take over tribal territories and resettle surviving members in reservations, where they became dependent on handouts and could no longer support themselves. A conscious policy of 'detribalizing' them was pursued by forcibly taking children away from their families and putting them in schools where any attempt to maintain traditional customs or speak tribal languages was punished, 'killing the Indian in them'—an example cited by Fenelon, who prefers the word 'culturicide' (1998). But this term is clumsy and does not conjure the appropriate sense of death and outrage. Cultural Genocide means essentially the killing of people's culture by uprooting them from their ancestral lands (Padel and Das 2008).

In popular usage now, 'culture' often means just 'the pretty bits', exemplified by tribal or classical dances or music. The main patrons of dance, music, painting, religious festivals, and even lawyers' seminars in Orissa now are the biggest mining companies, Vedanta and Tata. The original meaning of culture, from Latin *cultus*, refers to *cultivation* (Oriya *chaso*) of the soil and the *cult* of nature-deities, as well as the essential *culture* (traditions and values) at the heart of a society. In other words, tribal people's economic and political systems are fundamental to their culture, and when dispossessed of their land these systems are effectively destroyed. Meeting a Kond woman resettled by Vedanta, whose village was one of five bulldozed to make way for the Lanjigarh refinery, she said 'they even destroyed our gods!'—since the *darni penu* stones were obliterated along with people's houses and fields.

What has happened to the Konds around Lanjigarh has been traumatic to witness: the creating of a wasteland out of what till recently were unspoilt, fertile fields and villages, and a drastic drop in people's quality of life in dozens of villages around the refinery. Trucks carrying Bauxite, alumina, coal and oil have killed a lot of people in accidents and churned up the roads, creating a massive problem of dust. The Bansadhara river has been polluted at its source, by leaching of toxic red mud and illegal emissions that have killed people and animals.[30]

Yet even this is nothing compared to what will happen if Niyamgiri is mined: a nightmare enactment of Gopinath Mohanty's prophetic *Alora*. What is special about Niyamgiri is that, of all the twenty to thirty major Bauxite-capped mountains in south Orissa, this mountain preserves the best forest on its summit. Others, such as Gandhamardan—saved from Bauxite mining by a historic movement in the mid-1980s — have magnificent forests and waterfalls on their sides. The reason that Niyamgiri's summits have preserved primary *sal*-forest is that they are seen as the abode of Niyam Raja, Lord of the Law, who guarantees the land's fertility. The Dongria clear patches of forest to cultivate the steep hill-slopes, but in honour of Niyam Raja, have maintained a strict taboo against cutting trees on the summits. Niyam Dongar, the mountain in the northwest of the range, is widely recognized as the centre of one of Orissa's best remaining forests, with greatest biodiversity, which is why the CEC and Wildlife Institute of India wrote strong reports commissioned by the Supreme Court outlining an environmental disaster if the mountain is mined.[31]

When geologists named the rock of these mountains Khondalite, they recognized a symbiosis that exists between the Konds and their mountains. As the Dongria put it: 'We need the mountain, and the mountain needs us'. Niyam Raja has Hindu temples in the towns surrounding the range, such as Bissamcuttack, where Dongria used to sacrifice buffaloes (P.K. Nayak 1989 p.180).

Losing their land or mountains brings the death of everything most valued in tribal culture. The sacredness of nature, respect for elders' knowledge, ritual contact with the ancestors, growing their own food on family land and making their own houses and tools, exchanging food with neighbours in an egalitarian spirit: these things are swept away by corporate values which emphasize the mainstream world's prime value of financial profit. Orissa's mineral wealth is seen by many as an inert resource just waiting to be utilized for the state to become rich again.

What tribal culture recognizes that mainstream culture does not, is the way that mountains maintain the fertility of land for miles around. Bauxite acts as a sponge, holding monsoon water and releasing it gradually throughout the year in countless perennial streams, that dry up when the blasting starts and the bauxite is extracted—a process visible and attested to by Kond villagers all around Panchpat Mali, the mountain in Koraput that Nalco has exploited since the 1980s. The real value of Orissa's mineral wealth is the land's outstanding fertility. Mine the mountains, and this fertility is gone forever—a process painfully visible over large areas in Orissa and neighbouring states where the mining of coal, iron, chromite and Bauxite has taken over and created a wasteland.

This diminishing fertility from the desecration of mountains is compounded by an insane overuse of water for metal factories. This has been strongly resisted by a farmers' movement in west Orissa, which has drawn attention to the Hirakud reservoir's channelling of water to new aluminium smelters and iron/steel factories, away from the irrigation canals that never reached the areas they were meant to, whose water volume is receding alarmingly.[32] The Wuppertal Institute in Germany, among the world's top agencies for studying resource use, estimates that producing one ton of steel consumes about 44 tons of water—dangerously high considering the massive increase of steel production being promoted in Orissa. But in the case of aluminium, producing one ton consumes over 1,300 tons of water.[33]

These facts make a mockery of the 'Sustainable Development' being promoted by the aid industry as well as by the mining industry.

Almost more shocking than the deterioration of life around Lanjigarh is the attempt by Vedanta to deny this and turn the truth on its head, through its Sustainable Development reports and CSR claims (Corporate Social Responsibility), which are promoted by two London-based PR companies, Finsbury and CO3, and accredited by leading accountancy firms such as PriceWaterhouse Coopers and Ernst & Young. The claim to be benefitting people is based on large sums supposedly spent on building schools and hospitals, setting up Self Help Groups for women, and even teaching people improved methods of cultivation![34] The reality is a sordid tale of corruption by sub-contractors, empty buildings, schemes that enmesh people into debt, and intimidation by company-employed *goondas*. But Vedanta is only following a model laid out by the Mining, Minerals and Sustainable Development process (MMSD) and Global Reporting Initiative (GRI), through which the world's biggest mining companies sabotaged attempts to make them accountable, replacing them with an ineffective, unaccountable system that amounts to a PR exercise that masks the real facts.[35]

In other words, aluminium companies are mounting an invasion of the Kond area that forms a continuity with the colonial invasion a century and a half before, and sacrifices Konds' natural resources, culture and values to the same gods of 'progress' and market value. In this situation, what should be the role of anthropologists? Some serve the aluminium companies and World Bank or DFID, or government-sponsored development projects in India, following the role of the first anthropologists, who were often administrators or missionaries. But anthropology does not influence WB policy, which is dictated by economists and political/corporate pressure. Policy and practice remain separated by the reality gap, while the effect of anthropology at the WB is a 'Christmas-tree decoration' of politically sensitive language, which serves to mask the institution's real impact (Mosse 2005, 2009).

To have the influence they deserve, anthropologists need to reflect back to mainstream society a questioning of our own beliefs and customs, and above all to analyze the exercise of power in mainstream institutions, which is why my next book, with Samarendra Das, makes the aluminium industry into its object of study, analyzing the World Bank and NGOs alongside the mining companies. One of the uncomfortable things we realized while writing this is that this metal, obtained from deposits which lie on the Konds' mountain-tops and in remote, forested mountains in other lands, is of central importance to the arms industry. A 1951 text which is probably unique for its frankness, from a senior US expert about aluminium's link with arms as well as the prohibitive environmental and financial costs of producing it, reveals that

> Aluminum has become the most important single bulk material of modern warfare. No fighting is possible, and no war can be carried to a successful conclusion today, without using and destroying vast quantities of aluminum… Aluminum is needed in atomic weapons, both in their manufacture and in their delivery… Aluminum, and great quantities of it, spell the difference between victory and defeat…[36]

From what we have discovered, this is just as true now as it was in the Second World War. So the companies making most profits out of the War on Terror, including the wars in Iraq and Afghanistan, are not just the oil companies, but also the arms companies and the mining companies that supply them to make the hardware that is devastating civilian populations. From a life-giving, water-retaining role in the soil and Bauxite, aluminium becomes a spreader of pollution and death, both in the areas where it is manufactured, and where it is used in war.

Orissa's farmers are uniting as never before to protect their land and resources. In doing so, they present a challenge to the world's biggest mining companies, that look at East India's mineral and water resources with frustrated greed. It is significant that the area where the War on Terror has entered India most insidiously is in the tribal heartland of Bastar, where the *Salwa Judum* civil war assumes the features of a 'resource war'. Sometimes a resource war assumes the character of a Left-Right confrontation, at other times, a war of religion. How can Hindus and Christians, *adivasis and dalits*, come together again in the wake of the Kandhamal conflict? If God exists, would He or She want us to argue and kill each other about Him or Her? The idea is ludicrous. A step towards reconciliation started on 21st January 2009, with the formation of an Adivasi Harijan Surakhya Samiti (Adivasi-Dalit protection society), which held a rally in Phulbani.

Where tribal villagers confront mining companies, they recognize a joint cause with non-tribal farmers confronting Posco (South Korea's mammoth steel company) on Orissa's coast, and Dalit farmers who have managed to expel Tata and other companies from Singur and Nandigram (West Bengal)—struggles where many people lost their lives, and thousands of homes were destroyed, and which have in turn inspired a powerful, largely/originally non-violent Santal movement against police atrocities in West Midnapur district (N. Dutta 2009). These movements, against the power of foreign capital to sacrifice people's lives and standard of living, affect everyone, and raise the question for all of us: What is development?

When Dongria Konds visited Delhi in 2007, they were appalled at the dirt in the streets and air, and the danger and stress from the traffic. What right have Delhi- or Bhubaneswar-based administrators or intellectuals to classify Dongria as 'primitive'? To Dongria, our cities are primitive or debased in their dirt, dangerous traffic and congestion and it is they who preserve the proper values of a civilized lifestyle that can sustain for centuries. The small-scale pattern of self-sufficiency and restraint of Dongria villages offers a model of real sustainability much needed in today's world. Is the power of India's villagers to fight off corporate takeovers still as strong as it was during India's Freedom Struggle? The Gandhamardan movement in 1985–7 united *dalits* and *adivasis*, Hindus, Christians and atheists, to protect a mountain's life-sustaining power from the clutches of mining interests. A new phase of Freedom Struggle is in full swing today, and who knows, our survival as a species may well depend on the success of these movements in bringing about a turning point. Corporate greed has already sacrificed too much of the earth's resources we all depend on.

NOTES

Notes to the Text

Preface

1. The title of my doctoral thesis was *British rule and the Konds of Orissa: a study of tribal administration and its legitimating discourse*.

Chapter One. A Case Study of Colonialism

1. This identification between Nirantali and Darni Penu is explicit in some myths and writings about the Konds, e.g. Elwin's *Myths of Orissa* (1954, esp. pp.549–50) and invocations to the goddess under both names translated by Niggemeyer (1964, Appendix). For Kui Konds, Nirantali's place is taken by Amali Baeli, who is similarly identified with Darni Penu (WM, Boal 1982).
2. This is my own synthesis of several Kond myths collected by Verrier Elwin (1954, esp. myths I.9–12). In his introduction, Elwin despaired of making sense of the Konds' myths he had collected!
3. Another synthesis of Kond myths after Elwin 1954 (myths XVII.17–21). In other Kond myths, it is human sacrifice that makes the earth firm (Elwin 1949 myths I.21–2). Macpherson recorded a myth which tells how the Earth Goddess became the first Kond woman, Amali Baeli, who cut her finger while preparing vegetables: her blood fell on the earth, which became firm and fertile, so she offered herself up for sacrifice; but the Konds declined,

preferring the sacrifice of outsiders (WM p.96, Boal 1982 pp.52 & 91).

4. 'Not by refraining from action does man attain freedom from action.... The world is in the bonds of action, unless the action is consecration. Let thy actions then be pure, free from the bonds of desire. Thus spoke the Lord of Creation when he made both men and sacrifice: "By sacrifice thou shalt multiply and obtain all thy desires. By sacrifice shalt thou honour the gods and the gods will then love thee. And thus in harmony with them shalt thou attain the supreme good...."

   There are Yogis whose sacrifice is an offering to the gods; but others offer as a sacrifice their own soul in the fire of God.... Neither this world nor the world to come is for him who does not sacrifice....

   Thus in many ways men sacrifice, and in many ways they go to Brahman. Know that all sacrifice is holy work, and knowing this thou shalt be free.'

   The *Bhagavad Gita*, translated by Juan Mascaro, Penguin 1962, chapter 3 verses 4 & 9–11; chapter 4 verses 25 & 31–2.
5. Or, for that matter, the definitions of theologians. See Hubert and Mauss' classic essay (1898/1964), and a collection of essays edited by M.F.C. Bourdillon and Meyer Fortes (*Sacrifice* 1980).
6. Peter Berger's book *Pyramids of sacrifice* (1974), suggests that development along the capitalist (or Marxist) path, in the scale of its costs to human life, is essentially similar to the Aztecs' human sacrifice of captives taken from the surrounding peoples. For example, the terrible droughts that have recently affected large parts of Africa, many now see as man-made disasters, created through what developed countries, in collusion with local elites, have imposed on the mass of the population and their land.
7. The Aztecs are the most famous human sacrificing society. Fiji at the time of Captain Cook's voyages is another well-attested example. In most other cases, the evidence is highly questionable, since colonials legitimized their conquest by playing on stereotypes about it. For example, the Ashanti were said to practise it on a horrific scale by the British forces that conquered them (James Morris 1973/1979 Ch.20), but the British may have mistaken capital punishment for sacrifice (Wilks 1975). The Tupinamba on the coast of Brazil were also accused of it by the Portuguese who overwhelmed them, but this claim was used to

justify enslaving them, which led to the Tupinambas' virtual extermination (Paul Hemming 1978). Nigel Davies (1981) goes over the history of human sacrifice without, it seems to me, a critical awareness of the unreliability of much of the evidence, which stems from the power of stereotypes about the custom: I feel his book thus reinforces those stereotypes. More comparable to the Kond custom is the human sacrifice by Dayaks in Borneo (Nigel Davies Ch.8), as well as the custom of headhunting current among the Nagas and other tribes of Northeast India, which sometimes shaded into human sacrifice (Fürer-Haimendorf 1976, Gohain 1977). There is evidence that some of the Konds' neighbours practised it, such as the Konda Reddis (Fürer-Haimendorf 1944) and the Maria Gonds (Elwin 1943b). It may be that the Marias' name is related-to the word for the Konds' victims—*meriah*. But most tribes of Central India do not seem to have been human sacrificers.

8. The concept of the shadow was developed by Carl Jung: 'By shadow I mean the "negative" side of the personality, the sum of all those unpleasant qualities we like to hide, together with the insufficiently developed functions and the contents of the personal unconscious.... Everyone carries a shadow, and the less it is embodied in the individual's conscious, the blacker and denser it is.... Mere suppression of the shadow is as little of a remedy as beheading would be for a headache.'(quoted from Anthony Storr ed. 1983) The shadow is frequently projected onto others. The significance of this concept for understanding societies' stereotypes of each other is clear.
9. Macpherson 1842, summarized in his articles in the JRAS (1843 and 1852), and in WM Ch.6. For Campbell's ridicule see below pp.251–2.
10. Dalton 1872, Risley 1891, Thurston 1909, Russell and Hira Lal 1916, and the Census and Gazetteers, especially Maltby's *Ganjam District Manual* 1882, and Ollenbach in O'Malley 1908.
11. In the Archives of the Jawaharlal Nehru Memorial Library, Teenmurti.
12. The main Kond ethnographies are F.G. Bailey's *Tribe, Caste and Nation* 1960, Niggemeyer's *Die Kuttia Kond* 1964, S. Banerjee's

An ethnographic study of the Kuvi Kandhas 1968, and Barbara Boal's *The Konds* 1982.

13. Mentioned as such for example by Kaye 1853, Dalton 1872 (quoted above p.3), Hunter 1872, Hutton 1941, Woodruffe 1953.
14. *Kuvinga* or *Kuinga* are the words Konds use to refer to themselves (Israel 1979 p.350, Winfield 1928 p.20). 'Kond' is an anglicized form of the Oriya name for them, *Kondo*, *Khondo*, *Kondho* or *Kandha*, which Konds also often use. 19th Century sources mostly call them *Khonds* or *Kondhs*. I follow Bailey and Boal in using the form *Kond*. The Telugu derivation was first suggested by Macpherson. Konda Reddis are also described as Hill Reddis, and Konda Doras as 'Lords of the Hills'.
15. Winfield (1928) gives 600,000 as the Kond population, Ahmed (1961 Part I) gives 690,000, and Banerjee (1968) 800,000.
16. On the official separation of Kui from Kuvi see e.g. Burrow and Bhattacarya 1962–3, and Israel 1979 pp.xix–xxi. Most scholars say they are not mutually intelligible.
17. Macpherson described the Konds as 'a congeries of tribes' (as Evans-Pritchard describes the Nuer, 1940 p.5). In modern classification, the Konds are counted as a single tribe. But Konds are divided into many clans, which in Macpherson's time were referred to as separate tribes. What constitutes a tribe, and what is a clan, often owes more to anthropological custom than to how people see themselves. Bailey and Niggemeyer see the Konds as a number of tribes that have migrated to their present land in a 'retreat to the interior'.
18. The towns of Phulbani and Udayagiri. Kui also live in neighbouring parts of Ganjam and Puri Districts.
19. The Kuttias are mostly in southwest Phulbani, and the Dongrias in north Koraput.
20. Ahmed 1961 Part I. Jatapus live in eastern Koraput and neighbouring areas of Andhra Pradesh. Konda Doras and Konda Reddis are sometimes said to be another offshoot of the Konds (e.g. Thurston 1909 pp.349–54).
21. Following Oriya usage, the British called the Hill Konds *Maliah* Konds, and the Plains Konds *Sasi* or *Desia* Konds. Plains Konds were further divided into *Bettiah* Konds (those in complete subjec-

tion to Hindu *rajahs*), and *Benniah* Konds (intermediate between *Maliah* and *Bettiah* Konds).

22. Bailey 1960 p.121.
23. From searching the literature, the only systematic difference I found between Munda- and Dravidian-speaking tribes concerns menstruation. The Konds and other Dravidian tribes are similar to Hindus in that women sit apart during their periods; they are not allowed to cook or work, and are seen as dangerously polluting for men. Kond houses often have a special back door and room for women during their periods. The Munda-speaking tribes are largely without menstrual taboos (NB: Elwin 1950 & 1955 on the Bondos and Soras, and Archer's 1974 on the Santals). I wrote an M.Litt. thesis on the differences between Munda and Dravidian tribes. Robert Parkin's *The Munda of Central India* (1992) gives more detail on the Munda-speaking tribes.
24. Elwin 1955, Vitebsky 1993.
25. Elwin's *Bondo Highlander* (1950) is the classic description. Uma Guha et al. (1968) is the main account of the Didayi.
26. Thusu and Jha 1969.
27. According to Thurston (1909), Porojas see themselves as 'subjects in contradistinction to a free hill man'. There are several distinct groups of Porojas: according to Yeatts (1931) 'all that is certain is that the term covers several quite distinct tribes'. The Bondo, Didayi, Gadaba and Durva tribes have been classified as Porojas at various times. The Pengo Porojas merge with Konds near Kashipur; they call themselves *Jani*, the word for the Kond priest who performed human sacrifice; and Pengos sometimes serve Konds as priests (Thusu 1977). Gopinath Mohanty's Oriya novel 'Paraja' (1945, translated into English 1987) is a vivid account of tribal life in Koraput.
28. Bison-horn Maria, Hill Maria, Muria and Raj Gonds are the main groups in Bastar district. Altogether Gonds occupy an area of Central India larger than Britain. Grigson 1938, Elwin 1943b, 1947, Fürer-Haimendorf 1979.
29. Elwin 1948.
30. For understanding the Konds' incorporation in Hindu kingdoms, I have found Kulke's work most helpful (see below, chapter 4, and Bailey 1960 Ch.VII). On similar ritualized allegiance of other tribes

to Hindu *rajahs* see Elwin (1947) and Thusu (1980) for the Gonds, Roy (1935) for the Bhuiyas, and Elwin (1950) for the Bondos.

31. For discussion of the dividing line between tribe and caste see Dumont and Pocock (1959), Bailey (1961), etc.
32. E.g. Macpherson and Forbes both mentioned fighting between their own troops and Konds that was only averted because the women intervened. Also, the custom of brideprice rather than dowry gives women a positive rather than a negative value, and gives higher status to the wife's rather than to the groom's family.
33. Basham 1971 p.33.
34. Ghurye's *The Scheduled Tribes* (1959) was a longer edition of his book, *The Aborigines—'so-called'—and their future* (1943).
35. For a critique of the concept of 'tribe' see Fried 1975, Godelier 1978.
36. On social evolutionism see below p.255 ff.
37. I explore this theme in the final chapter. E.g. G. and M. Wilson in *The analysis of social change* (1945) take for granted a 'transition from primitive to civilized', and declare the 'problems of maladjustment' it leads to 'inevitable'. They divide the subject up into economic, political, 'technical and scientific', and religious change. To me the first, most basic step in understanding social change is to differentiate the elite that instigates change from the people on whom changes are imposed—a distinction that emerges immediately from a balanced summary of almost any tribe's history. Changes in clothing in tribal areas might seem to be change at a superficial rather than a 'structural' level (Leach 1953 pp.17 & 20), yet where the change is from handmade fabrics manufactured within the community, to machine-made fabrics manufactured in factories, and sold in markets by traders who are not locals, this is a shift that involves every domain of social life, and affects economic and political as well as ritual relationships. See also on 'social change': Firth 1954, Hogbin 1958, Monica Hunter 1961, and especially A.D. Smith *The concept of social change* 1973.
38. Elias 1939/1978, Hocart 1952, Elwin 1943a on tribal people's loss of vitality produced by too quick exposure to outside influences, Lyall on 'the gradual brahminizing of the aboriginal, non-Aryan, casteless or broken tribes' (quoted in Risley 1891), Sinha on

'Rajputization' 1962, and Kulke's article on 'Kshatriyaisation and social change' 1978.

39. The research by Kulke and Eschmann (1978–80) on Hindu kingdoms in tribal areas of medieval Orissa helped me understand the shift of power relations that took place under British rule. Sinha (1962) and K.S. Singh (1971) have also worked on precolonial tribal history. Others have concentrated on tribal rebellions against colonial rule: J.C. Jha (1964) on the Munda rebellion of 1832, K.S. Singh (1966, 1983) on that of 1899 and more recent tribal political movements, Ranajit Guha (1983a & b) on administrators' discourse on the great Santal uprising of 1856, and David Arnold (1982) on the Rampa rebellion among the Konda Dora and neighbouring tribes in the 1870s. C.P. Singh (1978) traces the early stages in the imposition of British rule on the Ho tribe that resisted it fiercely, like the Konds. Behara (1984) covers some of the most decisive events I am concerned with—the Ghumsur wars of 1836–7, and Chokra Bissoi's war in 1846–8—but by trying to fit the facts into the mould of the modern concept of 'India's freedom struggle', he clouds the basic outline of events, following the British perception of these wars as rebellions rather than resistance to the first stages of imposing British rule.

40. Kincaid 1968 pp.126 ff. & 237. The Mauryan empire embarked on a policy of deforestation on a major scale, displacing forest tribes (Kosambi 1970 p.124). Ashoka repented and became a Buddhist after his massive slaughter among the population of Orissa, yet continued to threaten forest tribes with punishment if they did not obey his laws (Basham 1971 p.55). Kautilya's *Arthashastra* recommended techniques for demoralizing forest tribes, as well as recognizing their uses, as did the *Amuktamalyada*, a Telugu book on statecraft in the kingdom of Vijayawada of about 1500: 'If the king grows angry with [the forest folk], he cannot wholly destroy them, but if he wins their affection by kindness and charity they serve him by invading the enemy's territory and plundering his forts.'(quoted by Basham 1971 p.200) The early medieval Tamil kingdoms fought periodic wars against border tribes, whom they drove further into the interior (Burton Stein 1980).

41. Hunter 1875 pp.14–20, 284–309. Cleveland was appointed Assistant to the Supervisor of Rajmahal in 1774. In 1777–8 the Paharia

were reported to have burnt 44 villages in raids under the leadership of zemindars, whom Cleveland dispossessed in 1782. He was made Collector in 1779, when Rajmahal was transferred to Bhagalpur, and began a campaign of pacification at once. 47 hill chiefs 'submitted voluntarily' to him in 1780, when he established a corps of 400 Paharia archers under eight *sirdars* dressed in purple jackets and turbans. These Paharia Hill Rangers continued until 1857. In 1780 he executed 10 chiefs for stealing 900 cattle; and in 1782 he held a great trial of 20 chiefs and 120 commoners, of whom several were hanged, and several more sentenced to life imprisonment. John Shore wrote a poem about Cleveland's pacification of the Paharias, and Kipling adapted it to a short story (Kaye 1853 pp.489–92, Woodruffe 1953).

42. James Outram was one of the heroes of the Bhil campaigns, subjugating them by force. He created a Bhil corps, like Cleveland's Paharia corps, drilling recruits himself. Campbell recruited Konds and *meriahs* into a corps on the same principle. Outram became a friend of S.C. Macpherson. See Graham 1843, Kaye 1853 pp.473–89, Goldsmid 1880 pp.54–5, 85–6, 105, 112, and Simcox [1920]. 'The great thing was to convert them, if it were possible, into an agricultural population....'(Kaye p.483)

43. Johnson 1982a. In Evans-Pritchard's classic study of the Nuer in southern Sudan (1940), he defined their political structure in a way that includes relations with non-Nuer: 'the Nuer political system includes all the people with whom they come into contact' (p.5), 'The political structure of the Nuer can only be understood in relation to a *whole structure* of which other people are a part' (p.190). In elucidating the rules by which groups of Nuer maintain structural distance with each other as well as with other tribes, he includes 'the Government operating from various centres' (in his diagram p.114); and he makes explicit a context of recent military action by the Anglo-Egyptian army, who had subdued and in effect conquered the Nuer only two years before his fieldwork. Yet he does not in fact analyse Government-Nuer relations as part of the Nuer political structure. In his own terms, therefore, he fails to analyse the Nuer political system as a whole, even though he was present among them in the very years when domination by outsiders became the main feature of their political system. Presumably, he

was reluctant to analyse the Government because his role as anthropologist there made him, in effect, part of it. Likewise, in *African political systems* (Fortes and Evans-Pritchard 1940), there is more effort than usual to include European rule and its effect in the models of social structure, but the emphasis again is on effects, or 'differences in response to European rule'. Analysis of European rule itself is blocked off as if it were an anthropological taboo.

In *The Sanusi of Cyrenaica* (1949) Evans-Pritchard did undertake to analyse a colonial administration together with a tribal organization, and he exposes Italian administrators' false conceptions about the Bedouin and the Sanusi order to which they gave religious affiliation, through quotations of Italian reports. But he fought against this Italian administration during the war: it is easy to expose an enemy's illusions. What about the conceptions of the British officials whom Evans-Pritchard served? Are British administrators' conceptions of the Nuer or Bedouin somehow beyond such analysis? Evans-Pritchard was no doubt aware of this problem, even though he did not make it explicit, for *The Nuer* is in part a dialogue with British administrators, correcting their impression of Nuer society as lawless disorder and a state of uncontrolled warfare.

44. I use the terms 'deep' or 'unconscious structure' as opposed to 'surface' or 'conscious structure' (esp. in Ch.5), on the idea that the formal or surface structure of a society corresponds to its members' conscious understanding of it; whereas they take for granted or remain largely unconscious of the deep or informal structure, which tends to generate the formal structure through powerful collective representations: myths, symbols, cultural values etc. Cf. Lévi-Strauss 1977 pp.281–2, Barthes 1972 & 1977, and Bordieu 1977 p.78 etc.
45. Even relations between tribal societies are structured in a way that calls conventional anthropological analysis of single societies into question. For example, Uberoi's study of the institution of *kula*, shows that it was an institution with great political significance for the structure of relations between the Trobrianders and neighbouring island tribes (1962). Malinowski failed to see this because his focus was fixed on the structure of relations *within* a society.
46. As Curtin explains this in relation to European stereotypes about Africa:

'Perhaps the most striking aspect of the British image of Africa in the early nineteenth century was its variance from the African reality, as we now understand it. There was also a marked lack of the kind of "progress" one might expect to find in a body of ideas that was constantly enlarged by accretions of new data. This is especially hard to explain, given the fact that nineteenth century social scientists were trying to be methodical, working to a standard that was conceived as rational investigation.

'One source of error [was that] reporters went to Africa knowing the reports of their predecessors and the theoretical conclusions already drawn from them. They were therefore sensitive to data that seemed to confirm their European preconceptions, and they were insensitive to contradictory data. Their reports were thus passed through a double set of positive and negative filters, and filtered once more as they were assimilated in Britain. Data that did not fit the existing image were often simply ignored. As a result, British thought about Africa responded very weakly to new data of any kind.

'It responded much more strongly to changes in British thought. The travellers (and even more the analysts at home) took the European *Weltanschauung* as their point of departure. They did not ask, "What is Africa like, and what manner of men live there" but, "How does Africa, and how do Africans, fit into what we already know about the world". In this sense the image of Africa was far more European than African.' (Curtin 1965 p.479)

47. On the relationship between textual structure and social structure, see Raymond Williams 1958, Guha 1973, Barthes 1977.
48. E.g. Macpherson's quarrel with MacViccar over missionaries (explored in Ch.6), and Brigadier General Dyce's dramatic condemnation of Macpherson's administration (Ch.3), as well as the diaries of the Meriah Agency, which contain the Agents' correspondence with Indian subordinates.
49. On 'muted group' see Shirley Ardener 1975. American Indians' speeches contrast eloquently with what contemporary American officials wrote about them in *Bury my heart at wounded knee* (Dee Brown 1975). In that situation, the conflict was starker, and unmediated by people of intermediate culture as in India, and the native American tradition is more outspoken than that of tribal

India, so individuals perceived many of the basic differences between Europeans' concepts and their own very clearly—about land and ownership, religion, education etc.—and expressed this powerfully.

50. Foucault once described his work as an ethnography of Western society (1979). His *Discipline and punish* (1977) helps us understand the crucial role which prisons and other punishments played in the authority structure which British officials imposed on the Konds and other tribes.

51. Ballhatchet (1957), Stokes (1959), Burrow (1969), Barber (1975). Cohn (1961) provides an introduction to the anthropological analysis of British Indian history. In studying the administrators' training, I have found most revealing the writings of: William Paley, whose *Principles of moral and political philosophy* (1786) was one of the main set texts at Haileybury, the EIC training college; Malthus, who was a tutor at Haileybury for a large part of his life; and James Mill, who was appointed to the EIC administration in London on the basis of his *History of British India* (1817), which marks a turning point in British involvement in India, since Mill's view of Indian society was exceedingly negative.

52. Said 1984 (a review of a book about Conrad). Wurgaft's study (1984) of the myths and imaginative complex that inspired British colonials in 19th century India through the writings of Kipling and others, and Gillian Beer's comparison of Darwin's discourse with Victorian fictional narrative (1983), illuminate the interface between scientific or official writing and imaginative writing. In chapter 5, I examine Defoe's narrative about Man Friday in *Robinson Crusoe* to illuminate the Government's attitude to the victims of Kond human sacrifice. The fiction that administrators consumed in their childhood fed their imagination and thinking about other cultures as profoundly as the great texts which Stokes et al. deal with, in a sense at a deeper level—the level of emotions and ideals and scenarios of action. NB: Fanny Penny's novel *Sacrifice* (1910) about the Kond custom and its suppression by the British (below, Ch.5).

53. Again, Foucault's studies of shifts in the fundamental patterns of Western culture from the Renaissance to the 19th century, provide a way in. The Christian origins of colonial forms of power will

emerge in chapters 5 and 6, where I emphasize that the missionary Church functioned as an authority structure. As a background to this, it is helpful to understand how the Church in the Middle Ages and Renaissance imposed the king's law directly over every individual in a kingdom. Also, the treatment of witches and of heretics in European history provides the paradigm for later Christian treatment of tribal religions, as well as for secular Governments of the modern age that have attempted to eradicate other features of a tribal way of life.

54. Paul Hemming's *Red gold* 1978.
55. Finkielkraut is one of these. He calls the process *The undoing of thought* (1988), and blames anthropology for setting it in motion. In a sense perhaps the process is precisely this—the undoing of thinking that is divorced from feeling.
56. The move away from evolutionism and the whole idea that tribes represent stages in a fixed pattern of progress, involved a shift towards seeing tribal societies as highly sophisticated. Functionalists began this trend by showing that tribal beliefs were not irrational or prelogical, but *made sense* as coherent, consistent world views, performing the function of ensuring the cohesion of society. Structuralists have taken this trend further by working out the internal coherence of tribal bodies of beliefs and actions.
57. I take this distinction from a talk by Amitav Ghosh. My teachers in Delhi, J.P.S. Uberoi and Veena Das, and their students, have pioneered the study of Western society from a non-western perspective, studying the social organization of scientific knowledge, etc. (e.g. Uberoi 1978, 1984).
58. On the relationship between objectivity and subjectivity, see Weber (1949), and J.P.S. Uberoi 1978 on Goethe's scientific method. Goethe formulated a scientific method that differed significantly from the mainstream method of Newton and other contemporary scientists which is characterized by a complete dissociation between experimenter and object of study. To Goethe, *objectivity*—the clear seeing of an object—is impossible without an accurate *subjectivity*—a clear seeing of oneself and one's relationship with the object.

    'The manifestation of a phenomenon is not independent of the observer—it is caught up and entangled in his individuality....'

'The process of measuring is a coarse one, and extremely imperfect when applied to a living object....'

'Thus when making observations it is best to be fully conscious of objects, and when thinking to be fully aware of ourselves.'

These quotations from Goethe's scientific writings are from various texts collected and edited by Jeremy Naydler in his forthcoming book *Goethe on science*. Goethe's main scientific works are his *Metamorphosis of plants* and *Theory of colour*. One could say that Goethe's botanical work rests on the same basis as tribal knowledge of plants: accurate observation of their stages of growth sustained over many years. This subject was a theme in a paper I presented at a Conference on the environmental history of South and Southeast Asia at NISTADS, New Delhi in February 1992: 'Forest knowledge: Tribal people, their environment, and the structure of power'.

59. Asad 1973, Berreman 1981, Bordieu 1977, Brody 1975, Clifford 1986 & 1988, Diamond 1974 & 1980, Edwards 1992, Fabian 1983, Godelier 1978, Kuklick 1978 & 1991, Kuper 1988, Marcus & Fischer 1986, Morrison 1984, Rynklewich 1976, Sanderson 1990, Stocking 1991.

Chapter Two. Conquest: The Ghumsur Wars

1. *The savage wars* is the title of a book by L. James (1985), focusing on British wars of expansion in Africa. In India the British had fought wars of conquest, usually conceived as suppressions of rebellions, against the Paharias, Bhils, Hos (C.P. Singh 1978), Mundas (Jha 1964). A series of similar wars came later, defeating great rebellions of the Santals in the 1850s (Guha 1983a) and Birsa Munda in the 1890s (K.S. Singh 1966), gradually displacing the Andaman Islanders through many small skirmishes (Portman 1899), and the campaigns against Nagas, Abors and other tribes in Northeast India which continued into the 20th century (Hamilton 1912, Elwin 1959).
2. M.N. Das 1959 and Behara 1984 also cover these campaigns from Archival sources. Bailey intended to write a history of the Meriah wars (1960 pp.176–7, 192).

3. On the relation of textual structure with social structure see above p.25 & Ch.1 note 47. Everything the British wrote down obviously existed in a context of spoken discourse: what British soldiers said to one another about the Konds remains a blank; there are only hints of it in the texts. Similarly, what Indian officials said; Seeta Ram's account of his life as a sepoy (1873/1911) gives some idea, as do the letters of Indian officials about the Konds, preserved in the diaries of the Meriah Agency. The Konds' discourse is a more significant blank. The whole Anglo-Indian discourse which I analyse in this thesis was counterposed, we must always remember, to what Konds were saying. Konds talked about the situation and came to an understanding of it in their minds just as much as the colonials did; they joked about the colonials every bit as much as the colonials expressed contempt for them. But as frames of understanding these two discourses were extremely remote from each other. The few sentences given in the texts as spoken by Konds are the tip of an iceberg: this was only what they thought the British could understand, and only what the British did understand enough to remember and write down. But it was the British perception of the relationship that became law, and officially recognized as history.
4. Sonepur and Boad were ruled by the Bhanja dynasty in the 9th century, which later rose to power as the Somavamsi kings, who moved to the coast and united Orissa under their power. On *rajahs'* inter-relationships see Eschmann et al. eds. 1978, Kulke's 1978 articles, B.C. Mazumdar 1926 and Mukherjee 1981 on the pre-British history of Orissa. Behara (1984) goes into considerable detail on the history of Ghumsur before 1835. See also on the history of Orissa under British rule: Stirling 1846, B.C. Ray 1960, Mukherjee 1964, Patra 1971, Samal 1977. On the Konds' incorporation in Hindu kingdoms see Ch.4.
5. There were British invasions of Ghumsur in 1768, 1778, 1799, 1801, 1815 and 1835, and periods of direct Company rule in 1779–81, 1789–95 and 1815–19. The dates of the last few rulers illustrate this:

   Krishna Bhanja: reigned until 1773 (died)
   Vikram Bhanja (Krishna's son): 1774–8.
   Lakshman Bhanja (Vikram's elder brother): 1778–9

Vikram: 1781–2 (died in Athgarh, 1792)
Lakshman: 1783–8 (died)
Shreekar Bhanja (Lakshman's son): 1788–9 (became a *sanyasi*)
Dhananjay Bhanja (Shreekar's son): 1789–95 (as a minor under EIC tutelage, expelled by Shreekar 1795)
Shreekar: 1795–1801
Dhananjay: 1801–1815
Shreekar: 1819–32 (deposed, died in Puri, 1845)
Dhananjay: 1832–5 (deposed by the British and died among the Konds)

The tribute was Rs 30,000/-in 1766, raised soon after to 50,000/-, again to 100,000/-in 1783 (when the EIC calculated that the *rajah*'s 'gross revenue exclusive of alienations' was Rs 166,140/-), and lowered to 70,000/-in 1801. (Maltby 1882)

6. Russell's Report of 12th Aug. 1836 par.11. (R—NB: *where a Report appears in a published collection, such as Russell 1856, I refer to this with a letter in brackets).*
7. Shreekar spent several years wandering and living in Benares as a *sanyasi*, before returning in 1795. 'From this period' according to Russell (Report of 12th Aug. 1836 par.13), 'the zemindary continued in a state of the utmost disorder and confusion.' Shreekar soon accused the *sahukars* of 'ill-treatment and fraud [and] absconded.... It were now impossible, even if it were of any use, to ascertain the real cause of his disaffection. It is sufficient for our present purpose to note that at length he openly rebelled and set the public authorities at defiance.' Unable to 'reclaim him to obedience', the Collector of Ganjam applied for military aid against him. British troops overran Ghumsur from May to December 1801, and finally installed his son Dhananjay again. Shreekar lived for two years in the mountains north of Ghumsur—probably in close contact with Konds. 'After this he wandered for many years in the garb of a religious mendicant,' He obtained an interview with the Governor of Madras in 1812, but was imprisoned by the EIC, escaping in 1818. Meanwhile, Dhananjay had been accused of violence and tyranny. A British force invaded Ghumsur in 1815 and deposed him on the grounds of resisting trial for the murder of a close female relative. In his place, they set up Jagannath Bhanja and Dora Bissoi as regents for Balabadra Bhanja, Dhananjay's infant son. On his

escape from prison, Shreekar exposed a fraud: Balabadra (his own grandson) had died, and the regents had got a girl to impersonate him for two years. Shreekar was reinstated, and at first paid the tribute. But by 1830 tribute was in arrears from his neglect of business, so the British made ḥim resign and appointed Dhananjay again.

8. Russell's 1836 Report par.32. (R)
9. Stevenson to GOM 15th Nov. 1835, GOM Rev.C. 8th. Dec. nos.4–5.
10. Taylor's Reports to GOM of 21–22nd Nov. & 5th Dec. 1835, GOM Mil.C. 15th Dec. 39 & 22nd Dec. 23–4.
11. Stevenson's Reports of 7th and 10th Dec. 1835, GOM Rev.C. 15th Dec. 56–59 & 22nd Dec. 1–2.
12. GOM to Stevenson 3rd & 15th Dec. (ref.s in notes 9 & 11)
13. GOM to Stevenson 17th Dec. (ref. in note 11) and Russell's Report of 11th May 1837 par.6.
14. Russell gave the size of his army at this time as 1,561, but the real number was probably larger, since Hodgson and Taylor had apparently commanded about 2,000 men.
15. Russell's Report of 12th Aug. 1836 par.51. (R)
16. Capt. Butler, Camp Oodiagherry, to Taylor 17th Feb. 1836, GOM Mil.C. 17th May 1836 no.69.
17. Russell 12th Aug. 1836 par.57. (R)
18. Russell 11th May 1837 par.s 16 and 64 (next quotation). (R)
19. Capt. A.C. Wight, Oodiagherry, to Col. Muriel in Gullery 7th March 1836, GOM Mil.C. 12th April 89.
20. Major W.Low, Durgaprasad, to Muriel 7th March. (same ref. as previous)
21. '[Low's letter] verifies the worst fears; the bodies of these unfortunate young officers were found in the pass, and were stripped naked, cruelly mangled, and it is I fear but too evident that they were basely deserted by their men, many of whom panic struck, threw down their arms, and ran into camp.' Taylor, Camp Gullery, to GOM 8th March (same ref. as previous).
22. Russell's Report of 11th May 1837 par.65. Of the 24 sepoys who survived and returned to camp, 7 were wounded; these and 6 others had lost their muskets. The *jemadar* (Indian officer), 5 privates and the drummer (who had lost his drum) were marched down from

Durgaprasad under an escort of 16 sepoys back to headquarters at Gullery for punishment. What this punishment was I have not been able to discover.

23. This and the following passage are from Taylor's Report, Camp Nowgam, to GOM of 11th March 1836 Mil.C. 12th April 89.
24. A new pass had just been discovered from Gullery to Udayagiri via Mujjagudda, so the advance supply depôt was moved from Baibully to Udayagiri (Lt Gordon, Nowgam, to GOM, 17th April. 1836 Mil.C. 14th June 15).
25. Lt-Col Anderson, Gullery, to Taylor, 18th March. 1836 Mil.C. 17th May 73, and Russell's May 1837 Report par.66.
26. Taylor to GOM 2nd April. 1836 Mil.C. 3rd May 60.
27. Russell's May 1837 Report par.66.
28. Taylor, Nowgam, to GOM, 12th April 1836 Mil.C. 17th May 71. Broondawana Bhanja was executed first, near Nowgam. Veerama Soonderay, Sunsam Sing and Hutteeram were executed within a few days. Twelve men had already been executed.
29. These surgeons sent learned reports from the field in May, after several had succumbed to fever themselves. 'The molaria [*sic*] from the hills and jungles are probably the chief cause of the great sickness' wrote Asst Surgeon Lyall—without connecting it with mosquitoes yet. Of the dead 21 were Indian officers, 123 were privates, 28 were 'public and private followers' (i.e. servants), and 19 were various other non-combatants: gun, regimental and tent *lascars*, drivers, artificers, '*puckullies*', drummers and a Persian boy. Lyall's Report from Muzzaguda to GOM of 30th July 1836 Mil.C. 30th Aug. 58, Butterworth's Report from near Berhampur of 7th July Mil.C. 23rd Aug. no.7, Taylor 23rd April Mil.C. 24th May 44.
30. 'I am aware that....the regulations of the service make no provisions for the families of men dying on any other than foreign service. But I hope His Excellency will take into consideration the peculiar nature of the service on which these men have lost their lives.' Major Dun, Camp Goomsoor, to GOM 25th August 1836 Mil.C. 20th Sept. 47.
31. This was Captain Butterworth, an officer noted for his 'zeal and activity'. All these officers and supplies of food and medicine were sent by sea. From the Orissa coast they were sent to headquarters

at Nowgam via Aska, then into the hills by elephant, camel and bullock cart. There were over 500 bullock carts in use, but they could only just manage the mountain trails. The camels had started to sicken and die. But the elephants were indispensable.

32. Taylor to GOM 30th April 1836 Mil.C. 24th May 48. The twelve elephants that had assured supplies were kept on, but the camels were declared unsuitable. 'Fourteen of these valuable animals have died' Taylor reported (13th June). Later, in November, 37 more elephants were supplied by the Madras and Bengal Governments, and 500 carriage bullocks.
33. Russell met the *rajah* of Daspalla and ventured into his kingdom, where he captured some 'rebels' who had taken shelter there, and their 'treasure'. The Bengal Government would not support him with troops, but sent Mr Wilkinson, the Collector of Cuttack, to ensure the *rajah* of Nyagarh's fidelity.
34. Capt. Butler, Camp Cormunjee, private note to Taylor of 24th April 1836, GOM Mil.C. 31st May 56.
35. The next attack, in which Butler had hoped to surprise Dora Bissoi, failed for this reason: 'I have further to add with much regret and vexation that the result of the movement I made last night was a complete failure owing to the guide who accompanied me proving I have every reason to think completely treacherous.'(Report to Taylor of 27th April, ref. as previous note) Another attack near Chalee on 29th–30th April was equally unsuccessful: the Kond guides led the soldiers astray during the night-march (one escaped at 3 a.m. after leading them into some precipitous rocks), and only an old woman and child were captured. 'That [these] unfortunate events should have occurred I deeply deplore' wrote Taylor to the Madras Governor (1st May, Mil.C. 24th May 46).
36. Casualties were taken to a field hospital at Vishnuchakram, and eventually by bullock cart to Berhampur.
37. Russell's Report of 12th Aug. par.74.
38. Capt. Morgan to Taylor 9th June, Mil.C. 26th July 108.
39. Russell ibid. par.78.
40. This and the next passage are from Taylor's Report to GOM of 30th May 1836, Mil.C. 21st June 76.
41. Russell ibid. par.76. He recalled the minimum formalities necessary for an execution in the ruthless campaign against the Pindaris

(Afghan mercenary horsemen), after the last Maratha war in 1815 (ibid. par.89). (R)

42. Russell's Report of 11th May 1837 par.15. (R)
43. Madras Gov. Minute of 9th Sept. 1836 (R).
44. Russell's Report of 3rd March 1837 par.6.
45. Surgeon J.T. Couran's Report, Aska, to GOM of 22nd May 1836, GOM Mil.C. 26th July 102.
46. '150 matchlockmen of Kassem Rangeet and Bhagwan Dulaberra, persons of note in the zemindery who have given strong proof of their desire to support Government' (Anderson Report to GOM of 1st Aug. 1836, Mil.C. 30th Aug. 58.
47. Taylor's Memo. of instructions to officers, Camp Nowgam 19th Nov. 1836, Mil.C. 13th Dec. 108.
48. Russell's Report of 11th May 1837 par.24. (R)
49. Capt. Roberts, Puttingah, to Taylor 26th Nov. 1836, Mil.C. 13th Dec. 65.
50. Capt. Byam, commanding detachment of Nizam's Horse, to Taylor 28th Nov. 1836, Mil.C. 20th Dec. 57.
51. Russell's Report of 3rd March 1837 par.s 8 & 10.
52. Campbell 1864. In all out of 180 prisoners tried during the second war, 43 were sentenced to death, 47 to life imprisonment or transportation, 48 to imprisonment from 5 to 8 years mostly 'with hard labour', 15 were pardoned (including 13 Kond chiefs) and 24 acquitted (Russell's Report of 11th May 1837 contains a full list). According to a Report by Stevenson of 17th June 1837, 48 prisoners had by then been sent to Bellary jail, 3 to Trichinopoly jail, and one, Soonia Sing, to Chingleput jail—all in South India. 56 were serving shorter sentences in Ganjam jail, mostly with hard labour in chain gangs. Ten had died, including three Kond chiefs—two died on the march from Ghumsur.
53. WM p.159. Stevenson had died, probably from malaria. His successor as Acting Collector of Ganjam, Mr Inglis, reported Dora Bissoi's arrival at Chatrapur on 30th Nov. 1837.
54. Examples in Dee Brown 1975 (including some famous photographs of some of the Indian chiefs dressed in soldiers' uniforms) and Reynolds 1982.
55. On British conceptions of legitimate authority, displacing an old order they did not recognize as legitimate, see Weber on the

transition from a 'religious' to a 'rational legal order', or from a 'traditional authority' to a 'legal authority' (1947 pp.124–32, 324–62).

56. Macpherson 1842 pp.41–2, WM p.81.
57. Bailey: 'Both Kond traditions and the reports written by soldiers during the Meriah wars make it clear that warfare was endemic in the Kond hills.... the general impression of a society lacking the benefits of large-scale law and order cannot be wrong' (1960 pp.60–2), and Boal on 'the Konds' predilection for warfare' (1982 p.12). NB: against this way of describing tribal warfare Evans-Pritchard's demonstration that behind the Nuers' seeming endemic warfare, their raids and feuds were small-scale and highly structured (1940).
58. WM pp.360–5 on Loha Penu.
59. WM pp.79–80, quoted e.g. by R.V. Russell & Hira Lal 1916 pp.470–1. NB: Bailey 1960 p.61.
60. 'The Khond feuds are conducted with this preference for the aspect of war over its sterner realities. The race has become divided into septs and rival communities; something leads to a quarrel between two of them, and perhaps a life is taken.... when once a man has been killed, his tribe feel bound to take a life in return, and at a convenient season a challenge is sent. A Khond herald mounts a hill overlooking the rival village, sounds a point of war on his horn, and shouts the challenge, naming time and place; usually a valley is selected on the sloping sides of which there are rocks and bushes affording convenient cover to both parties (they do not wish to see too much of each other). On the day of battle the opposing armies take up each its position (under cover); those who can afford it wear a sort of pinafore of thick buffalo hide, almost proof against an arrow, and some fix a pair of buffalo horns on their heads *terroris causâ*. On a sudden one party starts up and sends a flight of arrows across the valley, dropping under cover again at once. The enemy replies with a similar discharge. When no results follow upon prolonged fighting of this sort, a few braves of either side caper down into the bottom of the valley and a skirmish ensues which ought to lead to slaughter, but somehow this, too, often ends harmlessly, and so the war goes on for perhaps three weeks, until by some fortunate accident somebody is hit, and either the tribal

honor is satisfied, or a fresh score is incurred, to be settled on the next occasion.' (Forbes 1885 pp.139 & 253–5)

61. Russell's Report of 11th May 1837 par.4. A print in WM shows two Konds dressed for battle wearing buffalo horn or peacock-feather head-dress, carrying axes and bows and arrows.
62. Seeta Ram 1911 p.70.
63. Lt Hill's Report of 2nd July 1838 (C).
64. 'Nicely bloodied' is how Hamilton described the killing of several Abors in the first day of a British invasion of their land (1912).
65. 1864 p.76, just as James Outram hunted with the Bhils he was pacifying, killing 235 tigers between 1825 and 1834 (Goldsmid 1880 p.112).
66. For instance: the killing of a Major sparked off Russell's war in Parla Kimedi, 1833–4 (R); the 'outrage' when three British seamen were killed by Andaman Islanders in 1855 was one of the main reasons that Britain occupied their Islands in 1858 (Portman 1899 p.186); a Major killed by Nagas in 1875 provoked a sustained campaign to subject Nagas to British rule (Elwin 1959); and Hamilton's revenge expedition against the Abors in 1911 was in response to the killing of some high-ranking British officials (Hamilton 1912).
67. From a novel by W. Robert Foran, *The Izzat of the regiment*, 1929.
68. There has been some debate on the authenticity of Seeta Ram's autobiography, which he supposedly gave to Lt-Col Norgate in 1861. Norgate translated it from Urdu and *The Times* recommended it in 1863, but it was first formally published in Lahore, 1873. Most opinion favours its authenticity (Lunt 1988).
69. Mouat 1859. It required many recommendations before the tightness of uniforms could be eased a bit.
70. 'Perhaps in no service within the peninsula have the men performed harder or more harassing duties than during the campaign in Goomsoor, nor perhaps has any service been so detrimental to the discipline of the men. Nothing but the system which has obtained in the Madras army for years could have enabled these men to leave the field with even the appearance of sepoys and I may surely say that they will bear comparison with any troops in the world after such duties as they have been required to perform. They have been called upon at all times in all hours to carry their knapsacks and two

days' provisions up the most difficult passes and through a country in which they knew by experience it was next to impossible to escape fever.... But with all this never was a murmur. These men worked cheerfully and were at all times ready and willing to perform any and every duty at the shortest possible notice. I do not believe any troops in the world could have behaved better and I am satisfied that Europeans would have sunk under the duties performed by the sepoys. I need not mention what our men can and will do before an enemy, but this was never more fully displayed than by 19 men under Captain Morgan of the 50th Regiment who retired before 500 Khondes [at Nowgam], and by the well-directed fire of his party kept them at such a distance as not to lose a single man.'(Report of 7th July 1836, Mil.C. 23rd Aug. no.7)

71. 'The chief characteristics of the Madras Sepoy have always been his undeviating loyalty, a remarkable power of endurance, and devotion to his officers, but that devotion can only be won by those who deserve it.' (Lt-Col Phythian-Adams 1943 pp.114–15)
72. In the English campaign against the Scots after Culloden, a harsh discipline was similarly enforced over the army with flogging—a harshness that mirrored the army's brutality to the Scots. (Prebble 1967)
73. Prison inspectors recognized that jails did not always reform convicts as intended: 'That the prisons of Lower Bengal are....training schools of vice and crime, I entertain no doubt whatsoever' wrote F.J. Mouat, a Bengal army Surgeon as well as the Bengal Inspector-General of prisons. His aim was to steer between the traditional idea 'that a prisoner should be rendered a terror to evil-doers by the infliction of as much pain as can be inflicted without injury to health, or risk to life', and a graduated system of correction that eliminated pain; his aim was also 'the conversion of prisons into schools of industry'. In 1843 he did away with treadmills and 'all labor...that was not penal or profitable', arguing that focus should be on the 'reformation [and] improvement of the individual', so that a prison became 'a hospital for the treatment of moral diseases', with schoolteachers and religious instructors. Instead of maintaining discipline with 'inhuman' punishments, especially flogging, he suggested more 'individualization' and segregation. Prison clothes were still to be purposefully degrading, food intentionally poor,

sanitation dreadful, and convicts were 'deprived of all intercourse with friends, relatives, and the other inmates of the prison, until a small restitution of these indulgences has been earned by continual good conduct, cheerful obedience to prison rules, and satisfactory work, both in the school-room and in the work-room'. During imprisonment, therefore, the system of individual rewards and punishments was especially intense (Mouat 1872).

Transportation as a punishment by the British in India entered a new phase in 1858 when the Andaman Islands were permanently occupied and a penal colony established there (Portman 1899, Mathur 1984)—initiating a catastrophic series of encounters with the native Andaman Islanders. I have not discovered that any Konds were sent to the Andamans, though Bhils and Santals certainly were, but it represents the extreme type of penal regime many Konds were subjected to, of labour, a whole internal system of rewards and punishments and inculcation of discipline: an extreme conquest over convicts' bodies and minds. Foucault (1977) mentions the Panopticon as epitomizing the trend to use prison as a means of reforming individuals: this was the pride of British prisons in India, built around a central control room from which every part of the prison could be surveyed.

74. Russell's accounts included Rs 100/-as 'price of two pistols presented, on leaving Goomsur, to the Rajah of Hautghur [Athghar], as an acknowledgement of services rendered by him to the Sirkar', and Rs 150/-as 'value of a horse presented, on his visiting me to Peetambararoy, the son of the Rajah of Boad, by whom the information was given which led to the capture of the rebel chiefs Nunda Bisoye and Bauhoobalendra etc. in his territory'.(11th May 1837 par.s 44–7) (R)
75. Despite this claim not to be involved, Revd Brown used his articles to urge the Government to extend its rule over the Konds in order to stamp out human sacrifice (below pp.191–3).

Chapter Three. Suppressing Human Sacrifice: The Meriah Agency

1. Millar rescued twelve of these from around Gullery *mutah*. Of the 30 rescued, one escaped, ten were returned to their families, and

eighteen children, aged between three and ten were kept in British care. (C p.5)

2. Russell's Report of 11th May 1837 (C p.9).
3. Mr Ricketts, Commissioner for the Tributary Mahals, rescued *meriahs* from Daspalla and northeast Boad (Report Feb. 1837); and his successors Mills and Gouldsbury continued these operations in the 1840s (C pp.72–89).
4. See below Ch.7 p.247 ff.
5. Campbell became Assistant to Mr Stevenson, the Agent and Collector in Ganjam, during the second Ghumsur war, and his post as Russell's private secretary was taken by Captain MacDonald, who conducted most of the Court Martial trials. At first Campbell reported direct to Russell in Madras, but from 1840 as Principal Assistant to the Collector in Ganjam, he forwarded his reports through the Collector. A law was passed in 1839 exempting Kond areas in Madras and Bengal from the usual course of British law, and placing them under Campbell's control.
6. Campbell's Report on his tour to Udayagiri, Posora, and Chokapand, 17th Jan. 1838; Millar's of 13th Dec. 1837; GOM Minute of 15th Jan. 1838 (C).
7. Bannerman's Report of 20th July 1838, and Russell's Minute of 6 December 1837: 'The question here arises, who, among the parties concerned in [Lutcheman's] seizure and confinement are fit subjects for punishment? In considering this point we must bear in mind that the practice [of human sacrifice], however barbarous in our eyes, is considered by the Khondes to be a religious act, and is sanctioned by the superstitions of ages, and they are yet ignorant of its being regarded by us as a crime, and that, until lately, they knew nothing of us nor we of them. Mujjee is a Khonde, and, being so, must be acquitted of any criminal intention.' (C) 'Maji' simply means headman in Kuvi; his village was 'Mulleegudda'.
8. COD 24th Oct. 1838, GOM 15th Feb. 1842 (C). Four Dom traders who were convicted of selling *meriahs* in 1841 were sentenced to hard labour in irons for two years as well as one or two hundred 'stripes' each, but the High Court in Madras could not confirm this sentence for lack of proper witnesses.

9. *Except where indicated the reports quoted in this chapter are published in Carberry ed. 1854 (C).*
10. In fact, *Rajahs* and Hindu chiefs were heavily involved in patronizing these sacrifices. See below Ch. 4 pp. 126–32.
11. Hill went to northeast Jeypore and south Boad, and made friendly contact with the *rajah* of Kalahandi. The road being planned was to run through his capital town, Bhawanipatna. The seven *mutahs* included Ryabagi, Chandrapur (where he had information about ten *meriahs* in three villages), Bijapur, Shrirampur, Subernagiri, and Poorsingia. Report of 19th Dec. 1840 from Nowgam to Sir T.H. Maddock, Secretary to the GOB, GOI Foreign Political Consultations 11th Jan. 1841 nos.95–6.
12. Below pp.70 & 144–6. Twelve *meriahs* were employed or supported by Bannerman and Campbell, eleven by 4 Indian officials. Also two had been discharged and were supporting themselves. Campbell's Reports of 22nd Jan. 1841 (C & K) and 6th Jan. 1842 (K only).
13. Bannerman's Report of 28th Jan. 1842, GOI Rev, C. 31st May 1843 no.14.
14. Another servant who had been with Macpherson eight years had died in Ghumsur, and Macpherson himself 'never to the end of his days recovered the health he enjoyed before his visit to Ghumsur' (WM p.14 NB: *dated letters & Reports by Macpherson are taken from his posthumous memoirs, WM, unless otherwise stated*).
15. He submitted this Report on 21st June 1841, and it was published by the Indian Government in Calcutta in 1842.
16. Macpherson's Report of 22nd April 1843, WM p.188, note. He was accompanied by a force of 50 *sebundies* under the command of Gopi Singh, brother of Sundera Singh.
17. See Ch.4 pp.126–32. The 'four great tribes' of Ghumsur Konds mentioned on p.70 were Barah Mutah, Atharah Mutah, Hodzoghor and Tentilghor.
18. WM note pp.173–4 & pp.207–8. Baba Khan got his chronicle translated into English and sent it to a member of Macpherson's family.
19. The Konds were divided administratively between Ganjam and Vizagapatam Districts in Madras Presidency, and Cuttack and the South West Frontier Agency in Bengal Presidency.

20. 'Tributary Mahals' were the 'palaces' (i.e. kingdoms) that paid tribute to the EIC.
21. Missionaries were calling for its suppression, alongside that of other 'social evils' in India, as in Peggs' book, *India's cries to British humanity*, 1830 (below pp.186 & 191–3).
22. 'The belief that I possess exclusive authority in Souradah is so essential to the maintenance of my ascendance over its intractable tribes....'(Report of 20th Feb. 1846, GOI HP 14th March 1846 no.33.)
23. On this episode see below Ch.6 pp.195–8. MacViccar went on to become one of the Konds' main administrators, with an authoritarian outlook similar to Campbell's.
24. For more on the status of *meriahs* in a Kond village see Ch. 4 below pp.111 & 125. Campbell got Government permission to buy the *meriahs* from Kond headmen at Rs 20/-each (Report to GOM of 16th Dec.1837—C).
25. Sam Bissoi's village was also burnt, though against Macpherson's orders. Macpherson's only Reports to the GOI in Calcutta on these events—which significantly are *not* reproduced in Carberry (1854)—are from Camp Purnaguda of 20th Feb. 1846 (GOI HP 14th March 33), and of 17th May from back in his base at Nowgam (GOI HP 30th May 1846 no.1.D)
26. To some extent Macpherson recognized this, but he did not explore the paradox of recognizing that Konds were more or less the independent allies of Hindu *rajahs*, and the way that British rule transformed this relationship into one of ruler and subjects based on British ideas of authority. Below pp.130–2.
27. The newspapers, like the Konds, claimed that the Boad *meriahs* had been 'stolen from their parents and sold' to Macpherson (Macpherson's Report of 17th May 1846 note A, GOI HP 30th May no.1.D).
28. Lt Prinsdale, Russellkonda, to Major Bird 4th April 1846, GOI HP 9th May no.12.
29. Captain Moore, the military commander with Macpherson, described the battle of 1st April as follows: Cadenhead advanced to meet the attacking Konds with *sebundies* and Macpherson's original escort under *Subadar* Abdul Cawder. Moore tried to cut off the fleeing Konds but failed. The only British casualty was Sundera

Singh, 'the Agent's confidential man', who was wounded. (Report to Bird from Purnaguda of 3rd April 1846 GOI HP 9th May 13) Bird wrote to Welsh: 'I would wish to state that it is currently reported that Captain Macpherson either has or intends to go to the extent of burning some villages with the intent of carrying out some object he has in view. This I confess appears almost incredible, but should it so turn out I feel exceedingly anxious as to how far I am justified in permitting Macpherson to make use of part of the Regiment under my command in such service, without the sanction of higher authority. I have therefore earnestly to request instructions on the subject.' (6th April) These reports and queries were forwarded by Welsh to the Madras army HQ, whose Commander-in-Chief forwarded them to the Governor-General in Calcutta (J.F. Thomas 21st April 1846, GOI HP 9th May 11).

30. 'I turned out of my camp, as soon as they appeared, two agents sent by Koortibas to confer with me. I showed the Hindu chiefs, his confederates, that I could stop their valuable salt trade.... The Rajah, startled by my treatment of his messengers, ordered Koortibas to proceed to me, and then to the Khonds, but he obeyed neither order.' (17th May Report, ref. in note 25)

31. Letter from Boad *rajah* to Col Ouseley, April 1846, GOI HP 30th May 1.C. This is a translation from Oriya by Ouseley's Assistant Lt Haughton. '35th year' refers to the *rajah*'s own reign, 'Cheyt' is the Hindu month of *chait* in March-April. 'The ploughman raised at home' may refer to Kond sons-in-law who lived with their wives' families, whose status may have been similar or even shaded into that of *meriahs* (NB: Ch. 4 note 27, and Bailey 1960 pp. 27–38 on the importance of 'sisters' sons'). The *rajah* seems to be saying that many of the 172 were not *meriahs* at all. This is stated openly in the Kond letter quoted below pp.82–3.

32. 'It is to me very surprising that an officer of Captain Macpherson's experience should have imagined that he was not expected to keep the Government constantly informed of his proceedings even though they were unattended by unusual circumstances, but it is a very serious error in that officer to suppose that when he had been compelled to resort to measures most deprecated by Government in engaging in hostilities attended with lamentable consequences, and found it necessary to call for military support, he should still

have imagined that Government should feel satisfied....when the only accounts which it possessed of the position in which he was placed was from common rumour or newspaper reports.... he has put it out of our power to form a correct judgement on the whole subject.' (Maddock's Minute of 28th May 1846, GOI HP 30th May no.2)

33. Macpherson describes this as a fight between Hindu chiefs, 'having each an attached section of the Khond population....all their lives bitterly at feud' (Report of 21st June 1846, GOI HP 18th July 37). As during the Ghumsur wars, the Konds were usually fighting under the overall command of Hindu chiefs. Whether a feud was essentially between Kond clans, or between Hindu chiefs, is difficult to tell.
34. This was Chango Pater. Macpherson wrote: 'I shall inflict severe punishment' after making a full inquiry into the attack, and if he attacked again, 'you must expect prompt and condign punishment' (Nowgam 23rd June, in Diary for 18th–24th June, GOI HP 18th July 41). The *sirdar* Punda Naik wrote that to establish 'permanent peace' it would be necessary to take 'severe measures....towards those who have savagely broken it'.
35. Report of 25th June to GOI, HP 18th July 39.
36. 'I much regret to say that I have received intelligence that on the 10th instant the party which was lately expelled thence aided by a force from Bondoghor in Boad, retaliated upon its aggressor by burning seven villages and killing two men. The Government are aware that this contest derives its special importance from the circumstance that several of the tribes of Ghumsur are involved in it as allies.... The difficulty of converting barbarous men with whom revenge is a first duty, and who have heretofore maintained their rights by force, into peaceful expectants of justice, will not be underestimated by Government.' Report of 13th July 1846, GOI HP 1st Aug. 11.
37. Macpherson sent a *vakil* (lawyer or agent) to the Boad *rajah* with a letter threatening that if he did not come within ten days 'you will be considered to be in disobedience to the Government, when you must expect to be dealt with in the severest manner according to custom' (letter of 9th June, in Diary for 18th–24th June 1846 GOI HP 18th July 41). On 13th July, after learning that the *rajah*'s

mother had died, Macpherson reported that the *rajah* still had not come in, but that he 'had no thought but of obedience to the Government; and was anxiously exerting himself to bring in the chiefs to tender their submission and redeliver the victims but that he had been prevented from effecting his object by an open renewal of the power struggle between Koortibas and the Proraj.'

38. Diary for 30th July–7th Aug. 1846, GOI HP 22nd Aug. 36.
39. Diary for 15th–23rd August (GOI HP 12th Sept. 20), and Report of 15th October par.28 (GOI HP 21st Nov. 11).
40. In the first attack on 24th August, Ootan Singh, Dulbehra of Hodzoghor, who lived in Tentilghor, was wounded, and someone else was killed. The Konds were reported as saying after their attack: 'We shall fight and die here.... They say the Circar has now become acquainted with the conspiracies into which Koortibas and we lately entered. Koortibas has been seized and sent off to a distant country; if we go to the Circar we also shall be treated in like manner.' (Reported in a letter from Duffadar Sheik Sooltan Sing in Tentilghor of 24th August in Macpherson's Diary for 24th Aug.–2nd Sept., GOI HP 21st Nov. no.2). But I doubt if 'conspiracies' was how the Konds described their actions. In the second attack one of the villages burnt was Lienparra. 'On going away Bisa Bissye called out to the people of Lienparra "we shall burn the whole of your mootahs and in 7 or 8 days shall also burn Tentilghor. Tell this to the Circar." (letter from the same Duffadar of 26th August)
41. Quoted from letters Macpherson received from his Agents in Aug.–Sept. (Diaries for 24th Aug.–11th Sept., GOI HP 21st Nov. 2–4). The second quotation continues with a reported conversation between Bir Khonro and his Kond followers that illustrates their relationship: 'Damodan D---'s brother and Lamo Mahanti have told me that except the Hindoos of Bondoghor all the other Bissyes, Mullickos and Khonros met in consultation and said to Bir Khonro "The Rajah is our father, the Khonro is our mother, our father has now forsaken us, what do you our mother counsel?" Bir Khonro said "The knot is formed from the whole hair of the head. What can I do alone?" The Mullickos, Bissyes etc. said "We shall establish you like a pillar in the ground and shall continue to look towards you alone." Bir Khonro replied that such a pillar could only remain

firm by being well heaped up with earth, when all said that "they could agree to whatever he should determine on." Bir Khonro then said that "The Dulbehra [of Tentilghor] must be first attacked when the Saheb will come up and reconsider the whole matter." '

42. 'On the 23rd [Sept.] a great deal of firing was heard in the direction of Lienpurra. On enquiry it appeared that formerly the Dulbehra's people and the people of Bulscoopa had entered into a contract of brotherhood, and had engaged not to fight against each other. Now as the people of Bulscoopa had broken this agreement, the Dulbehra's people were making a pooja to their gods and freeing themselves from the bonds and doing this were firing off matchlocks. On hearing this 70 men of Sangrimendi went to Bengrekia and fired off 20 matchlocks and then returned home.' (a letter to Macpherson of 25th Sept. in Diary for 21st–29th Sept., GOI HP 17th Oct. 22)
43. Diary of 30th Sept.–8th Oct., GOI HP 24th Oct. 30.
44. Macpherson's request for reinforcement was granted reluctantly by higher authorities, as was his request for full revenue powers in Sorada, Bodogarh and Chinna Kimedi, which Bannerman and the Madras Government had opposed—an order that was soon reversed when the Government became doubtful about Macpherson's management of affairs.
45. Diary for 9th–20th October (GOI HP 21st Nov. 6). And a few days later: 'The all-important general movement towards the God of Light in Ghumsur received a fresh and powerful impetus from another appearance [in a woman's dream] of that God, accorded by the Goddess of increase in Tentilghor….' (Diary for 29th Oct.–5th Nov., GOI HP 21st Nov. 10)
46. Report of 15th Oct. 1846 GOI HP 21st Nov. 11. This Report, coming with an optimism that proved unfounded just before Kond resistance really took off, is not included in the published collections of Reports. If Macpherson identified the Earth Goddess herself with evil, then it is not surprising if those who worshipped her regarded him with suspicion: an attitude that proved well-founded when even animal sacrifices to her were forbidden a few years later.
47. 'It being ascertained that uninformed persons entertain serious misconceptions with respect to the intention of the Supreme Government in investing Captain Macpherson with authority as its

Agent for the suppression of the Meriah sacrifice and female infanticide in the Hill Tracts of Orissa and obstructions to his measures having thence arisen the Supreme Government resolves to declare for the removal of such misconceptions and for general information, its exact intentions in appointing such an Agent....' The Government was not going 'to abrogate or injuriously change the hereditary authority and privileges of the Rajahs, the Bissyes, the Mullickos, the Khonds, the Paters and other hill chiefs and to change the ancestral usages of the Orissa Hills Country'. Those who had opposed Macpherson's measures out of ignorance would go free. 'But all doubt as to these intentions being now removed', future opposition would meet with severe punishment. Macpherson released this proclamation in November 1846 in Oṛiya and English. (GOI HP 21st Nov. 1846 14–15)

48. Mills suspected the *rajah had* aided the rebels, but persuaded him to release a proclamation to the Kond chiefs telling them to go to the Sahib and give up the *meriah* sacrifice, so as to ensure that the Sahib would not 'hang, imprison or punish you'. (Mills in Tikripara to Macpherson 1st Dec. 1846, GOI HP 27th Feb.1847 53)

49. Macpherson had warned Mills on 27th November that these chiefs were at the head of 'a destructive mob' of Konds eight miles from his camp at Renteillghor. They received an offer of Government pardon on the 28th–29th, but attacked Macpherson nevertheless, leaving Maheshwar to negotiate with Mills. Maheshwar met Dunlop (who did not know about the attack yet) on 3rd December, and persuaded him to let him go back to Bir Khonro to get him to come in as well, so Maheshwar left his escort and failed to appear before Macpherson. According to Macpherson, Ḅir Khonro was plotting rebellion before Mills' eyes, 'using of course only the Khond language except when the [Government] Jemadar was to be played upon'. On Bir's arrest, 'Maheswar absurdly called upon the tribes to rise to liberate his brother, and has ever since endeavoured to supply his place, while Noboghon has continued in resistance....[So Bir Khonro's] detention did not involve the least semblance of a breach of faith in any quarter, and was the only course open to me.' (Report of 22nd Jan. 1847, GOI HP 10th April 1847 no.1)

50. Noboghon Khonro, his son Bir, and Bir's son Maheshwar, had formerly held the position of 'leader of all the fighting tribes of Boad', until the *rajah* had got another branch of the family to murder the leader and take over, 70 years before. Madhwa Khonro was from this rival branch. (Report of 22nd Jan. 1847)

    Chokra Bissoi was Dora Bissoi's nephew. Macpherson described him as 'a man of considerable ability and himself a Benniah Khond'; and in 1842, when Chokra had visited him, as: 'a very fine intelligent young man [living in Angul] where the family took refuge. I am very sorry to say that I could do nothing for him or them. I could not employ him as anything except *first*, and this would not suit existing arrangements. I sent the poor fellow to Bannerman with his petition for employment and subsistence for his family, amounting to 70 persons and living on charity—a disgrace to the Government! He was, of course, infinitely disgusted with his reception and dismissal—a mere cold order to return whence he came.'(Letter of 14 Sept. 1843) Bannerman reflected that he had thought Chokra 'a quiet inoffensive youth' five years ago, and doubted if he really had much influence over the Konds: 'I do not think it likely that individually he is of much importance, or likely to prove a dangerous leader.' (Bannerman's Report of 25th Dec. 1846, GOI HP 27th Feb. 1847 no.121).

51. This letter is dated November 1846. It is preserved in GOI HP 27th Feb. 1847 no.53, and was translated, probably from Oriya, for Mr Mills.

52. Cadenhead to Macpherson 19th Dec. 1846, GOI HP 27th Feb. 59.

53. Captain Dunlop had come from Cuttack with Mills and had been transferred to Macpherson's command. Lt Haughton had been Ouseley's Assistant in the SWFA; he met Macpherson at Bulscoopa in the middle of Boad, bringing more troops and cavalry from the Bengal army, as well as 40 *sowars* (horsemen) from the Sambalpur *rajah*'s army. The Calcutta Government also ordered limited reinforcements to be supplied from Cuttack (26th December): two companies under four British officers were sent off by Mills on the 31st December, and another regiment just back from fighting in Arracan (Assam) was deputed to follow by steamer, while Welsh sent 3 companies of the Madras Army by steamer from Waltair to

Berhampur in December, and a whole regiment more in January. (GOI HP 27th Feb. 1847)

54. Bannerman to GOM 18th Dec. 1846, GOI HP 27th Feb. 64.
55. Mr C.J. Shubrik, Assistant to the Agent in Ganjam, reported to Bannerman that Cadenhead had asked him to send troops against Kond hideouts and to arrest a Kond chief, and that he had refused to do so. Bannerman approved: 'I perceive that you participate in my sentiments as to the impolicy of issuing peremptory orders to these hill chiefs (NB: semi-independent and rude) that in all probability would not be obeyed, and which under present circumstances there are no means of enforcing.'(Shubrik's Reports to Bannerman, and Bannerman to Shubrik 25th December) He wrote to the Madras Government that he was willing to aid Macpherson, 'but uninformed as I am how far a system of warfare against the Khond tribes in the interior of the hills has the approval of superior authority, I should not feel justified in participating in coercive measures of a questionable nature, undertaken without adequate means.' (Bannerman to GOM 25th December) Macpherson sent Bannerman a proclamation to publish (19th December) offering rewards of Rs 1,000 for the capture of Chokra Bissoi, and 100 or 200 for three other Kond leaders, one of them a *jani* (Earth Goddess priest). Chokra Bissoi claimed to have with him a son of the Ghumsur *rajah* by a wife concealed among the Konds, a legitimate heir to the Ghumsur *raj*. 'It is in my view positively certain that no such female did or could have existed as is now pretended' Bannerman affirmed, but without denying that the enemy believed this. On 15th January 1847 Bannerman reported that he was at last transferring Sorada, Bodogarh and Chinna Kimedi to Macpherson, but recorded his view that Macpherson's policy was a disaster. A copy of this letter, sent from Madras to Calcutta, caused the Indian Government to order the transfer suspended (Bushby to Bannerman 12th February 1847). All documents under GOI HP 27th Feb. 1847.
56. Welsh in Chetterpore to GOM, 16th & 19th Jan. 1847, GOI HP 27th Feb. nos.137–8.
57. Macpherson's Report of 26th Jan., GOI HP 27th Feb. 133.
58. Bannerman's Report of 17th Jan. (ibid. no.138), Dunlop's Report to Gouldsbury from Borogatza of 7th Feb. (GOI HP 10th April 38)

59. As Macpherson described Cadenhead's use of one tribe to fight another, 'These operations in Borogatza, Bengrekia and Bopalmendi gave to the Maha Mullicko and the chiefs of Chowpuddock power and confidence sufficient to enable them to deal according to their usages and without any aid from me with a chief and his adherents in resistance to the Government and his tribe.' (Report of 18th February 1847 from Sangrimendi to GOI, HP 10th April 4)
60. Macpherson to Green 10th Feb., GOI HP 10th April 5.
61. Cadenhead's Report to Macpherson from Harbunga of 24th Feb., ibid. 14.
62. The five tribes he had won over were Madhwa Khonro's, Bengrekia, Borogatza, Chowpuddock and Sangrimendi; the three still hostile were Ruttabari, Domasingi and Bondagorh (Report of 5th March, ibid. 12).
63. Secretary Bushby wrote to Macpherson expressing the Govt's 'utmost regret' at the violence he had resorted to (22nd Feb., GOI HP 10th April 38).
64. 'Several strongholds of the insurgents have been destroyed, villages and orchards have been plundered and burnt and the country ravaged equally by our own troops and by the insurgents. While the latter appear to have carefully avoided personal collision with the military....they have acted on the aggressive and have been able to harass and in one or two instances to gain the advantage over the troops without danger to themselves....

    [My conclusion from] the irregular, imperfect and confused reports from Captain Macpherson [is that his proceedings have been] managed with so little skill and prudence as to have brought about an insurrection among the Hill Tribes guided by the Hindu chiefs of the plains who possess an ill-defined authority over them....

    He began to concern himself with the petty feuds of rival chieftains and thus arrayed against himself as enemies the most influential men in the country....[and] pursued a system of intimidation and violence which naturally exasperated the Khonds against him....

    Our officers and troops are engaged in a series of petty warfare from which we have no object to gain and into which Captain Macpherson would seem to have been led more by the intrigues and animosities of rival parties in the country many of them inimical to him personally than from any combination against the British Government. Captain Macpherson throughout his proceedings seems to have raised up enemies from his disposition to favor one party and to repulse another and has thus given a political character to proceedings which had no concern with politics and ought to have been conducted in a spirit of conciliation and without any arrogance or assumption of power.' (Minute by Maddock 17th March 1847, GOI HP 10th April 39)

65. Dyce's Reports to GOM of 13th, 20th & 23rd (long quote) March 1847, GOI HP 10th April 39. 'The chief servants of [the Agency] have studiously avoided coming near me' he wrote. This is the point of greatest controversy in the Agency's history.
66. Bushby wrote to Dyce from the Government in Calcutta instructing him to open negotiations with the insurgents before withdrawing the troops, otherwise 'the hopes of pacification would become more distant than ever.' Dyce was to release all political prisoners arrested under Macpherson against whom nothing could be proved, and to pardon all except 'such as by any particular acts of treachery or atrocity may in your judgement have placed themselves beyond the pale of forgiveness.' (Macpherson to Dyce 25th March, Dyce to Macpherson 29th, Bushby to Dyce 19th & 27th, all under GOI HP 10th April 1847 no.39)
67. Private letter from Lt Phillips in Chalee of 19th March (ibid.). His Commanding officer, Major Rose, put up copies of Dyce's new proclamation, and tried to persuade thc Konds to return to their villages by leaving grain there that rival villagers had stolen. (Report to Col Green of 17th March, ibid.)
68. Dyce found minimal records of prisoners detained at the police *cutcherry* in Nowgam, some for 6 months without charge, and freed most of them. (Report of 9th April & Expenses for April-May, GOI HP 29th May 4 & 11th Sept. 25)
69. These were the chiefs of the Bengrekia, Bondagorh and Domasingi tribes. Dyce's Report to GOI of 25th April, and of 20th May (GOI HP 29th May 7 & 26).
70. GOI to Dyce 5th June (GOI HP 5th June 29). One of Campbell's first actions was to transfer some of the pacified districts back to

the jurisdiction of Ganjam (Report of 20th May, GOI HP 29th May 25).

71. Campbell and Dyce both commended Sooria Narain as 'an old and faithful servant of the Government', who had received 'the highest testimonials' from Russell; Campbell reinstated Sam Bissoi as chief of Hodzoghor (after a delay while Grant examined him for the enquiry on Macpherson's command), and Bannerman declared he had never believed Macpherson's allegations against Sam (letter to Dyce of 10th April, GOI HP 5th June 27).

72. GOI HP 29th May 26. Evidently Bir Khonro and Koortibas were not Chokra's allies, as Macpherson had assumed. Dyce and Campbell seem to have made the same mistake as Macpherson in trying to use hostile parties to mediate with each other.

73. Campbell's Diary of 1st–7th Aug. 1847 (GOI HP 11th Sept. 52) and Report of 3rd Sept. (GOI HP 9th Oct. 44).

74. Translation from Campbell's Diary of 8th–15th Aug., GOI HP 11th Sept. 60.

75. Maddock's Minute of 2nd Sept. 1847, GOI HP 11th Sept. 64. Campbell sent Bir Khonro and Koortibas a proclamation to circulate: 'This Chokra Bissye is not a great man. He is not a Rajah but a very common fellow indeed and why should such a person cause loss and injury to the whole of your country and to all the people; it is a great shame that you allow him to do it. This Chokra Bissye cannot always remain an insurgent, he will assuredly be shortly seized or else his life will be taken. To listen to his orders is not good but you must try and get hold of him and bring him either alive or dead to the Hoozoor and then you will not only receive 3,000 Rupees but expect the favor of the Circar.' (Diary for 15th–21st August)

76. Bir Khonro and his *paiks* were 'always ready promptly and powerfully to second our efforts' (Campbell's Report of 28th June 1848, GOI HP 22nd July 29).

77. Campbell's Report of 2nd October 1847, GOI HP 24th Dec. 81. The Chokapand Kond chiefs had submitted and Campbell entreated the Government on their behalf, declaring 'I firmly believe that in Chokapand and Boad they experienced wrongs and were driven to rebellion…. the Chokapand insurgents *had* a grievance, and that

grievance drove them to rob.' (Report of 19th April 1848, GOI HP 15th July 11).

78. Ouseley thought they should offer Chokra his life, but Campbell wanted him to 'throw himself on the well-known mercy of Govt.' (Campbell to Ouseley 26th July 1848, to GOI 5th Aug., Ouseley to GOB 10th Aug., Dalhousie's Minute of 21st Aug. GOI HP 19th Aug. 27, & 26th Aug. 8–10)

79. Campbell 11th Nov. 1848, GOI HP 25th Nov. 35. Macpherson had thought it possible there really was a son of the late Ghumsur *rajah*, but Bannerman had ridiculed this idea (note 55 above). Early in 1846 another, adopted son of the last *rajah* had arrived in Cuttack from Benares, where he had been pensioned off, with a certificate of good conduct from the British agent there. Gouldsbury politely but nervously forbade him from going into Ghumsur, for fear that he would reassert the cause of the Ghumsur *Raj*. (Gouldsbury in Pooree to GOB 2nd February 1847 & GOI Foreign Dep. to Gouldsbury 6th February, GOI HP 27th Feb. 1847 nos.111 & 115)

80. The *rajah* of Angul strongly denied Macpherson's charge that he was conspiring to stir the Konds to revolt (letter to Gouldsbury of 24th February), and the Calcutta Government was prepared to believe him innocent. But Gouldsbury stationed two companies at Barmul to watch over him. In late February nearly 1,000 soldiers crossed the Mahanadi river from Angul into Boad. Most went back before fighting, but a few attacked a couple of villages in Daspalla, killing 24 people, and came into conflict with Cadenhead, who said they were regular soldiers from Angul. The *rajah* denied this, saying they belonged to a refractory chief, who was against himself and in league with Noboghon Khonro. Reluctantly the *rajah* promised to supply the troops at Barmul, even though there were 'no rich merchants or ryots in my territory'. With the official letter offering this was a verbal message: 'Tell the Sahib to let the Govt know….I will produce these people [the men who had fought Cadenhead] within 15 days *provided* all troops are withdrawn except a small escort with Captain Dunlop and *provided also* that Beer Khonro and the Bushune [?] from my country whom Captain Macpherson imprisoned be freed.' This message Gouldsbury thought gave 'almost conclusive evidence of his complicity' in the rebellion (Report 9th March). The *rajah* gave three boatloads of

supplies but with 'suspicious tardiness' (Report of 24th March). So Gouldsbury summoned the *rajah* to Cuttack: 'I have assured him that if he appears before me he will not be subjected to any indignity' (26th March). On 16th March the *rajah* wrote to him: 'I beg to represent that if it can be proved that I have sent a single sepoy or armed man or horse or cannon....across the river to assist Nubbaghon Khonro....I will be liable to punishment.... Captain Macpherson is *sporting* (NB: misrepresenting) everything in this case, which will be made known. I have not assisted the Khonds nor given any advice to them, nor have I any enmity against the Govt. The whole is a tissue of falsehood. I beg that the matter may be fully enquired into.' (translation from Oriya into English sent by Gouldsbury 22nd March) But by the time Campbell took over, the *rajah's* guilt was considered certain. In any case, he had been on the Britons' black-list since a rumour that he had committed three murders in 1837 (GOI HP 10th April 1847 19 & 39).

81. Patra 1971 p.312. Angul was made a District in the Province of Bengal, and declared a Scheduled District in 1877. In 1894, the Hill Tracts of Boad (the Khondmals) were incorporated in it, even though the two areas were not contiguous.
82. In June 1849 Lt Frye reported another 'outrage' by Konds who attacked Government troops. Chokra was implicated in a rebellion in Parla Kimedi in 1856, but it was swiftly crushed, and Chokra's main lieutenant was captured the same year (below p.104).
83. Dunlop in Burmool to Gouldsbury 4th April 1847 (GOI HP 29th May no.3). On the other hand, Lt Haughton gave his opinion that Macpherson's policy of winning over tribal chiefs had been successful where he had seen it in Sangrimendi, that the expedition against Chokra Bissoi, which Macpherson had planned in March and Dyce had prevented, would have been successful, and that Macpherson had spared no pains for a 'peaceful submission' of the enemy. (Letters to Macpherson of 5th and 17th April, GOI HP 29th May nos.4 & 8)
84. GOI HP 5th June no.23, & 29th May no.5.
85. Grant in Berhampur to GOI 30th October 1847 (GOI HP 24th Dec. 1847 110) and final Report (GOI HP 7th Oct. 1848 28–168).
86. P. Mukherjee 1964 p.94.
87. Above pp.85–8.

88. Duff 1848, quoted in Boal 1982 pp.73–4.
89. Quoted in Anon. 1849 p.5.
90. E.g. the *Calcutta Englishman* of 9th June 1848: 'the disposition of the armed population of Ghumsur and Boad to rebel so far from being killed was barely scotched by Colonel Campbell's large military operations last year'—when Campbell claimed he had enforced complete peace! Dalhousie refused permission for a refutation at first: 'The Governor-General-in-Council observes that you should be content with the approval of your measures by the Govt, and not pay any attention to newspaper articles.' (GOI to Campbell 15th July 1848, HP 15th July 55). Campbell's next request, which I quote on pp.93–4, was granted (Campbell to GOI 14th Feb. 1849, HP 3rd March 15–16).
91. The anonymous author writes of a painful regret 'when we reflect on the character and position of the parties to whom, by the force of truth, we are in this instance constrained to be out and out, most unequivocally, though most reluctantly opposed.... while we lament that such a one should have so far forgotten the rights of his neighbour, we unhesitatingly asseverate that [his] account....is one elaborate fabrication of exaggerations and misrepresentations.' (1849 p.1)
92. Letter of 7th April 1863, WM p.399. William published his correspondence with Campbell in the *Edinburgh Courant.*
93. This theme of self-sacrifice also relates to the other main officers involved, several of whom died during service with the Konds, such as Frye and Stevenson. After his Kond posting, Cadenhead was made Assistant Agent of Sambalpur and its Munda population when it was taken over by the British in 1850. Within a few months he had fallen sick and died there. A school was established in his name as a memorial to him. His superior officer, J.H. Crawfurd recorded that 'The Indian Government has seldom been served more efficiently, and never more devotedly, than by our lamented friend' (WM p.290).

Campbell ended his final Report, of 9th February 1854, by commending MacViccar in words evocative of the power of this colonial theme: 'While I record these happy results, I may be permitted to bring before the Most Noble the Governor-General-in-Council the valuable services rendered by that able, active, and zealous officer, Captain MacViccar, who unflinchingly pursued his good work till fever in its most dangerous form compelled him to seek a change of climate.' (C)

94. When this incident came to his superiors' attention, Macpherson was sharply rebuked (Lt Macpherson in Vishnuchakram to GOM 17th July 1836, GOI HP 30th Aug. 1836 no.56).

95. Campbell wrote that the Konds of Domasingi and Jellingia *mutahs* 'had never before seen an European, and came in crowds to my tent'. Adingadikia was 'peculiarly a Kond muta', with no Hindu chiefs to mediate and translate. Reports of 25th March, 1st and 19th April (GOI HP 15th July 1848 nos.1, 3 & 11), & 7th June (GOI HP 22nd July 1848 14).

96. Above p.68. Campbell's Reports: GOI HP 22nd July 1848 no.18 & 12th August no.5. Dalhousie's Minute of 2nd August, GOI HP 12th Aug. no.8.

97. Campbell's Report of 17th March 1849 is reproduced in C. pp.109–113. Dalhousie commended Campbell's 'firmness, skill and judgement' (31st March). NB: *other Reports cited in this section are reproduced in C, K, or J, unless otherwise specified.*

98. Cadenhead in Calcutta to GOI, 5th July 1848 (GOI HP 22nd July no.31). For more on Frye's schoolbooks and missionary connections, see below, Ch.6.

99. 'In the house of the Tat Rajah, I discovered a youth that had been purchased by him for sacrifice, and who had undergone all the ceremonies preparatory to his immolation to the god of battles, Manicksoro.... This sacrifice is called "Junna", and is I believe performed by the Hill Rajas generally on important occasions, such as going to battle. I know it was performed by the Raja of Goomsur in 1835, on the eve of his rebellion against the Government.' (Report of 10th April 1852, C. p.121)

100. See below pp.144–7 on Campbell's strict 'care' of the *meriah* children.

101. Campbell recorded that on his tour in 1851–2, 'Several chiefs, on being asked to sign the pledge (which was always carefully explained, and much pains taken to make them understand its purport) to abandon the sacrifice, answered: "Many countries have forsaken the meriah sacrifice at the orders of the great Sirkar, why should we not do also." ' (Report of 10th April 1852) Even Oriya chiefs were

not always literate. As the missionary Goadby described the *rajah* of Bamanajar: 'He is a young man, and some time ago could neither read nor write, but as Colonel Campbell and other officers of the Meriah Agency who succeeded him, refused to acknowledge him until he had learnt to read and otherwise improve himself, he gave his mind to his letters, and can now read with fluency, and write with a good hand.' (*GBMS Report* 1865 p.26)

102. This illustrates Kulke's model of a shift in the legitimation of Orissa *rajahs* as Konds and Kond religion ceased to legitimize a *rajah*'s authority, and were displaced by the British and their Law (see Ch.4, 'The role of the Hindu *rajahs*', and Ch.5, 'Indian intermediaries: old and new elites'). The contracts British officials made with Konds are similar to those they made with independent Nagas, Mishmis and Abors in Northeast India, in the 1870s, which were recorded in photographs by Major-General Robert Gosset Woodthorpe during tours in the 1870s (see under Archival sources). These photographs show the impressive contrast of these formal occasions, as two different worlds meet on unequal terms: tribal chiefs squat in front of British officials who wear solar topis and sit in wicker chairs, surrounded by Indian scribes and servants, and soldiers standing guard. Major Butler, the Political Agent whose death in 1875 sparked off a vicious retaliation from the British, wears a kilt. The chiefs face the camera and posterity with a penetrating gaze.

Chapter Four. Human Sacrifice as a Kond and Hindu Ritual

1. By contrast, Captain Cook witnessed a human sacrifice in Tahiti (painting reproduced in Sahlins 1985), and Richard Burton witnessed them in Dahomey. Macpherson's informants on Kond affairs (listed in Report published in 1842) are mainly from the local Hindu elite. The chief one was Sundera Singh, son of the *rajah* of Sorada, who 'grew up among the Konds'. Campbell's chief informants were Sam Bissoi (who may well have authorized human sacrifices while ostensibly working to suppress them, above p.70) and Punda Naik, who had been chief of Baibully under the Ghumsur *rajah*, but came over to the British side and gave information that led to the capture and hanging of the Kond chief Baipatro. Campbell

reappointed him in his chiefship, stating that he was influential among the Konds, and 'a good counterpoise, should it be necessary to use him as such, to Sam Bissoye'.

2. Arens' questioning whether the custom of cannibalism has ever actually existed in his book *The man-eating myth* (1979) is important for emphasizing the extent to which such customs are fabricated to justify conquest, slavery, and genocide. But I feel it is important to separate two issues: on the one hand, colonialism itself, which legitimized its violence by dwelling on the violence of those it colonized, 'inventing' human sacrifice, headhunting or cannibalism—using ideas about them (whether or not they actually existed) to justify extreme oppression; and on the other hand, trying to understand the reality of forms of violence in other cultures free from any ulterior motive. To me the evidence on Kond human sacrifice seems too strong to say that the whole thing was a colonial invention, just as I question whether all accounts of cannibalism are unfounded.
3. The name Tari Penu is not generally recognized now. Possibly Tari is a variation or corruption of *darni*, or another word for 'earth' equivalent to the Hindi word *mitti*, in the sense of 'soil', as one Kuvi-speaker has suggested to me. The Konds in Bailey's and Niggemeyer's areas called her Tana Penu, *tana* being their word for 'earth'. Among Kuttia Konds her most familiar name is Bangu Penu. But Darni Penu is a name known in all Kond areas, although *darni* also refers simply to the stones planted in the earth that form her shrines (Boal 1982).
4. WM p.123. Macpherson gave a list of reasons why certain sacrificing Konds he had conversed with thought the British Government should recognize that 'it had no just right to interfere with it': it had been performed from the beginning; the *rajahs* sanctioned it, and Hindu rites allowed it; 'because it is essential to the existence of mankind in health, and to the continuation of the species'; and essential to the productive power of nature; and to the gods, who ordained it, for food; and the victims were bought for a fair price. (NB: *Reports quoted in this section are in Carberry 1854*.)
5. *Meriah* is the commonest British spelling. The Kond word is given in different areas as *meri, meroi, mervi, mrivi* (Bailey) and *mrimi* (Boal). Elsewhere Konds used the word *toka or toki*, which is

probably why early accounts called the occasion the 'Tonki' festival.

6. Above p.99. Campbell described the practice as 'rearing meriahs by bringing up women to prostitution' (10 April 1852), and 'Possia Poes' as 'labouring, living-in servants' or 'serfs' (1864 pp.53–4, 78–9).
7. This festival took place at a full moon that fell in the Hindu months of *Magh* or *Poos*, around January, which is a slack season, between most of the harvesting and sowing. Most accounts do not associate the *meriah* festival with any particular agricultural activity.
8. Arbuthnot (Report 1837) thought the sacrifice was to Jakeri Penu. 'Jakeri Penu' apparently refers to the village gods in general, and is used almost interchangeably with 'Darni Penu' for the piles of stones that serve as shrines in and around a village, and the beings which inhabit them. Boal translates Jakeri Penu as 'founding patriarch' (1982 p.91). Jakeri Penu is invoked in the same breath as Darni Penu at the buffalo sacrifices recorded by Niggemeyer (1964).
9. Campbell 1864 pp.51, 126, Boal 1982 pp.200–1, Watson and Kaye 1875.
10. WM pp.119–127; Boal 1982 pp.115–122.
11. Campbell's Report of 17th March 1849, GOI HP 31st March no.15 (K). Other descriptions (in WM, C etc.) included death by suffocation in a pit filled with pig's blood and burning alive. The *meriah's* tears were apparently taken as an omen of good rain in the year ahead.
12. Boal 1982 pp.114, 122–3, 129–131, 136–142. To me it seems likely that it was less frequent than Boal suggests, varying greatly in different areas and periods. The evidence is not clear on how frequent human sacrifices really were. Arbuthnot wrote of a twelve year cycle. Ricketts admitted, 'I was not successful in acquiring any good information as to the frequency of these sacrifices. One Khond of about 46 years of age told me he had witnessed fully 50. Other Khonds equally old would acknowledge to having been present only at two or three.'(23rd Feb. 1837) According to Campbell, 'On the most minute enquiry, I could not discover that more than four or five victims were sacrificed annually in the Goomsoor Maliahs,

or that any were sacrificed for private purposes, such as the restoration to health of a Moliko or headman.' (Jan. 1838)

13. Boal 1982, pp.108–9, and above p.106 on the increase in buffalo sacrifices to ward off epidemics and droughts. Many Konds blamed these on the suppression of the *meriah* sacrifice, which they believed angered Darni.
14. Occasionally a monkey or bullock was sacrificed instead (Boal 1982 pp.132–3).
15. Elwin's Report on tribes of Ganjam and Koraput Districts, addressed to the Education Dept of the Government of Orissa, 5th April 1945, in Elwin Papers, Teenmurti Library Archives, Misc.X no.147.
16. Boal makes a detailed comparison, 1982 pp.124–55, 238–61.
17. E.g. in sacrifices recorded by Elwin (1944) and Niggemeyer in 1956. Kuttias call one of the buffaloes dedicated for sacrifice the *duli* buffalo , named after the *duli* buffalo that was given to the Dom as part of the payment for the *meriah* victim.
18. 60,000 was Macpherson's estimate. He also thought that certain Kond areas were virtually free from female infanticide as well as from human sacrifice, but Campbell contradicted this, and found female infanticide in areas, such as Digi, that Macpherson had thought free of it, having been 'imposed upon....by designing natives.' (Report of 17th March 1849) Yet Macpherson also thought that no Kond area was entirely free of it (WM p.132).
19. The British Government publicized and took steps to suppress female infanticide in Rajasthan from the late 18th century onwards (although it is reported to still continue today). Rajputs of the highest sub-caste killed off female infants because giving their women in marriage to families from any other, lower, level was held to shame the group, as well as impoverishing it through the huge dowries (Duff 1844, Dumont 1980 p.118).
20. Campbell's Report of August 1848 (C p.108). Campbell implies that these marriage payments were dowries. Among most Konds, as with other tribes, a man 'buys' a woman with a brideprice—which at least places a positive value on women, unlike the Hindu custom of dowry, where the husband's family is of higher status and has to be persuaded to take the bride by the large dowry that accompanies her, often in effect as a bribe.

21. See above p.81, and below p.124.
22. Lord Elphinstone particularly stressed that human sacrifice should never be alluded to 'as a *Khond custom*—but as a custom prevalent among barbarous tribes in every part of the world', citing Hume to the effect that among 'civilized nations' only the Carthaginians had been guilty of it (Minute of 16th March 1841, C pp.32–3 & 39). E.g. Joseph Campbell (1959, 1962) as well as Nigel Davies (1981) take a similar view of human sacrifice as characteristic of 'primitive' societies.
23. Elwin often conveys a general feeling of tribal religion quite accurately. Piers Vitebsky (1993) describes that of the Lanjia Soras in much greater depth and accuracy. Among tribes outside India, I find Signe Howell's study of the spiritual life of a tribe in peninsular Malaya (1984) particularly helpful. She and Vitebsky take further the trend which Evans-Pritchard started, and Godfrey Lienhardt continued (1961), of giving close attention to the *language* of tribal religion, bringing out ways of understanding life that differ more radically from our own ways than earlier anthropologists comprehended.
24. Introduction to *Myths of Orissa* 1954. Niggemeyer says much the same (1964 p.147). Elwin's collection of Kond myths is from a relatively small area of Kuttia and Kuvi Konds.
25. Boal 1982 p.88. According to her *kuta gatanju* basically means 'diviner'. Some Konds use the term *dissari* for a diviner, like neighbouring tribes, and *gunia* for the most powerful of shamans (Elwin 1944). In having female as well as male shamans, Konds (Kuvis and Kuttias at least) resemble the Soras, but differ from most neighbouring tribes.
26. The title of Piers Vitebsky's book (1993). Elwin's field-notes go into some detail on Kond shamans, as does Niggemeyer (1964). For a deeper understanding I am indebted to Madhu Ramnath's and Vitebsky's accounts of neighbouring tribes, which is consistent with the Kond material.
27. On Northeast India see Fürer-Haimendorf 1976 Chs.14–15, Gohain 1977. On 'ploughmen raised at home', see letters from the Boad *rajah*, Chokra Bissoi and Kond chiefs, quoted in Ch.3. Bailey (1960) brings out the structural importance in Kond villages of 'sisters' sons'—men from poor families who lived with their wives'

families for the first few years of marriage, working for them instead of paying a brideprice. Perhaps they formed a class of 'ploughmen' who shaded into, or were sometimes confused with, *meriahs*.

28. Bailey 1960 pp.50–1 & 69. Boal supports Bailey's view on this matter. NB: what Macpherson calls 'tribes' and their 'branches', Bailey calls 'clans' and 'lineages'. Macpherson gave an outline of how this system corresponded to territorial divisions of *mutahs* (1842), although he admitted that an exact correspondence was 'never seen in fact'. See also Risley 1891 p.lv.
29. On Kond totemism see Friend-Pereira 1904, Bailey 1960 pp.42–3, and Boal 1982 pp.200–8. There are similar 'totemic' associations between exogamous clans or lineages with animals or plants in other Central Indian tribes (Ferreira 1965, Lévi-Strauss 1963).
30. Above p.80 & Ch.3 note 42. Bailey points to a connection between cult of the earth, human sacrifice, and brotherhood or peace pacts between clans (1960 pp.21–2, 40, 50–1, 81).
31. Above pp.54–6, and Ch.2 note 61. Macpherson said that wars were mainly disputes over territory and women.
32. Elwin 1947, Thusu 1980.
33. Roy 1935, Bailey 1960 p.179.
34. Tod 1829/1914 p.181, and Hari Sen, private communication.
35. Sinha 1962, K.S. Singh 1971.
36. 'For nine centuries the Konds lived under two different sets of political institutions: their own and the Oriya system.'(Bailey 1960 p.173) As Frye describes the Hindu chiefs: 'In each division [of a kingdom] is a village….[of] Uriya[s]….styled "godah" [or *garh*]…. [whose] head….is called…."Patro", and by Khonds…."Rajenju", equivalent to Raja. The Patros….also call each other Raja, when speaking of themselves with reference to the Khonds…. The Patro is….surrounded by a petty court.'(1860 p.5) The word *bissoi* is derived apparently from Sanskrit *vishayapati*, meaning 'one in charge of a district' (Mukherjee 1981 p.127).
37. Eschmann's research (1978 p.85) shows that this identification was widespread: 'Most of the tribal cults in Orissa, which are important enough to be Hinduized, are related to a female deity, who protects the men, [assures] the fertility, and accepts blood sacrifice…. The most frequent and in a way logical association or identification of

such goddesses is towards Durga.... Such a connection between a tribal goddess and Durga may start on a purely tribal level. In many Khond villages, for instance, there is no apparent Hinduization whatsoever, except for the fact, that when the post which represents the goddess, is renewed—which happens perhaps every thirty years—a Brahmin is called to impart the *prati-pratishta-mantra* of *Vana Durga* (the "Durga of the woods") and thus theoretically acknowledges the post as a *murti*.'

38. 'In Keonjhar, a Khond priest is still permitted as a relic of the past to perform rites to a rough hewn stone inside the chief's house, although the ruling family has long since been converted to Vaishnavism.'(Cobden-Ramsay 1910 p.30). The argument about legitimation is from Kulke's articles 1978a & b, which examine the layout of towns in central Orissa and documents of Orissa history, but without looking at the evidence on Kond human sacrifice.

39. Above p.70, WM p.202. Sam was of the *soodoo* caste, the *Dulbehra* of the *keont* caste, between which 'feelings of deep jealousy have always existed' (Macpherson's Report of 15th Oct. 1846, GOI HP 21st Nov. no.11). This rivalry shows the kind of conflicts that arose between Hindu chiefs, and the significance of Kond deities in this conflict: Sam and the *Dulbehra* both laid claim to the chiefship of Hodzoghor, of which Bura Penu's stone was a symbol.

40. Campbell reported that the *bissois* expressed their 'horror of human sacrifice' to him, but admitted they were 'wholly unable to coerce the Konds' to make them stop it. They requested the Government to make a proclamation threatening severe punishment for the *meriah* sacrifice. When Sam was first made a British prisoner in 1836, and was being taken as a guide and interpreter by Russell to help rescue *meriahs*, Russell was going to remove the chains that bound him, as a favour, but Sam kept them on, at his own request. *Bissois* were evidently anxious that Konds should know the order to stop human sacrifice came from the British: to appear constrained to relay this order, and not as ordering it themselves. For instance, Captain Hicks reported in 1844, 'I believe the sacrifices are still most numerous, that the few children sent in by the Rajas are intended as a mere blind, and that if they are able, they are most unwilling to attempt the rescue of the victims annually sacrificed in their territories.' (C p.77)

41. Campbell says this 'junna' sacrifice was made to Manecksoro, 'the god of war' (calling her a goddess in later reports).
42. Veena Das drew my attention to the inclusion in ancient Hindu texts of human beings among potential offerings of sacrifice (NB: her article on the language of sacrifice, 1983).
43. Letter from *vakul* to Macpherson 9th Sept. 1846, Diary for 3rd–11th Sept. GOI HP 21st Nov. no.4.
44. Gouldsbury Report to GOB 9th March 1847 GOI HP 10th April no.10.
45. Letter from *vakul* to Macpherson 27th June 1846, Diary for 25th June–1st July GOI HP 18th July 44.
46. MacViccar's Report of 26th April 1852 (C p.116).
47. Pfeffer's article 'Tribal social organisation and "Hindu" influence' 1982.
48. Above p.110, and Bailey p.98. Mills reported that Konds justified human sacrifice with reference to turmeric: 'they say that the blood of victims imparts a high colour and raises its value.' (June 1844, in C)
49. E.g. Elwin 1955. S. Banerjee (1968) records a custom, which continued until 1952, of a Kond village supplying a bucket of turmeric to the Maharaja of Jeypore at his Dassehra festival.
50. Elwin Papers Misc.X 161. pp.50 & 57. NB: the case cited above p.65, where a Dom sold his own daughter as a *meriah* after the Government had removed the intended victim.
51. 1982 pp.153–5. However, in some myths it is the primeval woman (who is Tari Penu in human form) who offers herself for sacrifice (above p.120), which might be taken as supporting Frazer's idea. To me it seems clear that the *meriah* begins to merge with the goddess some time before sacrifice as his sacredness is heightened—while the basic view is that he is food for the goddess. Hubert and Mauss suggest that 'sacrifice *to* the god developed parallel to sacrifice *of* the god' (1898/1964 p.90).
52. On the Ashanti see Ch.1 note 7.
53. On the suppression of *thugee*, e.g. Morris 1973/1979 Ch.4.
54. Fürer-Haimendorf 1976 & Gohain 1977 on northeastern India; Nigel Davies 1981 pp.167–74 on Dayaks.
55. Tacitus records the Roman suppression of human sacrifice by Druids in Britain (*Annals of Imperial Rome*, Penguin 1971). On the

Portuguese use of the idea that the Tupinamba practised it see Hemming 1978.

56. This is persuasively argued in several recent works by feminist historians, notably Sjöö & Mor 1987, and Eisler 1987.
57. Ward 1953.
58. E.g. in the wars against the Marathas and Tipu Sultan, whom the British saw as tyrants similar to Napoleon. NB: Peggs' appeals to 'British humanity' (1846).

Chapter Five. The Colonial Sacrifice…

1. E.g. 'sepoys', as they were known in Bengal, were called 'privates' in Madras (Phythian-Adams 1958 p.274–5). In the case of the Kond Agency, the administrators were army men serving outside their regiments on public or political appointment, in distinction to the Collector of Ganjam District and the Commissioner in Cuttack, who were civil servants of Madras and Bengal.

   The Governments in Madras and Bengal (as well as the Government of India, also based in Calcutta) were divided horizontally into Departments, such as Military, Revenue, Medical and Home Departments. It is under the 'Public Consultations' of the GOI Home Department that all the Kond Agency correspondence is ultimately filed (copied laboriously into big volumes by Writers), since the Agent reported direct to the Governor-General. Each Department was headed by a high-ranking Secretary, and the Governor's Council was made up of Department heads, presided over by the President.
2. Cohn calls this 'history from the inside' (1961 Ch.1). One significant example of an informal structure is in the institutionalization of prostitutes for the army, studied by Ballhatchet in *Race, sex and class* (1979).
3. The conceptual structure of this discourse is where conscious and deep structure meet. The key concepts beneath the official classification of ranks and departments, as well as of the native population, reveal the unarticulated assumptions of British rule: the motives and ideals that generated officials' behaviour, and the polarities that structured their whole frame of thinking and acting—patterns of which they were largely unconscious. These generating

concepts—what Durkheim called 'collective representations'—were connected to culturally conditioned patterns of *feeling* as well as thinking, although their surface expression—the key words that triggered them—are often highly loaded and ambiguous, such as the concepts we examine in this book of 'peace', 'honour', 'sacrifice' and 'enlightenment'.

4. E.g. A list of meticulous details sent to the Government by Campbell (9th May 1848) was sent back to him with a demand for all the children's exact ages—as if this could be known! (GOI HP 15th July 1848 nos.24–8 & 52)
5. Campbell's Reports of 6th Jan. 1842 (K), 17th March 1849 (GOI HP 31st March no.25), and 9th Feb. 1854 (C). The Reports by Campbell quoted below are as follows: 5th August & 22nd October 1847 (GOI HP 24th Dec. 1847 nos.66–8 & 71), 19th April & 16th June 1848 (GOI HP 15th July 1848 nos.11 & 42).
6. Maddock authorized Campbell to send the children to Baptist orphanages at the cost of Rs 3 per child per month, while cautioning him to guard against the impression that they were being put into the missionaries' care in order to convert them. A few months later, Campbell again appealed for permission to start a *meriah* village, promising that it would become a source of profit, not loss, to the Government (Report of 19th April 1848). This request was discussed at a meeting of the Governor-General-in-Council on 6th July 1848, at which Lord Dalhousie declared the idea 'highly objectionable', since it would 'serve to keep alive in the minds of the population the recollection of a rite of which we wish to obliterate every trace.' (GOI HP 24th Dec. 1847 no.66, 15th July 1848 nos.11 & 42, 22nd July no.24)
7. The case referred to above p.66.
8. Above p.101, below p.230.
9. This novel by Mrs Penny, published in 1910, is discussed in the next section.
10. Defoe 1975 pp.129–30 & 132. The mainland is not named, but lies approximately in the position of Venezuela. The quotations in the next four paragraphs are from pages 133–81 of the novel.
11. Ibid. pp.181 & 217.
12. Ibid. p.76.

13. Ransford 1971 Ch.3. Britain took over the slave trade from the Dutch in the 17th century, when the scene of the novel is set.
14. Portman 1899, Chapter V.
15. On the image of Africans as racially inferior see Curtin 1965 Ch.2, Ransford 1971, Bolt 1984. The 'scientific' racism which Knox established in his *Races of Man* (1850) and the 'science of phrenology' were definitive Victorian statements of racist theory.
16. Quoted by the editor in Defoe 1975 pp.293 & 298.
17. 'Perhaps no event in a soldier's life gives rise to such varied feelings as his embarkation for India. To some men it is the fulfilment of the wish of many years, ever since they pored over the well-thumbed pages of *Captain Cook's voyages*, or Defoe's *Robinson Crusoe*, and thence imbibed a longing for adventure and foreign travel.' The opening statement of *The young soldier in India: His life and prospects* by 'H.S.', 1889.
18. When Frye died of fever in the Kond hills in 1851, Campbell wrote of him: 'I can safely say that the Government never had a more zealous servant, nor a more accomplished scholar. He worked with all his heart in this good cause, and was one of the best and truest friends the Khonds ever had.' (1864 p.176)
19. Morris 1973/1979 p.508, Johnson 1982b. The other inspiring hero of mythic proportions in this respect was Captain Cook, whose death at the hands of natives towards whom his own intentions were most 'benevolent', was an archetypal 'colonial sacrifice', that inspired thousands of imperial officials.
20. Mrs Fanny Emily Penny wrote over 20 popular novels about India, including *Caste and creed* (1890), *The romance of the Nautch girl (1895), A mixed marriage* (under her maiden name of Frank), *The sanyasi, The tea planter, The Rajah, The Malabar magician, The outcaste, Love in the hills, Love in a palace, Desire and delight* (1904–19), as well as non-fiction books on women's medical work, the Forest officer Jim Burns, and a history of Madras. *Sacrifice*, about the Konds, was dedicated 'to Colonel J. MacDonald Smith, Indian staff corps, who was Special Assistant to the Agent in Ganjam at Russellkonda from 1870 to 1878, in grateful recognition of his assistance.' Evidently he was one of her main sources, if not her model for the hero.

21. The dark side of British army life in India was brought out in William Arnold's novel *Oakfield, or Fellowship of the East* (1854), a critical appraisal of his own experiences in the Indian Army, like Orwell's even bleaker *Burmese days* (1934). These novels by disillusioned ex-officials help us understand the huge gulf between administrators' heroic self-image, and the common reality of violence, prejudice, and a great narrowness of outlook.
22. Kirke-Greene 1980. Even in the Ghumsur wars there were probably only about 60 Britons 'in the field', presiding over a force of several thousand Indians. Russell, Stevenson, General Taylor, 3 Colonels, 5 Majors, 10 Captains, 12 Lieutenants, 6 Sergeants or Ensigns, a Quartermaster, and a Surgeon with 8 Assistant Surgeons are all that I have found reference to.
23. Mayhew closes his book *Christianity and the Government of India* (1929) by quoting Curzon's 'call to service' for British officials in India around 1900: 'the Almighty has placed your hand on the greatest of His ploughs. To drive the blade a little forward in your time, and to feel that somewhere among the millions you have left a little justice or happiness or prosperity, a sense of manliness or moral dignity, a sprig of patriotism, a dawn of intellectual enlightenment, or a stirring of duty where it did not exist before—that is enough, that is the Englishman's justification in India.'

    Colonel Norgate, in his preface to Seeta Ram's *From sepoy to Subedar* (1873/1911), denied responsibility for 'the opinions contained in the work...: they are those of a Hindoo, not a Christian.' In the Victorian period it was 'beyond the pale' for a British official to become a Hindu or Muslim, or even to get too close to Hindus and Muslims, as some of Kipling's stories illustrate (Wurgaft 1983 pp.135, 138–9). By the Test Act, even Jews could not enter the elite.
24. On the relationship between administrators and missionaries, see Chapter six, below.
25. E.g. Macpherson's talk of 'converting' the Konds to peace, and their 'religious conquest' (above p.53, below p.250).
26. MacViccar Report of 21st May 1855 (K).
27. Seeta Ram found the suppression of the Santal uprising in 1858 'a curious war: at one part of the jungle we were firing on them, and at another the Sirkar was giving them cart-loads of rice' (1911 p.111)—which sounds similar to Macpherson's use of 'friendly'

Konds against 'enemy' Konds—and the way that 'friends' and 'enemies' virtually changed place when General Dyce took over!

28. Above pp.59 & 140. The pre-Christian religions of the Germans and Celts conflated capital punishment with human sacrifice. Criminals condemned for different classes of offences were sacrificed to different gods by different methods, among which were drowning, hanging, burial alive and the sword (Ward 1953). A similar differentiation is visible among the executions that are such a prominent feature of British and European history: hanging for commoners, beheading for nobles executed for treason, and burning alive for heretics and witches.
29. Wurgaft 1983 reproduces a photograph of a hanging (above p.59).
30. Mills in 1844 recommended a lenient punishment for one chief on the grounds that he had never given a pledge to refrain from it: Lt Hicks should secure his attendance and reprimand him; 'some days' detention as a prisoner, and, if found necessary, a transportation to Cuttack will probably be a suitable punishment for his refractory conduct' (Report of 16th June 1845—C). MacViccar mentioned Konds' abstention from human sacrifice after an exemplary punishment of Konds in 1852 for an attempted sacrifice, and commented: 'I fear some severe examples must be made 'ere these cruel practices are completely suppressed in Jeypore' (21st May 1855—K). 'Severe example' was a code for execution. McNeill punished cases of human sacrifice and infanticide with imprisonment, transportation, and hard labour in chain gangs (above pp.104–6). Several Maria Gonds convicted of performing human sacrifices in the 1930s–40s were executed (above p.113).
31. McNeill's Reports of 23rd Feb. 1858 (GOI HP 26th March no.23), and 16th April (K).
32. Orwell 1934/1970. Foucault, in *Discipline and punish* (1977), outlines the 'totalizing' control over the human body which was expressed by public executions, as well as through the prison system and military drill, in the order of power that evolved from the late 18th century.
33. Above p.104, below p.173.
34. Bengal also included Daspalla and other 'tributary states' which kept their *rajah* and nominal independence. Kalahandi and Patna were included in the Central Provinces, with its capital at Nagpur,

which came under Bombay. The Central Provinces were formed in 1861 under (Sir) Richard Temple as Commissioner. Kalahandi and other Oriya-speaking Districts were not formally joined to Orissa until 1905.

35. The hill tracts of Chinna Kimedi were annexed and added to Ganjam in 1872. Ganjam District was divided into plains and Hill Agency divisions, the latter still withdrawn from the jurisdiction of ordinary courts by Act XXIV of 1839. No land rent was demanded, though a plough tax soon had the same effect.

    The *taluqs* of Ganjam, Goomsur, Berhampur (which included Chinna and Pedda Kimedi), and Chicacole, each included Hill and Plains sections.

36. Forbes' Report to GOM of 17th Feb. 1863 (K).

37. Forbes was trying to settle a dispute between three *mutahs* within Sorada: Simanabadi *versus* Daringabadi and Grenobadi (above p.55). He described the resistance his soldiers met when they came to Daringabadi to request attendance at a meeting: 'the party was suddenly surrounded by 60 or 70 men armed with Tangis (a long-handled battle-axe in universal use) who threatened to cut them down, using at the same time the most abusive and seditious language against the "Circar". I then issued a warrant for the apprehension of the head men, and entrusted its execution to a party of 50 men under a Sirdar with orders to bring them in by force, and to use their weapons if attacked. They came accidentally, while passing through Tarabadi, on the head man of Gerandabadi (a notorious ruffian named Sifika Pudra) who was haranguing the Khonds of that village, and sent him to camp at once. On arriving at Daringabadi they found the whole male population of that mutah, some 2,000 men, assembled on the hills with various weapons, but succeeded in getting two of the head men to come down whom they apprehended. When the Khonds saw they were made prisoners they threatened to stone the party, but retired when the Sirdar loaded his muskets and announced that he had orders to fire. The two prisoners were immediately recognized by the men of the first party as the leaders of the Khonds who threatened to cut them down. They were tried under section 506 of the penal code and sentenced to six years' rigorous imprisonment—a sentence which will, I hope, have some effect on the very turbulent and vicious tribes of the Sorada

Maliahs.' Forbes sentenced Sifika Pudra to two years' rigorous imprisonment, and left the area after 'making what appeared to be a very hearty peace' between the two sides. (Report of 17th Feb. 1863—K) The next quotation is from the same Report.

38. Maltby gives a full list of 459 policemen in 6 grades, and where they were stationed (1882 Appendix 23). 'The force may seem unnecessarily large, but the advantages of immediate action in the hill districts is supreme.' (Ibid. p.92).
39. 'At a later date in the same year, 1882, a Khond landowner was convicted and executed for having offered a five-year-old girl as a Meriah sacrifice.' (Russell and Hira Lal 1916 vol.III pp.480–1). Thurston recorded the grisly details of Konds' killing of Koltas (1909 pp.411–12).
40. These ferocious axes and other items were presented by Strode-Wilson (1894–1905), the Minchin family (1902), Balfour (1916), and D. Gunn (1922). On the symbolic significance of these axes in the Oxford Museum see below p.254.
41. Ghurye documents the history of this process of excluding tribals from regular law, which he sees as a prime example of 'divide and rule' (1959 Chs. 4 & 5, pp.76–8 on the Konds).
42. 'The military classes who were our active opponents have given the best proof of their submission....by delivering up their own chiefs' (Russell, 3rd March 1837 par.10).
43. 'The struggle between the two brothers—invoked as a myth of tragic conflict—encapsulated much of the history of British India after the Mutiny' (Wurgaft 1983 p.89). One of the brothers favoured rule of Punjab through the established Sikh *sirdars*, the other annexation and direct rule through British-appointed officials. The point is, these two options defined what was thinkable for the British—and made relatively little difference for those who worked the land.
44. From Macpherson's Diary for 21st–29th Sept. 1846, GOI HP 17th Oct. no.22.
45. Macpherson's Report of 17th May 1846 pars.2 & 4, GOI HP 30th May no.1D.
46. 'There is no part of a Collector's duty which is more important than the supervision of the education of minors, and the charge of boys like the sons of the rebel Janardanasing of Sooradah [among them

Sundera Singh?], now living under the surveillance of the Police at Chicacole, who it may be hoped will, by kind and conciliatory treatment, be reclaimed from the lawless habits in which their youth has been passed and become useful members of society.' (Russell's Report of 1st Nov. 1834 par.154—R) Carmichael wrote similarly about the Jeypore aristocracy 30 years later: 'The Zemindars still indulge in much feudatory pomp in their retinues, but they no longer shut themselves up in their fastnesses….all speak English after a fashion…. I wish I could see them solicitous to secure an English education for their sons. I stirred them up to this end and extracted some promises….'(29th March 1863, in J)

47. Hunter ibid. pp.113–9. In between the great Juang uprising of 1868 and the great Kond uprising in Kalahandi of 1882, the Konda Doras (just south of Koraput District) made a similar uprising, or *fituri*, in 1879–80, which was suppressed with similar brutality by the British (David Arnold 1982). The problems that caused these risings continued, and in 1922–4 the Konda Doras rebelled again.

48. The pattern of promotion had the effect of binding a small number of local men closely to British interests. The petty nature of this system of punish-or-reward is illustrated in a letter from Macpherson of 9th July 1846 to Punda Naik, the *sirdar* of Ghumsur, who was in Gottingia after a local feud had just resulted in the death of twelve Konds: 'You have been my chief instrument in giving Ghumsur habitual peace in the place of war. The silver bangles which I promised you [for gallantry in the fight of 1st April] are lying ready and I intend to recommend you to the Government for further advancement if your future services shall bear the same character as the past. If you shall not stop this fighting all that you have done in Ghumsur for peace will be undone and the value of your services will be entirely changed.' (Diary of 2nd–13th July 1846, GOI HP 1st Aug. no.12)

49. As we have seen, Macpherson accused Sam of actually patronizing human sacrifices that he pretended Bannerman had sanctioned, a charge which Bannerman and Campbell did not believe. They trusted Sam and Sooria closely; but they and Dyce made similar accusations against Baba Khan and Macpherson's other subordinates, of extorting bribes from Konds, which Chokra Bissoi and many Konds endorsed. It seems likely that there was considerable

truth in the allegations of both sides: these accusations and counter-accusations show the extent to which Britons were drawn into and accentuated local factions, and did not truly know what went on 'beneath' them.

50. This, it seems to me, is one of the main faults with Dumont's classic study of Indian society under this title; for his work ignores not only ideas of equality that feature in Indian society, but also the principle of hierarchy in Western society, which the British brought to India, and which still has great currency, despite the ideal of equality formulated in the West.
51. Examples of a 'native establishment' at the Agent's *cutcherry* (headquarters) grade people by pay, from the chiefs and *munshis* at the top, to lesser *sirdars*, and the mass of *peons* (the foot-soldiers whose name gave rise to 'pawns'), and the cook and sweeper at the bottom. (Russell 11th May 1837, GOI to Macpherson 6th Dec. 1845 GOI HP 6th Dec. no.8C, and on Campbell's establishment 1848–49, GOI HP 31st March 1849 no.25)
52. 16th March 1841 (C). Campbell 'successfully encouraged the Khonds by every means in my power to frequent the markets in the plains' (Anon.1849 p.11). He also encouraged a larger trade: on a single day his camp at Kormingia was held up by 2,000 bullocks of Brinjari merchants carrying wheat from the Orissa plains to Sambalpur, for whom the British road meant a quick route, and maybe business on the way. These merchants payed a small toll to the British for every bullock at 21 stages on this route (Report of 6th Jan. 1842).
53. MacDonald's Report of 31st Jan. 1855 (in K).
54. There were many other tribal uprisings apart from the Santal, Juang, Konda Dora, Kond and Bastar ones just mentioned (above notes 27 & 47, and p.175).
55. From the start, in the 1830s, the British perceived the Konds' forest in terms of marketable products and cultivable land: 'The forest has no underwood; every inch of the land could be cultivated' (Kittoe 1839 p.678).
56. The present-day classification of many tribals as 'encroachers', on the grounds that they do not possess title deeds to their land, serves to justify displacing them with minimal compensation when the land is taken over for a dam or other project.

57. Thompson 1977, Prebble 1967. NB: above p.97.
58. Kond councils in 1871 and 1901 made oaths to give up drink because of its link with indebtedness. But the main drive clearly came from the administration (Ghurye 1943 p.118, Bailey 1957 ch.1).
59. Dalton 1872, Elwin 1948. At present, there is a 'Clothe the Bondos programme', with the identical aim of forcing an end to tribal 'nudity'.
60. Hugh Brody gives a telling example of the same stereotype from an administrator's description of the Inuit (Eskimo) in the 1940s: 'There is no learning to know the Eskimo through an exchange of ideas. Properly speaking, the Eskimo does not think at all. He has no capacity for generalization. He cannot explain himself to you, nor can he explain his people.' (1975 p.101)
61. Ghurye 1943 pp.90–1. On Ghurye see above pp.19–20 and below in Chs.7 & 8.
62. Thurston 1909 p.359, Griffiths 1967 pp.268–85.

Chapter Six. 'Soldiers Of Christ'

1. British Protestants first became interested in Mission work in connection with the American colonies. The chemist Boyle in the 1660s was Governor of a corporation for spreading the Gospel in New England, and a patron of bible translations, as well as a Director of the East India Company. At the same time in Massachusetts John Eliot, a Presbyterian, was translating the bible into native American languages and converting 'praying towns' of Indians to his faith. The Society for Promoting Christian Knowledge (SPCK, founded 1698) and the Society for the Propagation of the Gospel (SPG, founded 1701), both Anglican, also worked mainly in North America during the eighteenth century. But it was the Danish who led the Protestant world in Mission work between 1700 and 1800, and put the first Protestant Mission in India: Frederick IV established the Royal Danish Mission in 1705 by sending the German Lutheran missionary Ziegenbalg to Tranquebar. His work was publicized by the SPCK, who extended it into British territory after the EIC allowed two missionaries to work in Madras in 1728. The most

famous of these Danish missionaries was Christian Friedrich Schwartz, who worked in South India continuously from 1750 to 1798. The Moravian Missionary Society was also based in Denmark. It was started by Count Zinzendorf in 1732, with a Mission to the Eskimos in Greenland that clashed with the stricter work of the Danish Lutheran missionary Egede, who worked in Greenland 1722–36 (Neill 1964). The new missionary outlook apparently came to Britain through the Moravian influence on John Wesley, whose mass meetings in the 1740s had a huge impact on the Church of England as well as on Non-Conformists: Methodism began as an evangelical missionary revival.

Two major propaganda pieces were published around the time the BMS was founded: Carey's *An Enquiry into the Obligations of Christians to use Means for the Conversion of the Heathen,* and Charles Grant's *Observations on the state of Society among the Asiatic subjects of Great Britain, particularly with reference to morals and means of improving them.* After a great debate in Parliament in 1793, the EIC continued to exclude missionaries from its territory until the next renewal of its charter in 1813. Following the Baptist lead, the London Mission Society (LMS) was founded in 1795 by the Congregational sect in 1795, and the Church Mission Society (CMS) by Anglicans in 1799, both of which sent Missions to India after 1813.

Carey and his colleagues first supported themselves on an indigo farm in Bengal, but finally settled at Serampore. Wellesley patronized them despite official disapproval.

2. My sources on the Baptist missionaries include James Peggs (1830, and *History of the Orissa Mission* 1846), Pearce Carey's *Dawn on the Kond Hills* (1936), and Barbara Boal's writings (1966, 1973, 1982), as well as Reports of the GBMS and BMS, the former published in Cuttack specifically on the Orissa Mission, the latter in London on BMS Missions in general. These Reports I consulted at the headquarters of the BMS in Gloucester Place. Pearce Carey quotes other primary sources—missionaries' reports and diaries—which were apparently destroyed when the previous BMS premises were bombed in 1940.
3. Catholic Missions suffered during the Pope's suppression of the Jesuit order 1773–1814. In the 1830s the Pope appointed the first

four vicars apostolic to India, who coexisted uneasily with bishops appointed to sees in India by the Portuguese. By 1859 16 Papal vicars had been appointed (Neill 1964 & 1985). The Pope made Vishakapatnam a vicariate in 1845 and two fathers went from there to Sorada in 1850: Francois Sermet, who died soon after his arrival, and Father John Mary Tissot who remained there into the 1870s. In 1856–7 a Father Seigneur was attempting to convert Sorada's *brahmins*, on De Nobili's principles, without success. These Catholics were from Annécy, near Geneva, of the order of St Francis de Sales (1567–1622), who had been bishop there, and became famous for converting Huguenots to Catholicism. At least two major 'Salesian' missionary societies were founded in his memory. The elder of these, the Missionaries of St Francis de Sales, was founded in 1838, and sent Missions to China and Brazil as well as to India.

Like the Baptists, the Catholics worked hard at relief work during the great famine, and gained respect and recognition by doing so: 'The famous Orissa famine (1866–7) opened a new chapter for the church in Orissa. The selfless service of the missionaries attracted the attention of the people far and wide.' The sisters of St Francis of Annécy joined them in 1871, and built an orphanage for 200 children. A Father Upand was active on a series of unrecorded Kond tours in the 1880s. These and other details are from the historical introduction to a *Directory of the Diocese of Berhampur* 1984, which I consulted in the Catholic centre in Bhanjanagar (Russellkonda).

4. Oliver Millman, in *BMS Report* 1908 p.32. In 1914 he admitted that 'most of Udayagiri's 982 Christians are Roman Catholics'. Father Rey, transferred from Digi to Sorada in 1914, began work on a Kui translation of the Gospels etc. In 1919 Father Cyrile built an impressive church in Sorada, which still stands.
5. St Vincent de Paul (1580–1660) was a French churchman who founded a Mission for the poor, and lived at the royal court in Paris. The Congregation of St Vincent de Paul, founded 1833, revived this saint's Mission, which had been active in Scotland in the 18th century. Vincentian missionaries, or 'Lazarists', spread all over Europe soon after 1833, founding a house in Spain in 1850.

Sorada was the centre of this Spanish Mission 1923–49, whence stations were established in the Kond hills at Katingia, as well as in Russellkonda, Cuttack, Berhampur and Gopalpur, which became the headquarters in 1949. In 1935 a seminary was built in Russellkonda, and beside it, a church which has a dormitory for the training priests above the nave. In 1938 a bishop of Berhampur was ordained, and became head of the Mission, making it independent of Vishakhapatnam. In 1940 the male priests were joined by a group of nuns, the Daughters of Charity of St Vincent de Paul. Berhampur is now one of five bishoprics in Orissa, under an archbishop in Puri.

6. The Mission HQ was in Breklum. Its first two seminary-trained missionaries came to India in 1881. They went first to a Lutheran mission in Rajahmundry, and after trying to form a Mission in Bastar and being refused permission by the *rajah*, they settled in Salur. From there, later arrivals established stations at Jeypore, Koraput, Kotapad and Nowrangpur. These missionaries also suffered from bad health: 'In those early times malaria fever proved to be a great hindrance to Mission work. The Revd Reimers and his wife died at Koraput. The Revds Harlers, Kuhlman and Timm also died, the last from cholera at Kotapad.' These details are from the *Yearbook of Evangelical Lutheran Missions* for 1931 published by the Federation of Lutheran Christians in India, of which there is a copy in the India Office Library. Danish missionaries also had Missions to the Mundas, Santals and Gonds at this time. The Lutheran Mission to the Mundas of Chota Nagpur, which began in 1845, had 900 converts and 2,000 enquirers living in 50 Christian villages just before the Mutiny in 1857. After the Mutiny, conversions multiplied (S.C. Roy 1912).
7. I first visited this hospital in December 1986, when its founder, Dr. Elizabeth Madsen, was still its director, but lived at some distance and worked on her own in Kond villages. I also visited Agnes Hertz, who lived at an orphanage in Rayagadha, translating one of the Gospels.
8. Missionaries were divided at first on the question of how far to act on the Government's behalf. William Carey declared that his son Felix, who was a missionary in Burma, had 'shrivelled from a missionary into an ambassador' by acting as Government spokesman there (Myers 1892 p.69).

9. 'Nobody was sure whether [the British colonies were] truly a Christian empire, or merely an empire mostly run by Christians.' (James Morris 1973/1979 p.322). But the ideology was often unambiguously Christian, both in the 1830s–50s, before the Mutiny, when a flood of missionary influence was entering India, and at the height of empire in late-Victorian times, when Curzon epitomized this trend.
10. EIC ships were one scene of conflict. Peggs wrote of the elder Goadby's voyage out in 1830: 'As Commanders of East India ships are generally so unfavourable to religious worship, it should be known that Captain Renner manifested a very different spirit.' (1846 p.242) William Golding illustrates this conflict in his novel *Rites of Passage* (1980), set on a ship bound for Australia during the early 19th century. One of the central characters is a self-righteous Anglican clergyman, who is mocked by the captain, crew, and other passengers.
11. On this concept of 'Providence', referred to by Peggs (1846 pp.143–4, 149), the United States provides copious examples during the same period, since the displacing of Indians from their land tended to be justified by 'Providence' or 'Manifest Destiny' (Dee Brown 1975).
12. 1st July 1841 (pp.400–1), entitled 'Murder of children by the Khunds': '....We have been told that (if we do not mistake the number) upwards of 100 victims who were to have been sacrificed in January, the Agent of the Madras Government could have rescued with half a dozen burkandazes; but he was obliged to relinquish them to their unhappy fate on receiving orders from head-quarters that nothing but persuasion should be employed. Surely the case is too dreadful to be committed to these most ignorant and brutal of the Honourable Company's subjects: men who would as soon kill a child as a chicken.'
13. Cust, at a speech on behalf of the Church Missionary Society in Balliol College Oxford, 1895 (Beidelman 1982 pp.51–2). Similarly, at a public meeting in London, 1829, a Col Phipps referred to the BMS efforts in Puri in the wake of the British conquest of Orissa: 'Thus the planting of the standard of England in....the district of Cuttack, was followed, in the providence of God, by the lifting up of the cross.' (Peggs 1846 p.158)

14 *GBMS Report* 1860 p.60: Goadby affirmed that Angul's tribute had increased 20 times within five years of annexation, and 'While staying here I heard that the late Raja had 900 concubines!' As a Christian missionary, Peggs cannot actually approve of the war and 'looks forward to peace', but makes clear a reliance on the Government to enforce peace so that the Mission can go in (1846 p.196).

15. Some came to the missionaries' services in the 1820s (above pp.190–1), and the elder Goadby called the Judge of Cuttack and his wife 'truly the friends of religion' for their patronage in the 1830s (Peggs 1846 p.238). By the 1900s, it was normal for missionaries who came to Russellkonda for their quarterly meetings to be the Government Agent's guests. On one occasion, 'An English service was held in the bungalow of the agent of Government for the hill tracts (J.S. Maloney, I.C.S.), for the benefit of the European residents, but a number of Indian officers also attended.... The Tahsildar, a Hindu gentleman, was particularly struck with the fact that we Europeans gathered from all quarters were all equally well acquainted with the hymns.' (*BMS Report* 1903 p.31)

16. Goadby reported from a tour in 1860: 'We had received an invitation to spend a few days with a pious officer of the 43rd Madras Native Infantry. Major Y---was brought to a knowledge of the truth by Captain M---, a European officer baptised by Mr Stubbins twenty years ago.... We were pleased to learn that he regularly conducted a prayer meeting in the regiment and that he had been successful both here and elsewhere in leading sinners to Christ.' (*GBMS Report* 1860 p.22)

17. From Macpherson's letter to GOI explaining the whole affair, 9th Feb.1846. These letters are listed as GOI Home, Public, 14th March 1846 Nos.33–7, and have not, I think, been published in any form before. A famous parallel case occurred at a higher level in 1859, when the Governor-General rebuked the Lieutenant-Governor of Punjab for allowing the Commissioner of Amritsar to attend a missionary baptism. But the Mutiny had changed the climate of opinion about missionaries, and this time the Lieutenant-Governor answered back and justified his subordinate's action. (Neill 1966 p.99).

18. Peggs 1846 p.241. Miss Kirkman married Isaac Stubbins shortly after his first wife died, and worked with him in the Mission until 1865.
19. Pearce Carey chapter VII. The inscription read:

    '-ris, daughter of Mrs Millman
    1914'

    Most surviving tombstones belong to soldiers and administrators of the years after the Agency.
20. Letter to Miss Bowse of 29th October 1935, in Evans' file in the BMS archives.
21. Peggs 1846 p.245, describing the ordination of one of the first missionaries to go to Orissa, just before he left in 1838.
22. The Anabaptist movement got under way with the circulation of a document called the Anabaptist Confession of Schleitheim in 1527. But Anabaptists were widely regarded as extremists, partly in memory of the violent Anabaptist regime that arose in Munster in 1533–5. In Britain as elsewhere in Europe, 'the name Anabaptist was applied loosely and widely as a term of abuse. It covered a multitude of different opinions.... The outside world eyed Anabaptists with horror.'(Chadwick 1964 p.189) For this reason, some Baptists dissociate their origins from the Anabaptists, and consider that their sect arose independently out of the Congregational movement (A. Taylor 1818).
23. Potts 1967 p.59. The BMS view was set forth by William Carey's associate, Ward, who accompanied Bampton and Peggs to India, in *A Protestant's reasons why he will not be a papist*, Serampore 1802. According to Neill, 'the friendly toleration, which existed between the various Protestant [mission] agencies, was not in general extended to the Roman Catholics.'
24. For instance, Father Constant Lievens baptized 65,000 Mundas in the space of four years in the 1880s. The Catholic missionaries apparently told Konds that they were 'not bidden' to distribute the Gospels in Kui, which Baptist missionaries considered one of their main aims.

    Baptists did sometimes come into conflict with other Protestants in India, on account of their extreme strictness: 'The Baptists have never been easy neighbours for Christians of other communions.... [since, to Baptists,] only those who have been baptized by immersion on profession of faith may be admitted to the Lord's Supper.' (Neill 1984 p.209) From the other side, some Anglicans expressed hostility to Baptists for excluding children who die young from salvation by not baptizing them at birth, the theme of an anonymous pamphlet published in 1850, *Reasons for not supporting the BMS, by a Paedo-Baptist* (i.e. by someone baptized in infancy, and therefore not a Baptist).

25. From *India and Indian Missions* by Alexander Duff, 1839, quoted by Sen Gupta 1971 p.179. Duff went to India from Scotland in 1830 as the first missionary of the General Assembly on Foreign Mission.

    But some of the strongest statements are in the early Baptist literature by Carey and others (note 1.), notably Ward in his pamphlet *An account of writings, religion, and manners of the Hindoos, with translations* in two volumes, 1811: 'Suffice it to say, that fidelity to marriage vows is almost unknown among the Hindoos; the intercourse of the sexes approaches very near to that of irrational animals.' (Sen Gupta 1971 p.67)

    Katherine Mayo's *Mother India* (New York 1927) is a book in the same genre that was very influential and aroused strong reactions, propagating a similar negative stereotype of Hindu women as essentially unchaste, and sexual excess as an essential part of Hindu family life. Though full of missionary zeal, it is a secular piece of journalism, and fastens on the issues of public health and the position of women, in a clear development from missionary discourse. Veena Das has drawn my attention to this subject.

26. These topics figure large in Peggs' two books, whose engravings include infanticide, suttee, and several illustrations of the 'iniquities of Juggernaut' as well as 'infanticide among the Khunds in Goomsur'. Later, in the 1870s, the Government considered preventing the Jagannath festival to combat the spread of cholera. Yet Hunter wrote scathingly of the 'piety of missionaries' who greatly exaggerated the extent of these infamous immolations.

    The *GBMS Report* for 1873 answered him by admitting there had been some exaggeration, but quoting eye-witness accounts by missionaries from the 1820s and Buchanan in 1806, who recorded the following entry in his diary: 'I have returned home from witnessing a scene which I shall never forget.... The characteristics of Moloch's worship are obscenity and blood.... After the tower had proceeded some way, a pilgrim announced that he was ready to offer himself a sacrifice to the idol. He laid himself down in the road before the tower as it was moving along, lying on his face with his arms stretched forward; the multitude passed round him, leaving the space clear, and he was crushed to death by the wheels of the tower. A shout of joy was raised to the god; he is said to *smile* when the libation of blood is made.' The missionary writer concluded: 'We hope that none of our readers will be so deluded as to suppose that the benevolent teaching of Chaitanya or "the gentle doctrines of Jaggernath," have occasioned the suppression of these revolting sacrifices. No mistake could be greater. The Ethiopian has not changed his skin, nor the leopard his spots. No more have the priests of the ugly god become patterns of meekness and mildness. It is British authority, and that alone, that keeps these evil-doers in check. We deeply regret the tone of Dr. Hunter's references to idolatry.... there is no fact in the history of the world better established than that idolatry has everywhere and always been the parent of pollution, selfishness, cruelty, and blood.'(*GBMS Report* 1873 pp.31–4)

27. A Miss Harriet Leigh, quoting an unnamed earlier source, *BMS Centenary Celebrations* 1892–3 p.400.
28. Peggs' final chapter in *India's cries to British humanity* (1830) is on this topic, as well as an article in the *Calcutta Christian Observer* for 1840 on how to missionize the hill tribes.
29. Innes 1895 pp.4 & 7. William Carey's parting words to Andrew Fuller, the first secretary of the BMS, were often repeated: 'I will venture to go down, but remember that you must hold the ropes.'(Myers 1892 p.8) The society was headed by a secretary, who met with a central committee of 25 once a month in London. A general committee of 80 met once a year. Subscriptions were collected by county.
30. 'Khond mothers object to their boys being taught Oriya, and would, I was assured, make them come to school if they were taught in their own language. I had several Khond school books with me prepared by the late lamented and gifted linguist Captain Frye. On my reading a fable or two to the boys, they laughed and grinned with delight, remarking that they could understand these books,

while the Oriya fables they could not understand even after they had got them all by heart.' (*GBMS Report* 1865 p.21)

31. The titles of books printed in Oriya by the Orissa Mission in the 1830s–60s include others entitled *Dawn of Knowledge, Baxter's call to the unconverted, Alleine's alarm, Jewel mine of salvation* and a *Moral Class Book*, as well as the Bible. The Religious Tract Society gave annual grants of paper for these tracts, which were distributed in their thousands. In the report for 1891, the missionaries described a 'Hindu Oriya tract attacking Christianity' that had appeared: it was a 'scurrilous' piece, but evidence of the progress Christianity was making against Hinduism.
32. Vivian Meik in *The People of the leaves*, London 1931 p.193. This book was written after a short visit, and presents an extremely distorted view of the Juang (Elwin 1948 p.11). The author mentions that she was stationed at Sambalpur, but not with which Mission.
33. The hospital was just taking off as Pearce Carey published his book. Medical work was slow in starting, in spite of repeated appeals for a medical missionary. Dr Fletcher Moorshead, a senior BMS administrator in London, campaigned for a Medical Mission to the Konds after visiting Arthur Long in 1906. 'With more mystery than mercy' the project was not fulfilled within his lifetime (Pearce Carey p.113). A Dr Craig and his wife hardly began before they got malaria and left India for good. The Moorshead Memorial Hospital was finally opened at the Udayagiri Mission in 1935, with the arrival of Dr Wilkins, a descendant of Pike, who founded the GBMS. Dr Stanley Thomas joined him in 1938, but went to serve with Konds in the army during the War. Several missionary nurses came to the hospital in the 1930s and 1940s, who gradually trained several Kond women as nurses. From the 1930s a considerable proportion of the male missionaries were doctors, and a considerable proportion of female missionaries were nurses.
34. 'Despite the fear attached to these violent deaths, two positive and helpful elements in daily living result from awareness of constant contact with the more settled members of the family ancestors. They "keep one in community" and they underline the conviction that one's personality will not be destroyed at death. Nevertheless,

the desire to remain in right relationship with them is of a limited kind. It arises more from fear of giving offence and from the need to placate than from the desire to be in deeper communion for its own sake.... it is not essentially personal. Also it is centred on well-being in *this* life.... Again this raises the question for the Kui Church, founded as it is on the approach to the individual so stressed by Nonconformist-Evangelical tradition: Is Christianity confronting the whole man in the wholeness of his community-understanding?' (Boal 1973 pp.180–1)

35. A powerful example from the Reformation is the law passed in 16th century England, in association with the first official prayer book in English (1549), that a priest must put the wafer directly into each communicant's mouth, to avert the risk of its use in sacrilegious acts, such as witchcraft. This was part of a long process of king and state establishing a monopoly over the religious life of every individual through the priesthood of the Anglican Church. Keith Thomas (1973 pp.38–9) cites this as an example of survival of superstition in the Church. To me it seems more to represent an example of the state's increasing power and control over the individual during the Reformation: symbolically, the king's priests were placing the host into the mouth of everyone in the kingdom. In the missionary case, the monopoly is of a similar nature, except that it works through the rules of Mission Societies like the BMS, and the Church Councils these have established.
36. Survival International's *Urgent Action Bulletin on Paraguay*, 1st Feb. 1987. The New Tribes Mission is based in Florida. Its missionaries are fundamentalist, evangelical, born-again Christians, whose aim is to convert all remaining tribal peoples to Christianity.
37. Frank Waters, on Hopi children who were taken by force to schools far from their Indian families, whom they were not allowed to see for four years (1963 pp.293–4).
38. John Fire/Lame Deer 1980 [1972] pp.33–7.
39. Dee Brown 1971 p.252. Black Elk, one of the last great Lakota medicine-men of the old order, became a Catholic catechist, and transmitted his vision to posterity after he was supposedly a Christian, living a life that expressed a strict renunciation of the old religion (Niehardt 1961).

Chapter Seven. Merchants of Knowledge…

1. Among the best and most human anthropology of tribal India I would particularly recommend W.G. Archer's work on the Santal, *The hill of flutes* (1974), and Piers Vitebsky's *Dialogues with the dead* (1993). Elwin's work is relatively unsystematic, as Vitebsky points out, but in its human aliveness it gives a much more accurate picture of tribal cultures than most seemingly 'objective' anthropology does.
2. Said's classic, *Orientalism* (1978), examines under this concept the domination of non-western cultures by Western (or Western-style) scholar-specialists who create a way of 'knowing' other cultures that has superior status and tends to denigrate or discount those cultures' own forms of knowledge.
3. This is evident in such works as Talal Asad's *Anthropology and the colonial encounter* (1973), the journal *Critique of anthropology*, as well as the other works cited in Ch.1 note 59.
4. For instance, Tylor, MacLennon and Frazer drew on Macpherson's and Frye's Kond ethnography for their larger theoretical works. Ethnology, 'culture science', also refers to an abstract and comparative level of analysis. When I speak of the role of the anthropologist I am therefore grouping all of these other '-ologies', as well as physical anthropology, with social anthropology.
5. John Fire/Lame Deer (1972/1980) p.150.
6. Articles by Taylor and Maxwell in *MJLS* for July 1837 and January 1838.
7. I.e. human sacrifice in Fiji and its vicinity, on which see e.g. James Morris 1973/1979 pp.361–7.
8. Apparently not the same as the John Campbell who was later to become the Kond Agent, who was a Captain at this time and played a major role in the wars, as described in Ch.2.
9. Lt Kittoe's journal of his survey of a road through the Kond country, published in the *JASB* in 1839, may be considered as part of this early series of published writings on the Konds. It is more geographical than ethnographic. Its main argument is a call for the extension of British rule.
10. S.C. Macpherson 1842—one of the best early ethnographies of a tribe in India, comparable with D.C. Graham's monograph on the Bhils (1843) and a few earlier writings on the Paharia and Munda.

11. The first was published prematurely, without his permission—he had sent it to a relative in Britain while recuperating in South Africa—the Kond Earth Goddess is here referred to as 'the earth god'. The second article is considerably longer (60 pages instead of 20); he submitted it during his leave in Britain after the end of his Kond adventures.
12. 'Now, our leading objects with respect to these tribes are, I conceive, necessarily these—1st, as a matter of policy to induce their acknowledgement of our supremacy, and to establish relations with them as subjects which shall supersede their exclusive relations with the zeminderies as allies—2ndly, with reference to their religion, to effect the abolition of the rite of human sacrifice; and it is plain that the first condition of the accomplishment of these objects is peace.' (WM p.82) Macpherson's superiors left this point highly ambiguous as we have seen (above pp.52–4, 64, 72–3).
13. Especially Elwin 1955 and Vitebsky 1993 on Sora religion, but also Elwin's fieldwork notes and Niggemeyer (1964) on the Konds.
14. '...in the attempt to present in exact language and systematic form, a body of traditional ideas, I fear I have, perhaps unavoidably, imported to the subject an appearance of completeness and consistency that does not strictly belong to it.' (1852 p.273) It is true that this classification is highly alien to Kond ideas and destroys the *feeling* of their religion.
15. First Temple's *Gazetteer of the Central Provinces* (1867) and Carmichael's *Manual of Vizagapatam district* (1869), followed by Maltby's *Manual of Ganjam district* (1882), Cobden-Ramsey's *Gazetteer of the Orissa Feudatory Estates* (1910), O'Malley's of *Angul district* (1911), of which Ollenbach wrote the main part, and later volumes on the same Districts (starting with Francis 1907).
16. The Census was incorporating the same ethnographic material in a more condensed form at intervals of ten years from 1871, as part of its aim of counting and defining the whole population of India for administrative purposes.
17. Hunter's *Annals of rural Bengal* (1872) concentrated on Orissa and included many pages on the Konds. His *Statistical account of Bengal* in over 20 volumes, incorporated the Konds in a volume on the Orissa Feudatory Estates (1877).

18. Also with extensive articles on the Konds are Thurston's volumes on South India (1909; cf. Thurston 1907 & 1912), and Russell and Hira Lal's on the Central Provinces (1916). Baines, the Census Commissioner in 1891, was one of the first to attempt a handbook of all the tribes and castes of India (1912).
19. On social evolutionism see particularly Sanderson 1990, as well as Stocking 1991 and Kuklick 1978 & 1991.
20. Campbell's unquestioned faith in mainstream theories of political economy etc. shows in his use of the word 'fact': he attributes the same 'savage' features to Kond society as were attributed to all other societies of the same 'rudimentary stage'. For example, his perception of Kond women was predetermined by the low status currently attributed to women in savage societies in general: 'Their wives are used as servants, and exercise no influence over their lords in any part of Khondistan that is known to me. The reverse has been asserted [by Macpherson], but is opposed to fact. In all my intercourse with the Khonds, I never saw or heard of a woman present or taking part in any deliberation or assembly.... She is here, as in many other barbarous nations, the drudge and the slave of man.'(Report of 17th March 1849) Campbell clearly failed to realize that, though Kond women do not take a formal part in councils, they often influence decisions decisively (e.g. above p.166). The idea that women have a low status among the Konds, or among the other tribal peoples of Central India, is contradicted by all detailed recent anthropology.
21. E.g. 'Among savage tribes the state of war is universal. At a more advanced stage [to which the Khonds belong] hostility is limited....by contracts' (above pp.54–5).
22. Caldwell (*Comparative Dravidian Grammar* 1875 pp.516–17) and Grierson (*Linguistic Survey of India* 1906 vol.IV pp.457–71) had published encyclopaedic linguistic studies similar to the grand ethnographies of Risley etc., which classified the Kond language in relation to all India's other languages.

The first Europeans to learn the Konds' language were Cadenhead and Frye. Frye apparently wrote a grammar (which I have not been able to trace). His Indian assistant in this linguistic research published another (Letchmajee 1902), and so did Macdonald Smith (1876), before Friend-Pereira (1909). The first grammars of the southern Konds' language were those of Schulze (1911) and Fitzgerald (1913).

23. See Morrison (1984) on the similar range of social theorists referred to by Ibbetson in his ethnographic writings on Punjab. Richard Temple (like Campbell) wrote without referring to other theorists, but was clearly influenced by current social theory such as Maine's.
24. This is from the long essay 'Caste in relation to marriage' that introduces Risley's volumes, where he surveys current theoretical trends in anthropology. In the article on the Konds (vol.III pp.397–414), he begins with an account of villages, *gochis* or clans, and *klambus* or sub-septs; goes on to brideprice and childbirth, religion (where he comments on Macpherson's attribution to them, wrongly he thought, of 'a very advanced religion') and human sacrifice (concentrating on Campbell's account of it), before dealing with death, witchcraft and ordeals to discover witches, clothes, hair and tattooing, agriculture, and headmen, ending with a list of kinship terms.
25. Duff's reference to civilization at the time of Noah, cited above pp.212–3.
26. On racist ideology see above p.213. In Britain the theory of innate difference in racial capabilities was being developed by Hunt and Robert Knox (Lienhardt 1964 p.7, Bolt 1984). But it also connects with the theory of a deep cultural as well as racial divide between Hindus and 'aboriginal' or 'wild tribes', which was first expressed as a specific theory by Lt-Gen Briggs (1852). The administrator-anthropologists' use of the word *race* does not necessarily have the connotation of fixed innate mental capacity that Hunt and Knox attributed to differences between races—the theory we call racism. Nevertheless, an intrinsic inferiority or degeneracy is often implied. There does seem to be a real conflict with evolutionism here. It rarely surfaces in the ethnographic literature, though it was much debated by anthropologists in Britain.
27. E.g. Risley's statement that 'it is scarcely a paradox to lay down as a law of the caste system of Eastern India that a man's social status varies in inverse ratio to the width of his nose' (1891 p.xxxiv).
28. This belief that to be counted is inauspicious is widespread in many cultures, including ancient Roman civilization. The Latin poet

Catullus provides an example in a lighter vein in one of his most famous poems, which is based on the idea that in order to avoid the danger that someone will count the kisses he exchanges with his beloved and use that information to cast an evil spell on them, they should exchange an uncountable number of kisses:

Da mi basia mille, deinde centum,
Dein' mill' altera, dein' secunda centum....
'Give me a thousand kisses, then a hundred,
Then another thousand, then a second hundred....'

29. Lt-Col Marshall had already written *A phrenologist among the Todas* (1873), which contains measurements of Todas' heads and bodies, and photographs of their profiles. Marshall declares their former practice of female infanticide 'the crime of weak races, of Dolichocephali' (1873 p.190). The Hungarian anthropologist Von Ujfalvy was the first to practise 'anthropometry' in India (K. Sharma 1979 p.9).
30. E.g. Uma Guha et al. did fieldwork among the small Didayi (or Gataq) tribe when it was clear that much of it was going to be displaced by the Machkund dam in south Koraput District (1968).
31. Vidyarthi 1978, Sinha 1991. The colonial anthropologists mentioned were also instrumental in encouraging S.C. Roy, 'the father of Indian anthropology', to develop his interest in tribal culture while practising as a lawyer in Ranchi, where he acted on behalf of *adivasis* in legal disputes. Roy's first monograph, *The Mundas and their country* (1912) is unusual for its detail on a tribe's history—precolonial, as well as under British rule—and the impact of missionaries, which he saw as beneficial.
32. Essays by Shiv Visvanathan in Nandy ed. 1990 document this connection: 'The concentration camp was an industrial research laboratory organized completely by doctors and scientists' (p.269); the US authorities set up laboratories in Japan to study the effects of the atom bomb they had dropped (pp.135–7), and since the war, have carried out a cynical study of Pacific Islanders who were exposed to radiation from nuclear tests, as well as medical studies on unsuspecting subjects within the US, as journalists and others have documented.
33. E.g. on tribal peoples in Malaya and the Philippines, Signe Howell's *Society and Cosmos* (1984) and Thomas Gibson's *Sacrifice and*

sharing in the Philippines highlands (1986); Colin Turnbull's *The forest people* (1961/1976) on the Mbuti in Zaire; and Elwin's *The Muria and their ghotul* (1947), W.G. Archer's *The hill of flutes* (1974), and Piers Vitebsky's *Dialogues with the dead* (1993) on tribal peoples of Central India.

34. E.g. as outstanding recent examples of the anthropological analysis of tribal peoples' conceptual world: Michelle Rosaldo's *Knowledge and passion* (1980), Signe Howell (1984) and Piers Vitebsky (1993). An appreciation of tribal knowledge is the theme of *Wisdom of the elders: Honoring sacred native visions of nature* by Suzuki and Knudtson (1992).
35. Jean Liedloff: *The Continuum Concept* (1986); Ivan Illich: *Deschooling society* (1973).

Chapter Eight. In the Name of Development

1. Fürer-Haimendorf (1982) touches on the cycle of exploitation, as did Grigson in *The challenge of backwardness* (1947). A paper which Piers Vitebsky presented to the NISTADS conference on environmental history in 1992 (mentioned in Ch.1 note 58) shows in more detail how institutionalized extortion and the related state of chronic indebtedness have forced Soras into the position of constantly having to create a large surplus which outsiders 'milk' them of, resulting in the deforestation of their hills.
2. This plan for a European colonization of the remote, forest areas where tribal people live 'to make them more productive' was widely talked about in the 1840s–50s, and is expressed in many books and articles, e.g. the last section of Peggs' *India's cries to British humanity* (1832).
3. Apart from the examples of the World Bank and multinational companies' involvement in industrial development cited below pp.307–9, the British Government's involvement in the Singrauli industrial complex (a series of power stations and mines associated with the Rihand dam in southeast Uttar Pradesh) is particularly significant. *In the name of progress: the underside of foreign aid* (Adams and Solomon 1985) explores the connection between Western countries' 'aid' to third world countries and the vested interests that lie behind it, through an examination of the *myths of*

foreign aid: the beliefs behind Western attempts to 'develop' the third world which intermesh with beliefs about 'development' in countries such as India.

4. I.e. the genocidal treatment of Karens in Burma, of the Chakmas and Garos in Bangladesh, of the East Timorese by the Indonesian army, and of the Nuba peoples in Central Sudan.
5. NB: Rabindra Ray's study of the Naxalites' ideology (1988). For a more open intolerance of tribal cultures by Marxist rebels, one can cite the pressure which Sendero Luminoso has brought to bear on Indians in the Peruvian Amazon, which includes massacring those who do not join them.
6. Above pp.185–6, 198–9, 227–8. A.D. Nock (1933) traces the history of the idea of religious conversion and the accompanying claim that a particular religion is the only true one or the only way to salvation: an idea integral to much of official Christianity, but which is also to be found in the *Old Testament*. Moses' massacre of 3,000 of his people for making the golden calf (*Exodus* 32) initiated a kind of religion that, in its intolerance and exclusiveness, was quite new in the history of the world.
7. NB: Ivan Illich *Deschooling society* (1973). Many schools in India (as well as the West) still follow a concept of education as a more or less blind learning of 'facts'—'facts' that no longer appear as certain as they once did. A much broader vision of education as learning to think for oneself and to base one's life on the principles of a larger awareness than the competitive view of success which many schools embody, are to be found in the alternative school systems founded on the thinking of Krishnamurti and Rudolf Steiner.
8. On 'applied anthropology' Sengupta cites H.G. Barnett (*Anthropology in Administration*, Illinois 1956), G. Dalton (*Economic Anthropology and Development*, New York 1971), and an article by Lucy Mair (in the *International Encyclopaedia of the social sciences* 1968 pp.326–30).
9. Esteva's article in *The development dictionary* (1992) is part of a large discourse that offers a critique of the concept of 'development': e.g. Ivan Illich *Toward a history of needs*, R. Nisbet *A history of the idea of progress* (1980) and Glynn Roberts *Questioning development* (1984).

10. *Sardar Sarovar: The report of the independent review* (Morse & Berger 1992) is the most detailed study of the social and environmental impact of a large dam in India, and makes clear its destructiveness on many levels.
11. Quoted in the Indian Press, October 1988.
12. Russell Means 1982:' We are resisting being turned into a National Sacrifice Area. We are resisting being turned into a national sacrifice people. The cost of this industrial process in not acceptable to us. It is genocide to dig uranium here [South Dakotal] and drain the water table no more, no less.'
13. From Alan Ereira, *The heart of the world* 1990 p. 113.

Chapter Nine. Questioning the Sacrifice: A Postscript

1. *Alora* was apparently not published during Gopinath's life. *Samadrusti* has published it (2007), but there is currently no translation of it.
2. 'Tribals plan to stop Vedanta vehicles,' in *The Hindu* 12.1.2009 p.8.
3. The Upper Indravati reservoir is covered in chapter 4 of *Out of This Earth* and is the main subject of Subrata Sahu's 2009 documentary film *DAM-aged.* Subrat interviewed a man who was the sole survivor of a team of about 20 people who were working at the tunnel mouth at the time of the accident.
4. PUDR 2006, Padel 2007. See also Nandini Sundar's powerful Afterword to the new edition of her book on Bastar (2007).
5. 'Flooding us out with money' was a phrase which a tribal elder used talking to me and Samarendra Das, about the company's actions. This and the children's song are quoted in chapter 6 of our forthcoming book, *Out of This Earth.*
6. Moody 2007a p.127. This is the area where Utah, Colorado, Arizona and New Mexico meet.
7. Gopinath Mohanty *Sroto Swati,* 2000 (his autobiography), Part III p.324.
8. This subject is also explored in my essay 'Mining Projects & Cultural Genocide: Colonial Roots of Present Conflicts' in a forthcoming book edited by Biswamoy Pati, *Adivasis in Colonial India.*

9. The fuller picture is explored in the two 2008 essays by Padel & Das in the bibliography.
10. A piece on the CPI-ML website (Communist Party of India—Marxist-Leninist) dated July 2007, gives the following figures: 317 mining leases granted during 1980-97 surrendered 34,527 hectares of forest, as against 881 mining leases granted for 60,476 hectares of forest during 1997–2005—a nearly fourfold increase (www.cpiml.org/liberation/year_2007/July/mining_policy). In chapter 7 of *Out of This Earth* we discuss the New Mineral Policy and show the influence of Rio Tinto, etc.
11. Vedanta's infringements of law are covered in chapters 6–7 of *Out of This Earth*, and in many other publications such as Nostromo 2005 and Moody 2007b, while Surya Dash has made a film (2008).
12. N.R. Patnaik 1992, and P.K. Pattanaik 2006 on the story of Rindo Majhi.
13. The National Minorities Commission made two reports in January 2008, one by Dr John Dayal, who visited Kandhamal twice between 29 Dec and 3 Jan (released 5th Jan), the other by Zoya Hasan and Dileep Padgaonkar, based on a visit of 6–8 Jan (available at http://ncm.nic.in/pdf/orissa%20report.pdf, consulted January 2009). Saraswati's incendiary language is described in section 1.26 of Dayal's report. NB articles by Kanungo and Pradhan & Padhi in *Economic and Political Weekly*.
14. E.g., in the villages of Brahminigaon and Gadapur, 1.6 in Dayal's report.
15. 1.20 in Dayal's report, p.2 in Hasan & Padgaonkar's report, and an article showing the continuation of this dispute a year later in *The Hindu* on 12.1.09 p.8, 'Kui Samaj opposes TAC suggestion': 'Leaders of the Kui Samaj of Kandhamal district are not satisfied with the way in which the Tribal Advisory Council has suggested addition of the term "Kandha" with "Kui" in the Scheduled Tribes list.' Chapter 6 of this book show instances where missionaries blurred the Kond-Dom distinction and called Dom converts Konds (e.g., pp.231-2).
16. The National Minorities Commission report, based on a visit on 11–13 September 2008, is available at http://kuidina.blogspot.com/2008/10/national-commission-for-minorities-full.html.

A report by the CPI-ML estimated deaths at over 500 (*India Today* 5.11.08).

17. http://pbaptist.wordpress.com/2008/09/17/india-violence-spreads-to-five-more-states/ citing local news reports.
18. *Tehelka* devoted an issue (3.11.07) to exposing precisely how the killing of Muslims was orchestrated in Gujarat after Hindu activists had been burnt at Godhra. The comparison between what happened in Gujarat in 2002 and Orissa in 2008 was widespread, and is brought out, for example, in an interview with Naveen Patnaik by Karan Thapar at http://cpiarticles.blogspot.com/2008/10/devil-advocate-interview-of-naveen.html
19. E.g., *Sambad* 11th July 2008.
20. *The Hindu* 12.7.08 (http://www.hinduonnet.com/businessline/blnus/27121906.htm). The mountains in question have various names. This article calls them the Ushabali plateau.
21. January 2009: 'Rail link may pacify situation in Kandhamal,' at http://hotnhitnews.com/Rail_Link_may_pacify_situation_in_Kandhamal_JVM_001_09008.htm
22. *Indian Express* 30 Oct 2008: 'Taking a leaf out of the much-criticized Salwa Judum campaign of neighbouring Chhattisgarh, the Orissa Government would start a similar scheme of deploying 2,000 armed tribal youths as special police officers in five Maoist-infested districts to fight the Naxals.'
23. Complaint Petition by Tribal Welfare Society, Bilaspur, before the National Commission for STs, GoI, in Delhi.
24. Samarendra Das has drawn my attention to the long-term protection which Ollenbach assured for forest in Kandhamal district, and the existence of extensive research on this subject. The history of forestry in Orissa, and the special circumstances which preserved Kandhamal's forests so well is the subject of a doctoral dissertation by V.P. Singh in the University of British Columbia, Canada.
25. From interviews in the documentary *Matiro Poko, Company Loko (Earth Worm, Company Man)* by Amarendra & Samarendra Das, 2005 (available from sdasorisa@rediffmail.com), reproduced in our forthcoming book *Out of This Earth*.
26. Mathur ed. 2006 p.2, David Pearce quoted by Cernea in Mathur ed. 2006 p.22.
27. On this debate, see Archana Prasad (2003), and Ram Guha (1999)—a debate little if at all informed by tribal people's perceptions.

While she is polemical against one strand of colonial discourse about tribal people, there seems a real danger that Prasad's work contributes to hardening the negative colonial stereotypes about them, which have had a massive, pernicious influence in India, and worldwide (Meek 1976). Her work reinforces these negative stereotypes among those on the Left.

28. A.K. Ganugo: 'Ethnic healers among the Dongria Kondhs of Orissa,' in *Adivasi* 2007, vol.47 p.139.
29. Above p.97, where Macpherson wrote that he was being 'my own General Wade', following the example of the roads which Wade built to conquer the Scottish Highlands. The Romans built roads in Britain and throughout their empire to facilitate conquest and the extraction of resources.
30. The CEC report of September 2005 warned that Vedanta's refinery was being built right next to the Bansadhara and was bound to pollute it, and indeed, within a few weeks of starting up, this had happened. The Orissa State Pollution Control Board (OSPCB) regional office at Rayagada wrote a strong letter to Vedanta at Lanjigarh on 23.11.07 (the very day the SC passed judgement, effectively clearing Niyamgiri for mining) pointing out a number of serious deficiencies in the refinery's pollution control measures, based on a site visit of 3th–4th November. Residue from the red mud lake was seeping continuously into the Bansadhara river, the lake's lining was leaking, the slurry mix was too alkaline, and boiler no.3 was leaking noxious gases and should be stopped. A subsequent site visit on 29th–30th January 2008 revealed non-compliance with these orders: the slurry was still too alkaline, the red mud lake lining was eroded and still leaking. Also, a storm water drain within the refinery compound, near the railway crossing, was diverting polluted waste slurry to the clean water pond, from where it was discharging into the Bansadhara. Long before this, and repeatedly since, residents of Chatrapur and other villagers have attested that the refinery regularly discharges highly toxic chemicals into the river. On 9.9.08 they sent a letter to the OSPCB about this. Many people and animals have developed body sores after bathing in the river, and at least two people have died, covered in sores. Meanwhile, residents of Bondhaguda and other villages close to the refinery and approach road are suffering from lung diseases due to air pollution (Mishra 2008).

31. To summarize the reports commissioned by the Supreme Court, in a case lasting from 2004–8: the Central Empowered Committee (CEC) made two reports, the second of which, submitted in September 2005, was a long and thorough examination of the evidence, concluding that Niyamgiri should not be mined, and construction of the Lanjigarh refinery should be stopped. To circumvent this report, more studies were commissioned from the Wildlife Institute of India (WII) and the Central Mining Planning & Design Institute (CMPDI). The WII report of mid-2006 (available on the website of the Environment Protection Group of Orissa, freewebs.com/epgorissa) also strongly opposed mining, while the CMPDI advocated it—not surprising from an institution designed to serve the mining industry. The WII, based in Dehra Dun, was forced to add notes which accommodated the pro-mining view, without changing the substance of their earlier argument. After this, a Note on Bauxite Mining in Koraput & Kalahandi districts was commissioned from the Ministry of Environment and Forests, which is full of distortions and concluded that mining would not harm the environment.
32. The Paschim Orissa Krishak Sangathan Samanbaya Samiti (W.Orissa farmers' organization) has held several huge demonstrations at Hirakud since 2006. One of their main Oriya publications, in Feb. 2008, is *Chashiro Rekha* [*Farmers' Line*]. Sambalpur: POKSSS.
33. Ritthoff, Rohn & Liedtke 2002.
34. Anil Agarwal's main company was Sterlite Industries India Ltd. until December 2003, when he registered Vedanta Resources plc on the London Stock Exchange, to gain finance for his Orissa and Chhattisgarh projects. This company's annual reports from 2006 include a Sustainability Report: *Creating Value 2006, World Class Resources + Accelerating Growth = Delivering Value 2007,* and *Enduring Value through Values 2008*. In this year the Sustainable Development Report was released separately. The company's PR campaign is analyzed more fully in chapter 19 of *Out of This Earth.*
35. Moody 2007a.
36. Dewey Anderson, 1951: *Aluminum for Defence and Prosperity.* Washington: US Public Affairs Institute. This text sold for just 50 cents, but no copy was available in a British library and it had to be ordered from America!

Glossary

Adivasi	Aboriginal, tribal (noun and adjective)
Anna	A sixteenth of a rupee
Begar	A Labourer forced into service by government Coolie officials (as coolie, constructing roads etc.)
Bissoi	Oriya chief (of a *mutah* or other unit)
Brahmin	The Hindu priestly caste at the top of the caste system
Chaprassi	Government messenger or servant
Coolie	Baggage carrier or labourer
Cutcherry	Office, a senior official's headquarters or 'establishment'
Dalit	The modern, politically correct term for untouchable, Harijan, SC, Pano, Dom
Dassehra	Hindu festival associated with kingship
Dewan	Minister of a Hindu kingdom
Dhobi	Washerman
Dom or Pano	An 'untouchable' caste of weavers/traders who live among Konds
Duffadar	Indian officer with the rank of sergeant
Dulbehra	A particular kind of chief in the Kond area
Feringhee	Indian word for foreigner or Englishman
gherao	surround, demonstrate

Gomastah	An Indian serving as a Government Agent (at a Hindu court etc.)
Haldi	Turmeric (Hindi)
Havildar	Indian officer with the rank of sergeant
Huzzoor	'Your Honour', 'Sir', 'Excellency'
Izzat	Honour
Jani	Kond priest, or particularly a priest of the earth goddess
Jemadar	Indian officer senior to *duffadar* but below *subedar*
Khonro	Kond chief over a wide area
Kui, Kuvi	The northern/eastern and southern/western Kond languages and peoples
Lascar	Indian sailor or orderly
Mahal	Palace, i.e. kingdom
Mahua	The drink distilled from flowers of the *mahua* tree, *Bassia latifolia* or *Madhuca indica*
Maji	Headman or chief of a Kuvi or Kuttia Kond village
Maliah	Mountains (Hindi, Oriya)
Meriah	A person purchased or kept by Konds apparently for human sacrifice
Moliko	Kond headman or village chief (NB: Hindi *malik*, master)
Munshi	Indian scribe or secretary
Mutah	A territorial unit of allied villages
Naik	Indian officer with rank of corporal (below *duffadar*)
Oriya	The Hindu people of Orissa and their language
Paik	Foot-soldier, militia-man
Patro	Kond chief
Penu	Kond deity or spirit
Peon	Foot-soldier (whence 'pawn')
Poosiah	A female *meriah*, wife or mistress of a Kond
Pro raj	A royal official at the court of the *rajah* of Boad

Puja	Hindu word for ritual of worship or sacrifice
Rajah	Hindu king
Rani	Queen
Ryot	Cultivator
Sahukar, soucar,	Moneylender
Sanyasi	A holy man who has renounced social life
Sarkar, Sircar, Circar	Government
Sebundies	Militia of irregular troops
Sepoy	Indian regular troops under British command
Sirdar	Chief
Subedar	Highest rank of Indian officer, commanding acompany
Sundi	Distiller caste in Kond area
Tahsildar	Government head of *tahsil* (administrative unitof a District) in charge of revenue
Taluq	Administrative unit of District similar to *tahsil*
That rajah	A subordinate *rajah*
Thugs	A sect of Kali devotees who murdered and robbed travellers, suppressed in the 1820s
Vakil, vakul	Attorney, lawyer, or Government legalrepresentative
Zemindar	Landlord or *rajah*

Bibliography

Published Works

Adams, Patricia & Lawrence Solomon 1985. *In the name of progress: The underside of foreign aid.* London: Earthscan publications.

Ahmed, M. 1961. *Census of India, vol.XII (Orissa),* Part I (Report), and Part VI (village monographs) no.3, *Lakhrish: A village of Kandhas.*

Ames, Michael 1992. *Cannibal tours and glass boxes: The anthropology of museums.* Vancouver: University of British Columbia Press.

Anon 1849. *The Khond Agency and the Calcutta Review, being a reply in refutation of the misrepresentations and distortions of facts contained in several articles on Khond affairs....in the Calcutta Review.* Madras: Athenaeum Press.

Anon. 1850. *Reasons for not supporting the BMS,* by a paedo-baptist. Norwich: Charles Muskett.

Anon. 1889. *The young soldier in India, his life and prospects,* by H.S. London: W.H. Alien.

Anon. 1942. *The BMS in India: 'Ye are my witness'.* Calcutta: Baptist Mission Press.

Archer, W.G. 1974. *The hill of flutes: Life, love and poetry in tribal India.* London: George Alien & Unwin.

Archer, W.G. & W.J. Culshaw 1945. The Santal rebellion. *MII* vol. 25 pp.218-39. Ranchi: Sudarshan Press.

Ardener, Shirleyed. 1975. *Perceiving women.* London: Malaby Press.

Arens, W. 1979. *The man-eating myth: Anthropology and anthropophagy.* New York: OUP.

Arnold, David 1982. Rebellious hillmen: The Gudem Rampa risings 1839–1924. In R.Guha ed. *Subaltern studies* vol.I. Delhi: OUP

Arnold, William 1854. *Oakfield, or Fellowship of the East.* Leicester University Press.

Asad, T. ed. 1973. *Anthropology and the colonial encounter.* London: Ithaca Press.

Bailey, F.G. 1957. *Caste and the economic frontier: A village in highland Orissa.* Manchester University Press.

——— 1960. *Tribe, Caste, and Nation: A study in political activity and political change in highland Orissa.* Manchester University Press.

——— 1961. 'Tribe' and 'caste' in India. *CIS* vol.5 pp.7-19.

Baines, Sir J.A. 1912. *Ethnography (tribes and castes).* Strasbourg: Karl J. Trübner.

Balagopal, K. 2008. 'The NHRC on Salwa Judum,' in *Economic & Political Weekly* vol.43 no.51, 20th Dec. pp.10–14.

Ballhatchet, K.A. 1957. *Social policy and social change in Western India, 1817–1830.* London: OUR London Oriental Studies Series vol.5.

——— 1979. *Race, sex, and class under the Raj: Imperial attitudes and policies and their critics 1793–1905.* Delhi: Vikas.

Berger, Peter L. & Thomas Luckmann 1971. The Social Construction of Reality: A Treatise in the Sociology of Knowledge. Penguin. [1966]

Banerjee, Sukumar 1968. *An ethnographic study of the Kuvi Kandha of Orissa.* Calcutta: ASI, monograph no.24.

Baptist Herald: The journal of the BMS. 1912 ff. London: BMS.

BMS. 1893. *Centenary celebration 1892–3.* London: BMS.

BMS Reports 1890–1950. London: Carey Press.

Barber, W.J. 1975. *British economic thought and India 1800–1858: A study in the history of development economics.* Oxford: Clarendon Press.

Barnes, J.A. 1977. *The ethics of inquiry in social science.* Delhi: OUP.

Barthes, Roland 1972 [1957]. *Mythologies.* London: Jonathan Cape.

——— 1977. Introduction to the structural analysis of narratives. *Image—Music—Text,* pp.79–124. New York: Wang & Co.

——— 1984 [1980]. *Camera Lucida.* London: Fontana.

Basham, A.L. 1971 [1954]. *The wonder that was India.* London: Fontana.

Bearce, George D. 1961. *British attitudes towards India 1784–1858.* Oxford: OUP

Beer, Gillian 1983. *Darwin's plots: Evolutionary narrative in Darwin, George Eliot, and I9th century fiction.* London: Routledge & Kegan Paul.

Behara, Dandapani 1984. *Freedom movement in the state of Ghumsar in Orissa 1836–1866.* Calcutta: Punthi Pasthak.

Beidelman, T.O. 1982. *Colonial evangelism: A socio-historical study of an East African mission at the grassroots.* Bloomington: University of Indiana Press.

Berger, Peter 1974. *Pyramids of sacrifice.* Harmondsworth: Penguin.

Berger, Peter L. & Thomas Luckmann 1971. *The Social Construction of Reality: A Treatise in the Sociology of Knowledge.* Penguin. [1966]

Berkhofer, R.F. 1965. *Salvation and the savage: An analysis of Protestant missions and American Indian response, 1787–1862.* New York: Athenaeum.

Berreman, Gerald D. 1981. *The politics of truth: Essays in politicalanthropology.* Delhi: South Asian Publishers.

Béteille, André 1987. 'The concept of tribe with special reference to India.' In *Archives Européenes de sociologie* vol.26 no.2 pp.297–318.

Bettelheim, Bruno 1986 [I960]. *The informed heart: A study of the psychological consequences of living under extreme fear and terror.* New York: Viking Penguin.

Boal, Barbara M. 1966. 'The Church in the Kond hills: An encounter with animism.' In Hayward, V.E.W. ed. *The Church as Christian community,* pp.223–50. London: Butterworth.

———1973. *Fire is easy: The tribal Christian and his traditional culture.* Manila: Christian Institute for ethnographic studies in Asia.

——— 1982. *The Konds: Human sacrifice and religious change.* War-minster: Aris and Phillips.

Bolt, G.C. 1984. 'Race and the Victorians.' In C.C. Eldridge ed. *British Imperialism in the 19th century,* London: Macmillan.

Bordieu, Pierre 1977. *Outline of a theory of practice,* tr. Richard Nice. Cambridge: CUP.

Bourdillon, M.F.C. & Meyer Fortes eds. 1980. *Sacrifice.* London & New York: Academic Press for the RAI.

Bradley, I. 1976. *The call to seriousness: The evangelical impact on the Victorians.* New York: Macmillan.

Briggs, Lt-Gen. 1852. 'Two lectures on the aboriginal races of India', *JRAS,* vol.XIII pp.275–309.

Brody, Hugh 1975. *The people's land: Whites and the Eastern Arctic.* Harmondsworth: Penguin.

Brown, Dee 1975 [1970]. *Bury my heart at wounded knee.* London: Pan.

Brown, W. 1837. 'Description of the Khunds or Khundas.' *Calcutta Christian Observer,* April pp.157–68, July pp.337–47.

Buckland, C.E. 1971. *Dictionary of Indian biography.* Varanasi: Indologi-cal Book House.

Burrow, J.W. 1969. *Evolution and Society: A study in Victorian social theory.* Cambridge: CUP.

Burrow, T.W. & S. Bhattacarya 1962–3. 'Notes on Kuvi, with a short vocabulary.' *Indo-Iranian Journal* vol.VI pp.231–89. The Hague: Mouton.

Calcutta Christian Observer [CCO]. Volumes for 1836–1844. Calcutta: Baptist Mission Press.

Campbell, Sir Duncan 1925. *Records of Clan Campbell in the EIC 1600–1858.* London: Longmans.

Campbell, George 1866. Speeches in *Proceedings of the Asiatic Society of Bengal* pp.71–2 & 87–91.

Campbell, Lt John 1837. 'Meteorological experiments made on the Goomsoor mountains.' *MJLS* vol.VI no.17 (Oct.) pp.295–9. Madras: Athenaeum Press.

Campbell, Maj.-Gen. John. 1861. *Narrative of the operations in the hill tracts of Orissa for the suppression of human sacrifice and infanticide.* London, for private circulation.

——— 1864. *A personal narrative of 13 years' service among the wild tribes of Khondistan, for the suppression of human sacrifice.* London.

Campbell, Joseph 1959. *The masks of God: Primitive mythology.* New York: Viking Penguin.

——— 1962. *The masks of God: Oriental mythology.* New York: Viking Penguin.

Carberry, F. ed. 1854. *History of the rise and progress of the operations for the suppression of human sacrifice and female infanticide in the hill tracts of Orissa.* Selections from the records of the GOI (Home Dep.) no.V. Calcutta: Bengal Military Orphan Press.

Carey, S. Pearce 1936. *Dawn on the Kond hills.* London: Carey Press.

Carmichael, D.F. 1869. *A manual of the district of Vizagapatam in the Presidency of Madras.* Madras: Asylum Press.

Castleden, Rodne 1989. *The Knossos labyrinth: A new view of the palace of Minos.* London: Routledge.

Centre for Science and Environment 2008 *Rich lands poor people: Is sustainable mining possible? State of India's Environment 6, a Citizen's report.* Delhi: CSE.

Cernea, Michael M. 2006. 'Resettlement management: Denying or confronting risks,' in Mathur ed. 2006.

Chattopadhyaya, K. 1978. *Tribalism in India.* Delhi: Vision Publishing House.

Chomsky, Noam & Edward Herman 1988. *Manufacturing Consent.* NY: Pantheon.

Clifford, James 1988. 'On ethnographic authority.' Ch.1 in *The predicament of culture.* Cambridge Massachusetts: Harvard University Press.

——— & George E. Marcus eds. 1986. *Writing culture: The poetics and politics of ethnography.* Berkeley: University of California Press.

Cobden-Ramsay, L.E.B. 1910. *Feudatory States of Orissa.* Bengal District Gazetteers no.XXI. Calcutta: Bengal Secretariat Book Depôt.

Cohen, S.P. 1971. *The Indian army: Its contribution to the development of a nation.* Berkeley: University of California Press.

Cohn, B.S. 1961. *The development and impact of British Administration in India: A bibliographic essay.* Delhi: Indian Institute of Public Administration.

——— 1972. *India: The social anthropology of a civilization.* New Jersey: Prentice Hall.

Currie, Bob 2000. *The politics of hunger: A study of democracy, governance and Kalahandi's poverty*. London: Macmillan.

Curtin, Philip D. 1965. *The image of Africa: British ideas and action 1780–1850.* London: Macmillan.

Dalton, E.T. 1855. 'Journal of a tour in the Abor country.' *Selections from the Records of the Bengal Government no.23. Papers relating to some frontier tribes on the North-East border of Assam,* pp.151–69. Calcutta: 'Calcutta Gazette' Office.

——— 1872. A *descriptive ethnology of Bengal.* Calcutta: Asiatic Society of Bengal, for the Government of Bengal.

Das, M.N. 1959. 'The suppression of the meriah system among the hill tribes of Orissa.' Ch. 10 in his *Studies in the economic and social development of modern India,* 1848–1856. Calcutta: Firma KLM.

Das, Veena 1983. 'The language of sacrifice.' *MAN* vol.18 pp.445–62. (Myers lecture, London 1982)

——— ed. 1992. *Mirrors of violence: Communities, riots and survivors in South Asia.* Delhi: OUP.

Davies, Nigel 1981. *Human sacrifice in history and today.* London: Macmillan.

Defoe, Daniel 1975 [1719]. *Robinson Crusoe,* ed. Michael Shinagel. New York: W.W. Norton & Co.

Diamond, Stanley 1974. *In search of the primitive: A critique of civilization.* New Brunswick: Transaction.

——— ed. 1980. *Anthropology: Ancestors and heirs.* The Hague: Mouton Publishers.

Dictionary of National Biography 1888. Entries on Sir John Campbell, Augustus Cleveland, Alexander Duff, Sir John Elphinstone, Samuel Charters Macpherson et al. London: Smith, Elder & Co.

Directory of the Diocese of Berhampur 1984. Berhampur: Bishop's House.

Duff, Alexander 1842. 'An analysis of Lt Macpherson's Report on the Khonds of Ganjam and Cuttack, Orissa.' *CCO,* October pp.567–90.

——— 1844. 'Female infanticide.' *CR* vol.II (May–August) pp.372–448.

——— 1846a. 'Goomsur; the late war there—the Khonds or Hill Tribes.' *CR* vol.VI (Jan.–March) pp.1–85.

——— 1846b. 'The first series of Government measures for the abolition of human sacrifice among the Khonds.' *CR* vol. VI (July–Sept.) pp.45–108.

——— 1847. 'Captain Macpherson and the Khonds of Orissa.' *CR* vol. VIII (July–Sept.) pp.1–51.

——— 1848. 'The Khonds—abolition of human sacrifice.' *CR* vol.X pp.273–341.

Dumont, Louis 1980 [1966]. *Homo Hierarchicus: The cnste system and its implications.* Revised English edition. University of Chicago Press.

——— & D.F. Pocock. 1959. 'Possession and priesthood.' *CIS* vol. III pp.55–74.

Edwards, Elizabeth 1992. *Anthropology and photography 1860–1920.* Newhaven & London: Yale University Press in association with the RAI.

Eisler, Riane 1987. *The chalice and the blade: Our history, our future.* San Francisco: Harper & Row.

Elias, Norbert 1978 [1939]. *The Civilizing Process, 1. A history of manners.* Oxford: Blackwell.

——— 1982 [1939]. *The Civilizing Process, 2. State formation and civilization.* Oxford: Blackwell.

Elwin, Verrier 1939. *The Baiga.* London: John Murray.

——— 1943a. *The Aboriginals.* Oxford: OUP, Pamphlets on Indian affairs no. 14.

——— 1943b. *Maria murder and suicide.* Bombay: OUP.

——— 1944. 'Notes on a Kondh tour.' *Mil* vol.24, pp.40–58.

——— 1947. *The Muria and their ghotul.* Bombay: OUP.

——— 1948. 'Notes on the Juang.' *Mil* vol.28 pp.7–146.

——— 1949. *Myths of Middle India.* Bombay: OUP.

——— 1950. *Bondo Highlander.* Bombay: OUP.

——— 1954. *Tribal myths of Orissa.* Bombay: OUP.

——— 1955. *The religion of an Indian tribe.* Bombay: OUP.

——— 1959. *India's North-East Frontier in the nineteenth century.* Bombay: OUP.

——— 1964. *The tribal world of Verrier Elwin: An autobiography.* London: OUP.

Ereira, Alan 1990. *The heart of the world.* London: Jonathan Cape.

Esteva, Gustavo 1992. 'Development', in Wolfgang Sachs ed. *The development dictionary: A guide to knowledge as power.* London: Zed books.

Eschmann, A. 1978. 'Hinduization of tribal deities in Orissa: The 'Sakta and 'Saiva typology.' Ch.4 in Eschmann et al. eds. *Cult of Jagannath....*

Eschmann, A., H. Kulke, & G.C. Tripathi eds. 1978. *The Cult of Jagannath and the regional tradition of Orissa.* The South Asia Institute, Delhi: Manohar.

Evans-Pritchard, E.E. 1940. *The Nuer.* Oxford: Clarendon.

——— 1949. *The Sanusi of Cyrenaica.* Oxford: Clarendon.

Fabian, Johannes 1983. *Time and the other: How anthropology makes its object.* University of Columbia Press.

Fawcett, F. 1901. The Dômbs of Jeypore, Vizagapatam District, Madras.' *MAN* vol.1 pp.34–8. London: RAI.

———— 1902. 'Note on the recent immigration of Khonds and other Central Indian tribes into the jungle-country of Assam.' *MAN* vol.II p.40.

Federation of Lutheran Christians in India 1931. *Yearbook of Evangelical Mission Societies and Churches in India.* Bezwada: Vani Press.

Fenelon, James 1998. *Culturicide, resistance and survival of the Lakota.* NY: Garland.

Ferreira, J. 1965. *Totemism in India.* London: OUP.

Fire, John (Lame Deer) and Richard Erdoes 1980 [1972]. *Lame Deer: Sioux medicine man.* London: Quartet books.

Firth, Raymond 1954. 'Social organisation and social change.' *JRAI* vol.84 pp.1–20.

Finkielkraut, Alain 1988 *The undoing of thought.* London: Claridge Press.

Fitzgerald, A.G. 1913. *Kuvinga bassa: The Khond language as spoken by the Parjas and kindred tribes of the Madras Presidency.* Calcutta: Catholic Orphan Press.

Forbes, Gordon S. 1885. *Wildlife in Canara and Ganjam.* London: Sonnenschein.

Forsyth, M. A. 1871. *The highlands of Central India: Notes on their forests and wild tribes, natural history and sports.* London: Chapman & Hall.

Fortes, Meyer & E.E. Evans-Pritchard eds. 1940. *African political systems.* London: OUP, for the International African Institute.

Foucault, Michel 1977. *Discipline and punish: The birth of the prison.* London: Alien Lane.

———— 1979. 'Truth and power: An interview with Michel Foucault', in *Critique of Anthropology* vols.13–14 pp.131–7.

———— 1982. 'Why study power: The question of the subject', in Dreyfus & Rabinow, *Michel Foucault: Beyond structuralism and her- meneutics.* Brighton: Harvester Press.

Francis, W. 1907. *Vizagapatam District Gazetteer.* Madras: Government Press.

Frazer, J.G. 1941 [1890]. *The Golden Bough: A study in magic and eligion,* abridged edition. London: Macmillan.

Fried, Morton H. 1975. *The notion of tribe.* Philippines.

Friend-of India. Weekly journal, 1835–76. Serampore.

Friend-Pereira, I.E. 1899. 'Some Khond songs.' *JASB,* LXVIII, III, pp.1–13. Calcutta: Bishop's College Press.

——— 1902. 'Marriage customs of the Khonds.' *JASB,* LXX, III, pp.18–28.

——— 1904. Totemism among the Khonds.' *JASB,* LXXII, III, pp.39–56.

——— 1909. *A grammar of the Kui language.* Calcutta: Bengal Secretariat Book Depot.

Frye, Lt J.P. 1860. 'On the Uriya and Kondh Population of Orissa.' *JRAS* vol.XVII, pp.1–38. London.

Fuchs, Stephen 1977. *The Aboriginal tribes of India.* London: Macmillan. [1973]

Fürer-Haimendorf, Christoph von 1944. 'Beliefs concerning human sacrifice among the Hill Reddis.' *MII* no.24 pp.15–41.

——— 1976. *Return to the Naked Nagas.* London: John Murray, [a revised edition of *The Naked Nagas,* 1939]

——— 1979. *The Gonds of Andhra Pradesh.* Studies on Modern Asia and Africa no.12. London: George Alien & Unwin.

——— 1982. *Tribes of India: The struggle for survival.* Berkeley: University of California Press.

Gadgil, Madhav & Ramachandra Guha 1992. *The fissured land: An ecological history of India.* Delhi: OUP.

GBMS Reports, 1860–66. London (1860–62), Derby (1863–66).

Ghurye, G.S. 1943 *The aborigines—'so-called'—and their future.* Poona: Gokhale Institute of Politics and Economics.

——— 1959. *The Scheduled Tribes.* Bombay: Popular Book Depot. [Revised edition of 1943]

Gibson, Thomas 1986. *Sacrifice and sharing in the Philippines highlands: Religion and society among the Buid of Mindoro.* London School of Economics, monograph no.57.

Girard, Rene 1977 [1972]. *Violence and the sacred.* Baltimore & London: Johns Hopkins University Press.

Gluckman, Max 1971 [1940]. *Analysis of a social situation in modern Zululand.* Manchester University Press.

Godelier, M. 1978 [1973]. *Perspectives in Marxist anthropology.* Cambridge: CUP.

Gohain, B.C. 1977. *Human sacrifice and head-hunting in Northeast India.* Calcutta & Gauhati.

Goldsmid, Sir F.J. 1880. *James Outram—a biography.* London: Smith Elder & Co.

GOM 1864. *A selection and precis of papers about Jeypore.* Selections from the records of the Madras Government no.LXXXI. Madras: United Scottish Press.

Goodland, Robert March 2007. *Utkal bauxite and alumina project: Human rights & environmental impacts.* (Washington, *RbtGoodland@aol.com).*

Graham, D.C. 1843 *A brief historical sketch of the Bheel tribe of Khan desh.* Bombay.

Grigson, W.V. 1938. *The Maria Gonds of Bastar.* London: OUP.

——— 1947. *The challenge of backwardness.* Hyderabad: Government Press.

Griffiths, Sir Percival 1967. *The history of the Indian tea industry.* London: Wiedenfeld & Nicolson.

——— 1971. *To guard my people: The history of the Indian police.* London: Ernest Benn.

Guha, Ram 1999. *Savaging the civilized: Verrier Elwin, his tribals and India.* Chicago: University of Chicago Press.

Guha, Ranajit 1963. *A rule of property for Bengal: An essay on the idea of permanent settlement.* Paris: Mouton.

——— 1983a. *Elementary aspects of peasant insurgency in colonial India.* Delhi: OUP.

——— 1983b. The prose of counterinsurgency.' In R. Guha ed. *Subaltern studies: Writings on South Asian history and society* II, pp.1–43. Delhi: OUP.

Guha, Uma et al. 1968. *The Didayi: A forgotten tribe of Orissa.* Calcutta: ASI, monograph no.23.

Gupta, Pabitra & Pratap C. Dutta 1966. *Anthropometry in India (1868–1961): A reference manual of somatological studies.* Calcutta: ASI memoir no. 10.

Hamilton, A. 1912. *In Abor jungles.* London: Eveleigh Nash.

Hardiman, David 2007. *Histories for the subordinated.* London: Palgrave Macmillan.

Hemming, John 1978. *Red gold: The conquest of the Brazilian Indians.* London: Macmillan.

Hibbert, C. 1980. *The great Mutiny: India 1857.* Harmondsworth: Penguin.

Hira Lal, Rai Bahadur 1922. 'The Aboriginals of Central India.' *MII* vol. II pp.12–32.

Hocart, A.M. 1952. 'Snobbery.' Ch. 13 in *The life-giving myth and other essays,* ed. Lord Raglan. London: Methuen.

Hodson, Col T.C. 1911. *The Naga tribes of Manipur.* London: David Nutt.

——— 1922. *The primitive culture of India.* Lectures delivered in 1922 at the School of Oriental Studies (University of London). London:

Royal Asiatic Society.

Hoffmann, Revd John 1930. *Encyclopaedia Mundarica,* vol. I (letter 'A'). Patna: Superintendent of Government Printing, Bihar and Orissa.

Hogbin, Ian 1958. *Social change.* London: Watts.

Howell, Signe 1984. *Society and cosmos: The Chewong of peninsular Malaysia.* Oxford: OUP.

Hubert, Henri & Marcel Mauss 1964 [1898]. *Sacrifice: Its nature and function.* University of Chicago Press.

Hunter [= Wilson], Monica 1961 [1936]. *Reactions to conquest: Effects of contact with Europeans on the Pondo of South Africa.* OUP for the International African Institute.

Hunter, Sir W.W. 1872. *Orissa.* vols.II & III of *The Annals of rural Bengal.* London: Smith, Elder & Co.

——— 1875. *Bhagalpur and the Santal Parganas,* vol.XIV of *A statistical account of Bengal.* London: Trübner.

——— 1877. *The district of Puri and the Orissa tributary states,* vol. XIX of *A statistical account of Bengal.* London: Trübner.

Hutton, J.H. 1941. 'Primitive tribes', in L.S.S. O'Malley ed. *Modern India and the West.* Oxford: OUP.

Hvalkof, Soren and Peter Aaby eds. 1981. *Is God an American? An anthropological perspective on the Summer Institute of Linguistics.* Denmark: IWGIA and Survival International.

Illich, Ivan 1973. *Deschooling society.* Harmondsworth: Penguin.

——— 1977. *Toward a history of needs.* New York: Pantheon books.

Indian People's Tribunal on Environment and Human Rights Oct. 2006, *Kashipur: An enquiry into mining and human rights violations in Kashipur, Orissa (www.iptindia.org).*

Innes, Alexander 1895. *More Light...: The Cameroons and the Baptist Mission. The only true biography of Alfred Saker and his cruelties, by eye witnesses. Also a complete refutation of statements made in the 'centenary volume' of the BMS.* Liverpool: E. Howell.

Israel, M. 1979. *A grammar of the Kuvi language.* Trivandrum: Dravidian Linguistics Association.

James, L. 1985. *The savage wars: British campaigns in Africa 1870–1920.* London: Robert Hale.

Jena, Mihir, Padmini Pathi, Jagganath Dash, Kamala Patnaik, Klaus Seeland 2002. *Forest tribes of Orissa. Vol.1 The Dongaria Kondh.* Delhi: DK Printworld.

Jha, J.C. 1964. *The Kol insurrection.* Calcutta: Thacker and Spink.

Johnson, Douglas H. 1982a. 'Evans-Pritchard, the Nuer, and the Sudan political service.' *African Affairs* vol.81 pp.231–46. London: Royal African Society.

——— 1982b. 'The death of Gordon: A Victorian myth.' *Journal of Imperial and Commonwealth History* vol.X pp.285–310. London: Frank Cass.

Joshi, Ramsharan 1984. *Tribals: Islands of deprivation.* Delhi: National Book Shop.

Journal of the Ethnological Society of London 1854. A Manual of ethnological enquiry, adapted from Pritchard's address to the British Association at Birmingham in 1839. Vol.III pp.193–208. London: Ethnological Society.

Kanungo, Pralay 2008. 'Hindutva's fury against Christians in Orissa,' in *Economic & Political Weekly* vol.43 no.37, 13th Sept. pp.16–19.

Kaye, Sir J.W. 1853. *The administration of the EIC: A history of Indian progress.* London: Richard Bentley.

Keys, E. ed. 1885. *Reports of the Meriah Agents (Ganjam) from 1837 to 1861.* Madras: Government Press.

Kincaid, C.A. & Rao Bahadur D.B. Parasnis 1968. *A history of the Maratha people to the death ofShivaji.* Delhi: S. Chand.

Kirke-Greene, A.H.M. 1980. The thin white line: The size of the British colonial society in *Africa.' African Affairs* vol.79 pp.25–44.

Kittoe, Lt M. 1839. 'Journal of Orissa.' In *JASB* vol.VIII pp.367–85, 474–80, 606–20, 671–81.

Kosambi, D.D. 1970. *The culture and civilization of ancient India in historical perspective.* Delhi: Vikas.

Kuklick, Henrika 1978. The sins of the fathers: British anthropology and African colonialism. In R.A. Jones ed. *Research in the sociology of knowledge,* no.I. Connecticut. Wesleyan University Press.

——— 1991. *The savage within: The social history of British social anthropology 1885–1945.* Cambridge: CUP.

Kulke, H. 1978a. 'Early state formation and royal legitimation in Eastern Indian tribal areas.' In Moser & Gautam eds. *Aspects of tribal life....* Bern.

——— 1978b. Tribal deities at princely courts.' In Sitakanta Mahapatra ed. *Proceedings of the international seminar on folk culture.* Cuttack.

——— 1978c. 'Kshatriyaisation and social change: Orissa.' In Devadas Pillai ed. *Aspects of changing India....for G.S. Ghurye.* Bombay.

——— 1980. 'Legitimation and town planning in the feudatory states of Central Orissa.' In J. Pieper ed. *Ritual space in India: Studies in architectural anthropology.* London: Art and archaeology research papers no. 17, pp.30–40.

Kuper, Adam 1988. *The invention of primitive society.* London: Routledge.

Leach, E.R. 1953. *Political systems of Highland Burma: A study of Kachin social structure.* London: Bell.

Leigh-Stutchbury, Elizabeth 1982. Blood, fire and mediation: Human sacrifice and widow-burning in 19th century India, in M. Alien & S.N. Mukherjee eds. *Women in India and Nepal,* pp.21–75. Canberra: Australian National University, monographs on South Asia no.8.

Letchmajee, L. 1902. *Introduction to Kui or Kandh grammar.* Calcutta.

Lévi-Strauss, Claude 1977 [1963]. 'Social structure.' In *Structural anthropology,* 1. pp.277–323. Harmondsworth: Penguin.

——— 1978 [1961]. 'Cultural discontinuity and economic and social development.' In *Structural anthropology, 2.* pp.312–22. Harmondsworth: Penguin.

Liedloff, Jean 1986 [1975]. *The continuum concept.* London: Penguin.

Lienhardt, Godfrey 1961. *Divinity and experience: The religion of the Dinka.* Oxford: Clarendon Press.

——— 1964. *Social anthropology.* Oxford: OUP.

Lord, F. Townley 1942. *Achievement: A short history of the BMS 1792–1942.* London: The Carey Press.

Low, D.A., J.C. Iltis, & M.D. Wainwright eds. 1969. *Government archives in South Asia: A guide to national and state archives in Ceylon, India and Pakistan.* Cambridge: CUP.

Lunt, James 1988 [1970]. 'Introduction' to an edition of Seeta Ram 1873/1911. London: Papermac.

Maccoby, Hyam 1982. *The sacred executioner: Human sacrifice and the legacy of guilt.* London: Thames and Hudson.

MacLeod, W.C. 1967. 'Celt and Indian: Britain's Old World frontier in relation to the New.' In Paul Bohannan & Fred Plog eds. *Beyond the frontier: Social process and cultural change* pp.25–41. New York: Natural History Press, American Museum sourcebooks in anthropology.

MacMunn, Major G.F. 1911. *The armies of India.* Bristol: Cathedral Publishing.

Macpherson, S.C. 1838. 'Report on the Goomsur, Duspullah and Boad zeminderies. Section One. On the configuration and superficial characteristics of the country in the plain.' *MJLS* vol.VII no.19 (April) pp.400–12. Madras.

——— 1842. *Report upon the Khonds of the districts of Ganjam and Cuttack.* Calcutta: G.H. Hutterman at the Bengal Military Orphan Press.

——— 1843. 'An account of the religious opinions and observances of the Khonds of Goomsur and Boad.' *JRAS* vol.VII pp.172–99.

——— 1852. 'An account of the religion of the Khonds in Orissa.' *JRAS* vol.XIII pp.216–75.

Macpherson, W. ed. 1865. *Memorials of service in India, from the correspondence of the late Samuel Charters Macpherson, C.B., Political Agent at Gwalior during the Mutiny and formerly employed in the suppression of human sacrifice in Orissa, edited by his brother.* London: John Murray.

[Maitland, Julia] 1843. *Letters from Madras during the years 1836–9. By a lady.* London: John Murray.

Maltby, T.J. 1882. *The Ganjam District Manual,* ed. G.D. Leman. Madras: W.H. Moore at the Lawrence Asylum Press.

Marcus, George E. & M.M.J. Fischer 1986. *Anthropology as cultural critique: An experimental moment in the human sciences.* University of Chicago Press.

Marshall, William E. 1873. *A phrenologist among the Todas, or the study of a primitive tribe in South India: History, character, customs, religion, infanticide, polyandry, language.* London: Longmans, Green & Co.

Mason, Philip 1974. *A matter of honour: An account of the Indian army, its officers and men.* London: Jonathan Cape.

Mathur, H.M. 2006. 'Resettling people displaced by development projects: Some critical management issues,' in *Social Change* vol.36 no.1, pp.48 & 69–70.

———— 2006 ed. *Managing resettlement in India: Approaches, issues, experiences*. Delhi: OUP.

———— 2008 ed. *India: Social Development Report 2008. Development and displacement.* Delhi: OUP for Council for Social Development.

Mathur, L.P. 1984. *Kala Pani: History of the Andaman and Nicobar Islands with a study of India's freedom struggle.* Delhi: Eastern Book Corporation.

Mathur, Shubh 2008. *The everyday life of Hindu Nationalism: An Ethnographic Account.* Gurgaon: Three Essays Collective.

Maxwell, W.G. 1838. 'Cursory notes on Wodhiahghur and the adjacent part of Goomsoor, and on the people of that country.' *MJLS* vol.VII no. 18 (Jan.), pp.134–42.

Mayhew, Arthur 1929. *Christianity and the Government of India: An examination of the Christian forces at work in the GOI and of the mutual relations of the British Government and the Christian Missions 1600–1920.* London: Faber & Gwyer Ltd.

Mazumdar, B.C. 1926. *Orissa in the making.* University of Calcutta.

Mazumdar, Kanchanmoy 1984. 'British Baptist missionaries in Orissa, 1822–58: A study in Western impact on 19th century society.' In Binod S. Das ed. *Life and culture in Orissa,* 108–16. Calcutta: Minerva Associates.

Means, Russell 1982. 'On a new consciousness of the American Indian Movement.' *Lokayan Bulletin* no.7 (August), Delhi. [A partial transcript of an address at a gathering at Pine Ridge Lakota reservation, South Dakota, July 1980]

Meek, R.L. 1976. *Social Science and the ignoble savage.* Cambridge: CUP.

Mill, James 1817. *A history of British India.* London: Baldwick, Chadock & Joy.

Minchin, A.A.F. 1920. *The sal forests of Ganjam, South India.* Madras: Government Press.

Mishra, Ashutosh 2008. 'Extracting a cost: Vedanta's refinery pollutes river, sickens people in Orissa,' in *Down to Earth* 17th Nov. Delhi.

Mohanty, Gopinath 1987 [1945]. *Paraja.* London: Faber & Faber. Translated from Oriya by Bikram K. Das.

——— 2000a. *Sroto Swati.* Cuttack: Vidyapuri. [autobiography, in Oriya]

——— 2006b. 'Tadpa,' translated by Sitakant Mahapatra, in *Oriya Short Stories.* Delhi: Srishti.

——— 2007. 'Alora,' In *Samadrushti* journal for 1–15 May. Bhubaneswar. [in Oriya]

——— 1987 [1949]. *Amritara Santaana.* Cuttack: Vidyapuri. ['Sons of nectar', a novel in Oriya about the Konds]

Mohanty, K.K. 2007. 'Primitive Tribal Groups and Biodiversity Conservation,' in *Adivasi* vol.47 nos.1–2 pp.13–24. Bhubaneswar: SC & ST Research & Training Institute.

Moody, Roger 2007a. *Rocks and Hard Places: The Globalization of Mining.* London: Zed.

——— 2007b. 'The Base Alchemist,' in Rakesh Kalshian ed. *Caterpillar and the Mahua flower: Tremors in India's mining fields.* Delhi: Panos, pp.83–102.

Morris, James 1979 [1968]. *Pax Britannica.* Harmondsworth: Penguin.

——— 1979 [1973]. *Heaven's command.* Harmondsworth: Penguin.

Morrison, Charles 1984. Three styles of imperial ethnography: British officials as anthropologists in India.' In *Knowledge and Society: Studies in the sociology of culture, past and present* [research annual] vol.5.

Morse, Bradford & Thomas Berger 1992. *Sardar Sarovar: Report of the independent review.* Ottawa: Resource futures international.

Mosse, David 2005. *Cultivating development: An ethnography of aid policy and practice.* London: Pluto.

——— 2009. 'Social analysis as corporate product: Non-Economists/ Anthropologists at the World Bank in Washington DC,' in Mosse ed. *Travelling rationalities: The anthropology of expert knowledge and professionals in international development.* Oxford: Berghahn.

Mouat, F.J. 1859. *The British soldier in India.* London: R.C. Lepage & Co.

——— 1872. 'On prison discipline and statistics in Bengal.' *Journal of the Statistical Society of London,* March, pp.57–106.

Mukerji, Bithika 2008. *Neo-Vedanta and Modernity.* Varanasi: Ashutosh Prakashan Sansthan. [1983]

Mukherjee, P. 1964. *History of Orissa in the 19th century.* Bhuvaneshwar: Utkal University Press.

——— 1981. *The history of the Gajapati kings of Orissa and their successors.* Revised ed. Cuttack: Kitab Mahal.

Muthayya, B.C. *et al.* 1984. *Rehabilitation of Displaced Villages: A Study in Nalco Complex, Damanjodi, Koraput District, Orissa.* Hyderabad: National Institute of Rural Development.

Myers, John Brown ed. 1892. *The centenary volume of the BMS 1792–1892.* London: BMS.

Nandy, Ashish 1990 [1988]. *Science, hegemony and violence: A requiem for modernity.* Tokyo: United Nations University, & Delhi: OUP.

Nayak, P.K. 1989. *Blood, honour, and territory: An analysis of blood feuds of Dongria Kondhs.* Delhi: Reliance.

Nayak, Ramesh C. and Joseph M. Kujur 2007 *State aggression and tribal resistance: A case of the police firing at Kalinga Nagar.* Delhi: Indian Social Institute.

Needham, R. ed. 1973. *Right and left: Essays on dual symbolic classification.* University of Chicago Press.

Neihardt, John G. 1961. *Black Elk speaks.* Lincoln: University of Nebraska Press.

Neill, Stephen 1964. *A history of Christian Missions.* Harmondsworth: Penguin, Pelican history of the Church vol.VI.

——— 1985. *A history of Christianity in India: 2. 1707–1858.* Cambridge: CUP.

Niggemeyer, H. 1964. *Kuttia Kond: Dschungel-Bauern in Orissa.* Munchen: Klaus Renner.

Nisbet, R. 1980. *A history of the idea of progress.* London: Butterworth.

Nock, A.D. 1933. *Conversion.* Oxford: OUP.

Norberg-Hodge, Helena 1991. *Ancient futures: Learning from Ladakh.* London: Rider.

Nostromo Research 2005. *Ravages through India: Vedanta resources plc Alternative report,* London and the India Resource Center, Delhi. (www.minesandcommunities.org)

Ollenbach, J. 1908. 'The Khonds.' Ch. IV of O'Malley 1908.

O'Malley, L.S.S. 1908 *Angul. Bengal District Gazetteers* vol.XI. Calcutta: Bengal Secretariat Book Depôt.

Orissa Baptist Mission Reports 1872–1905. Cuttack: Orissa Mission Press.

Orwell, George 1949 [1934]. *Burmese days.* London: Seeker & Warburg.

——— 1970. A hanging. In *The collected essays, journalism, and letters, vol.1. 1930–1940,* pp.66–71. Harmondsworth: Penguin. [1934 as Eric Blair]

Ota, A.B. 2007. Primitive tribal groups of Orissa: An overview. *Adivasi* vol.47. nos.1–2. Bhubaneswar: SC & ST Research & Training Institute.

Padel, Felix 2006. 22. Sept 2007. "A Cry Against the Hidden War: Bastar's Civil War," *Tehelka,* /www.tehelka.com/story_main34.asp?filename=cr220907A_CRY.asp

——— & Samarendra Das 2006. "Double death: Aluminium's links with genocide," *Social Scientist* no.394–5, pp.55–81. Delhi.

——— 2007. 'Agya, what do you mean by development?' pp.26–46 in Rakesh Kalshian ed. *Caterpillar and the Mahua flower: Tremors in India's mining fields.* Delhi: Panos.

——— 2008. 'Cultural genocide: The real impact of development-induced displacement,' in Mathur ed. 2008.

——— December 2008. 'Orissa's highland clearances: The reality gap in R & R,' in *Social Change* vol.38 no.4, pp.576–608.

——— (forthcoming, 2009). *Out of This Earth: East India Adivasis and the Aluminium Cartel.* Delhi: Orient BlackSwan.

Pagels, Elaine 1989 [1979]. *The Gnostic Gospels.* New York: Vintage.

Paley, William 1786. *The principles of moral and political philosophy.* 2nd ed. London: R. Faulder.

Pareek, R. 1977. *Tribal culture influx: The Jatapus of the Eastern Ghats.* Delhi: BR Publishing Company.

Parkin, Robert 1992. *The Munda of Central India: An account of their social organization.* Delhi: OUR

Parry, Jonathon 2007. 'The sacrifices of modernity in a Soviet-built steel town in Central India,' chapter 13 in Frances Pine & Joao De Pina-Cabral eds. *On the margins of religion.* Oxford: Berghahn.

Pati, Biswamoy 1993. *Resisting domination: Peasants, Tribals and the National Movement in Orissa, 1920–1950.* New Delhi: Manohar.

Patnaik, N. 1972. *Tribes and their development.* Hyderabad: National Institute of Community Development.

Patnaik, Nihar Ranjan 1992. *History and culture of Khond Tribes*. Delhi: Commonwealth Publishers.

Pattanaik, P.K. 2006. 'Tribal Resistance Movement under the leadership of Rindo Majhi,' in Nihar Ranjan Patnaik ed., *Glory of Indian tribes: A focus on Orissa.* Delhi.

Patra, K.M. 1971. *Orissa under the EIC.* Delhi: Munshiram Manoharlal.

Peggs, James 1832. *India's cries to British humanity, relative to infanticide, British connection with idolatry, Ghaut murders, suttee, slavery, and colonization in India; to which are added HUMANE HINTS for the melioration of the state of society in British India.* London: Simpkin & Marshall. 3rd edition.

——— 1846. *A history of the General Baptist Mission established in the Province (of Orissa).* In Stirling 1846, pp. 143-323. London: John Snow.

Penny, Mrs F.E. 1910. *Sacrifice.* London: Chatto & Windus.

People's Democratic Forum & People's Union for Civil Liberties—Karnataka, July 2003, *The struggle against bauxite mining in Orissa: Report of a citizens' visit to Orissa, Oct.–Dec. 2002.* Bangalore: PUCL-K.

People's Union of Democratic Rights (PUDR), April 2006, *Where the state makes war on its own people*, www.pudr.org/pages/salwa.judum.pdf

Pfeffer, G. 1982. 'Tribal social organisation and "Hindu" influence.' *International Asien Forum* pp.45–54. Miinchen.

Phythian-Adams, Lt-Col E.G. 1943. *The Madras Infantry 1748–1943.* Wellington: C.D. Qhody and sons at Defence Services Staff College Press.

Pinney, Chris 1992. 'The parallel histories of anthropology and photography.' In Elizabeth Edwards ed. 1992.

Portman, M.V. 1899. *A history of our relations with the Andamanese.* Calcutta: Office of the Superintendent of Government Printing in India.

Potts, E.D. 1967. *British Baptist Missionaries in India 1793–1837.* Cambridge: CUP.

Prasad, Archana 2003. Against primitive romanticism: Verrier Elwin and the making of an anti-modern tribal identity. Delhi: Three Essays Collective.

Pradhan, Pramodini & Ranjana Padhi 2008. 'Fear in Kandhamal,' in *Economic & Political Weekly,* 1st Nov. pp.11–14.

Pradhan, Satapathy Feb. 2006. *Police firing at Kalinganagar: A report by People's Union for Civil Liberties.* Delhi: PUCL.

Prebble, John 1967 [1961]. *Culloden.* Harmondsworth: Penguin.

——— 1969 [1963]. *The Highland clearances.* London: Penguin.

Radcliffe-Brown, A.R. 1922. *The Andaman Islanders.* Cambridge: CUP.

Ransford, Oliver 1971. *The slave trade.* London: John Murray.

Rath, Govinda Chanda ed. 2006. *Tribal development in India: The contemporary debate.* Delhi: Sage.

Ray, B.C. 1960. *Foundations of British Orissa.* Cuttack.

Ray, G. 1949. A study of the physical characters of the Kondhs. *Eastern Anthropologist* vol II pp.138–44. Lucknow: Universal Publishers.

——— 1950. Characteristic features of Kondh kinship terminology. *Eastern Anthropologist* vol.III pp.151–7.

Ray, Rabindra 1988. *The Naxalites and their ideology.* Delhi: OUP.

Reynolds, Henry 1982. *The other side of the frontier: Aboriginal resistance to the European invasion of Australia.* Harmonds worth: Penguin.

Risley, Sir H.H. 1891. *Tribes and castes of Bengal. Ethnographic Glossary. Vol.1 (A-K).* Calcutta: Bengal Secretariat Press.

Ritthoff, Michael, Holger Rohn & Christa Liedtke 2002. *Calculating MIPS: Resource productivity of products and services.* Wuppertal spezial 27e. Germany: Wuppertal Institute for Climate, Environment and Energy.

Rivers, W.H.R. 1906. *The Todas.* London: Macmillan.

Roberts, Glynn 1984. *Questioning development.* Paris: Co-ordinating Committee for International Relations Service, UNESCO.

Robins, Nick 2006. *The corporation that changed the world: How the East India Company shaped the modern multinational.* London: Pluto.

Rosaldo, Michelle 1980. *Knowledge and passion: Ilongot notions of self and social life.* Cambridge: CUP.

Rosaldo, Renato 1980. *Ilongot headhunting 1883–1974: A study in society and history.* Stanford University Press.

——— 1986. 'From the door of his tent: The fieldworker and the inquisitor.' In Clifford & Marcus 1986.

Rowney, H.B. 1884. *The wild tribes of India.* London: Thomas de la Rue.

Roy, S.C. 1912. *The Mundas and their country.* Calcutta: Kuntaline Press.

——— 1921. 'Anthropological research in India.' *MII: A Quarterly Record of Anthropological Science with special reference to India,* vol.1 no.l pp.11–55.

——— 1922. 'Ethnography in the old official records: Khond human sacrifices.' *MII* vol.11 pp.66–81.

——— 1935. *The Hill Bhuiyas of Orissa.* Ranchi: "Man In India" Office.

Russell, The Hon. G.E. 1856. *Reports on the disturbances in Purla Kimedy, Vizagapatam and Goomsur in 1832–1836.* Selections from the records of the Madras Government no.XXIV. Madras: United Scottish Press.

Russell R.V. and Hira Lal 1916. *Tribes and castes of the Central Provinces, vol.111 (G-Ko).* London: Macmillan.

Rynklewich, M.A. 1976. 'The underdevelopment of anthropological ethics.' In Rynklewich & J.J. Spradley eds. *Ethics and anthropology: dilemmas infieldwork.* New York: John Wiley & sons.

Sa, Fidelis de 1975. *Crisis in Chotanagpur.* Bangalore: Redemptionist Publications.

Sahlins, M. 1968. *Tribesmen.* New Jersey: Prentice Hall.

——— 1985. *Islands of history.* University of Chicago Press.

Sahoo, A.C. 2007. 'Life and Culture of the Dongria Kondhs,' in *Adivasi* vol.47 nos.1–2 pp.98–107. Bhubaneswar: SC & ST Research & Training Institute.

Sahu, L. 1942. *The hill tribes of Jeypore.* Cuttack: Revd E.R. Lazarus at the Orissa Mission Press.

Said, W. 1978. *Orientalism.* London: Routledge and Kegan Paul,

——— 1984. A review of Benita Parry's 'Conrad and imperialism'. *TLS* for 12th October, p.1149. London.

Sainath, P. 1996 *Everybody likes a good drought: Stories from India's poorest districts.* Delhi and London: Penguin.

Samal, J.K. 1977. *Orissa under the British crown 1858–1905.* Delhi: S. Chand.

Sanderson, Stephen 1990. *Social evolutionism: A critical history 1860–1920.* Oxford: Blackwell.

Sarangi, Deba Ranjan 2002 'Surviving against the odds: Case of Kashipur'. *Economic & Political Weekly* 3 August.

Saumarez-Smith, Richard 1985. 'Rule-by-records and rule-by-reports: Complementary aspects of the British imperial rule of law.' *CIS* vol.29 pp. 153–96.

Schulze, F.V.P. 1911. *A grammar of the Kuvi language, with copious examples*. Madras: Graves Cookson & Co.

——— 1912 *The religion of the Kuvi-Konds*. Madras: Graves Cookson.

——— 1913. *Vocabulary of the Kuvi-Kond language, with short sentences on general subjects for conversational purposes*. Madras: Graves Cookson.

Seeta-Ram 1911 [1863/1873]. *From sepoy to subedar, being the life and adventures of a native officer of the Bengal army written and related by himself*. Translated from Urdu by Lt-Col Norgate. 3rd ed. by Lt-Col Phillott. Calcutta: Baptist Mission Press.

Sengupta, K.P. 1971. *The Christian Missionaries in Bengal 1793–1833*. Calcutta: Firma KLM.

Sengupta S. 1977. *Applied anthropology: Meaning and necessity*. Calcutta: Firma KLM.

Sharma, B.D. 1990. *29th Report of the Commissioner for Scheduled Castes and Scheduled Tribes, 1987–1989*. Delhi: Government of India.

Sharma, Krishan 1979. *The Konds of Orissa: An anthropometric study*. Delhi: Concept Publishing House.

Shiva, Vandana 1990. 'Reductionist science as epistemological violence.' In Ashish Nandy 1990.

Simcox, A.H.A. [1920]. *A memoir of the Khandesh Bhil corps 1825–1891*. Bombay: Thacker & Co.

Singh, C.P. 1978. *The Ho tribe of Singhbhum*. Delhi: Classical Publications.

Singh, K. Suresh 1966. *The dust-storm and the hanging mist: A study of Birsa Munda and his movement in Chhotanagpur*. Calcutta: KLM.

——— 1971. 'State formation in tribal society: Some preliminary observations.' *Journal of the Indian Anthropological Society* vol.6 pp.161–81.

——— ed. 1972. *Tribal situation in India: Proceedings of a seminar*. Simla: Institute of Advanced Study.

———1982. 'Transformation of tribal society: Integration vs. Assimilation.' *Economic and Political Weekly* vol.XVII no.33 (14th August) pp.318–25.

——— ed. 1983. *Tribal movements in India*, vol.2 [Central India]. Delhi: Manohar.

——— 1984. 'Colonialism, anthropology and primitive society: The Indian scenario (1928–47).' *MII* vol.64 pp.399–413.

Sinha, A.C. 1991. 'Indian social anthropology and its Cambridge connections.' *Eastern Anthropologist* vol.44 no.4.

Sinha, S. 1962. 'State formation and Rajput myth in tribal Central India.' *MII* vol.42 pp.35–80.

Sjöö, Monica and Barbara Mor 1987. *The great cosmic mother: Rediscovering the religion of the earth.* San Francisco: Harper & Row.

Smith, A.D. 1973. *The concept of social change: A critique of the functionalist theory of social change.* London: Routledge & Kegan Paul.

Smith, Lt-Col E. Clementi 1945. The Bastar rebellion, 1910.' *MII* vol.25 pp.240–53.

Smith, J. Macdonald 1876. *A practical handbook of the Khond language.* Cuttack: Orissa Mission Press.

Sontag, Susan 1979. *On photography.* Harmondsworth: Penguin.

Stein, Burton 1980. *Peasant state and society in medieval South India.* Oxford and Delhi: OUP.

Stephens, H. Morse 1900. 'The East India College at Haileybury (1806–1857).' In A. Lawrence Lowell: *Colonial Civil Service: The selection and training of colonial officials in England, Holland, and France,* pp.233–346. New York: Macmillan.

Stirling, Andrew 1846. *Orissa, its geography, statistics, history, religion, and antiquities.* London: John Snow.

Stocking, George W. 1991. *Colonial situations: Essays in the contextualization of ethnographic knowledge.* Wisconsin University Press, History of Anthropology vol. 7.

Stokes, Eric 1959. *The English utilitarians in India.* Delhi: OUP.

Storr, Anthony ed. 1983. *Jung's selected writings.* Part 4. 'Archetypes: Shadow...' London: Fontana.

Street, Brian 1975. *The savages in literary representations of 'primitive' society in English fiction 1858–1920.* London: Routledge & Kegan Paul.

Sundar, Nandini 2007. *Subalterns and sovereigns: An anthropological history of Bastar 1854–2006.* Delhi: OUP. (2nd edition)

Sunday Statesman, weekly from 1939. Calcutta.

Suzuki, David & Peter Knudtson 1992. *Wisdom of the elders: Honoring sacred native visions of nature.* New York: Bantam.

Taub, Richard 1969. *Bureaucrats under stress: Administrators and administration in an Indian state* [Orissa]. Berkeley: University of California Press.

Taylor, Adam 1818. *The history of the General Baptists in the 17th century.* London.

Taylor, Revd W. July 1837. 'On the language, manners, and rites of the KHOONDS or KHOIJATI, of the Goomsoor mountains; from descriptions furnished by J.A.R.STEVENSON, ESQ., Commissioner in Goomsoor, and W.G.MAXWELL, ESQ., MD: with illustrative and connecting observations.' *MJLS* vol.VI pp. 17–46.

——— Jan. 1838. 'Some additional notes on the hill inhabitants of the Goomsoor mountains, with a translation of a Telugu paper, containing a historical narrative of the B'hanga family, feudal chieftains of Gumsara.' *MJLS* vol.VII pp.89–104.

Temple, Sir Richard 1862–3. *Reports on the Central Provinces.* Nagpur.

——— 1867. *Gazetteer of the Central Provinces.* Nagpur: Chief Commissioner's Office Press.

Thomas, Keith 1973. *Religion and the decline of magic.* Harmondsworth: Penguin.

Thompson, E.P. 1977. *Whigs and hunters: The origin of the Black Act.* Harmondsworth: Penguin.

Thurston, Edgar 1907. *Ethnographic notes of Southern India.* Madras: Government Press.

——— & Rangacharya 1909. *Castes and tribes of Southern India, vol.III (K).* Madras: Government Press.

——— 1912. *Omens and superstitions of Southern India.* London: T. Fisher & Unwin.

Thusu, K.N. 1977. *The Pengo Porojas of Koraput.* Calcutta: ASI, monograph no.39.

——— 1980. *The Gond kingdom of Chandra.* Calcutta: ASI, monograph no.40.

——— & Jha 1969. *The Ollar Gadabas of Koraput.* Calcutta: ASI, monograph no.27.

Tierney, Patrick 1989. *The Highest Altar: The story of human sacrifice.* London: Bloomsbury.

Tod, James 1914 [1829]. *Annals and antiquities of Rajasthan.* London: Routledge & Kegan Paul.

Torbert, Robert G. 1950. *A history of the Baptists.* USA: Judson Press.

Tournier, Michel 1974. *Friday or the other island,* tr. Norman Denny. Harmondsworth: Penguin, [in French 1967]

Trager, Helen G. 1966. *Burma through alien eyes: Missionary views of the Burmese in the 19th century.* London: Asia Publishing House.

Turnbull, Colin 1973. *The mountain people.* London: Pan Books.

——— 1976 [1961]. *The forest people.* London: Pan Books.

Tylor, Edward B. 1871. *Primitive Culture: Researches into the development of mythology, philosophy, religion, art and custom.* London: John Murray.

Uberoi, J.P.S. 1962. *The politics of the Kula Ring.* Manchester University Press.

——— 1978. *Science and culture.* Delhi: OUP.

——— 1984. *The other mind of Europe: Goethe as a scientist.* Delhi: OUP.

Vidyarthi, L.P. 1978. *Rise of anthropology in India: A social science orientation* (2 volumes). Delhi: Concept Publishing Company.

Visvanathan, Shiv 1990a. 'Atomic physics: The career of an imagination.' In Ashish Nandy 1990.

——— 1990b. 'On the annals of the laboratory state.' In Ashish Nandy 1990.

Vitebsky, Piers 1993. *Dialogues with the dead: The discussion of mortality among the Sora of Eastern India.* Cambridge: CUP.

Walker, T.L. 1902. "The Geology of Kalahandi State, Central Provinces," *Memoirs of The Geological Survey of India,* vol.XXXIII part III pp.1–22. Calcutta: GSI.

Wallerstein, Immanuel 1966. *Social change and the colonial situation.* New York: John Wiley.

Ward, Donald J. 1953. "The three-fold death: An Indo-European trifunctional sacrifice?' In *La Saga de Hadingus* pp.118–59. Paris.

Ward, William 1863. *A view of the history, literature, and religion of the Hindoos.* Madras: J. Higginbotham.

Waters, Frank 1963. *Book of the Hopi.* New York: Viking Penguin.

Watson, J. Forbes, and Sir J.W. Kaye 1875. *The people of India: A series of photographic illustrations of the races and tribes of Hindustan, with descriptive letterpress by Col Meadows Taylor,* vol. VIII. London: India Museum.

Watt, Ian 1975. ' "Robinson Crusoe" as a myth.' In Defoe 1975, pp.311–32. [1951]

Watts, N.A. 1970. *The half-clad tribals of Eastern India.* Bombay: Orient Longman.

Weber, Max 1947. *The theory of social and economic organisation,* ed. Talcott Parsons. New York: OUP. [1913]

——— 1949. *The methodology of the social sciences.* New York: The Free Press.

——— 1976. *The Protestant ethic and the spirit of Capitalism,* ed. Talcott Parsons. London. [1904]

White, B.R. 1983. *The English Baptists of the 17th century.* London: The Baptist Historical Society.

Wilks, Ivor 1975. *The Asante in the 19th century.* Cambridge: CUP.

Williams, Raymond 1958. *Culture and society 1780–1950.* Harmondsworth: Penguin.

Wilson, G. & M. 1945. *The analysis of social change.* Cambridge: CUP.

Winfield, W.W. 1928. *A grammar of the Kui language.* Calcutta: The Asiatic Society of Bengal, at the Baptist Mission Press.

——— 1929. *A vocabulary of the Kui language.* Calcutta: The Asiatic Society of Bengal, at the Baptist Mission Press.

Wolf, Eric 1982. *Europe and the people without history.* Berkeley: University of California Press.

Woodruffe [= Mason], Philip 1953. *The men who ruled India: I. The founders.* London: Jonathan Cape.

Wurgaft, Lewis D. 1984. *The imperial imagination: Magic and myth in Kipling's India.* Connecticut: Wesleyan University Press.

Yeatts, M. 1931. *Census of India,* XIV (Madras), Part I (Report).

Yule, Col. Henry & A.C. Burnell 1903. *Hobson-Jobson: A glossary of Anglo-Indian words and phrases.* A new ed. by William Crooke. London.

Unpublished Material

A. MISSIONARY AND ANTHROPOLOGICAL MATERIAL

BMS Archives, BMS headquarters, Gloucester Place, London. Evans, E.E. 1911–1935. File.

Millman, Oliver. 1939. *Among the Konds.* A transcription of a pamphlet published at the Orissa Mission Press, Cuttack. 20 pages.

NB: *GBMS Reports* for 1860–66, *BMS Reports* for 1890–1950, and the *Baptist Herald* are listed under published works.

Pitt-Rivers Museum and its Archives, Oxford.

Kond axes, ornaments, and other objects, presented by J. Strode Wilson (1894 & 1905), F.J.V. & E.A. Minchin (1902), the BMS (1902), the Folklore Society (1900), Balfour (1916) and D. Gunn (1922). Hutton, J.H. 1938. *Anthropology as an imperial study.* Unpublished lecture. Archive collection of the Pitt-Rivers Museum.

Woodthorpe, Maj.-Gen. R.G. 1871–6. Collection of photographs and tour diaries of tribes on the North-East Frontier, and Report 1875.

India Office Library, London.

BMS. n.d. *Catalogue of papers relating to South Asia 1813–1914,* by Mary M. Evans. Printed in London in the BMS. London: India Office Library.

Archives of the Jawaharlal Nehru Memorial Library, Teenmurti, New Delhi. Elwin Papers:

Misc. X. no. 147 Report on tribals of Ganjam and Koraput 5th April 1945

Misc. X. no. 160 Notes on the Konds (handwritten fieldnotes, 480 pages)

Misc. X. no. 161. Notes about Meriah Tribes (53 pages)

B. GOVERNMENT REPORTS AND MINUTES

India Office Library, London; and National Archives of India, New Delhi. NB: The documents cited, especially in chapters two and three, are available in these two Archives, where they have been copied by hand into large volumes that are catalogued under the following entries. GOI documents exist in both Archives, but documents of the Madras Government (GOM) are not necessarily available in Delhi. Not included here are Reports available in published collections, especially Carberry 1854 (C) and Russell 1856 (R), but also Keys 1885 (K) and GOM 1864: *...Papers about Jeypore* (J).

GOI Foreign Department, Political Consultations Jan. 1841
" Home Department, Public Consultations Aug. 1836
Dec. 1845–Nov. 1848
Jan.–March 1858
Oct. 1863
" Home Department, Revenue Consultations May 1843
GOM Military Consultations Dec. 1835–Dec. 1836.
" Revenue Consultations Dec. 1835–Oct. 1838.

Films

Das, Amarendra & Samarendra 2005. *Wira Pdika* or *Matiro Poko Company Loko* (Earth Worm, Company Man, in Kui/Oriya with English subtitles), available from sdasorisa@rediffmail.com

Dash, Surya Shankar 2008. *Niyamgiri, Mountain of Law* (in Oriya with English commentary & subtitles). Bhubaneswar: Samadrusti, available from dash.suryashankar@gmail.com

Index